BUSINESS ANALYTICS

BUSINESS ANALYTICS

Applied Modelling & Prediction

James Abdey

1 Oliver's Yard
55 City Road
London EC1Y 1SP

2455 Teller Road
Thousand Oaks
California 91320

Unit No 323-333, Third Floor, F-Block
International Trade Tower
Nehru Place, New Delhi – 110 019

8 Marina View Suite 43-053
Asia Square Tower 1
Singapore 018960

Editor: Ruth Stitt
Development editor: Jessica Moran
Editorial assistant: Charlotte Hegley
Assistant editor, digital: Benedict Hegarty
Production editor: Ian Antcliff
Copyeditor: Richard Leigh
Marketing manager: Lucia Sweet
Cover design: Francis Kenney
Typeset by: C&M Digitals (P) Ltd, Chennai, India
Printed in the UK

Library of Congress Control Number: 2023933185

British Library Cataloguing in Publication data

A catalogue record for this book is available from the British Library

ISBN 978-1-5297-7410-8
ISBN 978-1-5297-7409-2 (pbk)

CONTENTS

ACKNOWLEDGEMENTS

In the spirit of brevity, I'll keep it short.

My sincere thanks to all those who made this book possible. The Sage publication team for their sage advice, support, encouragement, patience, and Oscar-worthy performances of hiding disappointment with repeated delays.

Special mentions, of course, go to Bayes, Bernoulli, Poisson, Monty (Hall), Monte Carlo and all things Monégasque. The number 7. LaTeX. GMT. WFH. FFS (fat finger syndrome). Nespresso. 3am ideas. Excellent Excel cells. Tableau. S^3P. R. r. R^2 (including adjusted). Aha moments. p-values. The 4 Ps. z-values. t-values, F-values. n and any values. Indeed, the entire alphabet – Latin and Greek (*ευχαριστώ*). Cryptocurrency. Procrastination. Bias. Covid. Lockdowns. *Ceteris paribus*. Colours. Probability. Brexit. π. 1.96. e. Infinity.

The unit interval. Lines (metro and straight). Curves. Chocolate. Hypotheses. All things binary. It depends. Errors – Types I and II. Time. The Bank of England's Monetary Policy Committee. Spring and summer. October. Data, and its sibling Big. Self-doubt. Confidence: 95% and 99%, but not 90% (who did not help). Standardisation. Heads and Tails, but mostly Heads. The *Ever Given*. Events. `=RAND()`.

And last, but not least, me.

James Abdey
London, 2023

ABOUT THE AUTHOR

Dr James Abdey, Associate Professor (Education), Department of Statistics, London School of Economics and Political Science.

James is an Associate Professor (Education) in Statistics, having gained his PhD in 2010 from LSE, asking 'To p, or not to p?' He teaches the Department's large service-level undergraduate courses in mathematical statistics and quantitative methods, as well as elective courses in market research. His research interests include market research techniques and forensic statistics – the interplay of statistics and the law.

James has been closely involved with the University of London International Programmes for a number of years, for which he serves as Associate Academic Director, and helped launch the BSc Data Science and Business Analytics programme. James is a convenor for some courses in the LSE Online portfolio of programmes, and lectures during LSE's Summer School. Outside of academia, he has also worked on various quantitative-based consultancy projects in areas including the art market and the World Gold Council.

Answer: p. With probability 1.

PREFACE

A warm welcome to Business Analytics: Applied Modelling and Prediction!

I predict, with at least 95% confidence, that you will enjoy the analytics journey ahead of you in the following chapters.

While I am no doubt biased in my assertion that all chapters are super interesting, inevitably among the reader population of this text there will likely be variation in interest levels for different topics, plus a constraint on your time. As such, an element of signposting is desirable so you can maximise your skills acquisition subject to your time constraints – indeed, this is at the heart of Chapter 19!

0.1 A NON-RANDOM WALK DOWN ANALYTICS STREET

Chapter 1: Decision-making under uncertainty

Level: Beginner

The opening chapter is strongly recommended as the starting point for all readers. All subsequent topics arguably build on Chapter 1 content with an emphasis on viewing models as deliberate simplifications of reality, often built on assumptions. Notions of cause and effect are introduced, which themselves link directly to Chapters 11–14. It is important for any business analyst to recognise that decision-making is done under uncertainty, such that a proper appreciation that we operate in an uncertain environment is crucial.

Chapter 2: Descriptive statistics

Level: Beginner

Empirical work begins with exploratory analysis, literally exploring data to identify any interesting initial features. The mean and standard deviation are offered up as the best two-number summary of a quantitative variable, describing the central tendency and spread of such variables. Readers who have prior knowledge of 'the basics' could skip this chapter without significant detriment. Equally, reinforcing such fundamentals would also be time well spent. All in my humble opinion.

Chapter 3: Data visualisation

Level: Beginner

An introduction to the powerful data visualisation tool that is Tableau. For readers with more creative tendencies (rather than theoretical) who like to experiment with data, this is a must-read. 'Data viz' is an art as much as a science, and polishing your dashboard-building skills is definitely worthwhile as communication skills are in high demand. Besides, storytelling through data is an enjoyable activity.

Chapter 4: Probability

Level: Intermediate

Probability is our means for quantifying uncertainty. All probabilities are between 0 and 1, inclusive, but how are the numerical values of probabilities determined? This chapter focuses on probability fundamentals, as well as the different ways that probabilities can be determined (subjectively, by experimentation, and theoretically). This chapter is a bit more formula heavy, especially when working with Bayes' formula. However, Bayesian updating (revising probabilistic beliefs in light of new information) is at the heart of data-driven decision-making, such that investing the time to master these (admittedly quite abstract) concepts is worthwhile.

Chapter 5: Probability distributions

Level: Intermediate

Where possible, we seek to model a real-world variable as following a specific probability distribution. There are many 'families' of probability distributions, and this chapter reviews the main attributes of some of the most common families. Note that we use a probability distribution as an 'approximating model' of real-world variables, such that we choose a distribution which most closely reflects the stylised facts of the observed variable. This material can be a bit dry and repetitive, but the benefit is being aware of a wide range of distributions, which are at the heart of simulation models covered in Chapter 20. If you are tempted to skip this chapter, at least review Appendix B which provides a compendium of several distributions – think of this as a quick reference resource.

Chapter 6: Decision tree analysis and game theory

Level: Advanced

Decision trees model decision-making under uncertainty for unilateral (i.e. single) decision-makers. Under the assumption of risk neutrality (being indifferent to risk) decisions can be taken simply by comparing expected payoffs. Sometimes we can obtain 'expert opinions' which we model as imperfect information (since no one has perfect foresight). Information is power, so has value, and we determine the maximum willingness to pay for information. This draws on Bayes' formula (Chapter 4). The material on game theory is heavily theoretical, and is not essential for the remaining chapters. However, if you like a challenge, game theory is a fascinating topic to study the strategic decision-making of multiple 'players'. The emphasis is on price-setting and quantity-setting decisions.

Chapter 7: Sampling and sampling distributions

Level: Beginner

The first half of this chapter looks at different sampling techniques, that is, methods for drawing samples from populations. Inevitably, each approach has merits and limitations, and these are reviewed. Other things being equal, we seek a representative sample so that our statistical inferences are fairly accurate. The second half delves deeper into descriptive statistics (from

Chapter 2), in particular the sample mean. We explore the statistical properties of the 'sampling distribution' of the sample mean, and the important role of the sample size. This theory is drawn upon in Chapters 9 and 10, so studying it in preparation for estimation and hypothesis testing will make the methods used in those chapters easier to understand.

Chapter 8: Opinion research

Level: Beginner

This is a short standalone chapter looking at the issues of measurement and scaling. Any readers interested in market research surveys would benefit from studying it, especially those looking to design questionnaires. Some examples in later chapters on multivariate analysis will draw on survey response data, so it is interesting to study the types of scales from which such data were drawn.

Chapter 9: Estimation

Level: Intermediate

Variables of populations of interest typically have parameters associated with them. When the parameter values are unknown we estimate them using sample data. Estimation error is highly likely in practice. This chapter examines the desirable properties of a good 'estimator' of a parameter, and then proceeds to construct confidence intervals for means and proportions. In short, such intervals provide a quantitative margin of error around any estimate. These are very important concepts to grasp, so this chapter is highly recommended.

Chapter 10: Hypothesis testing

Level: Intermediate

Any theory or claim without supporting data evidence has little or no credibility. Hypothesis testing allows us to interrogate data in the pursuit of evidence to support or refute a theory or claim. Chapters 11–14 and 16–17 employ hypothesis testing, so this chapter is essential to understand the mechanics of how a statistical test works in order to get the most out of these later chapters. In particular, knowing what a p-value is and how to interpret one is a 'must-have', analytically speaking.

Chapter 11: Bivariate analysis

Level: Beginner

This chapter looks at the simplest cases of relationships between variables – 'bivariate' means two variables, so we do not have to worry about multiple pairwise comparisons when there is only one pairing. The main emphasis is on looking at the cases of two categorical variables (using cross-tabulations) and two measurable variables (using scatter plots and correlations). Chapters 12 and 13 draw heavily on this material.

Chapter 12: Analysis of variance

Level: Intermediate

The clue is in the chapter name, in that here we seek to analyse (and explain) the variation seen in an observed variable. Specifically, this variable of interest is called the dependent variable, and we attempt to explain it using one or two categorical variables, known as factors. In the latter case, we explore possible interactions between the two factors to see if the effectiveness of one on the dependent variable depends on the level of the other factor. Hypothesis testing features heavily, which leverages the mechanics of hypothesis testing seen in Chapter 10.

Chapter 13: Linear regression

Level: Intermediate

Extending Chapter 11, if we observe a correlation between two variables and suspect there is a causal relationship, we can run a linear regression. This is a popular technique for quantifying and testing how sensitive y is to a unit change in x. Essentially we compute the equation of the best-fitting line through a data cloud. Estimation and hypothesis testing feature heavily, for which Chapters 9 and 10 are excellent preparation.

Chapter 14: Multiple regression

Level: Intermediate

This chapter follows on from Chapter 13 as we extend the number of independent variables from 1 to k, for $k \geq 2$. Our objective remains to explain the variation in the dependent variable, but now with a more complex (yet likely more realistic) model. Some special considerations include omitted-variable bias, interactions, dummy variables, multicollinearity and model selection techniques. Note that multiple regression is a substantial topic area, and any readers particularly interested in this field would benefit from studying an econometrics text afterwards where these issues would be explored in much greater depth.

Chapter 15: Time-series analysis and forecasting

Level: Intermediate

Many variables in business will be time series (i.e. they vary over time), such as sales and market share. This chapter seeks to decompose a time series into its constituent parts, with a strong focus on trends and seasonality. When forecasting the future we can never be certain, but we still want a sense of how reliable our forecasts are likely to be. A selection of ways of assessing forecast accuracy is presented. This is somewhat of a standalone chapter, but highly recommended if you ever wish, or need, to forecast the future.

Chapter 16: Discriminant analysis

Level: Advanced

Our objective in this chapter is to classify cases (such as customers) based on a set of predictor variables. There are some similarities to, but also differences from, multiple regression in

Chapter 14. For convenience we make use of a software package called SPSS to run discriminant analysis (as we will in Chapters 17 and 18). Whenever a model classifies a case, there is a risk of misclassification. We consider how errors may differ in terms of their severity, so comparing the predictive accuracy of different models should take into account the different error rates.

Chapter 17: Factor analysis

Level: Advanced

Factor analysis is one of two types of data reduction (the other is cluster analysis in Chapter 18). We seek to exploit the interdependencies (correlations) found among a set of observed variables to extract the underlying factors or 'constructs'. By their nature, factors are quite 'fuzzy', so we have to work hard to find a practical interpretation for any extracted factors.

Chapter 18: Cluster analysis

Level: Intermediate

This chapter is concerned with another form of data reduction, this time looking for naturally occurring groups called clusters. A natural application is that of market segmentation, identifying similar groups of consumers who share some common attributes. Analytically, cluster analysis is quite straightforward. Using SPSS, we look to 'merge' cases that are sufficiently similar, or 'homogeneous'. Profiling of clusters simply makes use of descriptive statistics, as introduced in Chapter 2.

Chapter 19: Constrained optimisation models

Level: Advanced

You are reading this sentence as you are deciding which chapters of this text to study. You will likely be time-constrained, so you want to make the best use of your time. This chapter looks at how to make the 'best' or 'optimal' decision subject to at least one constraint being imposed. We will focus on the product mix problem where a manufacturer has to decide production levels subject to certain constraints. We deep-dive into sensitivity analysis reports to judge how sensitive the optimal solution is to changes in the model. We use Excel Solver, and see an interesting marketing application in the form of conjoint analysis.

Chapter 20: Monte Carlo simulation

Level: Advanced

Simulation models provide a safe space for experimentation. Each simulation, or scenario, results in one or more outputs. We introduce randomness into the system by modelling the input variables as random variables following probability distributions (which links with Chapter 5). We simulate multiple possible future worlds, resulting in a distribution of outcomes, for which we can then form an expectation of the future and quantify the risk of bad outcomes. A suitable final chapter!

ONLINE RESOURCES

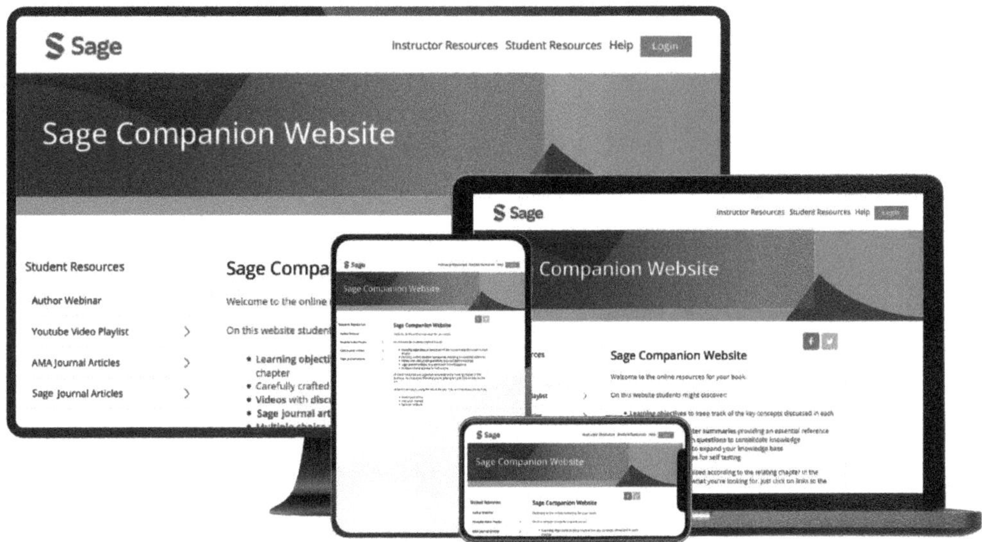

Visit **https://study.sagepub.com/abdey** to access a range of online resources that have been carefully developed to aid study and support teaching. *Business Analytics* is accompanied by:

For students

- **Excel examples** and **datasets** to help you master your analytics skills through hands-on learning.
- **Screencasts** of worked examples from Excel and Tableau demonstrating how the programs can be used.

For lecturers

- A **Teaching Guide** providing ideas and inspiration for using the book in teaching, including tips for helping students to grasp tricky concepts.
- **Solutions** for all end-of-chapter exercises.
- **PowerPoint Decks** for each chapter, which can be adapted and edited to suit individual teaching needs.
- A **Testbank** of questions that can be used to assess students' understanding and help them to prepare for exams.

All resources are available for easy upload to your **LMS** or **VLE**. Visit **https://study.sagepub.com/abdey** for more details.

1

DECISION-MAKING UNDER UNCERTAINTY

Chapter contents

Chapter level: *Beginner*

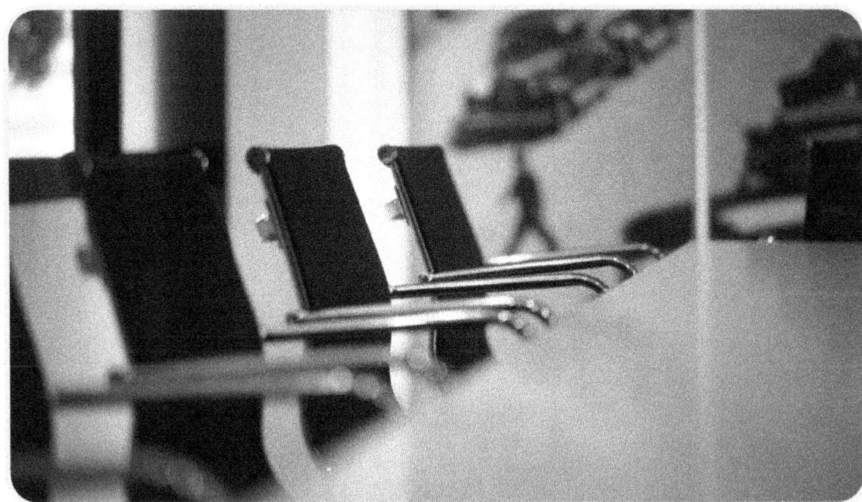

Source: Photo by @michaelfousert via Unsplash.

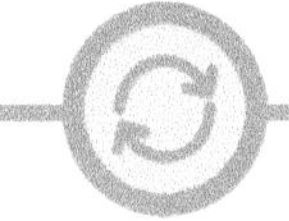

Key concepts

- Decisions
- Uncertainty
- Models

Chapter value

Appreciate that decisions are made under uncertainty, and hence are risky.

Key takeaway

A model is a deliberate simplification of reality.

Chapter outline

Welcome, Business Analytics Superstars! We begin by considering decision-making under uncertainty. Decisions are taken in the present, with uncertain future outcomes. In business, decision-making is problematic precisely because the outcomes of decisions are unknown at the time the decision is made. Will the advertising campaign be successful? Will a revamped website boost online sales? Will a start-up acquisition add value to justify the purchase price? Decisions, decisions.

To assist us, we construct *models* to simplify the (very complex) real world, hopefully retaining the most important aspects of reality such that we do not depart from reality too much. Decision-making involves perpetual trade-offs, such as our need to balance simplicity with reality. Resolving such trade-offs typically requires a degree of judgement, which can be subjective.

Learning outcomes

After completing this chapter, you should be able to:

- describe how decisions taken in the present have uncertain future outcomes
- think about how data-driven models can have a tangible impact on managerial decision-making
- discuss the features of a good model, in that it should achieve maximum simplicity with only a minimal departure from reality.

1.1 INTRODUCTION

To study, or not to study? To invest, or not to invest? To marry, or not to marry?

Also, 'To *p*, or not to *p*?', my PhD thesis - a guaranteed cure for insomnia! Have difficulty sleeping? Simply download and start reading. Deep sleep guaranteed within 60 seconds. http://etheses.lse.ac.uk/31/

For those curious, '*p*-values' are useful probabilities used in the pursuit of evidence in data. More on these statistical gems in Chapter 10.

These, among others, are decisions many of us face during our lives. Of course, decisions must be taken in the present, but the outcomes of those decisions lie in an uncertain future.

Presumably, we would always wish to make the best decision among the set of all possible alternatives. However, what do we mean by 'best'? The term needs to be qualified in the context of the decision at hand. To answer this, we would need to specify the objectives(s) that we are trying to optimise. This could be, for example, ***maximising*** the return on an investment, or predicting future sales while ***minimising*** the prediction error. Note that an *optimisation* problem is not always a maximisation problem, it could be a minimisation problem. 'Good' things – like market share – are desirable (hence maximisation), while 'bad' things – like losses – are undesirable (hence minimisation).

In practice, our decisions have to be made subject to one or more *constraints*. A classic example which we all face is what to do with our time. Each of us has only 24 hours in a day for which our objective may be to maximise productivity – or perhaps maximise our leisure time, in retirement at least. The more constraints we face, the more restricted our set of possible decisions becomes. Chapter 19 showcases how to work with 'constrained optimisation models'. Fun stuff.

1.2 UNCERTAINTY: FRIEND OR FOE?

Chance is what makes life worth living – if everything was known in advance, imagine the disappointment! Never an element of (good or bad) surprise. If decision-makers had *perfect information* about the future as well as the present and the past, there would be no need to consider the concept of uncertainty and the act of decision-making would be straightforward. (There would also be no need for this book, so I have a vested interest in uncertainty existing. QED.) However, it is usually the case that uncertainty cannot be eliminated and hence its presence should be recognised and used in the process of making decisions.

So, uncertainty makes life exciting. Think about every time your heart beats a little faster when an unexpectedly positive event happens (like winning the lottery).

Gambling, whether playing a lottery or high-rolling it in a casino, is statistically *not* an optimal decision due to the 'house edge'! Media outlets are all too keen to report on jackpot winners shedding happy tears, but less keen to report on the (far more numerous) non-winners shedding sad tears.

Businesses crave certainty in their decision-making, so uncertainty frustrates managerial decisions.

In the workplace, for example, making decisions is the most important task for any executive or manager. However, it is arguably also the toughest and riskiest activity. Bad decisions can damage a business, a reputation, even a career – sometimes irreparably and irrevocably. Just ask (the late, so perhaps don't ask) Bernie Madoff, master of the Ponzi scheme – until he got caught. Good decisions, by contrast, can result in that sought-after promotion, a strong reputation, and making money – I would expect with a high *probability* that making money is one of your motivations for studying business analytics! Of course, money is not necessarily the only variable we may be interested in maximising in life. (Yeah, right.) Nonetheless, *in*come could be a natural *out*come variable from your pursuit of this field!

Most of you reading this book will likely be pursuing a degree (a realistic *assumption*). Think back to when you were submitting your university or business school applications, when no doubt you were stressing over your personal statements! As you considered your university options you faced *opportunity costs*, a term beloved by economists. You could only enrol in one degree programme at one institution. You could not take multiple degrees at the same time (dual-degree programmes aside), so you had to decide *which* discipline to study and *where* to study. Some career destinations may require a certain type of degree. For example, if you want to become a (medical) doctor (I'm one of those fake PhD 'doctors') you will need to study medicine, whereas if you aspire to appear splashed on the cover of a business magazine as one of the latest '30 under 30' (or some other 'n under n', for a suitable integer n) entrepreneurs or corporate gurus, then a business analytics degree would seem more appropriate.

A degree is not just for three or four years, a degree is for life. It will be on your CV/résumé for the rest of your career. So, your choices of institution and discipline(s) are probably among the most important and life-defining decisions you have made to date (to study, or not to study). However, did you make the *right* decision? 'Well, James, it depends' – warning, I offer this as an answer to many questions, mainly because things in life are often *conditional* on other things!

To judge whether you have made the right decision, we would need to establish the best metric(s) to judge success. Clearly, there are many benefits to study – gaining knowledge about the world, expanding your network through your classmates, etc. – but realistically I would expect most of you to judge success in monetary terms. Your career lifetime earnings would be an obvious (and, in time, observable) metric to quantify your return on investment (degrees are rarely free, as universities love tuition fees – students love tuition fees less). That said, even this is arguably fraught with difficulty. For example, is it possible to attribute *all* of your earnings to your degree? Would you really have earned no money without a degree? What if you had studied a different subject, or attended a different university? Even if we ignored these issues, you would have to wait a very long time to *know* your lifetime earnings. So, how would we judge the quality of your degree decision today?

In short, we can't with certainty. Indeed, x months or years ago when deciding which of (possibly several) offers of admission to accept, you were having to commit to a programme of study (with the associated time, cost and effort) without certainty about what the payoff would be. Did you make this decision arbitrarily? Unlikely. Did you research the employment statistics and destinations of previous graduates of your programme? Hopefully!

'Do as I say, not as I do' is an appropriate proverb here. Ever the rebel, I decided not to heed my own advice when choosing whether to pursue a PhD in Economics *or* a PhD in Statistics. I was torn. So, to decide I resorted to *flipism* - a pseudo-philosophy of life whereby you make the most important decisions by flipping a (fair!) coin - credit to Donald Duck. 'Economics' was 'heads' and 'Statistics' was 'tails'. I got tails, and the rest is history. True story.

As we shall see, the past should not be considered a perfect predictor of the future, but by its very nature all data collected reflect the past. So, since we have no future data (yet) the past at least offers *some* indication of what we might expect to happen in the uncertain future. If your predecessors on your degree had a *median* salary of x (meaning 50% of graduates had salaries greater than or equal to x (i.e. $\geq x$) and the other 50% had salaries less than or equal to x (i.e. $\leq x$)) then this could form the basis of your personal expectation of your salary after you graduate. Of course, it is likely that many factors contribute to your salary (grades achieved, sector you work in, job role, country, etc.) and incorporating these would likely allow us to come up with a more accurate prediction.

We will formally define the *median* in Chapter 2 as a measure of central tendency. Compared with the *mean*, the median is often preferred to summarise income since it is a heavily positively skewed distribution, with a long right-hand 'tail', such that the median is less sensitive to *outliers*.

In summary, we cannot be *certain* today about whether your decision to study a particular programme will ultimately be vindicated, but the (circumstantial) data evidence out there would indicate that you are increasing your *probability* of success! More on this later.

Inevitably, discussions of money will feature heavily in the chapters ahead if we assume, for simplicity, a profit-maximising company (a favourite phrase of economists) as business owners (whether private or, in the case of public companies, shareholders) will want the managerial decision-makers to act in the best interests of the owners. Okay, in public companies there is always a risk of moral hazard in corporate governance, that is to say, non-aligned interests of managers who are obsessed with empire building or pocketing bonuses in the short run versus the shareholder owners who demand long-run profitability, although such risks can be mitigated with suitable remuneration packages such as stock options with possibly a delayed period before execution to disincentivise myopic, or short-sighted, decisions.

1.3 MODERN DECISION-MAKING

Decision-making should be viewed as a process where the decision-maker is faced with a problem or decision with *at least* two possible (but uncertain) outcomes. 'Possible' in the sense that each outcome can occur with a strictly positive *probability*, meaning a probability greater than zero (or > 0%). 'Uncertain' in the sense that no outcome is certain to occur, meaning each has a probability strictly less than one (or < 100%). The outcomes of interest are those of one or more **dependent variables**. These dependent variables *depend* (hence the name!) on a combination of **independent variables** that can be divided into:

Internal, or controllable, variables, that are under your control (in that you can decide on the levels or values of these)

External, or uncontrollable, variables, that are not under your control (in that the levels or values of these are determined by external forces). These can be summarised as situational factors.

Example 1.1

In marketing, decisions often relate to one or more of the **four Ps**, known as the marketing mix variables:

Product - what the business is selling (which could be a tangible good, or intangible service). 'Product' can comprise aspects such as the product's design, attributes, new product testing, product improvement, packaging and warranties.

Price - what price to sell at and whether to offer a discount. 'Price' can be considered an indicator of a product's quality (the adage 'you get what you pay for'), but also subject to price elasticity of demand and competitors' prices.

Placement - the provision of customer access and convenience. 'Placement' involves decisions such as the distribution channel, logistics and franchising.

Promotion - the choice of marketing communications. 'Promotion' involves decisions about advertising channels, frequency and mix of promotion types.

Figure 1.1 shows a flow chart linking the marketing mix variables (under the control of the decision-maker) with some high-level *situational factors* and some illustrative examples of possible dependent variables of interest split between *behavioural* and *performance measures*. Note that the arrows indicate what affects what. In particular, note the *interdependency* which is likely to exist between the controllable and uncontrollable variables. For example, actions by your competitors about their prices may then influence your price decisions when consumers face similar goods (known as substitute goods); also, your pricing decisions may then influence your competitors' behaviour. In due course, we will be able to model such *interactions*.

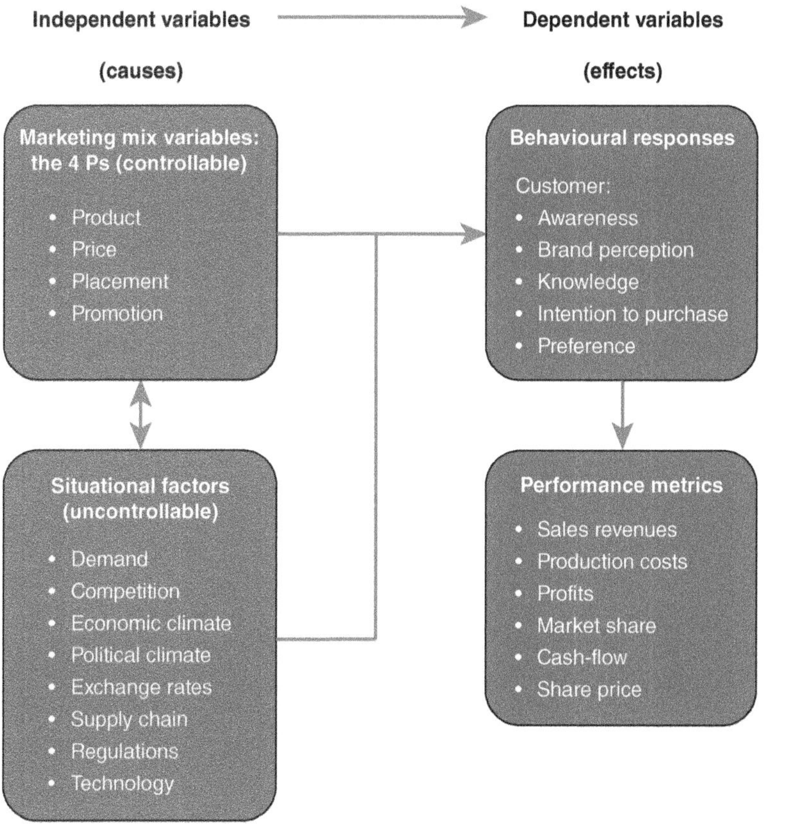

Figure 1.1 Flow chart illustrating the relationships between independent and dependent variables.

This strategic interaction will be considered in Chapter 6 through *game theory*, which looks at strategic decisions between two or more decision-makers (a bit like playing chess). With this exception of bilateral and multilateral decisions, the rest of our decision-making will be unilateral, that is, a single decision-maker acting in isolation. For example, you!

1.4 ADVANCES IN TECHNOLOGY

Recent advances in technology have resulted in two important consequences for individuals and businesses in terms of decision-making.

- The rate of collection of digital data has opened up the era of *big data*.
- Access to technology has allowed more people to be empowered to analyse data and make *data-driven decisions*.

While estimates vary, it is possible that the amount of data collected digitally could be doubling every 2-3 years. Depending on the length of your degree programme, it is possible that by the time of your graduation the amount of new data generated throughout your degree could exceed all data recorded in human history prior to your registration!

Big data, big potential, big business.

Extrapolating, we can confidently predict that the amount of data collected will continue to increase (albeit with uncertainty about the *rate* of increase). Businesses are increasingly realising that data-driven decisions represent a source of competitive advantage. Data-driven business decisions can help drive increases in productivity and profitability. The more competitive the industry, the tighter are profit margins, so any competitive edge becomes even more sought-after.

Today, the demand for people with quantitative skills far exceeds supply, creating a skills deficit. With demand set to increase further, and supply failing to keep pace with demand, any Economics 101 course will tell you that the price increases whenever demand exceeds supply. Of course, the 'price' being referred to here is that of an employee – the salary which quantitative staff can command (already high) is set to rise even further, which is good news for you!

1.5 DATA: THE NEW OIL?

The Economist magazine once postulated that 'the world's most valuable resource is no longer oil, but data'. The thesis was that the application of data in business decisions amounted to 'the new oil'. As a result, the phrase 'data is the new oil' emerged.

Analogies are rarely perfect. Viewing data like oil fails to acknowledge that oil is a *finite* natural resource, while (big) data is near *infinite*. Nonetheless, the analogy does hold up well from another perspective. Crude oil, as extracted direct from the ground, is of limited value. Only after it has been *refined* (into aviation fuel, petrol, etc.) does it gain significant value.

The same can be said of data: the requirement for *refinement*. Raw data, in and of itself full of noise, is also of limited value. Only after the data has been effectively processed, through analysis and 'making sense' of it, does it become truly valuable. Hence our objectives are to transform data into information, and ultimately knowledge and insights which can then inform our wise decision-making.

More formally, we should think about the DIKW pyramid, as shown in Figure 1.2. The pyramid models the conversion of data into information, from which we gain knowledge, leading to our enlightenment with wisdom. In each chapter of this book, we seek to make wise decisions, with their origins drawn from data.

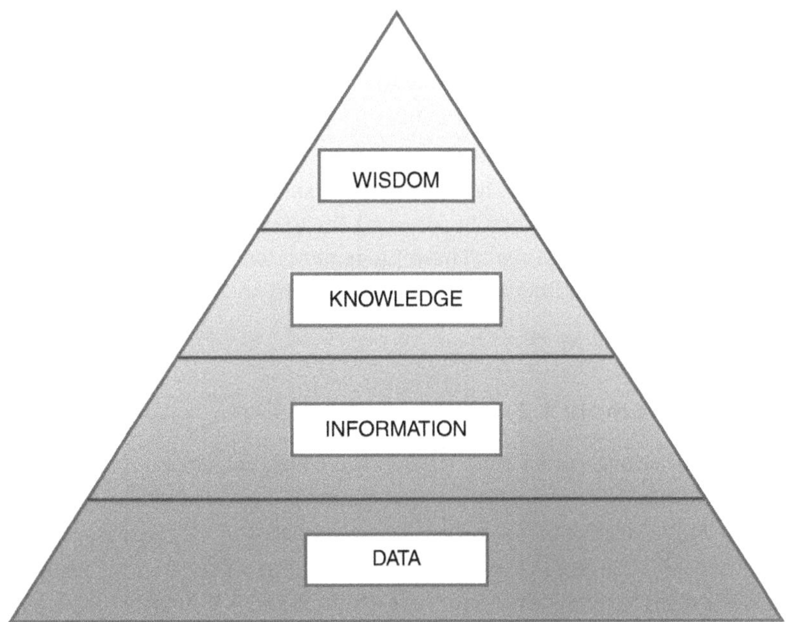

Figure 1.2 The DIKW pyramid.

1.6 QUALITATIVE VERSUS QUANTITATIVE ANALYSIS

As one of the main marketing mix variables, setting the price of your product is an important task. Suppose your company has designed a new version of an existing successful product and wishes to launch it on the market. What price should the company charge?

To keep things simple, suppose this is a small-ticket item, such that the company could sell it for any price from £10 up to £40, in increments of £5. In practice, a more granular set of prices would be feasible, down to the nearest unit of currency, such as down to increments of £0.01.

A price of £39.99 has the psychological benefit of 'appearing' much less expensive than a price tag of £40. Such *charm pricing* creates the illusion of a bargain! However, how much additional happiness would you really gain from, say, *one* penny sweet?

We need to determine the relevant criteria to judge the relative merits of these alternative prices using either a *qualitative* analysis, or a *quantitative* one, or – most likely – a combination of the two (adopting a quantitative approach with qualitative insights, such as *market intelligence*). In a qualitative analysis, the factors which are thought to influence the consumer's 'to buy, or not to buy?' decision would be listed and evaluated ahead of a final decision being taken. In a quantitative analysis, the factors are in numerical form and analysed to inform the decision.

1.6.1 Qualitative analysis

Taking a qualitative approach, suppose the previous version of the product was launched at a price of £20, and retailers reported selling their entire stock on the first day it was offered for sale. Treating this first-day sellout as a signal of excess demand, we decide to choose a higher price point for the new product. Fair enough, but by *how much* should we increase the price – by 50% to £30, or by 100% to £40? On what basis would you argue for a specific increase?

By brainstorming and listing all variables managers consider relevant to the price-setting problem, management can qualitatively judge how each variable could affect the outcome of interest (such as sales revenues or total profits) by assessing the expected influence on the outcome as, say, 'positive', 'neutral' or 'negative'. These judgements would then be considered by the decision-maker ahead of executing the decision. These steps are summarised in Figure 1.3.

Example 1.2

Let us set up a qualitative analysis for our price-setting problem. For simplicity, assume that there are only two factors that will affect profitability, and hence the price: (i) the manufacturing cost, and (ii) advertising expenditure. Relative to the previous launch (at £20 with the product sold out on the first retail day), the changes in the levels of (i) and (ii) are classified as 'increase', 'no change' or 'decrease'. With three classifications for both factors, there are a total of $3 \times 3 = 9$ possible combinations of levels of the two factors. We could visualise these using a simple decision tree, as shown in Figure 1.4, using the previous selling price of £20 as a starting point.

Since the manufacturing cost is likely to be known by the company, and its advertising expenditure is under its control (a form of promotion, one of the four Ps), then if, for example, production costs increased (perhaps due to supply chain disruption), with no change to advertising (due to the high demand last time), the decision-maker might settle on a price of £30. Note that for this scenario a price range of £25–£35 is indicated. So, why £30 and not £25 or £35?

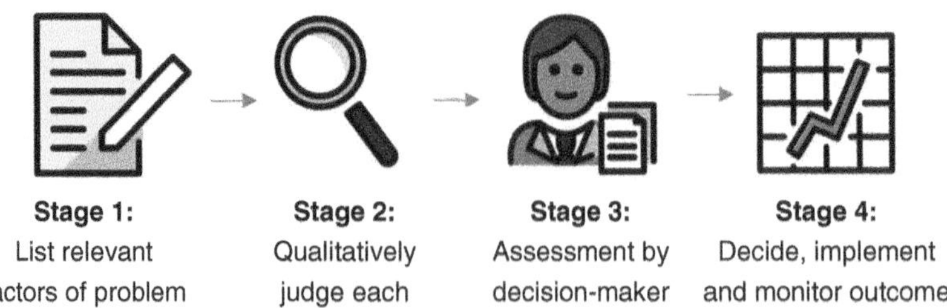

Figure 1.3 Stages in qualitative analysis.

With an increase in manufacturing cost, the company would be keen to pass this cost on to the consumer, rather than absorbing the cost internally. The 'increase' in manufacturing cost does not tell us the monetary value of the cost increase. The greater the increase, the higher we would wish to set the price to preserve our profit margin. However, our ability to pass any cost increase on to the consumer in full would depend on the *price elasticity of demand* of the 'typical' consumer - something our naïve model has failed to incorporate.

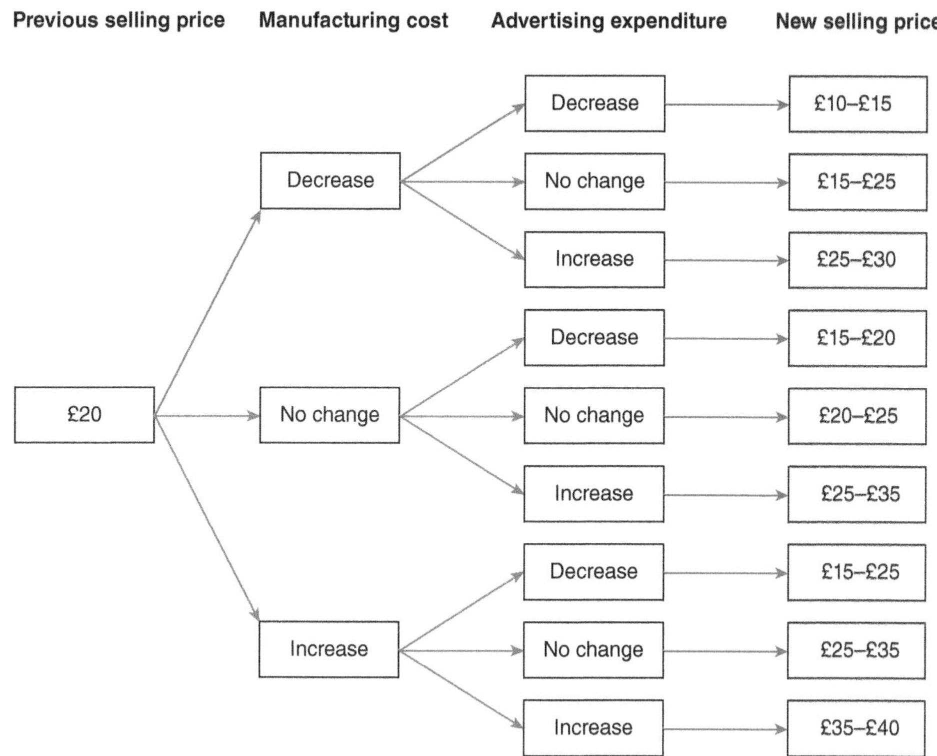

Figure 1.4 Decision tree for a qualitative approach to the price-setting decision.

As well as the naïvety of the model in Example 1.2, the qualitative approach in general is inevitably affected by the judgemental biases of the decision-makers. Such a 'gut instinct' approach to decision-making can, of course, result in 'good' or even optimal outcomes *occasionally*, but can be expected to be sub-optimal in the long run.

1.6.2 Quantitative analysis

Turning to a quantitative approach, our analysis would begin with asking pertinent questions such as:

- What is known about current market demand for this type of product?
- What is known about the competitive landscape?
- How and where will the product be manufactured?
- How much will it cost in advertising to launch the product?

This list is not collectively exhaustive, but market demand, the level of competition, production and advertising costs would be expected to be some of the most important factors in the context of a price-setting decision.

More generally, when faced with any decision, we need to establish what are considered to be the most important independent variables. Recall that these are either *internal* (under the decision-maker's control, such as factor inputs like labour and capital equipment) or *external* (outside the decision-maker's control, such as market demand and the competitive landscape). Combining the independent variables allows us to determine *expected outcomes*.

How do we assess which are the relevant independent variables? While not necessarily always straightforward, in practice we can appeal to basic economic theory (such as relationships governed by the law of demand, markets for substitutes, as well as the type of market structure, i.e. whether the company is a monopoly, or competing in an oligopoly – meaning a small number of dominant firms – or in a perfectly competitive environment), judgement and experience. Because of the cumulative effect the independent variables have on the outcome, it is important to give due thought and consideration to these.

Having determined the list of preliminary factors that you are confident would affect the outcome variable(s), you then need to ask:

- What do we know already?
- What data can be 'mined' to better understand the nature of the effect each factor exerts on the outcome?

Using a combination of mathematical and statistical techniques (introduced in subsequent chapters), we seek to model predictive relationships among the set of variables, the possible outcomes of interest, and, ultimately, the decision that needs to be taken.

Example 1.3

Revisiting our price-setting dilemma, now we take a quantitative approach.

We already know that the previous product launch immediately sold out at a price of £20. Given this starting point, a quantitative understanding of how each relevant factor influences the price would allow a data-driven decision to be reached. Having sourced relevant data, we could then address the following questions:

- Based on experience, has greater advertising expenditure led to higher sales?
- If so, was the increase linear or nonlinear?
- Did the relationship change over time?
- Was the return on advertising expenditure positive?
- What is the (estimated) probability that a customer would buy the new product instead of a close substitute?
- Does the probability vary across different customer segments or demographic groups?
- How sensitive are sales forecasts to different price points?
- Is there a seasonal effect evident in past sales?
- What is the best way to visualise and communicate the relevant data to the decision-maker?

To answer such questions, we need to define mathematically the relationships we suspect exist using a *model* – a deliberate simplification of reality. Typically, these models will involve one or more *parameters* – for example, the sensitivity of one variable to another – which will need to be estimated using our collected data. Next, the *statistical* significance (and *practical* significance) of the parameter estimates will need to be examined. A rigorous assessment of these relationships then allows you to articulate the results and/or consequences of the decision being made quantitatively.

1.7 UNCERTAINTY IN THE NEWS

'*News*' is not '*olds*'. News reports and articles disseminate new information about events taking place in the world – ignoring fake news, of course!

Especially in business news, you will find numerous reports discussing the many uncertainties currently being faced by business. While uncertainty certainly(!) makes life exciting, remember that it makes decision-making particularly challenging. Should a firm increase production? Advertise? Cut back? Merge?

We have already noted that decisions are made in the present, with uncertain future outcomes. Hence many media reports will comment on the uncertainties being faced.

Of course, some eras are more uncertain and volatile than others. As Lenin said: 'There are decades where nothing happens; and there are weeks where decades happen.'

Indeed, 2016 was arguably the year of the black swan – low-probability, high-impact events apparent only with the benefit of hindsight (or perhaps the grey rhino, if you feel the events were predictable in advance) – with the UK's referendum vote on its membership of the European Union (EU) and the US presidential election being the main geopolitical stories that year.[1] The ultimate outcomes of a vote to leave the EU and the election of Donald Trump to the White House were both deemed *improbable*, which is very different from their being *impossible*!

Both outcomes were considered unlikely (by most commentators), yet they both happened in quick succession. Some prediction markets actually priced in a 25% probability of each of these outcomes, but a simple probability calculation would equate this to tossing a fair coin twice and getting two heads – perhaps these were not such surprising results, indeed perhaps they were grey rhinos after all!

Prediction markets are often thought of in terms of sport – which team will win a match, for example. However, prediction markets exist for political outcomes, among other events. What is fascinating about the 2016 UK referendum on its EU membership and the US presidential election of the same year is the near carbon-copy of movement in the probabilities of the different possible outcomes during the hours of vote counting. In both cases the votes had binary outcomes: 'Leave' versus 'Remain', and 'Trump' versus 'Clinton'. (While other presidential candidates were on the ballot papers, in practice it was only a two-horse race between the candidates of the two major US political parties – Trump for the Republicans, and Clinton for the Democrats.)

Figure 1.5 shows comparisons of the prediction market percentage probabilities of winning during the early hours of vote counting. As Mark Twain said, 'history never repeats itself but it rhymes'. With near-perfect symmetry, this is perhaps the best example of such a dramatic

[1]And, in sport, Leicester City Football Club winning the English Premier League, defying most pundits' expectations!

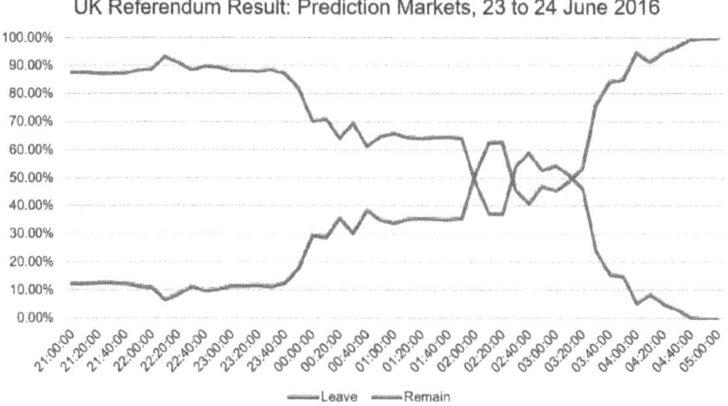

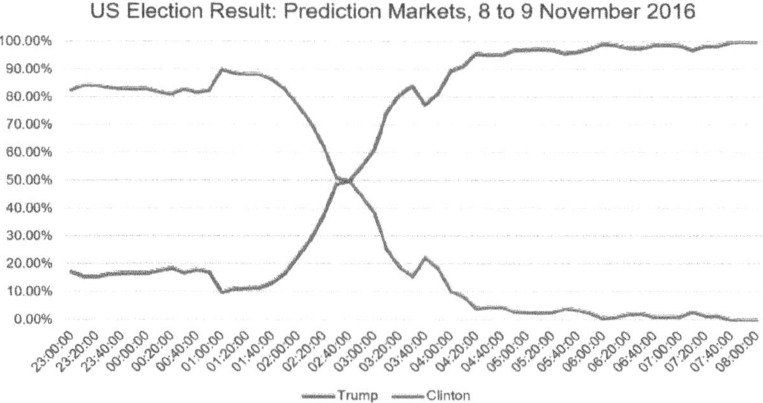

Figure 1.5 Changes in winning probabilities of Leave/Remain in the 2016 UK referendum on European Union membership (upper), and Trump/Clinton in the 2016 US presidential election (lower), based on prediction markets during the early hours of vote counting.

reversal of (political) fortunes in a matter of just a few hours. Note that the probabilities of the respective outcomes changed *upon receipt of new information* – here the continual reporting of counted ballots during the early hours after polling stations closed. Going into the close of polls, Remain and Clinton had probabilities of over 80% of victory (and hence Leave and Trump were both below 20%, as the respective combined probabilities must sum to 100%). Within just a few hours the view changed to a 50:50 split, and we all know the ultimate outcomes in each case by (very) early morning!

While these represent political examples, both votes were of major significance for business. Outcomes of political polls affect the tax, legal and regulatory environments in which businesses must operate. For example, the UK's departure from the EU ('Brexit') has had a huge impact on UK–EU trade arrangements. Indeed, immediately after the June 2016 referendum result was known, uncertainty arose about exactly what 'Brexit' meant. Exiting the single market? Exiting the customs union? Or perhaps it was as simple as 'Brexit means Brexit' according to the tautological former UK prime minister, Theresa May.

Financial markets, in particular, tend to be very sensitive to news. Even stories reporting comments from influential people, such as politicians, can move markets – sometimes dramatically!

Example 1.4

In early October 2016, there was a 'flash crash' of the UK pound following comments by the then president of France, François Hollande, who demanded 'tough Brexit negotiations' (he probably said it in French, *n'est ce pas*?). This negative sentiment (from the UK's perspective) caused a reaction in foreign exchange markets such that GBP fell by as much as 6% against the US dollar to $1.1841, which is a huge movement in exchange rate terms.

The root cause of the dramatic change was not immediately clear, although speculation was that a main driver was automated trading systems programmed to sell sterling if negative news stories about Brexit were discovered.

Increasingly, quantitative hedge funds and asset managers will trade algorithmically, with computers designed to scan the internet (known as *web scraping*) for news stories and interpret whether news reports contain any useful information which would allow a revision of probabilistic beliefs - more on this shortly when we play the 'Monty Hall' game!

Here, the demand for 'tough Brexit negotiations' by the then French president would be interpreted as being bad for the UK, which would lead to a further depreciation in the pound.

So, from now on, when you read (or listen to) the news, keep an eye out for (or ear open to) the word 'uncertainty' and consider what kinds of decisions are being made in the face of uncertainty. Relatedly, any reference to 'expectations' should be interpreted as what people (or the market) *think* will happen. Note that while expectations can be met, they are often either exceeded or not reached at all!

1.8 SIMPLICITY VERSUS COMPLEXITY - THE NEED FOR MODELS

A question for you. Is the real world:

(a) nice, easy and simple?
(b) nasty, difficult and complicated?

Answer: (b), but we wish it was (a)!

Although we care about the real world, seek to understand it, and make decisions in it, we have an inherent dislike of complexity. Indeed, in the world of the social sciences (studying the behaviour and decision-making of people) the real world is a highly complex web of interdependencies between countless variables.

For example, in economics, what determines the economic performance of a country? From national income accounting in Economics 101 you might say consumption, investment, government spending and net exports. But what affects, say, consumption? Consumer confidence? Perhaps, but what drives consumer confidence? Consumers' incomes? Consumers' inflation expectations? Fears of job insecurity? Perceived level of economic competency of the government? The weather? ...

So, in order to make any sense of the real world, we will inevitably have to *simplify reality*. Our tool for achieving this is a **model**.

Definition: A model

A model is a deliberate simplification of reality.

A *good* model retains the most important features of reality and ignores less important details. Immediately we see that we face a *trade-off* (a bit like an opportunity cost in Economics 101). The *benefit* of a model is that we simplify the complex real world. The *cost* of a model is that by simplifying reality we engineer a departure from reality. Broadly speaking, we would be happy if the benefit exceeded the cost, that is, if the simplicity made it easier for us to understand and analyse the real world while incurring only a minimal departure from reality.

1.8.1 Metro maps

The world-famous London Underground map is an excellent example of a model for getting people from point A to point B. Figure 1.6 shows a 1994 version of the London Underground network, with the familiar 'linear' landscape comprised of horizontal, vertical and 45-degree lines.

The map contains the most important pieces of information for reaching your intended destination:

- distinct names and colours for each line
- the order of stations on each line
- the interchange stations between lines

while less important details are ignored, such as:

- the depth of each tunnel
- the exact distance between stations
- the nonlinear nature of the tunnels under the ground.

Of course, an engineer would likely need to know these 'less important details' for tunnel maintenance, but for a tourist visiting London such information is superfluous and the map is very much fit for purpose. However, we said above that a model is a departure from reality, hence some caution should always be exercised when using a model. Blind belief in a model might be misleading. For example, the map in Figure 1.6 fails to accurately represent the precise geographic location of stations.

Figure 1.6 The London Underground map from 1994.

Source: © TfL from the London Transport Museum collection

Also, even line names can be a model – the Circle line (in yellow) is clearly not a true circle! Does it matter? Well, the Circle line forms a loop, and it is an easy name to remember, so arguably here the loop-related simplification of the name outweighs the slight departure in reality from a true circle!

Example 1.5

You are a tourist visiting London. What is the quickest route from Holborn to Temple? Should you go by Underground or walk?

Answer: Walk! However, Figure 1.6 suggests these two stations are far apart (can you locate them?). Geographic accuracy has been sacrificed, distorting the true distance between stations.

If we look at a geographically accurate map (Figure 1.7), we see that the map in Figure 1.6 can be very misleading in terms of where stations are located relative to each other.

Our key takeaway is that models inevitably involve trade-offs. As we further simplify reality (a benefit), we further depart from reality (a cost). In order to determine whether or not a model is sufficiently 'good', we must decide whether the benefit justifies the cost. Resolving this cost–benefit trade-off can be subjective – further adding to life's complexities.

Which representation of the London Underground do you prefer, Figure 1.6 or Figure 1.7? How important is it for the map to be geographically accurate? Could you improve on either map?

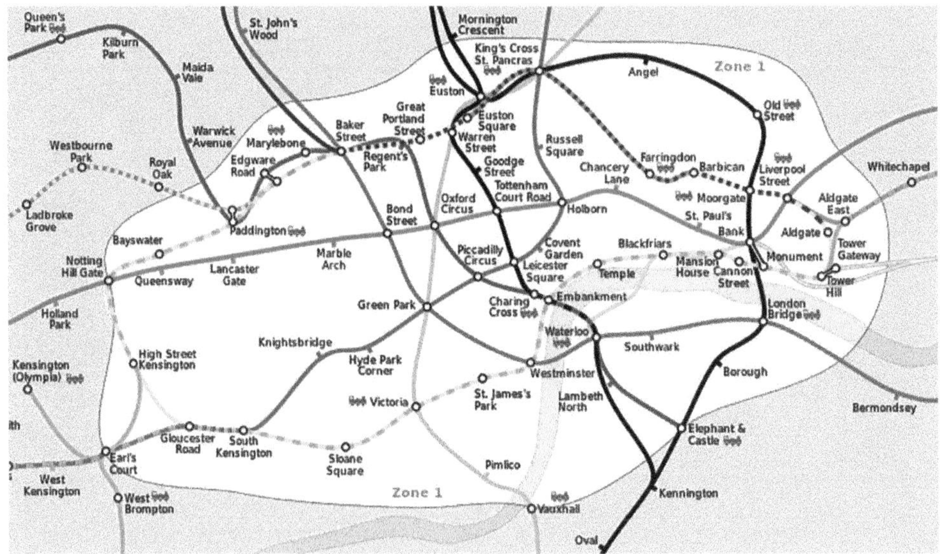

Figure 1.7 A geographically accurate London Underground map (Zone 1).

1.9 MODEL ASSUMPTIONS

We have defined a model to be a deliberate simplification of reality. To assist with the process of model building, we often make assumptions – usually *simplifying* assumptions.

Returning to the London Underground map, the Circle line (in yellow) is not a perfect geometric circle, but here it is reasonable to assume the line behaves like a circle as it does go round in a loop (as does a circle). So, adopting the name 'Circle line' assumes its path closely approximates a circle. I do not think anyone would seriously suggest the name 'Circle line' is inappropriate or particularly misleading!

Moving to statistical models, we make various kinds of assumptions. One such type is that of *distributional assumptions*, where we assume a particular probability distribution (a concept introduced in Chapter 5) for a particular variable. Data-driven models involve variables whose distributions take various 'shapes' (although not shapes like a circle, triangle or square!). By way of introduction, we explore some initial examples.

1.9.1 Probability distributions

'Probability' is our mechanism for quantifying uncertainty, allowing us to determine probabilities of various 'events' occurring – such as the probability that our sales decrease, or the probability that our cost of capital decreases, which can then inform our decision-making (whether we need to issue a profit warning, or whether we should borrow to invest). In Chapter 5 we will formally meet several common probability distributions which can be used in business modelling. One such distribution is the *Poisson distribution*, which is useful for modelling arrivals of customers (perhaps looking at footfall in a retail store, or the number of customer service enquiries received at a telephone call centre).

An example of Poisson probabilities is given in Figure 1.8. Here, the probability of receiving more than 6 customer enquiries per minute is less than 5%, which could be useful when making a decision about staffing levels at a call centre – assuming telephone enquiries are queued and dealt with by humans rather than an automated service!

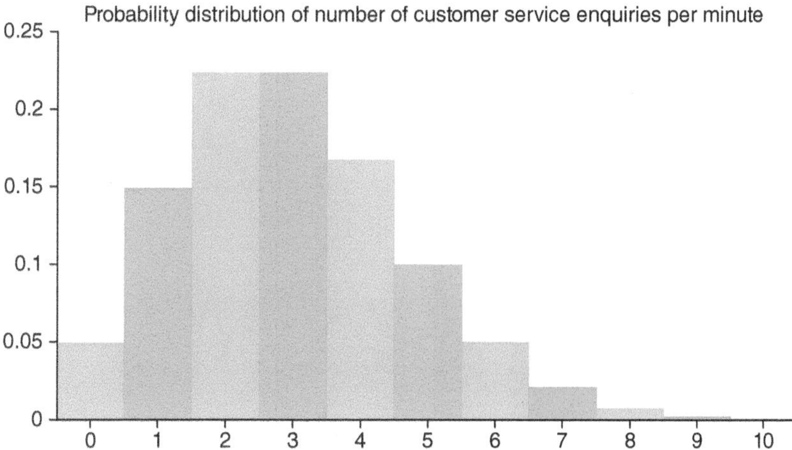

Figure 1.8 Poisson probability distribution to model volume of customer service enquiries.

1.9.2 Time-series analysis

Suppose we are interested in predicting the future – for example, the future sales of our product. This involves working with time-series data, which will be covered in detail in Chapter 15. For now, we briefly consider the example of sales forecasts shown in Figure 1.9. These illustrate *extrapolative forecasting* whereby *trends* and *seasonality* detected in historic data are projected (extrapolated) into the future. For the three client segments of 'Consumer', 'Corporate' and 'Home Office', a *linear* trend has been fitted. Clearly, this provides a very poor fit for the Consumer segment, but with some noticeable improvement for the other two segments. Note the shaded areas around the forecasts starting in 2024.

These are examples of *prediction intervals*, which provide 'error bars' to predictions, reflecting the degree of uncertainty attached to each prediction – wider bars indicate greater uncertainty.

Note that in Figure 1.9 the variable *time* (specifically the 'Order Date') is plotted on the horizontal axis (x-axis), with the sales of the respective segment on the vertical axis (y-axis). As such, we can think of 'sales' as the dependent variable and 'time' as the independent variable, hence sales are a function of time. Figure 1.9 displays a linear trend for each of three series, which is appropriate *if* there is a *linear* relationship between the dependent and independent variables.

Of course, 'time' is a very special variable in that time is never influenced by anything else. Therefore, time can often be used as a controllable variable to detect and measure *change*.

1.9.3 Regression analysis

Often, our interest is not explicitly in the time variable itself. Rather, we seek to explore the relationship(s) between two (or more) non-time variables. *If* these relationships are *linear*, then we may perform a linear regression analysis, covered in detail in Chapters 13 and 14. For now, consider Figure 1.10. This shows the sale price (in thousands, pounds sterling) of second-hand cars plotted against the cars' mileage. As we would expect, *ceteris paribus* (other things being equal) the more used a car is (the higher its mileage), the lower its second-hand retail price.

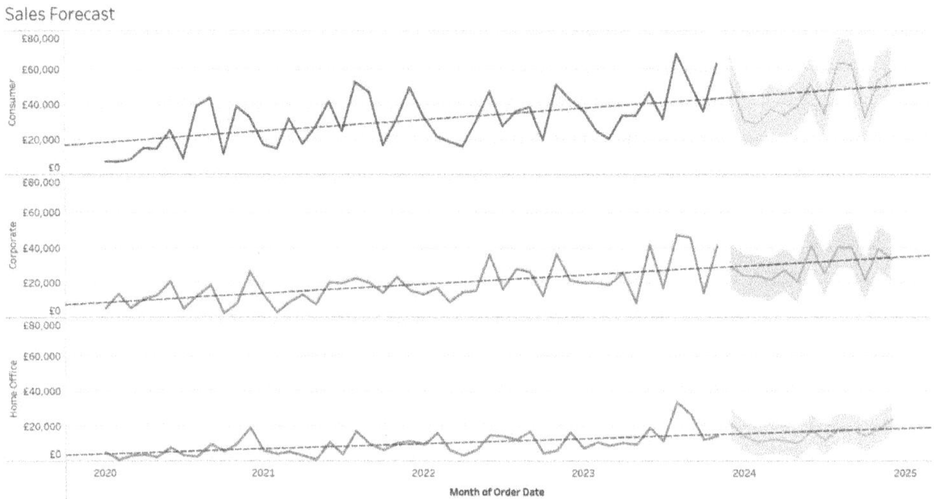

Figure 1.9 Sales forecasts, showing some evidence of trend and seasonality.

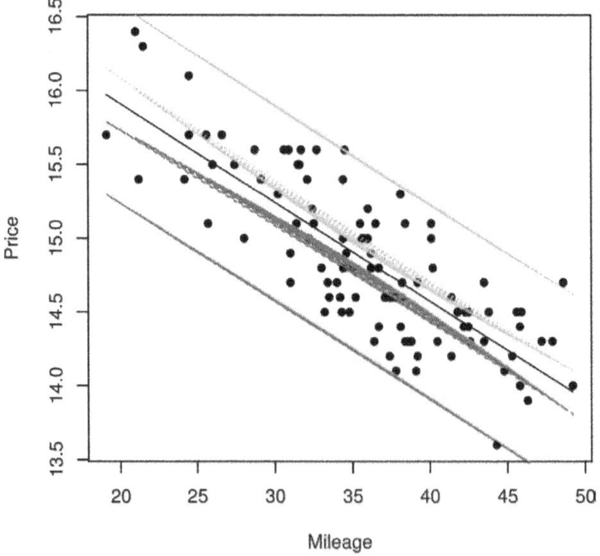

Figure 1.10 Line of best fit (black line) to relating prices and mileage of second-hand cars. The red and green limits indicate boundaries of 95% confidence intervals (inner pair) and 95% prediction intervals (outer pair) for a desired mileage value.

Definition: *Ceteris paribus*

Latin term for 'other things being equal'. This means that other things which could change are, for the moment, assumed not to. The term allows us to isolate the relationship between two variables, *controlling for* all other variables. For example, the 'demand curve' represents the effect of a price change on the quantity demanded, assuming all other determinants of demand (such as income, tastes or preferences) remain unchanged. Beware, though, that in the real world other things are rarely equal - when one variable changes there is usually a change in at least one other variable! Nevertheless, when conducting analysis, *ceteris paribus* is a very convenient way of investigating the effect of one variable on another without the complexity of worrying about other variables!

While the relationship is not perfect (relationships rarely are!), it can be well approximated by a linear relationship – see the black trend line, known as the line of best fit. ('Best' in what sense? All will be revealed in Chapter 13. Stay tuned.) The red and green lines represent two different types of interval. The inner red and green lines mark the boundaries of '95% confidence intervals' for estimating the *expected* price of a second-hand car for a given mileage. The outer red and green lines mark the boundaries of '95% prediction intervals' when estimating the *actual* price of a single second-hand car for a given mileage.

1.9.4 Normal distribution

Many of you will be familiar with the normal distribution, the well-known bell-shaped curve – which should ring a bell!

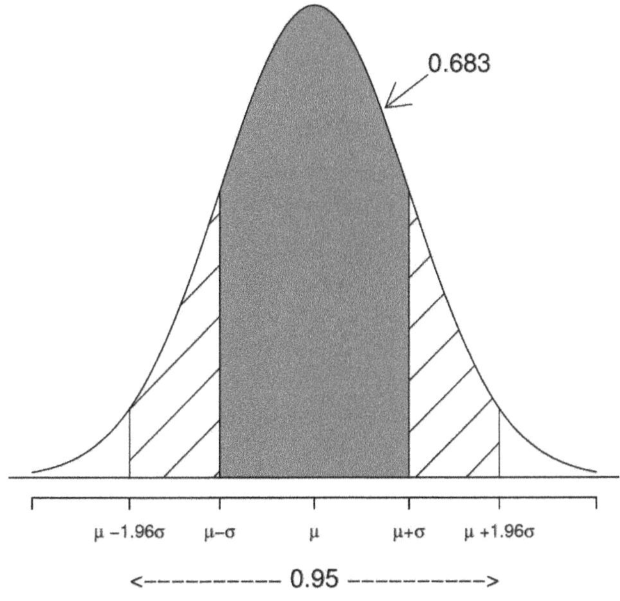

Figure 1.11 Some probabilities around the mean for the normal distribution.

The normal distribution (shown in Figure 1.11) is a popular choice of probability distribution when making distributional assumptions in modelling. For example, financial returns on assets are often assumed to be normally distributed. Under this assumption of normality, the probability of returns being *within two standard deviations of the mean* (the mean and standard deviation will be introduced formally in Chapter 2, but some of you may have encountered these terms previously) is *approximately* 95%. This means that the probability of returns being more than two standard deviations from the mean is *approximately* 5%. In Figure 1.11, the mean is denoted by μ and the standard deviation is denoted by σ. For *exactly* 95% probability, rather than *approximately* 95%, it is actually 1.96 standard deviations, as indicated in Figure 1.11.

Assuming market returns follow a normal distribution is fundamental to many models in finance, such as Markowitz's modern portfolio theory and the Black–Scholes–Merton option pricing model. However, this assumption does *not* typically reflect actual observed market returns since 'tail events', such as black swan (or even grey rhino) events – which are low-probability, high-impact events – tend to occur slightly more frequently than a normal distribution would predict!

For now, the moral of the story is to be wary of assumptions – if you make a wrong or invalid assumption, then decisions you make in good faith *may* lead to outcomes far from what you expected (remember expectations are not always met). As an example, the subprime mortgage market in the USA during the 2000s broadly assumed house prices would only ever increase – but what goes up usually comes down, at some point!

1.10 TO SWITCH, OR NOT TO SWITCH?

Congratulations, you have been selected to take part in a television game show!

This week's star prize is a brand new (electric) sports car. All you need to do to win the car is locate it behind one of three outwardly identical doors. Get it wrong, and you 'win' a sheep. Don't worry, no animals are harmed in the production of the show!

So behind one of the three doors is the car, behind the other two doors are sheep. Monty, the host of the show, knows where the car is (and hence also where the sheep are).

The rules are simple. You choose, but do not open, one of the three doors. After you have done so, Monty, who remember knows where the prize is, opens one of the two remaining doors. He always opens a door he knows will reveal a sheep, and randomly chooses which door to open when he has more than one option (which happens when your initial choice contains the car). Monty is a 'nice guy', appearing to help you by revealing a sheep, but not nice enough to help you find the car – he wants you to agonise over the choice of whether 'to switch, or not to switch?'. Cruel Monty.

After revealing a sheep, Monty gives you the choice of either switching to the other unopened door or sticking with your original choice. You then receive whatever is behind the door you choose. What should you do, assuming you want to win the car?

Note that the assumption that you want to win the car is reasonable. Even if you prefer public transport and like animals, it still pays to win the car (which is worth far more than a sheep), sell it, then buy lots of sheep! So, trying to win a sheep is a *baaad* decision!

So, consider three doors:

This is the (in)famous 'Monty Hall' problem which is a light-hearted way to begin appreciating the challenges of decision-making under uncertainty. We will solve this problem formally in Chapter 4 (using what is known as *Bayes' theorem*), but for now remember that at each round of the game you, as the player, do *not* know where the car is.

The controversy arose over the American game show *Let's Make a Deal*, and the *New York Times* (among others) devoted two pages to the problem, readers' letters, etc.

Bewildered game show players wrote to Marilyn vos Savant, an advice columnist for *Parade Magazine*, and asked for her opinion in her 'Ask Marilyn' column. Savant - who was credited by the *Guinness Book of Records* as having the highest IQ of any woman in the world (!) - gave her decision. She said, 'you should change your choice'. There then followed a long argument in the correspondence columns, some supporting Savant's decision and others saying that it was nonsense! What do you think?

To begin with, the only certainty you have is that the car must be behind one of the three doors. You may, or may not, initially chose the 'correct' door (assuming you want to win the prize!) but there is no certainty in your choice.

Without loss of generality,[2] let's assume you choose door 1. Monty is not allowed to open this door. Instead, suppose he opens door 3 to reveal, of course, a sheep.

[2]A useful expression to mean that what is assumed is arbitrary to demonstrate a specific case, but it does not affect the general result. Here we could assume you chose any of the three doors and the strategic choice of 'to switch, or not to switch?' is unaffected.

Upon revealing a sheep behind door 3, you still face uncertainty – the only certainty you have is that the car must be behind *either* door 1 *or* door 2 (door 3 has now been eliminated as a possible location of the car).

So, now it's 'make your mind up' time. To switch, or not to switch?

Well, what we would like to know is the *probability* of winning. We will formally introduce probability in Chapter 4, but for now we note the basics that probability is a number between 0 and 1, that is, defined over the *unit interval* [0, 1], which quantifies how likely an event is to occur. A *certain* event has a probability of 1; an *impossible* event has a probability of 0. All other events are 'maybe' events (which may or may not occur), becoming more likely (i.e. more probable) as the probability gets closer to 1. A simple illustration is provided in Figure 1.12.

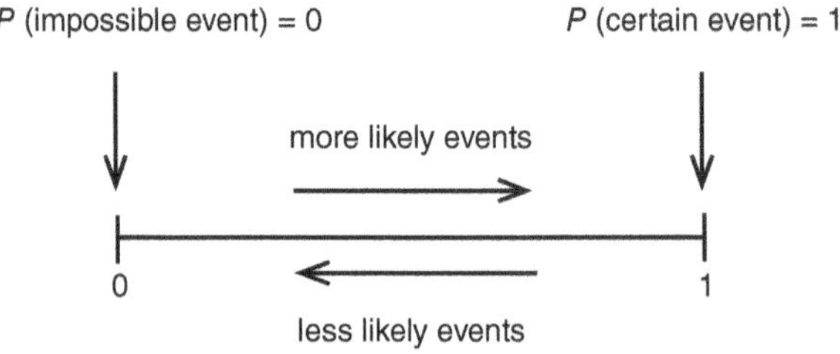

Figure 1.12 A simple illustration of probabilities.

So, let's now consider our door dilemma through a probability lens. Initially, when faced with three unopened doors, we have no information about the location of the car other than it must be behind one (and only one) of the three doors. Intuitively we attach an *equal* probability of 1/3 to the car being behind each door. Therefore:

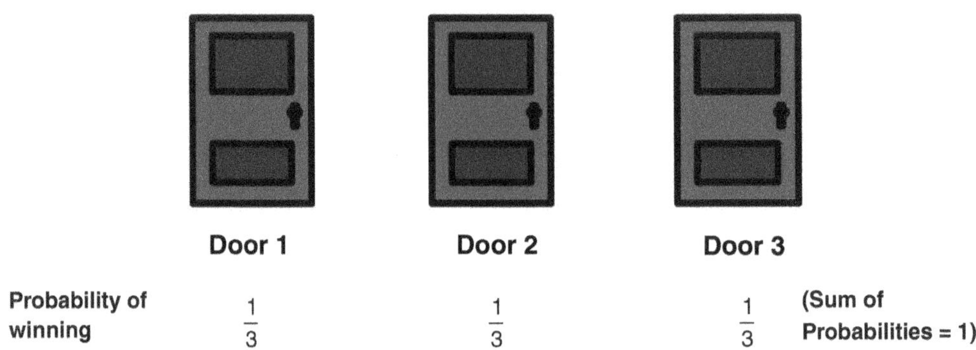

We have assumed you initially chose door 1, and then Monty revealed a sheep behind door 3, leaving just two doors unopened. So, what are the *revised* probabilities of winning, given the new information that there is a sheep behind door 3? These must be 1/2 and 1/2, as shown below, right?

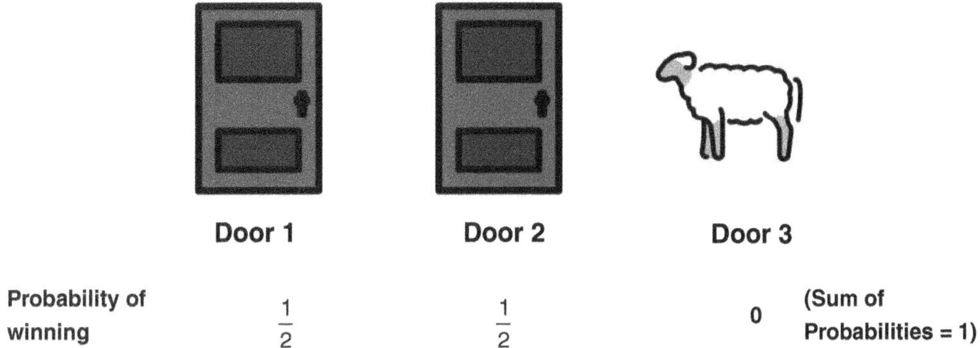

Wrong! If you thought it was a 50:50 split, then you're not alone! The Monty Hall problem has been called a 'cognitive illusion', because something about it seems to mislead most people's intuition. In experiments, around 85% of people tend to get the answer wrong at first. The most common incorrect response is that the probabilities of the remaining boxes after Monty's choice are both 1/2, so that you should not (or rather need not) switch. This is typically based on the reasoning of 'no new information'. Since we *know* in advance that Monty will open a door revealing a sheep, the fact that he does so appears to tell us nothing new and should not cause us to favour either of the two remaining doors – and so the argument is for a probability of 1/2 for each of the remaining two doors (noting that the probabilities must sum to 1).

Think of it this way, the *prior* (i.e. initial) probabilities of the car being behind each door are:

$$P(\text{door } 1) = (\text{door } 2) = P(\text{door } 3) = \frac{1}{3}$$

from which we may also write:

$$P(\text{door } 1) = \frac{1}{3} \text{ and } P(\text{door 2 or door 3}) = \frac{1}{3} + \frac{1}{3} = \frac{2}{3}.$$

Upon Monty revealing a sheep behind door 3, the above probabilities are still true, although we can now eliminate reference to door 3, since now $P(\text{door } 3) = 0$, and so $P(\text{door 2 or door 3}) = P(\text{door } 2)$.

Hence we have:

$$P(\text{door } 1) = \frac{1}{3} \text{ and } P(\text{door 2 or door 3}) = P(\text{door } 2) = \frac{2}{3}$$

so you *double* your chance of winning the car if you switch to door 2!

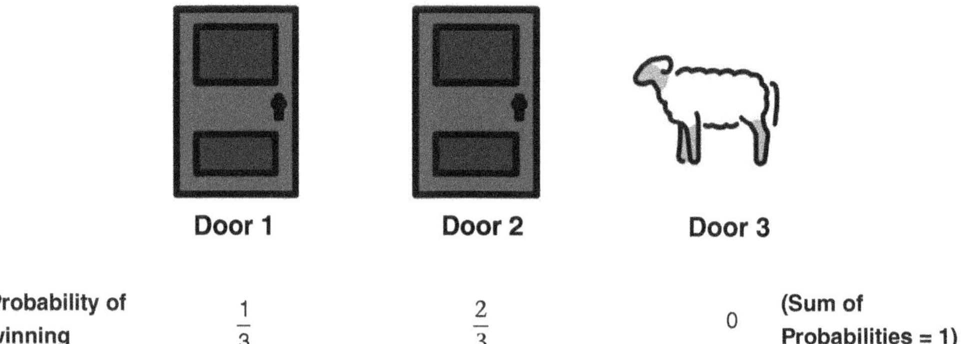

While it is true that Monty's choice tells you *nothing* new about the probability of your original choice, which remains at 1/3 since Monty was not allowed to open your initial door; it does tell us *a lot* about the other two doors. First, it tells us everything about door 3, namely that it does *not* conceal the car. Second, all of the probability of door 3 gets 'inherited' by the door neither you chose nor Monty chose to open (i.e. door 2), which now has the probability 2/3.

Note that the solution to the Monty Hall problem is *not* a probability, but a *strategy* – that is, a *decision* about *what we should do*. Here, the strategy is based on probabilities such that when faced with uncertainty it is rational to 'play to the probabilities' and choose the path which gives you the greatest probability of success. In this instance, the strategy 'to switch' is twice as likely to be successful compared with the strategy 'don't switch'. Hence let's suppose you maximise your chance of winning and decide to *switch to door 2*.

Let's see what you've won. . .

Oh no, you lost! What went wrong?!

Unfortunately, you have just experienced *bad luck*. A harsh lesson that life isn't always fair. However, there is another more important lesson: *in the long run, you cannot beat the laws of probability*.

In the *short run* you can, of course, as evidenced by the above game whereby had you been stubborn and stuck with your original choice of door 1 (with just a 1/3 probability of success) then you would have beaten the laws of probability, which we would attribute to *good luck*.

So how do we go from the short run to the long run? Answer: by playing the game repeatedly – effectively increasing the sample size. In Table 1.1 we consider 18 iterations of the game. Each round of the game is played independently, such that the location of the car randomises across the three doors across games. We will also randomise which door you (the contestant) initially choose. Round 1 is the game described above.

Monitoring the win rate, we see that there is a fairly quick convergence to 67%, as shown in Table 1.1. In general, though, we would not necessarily expect convergence quite so quickly (we were lucky here, albeit for illustrative purposes), rather convergence would occur as the number of *simulations* tends to infinity (which can be thought of as representing the 'long run'). Figure 1.13 shows an example of the convergence of the winning percentages from playing 'switch' and 'don't switch' to their theoretical values of 2/3 and 1/3, respectively.

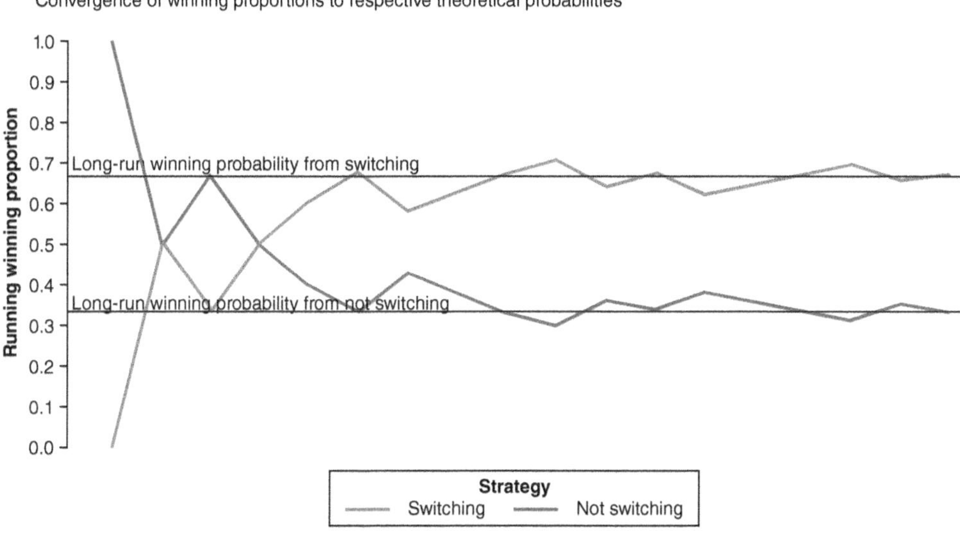

Figure 1.13 Winning percentage over several rounds in the Monty Hall problem by strategy.

The key takeaway from the Monty Hall problem is that when making decisions under uncertainty, there is *no guarantee* of success every time. Instead, we should be 'prepared to fail' on occasions (such as in our unfortunate round 1), while being confident that in the long run we win more often than we lose.

Of course, psychologically it can be difficult dealing with failure early on (such as we encountered in round 1), while we would experience misplaced euphoria initially with the strategy of not switching.

Note here that we are using updated probabilities to form a strategy – it is sensible to 'play to the probabilities' and choose as our course of action that which gives us the greatest chance of success (in this case we double our chance of winning by switching door). Of course, just because you pursue a course of action with the most likely chance of success *does not guarantee you success*!

If you play the Monty Hall problem and switch door, you can expect to win with a probability of 2/3, that is, you would win 2/3 of the time *on average*. In any single play of the game, you are either lucky or unlucky in winning the prize. So, you may switch and end up losing (and then think you applied the wrong strategy – hindsight is a wonderful thing!) but in the *long run* you can expect to win twice as often as you lose, such that in the long run you are better off by switching!

Table 1.1 Multiple independent iterations of the Monty Hall game, with running win rates.

Round	Your door choice (highlighted)	Monty opens a different door...	You choose to switch door	Result	Running win rate
1				Lose!	0/1 = 0%
2				Win!	1/2 = 50%
3				Lose!	1/3 = 33%
4				Win!	2/4 = 50%
5				Win!	3/5 = 60%
6				Win!	4/6 = 67%
7				Lose!	4/7 = 57%
8				Win!	5/8 = 63%
9				Win!	6/9 = 67%
10				Win!	7/10 = 70%
11				Lose!	7/11 = 64%
12				Win!	8/12 = 67%
13				Lose!	8/13 = 62%
14				Win!	9/14 = 64%
15				Win!	10/15 = 67%
16				Win!	11/16 = 69%
17				Lose!	11/17 = 65%
18				Win!	12/18 = 67%

Anyone can experience good luck and bad luck - not necessarily in equal proportions, since life is not always fair. :(

1.10.1 Increasing our probability of success

So, the moral of the story is that taking a data-analytic approach to decision-making does *not* guarantee success – we cannot eliminate uncertainty from our decision space, although we may wish to. The next best alternative is to quantify uncertainty to increase our probability of success, such that we are right more often than we are wrong. A 'batting average' is a suitable sporting analogy.

Take investing, for example. It is impossible to predict with certainty how stocks will perform. However, with due diligence and patient research, a skilled investor just needs to be right more often than they are wrong (or to have a few big winners to crowd out many small losers).

1.11 CHAPTER OVERVIEW

People in business are increasingly aware of the need to be able to handle a range of mathematical and statistical models. It must be admitted that many good managers are not very mathematically adept. However, they would be even more inquisitive, more precise, more accurate in their statements, more selective in their use of data and more critical of advice given to them if they had a better grasp of quantitative subjects. Modelling is an important tool which all good managers should appreciate.

When making decisions, it is easy to become overwhelmed trying to juggle and understand all of the different uncertainties associated with the decision problem. Out of necessity, simplification is required to construct a concise problem for which a data-driven model can be built. Formulating the problem can be a painstaking process, requiring many iterations as the model is 'fine-tuned'. Modelling effort, though, is rewarded with better decision-making.

While success cannot be guaranteed every single time, data-driven decisions can be expected to outperform in the long run. As the economist Keynes would say, in the long run we are all dead, nevertheless the pursuit of good decisions over bad ones is a noble one.

1.12 KEY VOCABULARY

Assumptions
Black swan
Ceteris paribus
Decisions
Dependent variables
DIKW pyramid
Expectation
Four Ps
Grey rhino
Independent variables
Linear regression analysis
Model
Normal distribution
Outcomes
Probability distribution
Sample size
Skills deficit
Strategy
Time-series data
Uncertainty

1.13 SUGGESTED READING

The Economist (2017). The world's most valuable resource is no longer oil, but data. 6 May. https://www.economist.com/leaders/2017/05/06/the-worlds-most-valuable-resource-is-no-longer-oil-but-data

Adam Payne (2016). These 2 betting charts show one way Brexit and Trump's victory were amazingly similar. *Insider*, 10 November. https://www.businessinsider.com/brexit-us-election-betting-markets-charts-similarities-2016-11?r=US&IR=T

1.14 EXERCISES

1.14.1 Test your understanding

1 What is meant by 'uncertainty'?
2 What is the difference between 'dependent' and 'independent' variables?
3 Identify examples of real-world dependent variables for any business problem of your choice.
4 For each dependent variable identified in Question 3, what are the likely independent variables? Briefly justify your choice.
5 What is meant by the 'four Ps'?
6 Explain the DIKW pyramid.
7 What is a model?
8 For a city other than London with a metro system, look at the official map of the network. Critique the map, noting any possible improvements you would recommend are made.
9 A friend of yours is a contestant on the Monty Hall game show. Your friend tells you 'No matter what, I will not switch door'. Would you support your friend's decision (to maintain your friendship!) or would you advise otherwise?
10 Suppose the producers of the Monty Hall show changed the format of the game. Instead of there being three doors, there are now $n > 3$ doors. The contestant chooses a door. Monty (who continues to know where the car is, and never reveals the car) opens $n - 2$ doors, leaving the contestant's original door and one other door unopened.

    (a) In terms of 'to switch, or not to switch?' what would you recommend is the optimal strategy and why?
    (b) Do you support the producers in increasing the number of doors to $n > 3$? Justify your view.

1.14.2 Case study corner

For a company or industry of your choice, formulate a possible quantitative business problem which could be analysed. In particular, think about the following.

- What is the specific business question to be addressed?
- What are the business objectives of the analysis?
- What are the dependent and independent variables?
- Are there any challenges in collecting relevant data to analyse the problem?
- Are there any uncertainties involved with the business problem? If so, what are they?

2

DESCRIPTIVE STATISTICS

Chapter contents

Chapter level: ***Beginner***

Source: Photo by Lukas Blazek via Unsplash.

Key concepts

- Exploratory analysis
- Descriptive statistics
- Mean, standard deviation

Chapter value

Data need to be simplified (i.e. 'reduced') to make variables easier to digest.

Key takeaway

The mean and standard deviation are an excellent two-number summary of quantitative variables.

Chapter outline

Business analytics involves dealing with *variables*. A variable is something that *varies* - easy to remember! However, variables come in different 'types' and from the get-go we need to study these types, known as *levels of measurement*. In due course, as we study a variety of analytical and modelling techniques, the suitability of each will depend on the levels of measurement involved, so stop, pause and think each time you encounter data about the types of variables you have, as this will affect what you can, and cannot, do with them!

We are often encouraged not to run before we can walk. Well, in matters of analysis, this saying definitely holds true. An essential starting point is to *describe* (or *summarise* or *reduce*) our datasets into easily digestible summaries. This can be done *visually* (our focus in Chapter 3) and *numerically*, covered in this chapter.

We introduce *descriptive statistics* and distinguish between measures of location, measures of dispersion and skewness. The main objective of descriptive statistics is to interpret key 'features' of a dataset numerically. All these statistics provide useful summaries of variables.

Learning outcomes

After completing this chapter, you should be able to:

- explain the concept of data reduction
- interpret and summarise raw data on variables numerically
- calculate basic measures of location and dispersion
- describe the skewness of a distribution and interpret box plots.

2.1 INTRODUCTION

And so we begin.

Our starting point is a collection of (usually numerical) data which has been collected in order to answer some questions of interest. Often the data forms a sample drawn from a larger population as depicted in Figure 2.1 (although for 'small', hence manageable, populations we would likely have the data in its entirety).

Our goal is to *make sense* of the data, which we proceed to do throughout subsequent chapters. Statistically, our analysis may have two broad objectives.

- Descriptive statistics: summarise the collected data in order to make it easier to understand.
- Statistical inference: use the observed data to draw conclusions about some broader population.

Sometimes (1) is the only aim. If we only require a high-level overview (i.e. an *exploratory analysis*) then descriptive statistics may suffice. However, even when (2) is the main aim, (1) is still an essential first 'exploratory' step, so there is no escape from descriptive statistics!

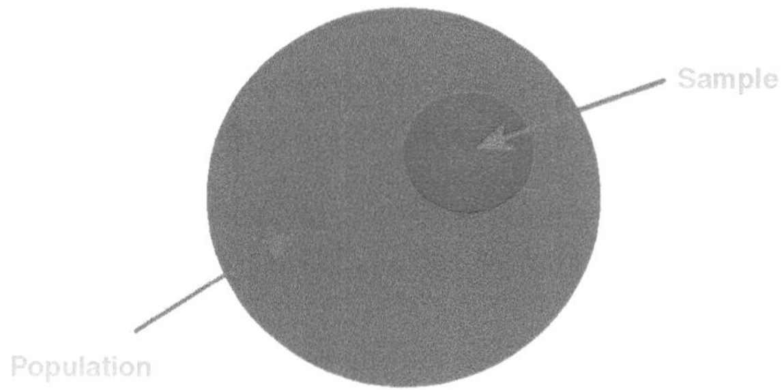

Figure 2.1 Sample as a subset of a population.

Keep it simple

If you ever read or watch the business news media, you rarely find numerical information beyond the descriptive. Often written for a non-technical audience, well-chosen simple statistics help to convey the message of the story without overcomplicating matters.

For example, 'Online sales rose *x*% year-on-year as lockdown-constrained households seek virtual retail therapy' or 'Commodity indices surge *y*%, signalling a commodity supercycle era'.

Percentages are a great way for communicating *changes* in numerical amounts.

Remember the DIKW pyramid in Figure 1.2? At the base is 'data'. Data does *not* just speak for itself. There are usually simply too many numbers to make sense of just by staring at them. Indeed, the human eye struggles to digest a spreadsheet of values, whether densely packed or sparse. Descriptive statistics (this chapter) and data visualisation (Chapter 3) attempt to summarise some key features of the data to make them digestible and facilitate clear communication to an audience. These summaries may be *numerical* (tables or individual summary statistics) or *graphical* (visualisations) or, if we are feeling generous, both!

2.2 QUALITATIVE AND QUANTITATIVE VARIABLES

As mentioned, variables come in different 'types', known by their **levels of measurement**. We distinguish between:

- **qualitative (or categorical) variables** – representing an attribute such that there is a non-numeric value assigned to that attribute. Examples include market sector, socioeconomic group and brand name.
- **quantitative (or measurable) variables** – representing an attribute which takes a numeric value. Examples include monetary amounts (revenue, costs, profits, sales) and proportions (market share).

Quantitative qualitative variables?

Can a qualitative variable be quantitative? Well, while qualitative variables are non-numeric, we may assign a numerical coding to each category level.

If the categories have *no rank order*, such as nationalities or brands (ignoring any personal brand preferences) then the numerical coding used is arbitrary. Such a categorical variable is **nominal**.

If the categories can be *ranked in order*, such as in market research opinion surveys (e.g. an itemised list with categories from 'strongly agree' to 'strongly disagree') then the coding must retain the ordering, so we could have 1 = strongly agree, 2 = agree, 3 = neither agree nor disagree, 4 = disagree and 5 = strongly disagree. Such a categorical variable is **ordinal**.

Example 2.1

We consider data for a sample of 80 countries on key geographic, macroeconomic and demographic variables for 2019 (i.e. pre-pandemic). This dataset can be accessed from *Data Planet* and is provided on the companion website. For each of the 80 countries, the following variables have been recorded.

- `Continent` of the country, by name and numerical code.
    - This is a *nominal* variable which has been coded (in alphabetical order, for convenience) as follows: 1 = Africa, 2 = Asia, 3 = Europe, 4 = North America, 5 = Oceania, 6 = South America. (Straddling Europe and Asia, Türkiye/Turkey has been classified as being in Europe but, of course, could have been classified as being in Asia. Ultimately, like many choices, it is a judgement call.)
- `Gross domestic product (GDP)` in 2010 US dollars, which is a *measurable* variable (specifically, a *ratio* variable, since the ratio of two values is meaningful).
    - Since GDP is a national aggregate, raw GDP values tend to be very large (i.e. with lots of zeros!), so expressing these values in billions of dollars (achieved through division by 1,000,000,000) results in easier-to-read values.
- `Population`, which is a *discrete* (countable) variable.
    - While China and India have populations in excess of a billion, although we could express this variable in millions, say, the order of magnitude of national populations is arguably at a level which can be easily read without changing the units.
- `GDP per capita` (i.e. per person, or per 'head' - yet more Latin) in 2010 US dollars, computed as `GDP` divided by `Population`.
    - By considering GDP per capita, rather than simply GDP, we have determined our first *average* (introduced later in this chapter). This is a great example to demonstrate the distinction between an *aggregate* (GDP) and a *mean* (GDP per capita). More on this later.

To GDP, or not to GDP?

For any students of economics, note that official macroeconomic statistics are often subject to measurement error and historical revisions. For example, it is notoriously difficult to accurately quantify GDP. Leaving aside the challenges of defining GDP, the underground economy, say, is - by its nature - *not* recorded in official statistics. These days so-called *high-frequency* economic indicators such as search engine queries, mobility and spending data provide more timely signals about economic activity (almost in real time), as demonstrated in monitoring the economic recovery from the Covid-19 pandemic. That said, GDP remains a popular and well-known variable which serves us well here for illustrative purposes.

How many zeros is that?

While the definition of a *million* is known by most people to have six zeros (i.e. 1,000,000), how many zeros are there in a billion? And a trillion? Answers: 9 and 12, respectively - assuming the 'short scale' naming system.

When numbers become very large it can be a challenge to conceptualise them. Hence the benefit of GDP per capita which is easier to relate to and arguably a better measure of economic prosperity. Two countries with similar GDPs, but very different population sizes, look very different when compared on a GDP per capita basis.

Back in 2011, in response to the ongoing global financial crisis of 2008-9, the eurozone's (one word) bailout fund reached 1 trillion euros (i.e. €1,000,000,000,000). At the time I was asked to contribute to an article about the use of such large numbers in reporting. I am especially proud of this quote from me: 'The first time someone hears the word trillion, they might not know the number of zeros but they know it's a big number.' So there you have it, folks - a trillion is a 'big number'. No doubt one of the most useless examples of an 'expert opinion'!

See Tom Geoghegan (2011). 'Is trillion the new billion?' *BBC News*, 28 October. https://www.bbc.co.uk/news/magazine-15478580

The statistical data in a sample are typically stored in a data matrix, as shown in Figure 2.2.

Rows of the data matrix correspond to different units (subjects/observations); here, each unit is a country. The number of units in a dataset is the sample size, typically denoted by n. Here, $n = 80$ countries (note only the first nine countries in the sample, ordered alphabetically, are shown).

Columns of the data matrix correspond to variables – different characteristics of the units. Here, `Country`, `Continent`, `Continent code`, `GDP`, `GDP in billions`, `Population` and `GDP per capita` are the variables.

	A	B	C	D	E	F	G
1	**Country**	**Continent**	**Continent code**	**GDP**	**GDP in billions**	**Population**	**GDP per capita**
2	Albania	Europe	3	15013330000	15.013	3066126	4896.51
3	Argentina	South America	6	4.16661E+11	416.661	45089492	9240.75
4	Australia	Oceania	5	1.50491E+12	1504.909	23705630	63483.19
5	Austria	Europe	3	4.68331E+11	468.331	8828456	53047.88
6	Bahrain	Asia	2	35128830000	35.129	1474016	23832.05
7	Belarus	Europe	3	60619540000	60.620	9503591	6378.59
8	Belgium	Europe	3	5.63422E+11	563.422	11647253	48373.78
9	Bolivia	South America	6	28113540000	28.114	11473676	2450.26
10	Botswana	Africa	1	17772860000	17.773	2283255	7784.00

Figure 2.2 Example of a data matrix. Note that the `red triangle` in cell `C1` indicates a cell note, which here has a record of the coding system used - a very handy aide-memoire. Comments can similarly be used.

2.3 CONTINUOUS AND DISCRETE VARIABLES

Different variables may have different statistical properties. These determine which kinds of statistical methods are suitable for the variables.

Continuous and discrete variables

A **continuous** variable can, in principle, take any real values within some interval. In Example 2.1, `GDP per capita` (for example) is continuous, taking any non-negative value (in principle).

A variable is **discrete** if it is not continuous, that is, if it can only take certain values, but not any others. In Example 2.1, `Population` is discrete, with possible values of 0, 1, 2, ... (in principle).

Many discrete variables have only a *finite* number of possible values. In Example 2.1, `Continent code` has six possible values. The simplest possibility is a **binary**, or **dichotomous**, variable, with just *two* possible values. For example, a person's sex at birth could be recorded as 1 = female or 2 = male.

Let's talk about sex (and analytics)

Sex is a nominal variable, hence the coding is arbitrary. We could have, for example, 0 = male and 1 = female, or 0 = female and 1 = male. However, it is important to remember which coding has been used!

(Continued)

A careful distinction between *sex* and *gender* should be made. How many genders are there? How many sexes are there?

The first question is hard to answer - there are many different gender identities. While gender is a nominal variable, the greater the number of gender identities classified, the more complex the coding system becomes. We face our usual trade-off between simplicity and complexity and the extent to which we wish to reflect reality.

The second question is (relatively) easier to answer - although there is not necessarily a settled answer. According to the Greek philosopher Plato there were/are three sexes: male, female and hermaphrodite. In practice, for administrative purposes and for convenience, birth certificates would usually stick with a two-group sexual taxonomy of 'male' and 'female'. However, biologically it could be argued there are more than two biological sexes. Perhaps, 'male', 'female' and 'intersex'.

To steer clear of any controversy, and for the sake of simplicity (recall our desire for simplifying assumptions in Chapter 1), here we shall consider sex at birth in examples with the binary classification of 'male' and 'female', rather than gender. Hence a binary 0-1 coding system can be used. The joy of ... stats.

A discrete variable can also have an unlimited number of possible values. For example, the number of visitors to a website in a day: 0, 1, 2, ... In practice, of course, there is a finite number of internet users in the world. However, it is reasonable to treat this variable as taking an unlimited number of possible values as an *approximating model*.

Example 2.2

In Example 2.1, suppose we wanted to visualise GDP geographically. Figure 2.3 shows GDP but *classified* according to the *level* of GDP using a six-point *ordinal* scale, defined as:

1 [$0, $3,000 billion)
2 [$3,000 billion, $6,000 billion)
3 [$6,000 billion, $9,000 billion)
4 [$9,000 billion, $12,000 billion)
5 [$12,000 billion, $15,000 billion)
6 [$15,000 billion, $19,000 billion).

Note that the class intervals above are **mutually exclusive** - meaning a country in the sample belongs to *at most one* of the intervals - and **collectively exhaustive** - meaning a country in the sample belongs to *at least one* of the intervals. The use of a square bracket, '[', indicates *inclusion* of the endpoint, while a round bracket, ')', indicates *exclusion* of the endpoint. So, for example, if a country had a GDP of $9,000 billion (precisely) it would be assigned to group 4, not group 3.

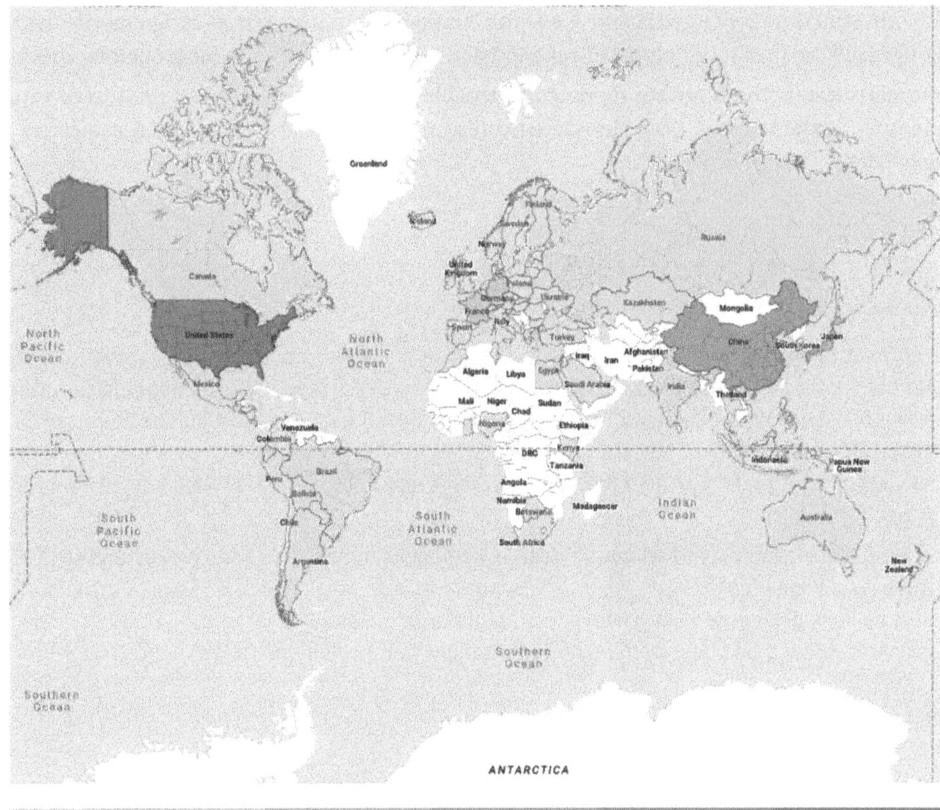

Figure 2.3 Colour brings visualisations to life. GDP is shown by country, but shaded according to the *level* of GDP, as indicated by the shading classification. Note that countries in white were not in the sample, hence no data were recorded.

Source: Based on Sage Data Planet.

MECE

Partitioning business problems using a 'MECE' (mutually exclusive and collectively exhaustive) approach can be effective. Management consultants, for example, may adopt this approach when thinking about *all* (collectively exhaustive) possible *distinct* (mutually exhaustive) scenarios.

In practice, thinking of distinct (mutually exclusive) possibilities is reasonably straightforward. The challenge is to think of all (collectively exhaustive) ways in which something may occur. More about this in Chapter 4.

In contrast, different continents (Africa, Asia, Europe, North America, Oceania and South America) do not have such an ordering. The numbers used for the continent coding variable are just labels for different continents. A different numbering (such as 6 = Africa, 5 = Asia, 1 = Europe,

3 = North America, 2 = Oceania and 4 = South America) would be just as acceptable as the one we originally used – but our alphabetical approach seems intuitively the most obvious choice.

Some statistical methods are appropriate for variables with both ordered and unordered values, some only in the ordered case. Unordered categories are *nominal* data; ordered categories are *ordinal* data.

To scale, or not to scale?

The map of the world in Figure 2.3 is the best-known world map projection, known as the *Mercator projection*. Think back to your geography class which probably used this familiar form. How good is it? Well, people are very familiar with this projection, but it suffers from severe distortions - notably Antarctica and Greenland are in fact far smaller in area than the map suggests! If you prefer correct relative sizes, then I recommend the Gall-Peters or Hobo-Dyer projections.

How *should* we represent the world? Just as in modelling, typically (and perhaps annoyingly) there is *no single right answer*. There are dozens of ways to map our home - Planet Earth, *Terra*. Just as in modelling, people will have to agree to disagree about what is 'best' or 'right'. What is important is to be able to articulate convincingly your arguments for your choice(s). Never forget this!

2.4 THE SAMPLE DISTRIBUTION

The sample distribution of a variable consists of:

- a list of the values of the variable which are observed in the sample
- the number of times each value occurs (the counts or frequencies of the observed values).

When the number of different observed values is small, we can show the whole sample distribution as a frequency table of all the values and their frequencies.

Example 2.3

Continuing with Example 2.1, the observations of the `Continent code` variable in the sample are:

3	6	5	3	2	3	3	6	1	6	3	4	6	2	6	4	4	4	3	1
3	3	3	3	3	4	3	3	3	6	1	3	3	2	1	2	2	3	2	2
3	3	2	3	2	6	4	3	3	3	1	2	3	3	2	3	6	1	3	3
2	2	3	3	3	3	2	6	6	3	1	4	5	3	1	4	3	2	3	2

We may construct a frequency table for the region variable as follows:

Region	Frequency (count)	Relative frequency (%)
(1) Africa	8	100 × 8/80 = 10.0
(2) Asia	16	20.0
(3) Europe	36	45.0
(4) North America	8	10.0
(5) Oceania	2	2.5
(6) South America	10	12.5
Total	80	100.0

Here '%' is the *percentage* of countries in a continent, out of the 80 countries in the sample. This is a measure of *proportion* (i.e. *relative frequency*).

2.4.1 Bar charts

A bar chart is the graphical equivalent of the table of frequencies. Figure 2.4 displays the `Continent` data as a bar chart. The relative frequencies of each continent in the sample are clearly visible. Note this is clearly not the most exciting of visualisations! We will consider this topic in greater depth in Chapter 3. The use of the bar chart here is just to show an example of a sample distribution graphically.

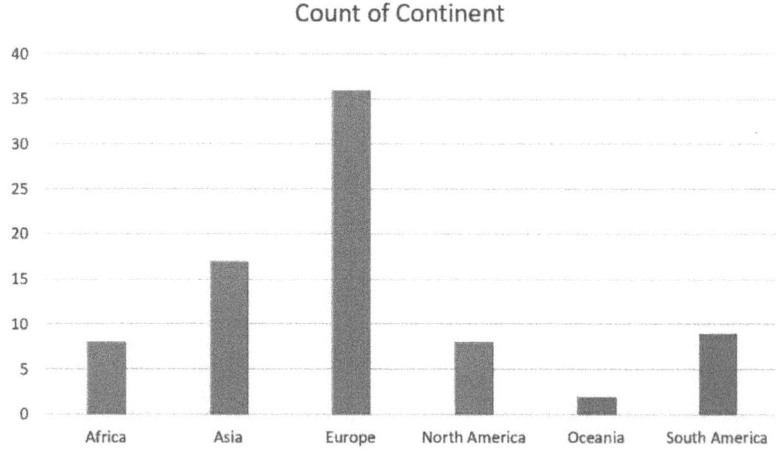

Figure 2.4 Example of a bar chart showing the `Continent` variable.

2.4.2 Sample distributions of variables with many values

If a variable has many distinct values, listing frequencies of all of them is not very practical.

A solution is to group the values into non-overlapping (MECE) *intervals* (or 'bins'), and produce a table or graph of the frequencies within the intervals. The most common graph used for this is a histogram.

A histogram is like a bar chart, but without gaps between bars, and often uses more bars (intervals of values) than is sensible in a table. Histograms are usually drawn using software, such as Excel or Tableau. You can let the software choose the bins or force them to your preferred choice.

Example 2.4

Continuing with Example 2.1, a table of frequencies for `GDP per capita` where values have been grouped into MECE intervals is shown below. Figure 2.5 shows a histogram of the data displaying the sample distribution.

GDP per capita (in $000s)	Frequency	%
[0, 10)	32	40.00
[10, 20)	14	17.50
[20, 30)	9	11.25
[30, 40)	4	5.00
[40, 50)	6	7.50
[50, 60)	9	11.25
[60, 70)	2	2.50
[70, 80)	0	0.00
[80, 90)	2	2.50
[90, 100)	1	1.25
[100, 110)	0	0.00
[110, 120)	1	1.25
Total	80	100.00

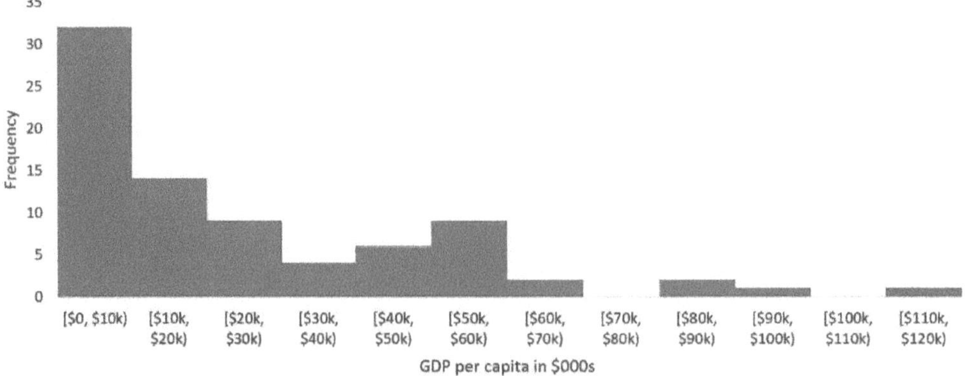

Figure 2.5 Histogram of `GDP per capita`.

2.4.3 Skewness of distributions

Skewness (asymmetry) and symmetry are terms used to describe the general shape of a sample distribution.

From Figure 2.5, it is clear that a small number of countries have much larger values of `GDP per capita` than the majority of countries in the sample. Luxembourg has the highest value at \$112,880 – lucky Luxembourgers!

The distribution of `GDP per capita` has a 'long right tail'. Such a distribution is called *positively skewed* (or skewed to the right). A distribution with a longer left tail (i.e. skewed towards small values) is *negatively skewed* (or skewed to the left). A distribution is *symmetric* if it is not skewed in either direction.

Example 2.5

Figure 2.6 shows a (slightly) negatively skewed distribution of marks in a statistics examination. Note that the data relate to all candidates sitting the examination. Therefore, the histogram shows the *population* distribution, not a *sample* distribution. The pass mark was 40, which explains the jump in bar height!

2.4.4 Missing values

For missing values (caused by non-response or no available data), as with outliers, there are two issues – how to identify missing values and what to do about them. Missing data can be coded in a variety of ways. Provided you know the code(s) in Excel, a global search can be conducted and all missing-value codes can be replaced with blanks.

More critically, what to do about missing values?

- The simplest (but not necessarily best) option is just to ignore them. In this case you need to be aware of how the missing values are dealt with by the software you use.
- Alternatively, the missing values could be replaced with averages of existing values, known as *imputation*.
- Subjective estimates are another possibility, based on judgement – but these are prone to bias.

Missing values, in the context of non-response, will be covered in Chapter 8.

2.5 MEASURES OF CENTRAL TENDENCY

Frequency tables, bar charts and histograms aim to summarise the *whole* sample distribution of a variable. Helpful, but we need more – we need *quantitative* summaries. Next we consider descriptive statistics, which summarise *one* feature of the sample distribution in a single number: summary statistics.

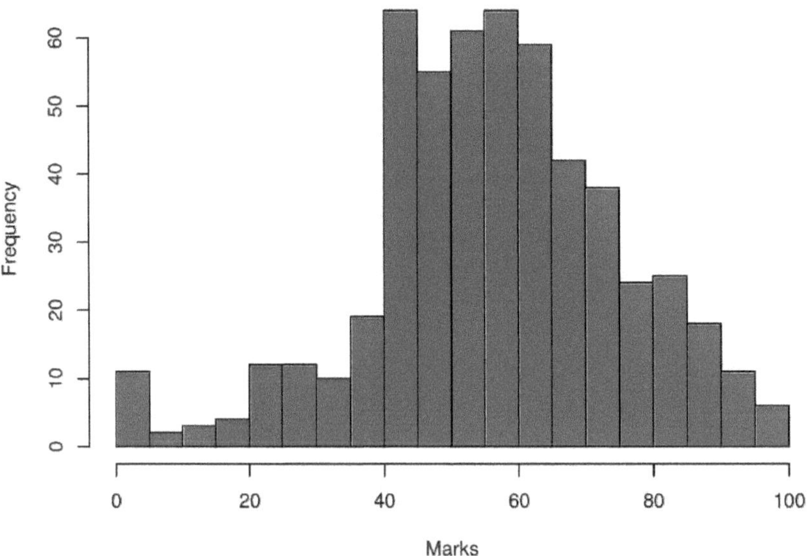

Figure 2.6 Final examination marks of a first-year statistics course.

We begin with measures of central tendency. These answer the question: where is the 'centre' or 'average' of the distribution?

We consider the following measures of central tendency:

- mean (i.e. the average, sample mean or arithmetic mean)
- median
- mode.

2.5.1 Notation for variables

In formulae, a generic variable is denoted by a single letter. In this text, when dealing with a single variable – i.e. a *univariate* analysis (the prefix 'uni' means one) – this is usually X. However, any other letter (Y, W, etc.) could also be used, as long as it is used *consistently*. A letter with a subscript denotes a single observation of a variable.

Example 2.6

We use X_i to denote the value of X for unit i, where i can take values 1, 2, ..., n, and n is the sample size. Therefore, the n observations of X in the dataset (the *sample*) are $X_1, X_2, ..., X_n$. These can also be written as X_i, for $i = 1, 2, ..., n$. So, if X was `GDP per capita`, then X_4 would be the GDP per capita of the fourth country in our sample.

2.5.2 Summation notation

Let $X_1, X_2, \ldots, X_n$ (i.e. X_i, for $i = 1, 2, \ldots, n$) be a set of n numbers. The sum of the numbers is written as

$$\sum_{i=1}^{n} X_i = X_1 + X_2 + \cdots + X_n$$

where i is the index of summation, taking integer values from the lower limit of 1 to the upper limit of n, inclusive. This may be written as $\Sigma_i X_i$, or just ΣX_i if the limits are obvious from the context. Other versions of the same idea are:

- infinite sums: $\sum_{i=1}^{\infty} X_i = X_1 + X_2 + \cdots$
- sums of sets of observations other than from 1 to n, for example (for even n):

$$\sum_{i=2}^{n/2} X_i = X_2 + X_3 + \cdots + X_{n/2}.$$

Excel function: SUM

Summing numbers in Excel is straightforward with the SUM function.

`=SUM(number1, [number2], ...)` adds all the numbers in a range of cells, where:

- `number1, number2, ...` are 1 to 255 numbers to sum. Logical values and text are ignored in cells, included if typed as arguments.

2.5.3 The sample mean

The sample mean (or arithmetic mean, 'mean' or 'average') is the most common measure of central tendency. The sample mean of a variable X is denoted by $\bar{X}$ (read as 'x bar'). It is the 'sum of the observations' divided by the 'number of observations' (sample size) expressed as:

$$\bar{X} = \frac{\sum_{i=1}^{n} X_i}{n} = \frac{1}{n}\sum_{i=1}^{n} X_i. \quad (2.1)$$

This is a simple conversion of an aggregate (the total) by *rescaling* the sum by dividing by n. While perhaps the simplest statistic in existence, personally I feel it is also one of the most (if not *the* most) important! If someone told you the value of a sum is 187,423, would you regard this as a 'large number'? Well, James, it depends! *Ceteris paribus*,[1] the value of the sum will be increasing in n (provided we are adding positive values). So, it makes a difference whether 187,423 was the result of adding just a few observations or many. Conversion to the mean through division by n makes it much clearer to judge whether a 'typical' observation is large or small.

[1]Remember this means 'other things being equal'.

Excel function: AVERAGE

For Excel datasets, the mean can be calculated with the `AVERAGE` function.

`=AVERAGE(number1, [number2], ...)` returns the average (arithmetic mean) of its arguments, which can be numbers or names, arrays, or references that contain numbers, where:

- `number1` is the required first number, cell reference or range for which you want the average;
- `number2,...` are optional additional numbers, cell references or ranges for which you want the average, up to a maximum of 255.

Example 2.7

The mean $\bar{X} = \sum_i X_i/n$ of the numbers $X_1 = 1$, $X_2 = 4$ and $X_3 = 7$ is:

$$\bar{X} = \frac{\sum_{i=1}^{3} X_i}{n} = \frac{1+4+7}{3} = \frac{12}{3} = 4.$$

Example 2.8

For the variables in Example 2.1, where $n = 80$, we have:

- `GDP` has $\bar{X}$ = $986 billion
- `Population` has $\bar{X}$ = 72,793,031
- `GDP per capita` has $\bar{X}$ = $24,565
- for `Continent code` the *mean* is not *mean*ingful(!), because the values of the variable do not have a *mean*ingful ordering!

Note that `GDP per capita` (for a country) represents a *population mean*, rather than a *sample mean* since it is the total national `GDP` figure divided by the national *population* size. It is customary to denote the population size by N and the population mean by the (Greek) letter μ.

Me, you, mew?

The correct pronunciation of μ in modern Greek is 'me', but (perhaps ignorantly) in the trade it is pronounced 'mew'. Sincere apologies to all Greek-speaking readers and phonetic enthusiasts.

Without drowning in the intricacies of how GDP is defined and measured, suppose for simplicity we treat GDP as the sum of the incomes of all N people in the country. GDP per capita would then be denoted by

$$\mu = \frac{\sum_{i=1}^{N} X_i}{N} = \frac{1}{N}\sum_{i=1}^{N} X_i.$$

Note when dealing with population data, it is important to define the population correctly. On a per-country basis, the population size would be the national population. If we wanted to know the average GDP per capita across all countries, then the population units are *countries*, not the number of citizens of a country.

It's all a guess

While we have been working with GDP and population data compiled by the World Bank and the US Census Bureau, respectively, these figures represent our best estimates - let's call them 'guesstimates' - since no one truly knows the exact size of an economy, nor the exact number of nationals of a country. Let alone the problems of dual/multi-nationalities. Remember, the real world is nasty, difficult and complicated!

If a variable has a small number of distinct values, $\bar{X}$ is easy to calculate from a frequency table. Consider, for example, the simple dataset of historic household saving rates in the UK in Table 2.1.

Table 2.1 Share of current savings to GDP, UK, 1950-2000.

Saving rate (% of GDP)	Frequency
12	1
13	0
14	2
15	1
16	4
17	7
18	12
19	9
20	3
21	3
22	6
23	2
24	1

Source: Based on Sage Data Planet.

The saving rate variable has just 13 different values which occur in the sample 1, 0, 2, ..., 1 times each, respectively.

Suppose X has K different values $X_1, X_2, \ldots, X_K$, with corresponding frequencies $f_1, f_2, \ldots, f_K$. Therefore, $\sum_{j=1}^{K} f_j = n$ (without loss of generality, using j as the summation index) and

$$\bar{X} = \frac{\sum_{j=1}^{K} f_j X_j}{\sum_{j=1}^{K} f_j} = \frac{f_1 X_1 + f_2 X_2 + \cdots + f_k X_k}{f_1 + f_2 + \cdots + f_K} = \frac{f_1 X_1 + f_2 X_2 + \cdots + f_k X_k}{n}.$$

Note that this is still the 'sum of the observations' divided by the 'number of observations'. In the saving rate example, the mean (where $K = 13$) is

$$\bar{X} = \frac{1 \times 12 + 0 \times 13 + \cdots + 1 \times 24}{1 + 0 + \cdots + 1} = \frac{12 + 0 + \cdots + 24}{51} = 18.6\%.$$

Excel function: SUMPRODUCT

In Excel, the numerator of such a mean can be calculated using the `SUMPRODUCT` function.

`=SUMPRODUCT (array1, [array2], [array3], ...)` returns the sum of the products of corresponding ranges or arrays, where:

- `array1, array2,` ... are 2 to 255 arrays for which you want to multiply and then add components. All arrays must have the same dimensions.

Why is the mean a good summary of the central tendency?

Consider the following small dataset:

		Deviations:			
		from $\bar{X}$ (= 4)		from the median (= 3)	
i	X_i	$X_i - \bar{X}$	$(X_i - \bar{X})^2$	$X_i - 3$	$(X_i - 3)^2$
1	1	−3	9	−2	4
2	2	−2	4	−1	1
3	3	−1	1	0	0
4	5	+1	1	+2	4
5	9	+5	25	+6	36
Sum	20 $\bar{X} = 4$	0	40	5	45

We see that the *sum of deviations* from the mean is 0, that is, we have

$$\sum_{i=1}^{n} (X_i - \bar{X}) = 0.$$

The mean is 'in the middle' of the observations $X_1, X_2, \ldots, X_n$, in the sense that positive and negative values of the *deviations* $X_i - \bar{X}$ cancel out, when summed over all the observations. (See the end of the chapter for the proof of this, if interested.)

Also, the smallest possible value of the sum of *squared* deviations $\sum_{i=1}^{n}(X_i - C)^2$ for any constant C is obtained when $C = \bar{X}$. So what? Well, this has implications for defining a useful measure of dispersion, discussed later. (Again, see the end of the chapter for the proof of this, if interested.)

2.5.4 The (sample) median

Let $X_{(1)}, X_{(2)}, \ldots, X_{(n)}$ denote the sample values of X when *ordered* from the smallest to the largest, known as the order statistics, such that:

- $X_{(1)}$ is the smallest observed value (the minimum) of X
- $X_{(n)}$ is the largest observed value (the maximum) of X.

Median

The (sample) median, q_{50}, of a variable X is the value which is 'in the middle' of the ordered sample. If n is odd, then $q_{50} = X_{((n+1)/2)}$.

- For example, if $n = 3$, $q_{50} = X_{(2)}$: (1) (2) (3)

If n is even, $q_{50} = (X_{(n/2)} + X_{(n/2+1)})/2$.

- For example, if $n = 4$, $q_{50} = (X_{(2)} + X_{(3)})/2$: (1) (2) (3) (4)

Excel function: `MEDIAN`

In Excel, the median can be calculated with the `MEDIAN` function.

`=MEDIAN(number1, [number2], ...)` returns the median, or the number in the middle of the set of given numbers, where:

- `number1, number2, ...` are 1 to 255 numbers or names, arrays, or references that contain numbers for which you want the median. `number1` is required, subsequent numbers are optional.

Example 2.9

Continuing with Example 2.1, $n = 80$, so $q_{50} = (X_{(40)} + X_{(41)})/2$. For `GDP per capita`, the median is $14,928.

2.5.5 Sensitivity to outliers

For the following small ordered dataset, the mean and median are both 4 (don't take my word for it, check for yourself!):

1, 2, 4, 5, 8.

Suppose we obtain one more observation to get the ordered sample

1, 2, 4, 5, 8, 100.

The median is now 4.5, and the mean is 20. In general, the mean is affected much more than the median by outliers, that is, unusually small or large observations. Therefore, you should identify outliers early on and investigate them – perhaps there has been a data entry error, which can simply be corrected. If deemed genuine outliers, a decision has to be made about whether or not to remove them.

An outlier is an extreme observation which departs greatly from 'typical' observations. Unfortunately, there is no universally agreed definition of an outlier. You might define an outlier as any value more than two or three *standard deviations* (to be introduced shortly) from the *mean*, but this is only a rule of thumb.

Sometimes an outlier is easy to identify and address. Sometimes a careful check of the variable values, one variable at a time, will not reveal any outliers, but there still might be unusual combinations of values. The best advice for dealing with outliers is to run analyses in two ways, *with the outliers and without them*, and see to what extent the outliers are influential. This is an example of a *sensitivity analysis* – if the outliers are influential to the conclusions you draw, then the analysis is *sensitive* to the outliers; if the conclusions are similar with and without outliers, then the analysis is *robust* to their presence, hence it makes no material difference whether the outliers are included or excluded – this makes our lives easier! In the above (deliberately artificial) example, the mean is very sensitive to the outlier of 100. If you wanted to use the mean, then careful consideration of the *representativeness* of 100 is required to decide whether or not to retain it. In contrast, if using the median then it makes little practical difference, that is, the median is fairly robust to the 100 value.

When summarising variables with skewed distributions, it is useful to report both the mean and the median.

Example 2.10

For our dataset in Example 2.1, the means and medians (suitably rounded) are:

	Mean	Median
`GDP`	$986 billion	$267 billion
`Population`	73 million	14 million
`GDP per capita`	$24,565	$14,927

It is evident that these are heavily skewed distributions (see, for example, Figure 2.5) with clear outliers, such as China and India (in terms of `Population`) and Luxembourg (in terms of `GDP per capita`). Which measure of central tendency would you recommend, and why?

Where do/will you fall in the income distribution?

Usually when studying incomes the *median* is used as a point of reference, due to the heavy positive skew of income distributions. For your home country you may wish to research what the median income is, although take care to check whether this is for an individual or a household.

Depending on your own future income expectations, you can then judge where you will end up in the income distribution. Top 10%? Top 1%?

2.5.6 Skewness, means and medians

Due to its sensitivity to outliers, the mean, more than the median, is pulled towards the longer tail of the sample distribution.

- For a positively skewed distribution, the mean is larger than the median.
- For a negatively skewed distribution, the mean is smaller than the median.
- For an exactly symmetric distribution, the mean and median are equal.

Excel function: `SKEW`

In Excel, a measure of skewness can be calculated with the `SKEW` function.

`=SKEW(number1, [number2], ...)` returns the skewness of a distribution, a characterisation of the degree of asymmetry of a distribution around its mean, where:

- `number1, number2, ...` are 1 to 255 numbers or names, arrays, or references that contain numbers for which you want the skewness. `number1` is required, subsequent numbers are optional.

Kurtosis has to do with the 'fatness' of the tails of the distribution relative to the tails of a normal distribution. A distribution with high kurtosis has many extreme observations.

Excel function: `KURT`

Kurtosis can be calculated in Excel with the `KURT` function.

`=KURT(number1, [number2], ...)` returns the kurtosis of a dataset, where:

- `number1, number2, ...` are 1 to 255 numbers or names, arrays, or references that contain numbers for which you want the kurtosis. `number1` is required, subsequent numbers are optional.

2.5.7 Mode

The (sample) mode of a variable is the value which has the highest frequency (i.e. appears most often) in the data. The mode is not very useful for continuous variables which have many different values, such as `GDP per capita` in Example 2.1. A variable can have several modes (i.e. be multimodal).

The mode is the only measure of central tendency which can be used even when the values of a variable have no ordering, such as for the (nominal) `Continent code` variable in Example 2.1. In most cases where a variable is essentially continuous, the mode is not very interesting because it is often the result of a few lucky ties.

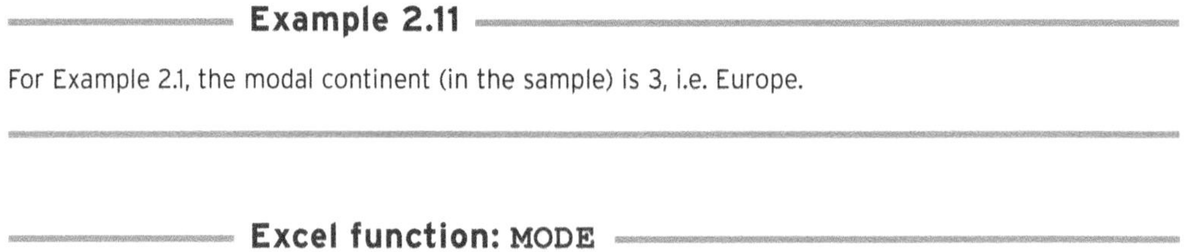

Example 2.11

For Example 2.1, the modal continent (in the sample) is 3, i.e. Europe.

Excel function: `MODE`

In Excel, the mode can be calculated with the MODE function.

`=MODE(number1, [number2], ...)` returns the most frequently occurring, or repetitive, value in an array or range of data, where:

- `number1, number2, ...` are 1 to 255 numbers, or names, arrays, or references that contain numbers for which you want the mode. `number1` is required, subsequent numbers are optional.

2.5.8 Minimum, maximum, percentiles and quartiles

Minimum and *maximum* values are, hopefully, self-explanatory. If there are any *outliers* in your data the minimum and/or maximum values would be among them, at a 'minimum'!

For any percentage p, the pth percentile is the value such that a percentage p of all values are less than it.

The quartiles divide the data into four groups, each with (approximately) a quarter of all observations. Naturally, the first, second and third quartiles are the percentiles corresponding to $p = 25$, $p = 50$ and $p = 75$, respectively. By definition, the second quartile ($p = 50$) is equal to the median, but the term 'median' is more commonly used.

Who are the top 1%?

Income inequality (the 'haves' and the 'have-nots') is a serious issue. However, while people may rail against the 'top 1%' (meaning those above the 99th percentile in the income distribution - from a global perspective, with a global population of $N \approx 8$ billion, there are by definition approximately 80 million such people, many of whom would probably be surprised to find they belong to that exclusive club!) perhaps the top 0.01% are the group of actual interest, typically the UHNWs (ultra-high net worth individuals).

The minimum and maximum values can be calculated with Excel's `MIN` and `MAX` functions, and the percentiles and quartiles with Excel's `PERCENTILE` and `QUARTILE` functions.

Excel function: `MIN`

`=MIN(number1, [number2], ...)` returns the smallest number in a set of values, ignoring logical values and text, where:

- `number1, number2, ...` are 1 to 255 numbers, empty cells, logical values, or text numbers for which you want the minimum. `number1` is required, subsequent numbers are optional.

Excel function: `MAX`

`=MAX(number1, [number2], ...)` returns the largest number in a set of values, ignoring logical values and text, where:

- `number1, number2, ...` are 1 to 255 numbers, empty cells, logical values, or text numbers for which you want the maximum. `number1` is required, subsequent numbers are optional.

Excel function: `PERCENTILE`

`=PERCENTILE(array, k)` returns the *k*th percentile of values in a range, where:

- `array` is the array or range of data that defines relative standing;
- `k` is the percentile value that is between 0 and 1, inclusive.

Excel function: `QUARTILE`

`=QUARTILE(array, quart)` returns the quartile of a dataset, where:

- `array` is the array or cell range of numeric values for which you want the quartile value;
- `quart` is a number: minimum value = 0; first quartile = 1; median value = 2; third quartile = 3; maximum value = 4.

2.6 MEASURES OF DISPERSION

Central tendency is not the whole story. The two sample distributions in Figure 2.7 have the same mean, but they are clearly not the same. In one (the red outline) the values have more **dispersion** (variation) than in the other case (the black outline).

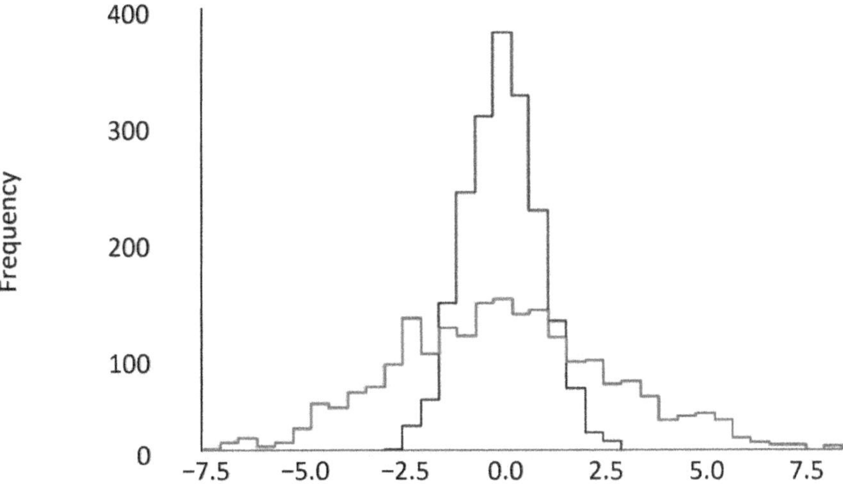

Figure 2.7 Two sample distributions.

What might the distributions in Figure 2.7 represent? Well, suppose these were the weekly *percentage returns* of two stocks. By construction these have zero means, hence *on average* the weekly return is 0%. However, the distributions of returns are obviously different. The red outline distribution is much more dispersed than the black outline distribution. In terms of returns we would say that the 'red stock' has greater *volatility* than the 'black stock', such that the red stock can be considered *riskier*. The advantage of holding the red stock is the greater probability of a large positive return, while the disadvantage is the greater probability of a large negative return (i.e. a loss). Upside potential means exposure to downside risk. Based on your risk appetite, which would you choose? Play it safe, or go for broke?

We now consider common formal measures of dispersion.

Example 2.12

Consider a small example determining the *sum of the squared deviations from the (sample) mean*, used to calculate common measures of dispersion.

			Deviations from $\bar{X}$	
i	X_i	X_i^2	$X_i - \bar{X}$	$(X_i - \bar{X})^2$
1	1	1	−3	9
2	2	4	−2	4
3	3	9	−1	1
4	5	25	+1	1
5	9	81	+5	25
Sum	20 $\bar{X} = 4$	120 $= \sum X_i^2$	0	40 $= \sum (X_i - \bar{X})^2$

2.6.1 Variance and standard deviation

The first measures of dispersion, the *sample variance* and its square root, the *sample standard deviation*, are based on $(X_i - \bar{X})^2$, the squared deviations from the sample mean.

Sample variance and standard deviation

The **sample variance** of a variable X, denoted by S^2 (or S_X^2, for clarity if dealing with multiple variables), is defined as

$$S^2 = \frac{1}{n-1}\sum_{i=1}^{n}(X_i - \bar{X})^2.$$

The **sample standard deviation** of X, denoted S (or S_X), is the positive square root of the sample variance:

$$S = \sqrt{\frac{1}{n-1}\sum_{i=1}^{n}(X_i - \bar{X})^2}.$$

Is the variance a mean in disguise?

We have seen that the sample mean, $\bar{X}$, is a sum (of values, X_i) divided by n. Well, S^2 is also a type of 'mean'. It is the mean of the squared deviations around $\bar{X}$, that is, it is a sum (of values, $(X_i - \bar{X})^2$), divided by $n - 1$.

'Why divide by $n - 1$, and not n? There must be a rational explanation, right?'

Since you ask, we divide by $n - 1$ to ensure that S^2 is an *unbiased estimator* of σ^2. Omitting technical details, this means that using the divisor $n - 1$ ensures that the *sample* variance, S^2, is equal to the *population* variance, denoted by σ^2, *on average*. Using the n divisor *systematically underestimates* σ^2, resulting in a *(negatively) biased estimator*. We would rather estimate something on average correctly, than incorrectly, *ceteris paribus*. Dividing by $n - 1$ ensures this.

Note that when we have a (very) large n, then $n \approx n - 1$, so there is minimal practical difference between a divisor of n and $n - 1$. Nonetheless, use $n - 1$ when working with sample data.

These are the most commonly used measures of dispersion. The standard deviation is easier to interpret than the variance, because the standard deviation is expressed in the *same units* as X (while the variance is expressed in squared units, i.e. $(\text{units})^2$). For example, the variance of returns is in $\%^2$ (per cent squared), which I at least would struggle to conceptualise!

A (very) useful rule of thumb for interpretation is that for many symmetric distributions, such as the 'normal' distribution (formally introduced in Chapter 5):

- about 2/3 of the observations are between $\bar{X} - S$ and $\bar{X} + S$, that is, within one (sample) standard deviation about the (sample) mean
- about 95% of the observations are between $\bar{X} - 2 \times S$ and $\bar{X} + 2 \times S$, that is, within two (sample) standard deviations about the (sample) mean.

Remember that standard deviations (and variances) are *never* negative, and they are zero *only* if all the X_i observations are the same (i.e. there is no variation in the data since $X_i - \bar{X} = 0$ for all i).

If we are using a frequency table, we can also calculate

$$S^2 = \frac{1}{n-1}\left(\sum_{j=1}^{K} f_j X_j^2 - n\bar{X}^2\right).$$

Example 2.13

Consider the following simple dataset:

			Deviations from $\bar{X}$	
i	X_i	X_i^2	$X_i - \bar{X}$	$(X_i - \bar{X})^2$
1	1	1	−3	9
2	2	4	−2	4
3	3	9	−1	1
4	5	25	+1	1
5	9	81	+5	25
Sum	20 $\bar{X} = 4$	120 $= \sum X_i^2$	0	40 $= \sum (X_i - \bar{X})^2$

We have:

$$S^2 = \frac{1}{n-1}\sum_{i=1}^{n}(X_i - \bar{X})^2 = \frac{40}{4} = 10 = \frac{1}{n-1}\left(\sum_{i=1}^{n} X_i^2 - n\bar{X}^2\right) = \frac{120 - 5\times 4^2}{4}$$

and $S = \sqrt{S^2} = \sqrt{10} = 3.16.$

To calculate the variance in Excel, the `VAR` (for samples) or `VAR.P` (for populations) function is used. To calculate the standard deviation, the `STDEV` (for samples) or `STDEV.P` (for populations) function is used.

Excel function: VAR

`=VAR(number1, [number2], ...)` estimates the variance based on a sample (ignores logical values and text in the sample), where:

- `number1, number2,` ... are 1 to 255 numeric arguments corresponding to a sample of a population. `number1` is required, subsequent numbers are optional.

Excel function: `VAR.P`

`=VAR.P(number1, [number2], ...)` calculates the variance based on the entire population (ignores logical values and text in the population), where:

- `number1, number2, ...` are 1 to 255 numeric arguments corresponding to a population. `number1` is required, subsequent numbers are optional.

Excel function: `STDEV`

`=STDEV(number1, [number2], ...)` estimates the standard deviation based on a sample (ignores logical values and text in the sample), where:

- `number1, number2, ...` are 1 to 255 numbers corresponding to a sample of a population and can be numbers or references that contain numbers. `number1` is required, subsequent numbers are optional.

Excel function: `STDEV.P`

`=STDEV.P(number1, [number2], ...)` calculates the standard deviation based on the entire population given as arguments (ignores logical values and text), where:

- `number1, number2, ...` are 1 to 255 numbers corresponding to a population and can be numbers or references that contain numbers. `number1` is required, subsequent numbers are optional.

2.6.2 Sample quantiles

The median, q_{50}, is basically the value which divides the sample into the smallest 50% of observations and the largest 50%. If we consider other percentage splits, we get other (sample) quantiles (percentiles), q_c.

Example 2.14

Some special quantiles are given below.

- The *first/lower quartile*, q_{25} or Q_1, is the value which divides the sample into the smallest 25% of observations and the largest 75%, or the 25%-75% split.
- The *third/upper quartile*, q_{75} or Q_3, gives the 75%-25% split.
- The extremes in this spirit are the *minimum*, $X_{(1)}$ (the '0% quantile', so to speak), and the *maximum*, $X_{(n)}$ (the '100% quantile').

These are no longer 'in the middle' of the sample, but they are more general measures of *location* of the sample distribution.

2.6.3 Quantile-based measures of dispersion

Range and interquartile range

Two measures based on quantile-type statistics are the:

- **range**: $X_{(n)} - X_{(1)}$ = maximum – minimum
- **interquartile range (IQR)**: IQR = $q_{75} - q_{25} = Q_3 - Q_1$.

The range is, clearly, extremely sensitive to outliers, since it depends on nothing but the extremes of the distribution, that is, the minimum and maximum values. The IQR focuses on the middle 50% of the distribution, so it is completely insensitive to outliers since it focuses on the 'core' of the distribution.

2.6.4 Mean absolute deviation

The **mean absolute deviation (MAD)** is another measure of variability – although some might think it 'mad' to use it! (The MAD is technically problematic as it is not differentiable, which is awkward if we want to optimise it by minimising it.)

For many variables, the standard deviation is approximately 25% larger than the MAD:

$$s \approx 1.25 \times \text{MAD}.$$

The formula for the MAD is:

$$\text{MAD} = \frac{\sum_{i=1}^{n} \left|X_i - \bar{X}\right|}{n} = \frac{1}{n}\sum_{i=1}^{n} | X_i - \bar{X} |.$$

So the MAD, like S^2, is also a mean (granted, the 'M' is a bit of a giveaway), formed from a sum (of absolute values, $\left|X_i - \bar{X}\right|$) divided by n (note, not $n - 1$).

Excel function: AVEDEV

To calculate the mean absolute deviation in Excel, the `AVEDEV` function is used.

`=AVEDEV(number1, [number2], ...)` returns the average of the absolute deviations of data points from their mean. Arguments can be numbers or names, arrays, or references that contain numbers, where:

- `number1, number2, ...` are 1 to 255 arguments for which you want the average of the absolute deviations. `number1` is required, subsequent numbers are optional.

2.6.5 Box plots

A box plot (in full, a box-and-whiskers plot) summarises some key features of a sample distribution using quantiles. The plot is comprised of the following.

- The line inside the box, which is the median (equivalently the second quartile, Q_2).
- The box, whose edges are the first and third quartiles (Q_1 and Q_3). Hence, the box captures the middle 50% of the data. Therefore, the length of the box is the interquartile range.
- The bottom whisker extends either to the minimum or up to a length of 1.5 times the interquartile range below the first quartile, whichever is closer to the first quartile.
- The top whisker extends either to the maximum or up to a length of 1.5 times the interquartile range above the third quartile, whichever is closer to the third quartile.
- Points beyond 1.5 times the interquartile range below the first quartile or above the third quartile are regarded as outliers, and plotted as individual points.
- Points beyond 3 times the interquartile range below the first quartile or above the third quartile are sometimes regarded as extreme outliers, and sometimes plotted as individual points using a different symbol.

A much longer whisker (and/or outliers) in one direction relative to the other indicates a skewed distribution, as does a median line not in the middle of the box.

Example 2.15

Figure 2.8 displays a box plot of `GDP per capita` using the sample of 80 countries introduced in Example 2.1. Some summary statistics for this variable are reported below.

	Mean	Median	Standard deviation	IQR	Range
GDP per capita	\$24,565	\$14,927	\$24,460	\$36,157	\$111,489

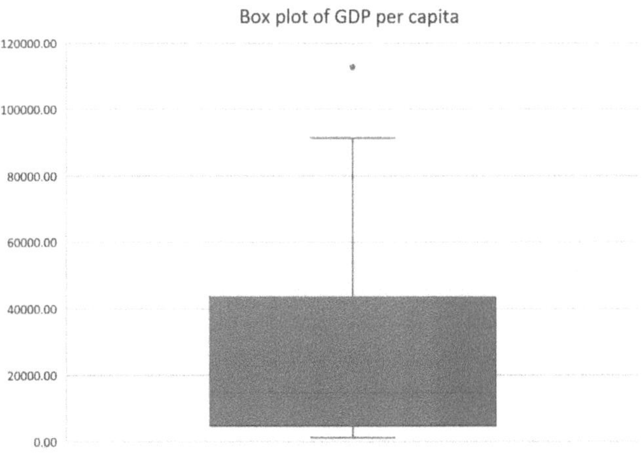

Figure 2.8 Box plot of `GDP per capita`.

2.6.6 Side-by-side box plots for comparisons

Box plots are useful for *comparisons* of how the distribution of a continuous variable varies across different groups, that is, across different levels of a discrete variable.

Example 2.16

Figure 2.9 shows side-by-side box plots of `GDP per capita` for the different continents in Example 2.1.

- GDP per capita in African countries tends to be very low.
- The median for Asia is not much higher than for Africa. However, the distribution in Asia is very much skewed to the right, with a tail of countries with quite high GDPs per capita.
- The distribution for Europe exhibits the most variation, with the outlier (Luxembourg again) clearly visible.
- The box plot for Oceania is not very useful, because it is based on very few countries (only Australia and New Zealand).

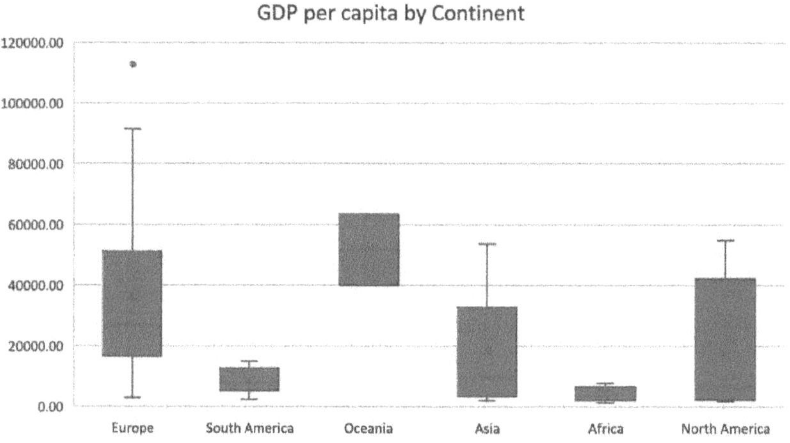

Figure 2.9 Side-by-side box plots of `GDP per capita` by `Continent`.

2.7 SUMMARY OF COMMON EXCEL FUNCTIONS

Appendix A summarises common Excel functions for calculating measures of central tendency and measures of dispersion and various other descriptive statistics.

2.8 CHAPTER OVERVIEW

This chapter has introduced some quantitative approaches to summarising data, known as descriptive statistics. We have distinguished measures of location, dispersion and skewness.

Although descriptive statistics serve as a very basic form of statistical analysis, they nevertheless are extremely useful for capturing the main characteristics of a dataset. Therefore, *any* statistical analysis of data should start with data visualisation (coming up in Chapter 3) and the calculation of descriptive statistics!

2.9 KEY VOCABULARY

Arithmetic/sample mean
Bar chart
Binary/dichotomous
Box plot
Collectively exhaustive
Continuous
Count/frequency
Data matrix
Descriptive/summary statistics
Discrete
Frequency table
Histogram
Interquartile range
Kurtosis
Levels of measurement
Maximum
Mean absolute deviation
Measures of central tendency
Measures of dispersion
Median
Minimum
Missing values
Mode
Mutually exclusive
Nominal
Order statistics
Ordinal
Outliers
Percentages
Percentile
Population
Qualitative/categorical variables
Quantile
Quantitative/measurable variables
Quartile
Range
Sample
(Sample) distribution
Sample size
Skewness
Standard deviation
Statistical inference
Sum
Symmetry
Unit
Variable
Variance

2.10 DATASETS

https://statisticaldatasets.data-planet.com/dataset/embed?id=17928BDD2CB14&type=static" "width="960" height="569" style="border:1px solid black;margin:auto;"

https://statisticaldatasets.data-planet.com/dataset/embed?id=17928D46E7D16&type= static""width="960" height="569" style="border:1px solid black;margin:auto;"

CICUP, University of Pennsylvania, Center for International Comparisons of Production, Income and Prices. 2013, September 4. Share of Current Savings to GDP: Share of Current Savings to GDP — United Kingdom, 1950–2000. Data Planet Statistical Datasets: A SAGE Publishing Resource. https://doi.org/10.6068/DP1792E876FEB5

2.11 EXERCISES

2.11.1 Test your understanding

1 Why do we tend to work with sample data rather than population data?
2 What are the different levels of measurement of variables?

3 Provide some real-world business examples of discrete and continuous variables.
4 What does MECE stand for, and what do these terms (ME and CE) mean in practice?
5 What is skewness, and what is the difference between positively skewed and negatively skewed?
6 What is the purpose of measures of central tendency, and what are the main measures (along with their Excel functions)?
7 Why is the mean a good summary of the central tendency?
8 What is an outlier, and how might you identify one?
9 What is the difference between a percentile and a quartile? Are they ever the same?
10 Why should we consider measures of dispersion in addition to measures of central tendency?
11 Which is better, the (sample) variance or the (sample) standard deviation? Briefly justify your view and state what the respective Excel functions are.
12 Why do we divide by $n - 1$ when calculating the sample variance?
13 Name two types of quantile-based measures of dispersion. Which do you prefer, and why?
14 What information can be deduced from a box plot?
15 For what purpose would we consider using side-by-side box plots?
16 In a population, would you expect the *mean* income to be greater than, less than, or equal to the *median* income?
17 For a set of n observations $x_1, x_2, \ldots, x_n$, with mean $\bar{x}$, show that

$$\sum_{i=1}^{n}(x_i - \bar{x}) = 0.$$

18 For a set of n observations $x_1, x_2, \ldots, x_n$, with sample mean $\bar{x}$, explain why it is *not* sensible to use the following as a measure of dispersion:

$$\frac{1}{n-1}\sum_{i=1}^{n}(x_i - \bar{x}).$$

19 For a sample of observations $x_1, x_2, \ldots, x_n$ on people's income, in UK pounds, would you recommend the *sample variance* or the *sample standard deviation* as the preferred measure of dispersion when explaining these results in a newspaper? Briefly justify your choice.
20 The annual before-tax earnings for a random sample of a company's employees, measured in thousands of UK pounds, produced the following summary statistics:

$$\sum_{i=1}^{12} x_i = 398 \quad \text{and} \quad \sum_{i=1}^{12} x_i^2 = 14{,}418.$$

(a) Calculate the sample standard deviation.
(b) Explain, without calculations, what the effect would be on the mean and standard deviation if each employee was given an annual bonus of £1,000.

21 Explain, by using a definition, why the range is influenced by extreme values.
22 Summary statistics of the performance of job applicants in a screening online aptitude test are as follows:

Question #	Number of attempts	Mean mark	Standard deviation
1	467	10.03 (out of 16)	2.93
2	465	9.48 (out of 12)	3.18
3	466	8.17 (out of 12)	2.21
4	224	9.37 (out of 20)	4.88
5	392	12.57 (out of 20)	5.41
6	273	10.51 (out of 20)	6.81
7	328	13.33 (out of 20)	6.10
8	330	12.51 (out of 20)	3.68

Here are box plots of the distributions:

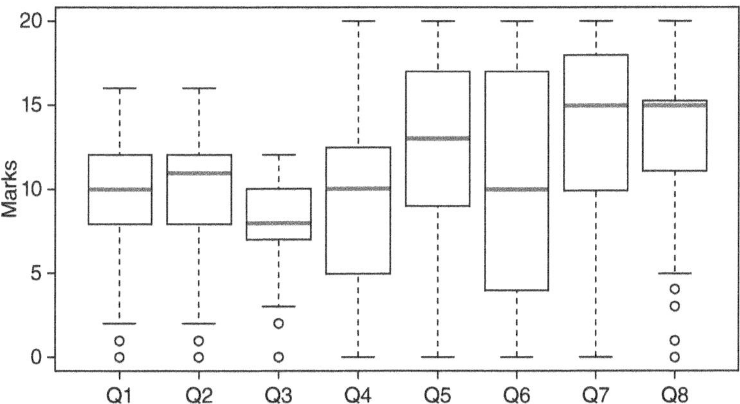

What can you deduce from this information? How might you use this information to inform the next stage of the job recruitment process?

2.11.2 Practice with Excel

Head over to the companion website for Excel examples and screencasts!

2.12 PROOFS

These proofs are not essential to review (or master), but are included for the 'interested reader'. A black square, ■, simply denotes the end of the proof. Enjoy.

The sum of deviations from the mean is 0

The mean is 'in the middle' of the observations $X_1, X_2, \ldots, X_n$, in the sense that positive and negative values of the *deviations* $X_i - \bar{X}$ cancel out, when summed over all the observations, that is:

$$\sum_{i=1}^{n}(X_i - \bar{X}) = 0.$$

Proof. The proof uses the definition of $\bar{X}$ and the properties of summation. Note that $\bar{X}$ is a constant in the summation, because it has the same value for all i.

$$\begin{aligned}
\sum_{i=1}^{n}(X_i - \bar{X}) &= \sum_{i=1}^{n}X_i - \sum_{i=1}^{n}\bar{X} && \text{(expansion of brackets)} \\
&= \sum_{i=1}^{n}X_i - n\bar{X} && (\bar{X} \text{ is a constant added } n \text{ times}) \\
&= \sum_{i=1}^{n}X_i - n\frac{\sum_{i=1}^{n}X_i}{n} && (\text{re-expressing } \bar{X}) \\
&= \sum_{i=1}^{n}X_i - \sum_{i=1}^{n}X_i && (\text{cancel the } n\text{s}) \\
&= 0. && \text{(et voilà!)}
\end{aligned}$$

The mean minimises the sum of squared deviations

The smallest possible value of the sum of squared deviations $\sum_{i=1}^{n}(X_i - C)^2$, for any constant C, is obtained when $C = \bar{X}$.

Proof.

$$\begin{aligned}
\sum_{i=1}^{n}(X_i - C)^2 &= \sum_{i=1}^{n}(X_i \overbrace{-\bar{X} + \bar{X}}^{=0} - C)^2 && \left(\text{introduce } \bar{X} \text{ terms}\right) \\
&= \sum_{i=1}^{n}\left((X_i - \bar{X}) + (\bar{X} - C)\right)^2 && \left(\text{add brackets to express as } (a+b)^2\right) \\
&= \sum_{i=1}^{n}\left((X_i - \bar{X})^2 + 2(X_i - \bar{X})(\bar{X} - C) + (\bar{X} - C)^2\right) && \text{(expand quadratic)} \\
&= \sum_{i=1}^{n}(X_i - \bar{X})^2 + \sum_{i=1}^{n}2(X_i - \bar{X})(\bar{X} - C) + \sum_{i=1}^{n}(\bar{X} - C)^2 && \text{(express as three summations)} \\
&= \sum_{i=1}^{n}(X_i - \bar{X})^2 + 2(\bar{X} - C)\overbrace{\sum_{i=1}^{n}(X_i - \bar{X})}^{=0} + n(\bar{X} - C)^2 && \text{(note the constant terms)} \\
&= \sum_{i=1}^{n}(X_i - \bar{X})^2 + n(\bar{X} - C)^2 && \text{(simplify)} \\
&\geq \sum_{i=1}^{n}(X_i - \bar{X})^2 && \text{(et voilà!)}
\end{aligned}$$

since $n(\bar{X} - C)^2 \geq 0$ for any choice of C. Equality is obtained only when $C = \bar{X}$, so that $n(\bar{X} - C)^2 = 0$.

■

An alternative formula for the variance

The sum of squares in S^2 can also be expressed as

$$\sum_{i=1}^{n}(X_i - \bar{X})^2 = \sum_{i=1}^{n}X_i^2 - n\bar{X}^2.$$

Proof. We have:

$$\sum_{i=1}^{n}\left(X_i-\bar{X}\right)^2=\sum_{i=1}^{n}\left(X_i^2-2X_i\bar{X}+\bar{X}^2\right) \qquad \text{(expand quadratic)}$$

$$=\sum_{i=1}^{n}X_i^2-2\bar{X}\overbrace{\sum_{i=1}^{n}X_i}^{=n\bar{X}}+\overbrace{\sum_{i=1}^{n}\bar{X}^2}^{n\bar{X}^2} \qquad \text{(note the constant terms)}$$

$$=\sum_{i=1}^{n}X_i^2-n\bar{X}^2. \qquad \text{(et voilà!)}$$

Therefore, the sample variance can also be calculated as

$$S^2=\frac{1}{n-1}\left(\sum_{i=1}^{n}X_i^2-n\bar{X}^2\right)$$

(and the standard deviation $S=\sqrt{S^2}$ again).

Sample moment

Let us define, for a variable X and for each $k = 1, 2, \ldots$, the following:

- the kth *sample moment* about zero,

$$m_k=\frac{\sum_{i=1}^{n}X_i^k}{n}$$

- the kth *central sample moment*,

$$m_k'=\frac{\sum_{i=1}^{n}\left(X_i-\bar{X}\right)^k}{n}.$$

In other words, these are sample averages of the powers X_i^k and $\left(X_i-\bar{X}\right)^k$, respectively.

Clearly,

$$\bar{X}=m_1 \quad \text{and} \quad S^2=\frac{n}{n-1}m_2'=\frac{1}{n-1}\left(nm_2-n(m_1)^2\right).$$

Moments of powers 3 and 4 are used in two more summary statistics which are described next, *for reference only*.

These are used much less often than measures of central tendency and dispersion.

Sample skewness

A measure of the skewness of the distribution of a variable X is

$$g_1=\frac{m_3'}{s^3}=\frac{\sum_{i=1}^{n}(X_i-\bar{X})^3/n}{\left(\sum_{i=1}^{n}(X_i-\bar{X})^2/(n-1)\right)^{3/2}}.$$

For this measure, $g_1 = 0$ for a symmetric distribution, $g_1 > 0$ for a positively skewed distribution, and $g_1 < 0$ for a negatively skewed distribution.

Sample kurtosis

Kurtosis refers to yet another characteristic of a sample distribution. This has to do with the relative sizes of the 'peak' and tails of the distribution (think about shapes of histograms).

- A distribution with high kurtosis (i.e. *leptokurtic*) has a sharp peak and a high proportion of observations in the tails far from the peak.
- A distribution with low kurtosis (i.e. *platykurtic*) is 'flat', with no pronounced peak and with most of the observations spread evenly around the middle and weak tails.

A sample measure of kurtosis is

$$g_2 = \frac{m_4'}{(m_2')^2} - 3 = \frac{\sum_{i=1}^{n}(X_i - \bar{X})^4 / n}{\left(\sum_{i=1}^{n}(X_i - \bar{X})^2 / n\right)^2} - 3.$$

$g_2 > 0$ for leptokurtic and $g_2 < 0$ for platykurtic distributions, and $g_2 = 0$ for the normal distribution (introduced in Chapter 5). Some software packages define a measure of kurtosis without the –3, which is called *excess kurtosis*.

Calculation of sample percentiles

This is how computer software calculates general sample percentiles (or how you can do so by hand, if you ever needed to).

Suppose we need to calculate the cth sample percentile, q_c, where $0 < c < 100$. Let $R = (n + 1)c/100$, and define r as the integer part of R and $f = R - r$ as the fractional part (if R is an integer, $r = R$ and $f = 0$). It follows that:

$$q_c = X_{(r)} + f(X_{(r+1)} - X_{(r)}) = (1 - f)X_{(r)} + fX_{(r+1)}.$$

For example, if $n = 10$:

- for q_{50} (the median), $R = 5.5$, $r = 5$, $f = 0.5$, and so we have

$$q_{50} = X_{(5)} + 0.5(X_{(6)} - X_{(5)}) = 0.5(X_{(5)} + X_{(6)})$$

as before;

- for q_{25} (the first quartile), $R = 2.75$, $r = 2$, $f = 0.75$, and so

$$q_{25} = X_{(2)} + 0.75(X_{(3)} - X_{(2)}) = 0.25X_{(2)} + 0.75X_{(3)}.$$

3

DATA VISUALISATION

Chapter contents

Chapter level: *Beginner*

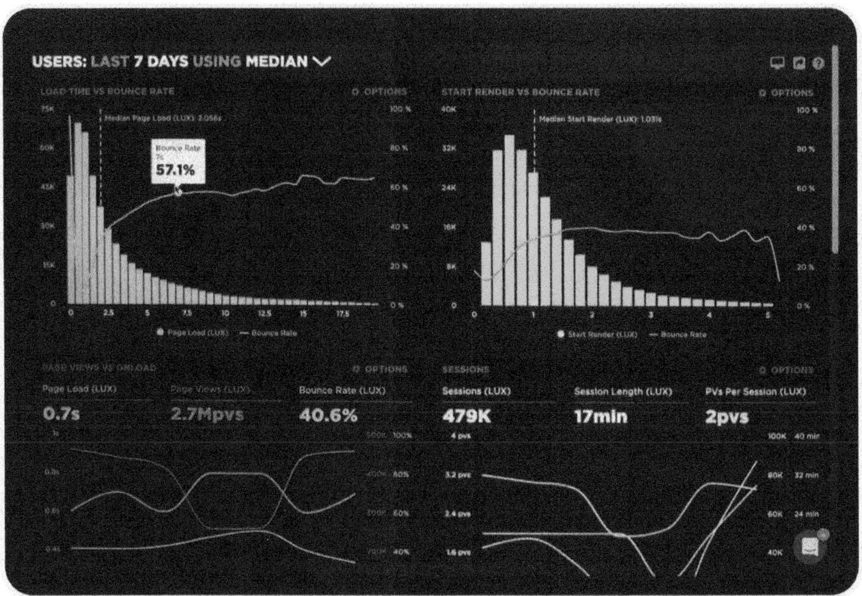

Source: Photo by Luke Chesser via Unsplash.

Key concepts

- Tableau
- Dashboards
- Storytelling with data

Chapter value

Bring data to life with data viz. Trends, patterns, relationships and outliers are ripe for discovery.

Key takeaway

Data visualisation is an art as much as a science.

Chapter outline

'Once upon a time. . .' is a classic opening to stories. In business analytics storytelling is important, but stories of fact rather than stories of fiction. *Tableau* is a very user-friendly, intuitive and powerful data visualisation tool with a strong focus on business intelligence. The ease of use with which it creates visualisations and its performance capabilities allow you to bring data to life through engaging and informative *dashboards* which can be merged into *stories* for publication and presentation. Combined with a compelling narrative, data-driven and evidence-based insights can emerge to assist with managerial decision-making. Pretty cool.

Data visualisation is an art as much as a science, such that there is no single right 'viz'. However, clarity of message is important, as well as knowing your audience. This chapter will introduce Tableau - how to get started, how to navigate it, how to get visualising. Be sure to add Tableau to the computing skills section of your CV and impress prospective employers. Equipped with these basics, you are then free to experiment and explore the power of Tableau developing your data viz skills and deliver that 'wow' factor, then live happily ever after.

Learning outcomes

After completing this chapter, you should be able to:

- appreciate the importance of data visualisation in bringing data to life
- understand, interpret and communicate data in a very practical way
- apply Tableau functionality to summarise a dataset.

3.1 INTRODUCTION

Twenty-first-century managerial strategies and corporate decisions can help to drive improved business efficiency, especially when adaptive, customer-centric and responsive to change. Our century is an age of information overload. Vast amounts of data are continually generated by people, computers and measuring instruments. Recall from Chapter 1 that it has been estimated that more data has been recorded digitally in the past 2–3 years than in the rest of human history combined!

Most businesses aren't short of data, but often lack the means to convert raw data into information and insights. Today our key challenge is not so much about *generating* data as how to *make sense of* and *analyse* data. Good managers are able to interrogate and understand data in a way which adds value to business performance.

Chapter 2 introduced basic examples of data reduction – summarising variables graphically and numerically. While looking at numbers and text can provide insights, for large quantities of data the sheer volume often makes this task impractical. One solution is to use data visualisation (*data viz* if we want to be trendy): tools which convert numbers and text into visual representations, often with interactive features.

Tableau is an excellent data visualisation tool used by many businesses. Data visualisation, as the name suggests, is concerned with converting numeric and non-numeric data into engaging images, which ultimately allows us to understand the data and the stories supported by data, adding real value to a business. People say a picture paints a thousand words. Data visualisation paints a thousand data points or more.

With data viz we can go data mining to look for interesting things, such as helpful geographic trends and patterns – for example, is a particular geographic or business unit losing money? Can data help tell us why? Data viz does *not* provide all the answers, rather it points you in the right direction. It's a bit like detective work. It's about identifying where to focus your energies to research promising leads further. Raw datasets are typically very 'noisy', so we need to find the 'signal'. With the right type of viz, and a little bit (or a lot) of luck, you can discover signals quite quickly, but sometimes it takes longer. Patience is a virtue.

This chapter introduces you to the basic functions of Tableau and how to navigate its interface. Upon launching Tableau you will reach the start page, which serves as the central starting point when using Tableau. From here you can connect to data, open previous workbooks, discover sample workbooks and gather information from resources. You will be shown various techniques for visualising data in Tableau, including the built-in Show Me function offering helpful suggestions for visualisation options which best fit the variables you are investigating, by their number and type. Very quickly you will be able to create simple yet powerful visualisations all by yourself!

Caveat emptor

Consumers of data viz should be cautious and sceptical. Have a critical eye and a questioning mind. Do not have blind trust nor faith in data, and always beware of it being presented in a sinister way. Distorted axes, truncated timespans, and confirmation bias effects, among others, could be deployed to mislead the viewer, whether intentionally or unintentionally. Look at the graph below, used to back up the following claim: 'Our management team have delivered stellar returns for our shareholders, justifying the record-breaking remuneration this year.'

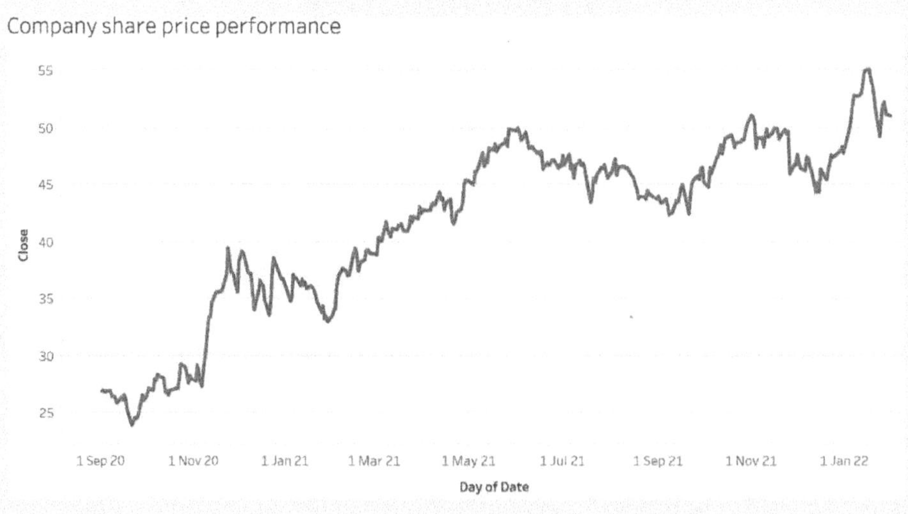

Now let's take a step back and look at the bigger picture:

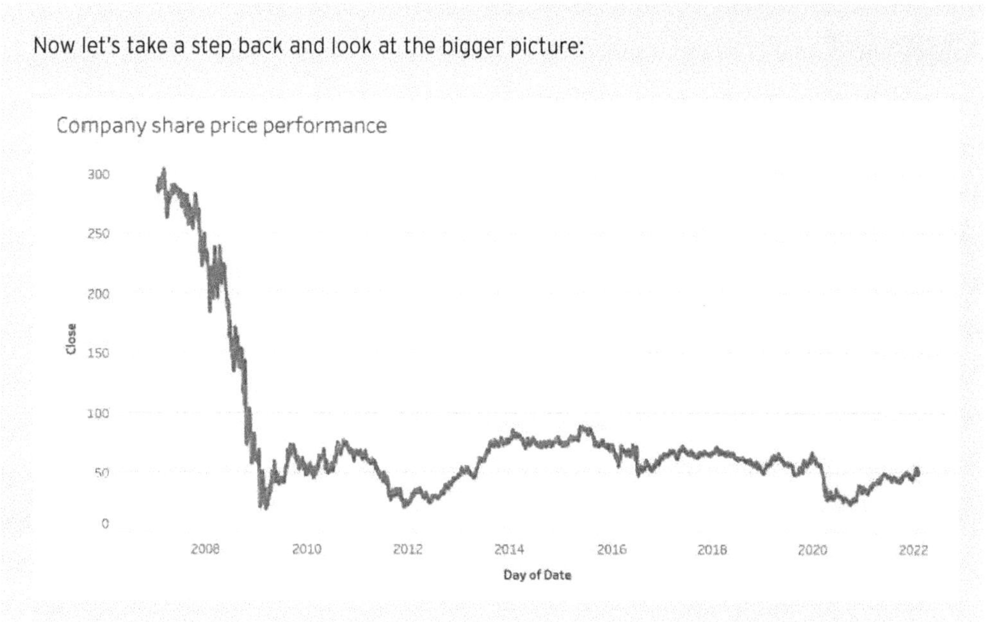

Is record remuneration really justified? Executives, marketers and politicians could all use data viz in an underhand way to promote a particular narrative. Lies, damned lies, and statistics.

3.2 GETTING STARTED

For any reader enrolled with an academic institution (university, business school etc.) *free* (yay!) one-year Tableau licences are available when you register with your institutional email address, or otherwise verify your student status, by visiting: https://www.tableau.com/en-gb/academic/

Let's dive straight into Tableau and explore its basic functions and interface navigation. Once installed, upon opening Tableau for the first time you are met with a fairly sparse start page as in Figure 3.1. The start page is, self-evidently, a natural place to start. Over time, your start page will fill up with thumbnails of recent workbooks that you will have worked on. See how quickly you can fill the space with project thumbnails signalling your data viz enthusiasm!

On the left you can import data from various sources by connecting to a file, such as a Microsoft Excel file. On the right there is direct access to an extensive library of Tableau's very own training resources, featuring numerous screencast videos guiding you through Tableau essentials. You are strongly encouraged to watch Tableau's own screencasts (each is very short) and then replicate and go and play with your own datasets.

To help you gain data viz confidence, Tableau installations come with some very useful built-in sample workbooks. These are fantastic as *templates* to study and perhaps inspire your own visualisations, albeit they are not collectively exhaustive of what can be created with Tableau, rather they consolidate a broad cross-section of possibilities.

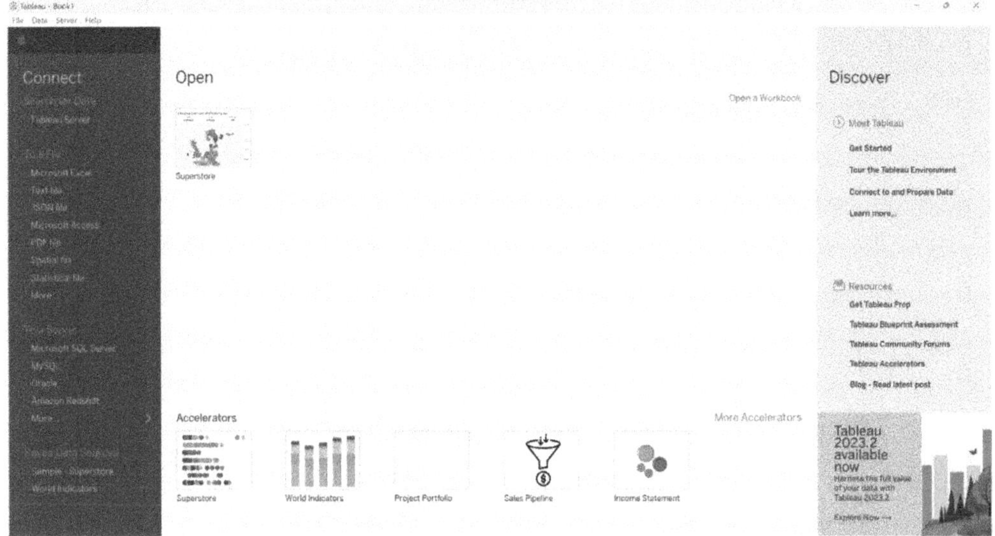

Figure 3.1 Start page of Tableau following installation.

Viz of the Day

Want to see the full power of Tableau? Want inspiration for your own visualisations? Want to share your stunning viz with the world?

If your answers are 'yes', 'yes' and 'yes', then check out (and subscribe to) Tableau Public's *Viz of the Day*. Here Tableau users come to share their creations with the world!

Imitation, after all, is the sincerest form of flattery.

In Tableau, we have the following hierarchy, all contained within a Tableau 'workbook':

Worksheet – where individual visualisations are created, starting from a blank canvas.

Dashboard – a collection of visualisations, formed by combining one or more worksheets (think of a dashboard like a single PowerPoint slide).

Story – a sequence of dashboards (think of a story like a full PowerPoint slide deck).

In terms of this hierarchy, 'Story' is our end destination which represents the final presentation. This is formed from a series of dashboards, which in turn are built from individual worksheets. Hence worksheets are the elementary building blocks. Dashboards in Tableau still maintain all of the functionality of a worksheet but consolidate all the information you want to report in one place. Dashboards can then be used to form stories, allowing you to bring data to life using an interactive presentation. However, one should be cautious when forming dashboards – while adding more worksheets to a single dashboard allows more information to be disseminated, there is a risk of *information overload*, so exercise sound judgement when creating dashboards.

3.2.1 Tableau's sample Superstore workbook

Depending on where you are in the world, the default sample workbooks visible to you may exhibit some geographic variations (Europe, USA, Asia–Pacific, etc.). For illustrative purposes, let's consider the sample European Superstore workbook – sales transactions based on a fictional superstore.

This example workbook contains many ready-made visualisations to give you ideas for creating engaging and informative dashboards of your own. These are named by tabs at the bottom (`Overview`, `Product`, `Customers`, etc.). Let's now briefly review the ready-made dashboards, identifying an interesting feature in each one.

Overview dashboard

Maps are visually appealing and can be suitable as an opening to a data viz presentation providing a high-level overview. Figure 3.2 shows the profitability for different European regions from where orders have been received. Here, `Profit Ratio` ranges from dark blue to dark brown (see the far right legend), distinguishing profit-generating areas from loss-making ones. A blue–brown spectrum circumvents issues for those prone to red–green colour blindness, a positive accessibility trait!

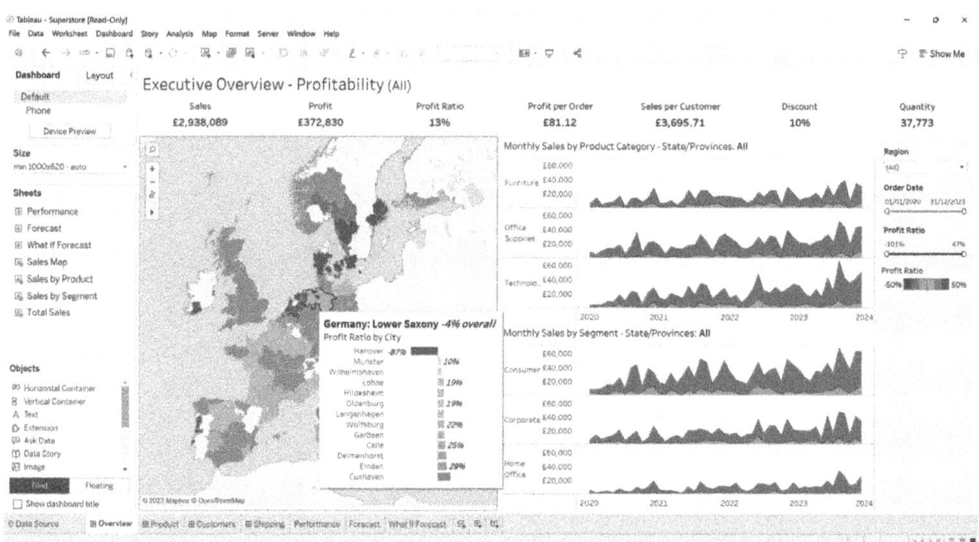

Figure 3.2 Overview dashboard of Tableau's sample Superstore dataset.

Note the interactive features of Tableau. By hovering over specific regions we can deep-dive into the headline picture indicated by the colouring. For example, Lower Saxony in Germany is shaded orange in Figure 3.2, suggesting poor profit performance – the only obvious area of concern in Germany since other German *Länder* (states) are shaded blue. However, looking at the region overall can be misleading as it may suppress interesting features which emerge through a more granular inspection. Indeed, on closer inspection, Hanover is the only problem area *within* Lower Saxony, with its –87% profit ratio crowding out the positive results elsewhere in Lower Saxony. Clearly, we would want to investigate the reason(s) behind Hanover's losses to (i) understand them, (ii) reduce them, and, failing that, (iii) cease selling there!

Product dashboard

Hovering over obvious outliers in the Product dashboard, shown in Figure 3.3, we can see the popularity of the Novimex Executive Leather Armchair (available in red!), which is the top-selling furniture item in the `Consumer` segment – perhaps there has been a pandemic-induced run on such chairs for all those 'work-from-home' executives needing ergonomic comfort and happiness?

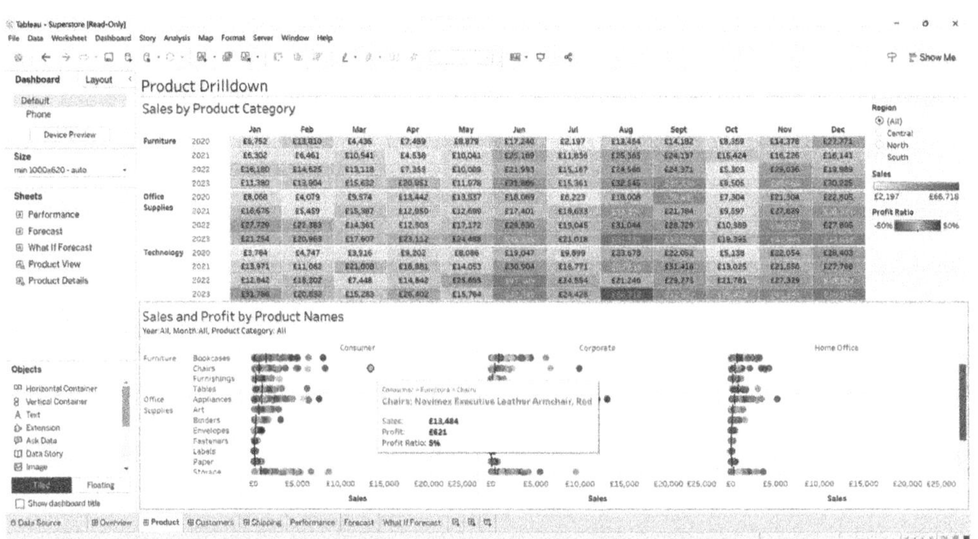

Figure 3.3 Product dashboard of Tableau's sample Superstore dataset.

Customers dashboard

In practice, all customers are not equal. Some are bigger spenders than others, and hence are more lucrative. Figure 3.4 presents a dashboard of customers. By some margin, Susan Pistek is the Superstore's best customer. Her likely high *customer lifetime value* marks Susan out as a prime target for the Superstore's customer relationship management team. Perhaps promotion beckons to the top tier of their loyalty programme to reward, and hopefully retain, her custom! We love Susan.

Shipping dashboard

Tableau has a powerful and intuitive filter mechanism, allowing us to refine what is visualised. For example, we may be interested in detecting any issues of concern in the shipment of orders. Figure 3.5 presents a dashboard of shipping-related variables. Consider the Q4 2022 first class dispatches. A staggering 77% were shipped late! While customers choosing `first class` are likely to be less impatient than those choosing `same day` delivery, they are probably not as patient as those choosing the `second class` and `standard class` options. Customer dissatisfaction is likely to rise if delayed first class deliveries persist – perhaps leading to increased customer complaints and demands for delivery fee refunds. (How frustrated have you been when your online order takes longer than expected to arrive? Patience may be a virtue, but it is often in short supply.)

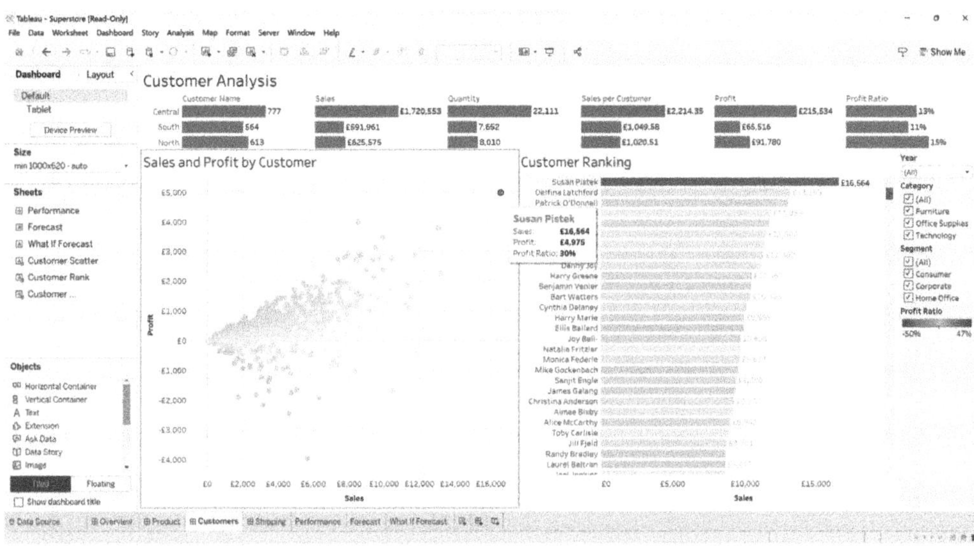

Figure 3.4 Customers dashboard of Tableau's sample Superstore dataset.

Notice how it is possible to provide a narrative (i.e. a story) around each discovered insight. Admittedly, these narratives are somewhat speculative, such as the surge in work-from-home practices being offered up as the primary *cause* of the Novimex armchair's popularity – it may have been due to a generous discount, or possibly a pricing error (it can, and does, happen).

Fat finger syndrome strikes again!

Electronic Arts may strive to offer customers a good deal, but a 99.9% discount on the FIFA 23 Ultimate Edition is a bit *too* generous.

India's Epic Games store listed pre-orders of the game at 4.80 rupees (about £0.05) instead of the intended 4,800 rupees (about £50), thanks to a misplaced decimal point. Oops.

Good news for those who spotted it - the 4.80 rupee price was honoured. For their good deed, I suggest a goodwill markup on their balance sheet to compensate for the, well, own goal!

3.2.2 Data Source

While impressive, actually creating the above dashboards yourself may seem somewhat daunting at first sight, so let's break things down. First, we examine the data on which the visualisations have been built. Click on 'Data Source' at the bottom left. You will then see (an equivalent of) Figure 3.6.

This somewhat resembles an Excel worksheet, indeed here the source data actually comes from an Excel file – itself formed of three worksheets: `Orders`, `People` and `Returns`, listed on the left. As usual with data management, variables are arranged columnwise, with observations rowwise. In Figure 3.6, the `Orders` worksheet is shown with the first 11 transactions (out of 10,000) visible. Each order is described by 20 initial variables (known as fields in Tableau parlance), such as `Order ID`, `Order Date`, `Dispatch Date` and `Delivery Mode`. The field list is also shown (left of centre in Figure 3.6).

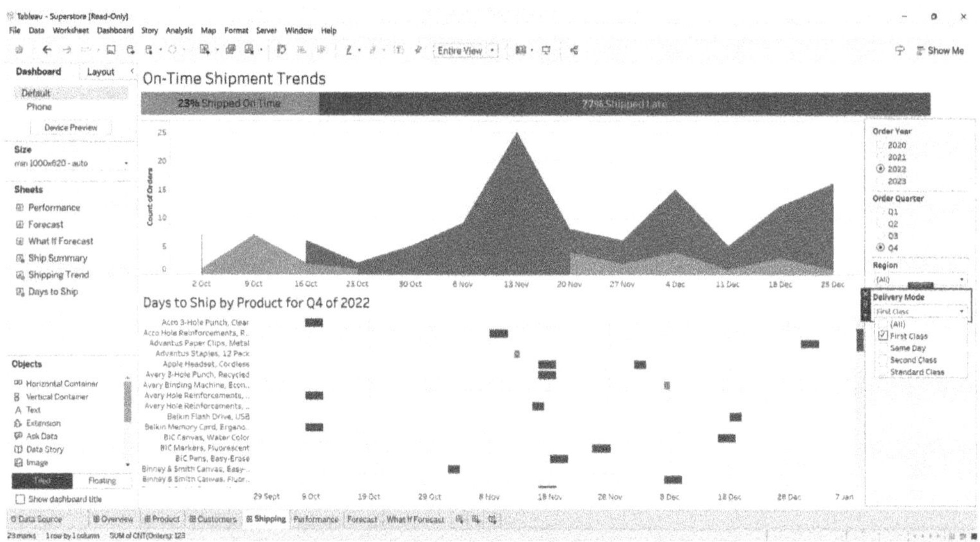

Figure 3.5 Shipping dashboard of Tableau's sample Superstore dataset.

If you were to scroll through the variable/field list and all the transactions, it is not really possible with the naked eye to spot any trends, patterns, relationships or outliers in the raw data. So, we need the help of data viz.

Relationships

Before we proceed, note that the top third of Figure 3.6 shows the relationships between the three source worksheets. In Tableau it is straightforward to define relationships between raw data worksheets, provided they share common fields. We deep-dive into these relationships in Figure 3.7.

Here we see that `Orders` and `People` are related, which is possible due to the common field of `Region`

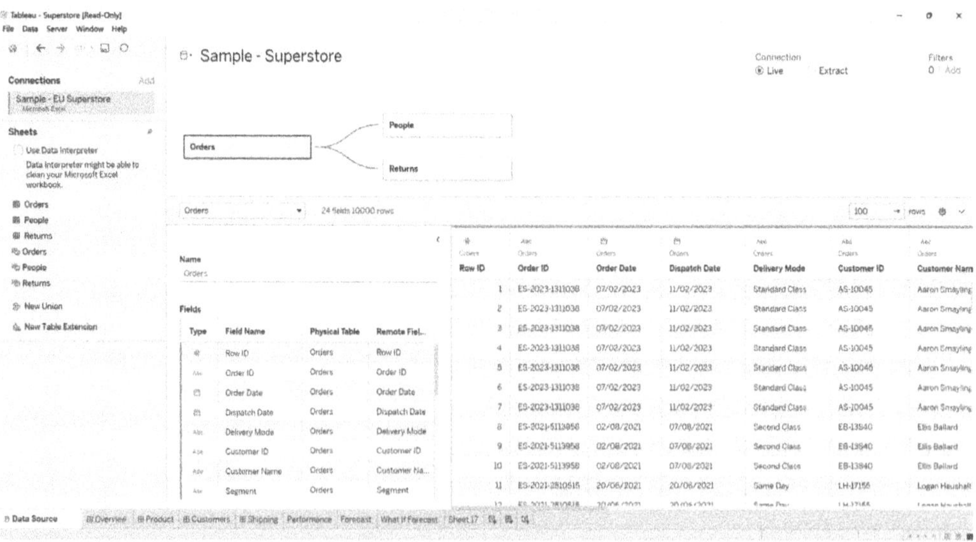

Figure 3.6 Data Source tab of Tableau's sample Superstore dataset.

in these two worksheets. Similarly, `Orders` and `Returns` are related, sharing the common field of `Order ID`. The cardinality of `many to many` allows multiple values of the shared field in one worksheet to be related to multiple rows in the other worksheet. For example, an `Order ID` can be an online shopping basket with multiple items purchased in a transaction, and multiple items can be returned.

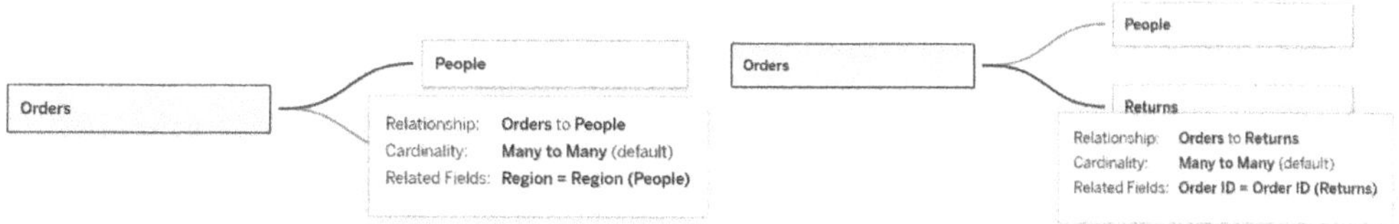

Figure 3.7 Relationships between the source worksheets of Tableau's sample Superstore dataset.

3.3 ON YOUR MARKS, GET SET, VIZ!

No doubt you are itching to get vizzing.

Earlier we noted the 77% of late-shipped first class items in Q4 2022 (in the Shipping dashboard, with appropriate filtering, shown in Figure 3.5). Was this a blip? Are there tardiness problems with other delivery modes? How much sales revenue and profit are derived from first class orders? To answer these questions, we need a viz. Et voilà, Figure 3.8!

To replicate this, click on `New Worksheet` (the icon third from right at the bottom of the screen,). In the worksheet view, we can see the complete field list in the `Data` pane on the left-hand side.

The expanded field list for `Orders` shows how Tableau distinguishes between dimensions and measures. What's the difference?

- A dimension is a variable that *cannot* be aggregated in some sense (taking the sum or average of a dimension field is meaningless).
- A measure is a variable that *can* be aggregated (summed, averaged, etc.).

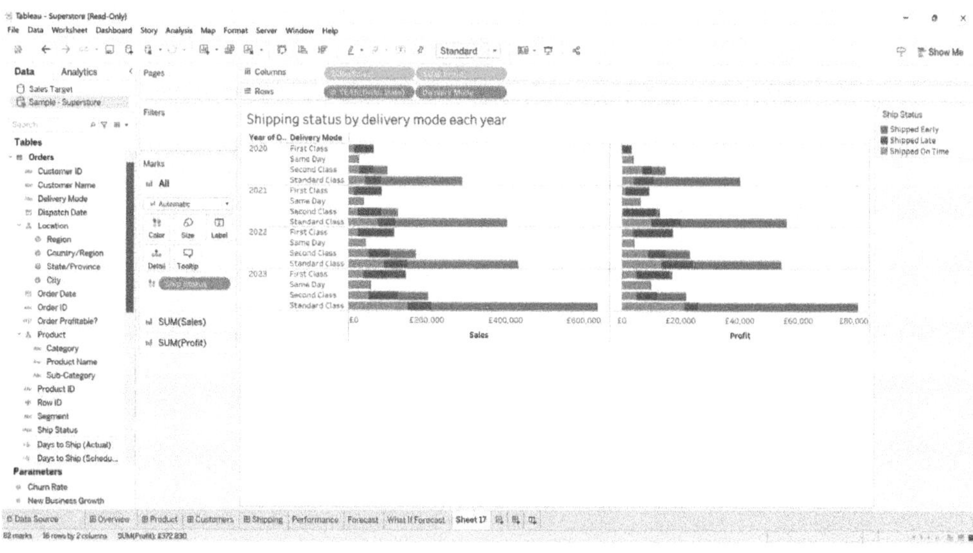

Figure 3.8 Worksheet showing shipping status by delivery mode each year using Tableau's sample Superstore dataset.

Example 3.1

In the `Orders` list:

- `Delivery Mode` is one of `first class`, `same day`, `second class` and `standard class`. This is a *dimension* because we cannot average `first class` and `same day`, for example.
- `Sales` is the revenue from a particular product in an order (note that the quantity of the product may be more than 1, such as a bulk purchase). This is a *measure* because we can aggregate and make sense of total sales, for example. Tableau features different types of aggregation: sum, average, median, count, minimum, maximum, percentile, standard deviation and variance. (You should recall these from Chapter 2!)

To create a viz, Tableau operates a *drag-and-drop* feature, where fields (variables) are placed on the Columns and Rows *shelves* at the top of a worksheet. In Figure 3.8, `Sales` and `Profit` (both measures) have been dragged and dropped onto the Columns shelf, while `Order Date` and `Delivery Mode` (both dimensions) have been placed on the Rows shelf, appearing as pills. It's clear that we have green pills (on the Columns shelf) and blue pills (on the Rows shelf). It is tempting to think, therefore, that green pills are measures and blue pills are dimensions. Wrong! This is a common misunderstanding (albeit most measures are green, and most dimensions are blue). The distinction is as follows.

- A blue pill is used for *discrete* data.
- A green pill is used for *continuous* data.

Example 3.2

Both `Sales` and `Profit` are measures, since they can be aggregated. They are also continuous, since sales and profit need not take integer values. We could compute the average, say, of either field, reporting the values to as many decimal places as we felt appropriate. In Figure 3.8 the (default) aggregation of `SUM` is used, with both fields showing as green pills in the Columns shelf:

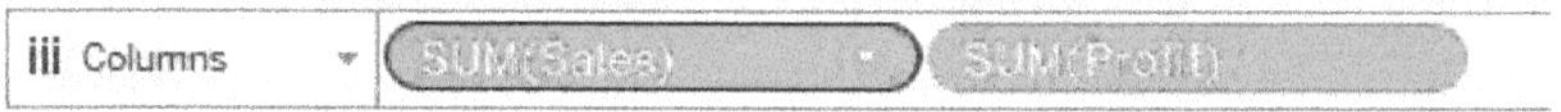

`Delivery Mode` is a dimension, since it cannot be summed nor averaged. It is also discrete, as we can only have one of the four modes (first class, same day, second class and standard class). A continuum of such names is not possible. In Figure 3.8 it is showing as a blue pill in the Rows shelf:

Of course, it is possible to aggregate `Delivery Mode` if we consider *frequency counts*, since counting is always possible for a categorical variable. As such, we can turn `Delivery Mode` into a green pill by converting it into a measure by setting the aggregation as `Count (Distinct)`, denoted by `CNTD`: CNTD(Delivery Mode) (achieved by left-clicking on the field in the field list, and selecting `Convert to Measure`).

Finally, we consider dates. These are dimensions that can be discrete (a blue pill) or continuous (a green pill). In our Figure 3.8 viz example, we have the `Order Date` visualised by year, with plotted values for the indicated years only. Hence in this context it is discrete, which is why `YEAR(Order Date)` is shown as a blue pill. However, if we wanted to conduct a *time-series analysis*, with `Order Date` on the horizontal axis (*x*-axis), then `Order Date` would be continuous with values being any specific date. As such, we can turn `Order Date` into a green pill by converting it to continuous: (achieved by left-clicking on the field in the field list, and selecting `Convert to Continuous`).

3.4 SHOW ME (WHAT WORKS!)

We have discussed the distinction between *dimensions* and *measures*. As we might expect, there are many different types of visualisation (histograms, box plots, scatter plots, treemaps, etc.). Which one(s) to use? Well, it depends! More specifically, it depends on whether you have dimensions and/or measures, as well as the number of each type of field.

Helpfully, Tableau has its Show Me feature which provides helpful suggestions for possible candidate visualisation types. In any worksheet, just click on 'Show Me' (top right) to see the gallery options, as shown in Figure 3.9.

Depending on which fields you have selected, it will make recommendations of suitable chart types (with greyed-out options being ill-suited). Think of Show Me as providing a helping hand; that said, use it in conjunction with your common sense!

Activity 3.1

Explore the Show Me function, experiment with different combinations of fields, and then 'show off' your data viz skills to an audience - captive or otherwise! Perhaps be a contender for *Viz of the Day*!

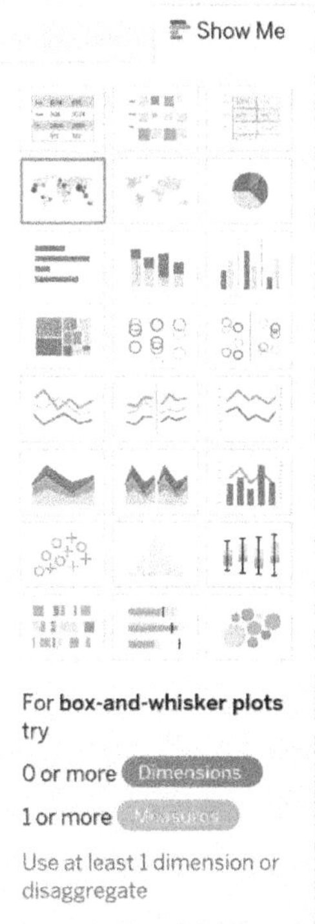

Figure 3.9 Tableau's Show Me gallery.

3.5 ADDING AND EDITING TEXT AND DYNAMIC TITLES

Here we focus on different ways to add and edit text in Tableau, followed by a walk-through of the more advanced option of using dynamic titles based on filters.

Let's begin with a familiar bar chart of sales, this time by `Country/Region`. Click on the `New Worksheet` icon. Note that the default chart title is the worksheet number. Clearly, we would wish to replace this with something more meaningful and informative. When someone is shown a chart, they often look at the title before anywhere else, so remember that titles should be precise and consistent, explain the relationship between the components, and be simplified text without redundancies. Likewise, all dimensions and measures should have meaningful names. Simply double-click the default `Sheet #` title to bring up the `Edit Title` dialog box. If we wish, we may add a caption but beware this takes up space on screen. Select **Worksheet** > **Show caption**.

In Figure 3.10 we have a static title of `Superstore Sales by Country/Region`, so if we viewed the data more granularly, by `State/Province`, say, (simply click the '+' on the left of the `Country/Region` pill in the Rows shelf to do this) the title does not update (bad), but the caption does (good), as shown in Figure 3.11.

Figure 3.10 Initial viz of sales using Tableau's sample Superstore dataset.

Showing mark labels is useful if you wish to display precise values (as shown in Figure 3.11). To show mark labels, click on `Label` in the `Marks` card, and then click on `Show mark labels`. However, you should use this sparingly to prevent overcrowding and needlessly confusing your audience.

Field names make it easier to interact with the data, so we really want to make sure we get those names correct. In the `Data` pane, right-click on the dimension or measure, and then click `Rename`. For example, we may change `Sales` to `Invoice value`, should we so wish.

Now let's add a filter for `Country/Region` and show the filter, and also break down by segment, generating a legend. The updated viz is shown in Figure 3.12. Note how the very high level of sales in England dwarfs that of other areas, making it harder to read non-England sales (suggestion: filter out England).

To update names of the filter or legend titles, click on the drop-down menu for the filter, and then click on `Edit Title`, and similarly for the legend. These titles look sensible as they are, so we can leave them. Note how the caption at the bottom auto-updates.

Now let's create a dynamic title that changes based on filter selections. This will help us produce clearer visualisations and improve the end user's experience. (Optimising user experience is always a good idea!) Suppose we are interested in sales for Austria, Finland and Spain, themselves broken down by segment. Simply select these countries using the filter. To create a dynamic title (which updates with any filter changes we subsequently apply) just double-click on the existing static title. Next, in the `Edit Title` dialog box, select **Insert** > **Country/Region**, and then click `OK`. The result is shown in Figure 3.13.

Great, we have now added a dynamic title! Your Tableau skillset is advancing quickly. Bravo.

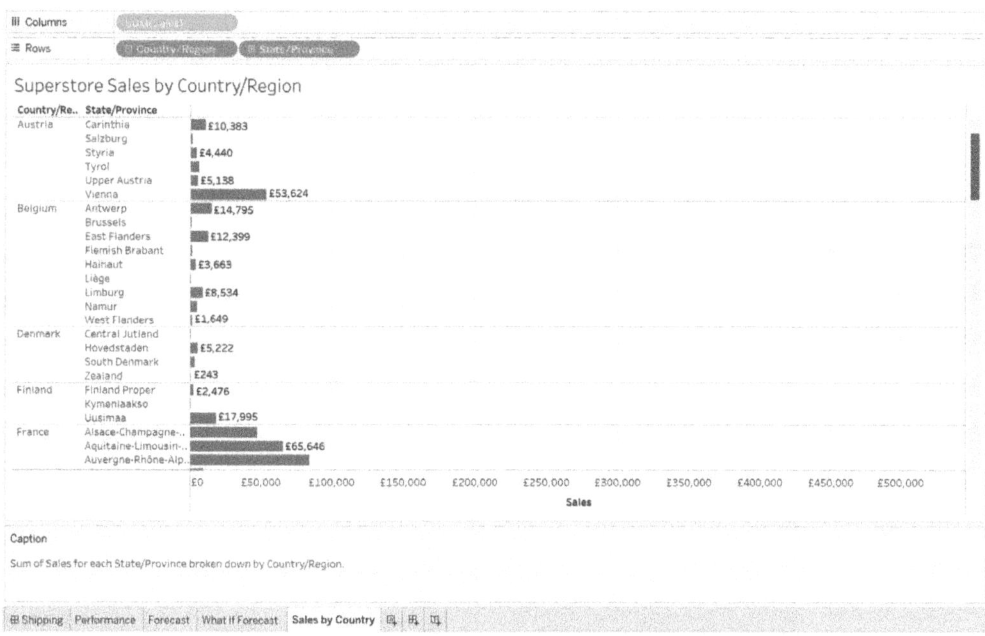

Figure 3.11 More granular viz of sales using Tableau's sample Superstore dataset.

3.6 MAPS

Let's look at creating maps in Tableau, again using the sample Superstore (European) dataset. Maps are great for showing quantitative geographic data, and Tableau provides powerful mapping tools for building accurate and clear visualisations.

Start with a new worksheet. In the `Data` pane, from the `Orders` table double-click on the `City` field. A map view is automatically created because `City` is a geographic field (as signalled by the globe icon: ⊕ State/Province). `Latitude` and `Longitude` appear in the Rows and Columns shelves, respectively. From here we can easily customise the shape, colour (UK spelling! 🇬🇧), and size of the points on the `Marks` card. Any changes made here should not be arbitrary, with the objective being to make the visualisation as clear and accessible as possible. For example, we can drag the `Sales` field to the `Color` (US spelling! 🇺🇸) and `Size` in the `Marks` card to emphasise where our sales are greatest. Doing so, the map auto*magically* changes the shading and size of the data points proportionately to the total sales amount. Fantastic. Unsurprisingly, capital cities dominate (notably London, Paris, Berlin, Madrid and Vienna), as shown in Figure 3.14.

Now let's apply a filter to show just the data for, say, France. Drag the `Country/Region` field to the `Filters` pane. Click on `None`, then `France` and `OK`.

Depending on the business problem you're solving, you can add or remove layers of geographic details to the visualisation. To add layers – or some style – select **Map** > **Background Maps** > **Streets**, say, if your human geography is a bit rusty. **Maps** > **Background Layers** is also worth exploring, especially if your physical geography is hazy. You may also like to experiment with the different colour palettes (double-click on the colour legend). Very quickly, we have modified the original viz quite dramatically, as shown in Figure 3.15.

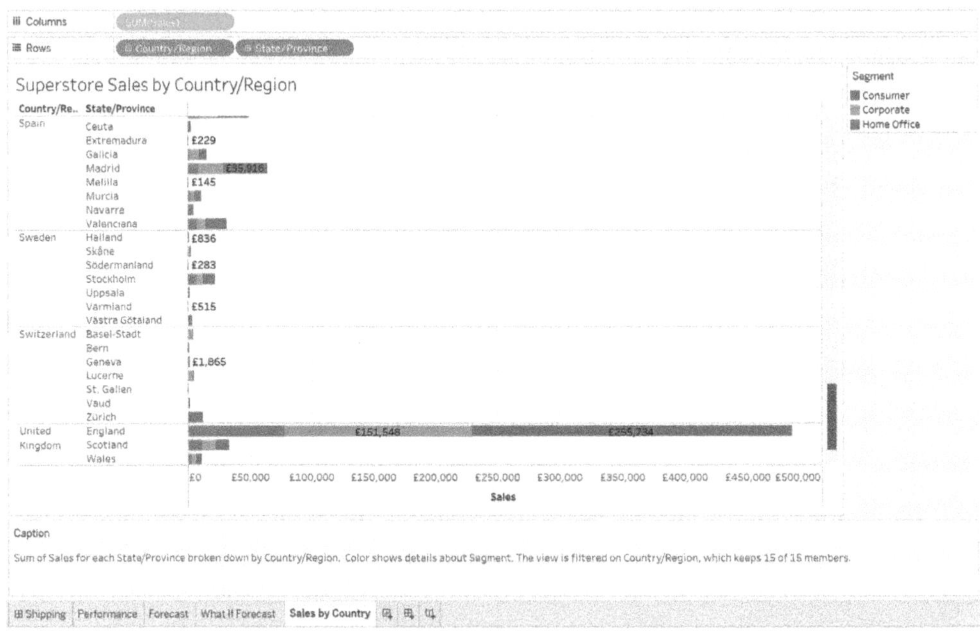

Figure 3.12 Even more granular viz of sales using Tableau's sample Superstore dataset.

It is possible to Zoom into a specific area, such as Paris, with different degrees of detail as shown in Figure 3.16.

Clearly, there are many possible permutations of map viz. In practice you would spend time fine-tuning to your specific requirements.

For US datasets, economic measures can also be added. How about median household income as well to give a sense of relative prosperity? Note the use of the *median*, rather than the *mean*, as income is positively skewed, so the mean can be distorted by a few high-income individuals (recall our discussion of outliers in Chapter 2).

As we have seen, maps are designed to help you visualise geographic data. So, make smart use of them and you'll never be lost. Now, go and play!

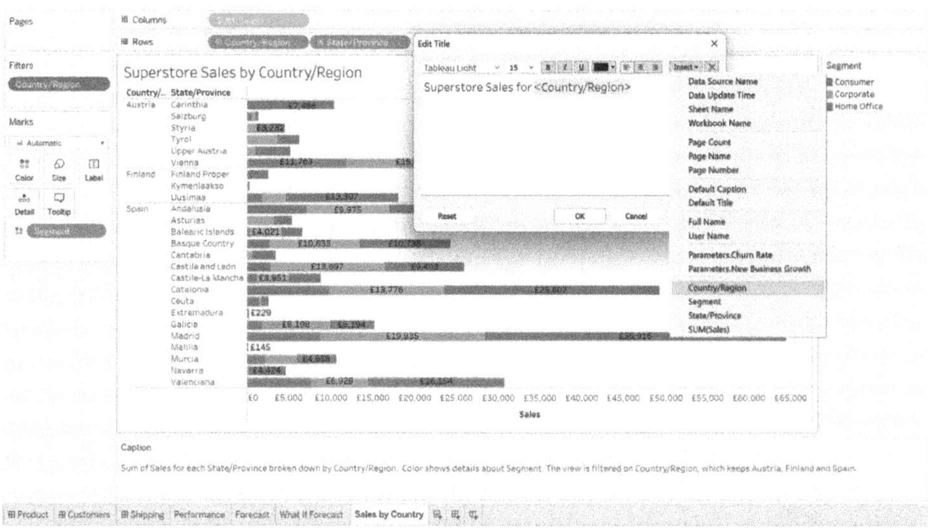

Figure 3.13 Our first dynamic title! Cue applause.

3.7 CALCULATED FIELDS AND PARAMETERS

Here we show how to create new fields known as calculated fields, essentially new variables calculated using a formula.

Remember that dashboards should be clear and accessible for the end user and adjusted to their needs (always keep in mind the user experience). Consider, for example, the What If Forecast dashboard in the sample Superstore dataset, shown in Figure 3.17.

Here sales forecasts are calculated using two parameters (listed bottom left in Figure 3.17):

- `Churn Rate` (the rate of customer attrition), which can be changed in increments of 0.1 percentage points between 0% and 25%, with a default/displayed value of 6.40%
- `New Business Growth` (the rate of business expansion), which can be changed in single percentage point increments between 0% and 100%, with a default/displayed value of 60%.

To see how these parameters have been created, right-click on the respective parameter name at the bottom of the data pane. We get Figure 3.18.

These are 'float' type parameters, meaning they are numeric and not restricted to being integers. Minimum and maximum values are specified, along with the incremental steps which are deemed suitable for any analysis. To create your own parameters simply right-click on the `Data` pane and follow **Create > Parameter....**

`Sales Forecast` is a calculated field returning forecasts of sales based on the churn rate and new business growth parameters. To create a new calculated field, navigate to **Analysis > Create Calculated Field....** However, let's analyse the pre-prepared `Sales Forecast` field. Note how Tableau indicates a calculated field using an equals sign before '#': =# **Sales Forecast**. Navigate to **Analysis > Edit Calculated Field > Sales Forecast...** from which we obtain Figure 3.19.

Here we see that the `Sales Forecast` formula is formed from sales (`[Sales]`) multiplied by the customer ***retention*** rate (which is 1 minus the churn rate, i.e. `(1-[Churn Rate])`), times a multiple of current business activity, representing business growth, as modelled by the new business growth parameter (`(1+[New Business Growth])`).

Note the syntax for creating a calculated field. Fields and parameters enter the formula within square brackets. A message, `The calculation is valid.`, confirms there are no syntax errors with the formula.

Example 3.3

If there is 0% churn (equivalently, 100% customer retention) and no new business growth, then `Churn Rate = 0` and `New Business Growth = 0`, such that `Sales Forecast` will just be current sales.

Ceteris paribus, the *higher* (*lower*) the churn rate, the *lower* (*higher*) sales are expected to be, as reflected by the `Sales Forecast` formula. The lower the churn, the greater the customer retention, which is a good thing.

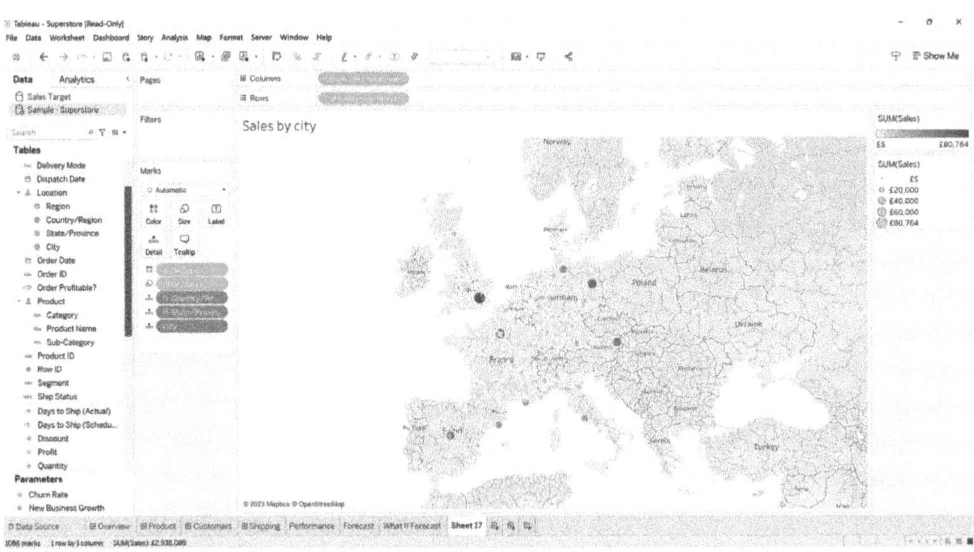

Figure 3.14 Our first map viz: sales by city using Tableau's sample Superstore dataset.

Ceteris paribus, the *higher* (*lower*) the new business growth, the *higher* (*lower*) sales are expected to be, again as reflected by the `Sales Forecast` formula. The more the business expands, the higher sales would be, also a good thing.

Example 3.4

With reference to Figure 3.17, the total January 2023 sales for the Consumer segment in the Central region were £19,614 (the top-left entry). Based on a churn rate of 6.40% and new business growth of 60%, the sales forecast calculation is:

$$£19{,}614 \times (1 - 0.064) \times (1 + 0.60) = £29{,}374$$

rounded to the nearest pound. Note that the parameter values enter the calculated field formula in decimal form rather than as percentages (i.e. 0.064 instead of 6.4%, and 0.60 instead of 60%).

While the `Sales Forecast` formula seems realistic (churn and business growth plausibly should feature in forecasts which, by their very nature, are forward-looking), what will the superstore's churn rate and new business growth *actually* be during the period being forecast? Well, being forward-looking, we just don't know! This is why a 'what if' dashboard has been created, allowing the business analyst to experiment with different combinations of the parameter values, starting with the default/displayed values of 6.40% (churn rate) and 60% (new business growth).

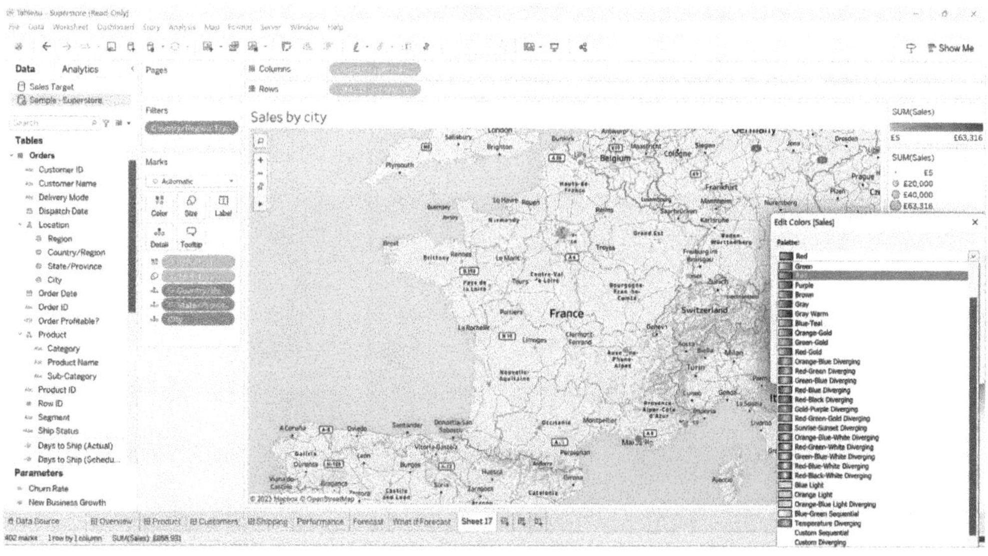

Figure 3.15 Our evolving map viz: sales by city with a focus on France using Tableau's sample Superstore dataset.

Clearly, the calculated value of `Sales Forecast` will depend on (i.e. be *sensitive* to) the values of these two parameters. By changing the parameter values (reflecting how optimistic or pessimistic we are), we will obtain different sales forecasts. Suppose the superstore plans to introduce a new loyalty scheme (with the expectation of lower churn) and a marketing drive (with the expectation of more business growth). How would the sales forecasts change? Let's *assume* churn of 3.50% and new business growth of 75%. Adjusting the parameter values using the sliders (on the right), we obtain Figure 3.20.

Example 3.5

With reference to Figure 3.20 the total January 2023 sales for the Consumer segment in the Central region are still £19,614 (unchanged, obviously). Based on a churn rate of 3.50% and new business growth of 75%, the `Sales Forecast` calculation is now:

$$£19{,}614 \times (1 - 0.035) \times (1 + 0.75) = £33{,}123$$

rounded to the nearest pound. The lower churn (which is good) and higher business growth (also good) have jointly resulted in a greater sales forecast, as expected.

Notice how the chart title in Figure 3.20 has updated with the revised parameter values. This was not achieved manually, but – yes, you've guessed it – by using a *dynamic title*. Double-click on the worksheet title to open the `Edit Title` dialog box, shown in Figure 3.21.

The grey-shaded components in the dialog box are the dynamic elements of the title. So, the year will adjust based on our filter setting (`All`, `2020`, `2021`, `2022` or `2023`). Similarly, we can feature parameter values in the title that automatically update to reflect the specific parameter values chosen (and, of course, in this worksheet the tabled `Sales Forecast` values automatically update as well).

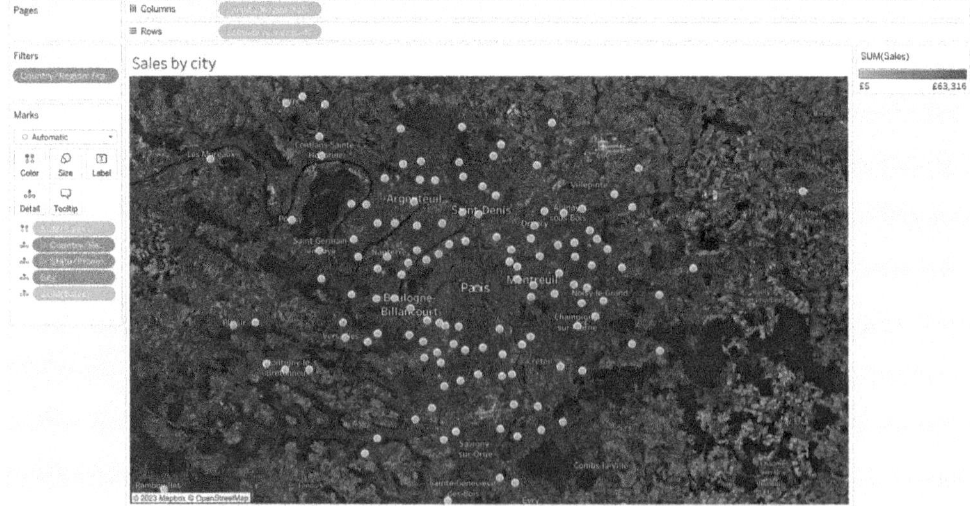

Figure 3.16 Paris, the city of love...and sales. Businesses love sales. Tableau, *je t'aime*.

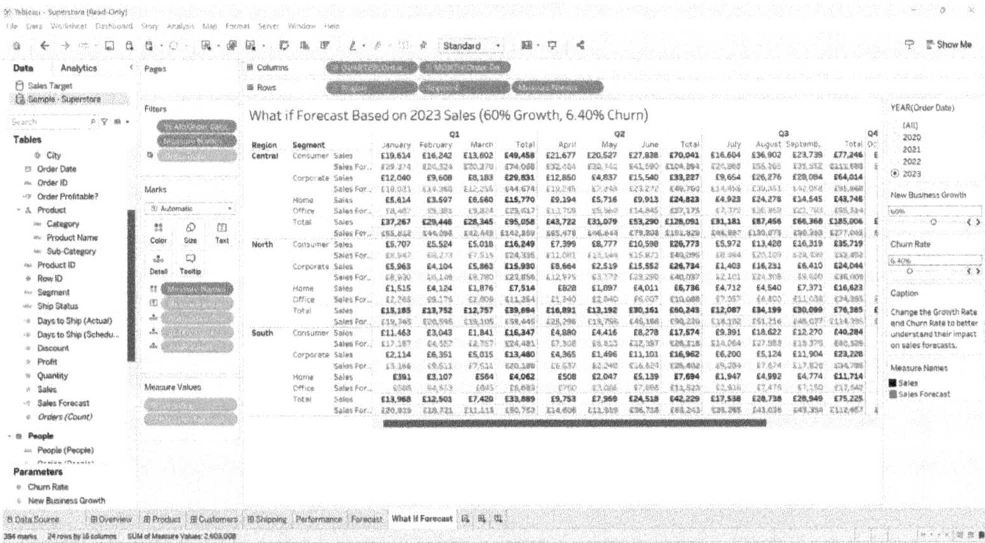

Figure 3.17 What If Forecast dashboard of Tableau's sample Superstore dataset.

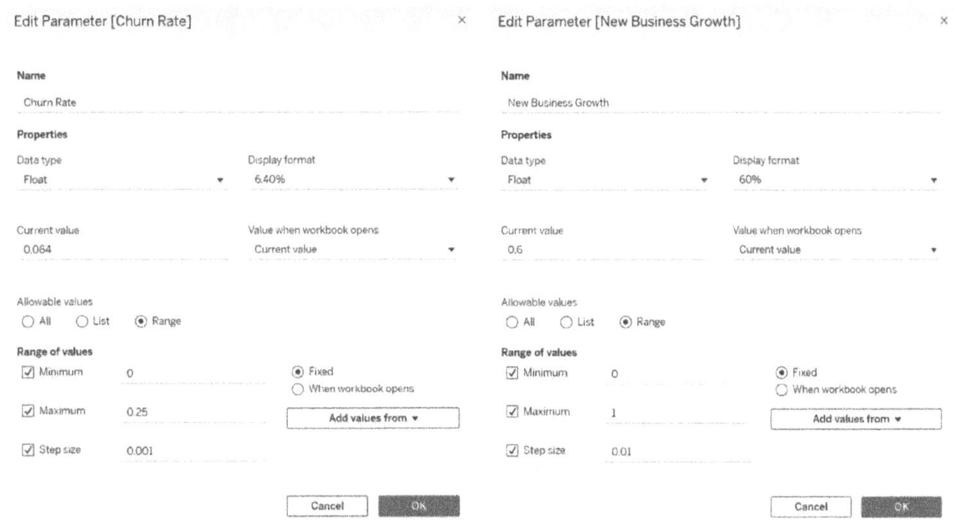

Figure 3.18 Examining the parameters `Churn Rate` and `New Business Growth` used in the What If Forecasts dashboard.

3.8 DIG DEEPER

Tableau's website contains a range of different tutorials and guides that are useful in gaining a comprehensive understanding of Tableau – far more comprehensively than is possible in this single chapter. Explore these self-study resources at your leisure (and for your pleasure) to gain mastery at extracting insight from data visually.

You can view the latest news, trends, tips and tricks by accessing the Whitepapers section on Tableau's website, https://www.tableau.com/learn/whitepapers.

Figure 3.19 Examining the calculated field of Sales Forecast.

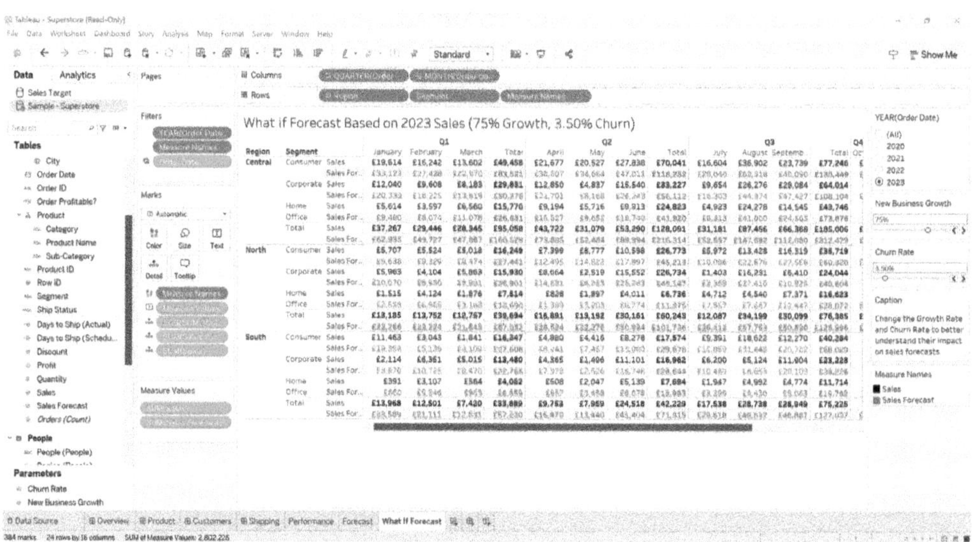

Figure 3.20 What If Forecast dashboard of Tableau's sample Superstore dataset with adjusted parameter values.

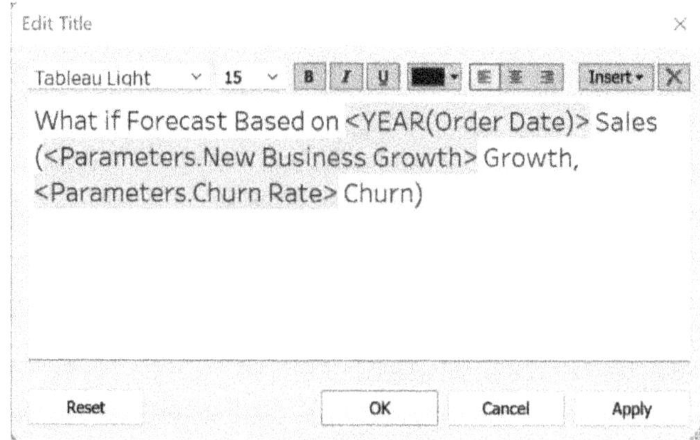

Figure 3.21 Examining the dynamic title used in Figure 3.20.

3.9 CHAPTER OVERVIEW

This chapter has introduced you to the powerful data visualisation tool which is Tableau. Understanding the fundamental functions of Tableau and being able to use them allows you to effectively communicate business insights extracted from data to a broad audience. Time and effort spent in constructing each viz will be rewarded with key takeaways being clearly digested by your audience. Had fun? If so, go and play, and keep vizzing.

3.10 KEY VOCABULARY

Calculated field
Caption
Dashboard
Data Source
Data visualisation
Dimension
Dynamic title
Field
Filter
Map
Measure
Parameter
Pills (blue and green)
Relationship
Show Me
Story
Tableau
Worksheet

3.11 EXERCISES

3.11.1 Test your understanding

1. Is data visualisation an art or a science? Briefly justify your view.
2. Should you always trust your first impressions when viewing data visualisations produced by others? If not, what might you wish to look at more closely?
3. Over time, what will you see on the start page in Tableau?
4. Distinguish between a 'worksheet', 'dashboard' and 'story' in Tableau.
5. How many worksheets should appear in a single dashboard? ('Well, James, it depends' is a fair answer, but explain on what basis 'it depends'!)
6. What is the purpose of a filter in Tableau?
7. What does the Data Source in Tableau show us?
8. Can multiple raw data worksheets be linked in Tableau? If so, how?
9. How do 'dimensions' and 'measures' differ in Tableau?
10. What is a 'blue pill'?
11. What is a 'green pill'?
12. What use is Show Me in Tableau?
13. What are some of the data visualisation types in the Show Me gallery? Which is your favourite, and why?
14. Is it possible for worksheet titles to update automatically, such as when filters are applied? If so, how?
15. If you wanted to create a map, how would you identify geographic fields in Tableau's list of variables?
16. What is a 'calculated field'?
17. Give an example of a parameter and how it could be used in a calculated field.
18. For the parameter suggested in Question 17, write the formula for the calculated field using Tableau syntax.
19. For the parameter used in Questions 17 and 18, what range of values would you suggest it takes, and what would be your choice of default value? Briefly justify your view.
20. Have you watched Tableau's own screencasts yet? If no, please do. If yes, proceed to the case study task below!

3.11.2 Case study corner

Source online any dataset of your choice (ideally with a large number of variables/fields). Experiment with creating some visualisations in Tableau, and produce a set of dashboards and an accompanying executive summary (a one-page document) summarising your findings. Are there any data-driven recommendations resulting from your data viz?

4

PROBABILITY

Chapter contents

Chapter level: *Intermediate*

Source: Photo by jakob5200 via Unsplash.

Key concepts

- Probability
- Events
- Bayes' theorem

Chapter value

Probability allows us to quantity uncertainty to assist with decision-making under uncertainty.

Key takeaway

All probabilities are between 0 and 1, reflecting how likely an event is to occur.

Chapter outline

Do you feel lucky? Well, do ya? Probability theory is the branch of mathematics that deals with uncertainty. Given our previous look at decision-making under uncertainty, now is the right time to formally explain what *probabilities* are, how we can calculate them, and the mechanism for 'updating' probabilities upon receipt of new information using the powerful result of *Bayes' theorem*.

Our study of probability is intrinsically linked to *risk*. Faced with uncertainty, it is important to have a clear sense of the risks involved, *manage* those risks, and *mitigate* risks as much as possible.

Many people may think of 'probability' and 'risk' as being synonymous, although it is better to be a little more precise, such that a probability measures, or estimates, the chance of an event - *any* event (good or bad) - of interest occurring in practice, while for business decisions we tend to think of risk as the chance of bad events, such as the risk of disruption to our supply chain.

Learning outcomes

After completing this chapter, you should be able to:

- explain the fundamental ideas of random experiments, sample spaces and events
- list the axioms of probability and all the common probability rules derived from them
- use the formulae for the number of combinations and permutations of k objects out of n
- explain conditional probability and the concept of independent events
- state Bayes' theorem and apply it to find conditional probabilities.

4.1 INTRODUCTION

Probability crops up in everyday life more than you may think. We use it to describe the likelihood of particular events, from games of chance to the weather and, as we saw during the Covid-19 pandemic, in the field of medicine when assessing the efficacy of vaccines.

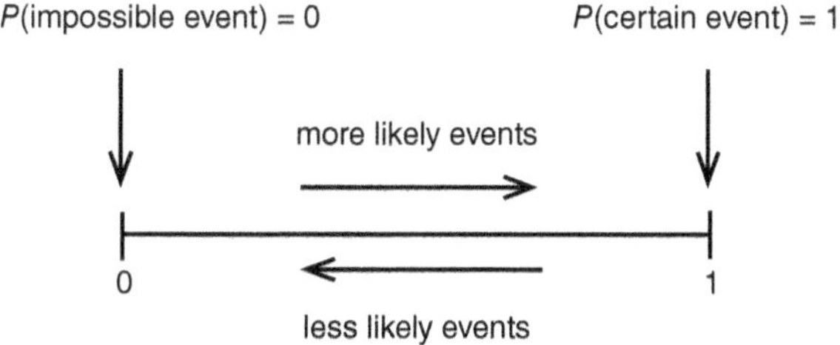

Figure 4.1 The range of probabilities and an indication of the relative likelihood of occurrence of an event.

We define probabilities to always lie in the **unit interval**, that is, all probabilities belong to the interval [0, 1]. We can easily convert these to percentages by multiplying by 100% if we wish, resulting in probabilities ranging from 0% to 100%. As a continuum, probabilities provide a measure of *how likely* a particular event of interest is to occur. By definition, an *impossible* event occurs with a probability of 0; a *certain* event occurs with a probability of 1. Probabilities strictly between 0 and 1, that is, in the interval (0, 1), can be thought of as *maybe* events – maybe they will occur, maybe they won't, with events becoming more likely, or more probable, as the probability gets closer to one. Figure 4.1 illustrates this basic premise.

Motivational case: Inferring customer satisfaction

A company conducted a survey of some of its customers to determine the level of satisfaction with its customer service. In total, 950 respondents participated in the survey which posed the question 'Are you satisfied with our customer service delivery?' with the binary set of response alternatives {Yes, No}. Their responses were recorded as follows:

	Answer		
	Yes	No	Total
Count	513	437	950
%	54%	46%	100%

However, we are not interested in just this *sample* of 950 respondents, but in the *population* which they represent, that is, *all* customers. **Statistical inference** will allow us to say things like the following about the population.

- 'A 95% confidence interval for the population proportion, π, of "satisfied" customers is (0.5083, 0.5717).' (Estimation will be covered in Chapter 9.)
- 'The null hypothesis that $\pi = 0.50$, against the alternative hypothesis that $\pi > 0.50$, is rejected at the 5% significance level.' (Hypothesis testing will be covered in Chapter 10.)

In short, the survey gives *statistically significant evidence* that satisfied customers are in the majority among all customers (management will be relieved). Such methods of statistical inference will be discussed later in Chapters 9 and 10. The inferential statements about the survey rely on the following assumptions and results. In the next few chapters, we will learn about the terms in bold, among others.

- Each response X_i is a realisation of a **random variable** from a **Bernoulli distribution** with **probability parameter** π.
- The responses $X_1, X_2, \ldots, X_n$ are **independent** of each other.
- The **sampling distribution** of the sample mean (proportion) $\bar{X}$ has **expected value** π and **variance** $\pi(1-\pi)/n$.
- By use of the **central limit theorem**, the sampling distribution is approximately a **normal distribution**.

4.1.1 The need for probability in analytics

In statistical inference, the data we have observed is regarded as a *sample* from a broader *population*, selected with a *random* process.

- Values in a sample are *variable*. If we collected a different sample we would not observe exactly the same values again (unless by chance).
- Values in a sample are also *random*. We cannot predict the precise values which will be observed before we actually collect the sample.

4.1.2 A preview of probability

The first basic concepts in probability will be the following.

- Experiment: For example, rolling a single die and recording the outcome.
- Outcome of the experiment: For example, rolling a 3.
- Sample space S: The *set* of all possible outcomes, here $\{1, 2, 3, 4, 5, 6\}$.
- Event: Any *subset* A of the sample space, for example $A = \{2, 4, 6\}$, that is, that an even score occurs.

Example 4.1

If the experiment is 'select a trading day at random and record the percentage change in the FTSE 100 index from the previous trading day', then the outcome is the percentage change in the FTSE 100 index.

The sample space is $S = [-100, +\infty)$ for the percentage change in the FTSE 100 index, as there is no upper bound, in principle! An event of interest might be $A = \{x \mid x > 0\}$, which is the event that the daily change is positive, that is, the FTSE 100 index gains value from the previous trading day.

4.2 QUANTIFYING PROBABILITIES

Ultimately, we need to determine the numerical value of $P(A)$, and we can judge the likelihood of the outcome by considering this value relative to the range of probabilities in Figure 4.1.

For now, we consider three alternative approaches to determining this probability.

1 **Subjective estimates.** One-off, rare or bespoke events like a pandemic, a stock market crash, a bank run, interest rate or inflation changes, and geopolitical shocks affecting supply chains represent huge potential risks for a business, yet typically the quantification of such probabilities falls to *subjective estimates* and (expert) *judgement*. Inevitably this approach is severely prone to *bias*, with probability estimates likely to show considerable variation among different experts due to their different opinions. Of course, we could simply average these estimates, with potentially different weights reflecting our degree of

confidence in each expert (more confidence equates to greater weight) – although this set of weights is itself rather subjective!

2 **Experimentation**. A *frequentist* approach to probability involves conducting an experiment under (seemingly) identical conditions a large number of times, and then simply counting how often the event of interest occurs. This is known as a *relative frequency* approach. It is intuitively appealing, but the ability to perform such a 'large number' of experiments may not always be feasible in practice. Chapter 20 explores Monte Carlo simulation which adheres to this frequentist approach, albeit these repeated experiments are performed as computer simulations.

3 **Theoretically**. Where possible, we seek to use theoretical probability distributions (such as the binomial, Poisson, exponential or normal) as *approximating models* of real-world phenomena. Since the properties of such distributions are well known, we may compute probabilities of events directly using these distributions which (provided the approximation to reality is sufficiently good) result in accurate probability values. An example might be using an exponential distribution to model 'times to service' of customers in a queue. We will study some of the most common probability distributions in Chapter 5.

Tick tock ... the Doomsday Clock

Finding the probabilities of events is one of the key goals when modelling uncertainty. For non-experimental situations (such as the likelihood of future geopolitical events) we have to resort to subjective estimates.

The *Doomsday Clock*, which features in the *Bulletin of the Atomic Scientists*, is a metaphor representing how close humanity is to destruction (an unhappy thought, I know!) based on the opinions of the judging panel. Expressed in terms of the number of minutes (or, in a highly volatile world, the number of seconds) to midnight, it was originally conceived due to the threat of nuclear war in the aftermath of World War II, but now also includes the threat posed by climate change and potentially even 'evil' artificial intelligence (think *The Terminator*!).

Check out: https://thebulletin.org/doomsday-clock/timeline/

To the moon!

For those with a finance career in mind, one way of developing a simple trading strategy based on the probability that a particular market may go up or down could be based on the relative frequencies of rises and falls for that market. Perhaps you might consider average daily returns (as a measure of central tendency), but also the volatility of returns, which could be measured using the standard deviation.

The probability of an event A, denoted by $P(A)$, will be defined as a *function* which assigns probabilities (real numbers between 0 and 1, inclusive) to events/sets. This uses the language and concepts of set theory, which we now review.

4.3 THE CONCEPT OF PROBABILITY

Probability can be viewed as a quantifiable measure of one's degree of belief in a particular event or set of events of interest. To motivate the use of the terms 'event' and 'set', we begin by introducing the concept of an *experiment*. An experiment can take many forms, but to keep things simple let us consider two mundane examples: the toss of a (fair) coin and the roll of a (fair) die.

Definition: Sample space

We define the sample space, S, as the set of all possible outcomes of an experiment.

Example 4.2

For a coin toss, we have $S = \{H, T\}$, where H and T denote 'heads' and 'tails', respectively, and are called the **elements** or **members** of the sample space.

For the roll of a die we have $S = \{1, 2, 3, 4, 5, 6\}$, with elements $1, 2, \ldots, 6$.

So the coin toss sample space has two elementary outcomes, H and T, while the score on a die has six elementary outcomes, 1, 2, ..., 6. These individual elementary outcomes are themselves events, but we may wish to consider events which are slightly more exciting. For example, for the die score, we may be interested in the event of obtaining an even score, or perhaps a score greater than 4. Hence we proceed to define an event.

Definition: Event

An *event* is a collection of elementary outcomes from the sample space S of an experiment and is a *subset* of S.

Typically, we can denote events by letters for notational convenience. For example, A = 'an even score', and B = 'a score greater than 4'. Hence $A = \{2, 4, 6\}$ and $B = \{5, 6\}$.

The universal convention is that we define probability to lie on a *scale* from 0 to 1 inclusive. Hence the probability of any event A, say, is denoted by $P(A)$ and is a real number somewhere in the unit interval, $P(A) \in [0, 1]$, where '$\in$' means 'is a member of'. Note the following.

- If A is an *impossible* event, then $P(A) = 0$.
- If A is a *certain* event, then $P(A) = 1$.
- For events A and B, if $P(B) < P(A)$, then A is more likely to occur than B.

Therefore, we have a probability scale from 0 to 1 on which we are able to *rank* events, as evident from the $P(B) < P(A)$ result above. However, we need to consider how best to *quantify* these probabilities.

Let us begin with experiments where each elementary outcome is *equally likely*, a criterion (conveniently) fulfilled by our (fair) coin toss and (fair) die score.

Determining event probabilities for equally likely elementary outcomes

For an experiment with *equally likely* elementary outcomes, let N be the total number of equally likely elementary outcomes, and let n be the number of these elementary outcomes which are favourable to our event of interest, A. Then

$$P(A) = \frac{n}{N}.$$

Example 4.3

We continue with Example 4.2.

For the (fair) coin toss, if A is the event 'heads', then $N = 2$ (heads and tails) and $n = 1$ (heads). So, for a *fair* coin, $P(A) = 1/2 = 0.50$. (Remember we are assuming *equally likely* elementary outcomes here, so a fair coin is required. If we had a *biased* coin, then this approach would fail to accurately quantify probabilities.)

For the (fair) die score, if A is the event 'an even score', then $N = 6$ (1, 2, 3, 4, 5 and 6) and $n = 3$ (2, 4 and 6). So, for a *fair* die, $P(A) = 3/6 = 1/2 = 0.50$.

Finally, if B is the event 'score greater than 4', then $N = 6$ (as before) and $n = 2$ (5 and 6). Hence $P(B) = 2/6 = 1/3$.

4.4 COMBINATORIAL THEORY: COUNTING

In the previous discussion concerning *equally likely* outcomes, it was crucial to know both n and N. For the (trivial) examples presented, it was (trivial) to obtain these values.

In small problems, just listing all possibilities is often quickest.

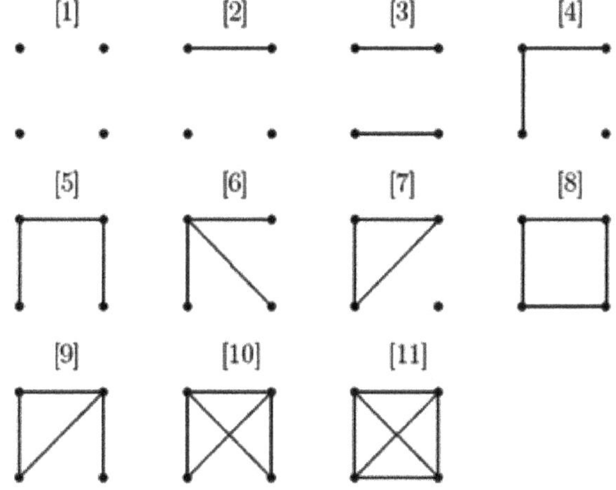

Figure 4.2 Friendship patterns in a four-person network.

Example 4.4

Consider a group of four people, where each pair of people is either connected (= friends) or not. Think of these as people connected on social media. How many different *patterns* of connections are there (ignoring the identities of who is friends with whom)?

The answer is 11. See the patterns in Figure 4.2.

For experiments with a much larger number of outcomes (your personal friendship network probably extends to many people), a useful tool to compute the number of possible outcomes is combinatorial theory. Some basic formulae are now summarised below.

4.4.1 Factorials

Definition: Factorial

The **factorial** of a non-negative integer n, denoted by $n!$, is the number of ways in which n different objects can be placed *in order*, where:

$$n! = n \times (n-1) \times (n-2) \times \cdots \times 3 \times 2 \times 1.$$

The exclamation mark, '!', is what we call 'factorial'.

In Excel, use the function `=FACT(number)`.

Example 4.5

We have:

$$3! = 3 \times 2 \times 1 = 6, \quad 5! = 5 \times 4 \times 3! = 120 \quad \text{and} \quad \frac{5!}{3!} = \frac{5 \times 4 \times 3!}{3!} = 20.$$

In addition, we define 0! = 1 in order to have compatibility with the formulae below.

4.4.2 Permutations

Definition: Permutation

The number of different groups of r objects which can be chosen *in order* from n different objects is called the number of **permutations** of r from n, defined as

$$^{n}P_{r} = \frac{n!}{(n-r)!}.$$

In Excel, use the function = `PERMUT(number, number chosen)`.

Example 4.6

The number of different queues (lines, i.e. in order) of 4 people which we can form from 6 people is:

$$^{6}P_{4} = \frac{6!}{2!} = 6 \times 5 \times 4 \times 3 = 360.$$

Note that in a queue, *where* you appear in the queue matters. We would rather be at the front of the queue than at the back of the queue! (Unless we are playing the glass bridge round of *Squid Game* (for those familiar with the show), where there is a clear first-mover *disadvantage*!)

4.4.3 Combinations

Definition: Combination

The number of different groups of r objects which can be chosen from n different objects (i.e. where *order does not matter*) is called the number of **combinations** of r from n, defined as

$$^{n}C_{r} = \binom{n}{r} = \frac{n!}{r!(n-r)!}.$$

In Excel, use the function = `COMBIN(number, number chosen)`.

Example 4.7

The number of different groups of 4 people (where order is irrelevant) which we can form from 6 people is

$$^{6}C_{4} = \frac{6!}{4!2!} = \frac{720}{24 \times 2} = 15.$$

Note that when you are a member of a group (or team), it is the *composition* of the group that matters, not the order in which individuals joined the group. (In the tug of war round of *Squid Game*, you just want to be on the winning team!)

Example 4.8

Consider a room with r people in it gathered at random. What is the probability that *at least two of them have the same birthday* (call this event A)? In particular, what is the smallest r for which $P(A) > 1/2$?

Assume that all days are equally likely.

Label the people from 1 to r, so that we can treat them as an ordered list and talk about person 1, person 2 and so on. We want to know how many ways there are to assign birthdays to this list of people. We note the following.

1 The number of all possible sequences of birthdays, allowing repeats (i.e. with replacement) is 365^r.
2 The number of sequences where *all birthdays are different* (i.e. without replacement) is $365!/(365 - r)!$.

Here (1) is the size of the sample space, and (2) is the number of outcomes which satisfy A^c, the **complement** of the case in which we are interested.

Therefore,

$$P(A^c) = \frac{365!/(365-r)!}{365^r} = \frac{365 \times 364 \times \cdots \times (365-r+1)}{365^r}$$

and

$$P(A) = 1 - P(A^c) = 1 - \frac{365 \times 364 \times \cdots \times (365-r+1)}{365^r}.$$

(Continued)

Probabilities, $P(A)$, of $r \geq 2$ people sharing a birthday are given in the following table:

r	$P(A)$	r	$P(A)$	r	$P(A)$	r	$P(A)$
2	0.003	12	0.167	22	0.476	32	0.753
3	0.008	13	0.194	23	0.507	33	0.775
4	0.016	14	0.223	24	0.538	34	0.795
5	0.027	15	0.253	25	0.569	35	0.814
6	0.040	16	0.284	26	0.598	36	0.832
7	0.056	17	0.315	27	0.627	37	0.849
8	0.074	18	0.347	28	0.654	38	0.864
9	0.095	19	0.379	29	0.681	39	0.878
10	0.117	20	0.411	30	0.706	40	0.891
11	0.141	21	0.444	31	0.730	41	0.903

This is the famous *birthday paradox*. Probability is littered with paradoxes such that the result seems to be counter-intuitive, and hence interesting. In this instance, if you told a room full of 23 people that it was more likely than not that at least two people shared a birthday, most people would probably not believe you! If you were one of those 23 people, it is not suggesting that you *personally* are more likely to share a birthday with someone else. Rather, there are 253 pairwise comparisons to consider

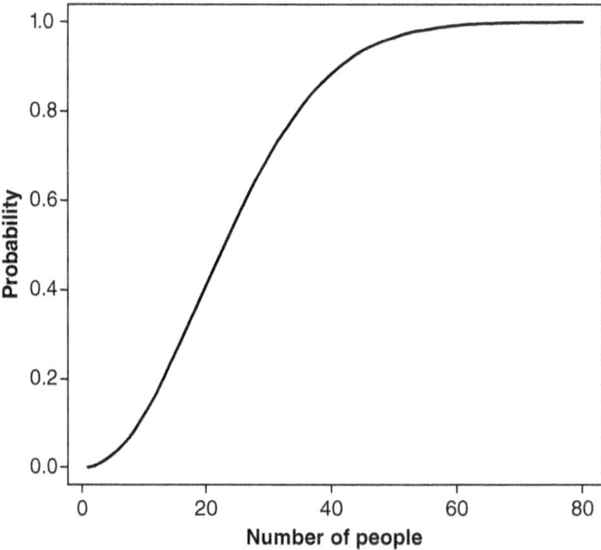

Figure 4.3 Probability of at least two people with the same birthday as a function of the number of people.

since we can compare person 1's birthday with the other 22, then compare person 2's birthday with the remaining 21, etc., giving 22 + 21 + ... + 2 + 1 = 253 possible pairings to consider. Once we appreciate the number of these pairwise comparisons it seems far more reasonable that at least two people share a birthday.

Figure 4.3 plots $P(A)$ against r for $r = 0, 1, 2, \dots, 80$.

Activity 4.1

For readers in a class, see if you can find some 'birthday twins' among you! Alternatively, among your personal friendship network see who among you share a common birthday. Many happy returns. (My birthday is 29 October.)

4.5 RELATIVE FREQUENCY

So far, we have only considered *equally likely* experimental outcomes. Clearly, to apply probabilistic concepts more widely, we require a more general interpretation – the relative frequency interpretation.

Relative frequency approach to probability

Suppose that the event A associated with some experiment either does or does not occur. Also, suppose we conduct this experiment *independently* a total of F times, representing the overall frequency of these repeated experiments. Suppose the event A occurs f times across the F repeated experiments. The 'frequentist' approach to probability would regard the probability of A as

$$P(A) = \frac{f}{F}$$

as $F \to \infty$.

Example 4.9

For a coin toss with event $A = \{H\}$, if the coin is fair we would *expect* that repeatedly tossing the coin F times would result in *approximately* $f = F/2$ heads, hence $P(A) = (F/2)/F = 1/2$.

Of course, this approach is not confined to fair coins!

Intuitively, this is an appealing interpretation and is extremely useful when we come to its use in statistical inference later on.

However, do be aware that I am not advocating that you perform all these experiments! Rather they are imaginary experiments, but the concept gives a meaning to numerical probability. (There is another 'school' of probability thought, known as the 'Bayesian' school. We will touch on this briefly via Bayes' theorem later in this chapter. In short, the Bayesian view is that probability is a degree of belief in an event's occurrence *based on the observer's knowledge of the situation*.)

4.6 RANDOMNESS

Statistical inference is concerned with the drawing of conclusions from data which are subject to *randomness*, perhaps due to the sampling procedure, perhaps due to observational errors, perhaps for some other reason.

Let us stop and think why, when we repeat an experiment under apparently identical conditions, we get different results.

The answer is that although the conditions may be as identical as we are able to control them to be, there will inevitably be a large number of uncontrollable (and frequently unknown) variables which we do not measure and which have a cumulative effect on the result of the sample or experiment. For example, weather conditions may affect the outcomes of field experiments.

Therefore, the cumulative effect is to cause variation in our results. It is this variation which we term *randomness* and, although we never fully know the true generating mechanism for our data, we can take the random component into account via the concept of probability which is, of course, why probability plays such an important role in data analysis!

4.7 PROPERTIES OF PROBABILITY

We begin this section by presenting three simple, self-evident truths known as **axioms** which list the basic properties we require of event probabilities.

Axioms of probability

1 For any event A, $P(A) \geq 0$.
2 For the sample space S, $P(S) = 1$.
3 If $\{A_i\}$, $i = 1, 2, \ldots$, are *mutually exclusive* events, then the probability of their 'union' is the sum of their respective probabilities, that is,

$$P\left(\bigcup_{i=1}^{\infty} A_i\right) = \sum_{i=1}^{\infty} P(A_i).$$

When the number of events is finite, say n, the **finite additivity** version of axiom 3 is

$$P\left(\bigcup_{i=1}^{n} A_i\right) = \sum_{i=1}^{n} P(A_i).$$

The first two axioms should not be surprising. The third may appear a little more daunting. Recall that events are mutually exclusive when they cannot occur simultaneously.

Example 4.10

When rolling a die once, the event A = 'obtain an even score' and the event B = 'obtain an odd score' are mutually exclusive.

Extending this, a collection of events is *pairwise* mutually exclusive if no two events can occur simultaneously. For instance, the three events A, B and C are pairwise mutually exclusive if A and B cannot occur together *and* B and C cannot occur together *and* A and C cannot occur together. Another way of putting this is that a collection of events is pairwise mutually exclusive if *at most one* of them can occur.

Related to this is the concept of a collection of events being *collectively exhaustive*, which recall means *at least one* of them must occur, that is, all possible experimental outcomes are included among the collection of events.

4.7.1 Notational vocabulary

Axiom 3 above introduced a new symbol. For the remainder of this chapter, various symbols connecting sets will be used as a form of notational shorthand. It is important to be familiar with these symbols, hence two 'translations' are provided – one informal, the other more formal.

Symbol	'Informal' version	'Formal' version	Example
$\cup$	or	union	$A \cup B$ = 'A union B'
$\cap$	and	intersect	$A \cap B$ = 'A intersect B'
^{c}	not	complement of	A^c = 'complement of A'
$\mid$	given	conditional on	$A \mid B$ = 'A conditional on B'

Also, make sure that you distinguish between a *set* and the *probability of a set*. This distinction is important. A *set*, remember, is a collection of elementary outcomes from S, whereas a *probability* is a number on the unit interval, [0, 1] (a consequence of Axioms 1 and 2). For example, A = 'an even die score', while $P(A) = 0.50$, for a fair die.

4.7.2 Venn diagrams

The previous coin and die examples were rather simple (for illustrative purposes). Hence it is highly likely (in fact with a probability of 1!) that you will encounter more challenging sets and sample spaces. Fear not, there is a helpful geometric technique which can often be used – we represent the sample space elements in a Venn diagram.

Imagine we roll a die twice and record the total score. Hence our sample space will be

$$S = \{2, 3, 4, 5, 6, 7, 8, 9, 10, 11, 12\}.$$

Suppose we are interested in the following three events:

- A = 'an even total', that is, $A = \{2, 4, 6, 8, 10, 12\}$
- B = 'a total strictly less than 8', that is, $B = \{2, 3, 4, 5, 6, 7\}$
- C = 'a total greater than 4 but less than 10', that is, $C = \{5, 6, 7, 8, 9\}$.

Having defined these events, it is therefore possible to insert every element in the sample space S into a Venn diagram, as shown in Figure 4.4.

The box represents S, so every possible outcome of the experiment (the total score when a die is rolled twice) appears within the box. Three (overlapping) circles are drawn representing the events A, B and C. Each element of S is then inserted into the appropriate area. For example, the area where the three circles all intersect represents the event $A \cap B \cap C$ into which we place the element '6', since this is the only member of S which satisfies all three events A, B and C. Note that '11' is the only possible outcome which does not feature in the definitions of A, B and C, so appears outside of $A \cup B \cup C$, but must lie inside S because it is a possible experimental outcome.

Example 4.11

Using Figure 4.4, we can determine the following sets:

- $A \cap B = \{2, 4, 6\}$
- $A \cap C = \{6, 8\}$
- $A \cap B \cap C = \{6\}$
- $(A \cup B \cup C)^c = \{11\}$
- $A \cap B \cap C^c = \{2, 4\}$
- $A^c \cap B = \{3, 5, 7\}$
- $(A \cup C)^c \cap B = \{3\}$
- $A \mid C = \{6, 8\}$.

Activity 4.2

Satisfy yourself that the sets of outcomes for each case in Example 4.11 are as claimed.

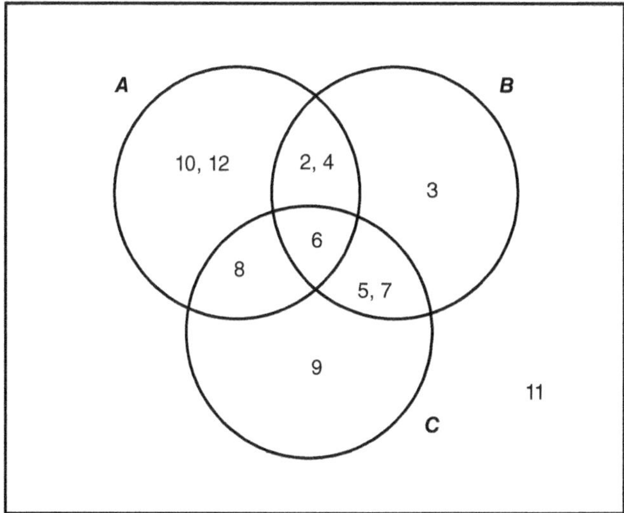

Figure 4.4 Venn diagram for pre-defined sets *A*, *B* and *C* recording the total score when a die is rolled twice.

4.7.3 The additive law

We now introduce our first probability 'law'.

Definition: The additive law

Let *A* and *B* be any two events. The **additive law** states that:

$$P(A \cup B) = P(A) + P(B) - P(A \cap B).$$

So $P(A \cup B)$ is the probability that *at least* one of *A* and *B* occurs, and $P(A \cap B)$ is the probability that *both A* and *B* occur.

Example 4.12

We can think about the additive law using a Venn diagram. The total area of the Venn diagram in Figure 4.5 is assumed to be 1, so area represents probability. Event *A* is composed of all points in the left-hand circle, and event *B* is composed of all points in the right-hand circle. Hence:

(Continued)

$P(A)$ = area x + area z,

$P(B)$ = area y + area z,

$P(A \cap B)$ = area z,

$P(A \cup B)$ = area x + area y + area z

and

$$P(A \cup B) = P(A) + P(B) - P(A \cap B)$$
$$= (\text{area } x + \text{area } z) + (\text{area } y + \text{area } z) - (\text{area } z)$$
$$= \text{area } x + \text{area } y + \text{area } z.$$

Therefore, to compute $P(A \cup B)$ we need to subtract $P(A \cap B)$, otherwise that region would have been counted twice.

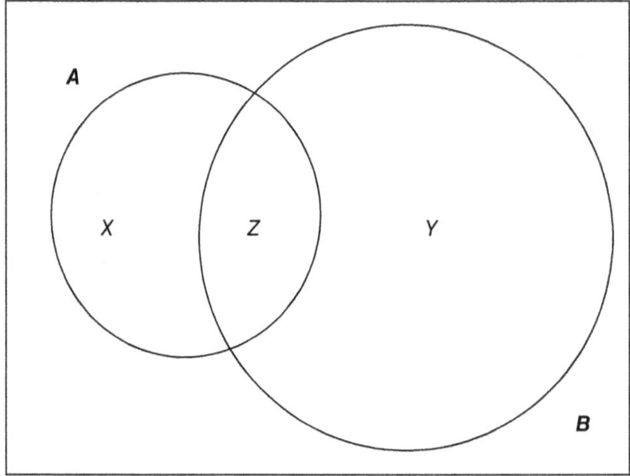

Figure 4.5 Venn diagram illustrating the additive law.

Example 4.13

Consider an industrial production situation in which a machine component can be defective in two ways such that:

- P(defective in first way) = $P(D_1) = 0.01$
- P(defective in second way) = $P(D_2) = 0.05$
- P(defective in both ways) = $P(D_1 \cap D_2) = 0.001$.

Therefore, it follows that the probability that the component is defective is

$$P(D_1 \cup D_2) = P(D_1) + P(D_2) - P(D_1 \cap D_2) = 0.01 + 0.05 - 0.001 = 0.059.$$

Example 4.14

Suppose that, on an average weekday, of all adults in a country:

- 86% spend at least 1 hour watching television (event A, with $P(A) = 0.86$)
- 19% spend at least 1 hour reading newspapers (event B, with $P(B) = 0.19$)
- 15% spend at least 1 hour watching television *and* at least 1 hour reading newspapers ($P(A \cap B) = 0.15$).

We select a member of the population for an interview at random. For example, we then have:

- $P(A^c) = 1 - P(A) = 1 - 0.86 = 0.14$, which is the probability that the respondent watches *less than* 1 hour of television
- $P(A \cup B) = P(A) + P(B) - P(A \cap B) = 0.86 + 0.19 - 0.15 = 0.90$, which is the probability that the respondent spends at least 1 hour watching television or reading newspapers (or both).

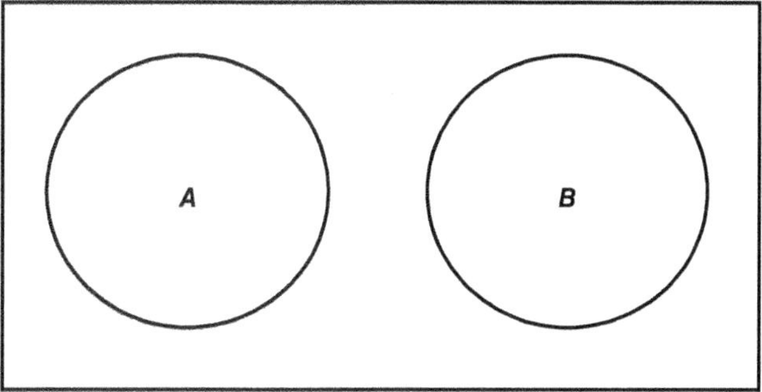

Figure 4.6 Venn diagram illustrating two mutually exclusive events.

Additive law: special case 1

If A and B are *mutually exclusive* events, i.e. they cannot occur simultaneously, then $P(A \cap B) = 0$. Hence,

$$\begin{aligned} P(A \cup B) &= P(A) + P(B) - P(A \cap B) \\ &= P(A) + P(B) - 0 \\ &= P(A) + P(B). \end{aligned}$$

Such events can be depicted by two non-overlapping sets in a Venn diagram, as shown in Figure 4.6. Now revisit Axiom 3 (finite additivity), to see this result generalised for n mutually exclusive events.

Additive law: special case 2

The probability of an event A *not* occurring, that is, its complement, A^c, is

$$P(A^c) = 1 - P(A).$$

We have actually already seen an application of $P(A^c) = 1 - P(A)$ in the context of the birthday paradox in Example 4.8.

4.7.4 The multiplicative law

The **multiplicative law** is concerned with the probability of two events occurring at the same time – specifically when the two events have the special property of **independence**. An informal definition of independence is that two events are said to be independent if one has no influence on the other.

The multiplicative law (for independent events)

Formally, events A and B are *independent* if the probability of their intersection is the product of their individual probabilities:

$$P(A \cap B) = P(A)\,P(B).$$

Example 4.15

Consider rolling two fair dice. The score of one die has no influence on the score of the other die. Therefore, the respective scores are independent events. Hence:

$$P(\text{two sixes}) = \frac{1}{6} \times \frac{1}{6} = \frac{1}{36}.$$

Example 4.16

Suppose that three components numbered 1, 2 and 3 have probabilities of failure π_1, π_2 and π_3, respectively. We determine the probability of a system failure in each of the following cases where component failures are assumed to be independent.

In a *parallel* system, the system fails if all components fail. Since the component failures are independent, the probability of system failure is $\pi_1 \pi_2 \pi_3$.

In a *series* system, the system fails unless all components do *not* fail. The probability that component i does *not* fail is $1 - \pi_i$, hence the probability that the system does *not* fail is $(1 - \pi_1)(1 - \pi_2)(1 - \pi_3)$, and so the probability that the system fails is $1 - (1 - \pi_1)(1 - \pi_2)(1 - \pi_3)$.

In a *mixed* system, the system fails if component 1 fails or if both component 2 and component 3 fail. Components 2 and 3 may be combined to form a notional component 4 with failure probability $\pi_2 \pi_3$. So the system is equivalent to a component with failure probability π_1 and another component with failure probability $\pi_2 \pi_3$, these being connected in series. Therefore, the failure probability is $1 - (1 - \pi_1)(1 - \pi_2\pi_3) = \pi_1 + \pi_2\pi_3 - \pi_1\pi_2\pi_3$.

Note that the multiplicative (or product) law does not hold for dependent events, which is the subject of conditional probability, discussed shortly. Also, take a moment to ensure you are comfortable with the terms 'mutually exclusive' and 'independent'. These are *not* the same thing, so do not get these terms confused!

For mutually exclusive events, $P(A \cap B) = 0$. For independent events, $P(A \cap B) = P(A)P(B)$. So since $P(A \cap B) = 0 \neq P(A)P(B)$ in general (except in the uninteresting case when $P(A) = 0$ or $P(B) = 0$), mutually exclusive events and independent events are different. In fact, mutually exclusive events are extremely *non*-independent (i.e. *dependent*). For example, if you know that A has happened, you know for certain that B has *not* happened. There is no particularly helpful way to represent independent events using a Venn diagram.

4.8 CONDITIONAL PROBABILITY AND BAYES' THEOREM

We have just introduced the concept of independent events – where one event has no influence on another. Clearly, there are going to be many situations where independence does not in fact hold, that is, the occurrence of one event has a 'knock-on' effect on the probability of another event occurring.

Example 4.17

For a single roll of a fair die, let the event A be 'roll a 6', and the event B be 'an even number'. The following probabilities are obvious:

$$P(A) = \frac{1}{6}, \quad P(B) = \frac{1}{2} \quad \text{and} \quad P(A \mid B) = \frac{1}{3}.$$

So, we see that the probability of a 6 *changes* from 1/6 to 1/3 once we are given the information that 'an even number' has occurred. Similarly, the probability of an even number *changes* from 1/2 to 1, conditional on a 6 occurring, $P(B \mid A) = 1$.

Example 4.18

In order to understand and develop formulae for conditional probability, consider the following simple example, representing the classification by sex and subject (where A, B, C and D are defined below) of 144 college students.

(Continued)

Subject	Female	Male	Total
A: Maths	4	14	18
B: Economics	17	41	58
C: Science	4	25	29
D: Arts	28	11	39
Total	53	91	144

Let F = 'Female' and M = 'Male' (obviously!). Then $P(A) = 18/144$, $P(F) = 53/144$ and $P(A \cap F) = 4/144$. Note that $P(A \cap F) \neq P(A)P(F)$, hence A and F are *not* independent events.

From the table we have the following probabilities:

$$P(A \mid F) = \frac{4}{53} \neq P(\mathrm{A}) \text{ and } P(F \mid A) = \frac{4}{18} \neq P(F).$$

The correct relationship of these *conditional* probabilities to the original *unconditional* probabilities is

$$P(A \mid F) = \frac{4/144}{53/144} = \frac{4}{53} = \frac{P(A \cap F)}{P(F)}.$$

Similarly,

$$P(F \mid A) = \frac{4/144}{18/144} = \frac{4}{18} = \frac{P(A \cap F)}{P(A)}.$$

Note that $P(A \cap F) = P(F \cap A)$.

Note also another important relationship involving conditional probability: the *total probability formula* (discussed in greater depth shortly). This expresses an unconditional probability in terms of other, conditional probabilities.

Example 4.19

Continuing with Example 4.18:

$$\begin{aligned} P(A) = \frac{18}{144} &= \left(\frac{4}{53} \times \frac{53}{144}\right) + \left(\frac{14}{91} \times \frac{91}{144}\right) \\ &= P(A \mid F)P(F) + P(A \mid M)P(M). \end{aligned}$$

4.8.1 Bayes' formula

Conditional probability

For any two events A and B, we define conditional probabilities as follows:

$$P(A \mid B) = \frac{P(A \cap B)}{P(B)} \quad \text{and} \quad P(B \mid A) = \frac{P(A \cap B)}{P(A)} \tag{4.1}$$

provided $P(A) > 0$ and $P(B) > 0$. In words, the probability of one event, given a second event, is equal to the probability of both, divided by the probability of the second (conditioning) event.

This is the simplest form of *Bayes' theorem*, and this can be expressed in other ways. Rearranging (4.1), we obtain:

$$P(A \cap B) = P(A \mid B)P(B) = P(B \mid A)P(A),$$

from which we can derive Bayes' theorem.

Bayes' formula

The simplest form of **Bayes' theorem** is

$$P(A \mid B) = \frac{P(B \mid A)P(A)}{P(B)}.$$

Example 4.20

Suppose we roll two independent fair dice again. Consider the following events.

- A = 'at least one of the scores is 2'.
- B = 'the sum of the scores is greater than 7'.

These are shown in Figure 4.7. Now $P(A) = 11/36 \approx 0.31$, $P(B) = 15/36$ and $P(A \cap B) = 2/36$. Therefore, the conditional probability of A given B is:

$$P(A \mid B) = \frac{P(A \cap B)}{P(B)} = \frac{2/36}{15/36} = \frac{2}{15} \approx 0.13.$$

Learning that B has occurred causes us to *revise* (update) the probability of A downward, from 0.31 to 0.13.

One way to think about conditional probability is that when we condition on B, we redefine the sample space to be B.

Example 4.21

In Example 4.20, when we are told that the conditioning event B has occurred, we know we are within the solid green line in Figure 4.7. So the 15 outcomes within it become the new sample space. There are two outcomes which satisfy A *and* which are inside this new sample space, so:

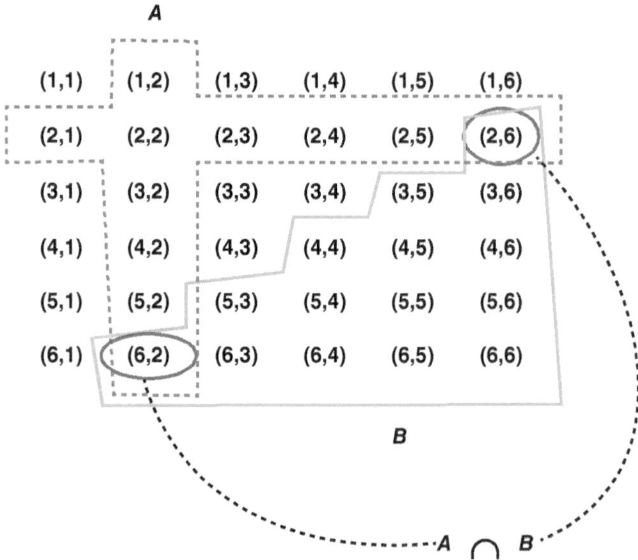

Figure 4.7 Events A, B and $A \cap B$ for Example 4.20.

$$P(A \mid B) = \frac{2}{15} = \frac{\text{number of cases of } A \text{ within } B}{\text{number of cases of } B}.$$

4.8.2 Independent events (revisited)

The terms 'dependent' and 'independent' reflect the fact that the probability of an event is changed when another event is known to occur only if there is some dependence between the events. If there is such a dependence, then $P(A \mid B) \neq P(A)$.

It follows from this that two events, A and B, are independent if and only if

$$P(A \mid B) = P(A).$$

Recall from the multiplicative law that under independence $P(A \cap B) = P(A)P(B)$. Substituting this into our conditional probability formula gives the required result:

$$P(A \mid B) = \frac{P(A \cap B)}{P(B)} = \frac{P(A)P(B)}{P(B)} = P(A)$$

provided $P(B) > 0$. Hence if A and B are independent, knowledge of B (i.e. '$\mid B$'), is of no value to us in determining the probability of A occurring.

4.8.3 Total probability formula

The simplest case of the total probability formula involves calculating the probability of an event A from information about its two conditional probabilities with respect to some other event B and its complement, B^c, together with knowledge of $P(B)$. Note that:

- B and B^c are mutually exclusive
- B and B^c are collectively exhaustive.

Fulfilment of these criteria (being mutually exclusive and collectively exhaustive) allows us to view B and B^c as a partition of the sample space.

The (simple form of the) total probability formula

The (simple form of the) **total probability formula** is

$$P(A) = P(A \mid B)P(B) + P(A \mid B^c)P(B^c).$$

In words, the probability of an event is equal to its conditional probability on a second event times the probability of the second event, plus its probability conditional on the second event not occurring times the probability of that non-occurrence.

There is a more general form of the total probability formula. Let $B_1, B_2, \ldots, B_n$ partition the sample space S into n pairwise mutually exclusive (at most one can occur) and collectively exhaustive (at least one must occur) events. For example, for $n = 4$, see Figure 4.8.

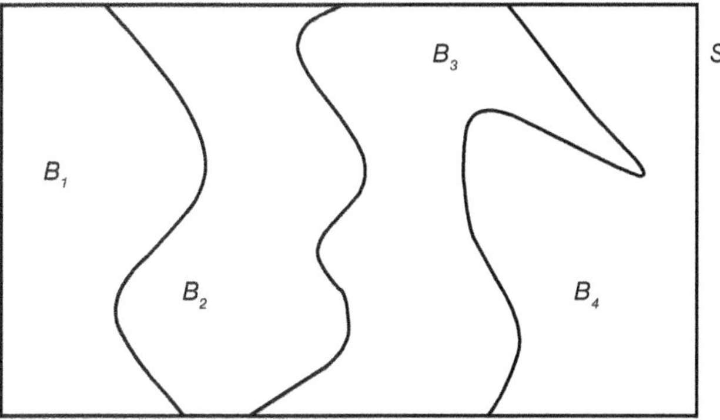

Figure 4.8 An example of a partitioned sample space.

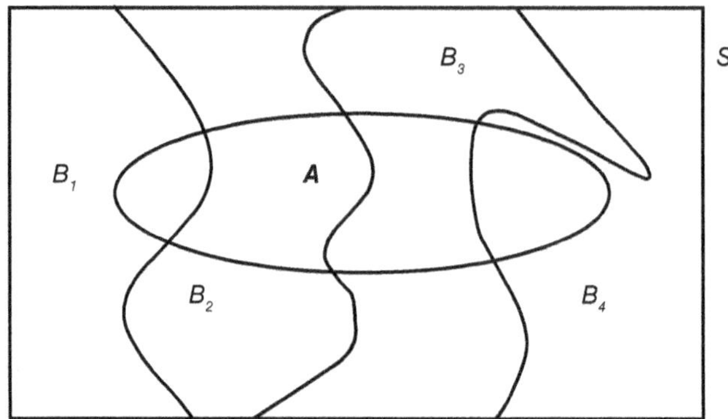

Figure 4.9 The event A within a partitioned sample space.

Figure 4.9 superimposes an event A. Extending the simple form of the total probability formula, we obtain

$$\begin{aligned} P(A) &= \sum_{i=1}^{n} P(A \mid B_i)P(B_i) \\ &= P(A \mid B_1)P(B_1) + P(A \mid B_2)P(B_2) + \cdots + P(A \mid B_n)P(B_n). \end{aligned}$$

Recall that $P(B \mid A) = P(A \cap B)/P(A) = P(A \mid B)P(B)/P(A)$, so assuming we have the partition B and B^c, then

$$P(B \mid A) = \frac{P(A \mid B)P(B)}{P(A \mid B)P(B) + P(A \mid B^c)P(B^c)}.$$

A more general partition gives us a more complete form of Bayes' theorem.

General form of Bayes' theorem

For a general partition of the sample space S into $B_1, B_2, \ldots, B_n$, and for some event A,

$$P(B_k \mid A) = \frac{P(A \mid B_k)P(B_k)}{\sum_{i=1}^{n} P(A \mid B_i)P(B_i)}.$$

Example 4.22

Suppose that 1 person in 10,000 (0.01%) has a particular disease. A diagnostic test for the disease has 99% *sensitivity* - if a person has the disease, the test will give a positive result with a probability of 0.99. The test has 99% *specificity* - if a person does not have the disease, the test will give a negative result with a probability of 0.99.

Let B denote the presence of the disease, and B^c denote no disease. Let A denote a positive test result. We first want to calculate $P(A)$. The probabilities we need are $P(B) = 0.0001$, $P(B^c) = 0.9999$, $P(A \mid B) = 0.99$ and $P(A \mid B^c) = 0.01$. Therefore,

$$\begin{aligned}P(A) &= P(A \mid B)P(B) + P(A \mid B^c)P(B^c)\\ &= 0.99 \times 0.0001 + 0.01 \times 0.9999\\ &= 0.010098.\end{aligned}$$

We now want to calculate $P(B \mid A)$, the probability that a person has the disease, given that the person has received a positive test result. Using the same probabilities as above, we obtain

$$P(B \mid A) = \frac{P(A \mid B)P(B)}{P(A \mid B)P(B) + P(A \mid B^c)P(B^c)} = \frac{0.99 \times 0.0001}{0.010098} \approx 0.0098.$$

Why is this so small? The reason is that most people do not have the disease and the test has a small, but non-zero, false positive rate $P(A \mid B^c)$. Therefore, most positive test results are actually *false positives*.

We now formally 'solve' the Monty Hall problem, introduced in Chapter 1!

Example 4.23

You are taking part in a game show. The host of the show, who is known as Monty, shows you three outwardly identical boxes. In one of them is a prize, and the other two are empty.

You are asked to select, but not open, one of the boxes. After you have done so, Monty, who knows where the prize is, opens one of the two remaining boxes. He always opens a box he knows to be empty, and randomly chooses which box to open when he has more than one option (which happens when your initial choice contains the prize).

After opening the empty box, Monty gives you the choice of either switching to the other unopened box or sticking with your original choice. You then receive whatever is in the box you choose. What should you do, assuming you want to win the prize?

Suppose the three boxes are numbered 1, 2 and 3. Let us define the following events.

- B_1, B_2, B_3: the prize is in Box 1, 2 and 3, respectively
- M_1, M_2, M_3: Monty opens Box 1, 2 and 3, respectively.

Suppose you choose Box 1 first, and then Monty opens Box 3 (the answer works the same way for all combinations of these). So Boxes 1 and 2 remain unopened.

What we want to know now are the conditional probabilities $P(B_1 \mid M_3)$ and $P(B_2 \mid M_3)$. You should switch boxes if $P(B_2 \mid M_3) > P(B_1 \mid M_3)$, and stick with your original choice otherwise. (You would be indifferent about switching if it was the case that $P(B_2 \mid M_3) = P(B_1 \mid M_3)$.)

Suppose that you first choose Box 1, and then Monty opens Box 3. Bayes' theorem tells us that:

$$P(B_2 \mid M_3) = \frac{P(M_3 \mid B_2)P(B_2)}{P(M_3 \mid B_1)P(B_1) + P(M_3 \mid B_2)P(B_2) + P(M_3 \mid B_3)P(B_3)}.$$

We can assign values to each of these.

(Continued)

- The prize is initially equally likely to be in any of the boxes. Therefore:

  $$P(B_1) = P(B_2) = P(B_3) = \frac{1}{3}.$$

- If the prize is in Box 1 (which you choose), Monty chooses at random between the two remaining boxes, Boxes 2 and 3. Hence $P(M_3 \mid B_1) = 1/2$.
- If the prize is in one of the two boxes you did *not* choose, Monty cannot open that box, and must open the other one. Hence $P(M_3 \mid B_2) = 1$ and so $P(M_3 \mid B_3) = 0$.

Putting these probabilities into the formula gives

$$P(B_2 \mid M_3) = \frac{1 \times 1/3}{1/2 \times 1/3 + 1 \times 1/3 + 0 \times 1/3} = \frac{2}{3}$$

and hence $P(B_1 \mid M_3) = 1 - P(B_2 \mid M_3) = 1/3$ (because also $P(M_3 \mid B_3) = 0$ and so $P(B_3 \mid M_3) = 0$).

The same calculation applies to every combination of your first choice and Monty's choice. Therefore, you will *always* double your probability of winning the prize if you switch from your original choice to the box that Monty did not open.

The *Monty Hall problem* has been called a 'cognitive illusion', because something about it seems to mislead most people's intuition. In experiments, around 85% of people tend to get the answer wrong at first.

The most common incorrect response is that the probabilities of the remaining boxes after Monty's choice are both 1/2, so that you should not (or rather, need not) switch.

This is typically based on 'no new information' reasoning. Since we know in advance that Monty *will* open one empty box, the fact that he does so appears to tell us nothing new and should not cause us to favour either of the two remaining boxes - hence a probability of 1/2 for each.
It is true that Monty's choice tells you nothing new about the probability of your *original* choice, which remains at 1/3. However, it tells us a lot about the other two boxes. First, it tells us everything about the box he chose, namely that it does not contain the prize. Second, all of the probability of that box gets 'inherited' by the box neither you nor Monty chose, which now has the probability 2/3.

Example 4.24

You are waiting for your bag at the baggage reclaim carousel of an airport. Suppose that you know that there are 200 bags to come from your flight, and you are counting the distinct bags which come out. Suppose that x bags have arrived, and your bag is not among them. What is the probability that your bag will not arrive at all, that is, that it has been lost (or at least delayed)?

Define A = 'your bag has been lost' and x = 'your bag is not among the first x bags to arrive'. What we want to know is the conditional probability $P(A \mid x)$ for any $x = 0, 1, 2, \dots, 200$. The conditional probabilities the other way round are as follows.

- $P(x \mid A) = 1$ for all x. If your bag has been lost, it will not arrive!
- $P(x \mid A^c) = (200 - x)/200$ if we assume that bags come out in a completely random order.

Using Bayes' theorem, we get

$$\begin{aligned} P(A \mid x) &= \frac{P(x \mid A)P(A)}{P(x \mid A)P(A) + P(x \mid A^c)P(A^c)} \\ &= \frac{P(A)}{P(A) + ((200 - x)/200)(1 - P(A))}. \end{aligned}$$

Obviously, $P(A \mid 200) = 1$. If the bag has not arrived when all 200 have come out, it has been lost!

For other values of x we need $P(A)$. This is the general probability that a bag gets lost, before you start observing the arrival of the bags from your particular flight. This kind of probability is known as the **prior probability** of an event A. (Prior probabilities and prior distributions are an integral part of Bayesian inference.)

Let us assign values to $P(A)$ based on some empirical data. Statistics by the Association of European Airlines (AEA) show how many bags were 'mishandled' per 1000 *passengers* the airlines carried. This is not exactly what we need (since not all passengers carry bags, and some have several), but we will use it anyway. In particular, we will compare the results for the best and the worst of the AEA in 2006: for Air Malta, $P(A) = 0.0044$, and for British Airways, $P(A) = 0.023$.

Figure 4.10 shows a plot of $P(A \mid x)$ as a function of x for these two airlines. The probabilities are fairly small, even for large values of x.

- For Air Malta, $P(A \mid 199) = 0.469$. So even when only one bag remains to arrive, the probability is less than 0.50 that your bag has been lost.
- For British Airways, $P(A \mid 199) = 0.825$. Also, we see that $P(A \mid 197) = 0.541$ is the first probability over 0.50.

This is because the baseline probability of lost bags, $P(A)$, is low.

So, the moral of the story is that even when nearly everyone else has collected their bags and left, do not despair!

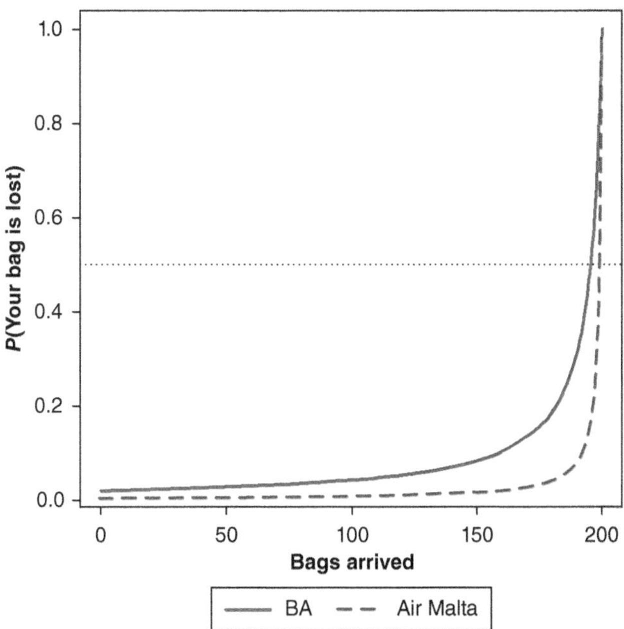

Figure 4.10 Plot of $P(A \mid x)$ as a function of x for the two airlines in Example 4.24, Air Malta and British Airways (BA).

Source: Author-created graph based on Association of European Airlines (AEA) data – AEA dissolved in 2016.

4.9 CHAPTER OVERVIEW

This chapter introduced some formal terminology related to probability theory. The axioms of probability were stated, from which various other probability results were deduced. There followed a brief discussion of counting rules (using permutations and combinations). The important concepts of independence and conditional probability were discussed, and Bayes' theorem was derived.

4.10 KEY VOCABULARY

Additive law
Axiom
Bayes' theorem
Combination
Combinatorial theory
Complement
Conditional probability
Element/member
Event
Experiment
Factorial
Finite additivity
Independence
Multiplicative law
Outcome
Partition
Permutation
Prior probability
Probability
Relative frequency
Sample space
Set theory
Total probability formula
Unit interval
Venn diagram

4.11 EXERCISES

4.11.1 Test your understanding

1 What values can probabilities take?
2 How do probabilities relate to the likelihood of occurrence of an event?
3 Distinguish between the following terms: 'experiment', 'outcome', 'sample space' and 'event'.
4 Probabilities can be determined (i) subjectively, (ii) by experimentation, and (iii) theoretically. Briefly explain the difference between these three approaches, and provide a practical example when each might be used.
5 When elementary outcomes of an experiment are equally likely, how is the probability of an event, such as A, determined?
6 How is a factorial calculated?
7 Provide expressions for the number of permutations and the number of combinations when choosing r objects from n.
8 When would permutations be used? When would combinations be used?
9 Explain the birthday paradox.
10 What is the relative frequency approach to probability?
11 What is meant by 'randomness'?
12 State the three axioms of probability.
13 Distinguish between the symbols '$\cup$', '$\cap$', '^{c}' and '$|$'.
14 State the general 'additive law' and two special cases of it.
15 What does it mean for two events to be independent?
16 State the multiplicative law.
17 How is the conditional probability $P(A \mid B)$ calculated?

18 What is the total probability formula?

19 State the simple and general forms of Bayes' theorem.

20 The successful operation of three separate switches is needed to control a machine. If the probability of failure of each switch is 0.1 and the failure of any switch is independent of any other switch, what is the probability that the machine will break down?

21 Suppose that 8 in every 100 people (i.e. 8%) have a particular disease. A diagnostic test for the disease has 76% sensitivity, that is, if a person has the disease, the test will give a positive result with a probability of 0.76. The test has 65% specificity, that is, if a person does not have the disease, the test will give a negative result with a probability of 0.65. Calculate the probability that a person does not have the disease, given that the person has received a negative test result.

22 A bank classifies borrowers as being either 'high risk' or 'low risk'. Twelve per cent of the bank's loans are made to high-risk borrowers. Overall, 7% of the bank's loans are in default, and 30% of loans in default were made to high-risk borrowers. What is the probability that a high-risk borrower will default?

23 A box contains 15 light bulbs, of which two are defective. If a person selects six light bulbs at random, without replacement, what is the probability that both defective light bulbs will be selected?

24 A firm produces electrical components using three non-overlapping shifts. It is known that 50% of the components are produced during shift 1, 20% during shift 2, and 30% during shift 3. A further look at product quality reveals that 6% of the components produced during shift 1 are defective. The corresponding percentages for shifts 2 and 3 are 8% and 15%, respectively.

(a) What percentage of all components are not defective?

(b) Given that a defective component is found, what is the probability that it was produced during shift 3?

25 Assume that a calculator has a 'random number' key and that when pressed generates an integer between 0 and 99 inclusive at random, all numbers being equally likely and generated independently of one another.

(a) Let X denote the random number generated when the key is pressed once. Write down the probability function of X.

(b) If two numbers are generated, what is the probability that the first number exceeds the second number?

(c) If five numbers are generated, what is the probability that at least one number occurs more than once?

26 Inventor A repeats an experiment three times, while inventor B repeats it twice. The probability of success of each experiment is 0.6 and the outcomes of different experiments are independent of each other.

(a) What is the probability that all three experiments of inventor A were successful and both experiments of inventor B failed?

(b) What is the probability that inventor B performed more successful experiments than inventor A?

(c) Given that inventor B performed more successful experiments than inventor A, what is the probability that both experiments of inventor B were successful?

(d) Inventor B is now planning to perform the experiment for a third time. Given that she had more successes than inventor A in her previous two experiments and given that both her previous experiments were successful, what is the probability she will also be successful next time?

27 James is a salesman for a company and sells two products, X and Y. He visits three different customers each day. For each customer, the probability that James sells product X is 1/3 and the probability that he sells product Y is 1/4. The sale of product X is independent of the sale of product Y during any visit, and the results of the three visits are mutually independent.

Calculate the probability that James will:

(a) sell both products, X and Y, on the first visit
(b) sell only one product during the first visit
(c) make no sales of product X during the day
(d) make at least one sale of product Y during the day.

4.11.2 Practice with Excel

Head over to the companion website for Excel examples and screencasts!

5

PROBABILITY DISTRIBUTIONS

Chapter contents

Chapter level: *Intermediate*

Source: Photo by PublicDomainPictures via Pixabay.

Key concepts

- Families of distributions
- Expected values and variances
- Parameters

Chapter value

Event probabilities can be calculated from a probability distribution.

Key takeaway

Probability distributions are used as approximating models of real-world variables.

Chapter outline

Know your Poisson from your normal? Your Bernoulli from your exponential? If not, then read on! Chapter 4 explained how probabilities can be quantified (i) using subjective estimates, (ii) by experimentation, and (iii) theoretically by way of 'established' probability distributions. This chapter considers a selection of the most common probability distributions, each of which can be used as an *approximating model* of real-world variables in business applications by capturing the *stylised facts* of such real-world variables.

For each distribution considered, we look at the *shape* of the probability distribution, as well as key statistical attributes - notably its *mean* and *variance*, capturing the central tendency and spread of the distribution, respectively. The distributions considered are actually *families* of distributions, where the different members of the families are distinguished by the *parameter(s)* of the distribution. In order to quantify the probabilities of events of interest (i.e. to determine $P(A)$), values must be specified for these parameters. For now, we may simply assume parameter values; in practice the parameter values themselves are often unknown and hence require *estimation*, covered in Chapter 9.

Learning outcomes

After completing this chapter, you should be able to:

- define a random variable and distinguish it from the values which it takes
- explain the difference between discrete and continuous random variables
- summarise basic discrete distributions such as the uniform, Bernoulli, binomial, Poisson, geometric and negative binomial
- summarise basic continuous distributions such as the uniform, exponential and normal
- work with linear functions of normal random variables.

5.1 INTRODUCTION

This chapter introduces the concept of *random variables* and *probability distributions*, extending our work on probabilities in Chapter 4. We will look at the most important distributions for discrete and continuous data. These distributions are all *univariate*, which means they are used to model a single numerical quantity ('univariate' meaning one variable).

While much of the content of this chapter may seem somewhat abstract and theoretical, we will be employing many of the distributions introduced here in later work. For example, the Monte Carlo simulation in Chapter 20 requires us to specify probability distributions for 'input' variables. Where possible, we seek to choose from existing (i.e. well-known) distributions for this task and so an exposure to, and awareness of, several distributions is a useful starting point.

Also, appreciate that this chapter does not provide a collectively exhaustive list of probability distributions. There are *many* families of distributions, many of which are related, with each useful for modelling specific real-world variables. Some of these are very niche, with specialist scientific applications. Our aim is to focus on the most common, and hence arguably some of the most useful, distributions.

5.2 RANDOM VARIABLES

A random variable is a 'mapping' of the elementary outcomes in the sample space, S, to real numbers, in $\mathbb{R} = (-\infty, \infty)$ (the real line). This allows us to attach probabilities to experimental outcomes. Hence the concept of a random variable is that of a measurement which takes a particular value for each possible trial (experiment). Frequently, this will be a *numerical* value.

Example 5.1

Suppose we sample five adults and measure their years of work experience. Then 'years of work experience' is the random variable (denoted by X, say) and the five (observed) values of this random variable are the realised measurements for the years of work experience of these five adults ($x_1, x_2, \ldots, x_5$).

Example 5.2

Suppose a fair die is rolled four times and we observe two 6s, a 3 and a 1. The random variable is the 'score on the die' (again, denoted by X), and for these four trials it takes the values 6, 6, 3 and 1 ($x_1 = 6, x_2 = 6, x_3 = 3$ and $x_4 = 1$). (If we do not know the true order in which the values occurred, we could also say that the results were 1, 6, 3 and 6, or 1, 3, 6 and 6, etc.)

An example of an experiment with non-numerical outcomes would be a coin toss, for which in Chapter 4 we wrote $S = \{H, T\}$. We can use a random variable, X, to convert the sample space elements to real numbers:

$$X = \begin{cases} 1 & \text{if heads} \\ 0 & \text{if tails.} \end{cases}$$

The value of any of the random variables in Examples 5.1 and 5.2 (as well as the coin toss) will typically vary from sample to sample, hence the name 'random variable'. Sensible enough!

So each experimental random variable has a collection of possible outcomes, and a numerical value associated with each outcome. We have already encountered the term 'sample space' which here is the set of all possible numerical values of the random variable.

Example 5.3

Examples of random variables include the following:

Experiment	Random variable	Sample space
Die is rolled	Value on top face	{1, 2, 3, 4, 5, 6}
Coin is tossed five times	Number of heads	{0, 1, 2, 3, 4, 5}
Twenty customers sampled	Number of satisfied customers	{0, 1, 2,..., 19, 20}
Machine operates for a day	Number of breakdowns	{0, 1, 2,...}
One adult sampled	Height in centimetres	{[150 cm, 200 cm]} (roughly)

5.3 PROBABILITY DISTRIBUTION

A natural question to ask is 'what is the *probability* of any of these values?'. That is, we are interested in the probability distribution of the experimental random variable.

Note that random variables come in two varieties – *discrete* and *continuous*. For completeness, mixture distributions (with discrete and continuous components) also exist.

Discrete and continuous random variables

- **Discrete:** Often synonymous with '*count* data', that is, random variables which take non-negative integer values, such as 0, 1, 2, ... For example, the number of customer complaints received in a month.
- **Continuous:** Synonymous with '*measured* data' taking any real-numbered values such as the real line, $\mathbb{R} = (-\infty, \infty)$, or some subset of $\mathbb{R}$, for example the unit interval [0, 1]. For example, in practice monetary amounts such as household income or expenditure are considered to be continuous.

The mathematical treatment of probability distributions depends on whether we are dealing with discrete or continuous random variables.

In Example 5.3, the sample spaces of various experiments are shown. In most cases there will be a higher chance of the random variable taking some values relative to others. Our objective is to express these chances using an associated *probability distribution*. In the discrete case, we can associate with each 'point' in the sample space a probability which represents the chance of the random variable being equal to that particular value. The probability is typically non-zero, although sometimes we need to use a probability of zero to identify impossible events.

To summarise, a probability distribution is the complete set of sample space values with their associated probabilities which, by Axiom 2 (Chapter 4), must sum to 1 for discrete random variables. The probability distribution can be represented visually by plotting the probabilities against the values of the random variable.

Finally, before we proceed, let us spend a moment briefly discussing some important issues with regard to the *notation* associated with random variables. For notational efficiency, we often use an *upper-case* (capital) letter to represent the random variable. The letter X is often adopted, but it is perfectly legitimate to use any other letter: Y, Z, etc. In contrast, a *lower-case* letter denotes a particular *value* of the random variable.

Example 5.4

Let X = 'the score of a fair die'. If the die results in a 3, then this is written as $x = 3$. The probability distribution of X is:

$X = x$	1	2	3	4	5	6
$P(X = x)$	1/6	1/6	1/6	1/6	1/6	1/6

This is an example of the (discrete) *uniform* distribution.[1] For discrete random variables, we talk about a *mass* of probability at each respective value. In the discrete uniform case this mass is the same (i.e. 1/6 for a fair die), and this is plotted to show the probability distribution of X in Figure 5.1.

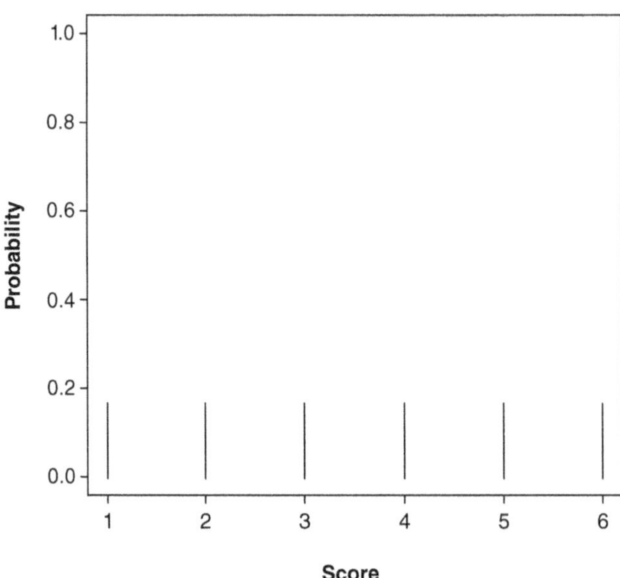

Figure 5.1 Probability distribution for the score on a fair die in Example 5.4.

[1]At most schools, 'uniforms' are worn, that is, all pupils wear the *same* clothes (with possibly slight differences across genders), hence when the term 'uniform' is applied to a probability distribution, we have the *same* probability of occurrence for each value of the random variable.

Discrete uniform distribution

A random variable X has a **discrete uniform distribution** if it has k possible outcomes, all of which are *equally likely*. If the distinct outcomes are 1, 2, ..., k, then the fact that k is finite means the distribution is 'discrete', and it is 'uniform' because all the probabilities are *equal*. The **probability mass function** (pmf) or simply **probability function** is:

$$P(X = x) = p(x) = \begin{cases} 1/k & \text{for } x = 1, 2, \ldots, k \\ 0 & \text{otherwise.} \end{cases}$$

For example, for the score on a fair die we have $k = 6$. Note that $P(X = x)$ and $p(x)$ mean the same thing, so we may use either.

Example 5.5

Let X = 'the number of heads when five fair coins are tossed'. The probability distribution of X is:

$X = x$	0	1	2	3	4	5
$P(X = x)$	0.03	0.16	0.31	0.31	0.16	0.03
	$= 0.50^5$	$= 5 \times 0.50^5$	$= 10 \times 0.50^5$	$= 10 \times 0.50^5$	$= 5 \times 0.50^5$	$= 0.50^5$

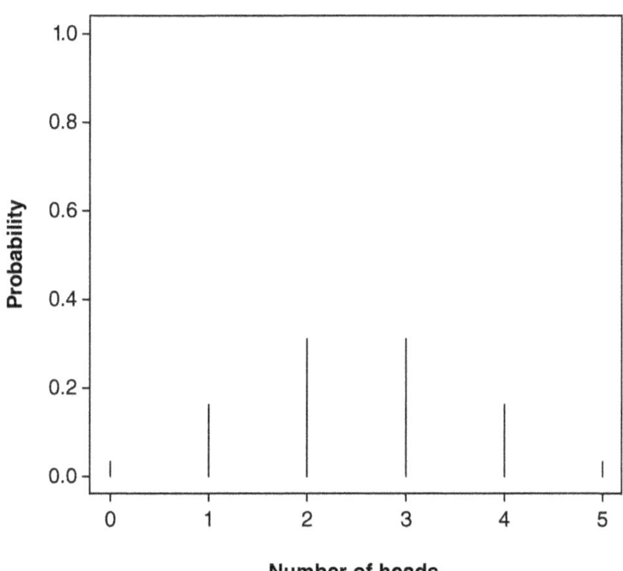

Figure 5.2 Probability distribution for the number of heads when five fair coins are tossed in Example 5.5.

(Continued)

This is an example of the *binomial* distribution (discussed shortly) and can be represented as:

$$p(x) = \binom{5}{x} \times 0.50^5, \text{ for } x = 0, 1, 2, \ldots, 5,$$

and 0 otherwise. The probability distribution of X is shown in Figure 5.2.

A probability distribution has a natural *relative frequency* interpretation: if the experiment is repeated a very large number of times, then the probability of any particular value of the random variable is equal to the limit of its relative frequency as the number of experiments becomes infinitely large.

There are many important probability distributions which describe the chances of real-life events, and these form the basis of statistical inference and data analysis. We now proceed to introduce some important discrete distributions.

5.4 BINOMIAL DISTRIBUTION

The *binomial distribution* is a series of n independent *Bernoulli trials*. Hence it makes sense to define a Bernoulli trial first of all! In fact, we have already seen an example of this – the single coin toss. The key features of a Bernoulli trial are as follows:

- A Bernoulli trial has only two possible outcomes (i.e. it is *dichotomous*) which are typically called 'success' and 'failure' – such as 'heads' and 'tails'. We usually code a success as '1' and a failure as '0'.
- There is a fixed probability of success, π, and, therefore, a fixed probability of failure, $1 - \pi$. So, for a fair coin, $\pi = 0.50$. Repeatedly tossing the same coin will not change π.
- Consequently, given a constant π, then successive Bernoulli trials are independent. Multiple coin tosses can be viewed as physically separate experiments, with the outcome of any single coin toss not affecting the outcome of any other coin toss.

Bernoulli distribution

The probability distribution for a Bernoulli trial is:

$X = x$	0	1
$P(X = x)$	$1 - \pi$	π

and the **Bernoulli distribution** can be expressed with the following probability function:

$$P(X = x) = \begin{cases} \pi^x (1-\pi)^{1-x} & \text{for } x = 0, 1 \\ 0 & \text{otherwise.} \end{cases}$$

Example 5.6

Other potential examples of Bernoulli trials are: (i) the sex of newborn babies (male or female), (ii) the classification of factory output (defective or not defective), (iii) voters supporting a candidate (support or not support), (iv) customer churn (whether a customer churns to a competitor or not), and (v) default status on a loan (default or not default).

In fact, many sampling situations become Bernoulli trials if we are only interested in classifying the result categorically in one of two ways. For example, we could classify customers according to age group, such that each is classified as being either 'young' or 'old'. Of course, this requires a threshold for when one goes from being 'young' to 'old', and this has to be decided in advance. Extending this idea, if we have n successive Bernoulli trials, then we define the *binomial distribution*.

Binomial distribution

Let X = 'the total number of successes' in a sequence of n independent and identically distributed Bernoulli trials. Then

$$X \sim \text{Bin}(n, \pi).$$

where the terms n and π are called **parameters**, since the values of these define which specific **binomial distribution** we have. Read '~' as 'is distributed as'. Its probability function is

$$P(X = x) = \begin{cases} \binom{n}{x} \pi^x (1-\pi)^{n-x} & \text{for } x = 0, 1, 2, \ldots, n \\ 0 & \text{otherwise.} \end{cases} \quad (5.1)$$

Here n is the number of Bernoulli trials, π is the (constant) probability of success for each trial, and $P(X = x)$ is the probability that the total number of successes in the n trials is equal to x. That is, we are seeking to count the number of successes, and each $P(X = x)$ is the probability that the discrete (count) random variable X takes the value x.

Equation (5.1) can be used to calculate probabilities for any binomial distribution, provided n and π are both specified. In Excel, we can compute these easily using the `BINOM.DIST` function.

Excel function: BINOM.DIST

`=BINOM.DIST(number_s, trials, probability_s, cumulative)` returns the individual term binomial distribution probability, where:

- `number_s` is the number of successes in trials
- `trials` is the number of independent trials
- `probability_s` is the probability of success on each trial
- `cumulative` is a logical value - for the cumulative distribution function (covered next), use 1 (or `TRUE`), and for the probability mass function, use 0 (or `FALSE`).

Note that a binomial random variable can take $n + 1$ different values, not n, since the variable represents the total number of successes. The smallest total number of successes in n trials is zero (i.e. if all trials resulted in failure) and the largest total number of successes is n (i.e. if all trials resulted in success), with the intervening total number of successes being 1, 2, ..., $n - 1$. Therefore, there are $n + 1$ different values in total.

Necessary conditions to apply the binomial distribution

- Each trial has only two possible outcomes, referred to as 'success' and 'failure'.
- A fixed probability of success, π.
- A fixed number of trials, n.
- All trials are statistically independent.

5.5 CUMULATIVE DISTRIBUTION FUNCTIONS

A probability function can be used to compute $P(X = x) = p(x)$, the probability of a single value x of the random variable. Of course, we may wish to know the probability that the random variable X is *less than or equal to x*. We call such a probability a *cumulative probability*, denoted by the cumulative distribution function (cdf):

$$F(x) = P(X \leq x). \qquad (5.2)$$

Cumulative distribution function for discrete random variables

For discrete random variables taking non-negative integer values, the cumulative distribution function is

$$\begin{aligned} F(x) &= P(X = 0) + P(X = 1) + P(X = 2) + \cdots + P(X = x) \\ &= p(0) + p(1) + p(2) + \cdots + p(x). \end{aligned}$$

It follows that we can easily find the probability function from the cumulative distribution function, or *vice versa*, using this relationship. Specifically, note that

$$P(X = x) = F(x) - F(x - 1).$$

Example 5.7

A pharmaceutical company was researching untreated bacterial growth. Consider 10 test tubes of bacterial solution and let us suppose that the probability of any single test tube showing bacterial growth is 0.20. Let X denote the total number of test tubes showing bacterial growth. Hence

$$P(\text{exactly 4 show growth}) = P(X = 4) = \binom{10}{4} \times 0.20^4 \times 0.80^6 = 0.0881$$

and

$$
\begin{aligned}
P(\text{more than 1 show growth}) &= 1 - F(1)\\
&= 1 - P(X = 0) - P(X = 1)\\
&= 1 - 0.810^{10} - \binom{10}{1} \times 0.20^{1} \times 0.80^{9}\\
&= 1 - 0.1074 - 0.2684\\
&= 0.6242.
\end{aligned}
$$

In Excel, we can compute this using `=1-BINOM.DIST(1,10,0.2,1)`.

Note that this technique also illustrates the advantage of computing the probability of an event by calculating the probability of it *not* happening and subtracting this from 1 (recall that $P(A) = 1 - P(A^c)$, a special case of the additive law in Chapter 4).

5.5.1 Cumulative distribution functions - another point of view

$X \sim \text{Bin}(n, \pi)$ is one of many distributions which take only non-negative integer values, and are typically about *counting*. It does not normally make sense to ask questions like 'What is $P(X = -3)$, $P(X = 1.5)$ or $P(X = \pi)$?' for the obvious reason that all such values are impossible, so the relevant probabilities are all zero. (Technically speaking for $n = 1$, if $\pi = 0$ or 1 then $P(X = \pi) = 1$, but this means a success is impossible or certain, respectively. Hence we no longer have two possible outcomes, but one certain outcome, a failure or success, respectively.)

However, it makes a lot more sense to ask questions like 'What is $P(X \le -3)$, $P(X \le 1.5)$ or $P(X \le \pi)$?'. The answers are 0, $F(1)$ and $F(0)$, respectively (using the notation in equation (5.2)). This illustrates why we can define the cdf of a counting-style random variable even for values of a *continuous* argument x as[2]

$$F(x) = P(X \le x).$$

With this convention, $F(x)$ is a function whose graph is a step function.

Example 5.8

If $X \sim \text{Bin}(2, \pi)$, then each time x reaches an integer value in the range [0, 2], the cdf 'jumps' by $P(X = x)$, until the sum of the probabilities reaches 1. This is shown in Figure 5.3.

(Continued)

[2]Note that the argument x is not the same as the random variable X, nor is it the same as a realisation or value of X. This is because X is not continuous, but takes only (selected) integer values. The x value simply tells us the range of values in which we are interested.

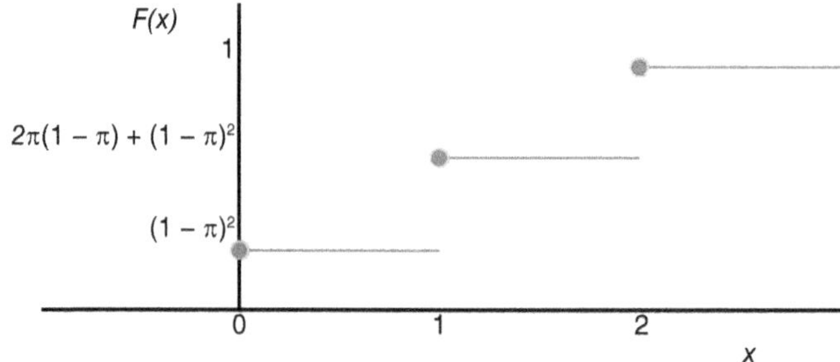

Figure 5.3 Step function showing the cdf of $X \sim \text{Bin}(2, \pi)$ in Example 5.8.

The same pattern shown in Figure 5.3 applies to any version of Bin(n, π), or indeed to any other distribution for which there is a largest possible integer value. For distributions like the Poisson (discussed next) which count, but which do not have a largest possible value, the pattern is similar, but the value 1 is never reached.

5.6 POISSON DISTRIBUTION

The *Poisson distribution* applies to random points occurring in a *continuous* medium such as time, distance, area or volume. The discussion here will concentrate mainly on one-dimensional cases, such as time or distance. In all cases, we are dealing with random points which have the following properties.

Properties of random points in a Poisson process

- Each point is *equally likely* to occur anywhere in the medium.
- The position taken by each point is completely *independent* of the occurrence or non-occurrence of all the other points.

In this situation the random variable X is the number of points in a particular unit of the medium.

Example 5.9

Examples of a Poisson process include:

- machine breakdowns per unit of time
- arrivals at an airport per unit of time
- flaws along wire per unit of length.

Poisson probability function

The probability function for the **Poisson distribution** is:

$$P(X = x) = \begin{cases} e^{-\lambda}\lambda^x / x! & \text{for } x = 0, 1, 2, \ldots \\ 0 & \text{otherwise} \end{cases}$$

where λ is the average number of points per unit of the medium, and is known as the *rate parameter*. Note that, unlike the binomial distribution, there is no upper bound on the value of x. A Poisson variable is hence countably infinite.

In Excel, we can compute Poisson probabilities using the `POISSON.DIST` function.

Excel function: POISSON.DIST

`=POISSON.DIST(x, mean, cumulative)` returns the individual term Poisson distribution probability, where:

- `x` is the number of events
- `mean` is the expected numeric value, λ, a positive number
- `cumulative` is a logical value - for the cumulative distribution function, use 1 (or `TRUE`), and for the probability mass function, use 0 (or `FALSE`).

Example 5.10

Consider a machine which breaks down, on average, 3.2 times per week, hence $\lambda = 3.2$ *per week*. The probability that it will break down exactly once next week is

$$P(X = 1) = \frac{e^{-3.2} \times 3.2^1}{1!} = 0.1304.$$

The probability that it will break down exactly four times in the next *two* weeks (hence λ is now 6.4) is

$$P(X = 4) = \frac{e^{-6.4}(6.4)^4}{4!} = 0.1162.$$

Note that if we know λ for one unit of time (here, per week) and we want to look at k units of time (in this example, $k = 2$), then we need to proportionally change λ to reflect this, and the revised rate parameter is $k\lambda$ (hence in this example the revised λ for a two-week period is $2 \times 3.2 = 6.4$). This proportional adjustment is extremely important to remember.

In Excel, we can compute these using `=POISSON.DIST(1,3.2,0)` and `=POISSON.DIST(4,6.4,0)`, respectively.

Example 5.11

Customers arrive at a bank on weekday afternoons randomly at an average rate of 1.6 customers per minute. Let X denote the number of arrivals per minute and Y denote the number of arrivals per 5 minutes.

We assume a Poisson distribution for both, such that

$X \sim \text{Poisson}(1.6)$

and

$Y \sim \text{Poisson}(5 \times 1.6) = \text{Poisson}(8)$.

1. What is the probability that no customer arrives in a one-minute interval? For $X \sim \text{Poisson}(1.6)$, the probability $P(X = 0)$ is

   $$p_X(0) = \frac{e^{-\lambda}\lambda^0}{0!} = \frac{e^{-1.6} \times 1.6^0}{0!} = e^{-1.6} = 0.2019.$$

   In Excel, either =POISSON.DIST(0,1.6,0) or =POISSON.DIST(0,1.6,1), since $P(X = 0) = P(X \leq 0)$ as X cannot take negative values.

2. What is the probability that more than two customers arrive in a one-minute interval? In this case we have

   $P(X > 2) = 1 - P(X \leq 2) = 1 - (P(X = 0) + P(X = 1) + P(X = 2))$,

which is

$$\begin{aligned} 1 - p_X(0) - p_X(1) - p_X(2) &= 1 - \frac{e^{-1.6} \times 1.6^0}{0!} - \frac{e^{-1.6} \times 1.6^1}{1!} - \frac{e^{-1.6} \times 1.6^2}{2!} \\ &= 1 - e^{-1.6} - 1.6e^{-1.6} - 1.28e^{-1.6} \\ &= 1 - 3.88e^{-1.6} \\ &= 0.2167. \end{aligned}$$

In Excel, =1–POISSON.DIST(2,1.6,1).

3. What is the probability that no more than one customer arrives in a 5-minute interval? For $Y \sim \text{Poisson}(8)$, the probability $P(Y \leq 1)$ is

$$p_Y(0) + p_Y(1) = \frac{e^{-8} \times 8^0}{0!} + \frac{e^{-8} \times 8^1}{1!} = e^{-8} + 8e^{-8} = 9e^{-8} = 0.0030.$$

In Excel, =POISSON.DIST(1,8,1).

5.7 POISSON APPROXIMATION TO THE BINOMIAL

Relationships exist between some probability distributions. Some of these relationships are *exact* (e.g. Bernoulli(π) = Bin(1, π)), while other relationships are *approximate* which hold well under certain 'limiting conditions'.

There are two commonly used such approximations to the binomial – one using the normal distribution (covered later), and another using the Poisson distribution. Clearly, any approximation is just that, an approximation, so we should only use this approximating procedure when we obtain a good (i.e. close) approximation.

Conditions for using a Poisson approximation to the binomial

To justify use of the Poisson as an approximating distribution to the binomial, the following conditions should hold:

- n greater than 30.
- π sufficiently extreme such that $n\pi < 10$.
- The approximation is only good for small values of x, relative to n.
- Set the Poisson rate parameter $\lambda = n\pi$.

Example 5.12

Suppose we sample 100 items at random from a production line which is providing, on average, 2% defective items. What is the probability of exactly three defective items in our random sample?

First, we have to check that the relevant criteria for using the Poisson approximation are satisfied. Indeed, they are: $n = 100 > 30$; $\pi = 0.02$ is sufficiently small such that $n\pi = 2 < 10$; and $x = 3$ is small relative to n. Hence

$$P(X=3) = \underbrace{{}^{100}C_3 \times 0.02^3 \times 0.98^{97}}_{\text{true binomial probability}} = 0.1823 \approx \frac{e^{-2} \times 2^3}{3!} = 0.1804.$$

In Excel, we can compute these using `=BINOM.DIST(3,100,0.02,0)` and `=POISSON.DIST(3,2,0)`, respectively.

Example 5.13

A classic example (from Ladislaus von Bortkiewicz, *Das Gesetz der kleinen Zahlen*, 1898) helps to remember the key elements of 'the law of small numbers'.

Figure 5.4 shows the numbers of soldiers killed by horsekick in each of 14 army corps of the Prussian army in each of the years spanning 1875-94.

Suppose that the number of men killed by horsekicks in one corps in one year is $X \sim \text{Bin}(n, \pi)$, where:

- n is large - the number of men in a corps (perhaps 50,000)
- π is small - the probability that a man is killed by a horsekick.

(Continued)

X should be well approximated by a Poisson distribution with some mean λ. The sample frequencies and proportions of different counts are as follows:

Number killed	0	1	2	3	4	More
Count	144	91	32	11	2	0
%	51.4	32.5	11.4	3.9	0.7	0

The sample mean of the counts is $\bar{x} = 0.7$, which we use as λ for the Poisson distribution. $X \sim \text{Poisson}(0.7)$ is indeed a good fit to the data, as shown in Figure 5.5.

	75	76	77	78	79	80	81	82	83	84	85	86	87	88	89	90	91	92	93	94
G	—	2	2	1	—	—	1	1	—	3	—	2	1	—	—	1	—	1	—	1
I	—	—	—	2	—	3	—	2	—	—	—	1	1	1	—	2	—	3	1	—
II	—	—	—	2	—	2	—	—	1	1	—	—	2	1	1	—	—	2	—	—
III	—	—	—	1	1	1	2	—	2	—	—	—	1	—	1	2	1	—	—	—
IV	—	1	—	1	1	1	1	—	—	—	—	1	—	—	—	—	1	1	—	—
V	—	—	—	—	2	1	—	—	1	—	—	1	—	1	1	1	1	1	1	—
VI	—	—	1	—	2	—	—	1	2	—	1	1	3	1	1	1	—	3	—	—
VII	1	—	1	—	—	—	1	—	1	1	—	—	2	—	—	2	1	—	2	—
VIII	1	—	—	—	1	—	—	1	—	—	—	—	1	—	—	—	1	1	—	1
IX	—	—	—	—	—	2	1	1	1	—	2	1	1	—	1	2	—	1	—	—
X	—	—	1	1	—	1	—	2	—	2	—	—	—	—	2	1	3	—	1	1
XI	—	—	—	—	2	4	—	1	3	—	1	1	1	1	2	1	3	1	3	1
XIV	1	1	2	1	1	3	—	4	—	1	—	3	2	1	—	2	1	1	—	—
XV	—	1	—	—	—	—	—	1	—	1	1	—	—	—	2	2	—	—	—	—

Figure 5.4 Numbers of soldiers killed by horsekick in each of 14 army corps of the Prussian army in each of the years spanning 1875-94. Source: L. von Bortkiewicz (1898). *Das Gesetz der kleinen Zahlen*. Leipzig: Teubner.

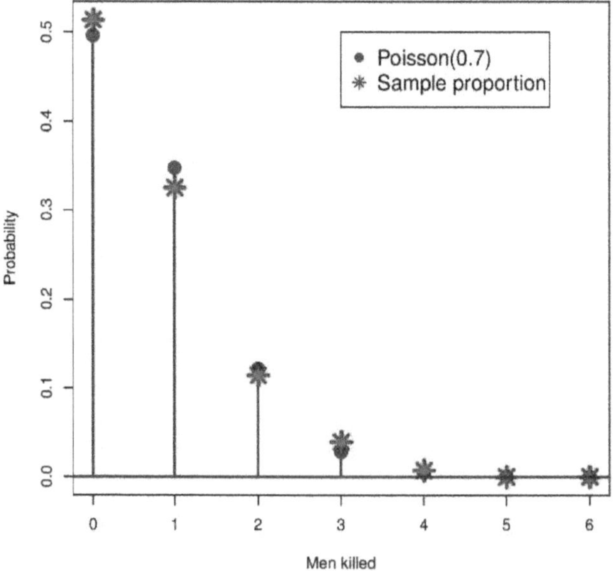

Figure 5.5 Fit of Poisson distribution to the data in Example 5.13.

Example 5.14

An airline is selling tickets for a flight with 198 seats. It knows that, on average, about 1% of customers who have bought tickets fail to arrive for the flight. Because of this, the airline overbooks the flight by selling 200 tickets. What is the probability that everyone who arrives for the flight will get a seat?

Let X denote the number of people who fail to turn up. Using the binomial distribution, $X \sim \text{Bin}(200, 0.01)$. We have

$$P(X \geq 2) = 1 - P(X = 0) - P(X = 1) = 1 - 0.1340 - 0.2707 = 0.5953.$$

In Excel, we can compute this using `=1-BINOM.DIST(1,200,0.01,1)`.

Using the Poisson approximation, $X \sim \text{Poisson}(200 \times 0.01) = \text{Poisson}(2)$.

$$P(X \geq 2) = 1 - P(X = 0) - P(X = 1) = 1 - e^{-2} - 2e^{-2} = 1 - 3e^{-2} = 0.5940.$$

In Excel, we can compute this using `=1-POISSON.DIST(1,2,1)`.

5.8 EXPECTED VALUE OF A DISCRETE RANDOM VARIABLE

Certain important properties of distributions arise if we consider *probability-weighted averages* of random variables, and of functions of random variables. (A function, $g(X)$, of a random variable X is, of course, a new random variable, say $Y = g(X)$.) For example, we might want to know the *average* value of a random variable.

It would be unwise to simply take the arithmetic average of all the values taken by the random variable, as this would mean that very unlikely values (those with small probabilities of occurrence) would receive the same weighting as very likely values (those with large probabilities of occurrence). The obvious approach is to use the probability-weighted average of the values of the random variable, known as the expected value of X.

Expectation of a discrete random variable

If $x_1, x_2, \ldots, x_N$ are the possible values of the random variable X, with corresponding probabilities $p_1, p_2, \ldots, p_N$, then

$$E(X) = \mu = \sum_{i=1}^{N} x_i p_i = x_1 p_1 + x_2 p_2 + \cdots + x_N p_N.$$

Note that the expected value is also referred to as the population mean, which can be written as E(X) (in words, 'the expectation of the random variable X'), or μ (in words, 'the (population) mean of X'). Also, note the distinction between the *sample* mean, $\bar{x}$, (introduced in Chapter 2) based on observed sample values, and the *population* mean, μ, of a probability distribution.

Example 5.15

If the 'random variable' X happens to be a constant, k, then $x_1 = k$, and $p_1 = 1$, so trivially $E(X) = k \times 1 = k$. This is a special case, known as the *degenerate distribution*.

Example 5.16

If $X \sim \text{Bin}(n, \pi)$, then

$$\begin{aligned} E(X) &= \sum_{x=0}^{n} xP(X = x) \\ &= 0 \times (1-\pi)^n + 1 \times \binom{n}{1} \pi^1 (1-\pi)^{n-1} + 2 \times \binom{n}{2} \pi^2 (1-\pi)^{n-2} + \cdots + n \times \binom{n}{n} \pi^n \\ &= n\pi. \end{aligned}$$

For the interested reader, a full proof of this result can be found at the end of this chapter.

Example 5.17

If $X \sim \text{Pois}(\lambda)$, then

$$\begin{aligned} E(X) &= \sum_{x=0}^{\infty} xP(X = x) \\ &= 0 \times \frac{e^{-\lambda}\lambda^0}{0!} + 1 \times \frac{e^{-\lambda}\lambda^1}{1!} + 2 \times \frac{e^{-\lambda}\lambda^2}{2!} + \cdots + k \times \frac{e^{-\lambda}\lambda^k}{k!} + \cdots \\ &= \lambda. \end{aligned}$$

For the interested reader, a full proof of this result can be found at the end of this chapter.

5.8.1 New random variables

Above we have labelled the population mean as the 'expectation' of the random variable and introduced the expectation operator, $E(\cdot)$. This operator, like the summation operator, Σ, is a *linear* operator and hence this property can be used to find the expectation of a new random variable, be it a *linear transformation* of a single random variable or a *linear combination* of two (or more) random variables.

Example 5.18

Suppose X is a random variable and α is a non-zero constant. Define $U = \alpha X$ to be a new random variable, that is, U is a linear transformation of X. What is the expected value of U? We have:

$$\begin{aligned}\mathrm{E}(U) = \mathrm{E}(\alpha X) &= \sum_{i=1}^{N}(\alpha x_i)p_i \\ &= \alpha x_1 p_1 + \alpha x_2 p_2 + \cdots + \alpha x_N p_N \\ &= \alpha(x_1 p_1 + x_2 p_2 + \cdots + x_N p_N) \\ &= \alpha \mathrm{E}(X).\end{aligned}$$

That is, $\mathrm{E}(\alpha X) = \alpha \mathrm{E}(X)$.

Example 5.19

Suppose X and Y are random variables. Let $Z = X + Y$ be a new, but clearly related, random variable, that is, Z is a linear combination of X and Y. What is the expected value of Z? To obtain this, simply exploit the linear property of the expectation operator. Hence

$$\mathrm{E}(Z) = \mathrm{E}(X + Y) = \mathrm{E}(X) + \mathrm{E}(Y).$$

We can combine these two approaches.

Expectation of linear combinations of random variables

Given random variables X and Y, and constants α and β (both non-zero), define $T = \alpha X + \beta Y$, it follows that

$$\mathrm{E}(T) = \mathrm{E}(\alpha X + \beta Y) = \alpha \mathrm{E}(X) + \beta \mathrm{E}(Y).$$

5.9 VARIANCE OF A DISCRETE RANDOM VARIABLE

The concept of a probability-weighted average (or expected value) can be extended to *functions* of the random variable.

Example 5.20

If X takes the values $x_1, x_2, \ldots, x_N$ with corresponding probabilities $p_1, p_2, \ldots, p_N$, then:

$$\mathrm{E}\left(\frac{1}{X}\right) = \sum_{i=1}^{N}\frac{1}{x_i}p_i \qquad \text{for all } x_i \neq 0.$$

$$\mathrm{E}(\ln(X)) = \sum_{i=1}^{N}\ln(x_i)p_i \qquad \text{for all } x_i > 0.$$

$$\mathrm{E}(X^2) = \sum_{i=1}^{N}x_i^2 p_i.$$

One very important 'average' associated with a distribution is the expected value of the square of the deviation of the random variable from its mean, μ. This can be seen to be a measure – not the only one, but the most widely used by far – of the *dispersion* of the distribution and is known as the *(population) variance* of the random variable.

Variance of a discrete random variable

If X takes the values $x_1, x_2, \ldots, x_N$ with corresponding probabilities $p_1, p_2, \ldots, p_N$, then the **(population) variance** of a discrete random variable is

$$\sigma^2 = \mathrm{E}\left((X-\mu)^2\right) = \sum_{i=1}^{N}(x_i-\mu)^2 p_i = \mathrm{E}(X^2)-\mu^2.$$

The (positive) square root of the variance is known as the **standard deviation** and is denoted by σ.

A proof of $\sigma^2 = \mathrm{E}(X^2) - \mu^2$ can be found at the end of this chapter.

Example 5.21

Let X represent the value shown when a fair die is thrown once. We now compute the mean and variance of X as follows:

$X = x$	1	2	3	4	5	6	Total
$P(X = x)$	1/6	1/6	1/6	1/6	1/6	1/6	1
$xP(X = x)$	1/6	2/6	3/6	4/6	5/6	6/6	$21/6 = 3.5 = \mu$
$x^2P(X = x)$	1/6	4/6	9/6	16/6	25/6	36/6	91/6
$(x - \mu)^2$	25/4	9/4	1/4	1/4	9/4	25/4	
$(x - \mu)^2P(X = x)$	25/24	9/24	1/24	1/24	9/24	25/24	70/24 = 2.92

Hence $\mu = \mathrm{E}(X) = 3.5$, $\sigma^2 = \mathrm{E}((X - \mu)^2) = 2.92$ and $\sigma = \sqrt{2.92} = 1.71$. Alternatively, $\mu = \mathrm{E}(X) = 3.5$, $\mathrm{E}(X^2) = 91/6$, so the variance is $91/6 - (3.5)^2 = 2.92$, as before. However, this method is usually easier.

5.9.1 Limits and special cases

A useful interpretation of population properties is to think of them as the *limiting equivalents* of the corresponding sample statistics. Suppose we sample n values of random variable X and get $x_1, x_2, \ldots, x_n$, then, as $n \to \infty$:

- the sample mean, $\bar{x}$, *tends to* the population mean, μ, i.e. $\bar{x} \to \mu$.
- the sample variance, s^2, *tends to* the population variance, σ^2, i.e. $s^2 \to \sigma^2$.

Variance of binomial and Poisson distributions

- If $X \sim \text{Bin}(n, \pi)$ then

  $\text{Var}(X) = n\pi(1 - \pi)$.

- If $X \sim \text{Pois}(\lambda)$, then

  $\text{Var}(X) = \lambda$.

Note that for the Poisson distribution the mean and variance are equal.

5.9.2 New random variables (again)

As in the case of the expected value, we might want to look at linear transformations and/or linear combinations of random variables.

Variance of functions of random variables

Given random variables X and Y and non-zero constants α and β, by defining two new random variables $U = \alpha X$ and $T = \alpha X + \beta Y$, we have

$$\text{Var}(U) = \text{Var}(\alpha X) = \alpha^2\text{Var}(X).$$

Assuming *independence* of X and Y, then

$$\text{Var}(T) = \text{Var}(\alpha X + \beta Y) = \alpha^2\text{Var}(X) + \beta^2\text{Var}(Y).$$

5.10 DISTRIBUTIONS RELATED TO THE BINOMIAL DISTRIBUTION

There are many useful distributions which are related to the binomial distribution. Two of these are summarised below. Each arises in similar contexts to the binomial distribution which, of course, is when we have a fixed number of independent Bernoulli trials with constant probability of success π.

5.10.1 Geometric distribution

The *geometric distribution* is used when we perform a series of Bernoulli trials until we get the first success. The random variable X is the trial number on which we obtain this first success. Hence $x = 1, 2, \ldots$. So $x = 1$ corresponds to the first success on the first trial, $x = 2$ corresponds to the first success on the second trial, etc.

If the first success occurs on the xth trial, then there must have been $x - 1$ failures prior to this, each with a probability of occurrence of $1 - \pi$. Given independence of the Bernoulli trials, we can derive the probability function.

Probability function of the geometric distribution

If

$$P(X=x)=\begin{cases}(1-\pi)^{x-1}\pi & \text{for } x=1,2,\ldots \\ 0 & \text{otherwise}\end{cases}$$

then X has a **geometric distribution**, denoted by $X \sim \text{Geo}(\pi)$. It can be shown that for the geometric distribution,

$$\text{E}(X)=\frac{1}{\pi} \quad \text{and} \quad \text{Var}(X)=\frac{1-\pi}{\pi^2}.$$

5.10.2 Negative binomial distribution

The *negative binomial distribution* extends the geometric distribution in that the Bernoulli trials are continued until the rth success is achieved. Hence the geometric distribution is a special case of this, when $r = 1$.

Define X to be the trial number of the rth success. Then the smallest number of trials is r, that is, when we obtain r consecutive successes from the very beginning. Of course, if x is the trial number of the rth success, then this means we have previously incurred $r - 1$ successes, S, and $x - r$ failures, F, which could have occurred in any order. Again, given the independence of the Bernoulli trials, we can derive the probability function, noting that

$$P(X=x)=\underbrace{{}^{x-1}C_{r-1}\pi^{r-1}(1-\pi)^{x-r}}_{P(r-1\ Ss \text{ and } x-r\ Fs)}\pi.$$

Probability function of the negative binomial distribution

If

$$P(X=x)=\begin{cases}\binom{x-1}{r-1}\pi^r(1-\pi)^{x-r} & \text{for } x=r,r+1,r+2,\ldots \\ 0 & \text{otherwise}\end{cases}$$

then X has a **negative binomial distribution**, denoted $X \sim \text{Neg. Bin}(r, \pi)$. It can be shown that for the negative binomial distribution,

$$\text{E}(X)=\frac{r}{\pi} \quad \text{and} \quad \text{Var}(X)=\frac{r(1-\pi)}{\pi^2}.$$

Example 5.22

Suppose we are conducting independent Bernoulli trials with success probability $\pi = 1/6$ (for example, we might be rolling a fair die and need to throw a 5 for 'success'). If we want to know the probabilities for it to take *k* trials (throws) to get seven successes, then the negative binomial distribution gives us

$$P(X=7)=\left(\frac{1}{6}\right)^7,$$

$$P(X=8)=\binom{7}{6}\times\left(\frac{1}{6}\right)^7\times\left(\frac{5}{6}\right)^1,$$

$$P(X=9)=\binom{8}{6}\times\left(\frac{1}{6}\right)^7\times\left(\frac{5}{6}\right)^2,$$

$$\vdots$$

$$P(X=k)=\binom{k-1}{6}\times\left(\frac{1}{6}\right)^7\times\left(\frac{5}{6}\right)^{k-7}.$$

5.11 WHAT IS A CONTINUOUS RANDOM VARIABLE?

So far, we have considered discrete distributions such as the binomial and Poisson. These have dealt with count (or frequency) data, giving sample space values which are non-negative integers. In such cases, as with other discrete distributions, there is always a 'gap' between two possible values *within which there is no other possible value*. Hence the probability of an event involving several possible values is just the sum of the relevant probabilities of interest.

In contrast, a continuous-valued random variable, say X, can take *any value over some continuous range* or *interval*. So suppose x_1 and x_2 are distinct possible values of X, then there is another possible value between them, such as the midpoint $(x_1 + x_2)/2$. Although *in practice* our measurements will obviously only have so many decimal places (a consequence of practical limits to measurement accuracy), *in principle* it is possible to measure continuous variables to infinitely many decimal places. Hence it is mathematically convenient to use functions which can take any value over some defined continuous interval.

Example 5.23

Possible examples of continuous random variables include:

- in economics, *measuring* values of inputs or outputs, workforce productivity or consumption
- in sociology, *measuring* the proportion of people in a population with a particular preference
- in engineering, *measuring* the electrical resistance of materials
- in physics, *measuring* the temperature or electrical conductivity of materials.

Note the recurrent appearance of *measuring* in the above examples. Hence continuous random variables deal with measured data, while discrete random variables deal with count data.

The main transition from the discrete world of thinking is that in the continuous world only *intervals* are of interest, not single (point) values.

5.11.1 A formal definition

The possible values of a continuous random variable lie in the domain of real numbers, $\mathbb{R}$. Sometimes a random variable X may take any real value, $-\infty < x < \infty$, while sometimes it may take just a subset of the real line, such as the positive real numbers, $0 < x < \infty$, or the unit interval, $0 \le x \le 1$.

Other subsets of $\mathbb{R}$ are possible, such as $x \in (0,1) \cup (2,3)$, but we will restrict ourselves to ranges of real numbers for which there are no 'gaps'. (We could, of course, refer to $x \in (0,1) \cup (2,3)$ by the single, continuous interval $0 < x < 3$, and treat the probability that the value is between 1 and 2 (inclusive) as being zero.) A range without gaps is known as an interval, with either finite or infinite length, for example $[0, 1]$ and $(-\infty, \infty)$, respectively.

Properties of continuous distributions

The random variable X has a continuous distribution if:

- there is an interval $S \in \mathbb{R}$ such that the possible values of X are the point values in S
- for any individual point value $x \in S$, we have

$$P(X = x) = 0 \tag{5.3}$$

- for any pair of individual point values u and v, say, in S with $u < v$ we can always work out $P(u < X < v)$.

A consequence of equation (5.3), that is, that in the continuous world the probability of a single point value is zero (seemingly counter-intuitive!), is that we can be somewhat blasé about our use of $<$ and $\le$ since

$$P(X \le x) = P(X < x) + P(X = x) = P(X < x) + 0 = P(X < x).$$

Hence for any constants a and b, such that $a < b$, all of the following are equivalent:

$$P(a \le X \le b) = P(a < X \le b) = P(a \le X < b) = P(a < X < b).$$

It is useful to have a broad understanding of this definition of a continuous random variable, although you will *not* need to reproduce this in detail. It is more important to be able to actually calculate various probabilities such as $P(a < X < b)$. This is possible using either the *probability density function* or the *cumulative distribution function*.

5.12 PROBABILITY DENSITY FUNCTION AND CUMULATIVE DISTRIBUTION FUNCTION

The probability properties of a continuous random variable, X, can be described by a *non-negative* function, $f(x)$, which is defined over the relevant interval S. $f(x)$ is called the probability density function (pdf). A pdf itself does *not* represent a probability (hence $f(x)$ is not bounded by 1), instead it is a *density* of probability at a point x, with probability itself corresponding to the *area* under the (graph of the) function $f(x)$.

Example 5.24

If we wanted $P(1 < X < 3)$, say, then we would compute the area under the curve defined by $f(x)$ and above the x-axis interval (1, 3). This is illustrated in Figure 5.6.

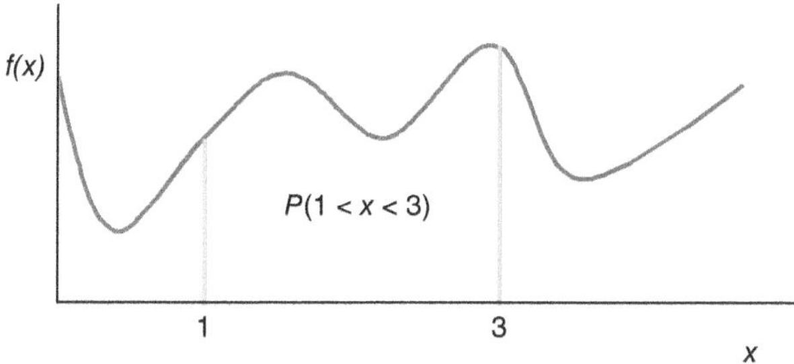

Figure 5.6 For an arbitrary pdf, $P(1 < X < 3)$ is shown as the area under the pdf and above the x-axis interval (1, 3).

In this way the pdf will give us the probabilities associated with *any* interval of interest, but there is never any interest in wanting the probability for a point value of a continuous random variable (which, remember, is zero). With this in mind, it is clear that *integration* is very important in the theory of continuous random variables, because of its role in determining areas. Hence the following properties for Example 5.24 should be readily apparent:

- $P(1 < X < 3)$ = the area under $f(x)$ above the x-axis interval (1, 3) = $\int_1^3 f(x)\,dx$.
- The total area under the curve is 1, since this represents the probability of X taking any possible value.

Formal properties of a pdf

Any function $f(x)$ defined on an interval $S \in \mathbb{R}$ can be the pdf for the probability distribution of a (continuous) random variable X, provided that it satisfies the following two criteria.

1. $f(x) \geq 0$ for all $x \in S$ (since you cannot have negative probabilities, from Axiom 1).
2. $\int_S f(x)\,dx = 1$, where S represents the sample space of x values. Hence the total area under the curve (i.e. the total probability) is 1, from Axiom 2.

So, if we want to calculate $P(a < X < b)$, for any constants a and b in S such that $a < b$, then

$$P(a < X < b) = \int_a^b f(x)\,dx.$$

Therefore, this integration/area approach helps explain why, for any single point $u \in S$, we have $P(X = u) = 0$. We can think of this probability as being the area of the (vertical) line segment from the x-axis to $f(u)$, which is $\int_u^u f(x)\,dx = 0$.

5.12.1 Attributes of a continuous random variable

Just as with a discrete random variable, for a continuous random variable we want to describe key features of the distribution. We now define various measures of location and dispersion. The main difference is the use of integrals instead of summations in the definitions.

Attributes of a continuous random variable

The relevant definitions are as follows.

- The **mean** of X is

$$E(X) = \mu = \int_S x f(x)\,dx$$

where, as before, S denotes the sample space of X.

- The **variance** of X is

$$\text{Var}(X) = \sigma^2 = E\left((X-\mu)^2\right) = \int_S (x-\mu)^2 f(x)\,dx.$$

However, recall we can also express the variance as

$$\sigma^2 = E(X^2) - \mu^2$$

where

$$E(X^2) = \int_S x^2 f(x)\,dx.$$

- The standard deviation of X is

$$\sqrt{\text{Var}(X)} = \sqrt{\sigma^2} = \sigma.$$

- The **median** of X is the value m in S such that $P(X \le m) = P(X \ge m) = 0.50$. Therefore, in general, we can compute m using

$$\int_{-\infty}^m f(x)\,dx = 0.50 \quad \text{or} \quad \int_m^\infty f(x)\,dx = 0.50.$$

If the sample space of X has a lower bound of a then substitute a for $-\infty$, and if the sample space of X has an upper bound of b, then substitute b for ∞.

- The **mode** of X is the value of X (if any) at which $f(x)$ achieves a *maximum*. Note that the pdf could be multimodal.

Occasionally statisticians need to look at the expected value of higher-order powers of $(X - \mu)$ than the second. For example, $\mathrm{E}((X - \mu)^3)$ is used to determine *skewness*, which you may recall from Chapter 2 is a measure of a distribution's departure from symmetry.

5.12.2 The cumulative distribution function

Just as for discrete distributions, we can think about cumulative probabilities in the continuous setting.

Cumulative distribution function of a continuous distribution

If X is a continuous random variable and $x \in \mathbb{R}$, then the cdf for X is the probability that X is less than or equal to x, such that

$$F(x) = P(X \leq x) = \int_{-\infty}^{x} f(t)\,\mathrm{d}t. \tag{5.4}$$

Note that the cdf is written $F(x)$, with an upper-case (capital) 'F', while the pdf is written $f(x)$, i.e. with a lower-case 'f'.

Hence we see an important relationship between the cdf and the pdf, that is, we obtain the cdf by *integrating* the pdf from the lower bound of X, $-\infty$ in equation (5.4), to x. Therefore, this implies we can obtain the pdf by *differentiating* the cdf with respect to x.

Relationship between pdf and cdf

Let $F(x)$ be the cdf of a continuous random variable. It follows that

$$f(x) = \frac{\mathrm{d}}{\mathrm{d}x} F(x) = F'(x).$$

5.13 (CONTINUOUS) UNIFORM DISTRIBUTION

Suppose X has a (continuous) uniform distribution from a to b, such that X is *equally likely* to be in any of the length-one intervals between a and b, and also that it is impossible for X to take a value outside this interval. We now define the pdf of X.

Continuous uniform pdf

If X has a *uniform distribution* over the continuous interval $[a, b]$, then

$$f(x) = \begin{cases} 1/(b-a) & \text{for } a \leq x \leq b \\ 0 & \text{otherwise.} \end{cases} \tag{5.5}$$

We can easily check that equation (5.5) is a valid pdf since, clearly, $f(x) \geq 0$ for all values of x, and it integrates to 1 since

$$\int_{-\infty}^{\infty} f(x)\,dx = \int_{-\infty}^{a} 0\,dx + \int_{a}^{b} \frac{1}{b-a}\,dx + \int_{b}^{\infty} 0\,dx = 0 + \left[\frac{x}{b-a}\right]_{a}^{b} + 0 = 1.$$

Example 5.25

Suppose X has a continuous uniform distribution over $[0, 10]$, such that $1/(b - a) = 1/(10 - 0) = 0.1$. We have

$$P(2 < X < 6) = \int_{2}^{6} 0.1\,dx = [0.1x]_{2}^{6} = 0.4$$

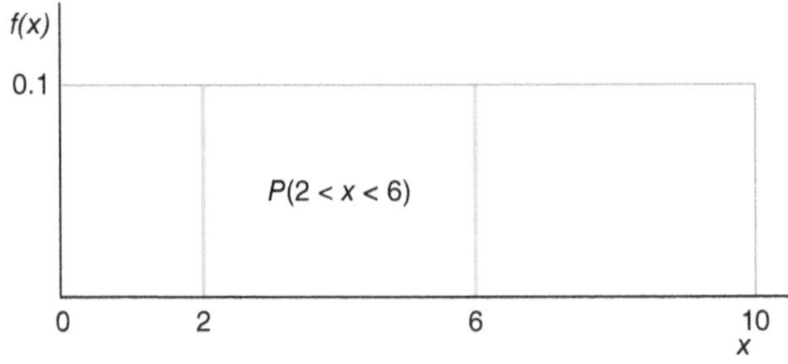

Figure 5.7 The pdf of X when X has a uniform distribution over [0, 10], showing the region denoting $P(2 < X < 6)$.

and

$$P(X < 8) = \int_{0}^{8} 0.1\,dx = [0.1x]_{0}^{8} = 0.8.$$

Of course, for this distribution these probabilities can simply be found geometrically as areas of appropriate rectangles, as illustrated in Figure 5.7 for $P(2 < X < 6)$. Also, note that geometrically we can determine the median to be 5.

For the distribution function we have

$$F(x) = \int_0^x f(t)\,\mathrm{d}t = \int_0^x 0.1\,\mathrm{d}t = [0.1t]_0^x = 0.1x \quad \text{for } 0 \le x \le 10.$$

In full we write this as

$$F(x) = \begin{cases} 0 & \text{for } x < 0 \\ 0.1x & \text{for } 0 \le x \le 10 \\ 1 & \text{for } x > 10. \end{cases}$$

Figure 5.8 displays the cdf of X.

The (population/theoretical) mean is

$$\mu = \mathrm{E}(X) = \int_0^{10} xf(x)\,\mathrm{d}x = \int_0^{10} 0.1x\,\mathrm{d}x = \left[\frac{0.1x^2}{2}\right]_0^{10} = 5.$$

The (population/theoretical) variance is

$$\sigma^2 = \mathrm{E}(X^2) - \mu^2 = \int_0^{10} 0.1x^2\,\mathrm{d}x - 5^2 = \left[\frac{0.1x^3}{3}\right]_0^{10} - 25 = 8.33.$$

5.14 EXPONENTIAL DISTRIBUTION

The *exponential distribution* arises in reliability theory and queuing theory. For example, in queuing theory we can model the distribution of *interarrival* times (if, as is often assumed, arrivals are treated as having a Poisson distribution with a rate parameter of λ). In this case, X is a positive-valued random variable following an exponential distribution.

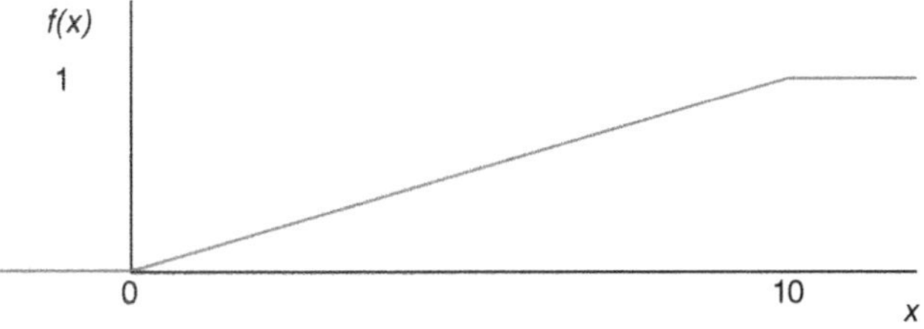

Figure 5.8 The cdf of X when X has a uniform distribution over [0, 10].

Exponential distribution

Let X be a non-negative continuous random variable. X follows an **exponential distribution**, denoted by $X \sim \text{Exp}(\lambda)$, if

$$f(x) = \begin{cases} \lambda e^{-\lambda x} & \text{for } x \geq 0 \text{ and } \lambda > 0 \\ 0 & \text{otherwise} \end{cases}$$

where $\lambda > 0$ is the (shape) parameter of the distribution. Its cdf is

$$F(x) = \begin{cases} 0 & \text{for } x < 0 \\ 1 - e^{-\lambda x} & \text{for } x \geq 0. \end{cases}$$

Its expected value and variance, respectively, are

$$\text{E}(X) = \frac{1}{\lambda} \quad \text{and} \quad \text{Var}(X) = \frac{1}{\lambda^2}.$$

Its median is $(\ln 2)/\lambda$.

The general shape of the pdf is that of 'exponential decay', as shown in Figure 5.9, hence the name! In Excel, we can compute probabilities for the exponential distribution using the `EXPON.DIST` function.

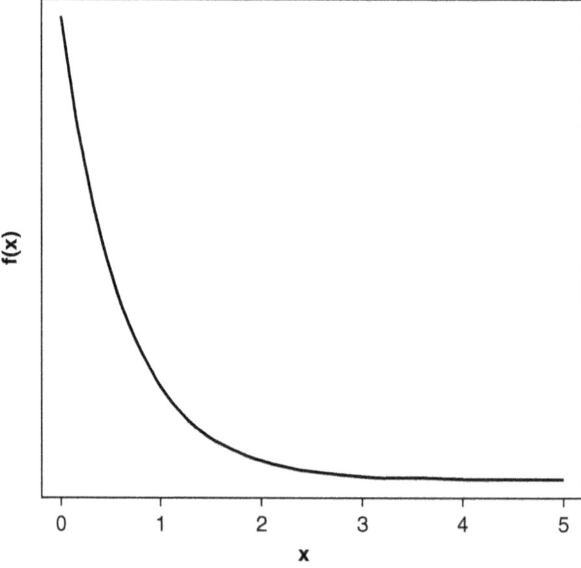

Figure 5.9 Exponential distribution pdf.

Excel function: `EXPON.DIST`

`=EXPON.DIST(x, lambda, cumulative)` returns the exponential distribution, where:

- `x` is the value of the function, a non-negative number
- `lambda` is the parameter value, a positive number
- `cumulative` is a logical value - for the cumulative distribution function, use 1 (or `TRUE`), and for the probability density function, use 0 (or `FALSE`).

Example 5.26

Suppose $\lambda = 3$. Then

$$P(3 < X < 5) = \int_3^5 3e^{-3x}dx = \left[-e^{-3x}\right]_3^5 = e^{-9} - e^{-15} = 0.00012$$

or in Excel, =EXPON.DIST(5,3,1)–EXPON.DIST(3,3,1), and

$$P(X < 6) = \int_0^6 3e^{-3x}dx = \left[-e^{-3x}\right]_0^6 = e^{0} - e^{-18} = 1 - e^{-18} \approx 1$$

or in Excel, =EXPON.DIST(6,3,1).

The distribution function can be calculated as follows:

$$F(x) = \int_0^x 3e^{-3t}dt = \left[-e^{-3t}\right]_0^x = e^{0} - e^{-3x} = 1 - e^{-3x} \quad \text{for } x \geq 0.$$

In full we write this as

$$F(x) = \begin{cases} 0 & \text{for } x < 0 \\ 1 - e^{-3x} & \text{for } x \geq 0 \end{cases}.$$

The (population/theoretical) mean is

$$\mu = E(X) = \int_0^\infty x\,3e^{-3x}dx = \left[-xe^{-3x} - \frac{e^{-3x}}{3}\right]_0^\infty = \frac{1}{3}.$$

The (population/theoretical) variance is

$$\sigma^2 = E(X^2) - \mu^2 = \int_0^\infty x^2 3e^{-3x}dx - \left(\frac{1}{3}\right)^2 = \frac{1}{9}.$$

Note that these last two results were obtained using a technique known as integration by parts.

Example 5.27

We extend Example 5.11.

The number of customers arriving at a bank per minute has a Poisson distribution with parameter $\lambda = 1.6$. Therefore, the time X, in minutes, between the arrivals of two successive customers follows an exponential distribution with parameter $\lambda = 1.6$.

From this exponential distribution, the expected waiting time between arrivals of customers is $E(X) = 1/1.6 = 0.625$ (minutes) and the median is calculated to be $(\ln 2)/1.6 = 0.433$.

We can also calculate probabilities of waiting times between arrivals, using the cumulative distribution function:

$$F(x) = \begin{cases} 0 & \text{for } x < 0 \\ 1 - e^{-1.6x} & \text{for } x \geq 0. \end{cases}$$

For example, the probability that two arrivals are at most 1 minute apart is

$$P(X \leq 1) = F(1) = 1 - e^{-1.6 \times 1} = 1 - e^{-1.6} = 0.7981.$$

In Excel, `=EXPON.DIST(1,1.6,1)`. The probability of a gap of 3 minutes or more between arrivals is very small:

$$P(X > 3) = 1 - F(3) = e^{-1.6 \times 3} = e^{-4.8} = 0.0082.$$

In Excel, `=1-EXPON.DIST(3,1.6,1)`.

5.15 NORMAL DISTRIBUTION

The normal distribution (also referred to as the Gaussian distribution, after Carl Friedrich Gauss (1777–1855)) is the most important probability distribution and is essential to much statistical theory and reasoning. It is, in a sense, the 'parent' distribution of all the *sampling distributions* which we shall meet in Chapter 7.

In order to get a feel for the normal distribution, let us consider the exercise of constructing a histogram of people's heights (assumed to be normally distributed). Suppose we start with 100 people, chosen at random, and construct a histogram using sufficient class intervals such that the histogram gives some representation of the distribution of the data. This will be a fairly 'ragged' diagram, but useful nonetheless.

Now, suppose we increase our random sample to 500 people and construct an appropriate histogram for these observations, but using more class intervals now that we have more data. This histogram will be smoother than the first, peaked in the centre, and roughly symmetric about the centre. The normal distribution is emerging! If we continue this exercise to random samples of 5000 people, or even 50,000, then we will eventually arrive at a very smooth bell-shaped curve as shown in Figure 5.10. Hence we can view the normal distribution as the smooth limit of the basic histogram as the sample size becomes very large.

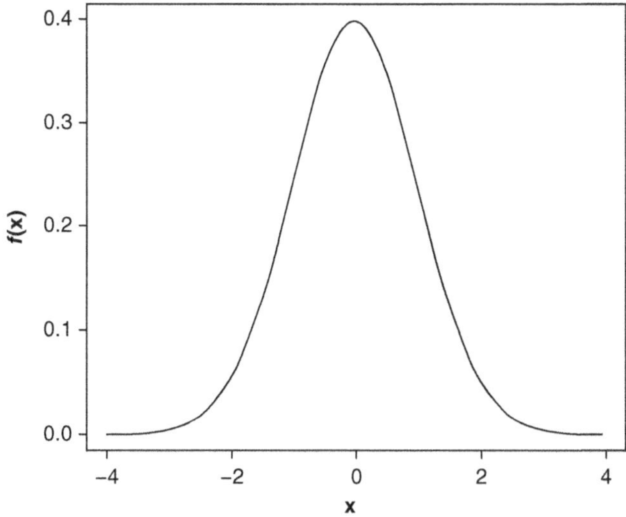

Figure 5.10 The (standard) normal distribution.

5.15.1 Relevance of the normal distribution

The normal distribution is relevant to the application of statistics for many reasons. A few of these follow.

- Many naturally occurring phenomena can be *modelled* as following a normal distribution. Examples include heights of people and dimensions of manufactured goods.
- A very important point is that averages of sampled variables (discussed in Chapter 7), indeed *any functions* of sampled variables, also have probability distributions. It can be demonstrated, theoretically and empirically, that, *provided the sample size is reasonably large*, the distribution of the sample mean, $\bar{X}$, will be (approximately) normal regardless of the distribution of the original variable. This is known as the *central limit theorem*, which we will return to later.
- The normal distribution is often used as the distribution of the error term in standard statistical and econometric models such as linear regression (covered in Chapters 13 and 14). This assumption can be, and should be, checked.

How tall? How fat?

Note the use of the word *modelled*. This is due to the *distributional assumption* of normality. Since a normal random variable X is defined over the entire real line, $-\infty < x < \infty$, we know that a person cannot have a negative height, even though the normal distribution has positive, non-zero probability over negative values. Also, nobody is of infinite height (the world's tallest man

(Continued)

ever, Robert Wadlow, was 272 cm), so clearly there is a finite upper bound to height, rather than ∞. Therefore, height does *not* follow a true normal distribution, but the approximation is good enough for modelling purposes.

More generally, in practice few (if any) real-world variables can be truly normally distributed. However, as an *approximating model* the normal distribution is well known, easy to work with, and hence a popular choice in many modelling situations.

Stock returns, for example, are often assumed to follow a normal distribution. However, the 'tails' of a normal distribution often underestimate the probability of extreme outcomes (such as large gains and large losses). Instead *fat-tailed* distributions such as the *t* distribution (introduced in Chapter 9) may be more suitable.

5.15.2 Consequences of the central limit theorem

The consequences of the central limit theorem are twofold.

- A number of statistical methods which we use have a *robustness* property, that is, it does not matter for their validity just what the true population distribution of the variable being sampled is.
- We are justified in assuming normality for statistics which are sample means, or linear transformations of them.

The central limit theorem was introduced above 'provided the sample size is reasonably large'. In practice a sample size of 30 or more is usually sufficient (and can be used as a rule of thumb), although the distribution of $\bar{X}$ may be (close to) normal for n much less than 30.

This depends on the distribution of the variable in the population. If this population distribution is in fact normal, then all sample means computed from it will be normal. However, if the population distribution is very non-normal, such as exponential (positively skewed, whereas the normal distribution is symmetric), then a sample size of at least 30 would be needed to justify normality.

5.15.3 Characteristics of the normal distribution

The pdf of the normal distribution takes the general form

$$f(x) = \frac{1}{\sqrt{2\pi\sigma^2}} \exp\left(-\frac{(x-\mu)^2}{2\sigma^2}\right).$$

The *shape* of this function is the bell-shaped curve as shown in Figure 5.10. Do not panic, you will not be dealing with this pdf explicitly! That said, do be aware that it involves *two parameters* – the mean, μ, and the variance, σ^2.

- Since the normal distribution is symmetric about μ, the distribution is centred at μ. As a consequence of this symmetry, the mean is equal to the median. Also, since the distribution peaks at μ, it is also equal to the mode. In principle, $-\infty < \mu < \infty$.
- The variance is σ^2, hence the larger σ^2, the larger the dispersion of the distribution. Note that $\sigma^2 > 0$.

If X has a normal distribution with parameters μ and σ^2, we denote this by $X \sim N(\mu, \sigma^2)$. Given the infinitely many possible values for μ and σ^2, and given that a normal distribution is *uniquely defined* by these two parameters, there is an infinite number of normal distributions due to the infinite combinations of values for μ and σ^2.

Some probabilities around the mean

The following results hold for all normal distributions, and are well worth remembering!

- $P(\mu - \sigma < X < \mu + \sigma) = 0.683$. In other words, about 68.3% of the total probability is within 1 standard deviation of the mean.
- $P(\mu - 1.96\sigma < X < \mu + 1.96\sigma) = 0.950$.
- $P(\mu - 2\sigma < X < \mu + 2\sigma) = 0.954$.
- $P(\mu - 2.58\sigma < X < \mu + 2.58\sigma) = 0.99$.
- $P(\mu - 3\sigma < X < \mu + 3\sigma) = 0.997$.

The first two of these are illustrated graphically in Figure 5.11.

The above results tell us that for any normal distribution we have (approximately) a 68%, 95% and 99.5% chance of being within 1, 2 and 3 standard deviations of the mean, respectively. Hence a '3-sigma' (3σ, i.e. three-standard-deviation) event, for example, would be a rare occurrence, and events beyond three standard deviations from the mean (i.e. $> 3\sigma$ events) would be even rarer.

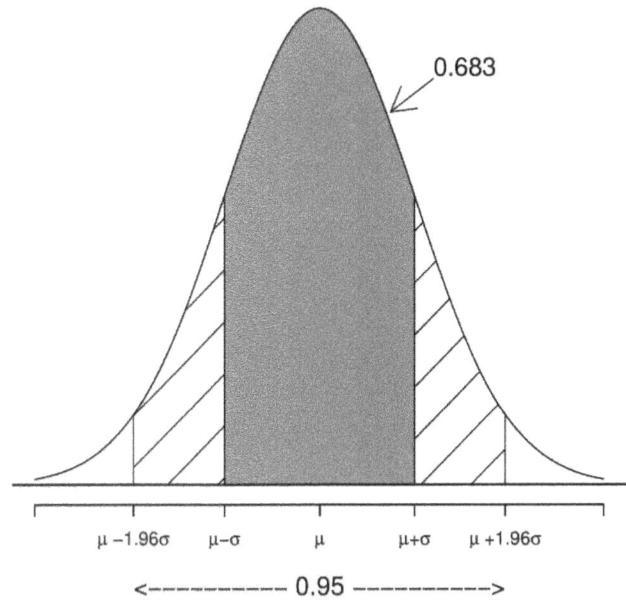

Figure 5.11 Some probabilities around the mean for the normal distribution.

The most important normal distribution is the special case when $\mu = 0$ and $\sigma^2 = 1$. We call this the standard normal distribution, denoted by Z, and we write $Z \sim N(0, 1)$. Note that the cdf for the

Z distribution, $F(z) = P(Z \leq z)$, is often denoted $\Phi(z)$ (special notation for a special distribution). We now consider some examples of working out probabilities from $Z \sim N(0, 1)$.

In Excel, we can compute these using the `NORM.S.DIST` function.

Excel function: `NORM.S.DIST`

`=NORM.S.DIST(z, cumulative)` returns the standard normal cumulative distribution (which has a mean of 0 and a standard deviation of 1), where

- `z` is the value for which you want the distribution
- `cumulative` is a logical value - for the cumulative distribution function, use 1 (or `TRUE`), and for the probability density function, use 0 (or `FALSE`).

Example 5.28

If $Z \sim N(0, 1)$, what is $P(Z > 1.2)$?

When determining probabilities, it is useful to visualise the specific area of probability which we are after.

So, for $P(Z > 1.2)$, we require the upper-tail probability red-shaded in Figure 5.12. This is simply $1 - \Phi(1.2)$, which is 0.1151.

In Excel, `=1-NORM.S.DIST(1.2,1)`, which returns $1 - \Phi(1.2)$.

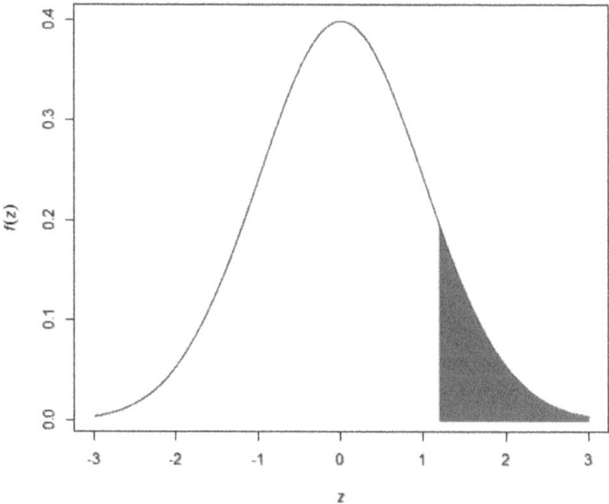

Figure 5.12 The standard normal distribution with the total shaded area depicting the value of $P(Z > 1.2)$.

Example 5.29

If $Z \sim N(0, 1)$, what is $P(-1.24 < Z < 1.86)$?

The probability we require is the sum of the blue and red areas in Figure 5.13. The red area is given by

$$
\begin{aligned}
P(0 \le Z \le 1.86) &= P(Z \le 1.86) - P(Z \le 0) \\
&= \Phi(1.86) - \Phi(0) \\
&= (1 - 0.0314) - 0.5 \\
&= 0.4686.
\end{aligned}
$$

The blue area is given by

$$
\begin{aligned}
P(-1.24 \le Z \le 0) &= P(Z \le 0) - P(Z \le -1.24) \\
&= \Phi(0) - \Phi(-1.24) \\
&= 0.5 - 0.1075 \\
&= 0.3925.
\end{aligned}
$$

Note that by symmetry of Z about $\mu = 0$, $P(Z \le -1.24) = P(Z \ge 1.24)$. Hence

$$P(-1.24 < Z < 1.86) = 0.4686 + 0.3925 = 0.8611.$$

In Excel, enter `=NORM.S.DIST(1.86,1)-NORM.S.DIST(-1.24,1)`, which returns $\Phi(1.86) - \Phi(-1.24)$.

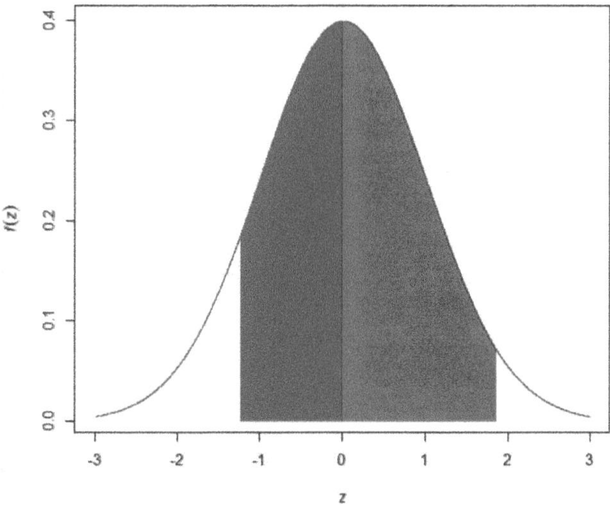

Figure 5.13 The standard normal distribution with the total shaded area depicting the value of $P(-1.24 < Z < 1.86)$.

5.15.4 The general normal distribution

We have already discussed that there exists an infinite number of different normal distributions due to the infinite pairs of parameter values since $-\infty < \mu < \infty$ and $\sigma^2 > 0$. It is helpful to use standardisation. This is a special (linear) transformation which converts $X \sim N(\mu, \sigma^2)$ into $Z \sim N(0, 1)$.

The transformation formula for standardisation

If $X \sim N(\mu, \sigma^2)$, then the transformation

$$Z = \frac{X - \mu}{\sigma}$$

creates a standard normal random variable, $Z \sim N(0, 1)$. So to standardise X we *subtract its mean and divide by its standard deviation.* See the end-of-chapter proof of why standardisation produces a zero-mean, unit-variance variable.

In Excel, we can compute these using the `NORM.DIST` function.

Excel function: `NORM.DIST`

`=NORM.DIST(x, mean, standard dev, cumulative)` returns the normal cumulative distribution for the specified mean and standard deviation, where:

- `x` is the value for which you want the distribution
- `mean` is the mean of the distribution
- `standard dev` is the standard deviation of the distribution, a positive number
- `cumulative` is a logical value - for the cumulative distribution function, use 1 (or `TRUE`), and for the probability density function, use 0 (or `FALSE`).

Example 5.30

Suppose $X \sim N(5, 4)$. What is $P(5.8 < X < 7.0)$? We have

$$\begin{aligned} P(5.8 < X < 7.0) &= P\left(\frac{5.8-5}{\sqrt{4}} < \frac{X-5}{\sqrt{4}} < \frac{7.0-5}{\sqrt{4}}\right) \\ &= P(0.4 < Z < 1) \\ &= P(Z > 0.4) - P(Z > 1) \\ &= 0.3446 - 0.1587 \\ &= 0.1859. \end{aligned}$$

In Excel, `=NORM.DIST(7,5,2,1)-NORM.DIST(5.8,5,2,1)`, which returns $P(X \leq 7) - P(X \leq 5.8)$.

5.15.5 Linear functions of normal random variables

We are often interested in linear functions of normal random variables (linear transformations and linear combinations). The following basic results are useful in dealing with such situations.

Linear transformations of normal random variables

If $X \sim N(\mu, \sigma^2)$ and a and b are constants (with $b \neq 0$), then

$$a + bX \sim N(a + b\mu, b^2\sigma^2).$$

Linear combinations of normal random variables

If X_1 and X_2 are *independent* normal random variables, such that we have $X_1 \sim N(\mu_1, \sigma_1^2)$ and $X_2 \sim N(\mu_2, \sigma_2^2)$, then

$$X_1 \pm X_2 \sim N(\mu_1 \pm \mu_2, \sigma_1^2 + \sigma_2^2).$$

Note that the variances are *added* even when dealing with the *difference* between independent random variables.

5.15.6 Transforming non-normal random variables

Even when the distribution of a random variable is clearly non-normal, a transformation can frequently be found such that the *transformed* random variable is normally distributed. This can be used, via the standard normal distribution, to calculate probabilities for the original random variable.

Example 5.31

For workers' incomes, if Y represents income, then the distribution of Y is very positively skewed and thus non-normal. However, if we transform this to $X = \ln(Y)$, then X is found to have a normal distribution. Any Y for which such a transformation leads to a normal random variable is said to have a **log-normal distribution**. Another common transformation which converts some non-normal distributions into normal distributions is taking the square root.

The following example illustrates the ways in which, with an appropriate transformation, we can calculate probabilities for the original distribution.

Example 5.32

Suppose that $X = \ln(Y)$ and $X \sim N(0.5, 0.16)$ and we seek $P(Y > 1)$. It follows that

$$\begin{aligned} P(Y > 1) &= P(e^X > 1) \\ &= P(X > \ln(1)) \\ &= P(X > 0) \\ &= P\left(Z > \frac{0 - 0.5}{\sqrt{0.16}}\right) \\ &= P(Z > -1.25) \\ &= 0.8944. \end{aligned}$$

In Excel, after standardisation, `=1-NORM.S.DIST(-1.25,1)`, which returns $1 - P(Z \leq -1.25)$.

5.16 NORMAL APPROXIMATION TO THE BINOMIAL

We discussed using a Poisson approximation to a Bin(n, π) distribution. Recall that the necessary conditions for this to be a 'good' approximation were:

- n should be greater than 30
- π should be sufficiently extreme such that $n\pi < 10$.

If these criteria are satisfied, then we use a Pois($n\pi$) approximating distribution.

An alternative approach to approximating desired binomial probabilities is the normal approximation to the binomial. As with the Poisson approximation, we require n to be 'large', greater than 30, say. However, the normal approximation is more suitable for *non-extreme* π. It can be shown (not here) that for large n and moderate π we have

$$\text{Bin}(n, \pi) \approx N(n\pi, n\pi(1 - \pi)).$$

However, there is one small caveat. The binomial distribution is *discrete*, but the normal distribution is *continuous*. To see why this is problematic, consider the following. Suppose $X \sim \text{Bin}(40, 0.4)$. Since X is discrete, such that $x = 0, 1, 2, \ldots, 40$, we have that

$$P(X \leq 4) = P(X \leq 4.5) = P(X < 5)$$

since $P(4 < X \leq 4.5) = 0$ and $P(4.5 < X < 5) = 0$ due to the 'gaps' in the probability mass for this distribution. In contrast, if $Y \sim N(16, 9.6)$, then

$$P(Y \leq 4) < P(Y \leq 4.5) < P(Y < 5)$$

since $P(4 < Y < 4.5) > 0$ and $P(4.5 < Y < 5) > 0$ because this is a continuous distribution.

The accepted way to circumvent this problem is to use a continuity correction which corrects for the effects of the transition from a discrete Bin(n, π) distribution to a continuous $N(n\pi, n\pi(1-\pi))$ distribution.

Continuity correction

This technique involves representing each discrete binomial value x, for $0 < x < n$, by the continuous interval $(x - 0.5, x + 0.5)$. Great care is needed to determine which x values are included in the required probability. Suppose we are approximating $X \sim \text{Bin}(n, \pi)$ with $Y \sim N(n\pi, n\pi(1-\pi))$. Then

$$P(X < 4) = P(X \leq 3) \Rightarrow P(Y < 3.5) \quad \text{(since 4 is excluded)}$$
$$P(X \leq 4) = P(X < 5) \Rightarrow P(Y < 4.5) \quad \text{(since 4 is included)}$$
$$P(1 \leq X < 6) = P(1 \leq X \leq 5) \Rightarrow P(0.5 < Y < 5.5) \quad \text{(since 1 to 5 are included).}$$

Example 5.33

A fair coin is tossed 100 times. What is the probability of getting more than 60 heads?

Let X be the number of heads, hence $X \sim \text{Bin}(100, 0.5)$. Here $n > 30$ and π is moderate, hence a normal approximation to the binomial is appropriate. We use $Y \sim N(50, 25)$ as the approximating distribution. So:

$$P(X > 60) \approx P(Y > 60.5) = P\left(Z > \frac{60.5 - 50}{\sqrt{25}}\right) = P(Z > 2.1) = 0.01786.$$

In Excel, =1−NORM.DIST(60.5,50,5,1).

5.17 SUMMARY OF PROBABILITY DISTRIBUTIONS

Appendix A summarises common Excel functions for working with some probability distributions, both discrete and continuous.

Appendix B provides a compendium of probability distributions, specifically summary information for the:

- discrete uniform distribution
- Bernoulli distribution
- binomial distribution
- Poisson distribution
- geometric distribution
- continuous uniform distribution
- exponential distribution
- normal distribution.

5.18 CHAPTER OVERVIEW

This chapter has introduced discrete and continuous random variables. In particular, some common families of probability distributions have been presented. In addition to the functional form of each of these distributions, important properties (such as the expected value and variance) have been studied. While much of the material has been theoretical, keep in mind that each of these distributions can be used as an *approximating* model of real-world variables.

5.19 KEY VOCABULARY

Bernoulli distribution
Binomial distribution
Continuity correction
Continuous
Continuous uniform distribution
Cumulative distribution function
Discrete
Discrete uniform distribution
Expectation operator
Expected value
Exponential distribution
Geometric distribution
Interval
Log-normal distribution
Mean
Median
Mode
Negative binomial distribution
Normal distribution
Parameter
Poisson distribution
Population mean
Population variance
Probability density function
Probability distribution
Probability (mass) function
Probability-weighted average
Random variable
Standard deviation
Standard normal distribution
Standardisation
Step function
Variance

5.20 EXERCISES

5.20.1 Test your understanding

1. In what sense is a variable 'random'?
2. What types of data would be represented with a discrete random variable? What types of data would be represented by a continuous random variable?
3. If X denotes a random variable, what is the difference between 'X' and 'x'?
4. What must be true about the possible outcomes of a discrete uniform distribution?
5. What is the 'relative frequency' interpretation of a probability distribution?
6. If a company classified its customers into two types – 'satisfied' and 'dissatisfied' – what would be the appropriate probability distribution to model these customer types, and why?
7. In a game show each contestant has two chances out of three of winning a prize, independently of other contestants. If six contestants take part, determine the probability distribution of the number of winners. Find the mean and variance of the number of winners.
8. Components for assembly are delivered in batches of 100, and experience shows that 5% of each batch are defective. On arrival, five pieces are selected at random from each batch and tested. If two or more of the five are found to be faulty, the entire batch is rejected. What is the probability that a 5% defective batch will be accepted?

9 One in ten of the new cars leaving a factory has minor faults of one kind or another.

(a) Assuming that a batch of ten cars delivered to a dealer represents a random sample of the output, what is the probability that:

(i) at least 1 will be faulty?
(ii) more than 3 will be faulty?

On receiving a delivery of ten new cars from the manufacturer, the dealer checks out four of these, chosen at random, before they are delivered to customers.

(b) If, in fact, two of the cars are faulty, what is the probability that both faults will be discovered?

10 Over a period of time the number of break-ins per month in a given district has been observed to follow a Poisson distribution with mean 2.

(a) For a given month, find the probability that the number of break-ins is:

(i) fewer than 2
(ii) more than 4
(iii) at least 1, but no more than 3.

(b) What is the probability that there will be fewer than ten break-ins in a 6-month period?

11 Arrivals at a supermarket are assumed to follow a Poisson distribution with a rate parameter of 120 per hour. If T is the time to arrival of the next customer (in minutes), calculate

$P(T > 1.0 \mid T > 0.5)$.

12 Two per cent of items of a particular type produced by a company are known to be defective. If a random sample of 100 items is selected for inspection, calculate the probability of getting no defectives by using:

(a) the binomial distribution
(b) the Poisson distribution.

13 Suppose $X \sim N(10, 4)$.

(a) Find:

(i) $P(X > 13.4)$
(ii) $P(8 < X < 9)$.

(b) Find the value a such that $P(10 - a < X < 10 + a) = 0.95$.
(c) Find the value b such that $P(10 - b < X < 10 + b) = 0.99$.
(d) How far above the mean of the standard normal distribution must we go such that only 1% of the probability remains in the right-hand tail?
(e) How far below the mean of the standard normal distribution must we go such that only 5% of the probability remains in the left-hand tail?

14 Your company requires a special type of light bulb which is available from only two suppliers. Supplier A's light bulbs have a mean lifetime of 2000 hours with a standard deviation of 180 hours. Supplier B's light bulbs have a mean lifetime of 1850 hours with a standard deviation of 100 hours. The distribution of the lifetimes of each type of light bulb is normal. Your company requires that the lifetime of a light bulb be not less than 1500 hours. All other things being equal, which type of bulb should you buy, and why?

15 The life, in hours, of a light bulb is normally distributed with a mean of 200 hours. If a consumer requires at least 90% of the light bulbs to have lives exceeding 150 hours, what is the largest value that the standard deviation can have?

16 A company manufactures rods whose diameters are normally distributed with a mean of 5 mm and a standard deviation of 0.05 mm. It also drills holes to receive the rods, and the diameters of these holes are normally distributed with a mean of 5.2 mm and a standard deviation of 0.07 mm. The rods are allocated to the holes at random. What proportion of rods will fit into the holes?

17 An investor has the choice of two out of four investments: X_1, X_2, X_3 and X_4. The profits (in thousands of pounds per annum) from these may be assumed to be independently distributed and

profit from $X_1 \sim N(2, 1)$,

profit from $X_2 \sim N(3, 3)$,

profit from $X_3 \sim N(1, 0.25)$,

profit from $X_4 \sim N(2.5, 4)$.

Which pair of investments should the investor choose in order to maximise the probability of making a total profit of at least £2000? What is this maximum probability?

18 An advertising agency claims that 40% of all television viewers watch a particular programme. In a random sample of 500 viewers, what is the probability that fewer than 170 will be watching the programme if the agency's claim is correct?

19 The number of newspapers sold daily at a kiosk is normally distributed with a mean of 350 and a standard deviation of 30.

(a) Find the probability that fewer than 300 newspapers are sold on Monday.
(b) Find the probability that fewer newspapers are sold on Tuesday than on Monday.
(c) Find the probability that fewer than 1700 newspapers are sold in a (5-day) week. What assumption have you made in order to answer this?
(d) How many newspapers should the newsagent stock each day such that the probability of running out on any particular day is 10%?

20 Explain the purpose of a continuity correction.

21 An electrical device contains 10 components connected in series. The device fails if any one of the components fails. For each component the probability that it survives a year of use without failing is π, and the failures of different components can be regarded as independent events.

(a) What is the probability that the device fails in a year of use?
(b) How large must π be for the probability of failure in (a) to be less than 0.1?

22 The possible annual percentage return of the stocks of ABC and DEF share a common probability distribution, given below.

Return of ABC	−7.3	−1.9	6.4	13.7	15.9	34.1
Return of DEF	38.9	25.6	16.3	5.6	−2.5	−5.3
Probability	0.05	0.20	0.25	0.25	0.20	0.05

(a) Determine the expected annual return of ABC and DEF.
(b) Determine the standard deviation of the annual return of ABC and DEF.
(c) If you could only invest in one of these two stocks, which would you choose and why?
(d) What can be concluded about the relationship of the annual returns of these two stocks? Would this impact your investment decision-making?

23 At a charity event, the organisers sell 100 tickets for a raffle. At the end of the event, one of the tickets is selected at random and the person with that number wins a prize. Person A buys ticket number 22. Person B buys tickets numbered 1–5. What is the probability of each of them winning the prize?

24 Towards the end of the financial year, James is considering whether to accept an offer to buy his stock option now, rather than wait until the normal exercise time. If he sells now, his profit will be £120,000. If he waits until the exercise time, his profit will be £200,000, provided that there is no crisis in the markets before that time; if there is a crisis, the option will be worthless and he would expect a net loss of £50,000. What action should he take to maximise his expected profit if the probability of crisis is:

(a) 0.5?
(b) 0.1?
(c) For what probability of a crisis would James be indifferent between the two courses of action if he wishes to maximise his expected profit?

25 The waiting time X (in minutes) of a customer at a taxi rank has the following probability density function:

$$f(x)=\begin{cases}0.25e^{-0.25x} & \text{for } x\geq 0\\ 0 & \text{otherwise.}\end{cases}$$

This is the exponential distribution with parameter $\lambda = 0.25$. For this distribution, calculate the probability that the waiting time is:

(a) 5 minutes
(b) at most 4 minutes
(c) at least 8 minutes
(d) at most 0.5 standard deviations from its expected value.

26 In a survey of the population of employed workers in the UK, respondents are asked how many hours they usually work per week in their main job. The average of the responses is 38.74 hours, with a standard deviation of 15.72 hours. In answering the following question, suppose that working hours in the population follow a normal distribution with these values of the mean and standard deviation.

(a) What percentage of people in the population work between 35 and 45 hours per week?
(b) How many hours do the middle 50% of people in the population work?
(c) What is the number of hours such that only 10% of people work that long or longer per week?

27 Each morning telephone calls arrive at a reception desk according to a Poisson process with on average three calls every 5 minutes. Let T denote the waiting time, in minutes, until the first call is received after 09:00.

(a) What is the distribution of T?
(b) Calculate $P(T > 4)$.

28 The times taken, in minutes, for three commuters to travel to work can be regarded as independent and normally distributed random variables with means and standard deviations as given in the following table:

Commuter	Mean	Standard deviation	Departure time
A	28	4	08:30
B	50	6	08:10
C	35	5	08:20

In order to arrive at work for a 09:00 start, the commuters leave home at the times shown in the right-hand column of the table. Let A, B and C be the random variables denoting the journey times, in minutes, of commuters A, B and C, respectively.

(a) Find the probabilities of the following events:

(i) Commuter A is late for work.
(ii) Commuter A arrives at work before Commuter B.
(iii) At least one commuter is late for work.
(iv) All three commuters are late for work, given that at least one commuter is late for work.
(v) Commuter C is late for work, given that exactly one commuter is late for work.

(b) At what time should Commuter C leave home if there is to be a 2.5% chance of her being late for work?

5.20.2 Practice with Excel

Head over to the companion website for Excel examples and screencasts!

5.21 PROOFS

These proofs are not essential to review (or master), but are included for the 'interested reader'. A black square, ■, simply denotes the end of the proof. Enjoy.

Derivation of E(X) for the binomial distribution

For E(X), we have

$$\begin{aligned}
E(X) &= \sum_{x=0}^{n} x\binom{n}{x}\pi^x(1-\pi)^{n-x} \\
&= \sum_{x=1}^{n} x\binom{n}{x}\pi^x(1-\pi)^{n-x} \\
&= \sum_{x=1}^{n} \frac{n(n-1)!}{(x-1)!((n-1)-(x-1))!}\pi\pi^{x-1}(1-\pi)^{n-x} \\
&= n\pi\sum_{x=1}^{n}\binom{n-1}{x-1}\pi^{x-1}(1-\pi)^{n-x} \\
&= n\pi\sum_{y=0}^{n-1}\binom{n-1}{y}\pi^{y}(1-\pi)^{(n-1)-y} \\
&= n\pi\times 1 \\
&= n\pi
\end{aligned}$$

where $y = x - 1$, and the last summation is over all the values of the probability function of another binomial distribution, this time with possible values 0, 1, 2, ..., $n - 1$ and probability parameter π. ■

Derivation of E(X) for the Poisson distribution

We have

$$\begin{aligned}
E(X) = \sum_{x=0}^{\infty} xp(x) = \sum_{x=0}^{\infty} x\frac{e^{-\lambda}\lambda^x}{x!} = \sum_{x=1}^{\infty} x\frac{e^{-\lambda}\lambda^x}{x!} = \lambda\sum_{x=1}^{\infty}\frac{e^{-\lambda}\lambda^{x-1}}{(x-1)!} &= \lambda\sum_{y=0}^{\infty}\frac{e^{-\lambda}\lambda^{y}}{y!} \\
&= \lambda\times 1 \\
&= \lambda
\end{aligned}$$

where we replace $x - 1$ with y. The result follows from the fact that $\sum_{y=0}^{\infty} e^{-\lambda}\lambda^y / y!$ is the sum of all non-zero values of a probability function of this form. ■

Alternative expression for the variance

We prove an alternative expression for the variance:

$$\begin{aligned}
\sigma^2 &= E\left((X-\mu)^2\right) \\
&= E\left(X^2 - 2\mu X + \mu^2\right) \\
&= E\left(X^2\right) - 2\mu\, E(X) + \mu^2 \\
&= E\left(X^2\right) - 2\mu^2 + \mu^2 \\
&= E\left(X^2\right) - \mu^2.
\end{aligned}$$

In words, 'the (population) variance is equal to the mean of the square minus the square of the mean'. Rearranging gives:

$$E(X^2) = \sigma^2 + \mu^2.$$

This representation is useful since we often want to know $E(X^2)$, but start by knowing the usual details of a distribution, namely, μ and σ^2.

Why standardisation achieves a zero mean and unit variance

To see why, first note that any linear transformation of a normal random variable is also normally distributed. Therefore, as X is normal, so too is Z, since the standardisation transformation is linear in X. It remains to show that standardisation results in a random variable with a zero mean and a unit variance.

Since $X \sim N(\mu, \sigma^2)$,

$$E(Z) = E\left(\frac{X-\mu}{\sigma}\right) = \frac{1}{\sigma}E(X-\mu) = \frac{1}{\sigma}(E(X)-\mu) = \frac{1}{\sigma}(\mu-\mu) = 0.$$

This result exploits the fact that σ is a constant, hence it can be taken outside the expectation operator. Turning to the variance,

$$\text{Var}(Z) = \text{Var}\left(\frac{X-\mu}{\sigma}\right) = \frac{1}{\sigma^2}\text{Var}(X-\mu) = \frac{1}{\sigma^2}\text{Var}(X) = \frac{1}{\sigma^2}\times\sigma^2 = 1.$$

This result uses the fact that we must square a constant when taking it outside the 'Var' operator.

6

DECISION TREE ANALYSIS AND GAME THEORY

Chapter contents

Chapter level: *Advanced*

Source: Photo by Ylanite via Pixabay.

Key concepts

- Strategic decision-making
- Decision tree analysis
- Game theory

Chapter value

Optimal strategic decisions are determined both unilaterally and bilaterally.

Key takeaway

Risk neutrality simplifies decision-making to maximising expected payoffs only.

Chapter outline

Decision-making is an uncertain art, as well as an uncertain science. Final *realised* outcomes cannot be known with certainty at the moment a decision is made. Nevertheless, the range of *possible* outcomes is typically known - for example, product demand must be a non-negative quantity! As we have seen in Chapters 4 and 5, *probability* is our mechanism for quantifying uncertainty such that we can attach a *probability distribution* to the possible outcomes. *Decision tree analysis* uses a tree-like structure (hence the name!) to visualise the time order of events, the set of decisions, the uncertain outcomes and their associated probabilities. Subject to an optimal criterion, a *unilateral* decision-maker can solve the decision tree for their optimal strategy set.

Game theory extends the problem to two or more 'players'. We focus on bilateral decision-making whereby one decision-maker must anticipate the response of the other (a bit like playing chess). Each player's actions could be taken either *simultaneously* or *sequentially* - the latter giving rise to a first-mover advantage. We examine competitive behaviour in terms of setting prices and quantities.

Learning outcomes

After completing this chapter, you should be able to:

- construct decision trees and solve them using backward induction to determine the optimal strategy set for the decision-maker
- define different risk attitudes - risk-averse, risk-neutral and risk-loving appetites
- monetise the value of information (whether perfect or imperfect) to determine its usefulness in assisting the decision
- construct simple game theory problems to model the strategic interaction of two decision-makers and solve for Nash equilibria in both pure strategies and mixed strategies
- model simultaneous quantity setting using the Cournot competition model
- model simultaneous price setting using the Bertrand competition model
- model sequential quantity setting using the Stackelberg leadership model.

6.1 INTRODUCTION

Managers need to know what actions to undertake, which could mean simply to 'do nothing' – a business equivalent of the *Hippocratic oath* of physicians, to 'first do no harm'. Of course, managers may have an urge to demonstrate their worth (and justify their salary!) by being active, rather than passive, but if this leads to an outcome which is inferior to the status quo, then harm has been done!

Faced with uncertainty, we proceed to construct simple decision trees which display the mutually exclusive and collectively exhaustive (MECE) paths which could stem from a *decision node*. Ultimate outcomes are at the mercy of chance, and we will explicitly incorporate such 'luck' as a *chance node* with a corresponding probability distribution attached to the different possible outcomes. Once the outcomes are also included, we can then solve the tree back to front (technically, right to left) using a technique called backward induction.

To motivate decision tree analysis, consider some *unilateral* managerial decisions (i.e. with a single decision-maker):

- hiring decisions – to hire, or not to hire?
- research and development (R&D) decisions – to invest, or not to invest?
- supplier decisions – to procure, or not to procure?

Decisions need not always be binary. For example, R&D expenditure could involve multiple amounts. However, for a choice we require *at least two* options – if there is only one option, then there is no choice!

6.2 TO ADVERTISE, OR NOT TO ADVERTISE?

Consider a confectionery company which has developed a new low-calorie chocolate bar – named *Chocolow* – aimed at guilt-ridden chocaholics. Having performed well in blind taste test trials, the company is ready to roll out these treats in supermarkets nationwide. The manufacturer is contemplating whether or not it should spend money advertising *Chocolow* to stimulate brand awareness and boost demand, or simply to let consumers discover the product on the supermarket shelves in the confectionery aisle.

To keep things simple, let us assume that sales of *Chocolow* bars in the first 6 months will either be 'high', grossing £1 million, or 'low', grossing £0.5 million. (In practice, there would be a continuum of units sold, but here we prioritise simplification using a binary set of sales levels.) Based on previous experience, the company thinks (rightly or wrongly) that high and low sales are equally likely, so that both occur with an assumed probability of 0.50.

While word-of-mouth advertising is free, the manufacturer is considering traditional paid-for advertising at a fixed cost of £100,000. Advertising is not guaranteed to be effective, although the fixed cost is not contingent on success. Instead, the benefit of advertising will be modelled as *increasing the probability* of high sales. The company assumes (again, rightly or wrongly) that with advertising, the probability of high sales increases to 0.80 (from 0.50 without advertising).

So, the decision facing the company is: to advertise, or not to advertise? Is the benefit of a 60% increase in the probability of high sales ((0.80 – 0.50)/0.50 = 60%) worth the fixed cost of £100,000? We proceed to answer this question by constructing a *decision tree*.

Elements of a decision tree

A decision tree consists of:

- **decision nodes**, denoted by squares (□), which represent points where the decision-maker decides which path to take
- **chance nodes**, denoted by circles (○), which represent points where there is resolution of uncertainty
- **branches** which connect the nodes
- **probabilities** which indicate the likelihood of each branch stemming from a chance node
- **payoffs** at the end of terminal branches which indicate the monetary outcome.

Figure 6.1 displays the decision tree for *Chocolow* advertising. We read decision trees from left to right. So, at the start we see a decision node – the square – showing the two possible paths. Note the decision is under the control of the decision-maker – they *choose* whether to advertise or not advertise. After this decision, chance (or fate, or destiny, call it what you will) takes over and 'decides' whether sales will be high or low. In practice, chance plays the role of all factors which influence consumers' purchasing decisions about *Chocolow* – what is important to recognise is that the company has no control over what chance (fate, destiny) has in store.

The probabilities reflect the likelihood of these outcomes and are conditional on which decision was taken at the start. Hence if 'not advertise' was chosen, high and low sales both occur with a 50% probability; if 'advertise' was chosen, high sales occur with an 80% probability while low sales occur with a 100% – 80% = 20% probability. Notice that the *sum* of all the probabilities of all branches to the right of a chance node *must* add up to 1, as these branches are MECE.

On the far right we see the payoffs, representing the sales revenues. Since the fixed cost of £100,000 is paid once 'advertise' is chosen regardless of outcome, then this amount must be subtracted from the sales revenues of £1 million and £0.5 million for high and low sales, respectively.

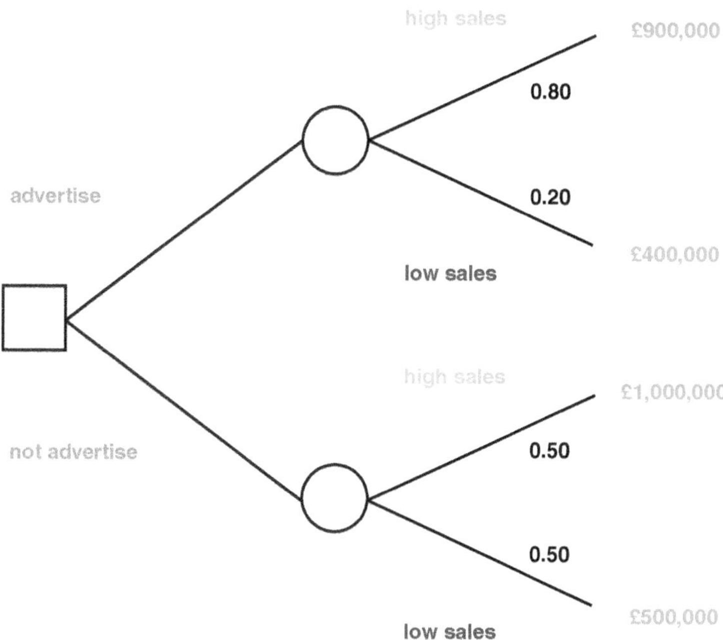

Figure 6.1 Decision tree for *Chocolow* advertising problem.

Having set up the decision tree in Figure 6.1, how do we decide whether to advertise, or not to advertise? To answer this, we will assume for simplicity that the company is risk-neutral. By conveniently ignoring risk, the problem reduces to a comparison of the expected monetary value (EMV) of each possible decision, and then the decision-maker simply chooses the option yielding the maximum EMV. Given the discrete nature of the branches following chance nodes, the EMV is just a *probability-weighted average* calculated as the sum of payoffs multiplied by their respective probabilities, analogous to Section 5.8 where the expected value of a discrete random variable was defined.

We now compute the EMVs for the two decision alternatives:

$$\text{EMV(advertise)} = £900{,}000 \times 0.80 + £400{,}000 \times 0.20 = £800{,}000$$

$$\text{EMV(not advertise)} = £1{,}000{,}000 \times 0.50 + £500{,}000 \times 0.50 = £750{,}000.$$

We see that:

$$\text{EMV(advertise)} > \text{EMV(not advertise)}$$

hence the payoff-maximising option is 'advertise'. It is arguably naïve to assume the company is risk-neutral (i.e. ambivalent or indifferent to risk), but the risk-neutral assumption allows us to ignore the *variation* of payoffs from the different decisions.

So, how should we interpret the EMV of £800,000? By choosing 'advertise' we never actually realise £800,000 – the only possible payoffs, after all, are £900,000 and £400,000. It is entirely possible (with a 20% probability) that we pursue the optimal path of 'advertise' and experience low sales through no fault of our own – chance is a cruel mistress – with the advertising proving ineffective, resulting in the *worst* of all possible payoffs at just £400,000. However, recall that an expected value represents a *long-run average*. That is, if we imagined playing this game independently a large number of times (say, once per year for several years), choosing 'advertise' on each occasion, then 80% of the time we would expect high sales of £900,000 to result (our good luck), and only 20% of the time we would expect low sales of £400,000 (our bad luck). Averaging this out produces an average payoff of £800,000 per year.

6.3 TO DRILL, OR NOT TO DRILL?

Despite the world hopefully transitioning to a greener economy, oil consumption is likely to continue for the foreseeable future. Suppose you are the director of operations for an oil exploration company. In your quest to find 'black gold', you have a potential site and are deciding whether to drill and hopefully discover abundant oil reserves. Suppose further that there is uncertainty not just about whether there is oil under the site, but even if so, its depth is unknown, with consequences for extraction costs. Figure 6.2 shows a decision tree for this drilling conundrum.

We observe the following:

- *Decision node 1*. Choosing 'drill' leads to chance node A where if oil is found (with 70% probability) a payoff of £900 million is realised (inclusive of drilling costs). Alternatively, choosing 'not drill' provides a payoff of £0.
- *Decision node 2*. This point is only reached if no oil is discovered at the shallow depth. Here the decision-maker can decide to 'stop', realising the non-recoverable drilling cost of £100 million (i.e. a negative profit), or choose to 'drill deeper' – at additional cost – leading to chance node B. If oil is discovered at this greater depth (with 20% probability) the payoff is £600 million (again, inclusive of drilling costs), otherwise if no oil is found the total drilling costs are £300 million.

- Oil found at a greater depth is more costly to extract to the surface, hence the payoff from oil at the greater depth is only £600 million, and it costs twice as much to drill to the greater depth, that is, the costs of a no-oil outcome increase from £100 million to a total of £300 million.

The decision tree in Figure 6.2 has two decision nodes, which are solved using *backward induction*; that is, we determine the optimal strategy for decision node 2 *first*, which then allows us to determine what to do at decision node 1. Again, we assume a risk-neutral decision-maker so we compute EMVs. From decision node 2 we have

EMV(drill deeper) = £600m × 0.20 – £300m × 0.80 = –£120m

EMV(stop) = –£100m.

Since

EMV(stop) > EMV(drill deeper)

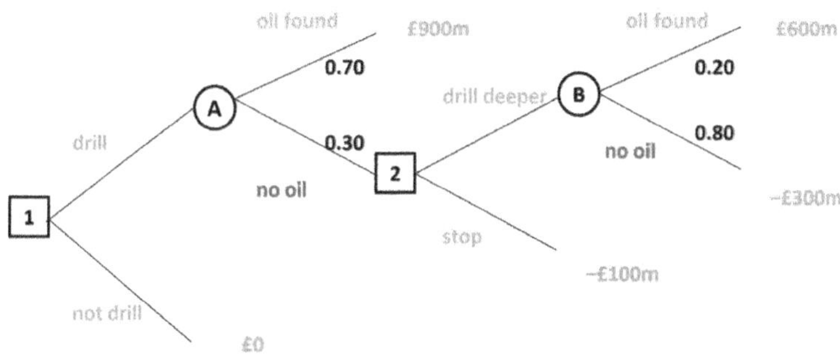

Figure 6.2 Decision tree for oil drilling problem.

the optimal choice at decision node 2 is to 'stop'. At first sight this might seem counter-intuitive. Why would a rational decision-maker choose a course of action with a (certain) loss of £100 million? Well, they would if the alternative (in EMV terms) is *worse*! Such is the case here, where the expected loss is £120 million from choosing to drill further. So, rather than *profit maximisation* we are opting for *loss minimisation* (the lesser of two evils). I would not enjoy losing £100 million, but it is less bad than losing £120 million (in expectation)!

What about decision node 1? Again, we compare EMVs:

EMV(drill) = £900m × 0.70 – £100m × 0.30 = £600m

EMV(not drill) = £0.

Since

EMV(drill) > EMV(not drill)

the optimal choice at decision node 1 is to 'drill'. Note the inclusion of –£100 million in the EMV(drill) calculation – we have already decided what we would do at decision node 2 ('stop') so we use the EMV from this as the 'payoff' in the EMV(drill) calculation. Therefore, we now have our strategy: drill, then if no oil is found, stop.

It is entirely possible that decision node 2 is never reached. If we are lucky (fingers crossed!), then we strike oil immediately and achieve a payoff of £900 million. If this happens, then what was the point of worrying about decision node 2? Well, we should think of this as *contingency planning*. In a decision tree with multiple decision nodes, we should *always* have a plan for every decision node, even if it may never be reached in practice. Better to know in advance what is optimal to do in every possible scenario before we actually encounter it, rather than 'panic' and end up making a rash or knee-jerk reaction which proves to be sub-optimal.

Contingency planning examples

Advice about what to do in emergency situations is a great example of contingency planning. Think about all the fire alarm drills you have experienced, or the pre-takeoff flight safety demonstrations you have heard (and probably ignored). One hopes, of course, that the information gained will never actually be needed in practice. However, such safety briefings tell you what to do *if* a fire, flight emergency, etc. takes place. Like decision node 2 in the oil drilling problem which may never be reached, it is better to prepare for all possible contingencies in advance. If an in-flight emergency occurs, you will probably wish you had paid more attention to the safety demonstration so that you know what action(s) you need to take to (hopefully) safely evacuate the aircraft. Brace, brace, brace.

6.4 RISK ATTITUDES

So far, we have assumed the decision-maker is risk-neutral such that they are *indifferent to risk*. This has allowed us to only have to consider the expected monetary value (i.e. the long-run average outcome) and ignore the *variation* in the possible outcomes. Here we consider different *risk attitudes*, which can be classified as (i) risk-averse, (ii) risk-neutral and (iii) risk-loving. Consider the simple investment decision between a safe asset (such as a government bond – effectively an IOU issued by the government) which returns a guaranteed (hence certain) £1000 (ignoring the possibility of a sovereign default since a government could simply choose to print more money to repay the debt, in theory at least – sovereign defaults have been known!), and a risky asset such as a corporate bond which returns £2000 if the firm repays, otherwise it returns £0 if it defaults. Suppose there is a 50% probability of default – an extreme 'junk bond'! The decision tree is shown in Figure 6.3.

From Figure 6.3 we see that:

$$\text{EMV(government bond)} = £1000$$

$$\text{EMV(corporate bond)} = £2000 \times 0.50 + £0 \times 0.50 = £1000.$$

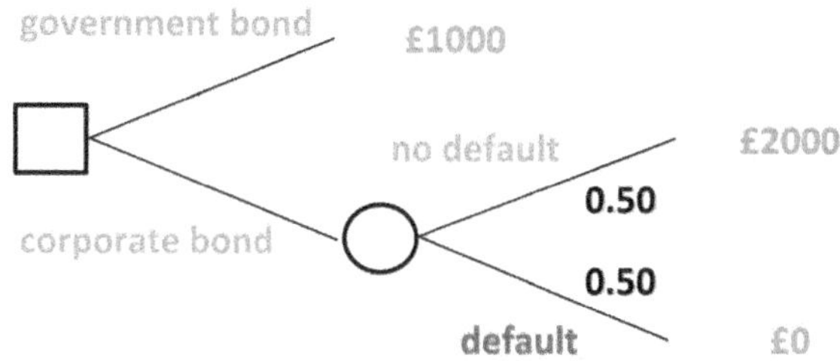

Figure 6.3 Decision tree for bond investment decision.

Hence

EMV(government bond) = EMV(corporate bond)

so the expected returns are equal. However, it is clear that the government bond carries no risk of default, returning £1000 to the investor, whereas the corporate bond carries substantial risk. The decision between the government bond and the corporate bond will now depend on the risk appetite of the investor:

- A risk-averse investor would choose the government bond since they are averse to risk so are worried about the risk of default for the corporate bond.
- A risk-neutral investor would be *indifferent* between the two bond types as they only care about EMVs, which here are equal. We can think of the investor using a randomisation device (such as tossing a *fair* coin) to make their choice.
- A risk-loving investor would choose the corporate bond since they are excited by risk and the potential to realise £2000.

More generally:

- a decision-maker is *risk-averse* if they strictly prefer the certain outcome of £x over a risky alternative with an EMV also of £x.
- a decision-maker is *risk-neutral* if they are indifferent between a certain outcome and an uncertain outcome with the same EMV.
- a decision-maker is *risk-loving* if they strictly prefer a risky alternative with an EMV of £x over the certain outcome of £x.

An individual's risk appetite will depend on the amount of money at stake. Consider again Figure 6.3. Which bond would you choose? What if we added some zeros to the payoffs such that the government bond yielded £1,000,000 and the corporate bond yielded £2,000,000 if there was no default? It is likely your degree of risk aversion would now be higher! Still risk-loving? Well, what about a game of Russian roulette? With your life at stake, although you are more likely to pull the trigger on an empty chamber, would you really accept the gamble? (An interesting application of the *geometric distribution* discussed in Chapter 5.)

6.4.1 Certainty equivalent

Definition: Certainty equivalent

The **certainty equivalent** (CE) of a risky alternative is defined as the amount of money that would make the decision-maker indifferent between receiving this amount with certainty and the risky alternative.

Example 6.1

A risky investment project pays out £2000 with a probability of 0.50 and £0 otherwise. The certainty equivalent, x, makes the decision-maker indifferent between the certain outcome x and the risky project. Figure 6.4 shows the decision tree.

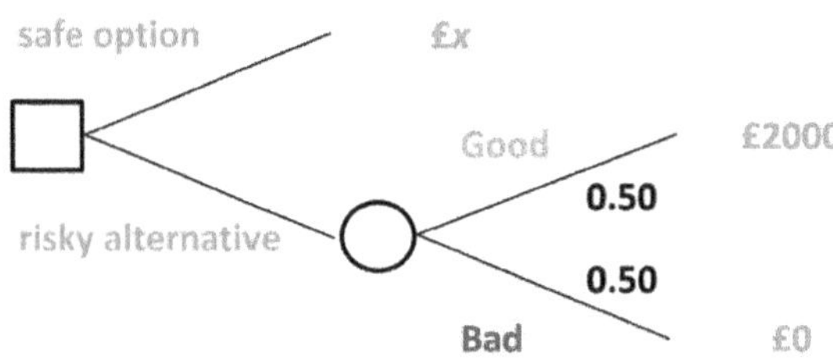

Figure 6.4 Decision tree where x is the certainty equivalent.

6.4.2 Risk premium

Definition: Risk premium

The **risk premium** of a risky alternative is defined as

$$\text{risk premium} = \text{EMV} - \text{CE}$$

and represents how much money the decision-maker is willing to pay to receive a certain payoff of x rather than face the risky alternative with an expected payoff of x. Risk attitudes can be determined as follows:

$\text{EMV} > \text{CE} \Rightarrow$ risk-averse, with positive risk premium

$\text{EMV} = \text{CE} \Rightarrow$ risk-neutral, with zero risk premium

$\text{EMV} < \text{CE} \Rightarrow$ risk-loving, with negative risk premium.

For risk-neutral decision-makers, we simply choose the maximum EMV option.

6.5 PUTTING A PRICE ON INFORMATION

Businesses crave certainty when making decisions. However, the world is uncertain. Decision trees visually represent how decisions have to be undertaken *before* the uncertainty is resolved. For example, in Figure 6.1 the decision of 'to advertise, or not to advertise?' had to be taken in advance of knowing whether sales would be high or low. If we knew sales would be high *before* we made the decision, then there would be no need to pay for advertising.

In practice we do not have access to a 'crystal ball' that can reveal what the future holds. Nevertheless, for now let's assume we do! We will call such a situation as being in receipt of *perfect information*. (We will then consider the more realistic case of *imperfect information*.)

Definition: Perfect information

Perfect information turns decision-making under *uncertainty* into decision-making under *certainty*. In a decision tree, chance nodes appear *before* decision nodes, such that the decision-maker has full knowledge of the 'state of the world' by the time they must make a decision.

Being in possession of such a crystal ball – effectively a clear window to the future – is clearly highly desirable, hence it must have value. Anything with value should come at a price, so what price should we be willing to pay for this perfect foresight? This price is known as the **expected value of perfect information** (EVPI).

Calculating EVPI

1. Calculate the EMV in the usual way from the problem of decision-making under uncertainty.
2. Determine the optimal decision under each possible state of the world and its associated payoff.
3. Calculate the expected payoff with perfect information as a probability-weighted average.
4. Then, under risk neutrality,

$$\text{EVPI} = \text{E(payoff} \mid \text{perfect information)} - \text{EMV}.$$

Example 6.2

Consider again the bond investment decision problem in Figure 6.3, for which the EMV is £1,000. Suppose we knew with certainty in advance whether or not the corporate bond would end up in default. If we knew the corporate bond would default (with a payoff of £0), it is rational to choose the government bond. If we knew the corporate bond would not default (with a payoff of £2000), it is rational to choose the corporate bond. This is shown in Figure 6.5.

(Continued)

If there is no corporate default (with a 50% probability), then choosing the corporate bond is rational (since £2000 > £1000), while if there is a corporate default (also with a 50% probability), then the government bond is chosen (since £1000 > £0).

Therefore, the expected payoff with perfect information is

$$\text{E(payoff | perfect information)} = £2000 \times 0.50 + £1000 \times 0.50 = £1500,$$

hence

$$\text{EVPI} = \text{E(payoff | perfect information)} - \text{EMV} = £1500 - £1000 = £500.$$

How should we interpret EVPI? Well, the monetary value of knowing the default status of the corporate bond with certainty *before* choosing the bond is £500, so this represents our *maximum willingness to pay* for this certainty. Suppose the price of this perfect information is £x. Then:

- for $0 \leq x < 500$, the perfect information will be bought, with the purchaser gaining a 'consumer surplus' (in economist speak) of £500 – £x.
- for $x = 500$, the decision-maker is indifferent between purchasing and not purchasing the perfect information - as this is the maximum willingness to pay, it is the price of indifference since the benefit is equal to the cost (the decision-maker is no better off, nor no worse off, by purchasing it).
- for $x > 500$, the perfect information is too expensive and so will not be purchased. (It would be irrational to purchase it!)

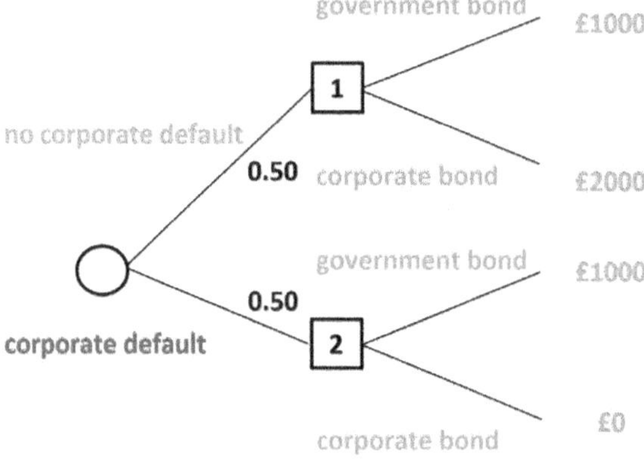

Figure 6.5 Decision tree with perfect information - decision nodes are positioned after the resolution of uncertainty.

Example 6.3

Consider again the oil drilling problem. Suppose we could hire a geologist who could tell us with certainty whether there is oil at the site and, if so, the depth at which it is located. What would be our maximum willingness to pay for this knowledge, that is, what is the EVPI?

From Figure 6.2, we see that there are three states of the world:

- oil found at the first depth, with probability 0.70
- oil found at the second depth, with probability 0.30 × 0.20 = 0.06 (note the multiplication of probabilities here: first there must be no oil at the first depth, and then oil found at the second depth)
- no oil, with probability 1 – 0.70 – 0.06 = 0.24 (since the probabilities of these three MECE events must sum to 1).

Figure 6.6 shows the decision tree with perfect information from the geologist. The optimal choice at:

- decision node 1 is 'drill' (since £900m > £0)
- decision node 2 is 'drill' (since £600m > £0)
- decision node 3 is 'don't drill' (since £0 > –£300m).

Hence

E(payoff | perfect information) = £900m × 0.70 + £600m × 0.06 + £0 × 0.24 = £666m.

and so (using the EMV calculated previously):

EVPI = E(payoff | perfect information) – EMV = £666m – £600m = £66m,

meaning we are willing to pay a maximum of £66 million for the geologist's (perfect) assessment of what is under the ground.

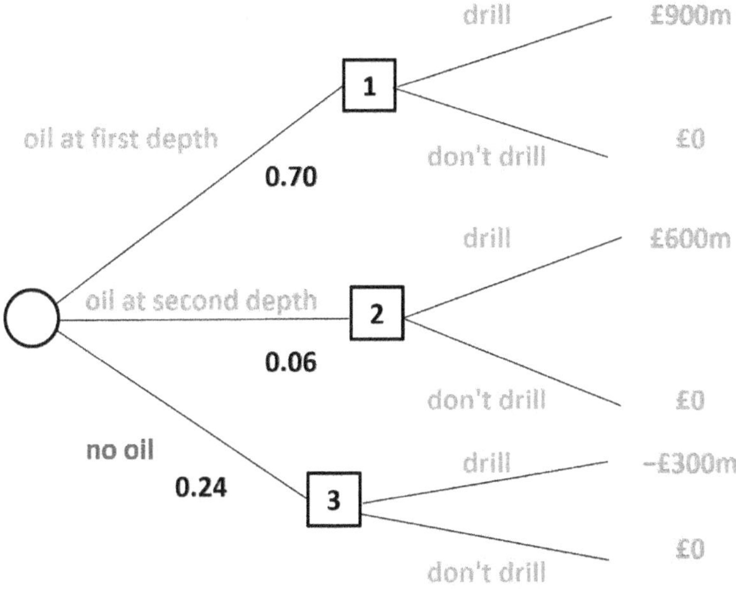

Figure 6.6 Decision tree with perfect information - decision nodes are positioned after the resolution of uncertainty.

Examples 6.2 and 6.3 assumed we could obtain *perfect* information. In reality, of course, no one has perfect foresight of the future (a prediction could be correct by chance, but it would be impossible to replicate correct predictions all of the time). However, 'experts' exist who can be thought of as having superior information sets, given their extensive knowledge about their field of expertise. For example, a debt analyst could provide their expert opinion on a company defaulting on its debt; an equity analyst could provide their expert opinion on future dividends per share; a geologist could undertake an exploratory survey to provide their expert opinion on whether there is oil under the ground.

So, information is available to us, but such expert opinions constitute *imperfect*, rather than *perfect*, information.

Definition: Imperfect information

Imperfect information is the receipt of an imperfect signal (such as an expert opinion) which reduces - but does not eliminate - the uncertainty in a decision tree. Bayes' theorem (see Chapter 4) updates the probabilistic beliefs in light of the new information, allowing the decision-maker to make a better-informed decision.

Relative to perfect information, we expect the *value* of imperfect information to be lower since it only reduces uncertainty rather than eliminates it, so we can effectively think of imperfect information as being a lower-quality 'product' compared to perfect information, hence its value and so its cost is lower (price can be thought of as a signal of quality). The price that we should be willing to pay for imperfect foresight is known as the **expected value of imperfect information** (EVII).

Calculating EVII

1. Calculate the EMV in the usual way from the problem of decision-making under uncertainty.
2. Determine the optimal decision under each possible predicted state of the world.
3. Calculate the expected payoff with imperfect information as a probability-weighted average.
4. Then, under risk neutrality,

$$\text{EVII} = \text{E}(\text{payoff} \mid \text{imperfect information}) - \text{EMV}.$$

Due to the lower quality of imperfect information relative to perfect information, then we would expect:

$$\text{EVII} < \text{EVPI}.$$

Example 6.4

Extending Example 6.2, instead of being able to obtain perfect information, suppose we could consult a debt analyst who has analysed the firm that issues the corporate bond. The analyst has a *reputation* for correctly predicting whether or not a corporate bond defaults 80% of the time, that is,

$$P(\text{predicts default} \mid \text{bond defaults}) = P(\text{predicts no default} \mid \text{bond does not default}) = 0.80,$$

and hence

$$P(\text{predicts default} \mid \text{bond does not default}) = P(\text{predicts no default} \mid \text{bond defaults}) = 0.20.$$

Since the prior probability that the bond defaults is 0.50, we have, using the total probability formula (see Section 4.8.3),

$$\begin{aligned} P(\text{predicts default}) &= P(\text{predicts default} \mid \text{bond defaults})\, P(\text{bond defaults}) \\ &\quad + P(\text{predicts default} \mid \text{bond does not default})\, P(\text{bond does not default}) \\ &= 0.80 \times 0.50 + 0.20 \times 0.50 \\ &= 0.50 \end{aligned}$$

and hence $P(\text{predicts no default}) = 1 - 0.50 = 0.50$. Now we seek the conditional probability of default, given the analyst's prediction of default. Applying Bayes' theorem, we have

$$\begin{aligned} P(\text{default} \mid \text{predict default}) &= \frac{P(\text{predict default} \mid \text{default})\, P(\text{default})}{P(\text{predict default})} \\ &= \frac{0.80 \times 0.50}{0.50} \\ &= 0.80 \end{aligned}$$

and hence $P\,(\text{not default} \mid \text{predict default}) = 1 - 0.80 = 0.20$. Similarly,

$$\begin{aligned} P(\text{default} \mid \text{predict default}) &= \frac{P(\text{predict not default} \mid \text{default})\, P(\text{default})}{P(\text{predict not default})} \\ &= \frac{0.20 \times 0.50}{0.50} \\ &= 0.20 \end{aligned}$$

and hence $P\,(\text{not default} \mid \text{predict not default}) = 1 - 0.20 = 0.80$.

The decision tree with imperfect information is shown in Figure 6.7. How to read this tree? We begin at chance node A, from which there are two branches corresponding to the possible predictions of the analyst. We have established from the total probability formula that both predictions (of default and no default) have probabilities of 0.50. Next, upon receipt of the prediction, the decision-maker chooses between the government and corporate bonds. The government bond leads to a

(Continued)

guaranteed payoff of £1000, while choosing the corporate bond leads to a further chance node. At chance node B we see the *conditional* probabilities of 0.80 and 0.20 for default and does not default, respectively, found using Bayes' theorem above. Similarly, at chance node C we see the *conditional* probabilities of 0.20 and 0.80 for default and does not default, respectively, also found using Bayes' theorem above.

What should the (risk-neutral) investor do at decision node 1? We compare the EMVs from the two options. We have:

$$\text{EMV(government bond)} = £1000$$

$$\text{EMV(corporate bond)} = £0 \times 0.80 + £2000 \times 0.20 = £400.$$

Since

$$\text{EMV(government bond)} > \text{EMV(corporate bond)}$$

the optimal choice at decision node 1 is to choose the government bond. Indeed, we can think of the analyst's prediction of default as a 'negative signal', effectively dissuading the investor from choosing the corporate bond. Given the analyst's reputation of 80% accuracy in correctly predicting default status, this negative signal has value. Notice how the *prior* probability of default of 0.50 *increases* to the *posterior* probability of 0.80. There is still uncertainty, since $0.80 < 1$, but the prediction of default makes this outcome more likely.

What should the (risk-neutral) investor do at decision node 2? Again, we compare the EMVs from the two options. We have:

$$\text{EMV(government bond)} = £1000$$

$$\text{EMV(corporate bond)} = £0 \times 0.20 + £2000 \times 0.80 = £1600.$$

Since

$$\text{EMV(corporate bond)} > \text{EMV(government bond)},$$

the optimal choice at decision node 2 is to choose the corporate bond. Here the analyst's prediction of no default is a 'positive signal', effectively persuading the investor to choose the corporate bond. This positive signal has value. Notice how the *prior* probability of no default of 0.50 *increases* to the *posterior* probability of 0.80. There is still uncertainty, since $0.80 < 1$, but the prediction of no default makes this outcome more likely.

We now compute the EVII. At chance node A we have that

$$\text{E(payoff} \mid \text{imperfect information)} = £1000 \times 0.50 + £1600 \times 0.50 = £1300.$$

Therefore

$$\begin{aligned} \text{EVII} &= \text{E(payoff} \mid \text{imperfect information)} - \text{EMV} \\ &= £1300 - £1000 \\ &= £300, \end{aligned}$$

meaning our maximum willingness to pay for the analyst's prediction is £300. Note that EVII < EVPI, since £300 < £500, which is a quick 'reality check'.

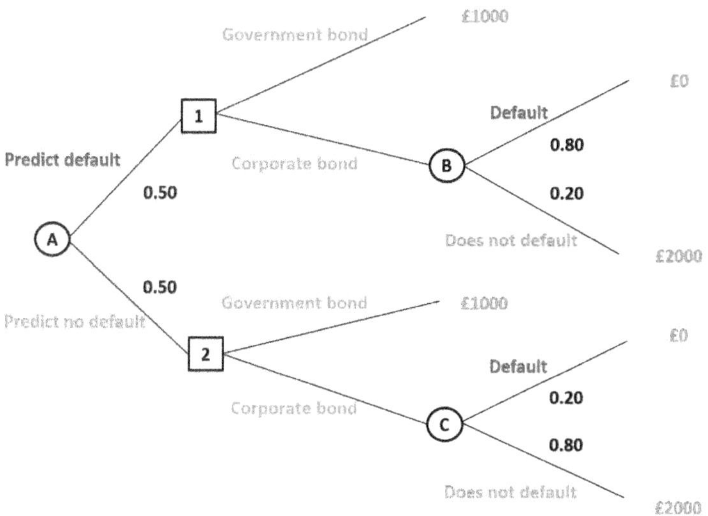

Figure 6.7 Decision tree with imperfect information - decision nodes are positioned after the expert's (imperfect) prediction is received.

Example 6.5

Extending Example 6.4, what if there was another analyst with a better reputation, that is, a better track record at correctly predicting default, say of 90% instead of 80%? We would expect the EVII in this case to be greater, reflecting the better 'quality' of information received from a more highly skilled analyst.

We can verify this by recomputing values but now using the fact that

$$P(\text{predicts default} \mid \text{bond defaults}) = P(\text{predicts no default} \mid \text{bond does not default}) = 0.90$$

and hence

$$P(\text{predicts default} \mid \text{bond does not default}) = P(\text{predicts no default} \mid \text{bond defaults}) = 0.10.$$

You should replicate the analysis in Example 6.4 with these new values and you should find that from chance node A we have

$$E(\text{payoff} \mid \text{imperfect information}) = £1000 \times 0.50 + £1800 \times 0.50 = £1400,$$

giving an EVII of £400. As we would expect, analyst skill is rewarded with a higher EVII, so the better analyst is justified in charging a higher price for their advice, even though the advice is still imperfect!

The moral of the story? You can convert your skill into monetary success!

Example 6.6

Consider again the *Chocolow* advertising problem. The confectionery company has decided to advertise. In addition, they are considering employing a market research agency to research whether sales for the *Chocolow* bars will be high or low.

The market research agency has been operating for many years, and based on its historical predictions of commercial success for previous new products, we can determine the probability of a correct prediction of high or low sales in this problem. Further, suppose there is asymmetry in the agency's skill. Specifically, the agency has:

- a 40% 'false positive' rate (predicting high sales when sales will be low)
- a 30% 'false negative' rate (predicting low sales when sales will be high).

Therefore

$$P(\text{predicts high sales} \mid \text{high sales}) = 0.70 \text{ and } P(\text{predicts low sales} \mid \text{high sales}) = 0.30,$$

and also

$$P(\text{predicts high sales} \mid \text{low sales}) = 0.40 \text{ and } P(\text{predicts low sales} \mid \text{low sales}) = 0.60.$$

With advertising, from Figure 6.1 the prior probabilities of high and low sales are 0.80 and 0.20, respectively. Using the total probability formula, we have

$$\begin{aligned} P(\text{predicts high sales}) &= P(\text{predicts high sales} \mid \text{high sales})\, P(\text{high sales}) \\ &\quad + P(\text{predicts high sales} \mid \text{low sales})\, P(\text{low sales}) \\ &= 0.70 \times 0.80 + 0.40 \times 0.20 \\ &= 0.64, \end{aligned}$$

and hence $P(\text{predicts low sales}) = 1 - 0.64 = 0.36$. Now we seek the conditional probability of high sales, given the market research agency's prediction of high sales. Applying Bayes' theorem, we have

$$\begin{aligned} P(\text{high sales} \mid \text{predict high sales}) &= \frac{P(\text{predicts high sales} \mid \text{high sales})\, P(\text{high sales})}{P(\text{predict high sales})} \\ &= \frac{0.70 \times 0.80}{0.64} \\ &= 0.875, \end{aligned}$$

and hence $P(\text{low sales} \mid \text{predict high sales}) = 1 - 0.875 = 0.125$. Similarly,

$$\begin{aligned} P(\text{high sales} \mid \text{predict low sales}) &= \frac{P(\text{predict low sales} \mid \text{high sales})\, P(\text{high sales})}{P(\text{predict low sales})} \\ &= \frac{0.30 \times 0.80}{0.36} \\ &= \frac{2}{3} (= 0.666\ldots), \end{aligned}$$

and hence $P(\text{low sales} \mid \text{predict low sales}) = 1 - 2/3 = 1/3\ (= 0.333\ldots)$.

Notice that the probability of high sales changes in response to the market research agency's prediction. The prior probability of high sales *increases* from 0.80 to 0.875 in response to a prediction of high sales (a *correct positive* signal; a *true positive*) and *decreases* from 0.80 to 0.666... in response to a prediction of low sales (an *incorrect negative* signal; a *false negative*). Similarly, the prior probability of low sales *decreases* from 0.20 to 0.125 in response to a prediction of high sales (an *incorrect positive* signal; a *false positive*) and *increases* from 0.20 to 0.333... in response to a prediction of low sales (a *correct negative* signal; a *true negative*).

The decision tree with imperfect information is shown in Figure 6.8.

Given the positive payoffs, regardless of sales level from 'launch product', the EMVs from launching will clearly be greater than the EMV of 'do nothing' (which is £0). At decision node 1, the EMV from launching is

$$£900{,}000 \times 0.875 + £400{,}000 \times 0.125 = £837{,}500$$

and at decision node 2 the EMV is (to the nearest pound)

$$£900{,}000 \times \frac{2}{3} + £400{,}000 \times \frac{1}{3} = £733{,}333.$$

We now compute the EVII. At chance node A we have that

$$E(\text{payoff} \mid \text{imperfect information}) = £837{,}500 \times 0.64 + £733{,}333 \times 0.36 = £800{,}000.$$

Therefore

$$\begin{aligned} \text{EVII} &= E(\text{payoff} \mid \text{imperfect information}) - \text{EMV} \\ &= £800{,}000 - £800{,}000 \\ &= £0, \end{aligned}$$

meaning our maximum willingness to pay for the market research agency's prediction is nothing!

Given the agency's skill, this might seem surprising. However, since 'launch product' is the optimal strategy regardless of the agency's prediction, there is *no value added* from the market research, so it is reasonable that we are not prepared to pay any amount for something which adds no value! So, beware hiring external consultants (and their hefty consultancy fees) if there is no possibility of their advice changing your course of action. Of course, if you aspire to be such a consultant, then make sure you are able to demonstrate your added value - your livelihood depends on it!

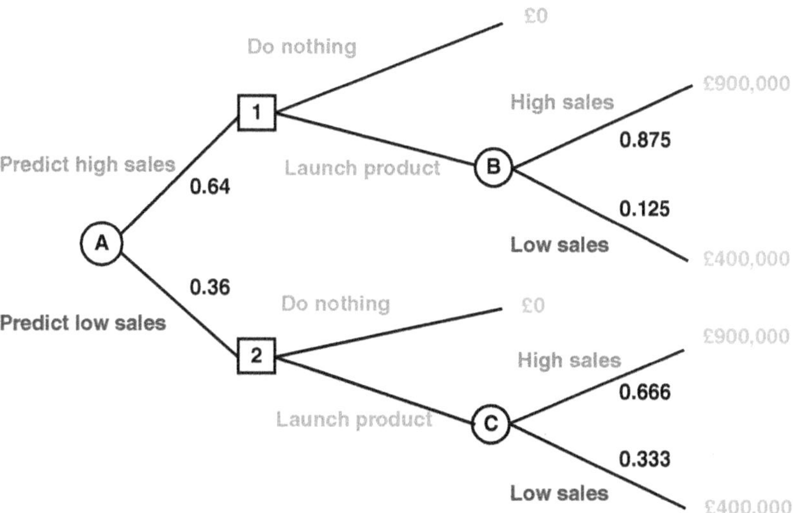

Figure 6.8 Decision tree with imperfect information - decision nodes are positioned after the agency's (imperfect) prediction is received.

6.6 GAME THEORY

The following material is algebra and calculus heavy!

In business, managers must act *strategically* by taking into account in their own decision-making the (expected) behaviour of their competitors. A limitation of our decision trees has been the focus on a single decision-maker acting *unilaterally*.

Game theory equips us with tools to model strategic interaction. We introduce simultaneous-move games and Nash equilibrium, followed by sequential-move games.

6.6.1 Simultaneous-move games

A simultaneous-move game (sometimes called a 'normal-form game') has three components:

1. A *set of players* (we will consider two players only – player 1 and player 2).
2. Each player's *set of strategies*, S_i for $i = 1, 2$ (the possible decisions they can make).
3. The *payoffs* for each player (typically these can be thought of as monetary payoffs, or at least a monetary equivalent).

A strategy profile is the set of strategies played by each player. For example, player 1 can choose between 'Left' and 'Right' (i.e. with strategy set S_1 = {Left, Right}) and player 2 can choose between 'Up' and 'Down' (i.e. with strategy set S_2 = {Up, Down}). With two strategies for each player, there are 2 × 2 = 4 possible strategy profiles: {Left, Up}, {Left, Down}, {Right, Up} and {Right, Down}.

Each strategy profile has a corresponding payoff profile. For our two-player game, let $\pi_i(s_1, s_2)$ denote the payoff of player i when players 1 and 2 play the strategies s_1 and s_2, drawn from strategy profiles S_1 and S_2, respectively.

Example 6.7

Assume player 1 has payoff profiles

$$u_1(\{\text{Left, Up}\}) = u_1(\{\text{Right, Down}\}) = 2 \text{ and } u_1(\{\text{Left, Down}\}) = u_1(\{\text{Right, Up}\}) = 1,$$

and assume the payoff profiles of player 2 are

$$u_2(\{\text{Left, Up}\}) = u_2(\{\text{Right, Down}\}) = 1 \text{ and } u_2(\{\text{Left, Down}\}) = u_2(\{\text{Right, Up}\}) = 3.$$

For clarity, we present these payoffs as a matrix, called the **normal form**. Each cell represents a specific *contingency*, where the first value is the payoff to player 1 and the second value is the payoff to player 2. Note that player 1 chooses a column and player 2 chooses a row.

		Player 1	
		Left	Right
Player 2	Up	2, 1	1, 3
	Down	1, 3	2, 1

If there are many players, n say, it is often convenient to express the strategy profile $\{s_1, s_2, \dots, s_n\}$ as $\{s_i, s_{-i}\}$, such that s_{-i} denotes the strategy profiles of all players *except* player i. For example, $s_{-i} = \{s_1, s_2, \dots, s_{i-1}, s_{i+1}, \dots, s_n\}$ where the element s_i is excluded. Using such notation, the payoff of player i is then $\pi_i(s_i, s_{-i})$. When there are only $n = 2$ players (as we will assume), this is a moot point.

We now proceed to 'solve' simple game theory problems for rational players, where we call solutions *equilibria*.

6.6.2 Dominant strategies

A special case is that of *dominance*. Assume a player has a particular strategy which *always* yields a greater payoff *regardless* of what the other player does. We call such a strategy a dominant strategy. When a player possesses a dominant strategy, then it is rational to *always* play this. If both players have a dominant strategy, then they each play their respective dominant strategies. This is illustrated in the famous Prisoner's dilemma, considered next.

Example 6.8

Two suspected criminals are arrested and held in separate interrogation rooms at the police station such that the suspects are unable to communicate with each other. Each suspect can either confess to the crime, 'Confess', or stay silent, 'Silent'. The four possible strategy profiles are therefore {Confess, Confess}, {Confess, Silent}, {Silent, Confess} and {Silent, Silent}.

Assume the following matrix of payoffs:

		Prisoner 1	
		Confess	Silent
Prisoner 2	Confess	-8, -8	-10, 0
	Silent	0, -10	-1, -1

We see that each prisoner has a dominant strategy of 'Confess'. For example, if Prisoner 2 plays 'Confess' then Prisoner 1 is better off by playing 'Confess' (since $-8 > -10$), while if Prisoner 2 plays 'Silent' then Prisoner 1 is still better off by playing 'Confess' , (since $0 > -1$). By symmetry, we reach the same conclusion for Prisoner 2. So the 'equilibrium' for this game is the strategy set {Confess, Confess}, with each prisoner receiving a payoff of −8. However, had both players played 'Silent' then they would both be better off, with each receiving a better payoff of −1 (i.e. a payoff that is less bad), although 'Silent' is never played because it is dominated by 'Confess'!

In this *one-shot game* (i.e. the game is only played once), the equilibrium is sub-optimal for both prisoners. It can be shown that in an infinitely repeated version of the Prisoner's dilemma, if the prisoners have sufficient patience, it is possible for {Silent, Silent} to result as the equilibrium. However, the one-shot version results in the prisoners being locked into the dominant strategy equilibrium, and also locked in a cell! Prison jumpsuits at the ready.

Let's exchange players who wear jumpsuits for those who wear just suits. We consider a business variant of the Prisoner's dilemma.

Example 6.9

Consider two rival smartphone manufacturers - for example, Apple and Samsung. Each firm has to decide whether or not to lower its prices in a particular market. In this application, 'Cut price' is the equivalent of 'Confess' and 'Maintain price' is the equivalent of 'Silent'. If one firm cuts its price and the other maintains its price, the price-cutting firm captures the entire market, giving the other firm a payoff of 0. Assume the following matrix of payoffs (Apple payoff, Samsung payoff):

		Apple	
		Cut price	Maintain price
Samsung	Cut price	100m, 100m	0, 500m
	Maintain price	500m, 0	300m, 300m

Regardless of Samsung's action, Apple's best response is to 'cut price'. Likewise, 'cut price' is the best response for Samsung. We see that the equilibrium is (Cut price, Cut price) resulting in both firms receiving payoffs of 100 million (you choose the currency!). However, if both maintained their prices, they would both be better off, with payoffs of 300 million.

Dominant strategy

Strategy s_i^* of player *i* is a *dominant strategy* if

$\pi_i(s_i^*, s_{-i}) > \pi_i(s_i, s_{-i})$ for all s_i different from s_i^* and for all s_{-i}.

This means that s_i^* is superior to any other strategy of player *i*, *regardless of the strategies of other players.*

6.6.3 Dominated strategies and iterated elimination

We now consider *dominated* strategies. These can occur even if there are no *dominant* strategies.

Definition: Dominated strategy

A **dominated strategy** results in a strictly *worse* payoff relative to any other strategy, *regardless of the strategies of other players.* Formally, strategy s_i for player *i* is a dominated strategy if another strategy, say s_i', results in a higher payoff no matter what other players do. Hence

$\pi_i(s_i) < \pi_i(s_i')$.

When a player has a dominated strategy, then they *never* play it (otherwise they are irrational as they lock in a worse payoff for themselves). Therefore, dominated strategies should be *eliminated*. This elimination may even be done iteratively, as the following example demonstrates.

Example 6.10

In this game, each player has three possible strategies with payoffs as shown in the normal form below:

			Player 1	
		Left	Centre	Right
	Top	4, 8	0, 7	2, 6
Player 2	Middle	5, 5	8, 1	9, 2
	Bottom	2, 3	0, 5	1, 4

Through a process of *iterative elimination* of strictly dominated strategies, we can then find the equilibrium of the game. We proceed in the following way.

1. For player 2 we see that 'Bottom' is dominated by 'Top' ($3 < 8$, $5 < 7$ and $4 < 6$), so we first eliminate 'Bottom'.
2. Focusing on the reduced game (with the 'Bottom' row deleted), we have that 'Centre' is dominated by 'Right' for player 1 ($0 < 2$ and $8 < 9$), so we now eliminate 'Centre'.
3. Focusing on the further reduced game, we have that 'Middle' is dominated by 'Top' for player 2 ($5 < 8$ and $2 < 6$), so we now eliminate 'Middle'.
4. Focusing on the further reduced game, we have that 'Right' is dominated by 'Left' for player 1 ($2 < 4$), so we finally eliminate 'Right'.

Hence (Left, Top) is the unique equilibrium.

We refer to a game as being *dominance solvable* if iterated elimination ends with each player having only one strategy, as in Example 6.10.

6.6.4 Nash equilibria

In many game theory problems there may not be dominant or dominated strategies. How to proceed? We seek a general equilibrium solution, applicable to all games regardless of whether or not they have dominance features. *Nash equilibrium* (developed by John Nash) provides the answer.

At this point it is appropriate to distinguish between a *pure* strategy and a *mixed* strategy.

Definition: Pure strategy and mixed strategy

A **pure strategy** is when a player chooses a single action that is a member of their strategy profile. For example, in the Prisoner's dilemma of Example 6.8, the pure strategies for each prisoner are 'Confess' and 'Silent'.

A **mixed strategy** assigns a *probability* to each pure strategy. For example, a prisoner could choose 'Confess' with probability π and 'Silent' with probability $1 - \pi$. Formally, a mixed strategy s_i is a *probability distribution* over the set of (pure) strategies.

There exists at least one Nash equilibrium (either in pure or mixed strategies) in every game for which there is a finite number of players with finite sets of strategies.

Definition: Nash equilibrium

A **Nash equilibrium** (in pure strategies) is a strategy profile $(s_1^*, s_2^*, \ldots, s_n^*)$ if each s_i^* is a *mutual best response*. This means that s_i^* is a best response to s_{-i}^* (the strategies of all players other than player *i*). As a best response, it is impossible for player *i* to be better off (in terms of their payoff) if they deviate from s_i^*. Formally,

$$\pi_i(s_i^*, s_{-i}^*) \geq \pi_i(s_i, s_{-i}^*)$$

for all strategies s_i in S_i.

Example 6.11

Consider the following game which has no dominant or dominated strategies:

			Player 1	
		Left	Centre	Right
	Top	6, 2	2, 6	8, 4
Player 2	Middle	2, 1	6, 2	1, 1
	Bottom	4, 6	4, 1	6, 5

By looking at the mutual best responses, we can deduce the Nash equilibrium (in pure strategies). To establish the mutual best responses, we determine each player's best response. For player 1, we have

Player 2's strategy	Player 1's best response
Top	Right
Middle	Centre
Bottom	Right

For player 2 we have

Player 1's strategy	Player 2's best response
Left	Bottom
Centre	Top
Right	Bottom

Hence we see that the only mutual best response is (Right, Bottom). This is the only Nash equilibrium in this game. This can be seen visually using the convention of placing a '*' next to the payoff which is the best response to another player's strategy.

		Player 1		
		Left	Centre	Right
	Top	6, 2	2, 6*	*8, 4
Player 2	Middle	2, 1	*6, 2	1, 1
	Bottom	4, 6*	4, 1	*6, 5*

For example, the '*' by 8 means that 'Right' is the best response for player 1 to player 2 playing 'Top'. A Nash equilibrium is identifiable from any cell(s) with two '*'s, which here is the single Nash equilibrium of (Right, Bottom).

Since no player can be better off by deviating from a Nash equilibrium unilaterally, in any position other than (Right, Bottom) at least one player can be better off from deviating, hence any other position cannot be a Nash equilibrium. For example, if we started at cell (Top, Centre), then player 1 could improve by changing to 'Right' since $(2 < 8)$. However, from (Right, Bottom) neither player can achieve better than their Nash equilibrium payoff. For example, player 1 cannot improve on 6 by switching to 'Left' or 'Centre' (either reduces the payoff to 4). Verify that player 2 also cannot improve!

A game can have more than one Nash equilibrium (in pure strategies).

Example 6.12

A Nash equilibrium is not necessarily unique. Consider the following game.

		Player 1	
		Left	Right
Player 2	Up	*3, 4*	1, 1
	Down	1, 1	*4, 3*

Here there are two pure-strategy Nash equilibria, namely (Left, Up) and (Right, Down).

Some games have no Nash equilibria in *pure* strategies.

Example 6.13

Consider the following game.

		Player 1	
		Left	Right
Player 2	Up	3, 2*	*5, 1
	Down	*5, 0	2, 6*

We see that there is no pure-strategy Nash equilibrium (there is no double incidence of '*').

However, it has been claimed above that a game always has at least one Nash equilibrium. This is true, although in games such as Example 6.13, the Nash equilibrium will be in *mixed* strategies. We have defined a mixed strategy above as being a probability distribution over the set of (pure) strategies.

Example 6.14

For the game in Example 6.13, player 1 could assign a probability distribution to their possible strategies of 'Left' and 'Right'. Suppose 'Left' is played with probability p and 'Right' is played with probability $1 - p$, for $0 < p < 1$. (The pure strategies of 'Left' and 'Right' occur when we set $p = 1$ and $p = 0$, respectively.) Similarly, player 2 could assign a probability distribution to their possible strategies of 'Up' and 'Down'. Suppose 'Up' is played with probability q and 'Down' is played with probability $1 - q$, for $0 < q < 1$. We can then identify a Nash equilibrium in mixed strategies, such that we determine the mutual best responses.

We work with *expected payoffs*, that is, *probability-weighted averages*. The expected payoff for player 1 from 'Left' is

$$E(\pi_1(\text{Left})) = 3q + 5(1 - q),$$

and the expected payoff for player 1 from 'Right' is

$$E(\pi_1(\text{Right})) = 5q + 2(1 - q).$$

Whenever

$$E(\pi_1(\text{Left})) \neq E(\pi_1(\text{Right}))$$

it pays for player 1 to play a pure strategy (e.g. if $E(\pi_1(\text{Left})) > E(\pi_1(\text{Right}))$, then play 'Left' as a best response, i.e. $p = 1$, but this would not be a mixed-strategy Nash equilibrium). Therefore, a mixed-strategy Nash equilibrium requires player 1 to be *indifferent* between 'Left' and 'Right', which requires that:

$$E(\pi_1(\text{Left})) = E(\pi_1(\text{Right})) \Leftrightarrow 3q + 5(1 - q) = 5q + 2(1 - q)$$

which solves for $q = 3/5$ (check this yourself!).

However, $q = 3/5$ refers to the probability that player 2 plays 'Up' (and hence 'Down' with the probability 2/5). So, likewise we require:

$$E(\pi_2(\text{Up})) = E(\pi_2(\text{Down})) \Leftrightarrow 2p + 1(1 - p) = 0p + 6(1 - p)$$

which solves for $p = 5/7$.

Hence the mixed-strategy Nash equilibrium can be written as:

$$\left(\left\{\frac{1}{2},\frac{1}{2}\right\},\left\{\frac{3}{5},\frac{2}{5}\right\}\right)$$

which represents the *probability distributions over strategies* for each player.

The games above have been (deliberately) basic in that the sets of strategies have been discrete. We proceed to special classes of games which introduce continuity in the strategies. Specifically, we will consider cases of simultaneous quantity setting (*Cournot competition*), simultaneous price setting (*Bertrand competition*), and sequential quantity setting (*Stackelberg leadership*).

6.7 COURNOT COMPETITION

In the Cournot competition model, there is competition in an industry, that is, there are $n > 1$ competitive firms. The firms produce a homogeneous (identical) product, for which the market price is p. The decision variable of firms is the *quantity* they produce; that is, firm i produces output q_i, for $i = 1, 2, \ldots, n$. Hence the strategy sets are essentially continuous.

Consumer preferences for the product determine the market demand function. For a 'normal' good, we will assume a linear (inverse) market demand function[1] of

$$p = a - bQ$$

with constants $a > 0$ and $b > 0$, where $Q = \sum_{i=1}^{n} q_i$ is the total industry production (or output) across the n firms (i.e. the industry supply). Note that the negative slope makes sense – as the industry

[1]'Inverse' because we have price as the left-hand-side variable. When we express quantity as a function of price, economists call it a *demand function*. So when we express price as a function of quantity, economists refer to an *inverse demand function*. This has links with dependent and independent variables which will be covered extensively in Chapter 13 on linear regression.

output increases, the market price must fall to stimulate enough consumer demand to buy the total industry supply. Each firm has a marginal cost of production of c (where marginal cost is the cost of producing one more unit of output). Assume $c < a$.

If we have a *duopoly*, then there are only two firms in the industry (the prefix 'duo' means two). In this case we have $n = 2$. We seek the *Cournot–Nash equilibrium*.

The firms are profit maximisers, hence their objective is to choose the level of output, q_i, that maximises their profit, conscious that the market price, p, is affected by their own production decision *and* that of their industry competitor. Profit is defined as total revenue minus total cost, which for firm 1 we represent as

$$\begin{aligned}\Pi_1(q_1,q_2) &= \underbrace{pq_1}_{\text{total revenue}} - \underbrace{cq_1}_{\text{total cost}} \\ &= (a - bQ)q_1 - cq_1 \\ &= (a - b(q_1 + q_2))q_1 - cq_1 \\ &= (a - bq_1 - bq_2)q_1 - cq_1 \\ &= (a - c)q_1 - bq_1^2 - bq_2q_1,\end{aligned}$$

noting that $Q = q_1 + q_2$.

Profit maximisation is an optimisation problem, which in mathematics is solved using *differentiation*. Differentiating with respect to q_1 (the decision variable for firm 1), we obtain the first-order condition

$$\frac{\partial \Pi_1}{\partial q_1} = a - c - 2bq_1 - bq_2.$$

At a maximum we set this first-order derivative equal to zero, and then solve for the optimum, denoted by q_1^* (keen readers may wish to verify that this is indeed a maximum by performing the second derivative test). We have

$$a - c - 2bq_1 - bq_2 = 0 \;\Rightarrow\; q_1^* = \frac{a-c}{2b} - \frac{q_2}{2}.$$

This is called the reaction function of firm 1, as it instructs firm 1 how to *react* to the output decision of firm 2. We see that q_1^* is decreasing in q_2, meaning that as firm 2 produces more, firm 1 produces less. Noting the symmetry of the problem, we immediately see that the reaction function of firm 2 (to firm 1) is

$$q_2^* = \frac{a-c}{2b} - \frac{q_1}{2}.$$

Therefore, we have that $q_1^* = q_2^* = q^*$ (i.e. we can drop the subscript) such that

$$q^* = \frac{a-c}{2b} - \frac{q^*}{2} \;\Rightarrow\; q^* = \frac{a-c}{3b}.$$

Hence the industry supply is

$$Q^* = q^* + q^* = \frac{2(a-c)}{3b}.$$

The market equilibrium price is then

$$p^* = a - bQ^* = a - b\frac{2(a-c)}{3b} = \frac{a}{3} + \frac{2c}{3}.$$

The profit of each firm is

$$\Pi_1 = \Pi_2 = pq^* - cq^* = \left(\frac{a}{3} + \frac{2c}{3}\right)\frac{a-c}{3b} - c\frac{a-c}{3b} = \frac{(a-c)^2}{9b}.$$

6.7.1 Non-identical firms

The above analysis assumed two identical firms, with identical marginal costs of production of c. In practice, marginal costs are likely to be different for the two firms (e.g. one may be able to source raw materials more cheaply), and we would expect the firm with lower marginal cost to benefit in terms of the profits they can make.

Let c_1 and c_2 be the marginal costs of firms 1 and 2, respectively, such that $c_1 \neq c_2$. Replicating the above analysis with c_1 and c_2 leads to the following reaction functions (you should check these):

$$q_1^* = \frac{a-c_1}{2b} - \frac{q_2}{2} \quad \text{and} \quad q_2^* = \frac{a-c_2}{2b} - \frac{q_1}{2}.$$

Solving simultaneously, by substituting the expression for q_2^*, we have

$$q_1^* = \frac{a-c_1}{2b} - \frac{a-c_2}{4b} + \frac{q_1^*}{4} \Rightarrow q_1^* = \frac{a-2c_1+c_2}{3b}.$$

Substituting into the reaction function of firm 2, we have

$$q_2^* = \frac{a-c_2}{2b} - \frac{a-2c_1+c_2}{6b} = \frac{a-2c_2+c_1}{3b}.$$

As expected, if c_1 increases, then q_1^* decreases and q_2^* increases, with corresponding effects on the firms' respective profits.

The moral of the story? It pays to be a cost minimiser!

6.7.2 Collusion

Consider again identical firms, where $c_1 = c_2 = c$. Would the firms benefit if they could *collude* and form a cartel?

We model this as a problem of maximising the *joint* profit of the firms. If we denote the total output produced under collusion by $Q^C = q_1 + q_2$, then the joint profit function is

$$\Pi^C(Q^C) = \underbrace{(a - bQ^C)Q^C}_{\text{total revenue}} - \underbrace{cQ^C}_{\text{total cost}}.$$

Differentiating to obtain the first-order condition, we solve for Q^{C*}, such that

$$\frac{\partial \Pi^C}{\partial Q^C} = 0 \Rightarrow Q^{C*} = \frac{a-c}{2b}.$$

This is *below* the Cournot–Nash equilibrium total industry supply derived previously. This demonstrates that collusive behaviour limits competition, resulting in a lower industry output.

The equilibrium market price is

$$p^{C*} = a - b\frac{a-c}{2b} = \frac{a+c}{2},$$

and industry profits are

$$\Pi^{C*} = \left(\frac{a+c}{2} - c\right)\frac{a-c}{2b} = \frac{(a-c)^2}{4b}.$$

Comparing industry profits with the Cournot case, we have that

$$\Pi^{C*} > \Pi_1 + \Pi_2 \quad \text{(from Cournot)},$$

and so we see that collusion increases the profits of both firms.

Of course, the trouble with cartels is that they rely on *trust*, with each cartel member agreeing to keep their promises and not renege (OPEC is a classic example of the challenges for members not to exceed their mutually agreed quotas for oil production). Indeed, collusive behaviour cannot be enforced if the firms play a one-shot game. Without a *credible* threat of punishment, a firm would simply renege and produce more as it would be their best response to the output of the other firm.

Is there any way to incentivise cartel members to collaborate for the benefit of all members such that they 'behave' and produce the cartel-optimum output? Yes, if the game is repeated an infinite number of times (i.e. for ever), provided that each cartel member is not too impatient!

For $n = 2$ identical firms (with $c_1 = c_2$) playing an infinitely repeated game, assume both firms produce the collusive output of $Q^{C^*}/2$, that is, they split industry production equally between themselves. We now introduce a discount factor, δ, such that $0 < \delta < 1$. The value of δ reflects how patient the firm is.

Let us consider a *trigger strategy* as follows. At the beginning (i.e. at time period $t = 0$), the firm abides by the cartel decision and produces the agreed output of $Q^{C^*}/2$. Remember that in a Cournot setting firms act simultaneously, so they cannot observe and react to the output decision of the other firm in the same time period, they can only react in the following time period. So, for each subsequent time period (i.e. for $t \geq 1$), the trigger strategy is as follows:

- if the other firm 'behaved' in period $t - 1$ and produced the agreed $Q^{C^*}/2$, then continue to also produce $Q^{C^*}/2$ in period t;
- if the other firm reneged on the agreement in period $t - 1$, then 'punish' the firm in retaliation by producing the Cournot–Nash output $q^* = (a - c)/3b$ in period *t and in all future time periods*.

So any instance of a firm reneging on the prior agreement triggers the punishment by the other firm in the next period and for evermore, even though this can be self-damaging – think about the phrase 'to cut off your nose to spite your face'!

Recall that the total industry output under the Cournot–Nash equilibrium is $Q^* = q_1^* + q_2^*$. A firm's best course of action in a single period is to renege and produce the one-shot best response to $Q^{C^*}/2$ produced by the other firm by using the reaction function. Let us call this Q^{Renege}.

In the time period in which a firm reneges, its payoff is $\pi_i(Q^{\text{Renege}})$. However, the short-run gain (in payoff terms) that period will be punished by the other firm when they retaliate by producing the Cournot–Nash quantity in all following time periods, receiving $\pi_i(Q^*)$. So, the total payoff starting from the deviation period is

$$\pi_i\left(Q^{\text{Renege}}\right) + \delta\pi_i\left(Q^*\right) + \delta^2\pi_i\left(Q^*\right) + \cdots = \pi_i\left(Q^{\text{Renege}}\right) + \frac{\delta}{1-\delta}\pi_i\left(Q^*\right).$$

By not reneging, the stream of payoffs would be

$$\pi_i\left(\frac{Q^{C*}}{2}\right) + \delta\pi_i\left(\frac{Q^{C*}}{2}\right) + \delta^2\pi_i\left(\frac{Q^{C*}}{2}\right) + \cdots = \frac{1}{1-\delta}\pi_i\left(\frac{Q^{C*}}{2}\right).$$

To disincentivise reneging we must have that

$$\frac{1}{1-\delta}\pi_i\left(\frac{Q^{C*}}{2}\right) \geq \pi_i\left(Q^{\text{Renege}}\right) + \frac{\delta}{1-\delta}\pi_i\left(Q^*\right).$$

This leads to

$$\pi_i\left(\frac{Q^{C*}}{2}\right) \geq (1-\delta)\pi_i\left(Q^{\text{Renege}}\right) + \delta\pi_i\left(Q^*\right),$$

and hence

$$\delta \geq \frac{\pi_i\left(Q^{\text{Renege}}\right) - \pi_i\left(Q^{C*}/2\right)}{\pi_i\left(Q^{\text{Renege}}\right) - \pi_i\left(Q^*\right)}. \qquad (*)$$

Because the payoff from collusion is higher than under Cournot competition, we must have that

$$\pi_i\left(\frac{Q^{C*}}{2}\right) > \pi_i\left(Q^*\right),$$

hence the expression on the right-hand side of (*) is less than 1. So provided the discount factor, δ, is sufficiently large the inequality is satisfied for all *i*, and hence it is possible to sustain collusion.

The moral of the story? Patience is a virtue!

6.8 BERTRAND COMPETITION

We now consider competition in prices between two identical firms (i.e. with identical marginal costs, $c_1 = c_2$) producing a homogeneous good. In the model of Bertrand competition, firms choose *prices* (whereas in Cournot competition they choose *quantities*).

Let the prices charged by firms 1 and 2 be p_1 and p_2, respectively. Suppose initially that $p_1 = p_2 > c$, such that both firms charge the same price above marginal cost. Now, if you are firm 1 you could capture 100% market share by lowering your price by a small amount, say $\epsilon_1 > 0$, such that

$$p_1 + \epsilon_1 = p_2 \text{ with } p_1 > c \Rightarrow c < p_1 < p_2.$$

Firm 2 is clearly unhappy since it has lost all its customers(!), who are now buying the (homogeneous) product from firm 1 since it is cheaper there. Firm 2 will *react* to recapture the entire market by lowering its price by a small amount below the new p_1, say $\epsilon_2 > 0$, such that

$$p_2 + \epsilon_2 = p_1 \text{ with } p_2 > c \Rightarrow c < p_2 < p_1.$$

Of course, now firm 1 is unhappy! This process of continually undercutting your competitor continues in a vicious circle until

$$p_1 = p_2 = c,$$

that is, both firms' competitive behaviour drives the price down to the marginal cost and this represents the Nash equilibrium, since this is the best price response to the other firm. This results in zero (economic) profit, known as the *Bertrand paradox*.

We saw that in the case of Cournot competition, collusion may be sustained if the firms had sufficient patience. Similarly, we can deduce a collusive benefit in the case of Bertrand competition with firms' patience resulting in a collusive price above c.

6.8.1 Bertrand competition with product differentiation

In practice, different firms do not produce identical products. Rather, there is some product differentiation (nothing to do with calculus!). For example, our *Chocolow* bars from earlier in the chapter were developed to be a lower-calorie alternative to regular chocolate bars. If you stand in the confectionery aisle at your local supermarket, you will see a wide array of chocolate bars – all chocolate, but all slightly different. These differences constitute the product differentiation.

Suppose two firms have differentiated products with the following demand functions (quantity expressed as a function of price):

$$q_1 = a - p_1 + p_2 \text{ and } q_2 = a - p_2 + p_1.$$

As differentiated products, these are *imperfect substitute* goods ('imperfect' due to the product differentiation). Notice that as the price of firm 2's product, p_2, increases then demand for firm 1's product, q_1, also increases as *some* consumers substitute towards the relatively cheaper product of firm 1. Some, not all, due to brand loyalty and consumer preference for firm 2's good (due to the product differentiation).

From the demand functions, we see that, unlike the Bertrand competition case with homogeneous products, *if*, say, $p_1 < p_2$ then firm 2 does not lose all of its customers to firm 1 – its brand, unique product characteristics, etc. are still attractive to some consumers. The more powerful this attraction, the *more* consumers it will retain, and customer *retention* is as important as (if not more important than) customer *acquisition*, due to the cost outlay typically involved in acquiring new customers. For example, cutting your prices to attract your competitor's customers incurs a cost to you. Of course, there is a limit to the customer retention. If $p_1 \ll p_2$, that is, the price difference is *very* large, then $q_2 \to 0$. From the second demand function above we can deduce that

$$0 = a - p_2 + p_1 \Rightarrow p_2 \geq a + p_1,$$

so if p_2 was at least $p_1 + a$ then firm 1 captures the entire market. Good for firm 1, bad for firm 2! We now derive the Nash equilibrium. Firm 1's profit is given by the profit function

$$\Pi_1 = \underbrace{p_1(a - p_1 + p_2)}_{\text{total revenue}} - \underbrace{c(a - p_1 + p_2)}_{\text{total cost}} = ap_1 - p_1^2 + p_1 p_2 - ca + cp_1 - cp_2.$$

Differentiating with respect to p_1 (the decision variable of firm 1 in the Bertrand model), we set the first-order condition equal to zero and solve for p_1. Hence

$$a - 2p_1 + p_2 + c = 0 \Rightarrow p_1 = \frac{a + c + p_2}{2}.$$

This is firm 1's reaction function to the price of firm 2. By symmetry of the demand functions, we have that $p_1 = p_2 = p^*$, and so

$$p^* = a + c,$$

which is the Nash equilibrium price of each firm. Substituting into the profit function, then each firm earns profits of a^2, that is, product differentiation allows the firms to earn positive profits, which is better than the case of zero profits with homogeneous products.

The moral of the story? Build a powerful brand with a distinct product!

6.9 STACKELBERG LEADERSHIP

In the Cournot competition model firms acted *simultaneously* when setting quantities. What if firms moved *sequentially*? In a two-firm context this would mean we have a *leader* (who sets their quantity first) and a *follower* (who 'moves' after observing the leader's decision). We consider Stackelberg leadership.

Suppose the firms are identical (with equal marginal costs). Without loss of generality, let firm 1 be the leader setting q_1, and let firm 2 be the follower setting q_2 (having observed q_1). The follower will rationally react to the leader by determining their best response to q_1, namely $q_2(q_1)$; that is, q_2 as a function of q_1. The leader is aware of this, and so sets q_1 optimally based on the follower's reaction function.

The reaction function of firm 2 is simply the Cournot solution of

$$q_2^* = \frac{a - c}{2b} - \frac{q_1}{2}.$$

Aware of this, the leader maximises their profit function:

$$\begin{aligned}\Pi_1(q_1, q_2) &= \underbrace{(a - bq_1 + bq_2^*)q_1}_{\text{total revenue}} - \underbrace{cq_1}_{\text{total cost}} \\ &= \left(a - bq_1 - \frac{a - c}{2} + \frac{bq_1}{2}\right)q_1 - cq_1 \\ &= \left(\frac{a - c}{2} - \frac{bq_1}{2}\right)q_1.\end{aligned}$$

Differentiating with respect to q_1 (the decision variable of the leader firm in the Stackelberg model), we set the first-order condition equal to zero and solve for q_1. Hence

$$q_1^* = \frac{a-c}{2b}.$$

We now substitute this into the reaction function of firm 2 to determine their best response:

$$q_2^* = \frac{a-c}{2b} - \frac{q_1}{2} \quad \Rightarrow \quad q_2^* = \frac{a-c}{4b}.$$

So we see that

$$q_2^* = \frac{q_1^*}{2},$$

meaning that the follower only produces half of the output of the leader. Hence the leader has larger market share, resulting in a clear first-mover advantage. Relative to the Cournot–Nash equilibrium, the leader produces more and the follower produces less.

Total industry supply is

$$Q = \frac{3(a-c)}{4b},$$

and this exceeds that in the case of Cournot competition. As total supply is higher, the equilibrium market price must be lower to stimulate enough consumer demand. Specifically, we have that

$$p = \frac{a}{4} + \frac{3c}{4}.$$

The leader's profit is

$$\Pi^{\text{Leader}} = \underbrace{p\frac{a-c}{2b}}_{\text{total revenue}} - \underbrace{c\frac{a-c}{2b}}_{\text{total cost}} = \left(\frac{a-c}{8b}\right)^2,$$

which is greater than the Cournot competition profit – this is the monetary benefit from having the first-mover advantage. Meanwhile, the follower suffers by realising lower profits of

$$\Pi^{\text{Follower}} = \left(\frac{a-c}{16b}\right)^2,$$

which is the monetary cost from having the second-mover disadvantage.

The moral of the story? Go first!

6.9.1 Sequential price setting

We conclude with examining price setting under the Stackelberg framework (i.e. sequential price setting rather than sequential quantity setting). Again, let firm 1 be the leader and firm 2 be the follower.

As before, having observed p_1, firm 2 will use its reaction function to maximise profits to determine their best response to p_1, namely $p_2(p_1)$; that is, p_2 as a function of p_1. Aware of this, the leader sets p_1 optimally based on the follower's reaction function.

The leader's profit function to be maximised is

$$\Pi_1 = \underbrace{p_1 q_1}_{\text{total revenue}} - \underbrace{c q_1}_{\text{total cost}} = (p_1 - c)\left(a - p_1 + \left(\frac{a + c + p_1}{2}\right)\right).$$

Differentiating with respect to p_1 (the decision variable of the leader firm), we set the first-order condition equal to zero and solve for p_1. Hence

$$p_1 = c + \frac{3a}{2}.$$

We now substitute this into the reaction function of the follower (firm 2) to determine their best response:

$$p_2 = c + \frac{5a}{4}.$$

Notice that the price of the follower is less than that of the leader. How do the profits of the leader and follower compare? We have

$$\Pi^{\text{Leader}} = (p_1 - c)(a - p_1 + p_2) = \frac{3a}{2}\left(a - \frac{3a}{2} + \frac{5a}{4}\right) = \frac{9a^2}{8}$$

and

$$\Pi^{\text{Follower}} = \frac{25a^2}{16}.$$

We observe that

$$\Pi^{\text{Leader}} < \Pi^{\text{Follower}}$$

such that in sequential price setting it is the *follower* who benefits! Quite a contrast to the sequential quantity setting when the leader had a clear first-mover advantage.

How can we explain this seemingly unexpected result? Well, in sequential price setting there is a first-mover *disadvantage*. To understand this, we need to recognise that once p_1 (the leader's price) has been set, the follower faces a less competitive landscape and is able to undercut the leader, as seen by $p_2 < p_1$.

The moral of the story? In a competitive marketplace of identical firms producing homogeneous goods it is better to let your competitors set their price first!

Admittedly, if firms were not identical, then a larger firm could move first and temporarily sell below cost, potentially forcing the follower out of business!

6.10 CHAPTER OVERVIEW

This chapter began by looking at decision-making under uncertainty using decision trees to assist unilateral decision-making. Under the simplifying assumption of risk neutrality, decision-makers compare expected monetary values to determine their best strategy. We also valued information (both perfect and imperfect), which allows better-informed decisions to be made. Thereafter, we modelled strategic interactions between players using game theory. Games were solved using Nash equilibria.

Discrete strategy sets were extended to continuous strategy sets allowing us to consider quantity-setting and price-setting decisions of firms both simultaneously and sequentially.

6.11 KEY VOCABULARY

Backward induction
Bertrand competition
Branch
Certainty equivalent
Chance node
Cournot competition
Decision node
Decision tree
Discount factor
Dominant strategy
Dominated strategy
Expected monetary value
Expected value of imperfect information
Expected value of perfect information
Game theory
Imperfect information
Mixed strategy
Nash equilibrium
Normal form
Payoff
Payoff profile
Perfect information
Prisoner's dilemma
Probabilities
Product differentiation
Pure strategy
Reaction function
Risk-averse
Risk-loving
Risk-neutral
Risk premium
Simultaneous-move game
Stackelberg leadership
Strategy profile

6.12 EXERCISES

6.12.1 Test your understanding

1 What are the elements of a decision tree?
2 How is an expected monetary value calculated?
3 Why should a risk-neutral decision-maker base their decision on a comparison of expected monetary values?
4 Explain why decision trees with multiple decision nodes should be solved using backward induction.
5 Distinguish between 'risk-averse', 'risk-neutral' and 'risk-loving' decision-makers.
6 Do you consider yourself to be risk-averse, risk-neutral or risk-loving? Why do you think this?
7 What is meant by the term 'certainty equivalent'?
8 Define the term 'risk premium' and explain how an individual's risk attitude can be determined from the risk premium.
9 What is the difference between 'perfect information' and 'imperfect information'?
10 How is the expected value of perfect information calculated?
11 How is the expected value of imperfect information calculated?
12 Suppose an expert predicts (imperfectly) whether a prospective borrower would default on a loan by classifying the prospective borrower as either a 'good credit risk' (resulting in loan approval) or a 'bad credit risk' (resulting in loan rejection). In qualitative/practical terms, distinguish between a:

(a) true positive
(b) false positive
(c) true negative
(d) false negative.

13 What is meant by 'strategic interaction' and how does this differ from unilateral decision-making?
14 Outline the components of a simultaneous-move game.
15 Assume player 1 has payoff profiles

$u_1(\{\text{Left, Up}\}) = u_1(\{\text{Right, Down}\}) = 4$ and $u_1(\{\text{Left, Down}\}) = u_1(\{\text{Right, Up}\}) = 2$,

and assume the payoff profiles of player 2 are

$u_2(\{\text{Left, Up}\}) = u_2(\{\text{Right, Down}\}) = 2$ and $u_2(\{\text{Left, Down}\}) = u_2(\{\text{Right, Up}\}) = 3$.

Construct the payoff matrix in normal form.

16 What is a dominant strategy?
17 How would you explain the Prisoner's dilemma to a friend?
18 What is a dominated strategy?
19 Explain the process of iterative elimination of strictly dominated strategies.
20 Distinguish between a 'pure strategy' and a 'mixed strategy'.
21 What is a Nash equilibrium?
22 In qualitative terms, briefly explain the Cournot competition model.
23 Is collusion desirable? (Ignore any legal implications!)
24 In qualitative terms, briefly explain the Bertrand competition model.
25 In qualitative terms, briefly explain the Stackelberg leadership model.
26 A (risk-loving?) individual decides to play Russian roulette. The revolver to be used has a cylinder with room for a maximum of six bullets. The cylinder is spun, and the revolver placed against the player's head. The possible outcomes are either 'survive with net worth' or 'die'.

(a) James decides to play. He places five bullets in the revolver's cylinder. James has the option of paying an amount of money, m_1, to remove one bullet (meaning there would only be four bullets). Construct James' decision tree.
(b) James decides to play. He places one bullet in the revolver's cylinder. James has the option of paying an amount of money, m_2, to remove the bullet (meaning there would be no bullets in the cylinder). Construct James' decision tree.
(c) Explain in qualitative terms how a solution could be reached for the decision trees in (a) and (b).

27 James, who is risk-neutral, is deciding whether to launch a new product to market. He also has an option to pilot test the new product (and observe whether the pilot test is successful) *before* committing to the full launch. Suppose that for both the pilot test and the full launch he judges commercial success and failure to be equally likely. Initially he has wealth of £100,000.

- If the pilot test is successful, James makes £10,000, but if the pilot test is unsuccessful he loses £5000.

- If the full product launch is successful (regardless of the outcome of any pilot test), James makes £1,000,000, but if the full product launch is unsuccessful he loses £500,000.

Draw the decision tree and determine James' optimal decisions.

28 A risk-neutral media executive is deciding whether to offer a new 'freemium' subscription service. If successful, the company will make £20 million. If unsuccessful, the company will make a loss of £5 million. Doing nothing costs nothing.

(a) It is (subjectively) estimated that there is a 25% chance of success. What should the executive do?

(b) For what probability of success, π, would the executive be indifferent in terms of their decision-making?

(c) The executive could undertake test marketing which would inform them with certainty about whether the freemium subscription service will be a success. Calculate the expected value of perfect information, and hence determine the maximum willingness to pay for the test marketing.

(d) Unfortunately, the test marketing is discovered not to be perfect after all. Suppose there is an 85% chance of a true positive (the test marketing correctly indicating success), and a 95% chance of a true negative (the test marketing correctly indicating failure). Calculate the expected value of imperfect information, and hence determine the maximum willingness to pay for the test marketing.

29 Consider the following normal form of a game.

		Player 1	
		Left	Right
Player 2	Up	1, 1	0, 2
	Down	2, 0	π_1, π_2

(a) Suppose that $\pi_1 = \pi_2$. For what values of π_1 do players 1 and 2 both have a dominant strategy? What are these dominant strategies?

(b) Suppose that $\pi_1 = \pi_2$. To make this game a Prisoner's dilemma, what would be the required values of π_1?

(c) Suppose that $\pi_1 > 0$ and $\pi_2 < 0$. Check whether there are any pure-strategy Nash equilibria.

(d) Do any values of π_1 and π_2 exist such that there is no pure-strategy Nash equilibrium?

30 Suppose that WFH (Work From Home) and WTF (Work Through Flexibility) are the only two firms facilitating remote working technology. If WFH and WTF each decide to enter the market, a price war is triggered, causing both firms to be loss-making. In the event that only one of WFH and WTF enters, both firms are profitable due to the non-entrant being a supplier to the entrant of some of its technology. The payoffs, in billions of pounds, are as follows, shown as (WFH, WTF).

		WTF	
		Enter market	Stay out
WFH	Enter market	-5, -5	6, 1
	Stay out	1, 6	0, 0

Assume the two firms make their decisions simultaneously.

(a) Identify any pure-strategy Nash equilibria.
(b) Identify the mixed-strategy Nash equilibrium.
(c) Suppose that, before deciding whether to enter, WTF signs a binding agreement with a remote recruitment agency. Business news media widely report the details of the agreement, so it is common knowledge. The agreement promises the remote recruitment agency compensation of £7 billion from WTF if WTF chooses not to enter the market. Find any pure-strategy Nash equilibria of the game in this case.

31 Suppose N competitor firms decide simultaneously whether or not they wish to enter a particular product market. Suppose that the overall market demand for the product is Q, where $Q < N$. If at most Q of the N firms choose to enter the market, suppose each entrant earns £1 million. If more than Q firms enter, each entrant earns nothing. Each non-entering firm earns £0.5 million. Determine whether there are any pure-strategy Nash equilibria.

32 An industry has two identical firms, producing output of q_1 and q_2, respectively. Hence industry output is $Q = q_1 + q_2$. Total production costs for firm i are $2 + q_i$, for $i = 1, 2$. Suppose the market demand curve is $Q = 10 - P$.

(a) Determine the Cournot–Nash equilibrium quantities for each firm, and the resulting market price, P.
(b) Could these two firms engage in collusion? Justify your answer.
(c) Suppose firm 1 moved first. Using the Stackelberg leadership model, how would this affect the quantities for each firm, and the resultant market price, P?

7

SAMPLING AND SAMPLING DISTRIBUTIONS

Chapter contents

Chapter level: *Beginner*

Source: Photo by dylan nolte via Unsplash.

Key concepts

- Sampling
- Sampling distributions
- Central limit theorem

Chapter value

Data varies from sample to sample, so we need the sampling distributions of descriptive statistics.

Key takeaway

As the sample size increases, a random sample is likely to be more representative of the population.

Chapter outline

Choose at random a number between 1 and 10 (to be continued). Conceptually, the idea of drawing a *sample* from a *population* is straightforward. For large populations, performing a census (a total enumeration of the population) is prohibitively expensive and hence infeasible in practice, necessitating the selection of a subset via a sample. However, to achieve valid 'inferences', the sample should be sufficiently *representative* of the population from which it is drawn. As we shall see, easier said than done!

There is a pervasive risk of a lack of sample representativeness, albeit we can try to mitigate (but not eliminate) this risk through our choice of sampling technique. Attributes of common sampling techniques will be discussed, and the term *sampling error* introduced. Any kind of error is undesirable (who would ever wish to be wrong?) but given this inevitable risk the best we can do is to *quantify* the chance of the sampling error exceeding some amount, for which *sampling distributions* are our key tool.

Learning outcomes

After completing this chapter, you should be able to:

- explain the sampling design process
- define the target population and determine the sampling frame
- compare non-random and random sampling techniques
- explain the concept of a sampling distribution and its role in statistical inference.

7.1 INTRODUCTION

Business analytics concerns data analytics, but to do any analysis first we need data! Central to this is the concept of sampling – the (possibly random) selection of a sample of members from an underlying population. Figure 7.1 demonstrates this basic premise.

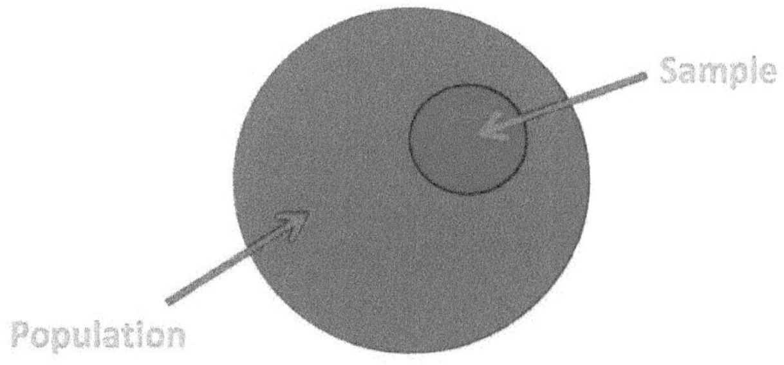

Figure 7.1 Drawing a sample from a population of interest.

From our sample we can then make *inferences* about the population. We begin by describing a range of sampling techniques, briefly outlining their relative advantages and disadvantages.

So, which number did you pick? I reckon '7' (otherwise another 'high' number). In general, people are *biased* towards 7 (and other high numbers) when asked to choose at random a number between 1 and 10. If you did choose a number between 1 and 10, it was not truly *at random*, due to an *unconscious bias* towards 7 and against lower numbers. Obviously, some readers would have chosen low numbers but, trust me, the modal value would have been 7. I recommend testing this out on a group of your friends. In case you're wondering, there was no subliminal nudging towards 7 because this happens to be Chapter 7. I swear this is a pure coincidence!

Motivational case: Death of opinion polling?

On 23 June 2016 the UK electorate was asked to vote in response to the following question: 'Should the United Kingdom remain a member of the European Union or leave the European Union?'

While a *referendum* is different from an *election*, in both cases until the votes are actually counted and the 'winner' declared, it cannot be known with certainty what the outcome will be. We could decide simply not to bother predicting the outcome in advance and simply enjoy the thrill of wait-and-see. However, businesses (let alone the politicians and the public!) would welcome an accurate prediction of the outcome to contingency plan for any significant change to the political (and hence regulatory) landscape. Ultimately, there was a significant change in the case of 'Brexit'.

Regardless of which side of the Brexit debate people were on, the eventual result of a 'Leave' victory over 'Remain' (by 52% to 48% of those who voted) was a surprise to many, if not all. But why?

A priori expectations for the most part were of a 'Remain' win, with these expectations arguably being reinforced by many opinion polls - notably polls conducted by *telephone*. Interestingly, *online* polls systematically tended to give around a six-percentage-point greater support level for Leave in the run-up to the vote. While this may not sound much, crucially this difference spanned the critical 50% threshold necessary to win in a winner-takes-all referendum, as shown in Figure 7.2.

Why the difference? Ultimately, this is an issue of representativeness in that online polls were better able to reach a *representative* sample of the electorate in terms of *relevant* demographic characteristics. Fail to achieve adequate representativeness, then no matter how large your sample, expect to be surprised!

If interested, see: https://yougov.co.uk/topics/politics/articles-reports/2016/06/28/online-polls-were-right

7.2 SAMPLING

Sampling is a key component in a business research design. The key to the use of statistics is being able to take data from a sample and make inferences about a large population. **Sampling design** involves several basic questions.

- *Should* a sample even be taken (over a census)?

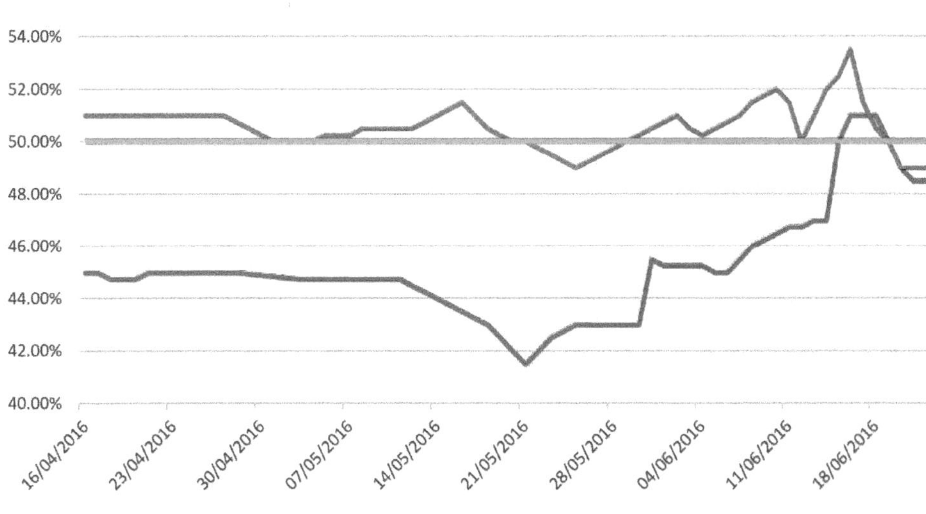

Figure 7.2 Telephone and online poll averages for Leave support in the run-up to the UK's EU membership referendum, with the 50% winning threshold in bold green. Source: Adapted from data in YouGov article: *The Online Polls Were RIGHT, and Other Lessons from the Referendum* by Freddie Sayers (June 28 2016).

- If we should draw a sample, what *process* should be followed?
- What *kind* of sample should be drawn?
- How *large* should the sample size, n, be?

We now consider how to answer some of these questions (we will discuss sample size determination in Chapter 9), although we first introduce some important terminology.

Sampling terminology

Target population - the collection of all population members, sharing some common set of characteristics, which comprises the universe for the purpose of the business analytics problem about which inferences are sought.

Members - 'objects' in which we are interested (such as customers, ex-customers, or potential customers).

Sampling unit - a member (such as a customer) or a unit which contains the member (such as a household).

Census - a complete enumeration of the members of a population of study 'objects' (such as customers, ex-customers, or potential customers).

Sample - a subgroup of the population members selected for participation in the study.

Sampling error (or estimation error) - the difference between an estimate of a population parameter and its true value. The less representative a sample is, the greater the risk of a large sampling error.

7.2.1 To sample, or not to sample?

To determine whether a sample or a census should be conducted, various factors need to be considered such as the following:

- *Population size.* 'Small' populations would make a census feasible, but in practice most populations of interest would be too large to enumerate in full and so a sample would be preferred.
- *Time horizon.* Samples are much quicker to perform, so if businesses wish to respond to research findings in a timely manner then speed is of the essence, strongly favouring a sample.
- *Budget.* For large populations, a census is very costly so a large budget would be required, whereas a small budget favours a sample because only some sampling units are selected.

Sidenote

Governments often perform a decennial census (i.e. once every 10 years) of households to assist governments in decision-making over the planning and funding of public services, such as health care, education and transport. However, replacing the logistically and administratively burdensome census with a well-designed sample of households could prove far more cost-effective, and possibly even more accurate given the diseconomies of scale from a census of a (very large) population.

- *Homogeneity of the population.* If the population characteristic of interest is expected to be homogeneous (i.e. has low variance, meaning population members are quite 'similar'), then a sample would likely be sufficient to represent the population, since variation in the sample would be expected to be low – if all members are similar, you do not need to observe that many of them. However, if the characteristic is likely to be heterogeneous, then a sample may fail to capture the large dispersion in the population, hence a census would be more appropriate.
- *Sampling errors.* When the commercial consequences of making sampling errors are significant (i.e. the 'cost' is high), then a census would be preferable due to the elimination of sampling errors entirely.
- *Non-sampling errors.* Non-sampling errors arise due to a systematic problem with the data collection, such as poorly worded questions in surveys resulting in response biases. Such errors are magnified the larger the sample size, so a sample is better because fewer resources would have been spent on collecting the data.
- *Type of measurement.* In a quality control setting of checking whether products are manufactured to desired specifications, if the check involved testing an item to destruction, such as the lifespan of a tyre, then a census is not feasible as there would be no tyres left to sell!

Of course, in practice, some of our factors may favour a sample while others favour a census, in which case a balanced judgement is required.

7.3 CLASSIFICATION OF SAMPLING TECHNIQUES

We now consider the different types of sampling techniques used in practice, which can be decomposed into *non-random* (or *non-probability*) sampling techniques and *random* (or *probability*) sampling techniques.

Non-random sampling techniques are characterised by the fact that some units in the population have an unknown probability or a zero probability of selection. There is also an inability to measure sampling error. Examples of such techniques are:

- convenience sampling
- judgemental sampling
- quota sampling
- snowball sampling.

Random sampling techniques mean every population member has a known, non-zero probability of being selected. Probability sampling makes it possible to estimate the margins of sampling error, and hence all statistical techniques (such as confidence intervals and hypothesis tests, covered in Chapters 9 and 10, respectively) can be applied. In order to perform random sampling, we need a sampling frame, which is a list of all population members. However, we need to consider whether the sampling frame is (i) adequate (does it represent the target population?), (ii) complete (are there any missing sampling units, or duplications?), (iii) accurate (are we researching dynamic populations with people migrating, domestically or internationally?) and (iv) convenient (is the sampling frame readily accessible?). Examples of such techniques are:

- simple random sampling
- systematic sampling
- stratified sampling
- cluster sampling.

We now consider each of the above listed techniques, explaining their strengths and weaknesses. To illustrate each, we will use the example of 50 consumers (numbered 1 to 50) who each happen to belong to one of five mutually exclusive demographic groups based on age as shown in Figure 7.3.

Admittedly, in this instance where the population size is only $N = 50$ a census would likely be feasible. However, the population size is kept deliberately small here for illustrative purposes of each sampling technique.

Age group	Consumer no.									
18–29	1	2	3	4	5	6	7	8	9	10
30–39	11	12	13	14	15	16	17	18	19	20
40–49	21	22	23	24	25	26	27	28	29	30
50–59	31	32	33	34	35	36	37	38	39	40
60+	41	42	43	44	45	46	47	48	49	50

Figure 7.3 A population of $N = 50$ consumers (numbered 1 to 50) arranged according to their age group.

7.4 NON-RANDOM SAMPLING TECHNIQUES

7.4.1 Convenience sampling

Convenience sampling attempts to obtain a sample of convenient members – hence the name! Typically, people are selected because they conveniently happen to be in the right place at the right time. Examples include taste-testing a new food item in a supermarket aisle and 'people-in-the-street' or *vox pop* interviews for broadcast media soliciting views on news topics of the day.

Suppose consumers who are aged 30–39 happen to shop at the same time of day and so tend to assemble at a convenient time and place, or perhaps they reside in a particular area of a town or city, such that only consumers in this age group are selected. Suppose a convenience sample of size $n = 6$ is required. An example of a possible resulting convenience sample consists of consumers 12, 14, 15, 17, 19 and 20, as shown in Figure 7.4.

Age group	Consumer no.									
18–29	1	2	3	4	5	6	7	8	9	10
30–39	11	12	13	14	15	16	17	18	19	20
40–49	21	22	23	24	25	26	27	28	29	30
50–59	31	32	33	34	35	36	37	38	39	40
60+	41	42	43	44	45	46	47	48	49	50

Figure 7.4 A convenience sample of size $n = 6$ (in red) drawn from the population of size $N = 50$.

Note that no consumers are selected from age groups other than those aged 30–39, hence the sample obtained is not representative *if* the characteristic of interest (such as consumer brand preferences) differs across consumers by age because it would be incorrect to generalise the preferences of those aged 30–39 to the other age groups.

Strengths of convenience sampling include being the cheapest, quickest and most convenient form of sampling – arguably the best for a 'quick-and-dirty' sampling scheme. Weaknesses include *selection bias* (due to the researcher choosing who is selected, and hence they will inevitably demonstrate bias in their selection – whether conscious or unconscious) and the lack of a representative sample. As such, this is really only suitable for exploratory types of research, as results can only be indicative, not conclusive.

7.4.2 Judgemental sampling

Judgemental sampling is a variant of convenience sampling whereby population members are chosen according to the judgement of an expert – hence the name!

Suppose a market researcher (and hence expert) judges (rightly or wrongly!) that age groups 18–29, 30–39 and 60+ are deemed to be sufficiently representative of all age groups – in terms of the characteristic of interest, such as consumer brand preferences. From each of these three age groups, suppose two consumers are chosen based on convenience, giving a total sample size of $n = 6$. Suppose the resulting judgemental sample here consists of consumers 3, 8, 16, 19, 44 and 46, as shown in Figure 7.5.

Age group	Consumer no.									
18–29	1	2	[3]	4	5	6	7	[8]	9	10
30–39	11	12	13	14	15	[16]	17	18	[19]	20
40–49	21	22	23	24	25	26	27	28	29	30
50–59	31	32	33	34	35	36	37	38	39	40
60+	41	42	43	[44]	45	[46]	47	48	49	50

Figure 7.5 A judgemental sample of size $n = 6$ (in red) drawn from the population of size $N = 50$.

Note that no consumers who are in the 40–49 or 50–59 age groups are chosen. Relative to the above convenience sample, the judgemental sample is more representative since three of the five age groups are represented, and hence a reasonable cross-section of ages is observed, but the absence of anyone from the 40–49 and 50–59 age groups means generalising inferences to these non-sampled groups is problematic – their brand preferences may significantly differ from those younger or older.

Strengths of judgemental sampling include being achieved at low cost, as well as being convenient, not particularly time-consuming, and good for exploratory research designs. Weaknesses are that it does not allow generalisations to excluded groups and suffers from subjectivity due to the judgement of the expert which may be biased (again, either consciously or unconsciously).

7.4.3 Quota sampling

Quota sampling attempts to obtain a representative sample through the specification of control categories, known as *quota controls*, of population members. The quota controls should be categorical variables (either nominal or ordinal) and chosen on the basis of control characteristics that are likely to be relevant to the research problem – for example, gender and age group might be considered relevant. Having established the quota controls, a sample size is chosen (possibly subjectively) and then population members are sampled from each group according to the assumed distribution of the control characteristics in the population (which has to be known, otherwise assumed). Selections are made from each group until these group quotas are met.

Suppose age (conveniently!) is thought to be relevant to the research study, such that our five age groups can be used as the quota controls. Suppose, from the decennial census, that the age distribution in the population was as per Table 7.1.

If we desire a sample size of $n = 10$, say, then we set quotas from each age group according to the distribution in the population. The quotas are shown in the final column of Table 7.1. From each age group, consumers are selected until the respective quotas are filled. Here suppose the resulting sample consists of consumers 2, 6, 11, 13, 18, 22, 29, 33, 38 and 45, as shown in Figure 7.6.

The key strength of quota sampling is that a quota sample can be controlled for certain characteristics in an attempt to obtain a representative sample in terms of the control characteristics, with samples from each group chosen in proportion to their distribution in the population. However, it suffers from selection bias as there is no guarantee of a representative sample due to the subjective nature by which the population members are selected. Also, while selection is done until quotas are filled, in opinion research those approached may choose not to respond, so selection continues until each group quota is met. This would then introduce *non-response bias* as those who refused to respond may hold different opinions from those who do.

Table 7.1 Example of using age group as a quota control.

Age groups	Population distribution	Sample distribution	Quota per age group
18–29	20%	20%	2
30–39	30%	30%	3
40–49	20%	20%	2
50–59	20%	20%	2
60+	10%	10%	1
Total	100%	100%	10

Age group	Consumer no.									
18–29	1	2	3	4	5	6	7	8	9	10
30–39	11	12	13	14	15	16	17	18	19	20
40–49	21	22	23	24	25	26	27	28	29	30
50–59	31	32	33	34	35	36	37	38	39	40
60+	41	42	43	44	45	46	47	48	49	50

Figure 7.6 A quota sample of size n = 10 (in red) drawn from the population of size N = 50.

7.4.4 Snowball sampling

In snowball sampling (which is not restricted to winter!) an initial group of population members is selected, which may be done randomly (covered in Section 7.5). After being selected, each is asked to recommend other members who are part of the target population that is of interest. Individuals who are recommended are then contacted.

Suppose consumers 8 and 32 are selected randomly. Consumer 8 refers consumers 12 and 20, while consumer 32 refers consumers 36 and 40. The resulting sample consists of consumers 8, 12, 20, 32, 36 and 40, as shown in Figure 7.7.

Age group	Consumer no.									
18–29	1	2	3	4	5	6	7	8	9	10
30–39	11	12	13	14	15	16	17	18	19	20
40–49	21	22	23	24	25	26	27	28	29	30
50–59	31	32	33	34	35	36	37	38	39	40
60+	41	42	43	44	45	46	47	48	49	50

Figure 7.7 A snowball sample of size n = 6 (in red) drawn from the population of size N = 50.

Note that there are no consumers in the 40–49 and 60+ age groups, hence it is a risk to generalise inferences to these age groups given their lack of representation. While the initial selection may be random (and hence free of selection bias), the referrals may be 'similar' to those referring if the referrers have a homogeneous network – as is the case for consumer 32 who refers two people in the same age group.

7.5 RANDOM SAMPLING TECHNIQUES

All random sampling techniques are *probability-based*, such that each population member has a known (but necessarily equal) probability of selection. To conduct random sampling a sampling frame is required in order for probabilities to be assigned.

7.5.1 Simple random sampling

In a simple random sample each population member has a *known* and *equal* probability of selection, with every member being selected *independently* of every other member. All possible samples of size n are equally likely to occur.

In order to perform simple random sampling we require a random number generator to randomly select (i.e. probabilistically select) which members are to be in the sample. In practice, we would appeal to a pseudo-random number generator, which generates numbers algorithmically, but for practical purposes the generated numbers have the appearance of being random.

Pseudo-random number generation (for the interested reader)

In matters of simulation (as studied in Chapter 20), random sampling is undertaken to eliminate any possible selection bias when drawing from particular (probability) distributions.

There exist many pseudo-random number generators which are algorithms. This means that if you know the algorithm and the starting point (known as the *seed*) you can determine with certainty which values will be generated, and hence the values are *deterministic* rather than *random*. However, for practical purposes the generated numbers have the appearance of being random, hence the use of the term 'pseudo', meaning 'false'.

Just by way of example, we outline one of the original and popular pseudo-random number generators to give you a sense of how they work. We consider the *linear congruential generator*. Let us define a sequence $\{x_i\}$ and set

$$x_{i+1} = (ax_i + b) \bmod M$$

for integer values a, b, M and x_0, where:

- a is the *multiplier*, such that $0 < a < M$
- b is the *increment*, such that $0 \leq b < M$
- M is the *modulus*, such that $M > 0$
- x_0 is the *seed* (the starting point), such that $0 \leq x_0 < M$

Then

$$\frac{x_i}{M} \sim \text{Uniform}[0,1],$$

that is, for large M the sequence of numbers $\{x_i\}$ generated by the algorithm satisfies statistical properties of random samples drawn from the continuous uniform distribution over the unit interval.

Suppose we select $n = 6$ random numbers (using a pseudo-random number generator) from 1 to 50. If random number generation is performed with replacement, we can simply choose to ignore any repeated values.

Excel function: RANDBETWEEN

`RANDBETWEEN(bottom, top)` returns a (pseudo-)random integer value where

- `bottom` is the smallest possible integer value returned
- `top` is the largest possible integer value returned

such that all integer values `{bottom, bottom+1, ..., top-1, top}` are equally likely to be returned.

Suppose the pseudo-random number generator returns 9, 13, 22, 25, 29 and 37 (arranged in order; the numbers might have been drawn as $x_1 = 29$, $x_2 = 13$, $x_3 = 9$, $x_4 = 37$, $x_5 = 29$, $x_6 = 25$ and $x_7 = 22$, with x_5 being ignored due to it being a duplication of x_1). Therefore, the resulting simple random sample consists of consumers 9, 13, 22, 25, 29 and 37, as shown in Figure 7.8.

Age group	Consumer no.									
18–29	1	2	3	4	5	6	7	8	[9]	10
30–39	11	12	[13]	14	15	16	17	18	19	20
40–49	21	[22]	23	24	[25]	26	27	28	[29]	30
50–59	31	32	33	34	35	36	[37]	38	39	40
60+	41	42	43	44	45	46	47	48	49	50

Figure 7.8 A simple random sample of size $n = 6$ (in red) drawn from the population of size $N = 50$.

Note that there is no consumer sampled from the 60+ age group, and there is excess representation of the 40–49 age group (if we assume the population distribution of age groups was as per Table 7.1).

Strengths of simple random sampling are that it is (hopefully!) *simple* to understand and results are readily generalisable. Weaknesses include possible challenges acquiring and/or constructing the sampling frame, and a truly representative sample cannot be guaranteed (as seen above, with no one selected in the 60+ age group). Also, relative to other random sampling techniques it can have lower precision.

7.5.2 Systematic sampling

In systematic sampling the sample is chosen by selecting a *random* starting point (making it a random form of sampling), after which every *i*th population member in succession is chosen from the sampling frame, where *i* is the *sampling interval*.

Sampling interval

For a population size N and sample size n, the **sampling interval** used in systematic sampling is

$$i = \left\lfloor \frac{N}{n} \right\rceil$$

where '$\lfloor \, \rceil$' indicates rounding to the nearest integer. For example, $\lfloor 6.7 \rceil = 7$.

Whenever the *order* of the population members in the sampling frame is related to the characteristic of interest, systematic sampling will *increase* the representativeness of the sample. For our age group example, if the 50 numbered consumers were arranged in age order (coincidentally with 10 members in each defined age group) then a systematic sample would guarantee a broad cross-section of ages, such that if brand preferences varied by age we would capture this variation in our sample.

However, whenever the order of the population members produces a *cyclical* pattern, systematic sampling may *decrease* the representativeness of the sample. For example, if our sampling frame consisted of daily sales figures of a supermarket (which is open 7 days per week) in chronological order, and we had a sampling interval of $i = 7$, if the random starting point happened to be a Monday, then we would only sample Monday observations (since every seventh day would be a Monday) and we might expect footfall for grocery shopping to be below average early in the week, producing an unrepresentative sample (many families would likely undertake a large weekly shop in the run-up to the weekend or during the weekend itself).

In our recurring 50-consumer example, we have $N = 50$ and suppose we choose $n = 6$. Hence the sampling interval is

$$i = \left\lfloor \frac{50}{6} \right\rceil = 8$$

since 8.33 is rounded (down) to 8. We now invoke our pseudo-random number generator (such as `=RANDBETWEEN(1,8)`) to obtain our random starting point, say 4. The systematic sample is then consumers 4, 12, 20, 28, 36 and 44 (i.e. every eighth consumer in our sampling frame after the fourth), as shown in Figure 7.9.

Age group	Consumer no.									
18–29	1	2	3	[4]	5	6	7	8	9	10
30–39	11	[12]	13	14	15	16	17	18	19	[20]
40–49	21	22	23	24	25	26	27	[28]	29	30
50–59	31	32	33	34	35	[36]	37	38	39	40
60+	41	42	43	[44]	45	46	47	48	49	50

Figure 7.9 A systematic sample of size $n = 6$ (in red) drawn from the population of size $N = 50$.

Note that all consumer age groups are represented, so we observe brand preferences (our assumed characteristic of interest) from a broad cross-section of ages.

Whether or not systematic sampling improves representativeness depends on the extent of any ordering in the sampling frame as well as whether there is any coincidence of the sampling interval with 'cyclicality' in the sampling frame (such as with our daily sales example).

Although once i is determined through pseudo-random number generation the rest of the systematic sample is 'fixed' (i.e. every ith member thereafter is sampled), this still constitutes a random sampling technique due to the random starting point.

Note that there are only i possible systematic samples which could result – far fewer than in the case of simple random sampling. For instance, in our consumer example with a sampling interval of $i = 8$, the eight possible systematic samples are:

(i) 1, 9, 17, 25, 33, 41
(ii) 2, 10, 18, 26, 34, 42
(iii) 3, 11, 19, 27, 35, 43
(iv) 4, 12, 20, 28, 36, 44
(v) 5, 13, 21, 29, 37, 45
(vi) 6, 14, 22, 30, 38, 46
(vii) 7, 15, 23, 31, 39, 47
(viii) 8, 16, 24, 32, 40, 48

as shown in Figure 7.10.

Age group	Consumer no.									
18–29	1	2	3	4	5	6	7	8	9	10
30–39	11	12	13	14	15	16	17	18	19	20
40–49	21	22	23	24	25	26	27	28	29	30
50–59	31	32	33	34	35	36	37	38	39	40
60+	41	42	43	44	45	46	47	48	49	50

Figure 7.10 All possible systematic samples of size $n = 6$ drawn from the population of size $N = 50$.

Note that since we had to round the sampling interval (down) from 8.33 to 8, consumers 49 and 50 do not feature in any of the eight possible systematic samples. If this concerned us, we could circumvent the problem by choosing a sample size n which resulted in $i = N/n$ being an integer without rounding, such as $n = 5$ or $n = 10$ for our case of $N = 50$. In practice, for very large populations (we have noted that $N = 50$ is a very small population) the exclusion of a small number of population members would not be problematic.

7.5.3 Stratified sampling

Stratified sampling is a two-stage technique such that the population is partitioned (divided up) into subpopulations called *strata* ('strata' is the plural of 'stratum'). The strata should be mutually exclusive and collectively exhaustive (MECE) in that every population member must belong to one, *and only one*, stratum and no population members are omitted. Next, members are randomly chosen from *each* stratum, such as by simple random sampling. Provided relevant stratification factors are used (and are feasible in practice, with stratum membership determinable), the accuracy of statistical inference is increased due to better expected representativeness.

Population members *within a stratum* should be as *homogeneous* as possible (i.e. as similar as possible), but members *between strata* should be as *heterogeneous* as possible (i.e. as different as possible). Ideally, the stratification factors should be related to the characteristic of interest to maximise the overall representativeness of the final sample. This sampling technique can be thought of as the random equivalent of quota sampling, where relevant quota controls serve as the stratification factors here.

However, a sampling frame is not required for quota (or indeed any non-random form of) sampling, unlike stratified (or indeed any random form of) sampling.

For our consumer example, the age groups serve as the obvious strata. Suppose we seek an overall sample size of $n = 10$. Since the strata are of equal sizes (each has 10 consumers), it seems reasonable to divide the required sample size of 10 equally among the strata, such that we draw a simple random sample of size 2 from each age group. For example, for the 18–29 age group we could use `=RANDBETWEEN(1,10)` twice (or as many times as necessary to avoid duplications with the first selection), similarly `=RANDBETWEEN(11,20)` twice for the 30–39 age group, etc. Suppose this resulted in the observed sample 6, 9, 11, 15, 24, 28, 31, 33, 45 and 50, as shown in Figure 7.11.

Note that, by construction, all age groups are represented. Stratified sampling, by its design, guarantees that all subgroups feature in the sample, resulting in more precise statistical inference. However, the technique is dependent on being able to create the strata in the first place – if you knew the identities of your customers, but not their ages, incomes, etc., then it would not be possible to determine stratum membership by age group or income group.

Finally, a comment on the sampling procedure when drawing the random samples from strata. Here we simply split the required 10 observations equally among the five age groups due to the equal-sized strata (10 consumers in each age group). Often, we would expect the strata to vary in size, such that in *proportionate* stratified sampling, the sample size drawn from each stratum is proportional to the relative size of the stratum. Therefore, larger strata have larger random samples drawn from them. In *disproportionate* (or optimal) stratified sampling, the sample size from each stratum is proportional to the relative size of the stratum *and* the standard deviation of the distribution of the characteristic of interest among all the elements in that stratum. By taking into account the standard deviation (in addition to stratum size), we sample more from heterogeneous strata to boost our chances of adequately capturing this variation, while we reduce our sample size requirement from more homogeneous strata as 'once you've observed a few, you've effectively observed them all'!

Age group	Consumer no.									
18–29	1	2	3	4	5	[6]	7	8	[9]	10
30–39	[11]	12	13	14	[15]	16	17	18	19	20
40–49	21	22	23	[24]	25	26	27	[28]	29	30
50–59	[31]	32	[33]	34	35	36	37	38	39	40
60+	41	42	43	44	[45]	46	47	48	49	[50]

Figure 7.11 A stratified sample of size $n = 10$ (in red) drawn from the population of size $N = 50$.

7.5.4 Cluster sampling

In cluster sampling, the target population is first divided into MECE groups known as *clusters*. A *random* sample of clusters is then selected, based on a random sampling technique such as simple random sampling, or with probability proportional to size (larger clusters having greater probabilities of selection). If the cluster sizes are equal, then simple random sampling and probability-proportional-to-size sampling are identical, as the equal-sized clusters would be assigned *equal* probabilities of selection. For each selected cluster:

- either *all* cluster members are included in the sample (known as '*one-stage* cluster sampling' – suitable for small cluster sizes)
- or a *random sample* of cluster members is chosen (known as '*two-stage* cluster sampling' – suitable for large cluster sizes).

Contrary to the characteristics of strata in stratified sampling, in cluster sampling the clusters themselves should be as *homogeneous* as possible, while *within* a cluster members are likely to be *heterogeneous* (but could be homogeneous). Ideally, each cluster should be a small-scale representation of the entire population. This justifies the sampling of only *some* clusters, not all, since the sampled clusters should be representative of the clusters not sampled.

On what basis would we wish to form the clusters? Typically, we would consider defining clusters based on geography – for example, cities or regions which are considered sufficiently similar (since clusters should ideally be homogeneous).

For our consumer example, it would *not* be appropriate to use age groups as clusters. Not only are age groups not geographically defined, but we would reasonably expect some heterogeneity in brand preferences across age groups, violating our desire for homogeneous clusters. As such, we will modify the example to consider five similar cities ('similar' in terms of, say, demographic composition). For simplicity, suppose the cities had the population sizes in Table 7.2, with clusters sampled with probability proportional to size.

Table 7.2 Example of cluster sizes and corresponding cluster sampling probabilities.

City	Size	Probability of selection
A	1 million	0.10
B	3 million	0.30
C	2 million	0.20
D	3 million	0.30
E	1 million	0.10

In this instance, suppose we randomly choose three cities (clusters): B, C and E. Given the large city population sizes, we would wish to use **multi-stage sampling**, where selection is performed in multiple successive stages. Our *primary* sampling units here are cities, after which we would choose appropriate *secondary* sampling units (such as boroughs or districts), and continue refining the sampling units in successive stages until finally the sampling units reduce to those of interest (such as consumers).

While multi-stage sampling is commonly used in cluster sampling so that we are at first sampling main clusters, and then clusters within clusters, etc., it is also possible to perform multi-stage sampling with mixed techniques, such as cluster sampling at the first stage and stratified sampling at the second stage. An example might be a national survey of salespeople in a company. Sales areas could be identified and a random sample taken from these. Instead of interviewing every person in the chosen clusters (which would be a one-stage cluster sample), only randomly selected salespeople within the chosen clusters would be interviewed.

Cluster sampling is relatively easy to implement and reasonably cost-effective. However, the technique suffers from a lack of precision and it can be difficult to compute and interpret results.

7.5.5 Contact method

Up to this point, our interest has been in the actual *sampling* method. We have not made reference to the choice of *contact* method, that is, the mode of administration of surveying individuals. As we saw in the opening motivational case concerning pre-referendum opinion polling, survey research results *can* be impacted by this choice – for example, telephone and online polls could return different results due to the online polls being better able to reach certain constituent groups. How would such polling be conducted in practice? Well, market research companies compile *access panels* of many different sociodemographic groups, allowing relevant target audiences to be reached quickly. However, response rates would vary among contact methods such as face-to-face surveys, telephone surveys and online/postal/mail (so-called 'self-completion') surveys. In most countries you can assume:

- an interviewer-administered face-to-face questionnaire will be the most expensive to carry out, but likely with a high response rate
- telephone surveys depend very much on whether your target population is on the telephone (and how good the telephone system is)
- self-completion questionnaires have low response rates.

7.6 SAMPLING DISTRIBUTIONS

As we have seen, a simple random sample is a sample selected by a process where every possible sample (of the same size, n) has the same probability of selection. The selection process is left to chance, therefore eliminating the effect of selection bias. Due to the random selection mechanism, we do not know (in advance) which sample will occur. Every population member has a known, equal, non-zero probability of selection in the sample, but no member is certain to appear.

Example 7.1

Suppose we have a population of size $N = 6$ members: A, B, C, D, E and F. We consider all possible samples of size $n = 2$ (*without replacement*, i.e. once an object has been chosen it cannot be selected again). There are 15 different, but equally likely, such samples:

AB, AC, AD, AE, AF, BC, BD, BE,
BF, CD, CE, CF, DE, DF, EF.

Since this is using simple random sampling, each *sample* has an equal probability of selection of 1/15.

As seen in Chapter 5, a population has particular characteristics of interest such as its mean, μ, and variance, σ^2. Collectively, we refer to these characteristics as *parameters*. If we do not have population data, the parameter values will be *unknown*.

Statistical inference has many branches, one of which is the process of estimating the (unknown) parameter values using the (known) sample data.

We use a statistic (called a (point) estimator) calculated from sample observations to provide a (point) estimate of a parameter.

Example 7.2

Continuing Example 7.1, recall that there are 15 different samples of size 2 from a population of size 6. Suppose the variable of interest is monthly income, such that:

Individual	A	B	C	D	E	F
Monthly income in £000s	3	6	4	9	7	7

If we seek the population mean, μ, we will use the sample mean, $\bar{X}$, as our estimator where, for a sample of size n, we have

$$\bar{X} = \frac{1}{n}\sum_{i=1}^{n} X_i.$$

For example, if the observed sample was 'AB', the sample mean is

$$\frac{3000+6000}{2} = £4500.$$

Clearly, different observed samples will lead to different sample means. Consider the *values* of $\bar{X}$ (i.e. $\bar{x}$), for all possible samples (in thousands of pounds):

Sample	AB	AC	AD	AE	AF	BC	BD	BE
Values	3, 6	3, 4	3, 9	3, 7	3, 7	6, 4	6, 9	6, 7
$\bar{x}$	4.5	3.5	6	5	5	5	7.5	6.5

Sample	BF	CD	CE	CF	DE	DF	EF
Values	6, 7	4, 9	4, 7	4, 7	9, 7	9, 7	7, 7
$\bar{x}$	6.5	6.5	5.5	5.5	8	8	7

So, the *values* of $\bar{X}$ vary from 3.5 to 8, depending on the sample values.

Since we have the population data here, we can actually compute the population mean, μ, in thousands of pounds, which is

$$\mu = \frac{1}{N}\sum_{i=1}^{N} X_i = \frac{3+6+4+9+7+7}{6} = 6.$$

So, even with simple random sampling, we sometimes obtain $\bar{x}$ values which are far from μ. Sampling error occurs whenever

$\bar{x} - \mu \neq 0$, or equivalently when $\bar{x} \neq \mu$.

Here, in fact, only one sample (AD) results in $\bar{x} = \mu$ such that if this was our observed sample then there would be no sampling error, but this would be purely by chance (with a probability of 1/15). In practice, if μ is unknown then even if we did observe AD *we would not know* that there was no sampling error!

Let us now consider the maximum possible *absolute deviations* of the sample mean from the population mean (i.e. the distance $|\bar{x} - \mu|$).

max $\lvert\bar{x} - \mu\rvert$	Range of $\bar{x}$	Number of samples	Probability
0	$\bar{x} = 6$	1	0.067
0.5	$5.5 \leq \bar{x} \leq 6.5$	6	0.400
1	$5 \leq \bar{x} \leq 7$	10	0.667
1.5	$4.5 \leq \bar{x} \leq 7.5$	12	0.800
2	$4 \leq \bar{x} \leq 8$	14	0.933
2.5	$3.5 \leq \bar{x} \leq 8.5$	15	1.000

So, for example, there is an 80% probability of being within 1.5 units (i.e. £1500) of μ.

We now represent this as a *frequency distribution*. That is, we record the frequency of each possible value of $\bar{x}$.

$\bar{x}$	Frequency, f	Relative frequency
3.5	1	1/15 = 0.067
4.5	1	1/15 = 0.067
5.0	3	3/15 = 0.200
5.5	2	2/15 = 0.133
6.0	1	1/15 = 0.067
6.5	3	3/15 = 0.200
7.0	1	1/15 = 0.067
7.5	1	1/15 = 0.067
8.0	2	2/15 = 0.133

The above frequency distribution is an example of the **sampling distribution** of $\bar{X}$. The sampling distribution is a central and vital concept in statistical inference. It can be used to evaluate how 'good' an estimator is. Specifically, we care about how 'close' the estimator is to the population parameter of interest (in this case μ).

As we have seen, different samples yield different sample mean values, as a consequence of the random sampling procedure. Hence estimators (of which $\bar{X}$ is an example) are random variables.

So, $\bar{X}$ is our (point) *estimator* of μ, and the observed value of $\bar{X}$, denoted by $\bar{x}$, is a (point) *estimate*.

7.7 SAMPLING DISTRIBUTION OF THE SAMPLE MEAN

Like any distribution, we care about a sampling distribution's *mean* and *variance*. Together, we can assess how 'good' an estimator is.

Here we consider the mean. We seek an estimator which does not mislead us *systematically*. So the 'average' (mean) value of an estimator, over all possible samples, should be equal to the population parameter itself.

Example 7.3

Continuing Example 7.2:

$\bar{x}$	Frequency, f	Product
3.5	1	3.5
4.5	1	4.5
5.0	3	15.0
5.5	2	11.0
6.0	1	6.0
6.5	3	19.5
7.0	1	7.0
7.5	1	7.5
8.0	2	16.0
Total	15	90.0

Hence the mean of this sampling distribution is

$$\frac{\sum_i \bar{x}_i f_i}{\sum_i f_i} = \frac{90}{15} = 6 = \mu.$$

An important difference between a sampling distribution and other distributions is that the values in a sampling distribution are summary measures of whole samples (i.e. statistics, or estimators) rather than individual observations.

Formally, the mean of a sampling distribution is called the *expected value* of the estimator, denoted by E(·). Hence the expected value of the sample mean is $E(\bar{X})$.

An *unbiased estimator* (formally defined in Chapter 9) has its expected value equal to the parameter being estimated. For Example 7.3, $E(\bar{X}) = 6 = \mu$.

Fortunately, the sample mean $\bar{X}$ is *always* an unbiased estimator of μ in simple random sampling, regardless of the:

- sample size, n
- distribution of the (parent) population.

This is a good illustration of a population parameter (here, μ) being estimated by its *sample counterpart* (here, $\bar{X}$).

The unbiasedness of an estimator is clearly desirable. However, we also need to take into account the *dispersion* of the estimator's sampling distribution. Ideally, the possible values of the estimator should not vary much around the true parameter value. So, we seek an estimator with a small variance.

Recall that the variance is defined to be the *mean of the squared deviations about the mean* of the distribution. In the case of sampling distributions, it is referred to as the sampling variance.

Example 7.4

Continuing Example 7.3:

$\bar{x}$	$\bar{x} - \mu$	$(\bar{x} - \mu)^2$	Frequency, *f*	Product
3.5	−2.5	6.25	1	6.25
4.5	−1.5	2.25	1	2.25
5.0	−1.0	1.00	3	3.00
5.5	−0.5	0.25	2	0.50
6.0	0.0	0.00	1	0.00
6.5	0.5	0.25	3	0.75
7.0	1.0	1.00	1	1.00
7.5	1.5	2.25	1	2.25
8.0	2.0	4.00	2	8.00
		Total	15	24.00

Hence the sampling variance is

$$\frac{\sum_i (\bar{x}_i - \mu)^2 f_i}{\sum_i f_i} = \frac{24}{15} = 1.6.$$

The population itself has a variance, the population variance, σ^2.

$\bar{x}$	$\bar{x} - \mu$	$(\bar{x} - \mu)^2$	Frequency, *f*	Product
3	-3	9	1	9
6	0	0	1	0
4	-2	4	1	4
9	3	9	1	9
7	1	1	2	2

Hence the population variance is

$$\sigma^2 = \frac{\sum_i (\bar{x}_i - \mu)^2 f_i}{\sum_i f_i} = \frac{24}{6} = 4.$$

We now consider the relationship between σ^2 and the sampling variance. Intuitively, a larger σ^2 should lead to a larger sampling variance. For population size N and sample size n, we note the following result when sampling without replacement:

$$\text{Var}(\bar{X}) = \frac{N-n}{N-1} \times \frac{\sigma^2}{n}.$$

Example 7.5

Continuing Example 7.4, we get

$$\text{Var}(\bar{X}) = \frac{6-2}{6-1} \times \frac{4}{2} = 1.6.$$

We use the term *standard error* (S.E.) to refer to the *standard deviation of the sampling distribution*, so

$$\text{S.E.}(\bar{X}) = \sqrt{\text{Var}(\bar{X})} = \sqrt{\frac{N-n}{N-1} \times \frac{\sigma^2}{n}} = \sigma_{\bar{X}}.$$

Some implications are the following.

- As the sample size n increases, the sampling variance decreases, that is, the *precision* increases. (Although greater precision is desirable, data collection costs will rise with n. Remember why we sample in the first place!)
- Provided the sampling fraction, defined as n/N, is small, the term

  $$\frac{N-n}{N-1} \approx 1$$

  so can be ignored. Therefore, the *precision depends effectively on the sample size only*.

Example 7.6

Continuing Example 7.5, the larger the sample, the less variability there will be between samples. Consider the sampling distributions of $\bar{X}$ for samples of sizes $n = 2$ and $n = 4$, respectively.

$\bar{x}$	$n = 2$	$n = 4$
3.50	1	-
4.50	1	-
5.00	3	2
5.25	-	1

$\bar{x}$	$n = 2$	$n = 4$
5.50	2	1
5.75	-	3
6.00	1	1
6.25	-	2
6.50	-	3
6.75	-	1
7.00	1	-
7.25	-	1
7.50	1	-
8.00	2	-

We can see that there is a striking improvement in the precision of the estimator, because the variability has decreased considerably for $n = 4$ relative to $n = 2$.

The range of possible $\bar{x}$ values goes from 3.5 to 8.0 down to 5.0 to 7.25. The sampling variance is reduced from 1.6 to 0.4.

The factor $(N - n)/(N - 1)$ decreases steadily as $n \to N$. When $n = 1$ the factor equals 1, and when $n = N$ it equals 0.

When sampling *without replacement*, increasing n must increase precision since less of the population is left out. In much practical sampling N is *very* large (e.g. several million), while n is comparably small (at most around 1000, say).

Therefore, in such cases the factor $(N - n)/(N - 1)$ is close to 1, hence:

$$\mathrm{Var}(\bar{X}) = \frac{N-n}{N-1} \times \frac{\sigma^2}{n} \approx \frac{\sigma^2}{n} = \frac{\mathrm{Var}(X)}{n}$$

for small n/N. When N is large, it is the sample size n that is important in determining precision, *not* the sampling fraction.

Example 7.7

Consider two populations: $N_1 = 3$ million and $N_2 = 200$ million (i.e. two markets where our product is sold), both with the same variance, σ^2. We sample $n_1 = n_2 = 1000$ from each population to assess brand awareness. Then

$$\sigma^2_{\bar{X}_1} = \frac{N_1 - n_1}{N_1 - 1} \times \frac{\sigma^2}{n_1} = 0.999667 \times \frac{\sigma^2}{1000}$$

(Continued)

and

$$\sigma^2_{\bar{X}_2} = \frac{N_2 - n_2}{N_2 - 1} \times \frac{\sigma^2}{n_2} = 0.999995 \times \frac{\sigma^2}{1000}.$$

So $\sigma^2_{\bar{X}_1} \approx \sigma^2_{\bar{X}_2}$, despite N_1 being much less than N_2.

7.7.1 Sampling from the normal distribution

The mean and variance of $\bar{X}$ are E(X) and Var(X)/n, respectively, for a random sample of size n from *any* population distribution of X. What about the form of the sampling distribution of $\bar{X}$?

This depends on the distribution of X, and is not generally known. However, when the distribution of X is *normal*, the sampling distribution of $\bar{X}$ is also normal.

Sampling distribution of $\bar{X}$ when sampling from normal populations

When sampling from $N(\mu, \sigma^2)$, the sampling distribution of the sample mean is such that

$$\bar{X} \sim N\left(\mu, \frac{\sigma^2}{n}\right).$$

So we note that $E(\bar{X}) = E(X) = \mu$.

- In an individual sample, $\bar{x}$ is not usually equal to μ, the expected value of the population.
- However, *over repeated samples* the values of $\bar{X}$ are centred at μ.

Notice that Var($\bar{X}$) depends on the sample size n. It is easy to see that as n increases (i.e. we take a larger sample), the variance of $\bar{X}$ gets smaller. That is, sample means are *less variable* than single values (individual observations) from the population. Indeed, as $n \to \infty$, Var($\bar{X}$) $\to 0$, and so the sample mean tends to the true value μ (the value we are trying to estimate). Hence the larger the sample size, the greater the accuracy in estimation (a good thing), but the greater the total data collection cost (a bad thing). As happens so often in life we face a *trade-off*, here between accuracy and cost.

Up to now, we have referred to the square root of the variance of a random variable as the standard deviation. In sampling theory, the square root of the variance of an estimator is called the *standard error*.

Standard error

The standard deviation of an estimator is called its **standard error**. For example, $\bar{X} \sim N(\mu, \sigma^2/n)$, so $\text{Var}(\bar{X}) = \sigma^2/n$, hence the standard deviation of $\bar{X}$, i.e. the standard error (S.E.), is

$$\text{S.E.}(\bar{X}) = \sqrt{\text{Var}(\bar{X})} = \sqrt{\frac{\sigma^2}{n}} = \frac{\sigma}{\sqrt{n}}.$$

Note that the standard error decreases as n increases.

To summarise, if $\bar{X}$ is the sample mean of a random sample of n values from $N(\mu, \sigma^2)$, then $\bar{X}$:

- is normally distributed
- has mean μ
- has variance σ^2/n and standard error $\sigma / \sqrt{n}$.

7.7.2 Central limit theorem

What if our sample is not from a normal distribution? For this, we can appeal to a remarkable mathematical result known as the central limit theorem (CLT). This concerns the sampling distribution of $\bar{X}$ when sampling from (nearly) *any* non-normal distribution. ('Nearly' because the CLT requires that the variance of the population distribution is finite. If it is not, the CLT does not hold – but such distributions are not common.)

Central limit theorem

When taking a random sample of size n from a non-normal population with finite mean μ and finite variance σ^2,

$$\bar{X} \sim N\left(\mu, \frac{\sigma^2}{n}\right)$$

approximately, as $n \to \infty$.

So the difference between sampling from normal and non-normal populations is that $\bar{X}$ is *exactly* normally distributed in the former case, but only *approximately* so in the latter case. The approximation is reasonable when n is at least 30, as a rule of thumb. Note that, because this is an *asymptotic* approximation (i.e. as $n \to \infty$), the larger n is, the better the normal approximation.

We can use standardisation to compute probabilities involving $\bar{X}$, but we must remember to divide by $\sigma / \sqrt{n}$, rather than σ, since the variance of $\bar{X}$ is σ^2/n, that is, we have

$$Z = \frac{\bar{X} - \mu}{\sigma / \sqrt{n}} \sim N(0,1).$$

How large is 'large *n*'?

The larger the sample size n, the better the normal approximation provided by the CLT is. In practice, we have various rules of thumb for what is 'large enough' for the approximation to be 'accurate enough'. This also depends on the population distribution of X. For example:

- for symmetric distributions, even small n is enough
- for very skewed distributions, a larger n is required.

For many distributions, $n \geq 30$ is sufficient for the approximation to be reasonably accurate.

Example 7.8

In the first case, we simulate random samples of sizes

$$n = 1, 5, 10, 30, 100 \text{ and } 1000$$

from the Exp(0.25) distribution (i.e. the exponential distribution with $\lambda = 0.25$, for which $E(X) = \mu = 1/\lambda = 1/0.25 = 4$ and $\text{Var}(X) = \sigma^2 = 1/\lambda^2 = 1/(0.25)^2 = 16$; see Appendix B). This is clearly a skewed distribution, as shown by the histogram for $n = 1$ in Figure 7.12.

Ten thousand independent random samples of each size were generated. Histograms of the values of $\bar{X}$ in these random samples are shown in Figure 7.12. Each plot also shows the pdf of the approximating normal distribution, $N(\mu, \sigma^2/n) = N(4, 16/n)$. The normal approximation is reasonably good already for $n = 30$, very good for $n = 100$, and practically perfect for $n = 1000$.

Example 7.9

In the second case, we simulate 10,000 independent random samples of sizes

$$n = 1, 10, 30, 50, 100 \text{ and } 1000$$

from the Bernoulli(0.2) distribution (i.e. the Bernoulli distribution with $\pi = 0.2$, for which $E(X) = \mu = \pi = 0.2$ and $\text{Var}(X) = \sigma^2 = \pi(1 - \pi) = 0.2 \times 0.8 = 0.16$).

Here the distribution of X itself is not even continuous, and has only two possible values, 0 and 1. Nevertheless, the sampling distribution of $\bar{X}$ can be very well approximated by the normal distribution, when n is large enough, that is, by $N(\mu, \sigma^2/n) = N(0.2, 0.16/n)$.

Note that since here $X_i = 1$ or $X_i = 0$ for all i, $\bar{X} = \sum_{i=1}^{n} X_i / n = m/n$, where m is the number of observations for which $X_i = 1$. In other words, $\bar{X}$ is the *sample proportion* of the occurrence of $X = 1$.

The normal approximation is clearly very bad for small n, but reasonably good already for $n = 50$, as shown by the histograms in Figure 7.13.

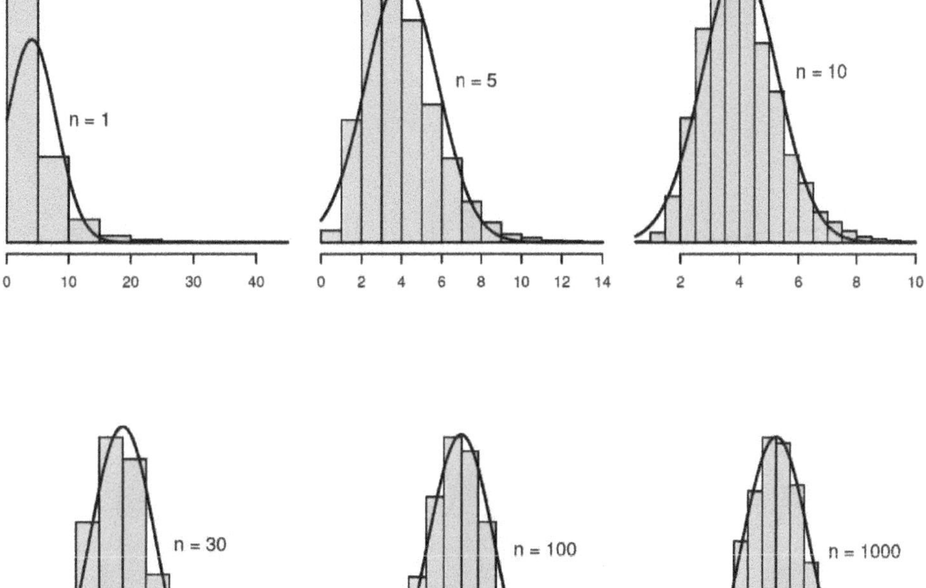

Figure 7.12 Sampling distributions of $\bar{X}$ for various n when sampling from the Exp(0.25) distribution.

7.7.3 Sample size effect

Figure 7.14 shows the sampling distribution of $\bar{X}$ for different sample sizes. As expected, the larger the sample size, the narrower and higher the peak, so that the effect of the sample size on the distribution of $\bar{X}$ is clear – a larger sample size leads to greater precision. However, note that a sample size of $n = 1$ (i.e. just a single observation) gives no extra information whatsoever about the variability or spread within the population being sampled because, for $n = 1$,

$$\text{Var}(\bar{X}) = \frac{\sigma^2}{n} = \frac{\sigma^2}{1} = \sigma^2,$$

that is, we end up with the variance of the original population, σ^2.

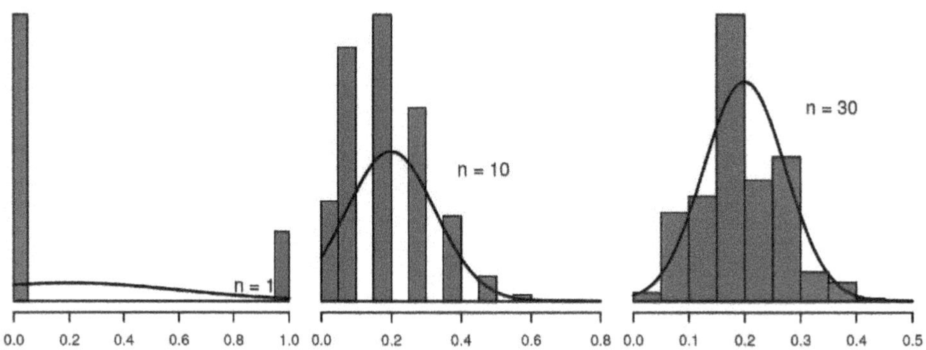

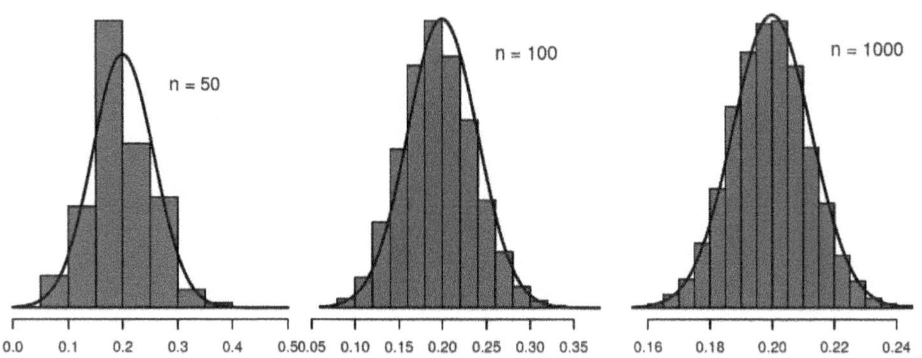

Figure 7.13 Sampling distributions of $\bar{X}$ for various n when sampling from the Bernoulli(0.2) distribution.

7.7.4 Modifications for finite populations

If sampling is *without replacement* from a finite population of size N, then it is immediately apparent that when $n = N$ (i.e. when the 'sample' *is* the population), the standard error of $\bar{X}$ has to be 0, not $\sigma / \sqrt{N}$, because we get the true value of the mean, not an estimate (since $\bar{x} = \mu$). A little thought shows that this is the extreme case of a more general rule. As $n \to N$, the smaller the standard error should be, compared to the one given by the formula for infinite populations. (Recall our previous hand-waving assumption that the population is 'large enough' to be treated as infinite.)

So, in this case, we ought in principle to use a better, more general, formula for the variance (hence standard error) of $\bar{X}$ taking into account the sampling fraction, which recall is n/N.

Finite population correction factor

When sampling n observations without replacement from a population of size N, we have

$$\mathrm{Var}(\bar{X}) = \frac{\sigma^2}{n}\left(1 - \frac{n}{N}\right)$$

and

$$\text{S.E.}(\bar{X}) = \frac{\sigma}{\sqrt{n}} \times \sqrt{1 - \frac{n}{N}}.$$

The factor $1 - n/N$ is known as the **finite population correction factor** (FPCF). If $n < 0.1N$, then the FPCF can be ignored as it is negligible.

The FPCF is negligible if the sample size is small relative to the population size, which justifies our treatment of 'large' populations as infinite for practical purposes. Therefore, in such situations we can ignore the FPCF. However, for 'small' populations, the FPCF adjustment should be used.

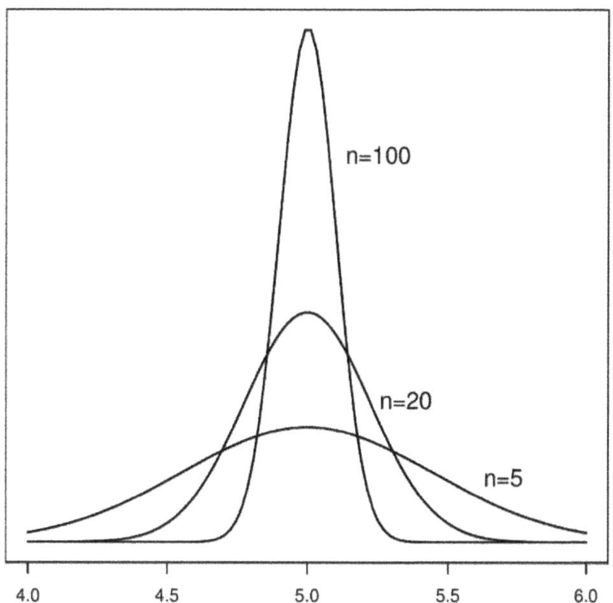

Figure 7.14 Sampling distributions of $\bar{X}$ when sampling from $N(5, 1)$.

Example 7.10

Suppose $X \sim N(5, 1)$, so that $\mu = 5$ and $\sigma^2 = 1$. Then

$$\bar{X} \sim N\left(\mu, \frac{\sigma^2}{n}\right) = N\left(5, \frac{1}{n}\right).$$

Figure 7.14 shows the sampling distribution of $\bar{X}$ for $n = 5$, $n = 20$ and $n = 100$. Note how all three sampling distributions are centred on 5, since

(Continued)

$E(\bar{X}) = E(X) = \mu = 5,$

while the sampling variance decreases as n increases since

$$\text{Var}(\bar{X}) = \frac{\text{Var}(X)}{n} = \frac{\sigma^2}{1} = \frac{1}{n}.$$

7.8 SAMPLING DISTRIBUTION OF THE SAMPLE PROPORTION

We often want to estimate a (population) *proportion*, π – for example, in surveys of consumer attitudes. Consider a poll in which we investigate consumers' perceptions of a brand. We ask, 'Do you have a positive perception of brand X?', to which the n respondents each answer 'yes' or 'no'. If r people respond 'yes', then the sample proportion, p, who have a positive perception is $p = r/n$. This is our point estimate of the true proportion of all consumers in the population, π, with a positive perception of brand X.

Obviously, we do not ask the same person more than once, so for a small population of size N (or for a sample size n which was large relative to N) we would need to consider the sampling fraction n/N, via the FPCF. However, in general, we will assume that the population is large enough to be regarded as infinite for practical purposes.

Let the random variable R denote the *total* number of 'favourable' responses in a random sample of size n, that is, those answering 'yes' to the survey question. Hence

$$R \sim \text{Bin}(n, \pi) \approx N(n\pi, n\pi(1 - \pi)),$$

where the approximation is justified subject to the conditions on n and N outlined above. Although this is an example of the normal approximation to the binomial, we will *not* worry about the continuity correction for proportions.

Let the random variable $P = R/n$ be the sample proportion. Note that the sample proportion is a special case of the sample mean, $P = \bar{X} = R/n$, where $R = \sum_{i=1}^{n} X_i$, where the X_i are binary (i.e. 0 or 1) for $i = 1, 2, \ldots, n$. Hence

$$\text{E}(P) = \text{E}\left(\frac{R}{n}\right) = \frac{1}{n}\text{E}(R) = \frac{1}{n}n\pi = \pi$$

and

$$\text{Var}(P) = \text{Var}\left(\frac{R}{n}\right) = \frac{1}{n^2}\text{Var}(R) = \frac{1}{n^2}n\pi(1-\pi) = \frac{\pi(1-\pi)}{n}.$$

Sampling distribution of the sample proportion

The sample proportion, P, is the estimator of the population proportion, π, such that

$$P \sim N\left(\pi, \frac{\pi(1-\pi)}{n}\right)$$

approximately, as $n \to \infty$, by the central limit theorem.

Note that P is a special case of $\bar{X}$ when X_i = Bernoulli(π), that is, when all observations are binary.

7.9 SAMPLING DISTRIBUTION OF THE SAMPLE VARIANCE

During the above discussions about $\bar{X}$ and P, we derived their respective sampling distributions as being (approximately) normally distributed. For example, application of the CLT meant the distribution of $\bar{X}$ was approximately normal *regardless* of the non-normal population distribution.

We briefly look beyond the population mean to consider the population variance, σ^2. Intuitively, we would wish to use the sample variance,

$$S^2 = \frac{1}{n-1}\sum_{i=1}^{n}(X_i - \bar{X})^2$$

(see Section 2.6.1) to estimate σ^2, since it is the sample counterpart. However, the sampling distribution of S^2 is sensitive to the underlying distribution from which the sample is drawn.

It can be shown that the sample variance, S^2, for a random sample of size n from $N(\mu, \sigma^2)$ has a known distribution with mean σ^2 and variance $2\sigma^4/(n-1)$, that is,

$$E(S^2) = \sigma^2 \text{ and } \operatorname{Var}(S^2) = \frac{2\sigma^4}{n-1}.$$

However, in almost all circumstances we are only going to want to use the sampling distribution of S^2 when we do not know the true variance σ^2, and that will mean that we cannot calculate $2\sigma^4/(n-1)$.

We can, however, remove the dependence of the standard error of S^2 on the unknown parameter σ^2 very simply, namely by taking a simple function of S^2

$$\frac{(n-1)S^2}{\sigma^2} \sim \chi^2_{n-1}$$

whose sampling distribution is a **chi-squared distribution** with $n-1$ *degrees of freedom*, denoted by χ^2_{n-1}. The degrees of freedom is the *parameter* of the chi-squared distribution.

In general, if $X \sim \chi^2_k$, then E(X) = k and Var = $2k$. Therefore, the sampling distribution of $(n-1)S^2/\sigma^2$ has mean $n-1$ and variance $2(n-1)$, that is,

$$E\left(\frac{(n-1)S^2}{\sigma^2}\right) = n-1 \quad \text{and} \quad \operatorname{Var}\left(\frac{(n-1)S^2}{\sigma^2}\right) = 2(n-1).$$

Hence for different sample sizes we will obtain fundamentally different distributions, since different values of n (and, therefore, of the degrees of freedom $k = n - 1$) affect the *shape* of the χ^2 distribution. (Compare this idea with the normal distribution, which always has a bell curve shape, regardless of the values of μ and σ^2.) Figure 7.15 shows the chi-squared distribution for various degrees of freedom, k.

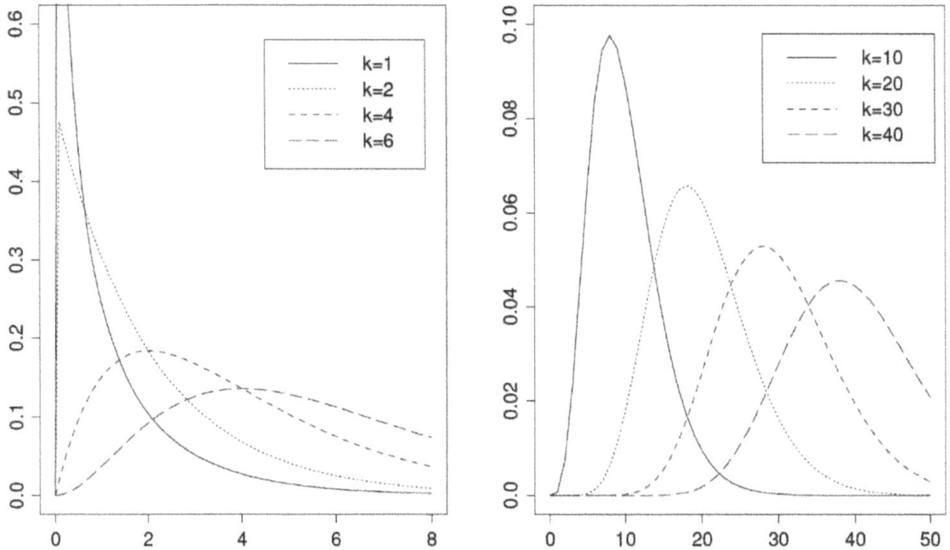

Figure 7.15 The chi-squared distribution for various degrees of freedom, k.

The χ^2 distribution can be used to find the probability of a sample variance lying in a given interval using the `CHISQ.DIST.RT` Excel function.

Excel function: `CHISQ.DIST.RT`

`=CHISQ.DIST.RT(x, deg_freedom)` returns the upper-tail probability of a chi-squared distribution, where

- `x` is the value of the chi-squared variable
- `deg_freedom` is the degrees of freedom.

Example 7.11

Suppose a machine is calibrated to produce components according to a $N(12, 2)$ distribution. What is the probability that the sample variance for a random sample of size $n = 15$ will exceed 6? Note that, conditional on $\sigma^2 = 2$, a sample variance exceeding 6 might lead us to incorrectly conclude that the machine produces components with too much heterogeneity, that is, we think σ^2 is larger than it really is. We have

$$P(S^2 > 6) = P\left(\frac{(15-1)S^2}{2} > \frac{(15-1)\times 6}{2}\right)$$
$$= P(X > 42)$$
$$= 0.00124$$

where $X \sim \chi^2_{14}$. Note this exact probability has been obtained using `=CHISQ.DIST.RT(42,14)`. Since this probability is *very* small (around 0.01%), it is *very* unlikely that we would observe such a large sample variance *if* the machine was calibrated correctly. Hence if we *did* observe a sample variance exceeding 6 we would rationally conclude that the machine calibration is wrong and seek to remedy it, since the probability of such an event is so small if $\sigma^2 = 2$. This logic links to hypothesis testing in Chapter 10.

7.10 CHAPTER OVERVIEW

This chapter has discussed different sampling techniques that may be employed when sampling from a population. Divided between non-random and random methods, the likely representativeness of different types of samples has been considered. The less representative the sample, the greater the sampling error is likely to be. Also, central to much work in statistical inference is the concept of a sampling distribution, whereby the values of a descriptive statistic – such as the sample mean – vary from (random) sample to (random) sample. We have looked at the sampling distribution of $\bar{X}$, noting its mean, variance and sensitivity to n. We briefly also considered sample proportions and sample variances. Our work in Chapters 9 and 10 will draw heavily on this chapter's material.

7.11 KEY VOCABULARY

Census
Central limit theorem
Chi-squared distribution
Cluster sampling
Convenience sampling
Estimate
Estimator
Finite population correction factor
Judgemental sampling
Member
Multi-stage sampling
Non-random sampling
(Pseudo-)random number generator
Quota sampling
Random sampling
Sample
Sample proportion
Sampling (design)
Sampling distribution
Sampling (estimation) error
Sampling fraction
Sampling frame
Sampling interval
Sampling unit
Sampling variance
Simple random sample
Snowball sampling
Standard error
Stratified sampling
Systematic sampling
Target population

7.12 EXERCISES

7.12.1 Test your understanding

1. What are the main considerations in sampling design?
2. Define each of the following terms: 'target population', 'members', 'sampling unit', 'census', 'sample' and 'sampling error'.
3. What factors determine whether a census or a sample is preferred?
4. What are the characteristics of non-random sampling techniques, and when would these be used in practice?
5. What are the characteristics of random sampling techniques, and when would these be used in practice?
6. Outline the features of a convenience sample, and provide a practical example when you would consider this the most appropriate sampling technique.
7. Outline the features of a judgemental sample, and provide a practical example when you would consider this the most appropriate sampling technique.
8. Outline the features of a quota sample, and provide a practical example when you would consider this the most appropriate sampling technique.
9. Outline the features of a snowball sample, and provide a practical example when you would consider this the most appropriate sampling technique.
10. Outline the features of a simple random sample, and provide a practical example when you would consider this the most appropriate sampling technique.
11. Outline the features of a systematic sample, and provide a practical example when you would consider this the most appropriate sampling technique.
12. Outline the features of a stratified sample, and provide a practical example when you would consider this the most appropriate sampling technique.
13. Outline the features of a cluster sample, and provide a practical example when you would consider this the most appropriate sampling technique.
14. In what sense are the techniques of quota sampling and stratified sampling similar? In what sense are they different?
15. What is a pseudo-random number generator?
16. Which Excel function could be used to select a simple random sample? Why is this function appropriate?
17. Why is a representative sample desirable, and to what extent do different sampling techniques achieve representative samples?
18. When conducting a survey, does the choice of contact method matter?
19. Explain what a sampling distribution is.
20. Distinguish between a (point) estimator and a (point) estimate.
21. What is a sampling fraction, and to what extent does this affect the sampling variance?
22. What is a standard error?
23. What is the sampling distribution of the sample mean, $\bar{X}$, when:
    (a) the random sample is drawn from a population with a $N(\mu, \sigma^2)$ distribution?
    (b) the random sample is not drawn from a population with a normal distribution?
24. How large does the sample size need to be for the central limit theorem to provide a good approximation to the sampling distribution of $\bar{X}$? 'Well, James, it depends' may feature in your answer, but explain what it depends on!
25. What is the purpose of the finite population correction factor?
26. 'The sample proportion is just a sample mean.' Do you agree? Briefly justify your view.

27 What is the (approximate?) sampling distribution of the sample proportion?

28 'All sampling distributions are normal distributions'. Do you agree? Briefly justify your view.

29 A random variable, X, can take the values 1, 2 and 3, each with equal probability. List all possible samples of size 2 which may be chosen when order matters, *without* replacement, from this population, and hence construct the sampling distribution of the sample mean, $\bar{X}$.

30 A perfectly machined regular tetrahedral (pyramid-shaped) die has four faces labelled 1 to 4. It is thrown twice onto a level surface and after each throw the number on the face which is downward is recorded. If the recorded values are x_1 and x_2, when order matters, then the observed sample mean is $\bar{x} = (x_1 + x_2)/2$. Write out the sampling distribution of the sample mean as a random quantity over repeated double throws.

31 Consider the population below with $N = 4$ elements:

A	B	C	D
3	6	9	12

(a) Calculate the population mean and variance.

(b) Write down the sampling distribution of the sample mean for samples of size $n = 2$ drawn without replacement, where order does not matter.

(c) Using the result in (b), calculate the mean of the sampling distribution.

(d) Using the result in (b), calculate the variance of the sampling distribution.

32 The weights of a large group of manufactured components have mean 8.2 kg and standard deviation 2.2 kg. What is the probability that a random selection of 80 components will have a mean weight between 8.3 kg and 8.4 kg? State any assumptions you make.

33 A random sample of 25 audits is to be taken from a company's total audits, and the average value of these audits is to be calculated.

(a) Explain what is meant by the sampling distribution of this average and discuss its relationship to the population mean.

(b) Is it reasonable to assume that this sampling distribution is normally distributed?

(c) If the population of all audits has a mean of £54 and a standard deviation of £10, find the probability that:

(i) the sample mean will be greater than £60

(ii) the sample mean will be within 5% of the population mean.

34 A country is about to hold a referendum about leaving the European Union. A survey of a random sample of adult citizens of the country is conducted. In the sample, n respondents say that they plan to vote in the referendum. These n respondents are then asked whether they plan to vote 'Yes' or 'No'. Define $X = 1$ if such a person plans to vote 'Yes', and $X = 0$ if such a person plans to vote 'No'.

Suppose that in the whole population 45% of those people who plan to vote are currently planning to vote 'Yes', and hence the referendum result would show a majority *opposing* leaving the European Union.

(a) Let $\bar{X} = \sum_{i=1}^{n} X_i / n$ denote the proportion of the n voters in the sample who plan to vote 'Yes'. What is the central limit theorem approximation of the sampling distribution of $\bar{X}$ here?

(b) If there are $n = 50$ likely voters in the sample, what is the probability that $\bar{X} > 0.5$? (Such an opinion poll would suggest a majority *supporting* leaving the European Union in the referendum.)

(c) How large should n be so that there is less than a 1% chance that $\bar{X} > 0.5$ in the random sample? (This means less than a 1% chance of the opinion poll *incorrectly* predicting a majority *supporting* leaving the European Union in the referendum.)

35 Suppose that we plan to take a random sample of size n from a normal distribution with mean μ and standard deviation $\sigma = 2$.

(a) Suppose $\mu = 4$ and $n = 20$.

(i) What is the probability that $\bar{X}$ is greater than 5?

(ii) What is the probability that $\bar{X}$ is less than 3?

(iii) What is $P(|\bar{X} - \mu| \leq 1)$ in this case?

(b) How large should n be in order that $P(|\bar{X} - \mu| \leq 0.5) \geq 0.95$ for every possible value of μ?

(c) It is claimed that the true value of μ is 5 in a population. A random sample of size $n = 100$ is collected from this population, and the mean for this sample is $\bar{x} = 5.8$. Based on the result in (b), what would you conclude from this value of $\bar{X}$?

7.12.2 Practice with Excel

Head over to the companion website for Excel examples and screencasts!

8

OPINION RESEARCH

Chapter contents

Chapter level: ***Beginner***

Source: Photo by Tumisu via Pixabay.

Key concepts

- Measurement
- Scaling
- Itemised rating scales

Chapter value

To better understand customers' opinions, we must ask them, using a well-designed survey.

Key takeaway

Itemised ratings scales are invaluable, but their design involves many trade-offs.

Chapter outline

'Share your feedback'. Survey fatigue is common, yet companies always want to better understand their customers. What is going well? What are the pain points? To get a proper sense of the overall customer journey, from awareness to loyalty, we typically need to ask people to respond to our survey questions. Designed well, good survey questions result in useful data for analysis.

Data on consumers can come in two broad types - *behavioural data* generated by day-to-day activities of consumers, such as transactions in their (digital) shopping baskets, and *attitudinal data* which is concerned more with the tastes and preferences of consumers.

While attitudes could be inferred from behavioural data, *ceteris paribus* it is preferable to collect such data explicitly through well-designed surveys. This chapter will consider some of the decisions to take into account when designing surveys to ensure the data generated is useful for analysis. A poorly designed survey may simply return useless data and be a waste of time, resources and effort.

Learning outcomes

After completing this chapter, you should be able to:

- explain the terms 'measurement' and 'scaling'
- explain the different levels of measurement, including how these may be analysed
- design survey questions using appropriate scaling techniques.

Motivational case: Doughy pizza sales knead help!

Pizzalicious is a supplier of popular pizzas. A few months ago it introduced a 'new and improved' recipe for its pizza bases following a positive response in blind taste test trials, and decided to rebrand this range as Pizzalush. However, it has noticed a fall in sales since the launch of the new recipe. The company is unsure whether the dip in sales is due to consumers not approving of the recipe change, the rebranding, or to other factors (or possibly a combination of these).

The company has commissioned a market research agency to target people who have purchased its products to survey their opinions on the new recipe pizzas and rebranding.

How should they design suitable survey questions to better understand the drop in sales?

8.1 INTRODUCTION

We begin by covering two main aspects, namely the fundamentals of *measurement* and *scaling*, followed by *comparative* and *non-comparative scaling*. Ahead of conducting multivariate analysis in Chapter 11 and beyond, it is extremely important to be clear on the different levels of measurement because the appropriateness, indeed the validity, of particular statistical methods will be dependent on the level of measurement of the variables that we have.

8.2 MEASUREMENT AND SCALING

Measurement is the assignment of numbers to characteristics of individuals (or objects) which adhere to pre-specified rules that are standardised and applied uniformly over time. In most business cases involving opinion research these individuals will be customers, ex-customers, prospective customers etc. in business-to-consumer settings, or representatives of companies in business-to-business settings. Here these individuals will be respondents to our market research survey. Observations could include demographic variables such as their age, gender or income group, or alternatively collecting attitudinal data such as on their preferences and tastes for different brands or products.

We require a *one-to-one correspondence* between the numbers and the characteristics being measured. So if, say, we were to have a categorical variable (such as age group) and we introduce a numerical coding for the different levels, there needs to be a one-to-one correspondence such that each time we observe the same level the same numerical value is assigned to it. If we undertake a *longitudinal* study (i.e. repeat observations over time), the measurement rules need to remain unchanged (with ideally exactly the same questions asked) so any *changes* can easily be detected, such as in brand-switching studies.

Example 8.1

As part of their market research, suppose Pizzalicious sought a respondent's age (as pizza preferences may vary by age). Given that age can be a sensitive matter for some people, if we asked for their exact age we would likely encounter *non-response*. By providing a set of mutually exclusive and collectively exhaustive (MECE) age *groups* this is less revealing of a respondent's exact age, so is more likely to elicit a response. Better to know someone's age group, than not know their age at all!
What is your age?

- Below 18
- 18-29
- 30-44
- 45-59
- 60+
- Prefer not to say.

Note the inclusion of 'Prefer not to say' to accommodate those even unwilling to reveal their age group.
In terms of assigning numeric codes to these response alternatives, it would seem appropriate to code as follows:

- Below 18 → 1
- 18-29 → 2

- 30-44 → 3
- 45-59 → 4
- 60+ → 5
- Prefer not to say → 6

albeit we should be careful not to incorrectly use the '6' responses in calculations. Here '6' indicates non-response.

Note that we are unable to distinguish the precise ages of respondents reporting the same age group. This is the trade-off we face between *response rate* and *granularity of data*.

Scaling involves creating a continuum. If working with a continuous variable, this could be over the real line, $\mathbb{R} = (-\infty, \infty)$. However, for many things which we may measure in practice, we might restrict ourselves to *positive* random variables whereby the characteristic being observed cannot take a negative value, such as income or age. So, for a continuum, rather than considering the whole real line we may just consider some subset of it, such as positive values, $[0, \infty)$. Examples of situations when we may encounter negative values are limited, such as *rates of change* or *percentage changes* over a particular time period, in which case values in percentage points could be $[-100, \infty)$, in principle. For example, if you were looking at change in income such that you suddenly became redundant, your income then goes down by 100% (ignoring any unemployment benefits).

For things like attitudes where perhaps the choice of scale is somewhat subjective, we could consider, for example:

$$1, 2, 3, 4, 5 \text{ or } -5, -4, -3, -2, -1.$$

Clearly, the former is more intuitive due to the use of positive values!

The extremes of the scale are called the anchors of the scale, such that there is some description about what those anchors represent, for example,

Strongly disagree	...	...	Strongly agree
1			5

so from 'strongly disagree' to 'strongly agree', and need not necessarily be a continuum. Care should be taken over the descriptors used for the anchors. Wording that is too extreme, such as 'completely agree' or 'absolutely agree' may be off-putting for some respondents, that is, there can be an aversion to extremist labels, reducing the likely response alternatives chosen by respondents, and hence limiting the variation in the data obtained (a bad thing).

How many points should such a scale have? Odd or even? Few or many? Well, James, it depends! Consider the choice of odd or even first. Provided the scale is *balanced* (i.e. symmetric), such as

Strongly disagree	Disagree	Neither agree nor disagree	Agree	Strongly agree
1	2	3	4	5

where 'strongly disagree' offsets 'strongly agree' etc., an odd number of points permits a *neutral response option* (the 'neither agree nor disagree' option above). If a neutral response was desirable, or considered realistic, then an odd number of points would be favourable. However, if it was felt a respondent *must* have a view – even if only a mildly positive or mildly negative sentiment – then an even number of points would be a *forced* scale, as it forces a non-neutral response, for example

Strongly disagree	Disagree	Slightly disagree	Slightly agree	Agree	Strongly agree
1	2	3	4	5	6

Turning to the choice of 'few or many', the benefit of fewer points is simplicity – you're giving the respondent fewer choices, making it easier to choose. However, there is always a trade-off whenever we gain simplicity – we typically lose some detail, and there is some loss of information. With a greater number of response options, this can generate greater *granularity* and greater *variation* in the answers which people might give. For example, all people who might answer '1' on a 1–5 scale would be indistinguishable from each other, yet on a 1–7 scale, say, the original '1' responses would likely be distributed across '1' and '2', making these (marginally) distinct.

Hence the number of scale categories is an important decision when constructing scales. We want as much variation in our observed variables as possible because the greater the variation, the easier it is to 'discriminate' (in a good sense) between individuals in that we recognise that consumers vary a great deal, and we may ultimately wish to segment our market and identify different groups of consumers. The more granular the information collected, the easier it is to segment. Chapter 18 discusses a technique called *cluster analysis* which can be used for market segmentation purposes.

8.3 LEVELS OF MEASUREMENT

A questionnaire will typically comprise several questions, resulting in the collection of multiple characteristics. So 20 questions, say, would produce information on 20 characteristics. For our purposes we will only consider structured questions which possess a fixed set of response alternatives, from which numerical data can easily be derived, as opposed to open-ended *unstructured* questions which pose challenges for coding responses and subsequent quantitative analysis (an example would be free-text comments).

Upon receipt of *multiple* characteristics, we will be able to perform various *multivariate* analyses. How these techniques are applied will depend on the levels of measurement of the variables (whether they are categorical or measurable) which will impact the kinds of statistical methods which can be applied to them. Recall that Chapter 2 introduced the measurement levels of *nominal*, *ordinal* and *measurable*.

8.3.1 Nominal variables

Note that with nominal-scale variables, we are extremely limited in the kinds of statistical analysis we can perform, such as frequency counts, percentages and modal categories. *Ceteris paribus*, that's a bad thing because we would like to be able to apply the most sophisticated statistical routines available to us, but some variables are inevitably nominal in nature, such as gender (even with multiple gender identities), or if we were conducting an anonymised survey such that a serial number was attached to each respondent – though numeric, ID numbers 0001, 0002, 0003, etc. are simply used to distinguish the different respondents.

8.3.2 Ordinal variables

Ordinal variables are also categorical, but with rank ordering, such as the age group variable in Example 8.1. All of the permissible statistical techniques applicable to nominal data extend to ordinal data, but we can also extend it to looking at percentiles, quartiles and also the median, but not the mean.

8.3.3 Measurable variables

For measurable variables, valid statistical techniques now extend to the mean and standard deviation. So if we have a simple univariate dataset, we can calculate the sample mean, $\bar{x}$, and the sample standard deviation, s, where the values have real-world meaning. We can use the sample mean as a point estimate of the population mean, μ; similarly, the sample standard deviation serves as a point estimate of the population standard deviation, σ.

Measurable variables can be split into those on an interval scale and those on a ratio scale, for which the latter has a *fixed zero point*. This means that a value of zero indicates absence of the attribute, and also that the ratio of two non-zero values has an interpretable meaning.

Example 8.2

Supermarkets could monitor weather forecasts due to the associations between temperatures and food/drink shopping habits. Historic weather data can be analysed alongside product and sales information to predict consumption patterns based on temperature forecasts. For example, a heatwave would increase demand for foods eaten outdoors, such as barbecue food and salads.

While temperature is measurable, is it interval or ratio? While conventions vary globally, temperature is usually reported in either degrees Celsius or degrees Fahrenheit. In either case a temperature of '0 degrees' does not mean an absence of temperature, regardless of unit type. 0°C is cold, while 0°F is very cold!

Let's work in Celsius. Suppose on 1 February it was 10°C in a location, while on 1 March it was 20°C. Taking the ratio, we have

$$\frac{20°\text{C}}{10°\text{C}} = 2 \text{ or } \frac{10°\text{C}}{20°\text{C}} = 0.5.$$

Does it make sense to say that 1 March was twice as hot as 1 February, or that 1 February was half as hot as 1 March? Clearly, no!

Suppose on 1 April it was 30°C. Similarly, it makes no sense to say that 1 April is three times as hot as 1 February. However, the 10-degree differential from month to month is fixed, so the increase in temperature month-on-month is equal. Hence temperature has an *interval* level of measurement.

(Continued)

Note that any positive linear transformation of the form $y = a + bx$ preserves the scale properties. For example, in the case of Celsius-to-Fahrenheit conversion, the transformations are (with obvious notation)

$$F = 32 + \frac{9}{5}C, \text{ or equivalently } C = -32 + \frac{5}{9}F.$$

Example 8.3

Suppose supermarkets wanted to research any association between product sales and age. While age is measurable, is it *interval* or *ratio*?

Consider two customers: one is 20, the other 40. Taking the ratio, we have

$$\frac{40}{20} = 2 \quad \text{or} \quad \frac{20}{40} = 0.5.$$

Here it *does* make sense to say the 40-year-old is twice as old as the 20-year-old, equivalently that the 20-year-old is half the age of the 40-year-old. Also, if someone had an age of 0 (i.e. at the exact moment of birth), then that would indicate absence of the attribute - the person's life is just beginning. Hence age has a *ratio* level of measurement.

Note that only proportionate transformations of the form $y = bx$, where $b > 0$, are allowed.

Table 8.1 summarises the basics of measurement levels.

Table 8.1 Summary of measurement levels, their properties and business examples.

Measurement level	Main properties	Business examples
Nominal	Identification and classification	Name, gender product type
Ordinal	Rank-ordered categories	Rank order of brands or television channels
Interval	Differences between values meaningful, no fixed zero point	Attitude scores, indices
Ratio	Fixed zero point, ratios have meaning	Market share, sales, income

8.4 SCALING TECHNIQUES

In market research survey design we often want to ask questions that require a response on a *scale*. Here we consider:

- comparative scales
- non-comparative scales.

In a comparative scale there is a direct comparison of stimuli, such as brands. We ask respondents to report their preferences for one brand over another. So it will be a comparison between these stimuli to say which one is strictly preferred to another (the respondent could be indifferent though). There will be a *rank order* of these stimuli objects, giving rise to data with an *ordinal* level of measurement. As seen above, this somewhat restricts us in terms of the statistical analysis we can perform on such data.

For a non-comparative scale the brands would be considered by the respondents such that they are rated independently of one another along some scale, giving rise to an *interval* level of measurement (rather than ratio, as typically there won't be a fixed zero point). So, from an analytical perspective, since we tend to favour interval- or ratio-level variables over nominal or ordinal ones, then on that basis alone, we would have a preference for non-comparative scales.

8.4.1 Comparative scales

Paired comparison scaling

As the name suggests, in a paired comparison scale a pair of objects (such as brands) is being compared according to some criterion (such as intention to purchase). For example, let's say we've got different brands of clothing. Do you prefer brand A or brand B? Which one would you be more inclined to purchase? Which brand are you more aware of? So, we need to clearly define what this criterion is.

Suppose we have n brands. How many paired comparisons are required? Consider an $n \times n$ matrix (i.e. with n rows and n columns)

$$\begin{pmatrix} x_{11} & x_{12} & \cdots & x_{1n} \\ x_{21} & x_{22} & \cdots & x_{2n} \\ \vdots & \vdots & \cdots & \vdots \\ x_{n1} & x_{n2} & \cdots & x_{nn} \end{pmatrix}$$

such that

$$x_{ij} = \begin{cases} 1 & \text{if object } i \text{ is preferred to object } j \\ 0 & \text{otherwise.} \end{cases}$$

Clearly, if we know x_{ij} then we know x_{ji} since it is the same two objects being compared. Saying i is preferred to j is equivalent to saying that j is less preferred to i. Also, the entries on the *leading diagonal*, the x_{ii} entries for $i = 1, 2, \ldots, n$, are not required since it is pointless to compare an object with itself.

So, in total the matrix has $n \times n = n^2$ entries, from which we subtract the n elements on the leading diagonal, then of the remaining off-diagonal elements we only need half of these (knowing x_{ij} means we know x_{ji}), resulting in

$$\frac{n^2 - n}{2} = \frac{n(n-1)}{2}$$

paired comparisons.

Note that the more brands we are asking respondents to compare (i.e. as n increases), the greater the number of paired comparisons required, which could be very time-consuming to get respondents to evaluate. This is due to the opportunity cost of time, and time is the number one reason for non-response in surveys. So, *ceteris paribus*, it's helpful to have paired comparisons on a greater number of brands because we then have more data, more information and hence insights that we can hopefully discover. However, if we make n too large, we are likely to dissuade the respondent from completing all of the $n(n - 1)/2$ paired comparisons. So probably $n \approx 10$ would likely be the maximum number, although even this would still require $10 \times 9/2 = 45$ paired comparisons!

We are assuming *transitivity* of preferences, a term which you may have covered in a microeconomics course setting. Suppose someone responded that for them brand A was strictly preferred to brand B based on whatever criterion was specified, and also that brand B was strictly preferred to brand C. Then it must be that brand A is strictly preferred to brand C. However, if the respondent said they also strictly preferred brand C to brand A, then we have a *violation of transitivity*. Indeed, if we detected this violation of transitivity in all of the responses from a particular respondent, then this would call into question the *integrity* of those responses. Consequently, we may perhaps delete that specific respondent's answers altogether, because it cannot be the case that you prefer A to B, B to C, and C to A. This would be irrational!

Example 8.4

Pizzalicious decides to run a paired comparison scaling survey of five pizza brands, including its old and new brand names.

For each pair of pizza brands, indicate which one of the pair you prefer. (An empty grid would then appear for the responses.)

Suppose the responses produced the following results.

	Pizzalicious	Pizzalush	Pizzapie	Pizza pro	Pizza yum	Total score
Pizzalicious	–	1	1	1	1	**4**
Pizzalush	–	–	0	0	0	**0**
Pizzapie	–	–	–	1	0	**1**
Pizza pro	–	–	–	–	1	**1**

Here a '1' indicates that the row brand is preferred to the column brand. Based on the respondent's answers, it is clear that they prefer the Pizzalicious brand over all others, including the new Pizzalush range. We also see that Pizzalush is the least preferred - indeed, all other brands are strictly preferred to it, suggesting an image problem.

Given the popularity of the original Pizzalicious brand, it's clear that something has negatively affected the perception of the Pizzalush brand. Further research would be needed to establish what this was.

8.4.2 Constant sum scaling

In constant sum scaling a constant sum of points must be allocated to a set of attributes, depending on the *relative importance* of those attributes to the respondent.

How many points should the respondent be endowed with? Should it be 10, 15, 50, 100? Well, James, it depends! The more points we give them, the more challenging the task, but we would have a more granular level of detail about just how much more preferred one attribute is relative to another.

One should also consider the contact method being used for this type of scale. For example, if this was conducted online, the computer could tell you your remaining balance of points to assign across the remaining attributes, such that there's no mental arithmetic required to ensure that the total points add up to the initial endowment. In contrast, if this was done in, say, a paper-based survey or done over the telephone, it would be (much) harder given the reliance on the respondent to perform mental arithmetic! Since mental arithmetic skills are likely to be generally lacking in the wider population, and especially if you have a very large number of points, the demands of the mental arithmetic to be performed would be far greater than if it was just 10 points being allocated. However, the fewer points you have, the fewer attributes you could ask the respondent to consider.

Example 8.5

Pizzalicious decides to use constant sum scaling to analyse consumer tastes and preferences towards pizzas (in general, not necessarily its own). Five attributes are considered, and suppose the table below reports the *average* number of points per attribute for three different consumer segments.

Attribute	Segment A	Segment B	Segment C
Price	15	61	16
Taste	18	11	8
Packaging	5	8	7
Nutrition value	48	11	6
Ease of preparation	14	9	63
Total	**100**	**100**	**100**

From the table we can *profile* the three segments based on the attribute that is most important to them. Clearly, segment A is the most health-conscious, due to the nutrition value having nearly 50% importance. Segment B seems to be formed of price-conscious consumers, given the importance of price to this group. Finally, segment C seems to value convenience above all else.

How could Pizzalicious make use of these results? Well, if we could also estimate the relative sizes of these segments, we would have a clear idea of the pizza consumer market and could try to position the Pizzalush brand for maximum appeal. For example, if segment C was dominant then emphasising the convenience factor of the brand (freezer storage, ease of cooking) could result in high(er) sales.

A reminder that Chapter 18 covers *cluster analysis* where we will consider in depth the issues of segmentation techniques.

8.4.3 Non-comparative scales

We shall consider three non-comparative scales:

- Likert scales
- Semantic differential scales
- Stapel scales.

Likert scales

A Likert scale is an itemised rating scale whereby attributes of interest are *rated* (note this is different from *ranking*).

Now, I'm sure you've seen or been asked to fill in questionnaires before, which will have a sort of grid format whereby you must report your level of agreement with various statements. Note the reference to *statements* rather than *questions*.

Strictly speaking, these choices have a rank order, so 'strongly agree' responses are from the most 'positive' people, while 'strongly disagree' responses are from the most 'negative' people, with differing degrees in between. We can assign numeric codes, such as '1 = strongly disagree' up to '5 = strongly agree'. Alternatively, in some cases we could reverse things round, so that '1 = strongly agree', and '5 = strongly disagree'. While the choice of coding doesn't really affect the respondent *per se*, for the person analysing the responses, they need to be clear about whether 1 was the best or worst answer!

Example 8.6

Pizzalicious could develop a series of Likert scale 'agree-disagree' statements to better understand attitudes to both the Pizzalicious and Pizzalush brands.

	Strongly disagree	Disagree	Neither agree nor disagree	Agree	Strongly agree
I regularly eat pizza	o	o	o	o	o
I eat pizza at home	o	o	o	o	o
I prefer to eat pizza at a restaurant	o	o	o	o	o
Eating pizza is healthy	o	o	o	o	o
I like to try different pizza toppings	o	o	o	o	o
Pizzalicious is a brand I trust	o	o	o	o	o
Pizzalicious is tasty	o	o	o	o	o
Pizzalush is a brand I trust	o	o	o	o	o
Pizzalush is tasty	o	o	o	o	o

If the survey was conducted online, these would be radio buttons (∘) and then with your mouse you would just click the appropriate response. In terms of consistency checks, if we have similar statements, then we might expect similar responses. If we had almost polar opposite responses for similar themed statements, this might call into question the reliability of the data collected.

Semantic differential scales

Semantic differential scales are *bipolar* scales, such that we have two poles (or ends) which are polar opposite adjectives. Often these are constructed as seven-point scales, and they are useful to assess brand image or product image.

Example 8.7

Pizzalicious wants to contrast the perceived image of the new Pizzalush range relative to its original name. It decides to use a semantic differential scale to achieve this.

Pizzalicious (and separately Pizzalush) is:

Tasty	—	—	—	—	—	—	—	Bland
Nutritious	—	—	—	—	—	—	—	Unhealthy
Trendy	—	—	—	—	—	—	—	Unfashionable
Value for money	—	—	—	—	—	—	—	Expensive
Popular	—	—	—	—	—	—	—	Unpopular

Comparing responses for both brand names would enable any significant differences to emerge. Note that Chapter 10 will introduce formal *hypothesis testing* to detect significant differences.

Stapel scales

Stapel scales are unipolar scales with 10 points, excluding a neutral point. These are useful for measuring attitudes, as well as images. We consider an example.

Example 8.8

Pizzalicious is interested in establishing which words consumers associate with its old and new brand names.

For each word below, indicate to what extent you feel the word describes the Pizzalicious (Pizzalush) brand. The more accurately you feel the word describes the brand, the higher the number you should choose; similarly, for words you feel do not accurately describe the brand, choose a negative number.

(Continued)

5	5	5	5	5	5	5
4	4	4	4	4	4	4
3	3	3	3	3	3	3
2	2	2	2	2	2	2
1	1	1	1	1	1	1
Tasty	**Convenient**	**Trendy**	**Healthy**	**Fair price**	**Filling**	**Stylish**
–1	–1	–1	–1	–1	–1	–1
–2	–2	–2	–2	–2	–2	–2
–3	–3	–3	–3	–3	–3	–3
–4	–4	–4	–4	–4	–4	–4
–5	–5	–5	–5	–5	–5	–5

Upon receiving survey responses, image perceptions can be established and the extent to which consumer perceptions differ from the intended perceptions quantified. Significant differences would suggest scope for developing an appropriate marketing message to 'correct' perceptions.

8.5 CHAPTER OVERVIEW

This chapter has considered aspects of opinion research. If we seek attitudinal data to better understand the tastes and preferences of our customers, this is best obtained directly through well-designed surveys. While designing a questionnaire is an art as much as a science, it is important to think about analytical considerations at the questionnaire design stage to ensure that the data collected adds value to a company. We have reviewed the different levels of measurement, and introduced some common scaling techniques. These have been framed in terms of a pizza supplier who is keen to understand the reason for a recent fall in sales, by better understanding consumers' attitudes towards pizza and their product's brand image.

8.6 KEY VOCABULARY

Anchor
Comparative scale
Constant sum scale
Interval scale
Itemised rating scale
Likert scale
Measurement
Non-comparative scale
Paired comparison scale
Ratio scale
Scaling
Semantic differential scale
Stapel scale
Structured questions

8.7 EXERCISES

8.7.1 Test your understanding

1 What is the difference between 'measurement' and 'scaling'?
2 In a survey, is it better to ask a respondent for their age or age group? Briefly justify your view.

3 When choosing the wording for anchors of a scale, what should you keep in mind?
4 When developing an itemised rating scale, outline the arguments for and against:
   (a) an odd number of points versus an even number of points
   (b) few points versus many points.
5 What are the analytical consequences of working with (a) nominal variables, (b) ordinal variables and (c) measurable variables?
6 Provide business examples of variables of each different measurement level.
7 Distinguish between 'comparative scales' and 'non-comparative scales'.
8 When comparing n brands using a paired comparison scale, how many distinct paired comparisons are required?
9 What is the objective of constant sum scaling?
10 What is a Likert scale and when would it be useful? Provide an example of such a scale.
11 What is a semantic differential scale and when would it be useful? Provide an example of such a scale.
12 What is a Stapel scale and when would it be useful? Provide an example of such a scale.

8.7.2 Case study corner

Suppose you are a marketing executive at the company of your choice. You have been tasked to create a market research survey to investigate consumer satisfaction levels. Create a short survey to fulfil this task, and prepare an executive summary explaining your choice of survey questions.

9

ESTIMATION

Chapter contents

Chapter level: ***Intermediate***

Source: Photo by Steinchen via Pixabay.

Key concepts

- Bias-variance trade-off
- Estimation error
- Confidence intervals

Chapter value

Estimates of unknown parameters are always uncertain, so we seek the best estimators.

Key takeaway

Confidence intervals allow us to quantify the likely extent of estimation error.

Chapter outline

Ignorance is *not* bliss. In the analytics world, when something is unknown we seek to *estimate* its value, which gives rise to the topic of estimation. More specifically, we seek to estimate *unknown parameters* using sample data drawn from a population.

Estimation is an imprecise art and there is always a risk of an estimate being wrong, known as the *estimation error*. While this risk is always present, we can specify the attributes of a desirable estimator based on its *bias* and *variance*. Thereafter, our point estimates (essentially 'best guesses') of parameters can be given error bounds to reflect the likely estimation error, giving rise to *interval estimation*. By setting our tolerance for how wide we are prepared for *confidence intervals* to be, we can then determine the minimum (and hence lowest-cost) sample size required.

Learning outcomes

After completing this chapter, you should be able to:

- summarise the performance of an estimator with reference to its sampling distribution
- use the concepts of bias and variance of an estimator
- define mean squared error and calculate it for simple estimators
- calculate sample means, standard deviations and proportions, and demonstrate their use as estimates
- construct a confidence interval for a population mean, a population proportion, the difference between two population means and the difference between two population proportions
- know when to use the Student's *t* distribution.

9.1 INTRODUCTION

Chapter 5 introduced several common probability distributions (summarised in Appendix B) which could be used as *approximating models* of business variables, such as the exponential distribution to model variation in waiting times, and the normal distribution to model variation in the manufacturing process. Such distributions are distinguished by one or more *parameters*, such as the rate parameter λ for the exponential distribution, and the mean and variance parameters μ and σ^2 for the normal distribution.

One of the main uses of statistics, and of sampling, is to *estimate* the value of *unknown* parameters. (Clearly, if the population parameter is *known*, then there is no need to estimate it!) Given a relevant set of data (an observed random sample) drawn from the population, the problem is to perform a calculation using these observed data values in order to arrive at a value which, in some sense, comes 'close' to the unknown population parameter which we wish to estimate.

Whatever it is that we are trying to estimate, this (numerical) statistic value which we calculate is known as a (point) estimate, and the general name for the process is (point) estimation. Note that, in principle, we might want to estimate *any* characteristic of the population distribution, but some will be far more common than others.

The statistic used to obtain a point estimate is known as a (point) estimator, each of which has a sampling distribution, as discussed in Chapter 7. Common estimators are the sample mean, $\bar{X}$, the sample proportion, P, and the sample variance, S^2, to estimate population means, population proportions and population variances, respectively.

Of course, in practice we do not realistically expect to achieve a point estimate which is *exactly* equal to the unknown population parameter, due to sample data being subject to randomness and, perhaps despite our best efforts, we cannot guarantee a truly *representative* sample (as discussed in Chapter 7 where several sampling techniques were presented). One can think of a point estimate as our 'best guess' of the parameter based on the available sample data. We would hope, of course, that this 'best guess' is reasonably close to the truth, that is, that our estimation error (the difference between the point estimate and the true parameter value) is small. This chapter will establish well-defined criteria for selecting a desirable estimator, as we may be faced with several competing estimators of a parameter and need to be able to identify the best one (where 'best' needs to be qualified). Once identified, we will then construct confidence intervals which allow us to compute a range of plausible values of a parameter reflecting the likely estimation error – essentially, to place error bounds around our point estimates. Sample size determination will also be discussed.

Motivational case: To coffee, or not to coffee?

Companies should make what they can sell, instead of selling what they can make. Assessing consumer tastes and preferences, and pre-empting their directional changes, can help companies produce what people are willing to buy, capture market share, and profit handsomely.

Take toothpaste. If you are good, you will brush your teeth twice a day - to keep the dentist away! The global market for toothpaste is huge, but there is product differentiation among the numerous toothpaste brands and types. Do you have sensitive teeth? Do you wish to banish cavities and plaque? Are you a heavy coffee-drinker who covets white shiny teeth? Maybe all three.

Estimating consumer appetites for different products is vital for manufacturers to ensure their output is sold. In the USA, 29 September is National Coffee Day, and in celebration Sensodyne launched *Repair and Protect with Deep Repair* in 2021, targeted at those with hypersensitive teeth. Diligent market research would have indicated a commercially viable market for the product. Why launch the product to coincide with National Coffee Day? Well, Sensodyne commissioned research into Americans' love of Americano...

> According to research conducted by OnePoll on behalf of Sensodyne, the 2000-person study... found that:
>
> **HOT, HOT, HOT**: 43% of people surveyed prefer hot coffee to the 34% of people who prefer iced coffee.
>
> **COFFEE TIME = ME TIME**: 55% of people surveyed prefer to enjoy their coffee alone, followed by grabbing a cup with friends or family, and then at a café.
>
> **CAFFEINE CRAZED**: 42% admitted that over the past year their daily coffee intake has increased.

Associating coffee and toothpaste seems a sensible marketing strategy. Note that the sample size of 2000 will be explained by our discussion of sample size determination in this chapter, and the percentages serve as point estimates when generalising to the US consumer population.

Source: https://prn.to/3HHeeBM

9.2 ESTIMATION CRITERIA: BIAS, VARIANCE AND MEAN SQUARED ERROR

Estimators are random variables and, therefore, have probability distributions, known as *sampling distributions* (see Chapter 7). As we know, two important properties of probability distributions are the *mean* and *variance* (see Chapter 5). Our objective is to create a formal criterion which combines both of these properties to assess the relative performance of different estimators, enabling us to choose the best out of a set of competing estimators. While we always want the 'best' of something, we need to clarify in what sense something is the best. 'Best' in terms of our choice of preferred estimator will be based on its mean and variance.

Bias of an estimator

Let $\hat{\theta}$ be an estimator of the population parameter θ. We define the **bias** of an estimator $\hat{\theta}$ as

$$\text{Bias}(\hat{\theta}) = E(\hat{\theta}) - \theta \tag{9.1}$$

An estimator is

positively biased if $E(\hat{\theta}) - \theta > 0$,

unbiased if $E(\hat{\theta}) - \theta = 0$,

negatively biased if $E(\hat{\theta}) - \theta < 0$.

The ^ (hat) notation is frequently used to denote an estimator of the symbol beneath the ^. So, for example, $\hat{\lambda}$ denotes an estimator of the Poisson rate parameter, λ.

A positively biased estimator means the estimator would systematically overestimate the parameter by the size of the bias, *on average*. An unbiased estimator means the estimator would estimate the parameter correctly, *on average*. A negatively biased estimator means the estimator would systematically underestimate the parameter by the size of the bias, *on average*.

In words, the bias of an estimator is the difference between the expected (average) value of the estimator and the true parameter being estimated. Intuitively, it would be desirable, *ceteris paribus*, to have an estimator with zero bias, called an *unbiased* estimator. Given the definition of bias in (9.1), an unbiased estimator of θ would satisfy

$$E(\hat{\theta}) = \theta$$

In words, the expected value of the estimator is the true parameter being estimated, that is, *on average* under repeated sampling the estimator correctly estimates θ.

Example 9.1

Suppose we use the sample mean, $\bar{X}$, as an estimator of the population mean, μ. Since

$$E(\bar{X}) = \mu,$$

$\bar{X}$ is an unbiased estimator of μ. Likewise suppose we use the sample proportion, P, as an estimator of the population proportion, π. Since

$$E(P) = \pi,$$

P is an unbiased estimator of π.

We view bias as a 'bad' thing so, *ceteris paribus*, the smaller an estimator's bias the better. In fact, we can view the bias as the *expected estimation error*, since we define the estimation error as $\hat{\theta} - \theta$, the difference between the point estimate and the true parameter value. However, since the value of θ is unknown (which is why we are estimating it!) we have no way of knowing the true estimation error, so instead we have to work with expectations:

$$\begin{aligned} \text{E(estimation error)} &= E(\hat{\theta} - \theta) && \text{(by definition)} \\ &= E(\hat{\theta}) - E(\theta) && \text{(properties of expectation operator)} \\ &= E(\hat{\theta}) - \theta && \text{(noting that } \theta \text{ is a constant)} \\ &= \text{Bias}(\hat{\theta}). && \text{(et voilà!)} \end{aligned}$$

Therefore, an unbiased estimator has zero expected estimation error, equivalent to point estimates being correct *on average*, while positively (negatively) biased estimators have positive (negative) expected estimation error, with the magnitude of the bias quantifying the extent of the systematic overestimation (underestimation).

So, the mean (expected value) of an estimator determines an estimator's bias. While this measure of central tendency of an estimator is extremely important, we should also take into account the *precision* of an estimator through its *variance*.

Variance of an estimator

The **variance** of an estimator of θ, denoted $\text{Var}(\hat{\theta})$, is obtained directly from the estimator's sampling distribution. The greater an estimator's variance, the less precise the estimator is.

Example 9.2

From Chapter 7, for the common estimators of the population mean (the sample mean, $\bar{X}$) and the population proportion (the sample proportion, P), we had the following estimator variances:

$$\text{Var}(\bar{X}) = \frac{\sigma^2}{n} \tag{9.2}$$

and

$$\text{Var}(P) = \frac{\pi(1-\pi)}{n}. \tag{9.3}$$

It is clear that in both (9.2) and (9.3) *increasing* the sample size n *decreases* the estimator's variance (and hence the standard error), so in turn *increases* the precision of the estimator. Remember, however, that this increased precision comes at a cost – namely the increased expenditure on data collection. We conclude that variance is also a 'bad' thing so, *ceteris paribus*, the smaller an estimator's variance the better.

So, we have two key estimator attributes – bias and variance. Figure 9.1 visualises these characteristics. *Ceteris paribus*, we prefer zero bias; *ceteris paribus*, we prefer low variance. However, in practice, other things are usually not equal, so we typically face a **bias–variance trade-off**. So, we seek a way to combine the bias and variance properties of estimators which will allow us to choose between competing estimators. One such approach is the *mean squared error*.

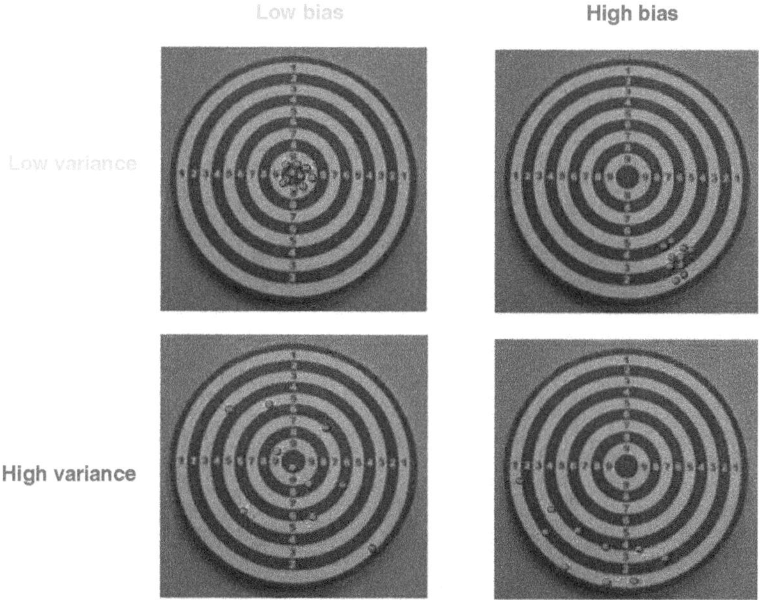

Figure 9.1 Visualising low and high bias, and low and high variance. Low bias (on target) is preferred to high bias (off target), and low variance (clustered points) is preferred to high variance (scattered points).

Mean squared error

The **mean squared error** (MSE) of an estimator is the average squared error. Formally, this is defined as

$$\text{MSE}(\hat{\theta}) = \text{E}((\hat{\theta} - \theta)^2) = \text{Var}(\hat{\theta}) + (\text{Bias}(\hat{\theta}))^2$$

The proof can be found at the end of the chapter.

We have already established that both the bias and the variance of an estimator are 'bad' things, so the MSE (being the sum of a bad thing and a bad thing squared) can also be viewed as a 'bad' thing. (Or, for that matter, a 'very bad' thing!) Therefore, when faced with several competing estimators, we prefer the estimator with the *smallest* MSE.

So, although an unbiased estimator is intuitively appealing, it is perfectly possible that a biased estimator might be preferred if the 'cost' of the bias is offset by a substantial reduction in the variance. This is represented by the 'high bias–low variance' pattern in Figure 9.1. Hence the MSE provides us with a formal criterion to assess the trade-off between the bias and variance of different estimators.

Example 9.3

The diameters of a manufactured component, X, are assumed to be normally distributed, $X \sim N(\mu, \sigma^2)$. Suppose we wish to estimate the population mean, μ, to assess whether the machine producing the components is calibrated correctly. We draw a random sample $\{X_1, X_2, \ldots, X_n\}$, such that these random variables are *independent and identically distributed* (IID).

Consider three candidate estimators of μ, denoted $\hat{\mu}_1$, $\hat{\mu}_2$ and $\hat{\mu}_3$, where

$$\hat{\mu}_1 = \bar{X} = \frac{1}{n}\sum_{i=1}^{n} X_i, \quad \hat{\mu}_2 = \frac{X_1 + X_n}{2} \quad \text{and} \quad \hat{\mu}_3 = \bar{X} + 3.$$

Which estimator should we choose? Intuitively, we would think $\hat{\mu}_1$ since it is the sample mean, but let's check using the 'minimum MSE criterion'.

We begin by determining the MSE of $\hat{\mu}_1$, noting that

$$\text{E}(\hat{\mu}_1) = \text{E}(\bar{X}) = \mu,$$

hence, using (9.1), we have that $\hat{\mu}_1$ is an unbiased estimator of μ (i.e. $\text{Bias}(\hat{\mu}_1) = 0$), and

$$\text{Var}(\hat{\mu}_1) = \text{Var}(\bar{X}) = \frac{\sigma^2}{n}.$$

So, the mean squared error of $\hat{\mu}_1$ is

$$\text{MSE}(\hat{\mu}_1) = \text{Var}(\hat{\mu}_1) + (\text{Bias}(\hat{\mu}_1))^2 = \frac{\sigma^2}{n} + 0^2 = \frac{\sigma^2}{n}.$$

Turning to $\hat{\mu}_2$, note (using Section 5.8.1) that

$$E(\hat{\mu}_2) = E\left(\frac{X_1 + X_n}{2}\right) = \frac{E(X_1) + E(X_n)}{2} = \frac{\mu + \mu}{2} = \mu$$

and, due to the *independence* of X_1 and X_n, we have (using Section 5.9.2)

$$\text{Var}(\hat{\mu}_2) = \text{Var}\left(\frac{X_1 + X_n}{2}\right) = \frac{\text{Var}(X_1) + \text{Var}(X_n)}{2^2} = \frac{2\sigma^2}{4} = \frac{\sigma^2}{2}.$$

Hence $\hat{\mu}_2$ is also an unbiased estimator of μ (i.e. Bias($\hat{\mu}_2$) = 0), hence

$$\text{MSE}(\hat{\mu}_2) = \text{Var}(\hat{\mu}_2) + (\text{Bias}(\hat{\mu}_2))^2 = \frac{\sigma^2}{2} + 0^2 = \frac{\sigma^2}{2}.$$

Finally, consider $\hat{\mu}_3$, noting that

$$E(\hat{\mu}_3) = E(\bar{X} + 3) = E(\bar{X}) + 3 = \mu + 3$$

and

$$\text{Var}(\hat{\mu}_3) = \text{Var}(\bar{X} + 3) = \text{Var}(\bar{X}) = \frac{\sigma^2}{n}.$$

Hence $\hat{\mu}_3$ is a biased estimator of μ, with a bias of

$$\text{Bias}(\hat{\mu}_3) = E(\hat{\mu}_3) - \mu = \mu + 3 - \mu = 3,$$

so

$$\text{MSE}(\hat{\mu}_3) = \text{Var}(\hat{\mu}_3) + (\text{Bias}(\hat{\mu}_3))^2 = \frac{\sigma^2}{n} + 3^2 = \frac{\sigma^2}{n} + 9.$$

We seek the estimator with the smallest MSE. Clearly, MSE($\hat{\mu}_1$) < MSE($\hat{\mu}_3$) so we can eliminate $\hat{\mu}_3$ immediately. Now comparing $\hat{\mu}_1$ with $\hat{\mu}_2$, we note that

- for $n = 2$, MSE($\hat{\mu}_1$) = MSE($\hat{\mu}_2$), since the estimators are identical
- for $n > 2$, MSE($\hat{\mu}_1$) < MSE($\hat{\mu}_2$), so $\hat{\mu}_1$ is preferred.

So $\hat{\mu}_1 = \bar{X}$ is our preferred estimator of μ, as we suspected! Note that, for $n > 2$, $\hat{\mu}_1$ uses all the *information* in the sample (i.e. all observations are used), unlike $\hat{\mu}_2$ which uses *only* the first and last observations. Of course, for $n = 2$, these two estimators are identical.

9.3 UNBIASED ESTIMATORS

Suppose unbiasedness is considered such a desirable estimator property that we decide to restrict attention to unbiased estimators only. Note that if $\hat{\theta}$ is an unbiased estimator of θ, we have that Bias($\hat{\theta}$) = 0, by definition. Hence

$$\mathrm{MSE}(\hat{\theta}) = \mathrm{Var}(\hat{\theta}) + (\mathrm{Bias}(\hat{\theta}))^2 = \mathrm{Var}(\hat{\theta}) + 0 = \mathrm{Var}(\hat{\theta}).$$

So, minimising the MSE of unbiased estimators is the same as choosing the estimator with the smallest variance, hence we term such an estimator the minimum variance unbiased estimator. Therefore, if we had two unbiased estimators of θ, say $\hat{\theta}_1$ and $\hat{\theta}_2$, then we prefer $\hat{\theta}_1$ if $\mathrm{Var}(\hat{\theta}_1) < \mathrm{Var}(\hat{\theta}_2)$. If this is the case, then $\hat{\theta}_1$ is called the more *efficient* estimator.

Examples of unbiased estimators of parameters include:

- $\bar{X}$ as an estimator of μ for data from $N(\mu, \sigma^2)$, since $\mathrm{E}(\bar{X}) = \mu$
- P as an estimator of π for Bernoulli sampling with success parameter π, since $\mathrm{E}(P) = \pi$
- S^2 as an estimator of σ^2 for data from $N(\mu, \sigma^2)$, since $\mathrm{E}(S^2) = \sigma^2$. (This explains why we use $n - 1$ as the divisor when computing the sample variance, since this results in an unbiased estimator of σ^2. See Section 2.6.1 for further discussion.)

9.3.1 Unbiased estimators of functions of parameters

It should be noted that unbiasedness is *not an invariant property*, by which we mean that if $\hat{\theta}$ is an unbiased estimator of θ there are important functions of $\hat{\theta}$ which are *not* unbiased. For example, if $\mathrm{E}(\hat{\theta}) = \theta$, it follows that (using Section 5.9 and noting that variances are never negative)

$$\mathrm{Var}(\hat{\theta}) = \mathrm{E}(\hat{\theta}^2) - \left(\mathrm{E}(\hat{\theta})\right)^2 > 0 \quad \Rightarrow \quad \mathrm{E}(\hat{\theta}^2) = \mathrm{Var}(\hat{\theta}) + \theta^2 > \theta^2.$$

Unbiased estimators of functions of parameters, when the parameter is drawn from the population distribution, can, however, often be found by an appropriate adjustment known as a *bias correction*.

Example 9.4

Suppose we have a random sample of n values from $N(\mu, \sigma^2)$, and we wish to find an unbiased estimator of μ^2. Since we know that $\bar{X}$ is an unbiased estimator of μ, we might think that $\bar{X}^2$ is an unbiased estimator of μ^2. However, if we try $\bar{X}^2$, then

$$\begin{aligned}\mathrm{E}(\bar{X}^2) &= \mathrm{Var}(\bar{X}) + (\mathrm{E}(\bar{X}))^2 \\ &= \frac{\sigma^2}{n} + \mu^2 \\ &\neq \mu^2.\end{aligned}$$

However, we know that $\mathrm{E}(S^2) = \sigma^2$, so that, by combining this with the above, it follows that

$$\mathrm{E}\left(\bar{X}^2 - \frac{S^2}{n}\right) = \mathrm{E}(\bar{X}^2) - \mathrm{E}\left(\frac{S^2}{n}\right) = \frac{\sigma^2}{n} + \mu^2 - \frac{\sigma^2}{n} = \mu^2.$$

Hence $\bar{X}^2 - S^2/n$ is an unbiased estimator of μ^2.

Finding unbiased estimators

Example 9.4 illustrates a somewhat rough-and-ready, but effective, method for finding unbiased estimators of parameters.

1 Guess at a sensible estimator.
2 Derive its expectation.
3 Adjust the estimator accordingly to remove the bias.

Unbiasedness is a very desirable property for estimators used in survey sampling, where the 'fairness' represented by the unbiased concept is regarded as being extremely important.

9.4 INTERVAL ESTIMATION

In data-driven decision-making, we are often making a decision which involves a population, such as a set of individuals or companies which constitute the market for a product, or it could consist of the items being manufactured from a production line. The sort of information needed for a decision may be a mean value (e.g. 'How many items does an individual purchase per year, on average?') or a proportion ('What proportion of items manufactured has a fault?'). The associated decision may range from setting up extra capacity to cope with expected demand, to stopping the production line for adjustment.

In most cases it is impossible to gather information about the whole population (due to time and financial constraints), so by necessity we have to collect information about a sample drawn from the population and infer the required information about the population. Chapter 7 discussed the reasons for sampling.

In order to carry out this type of exercise, one obvious decision needs to be made. How large should the sample be? The answer to this question is: 'Well, James, it depends!' Specifically, it depends on how variable the population is, on how accurate the input to the decision needs to be, and on how costly the data collection is.

We will now study and construct *confidence intervals*, as well as look at *sample size determination*. How does it affect accuracy when you estimate population means and proportions? How do you use this information? Note that inferring information about a parent (or theoretical) population using observations from a (random) sample is the primary concern of statistical inference.

9.4.1 Principle of confidence intervals

A point estimate is our 'best guess' of an unknown population parameter based on observed sample data. Due to the random nature of sample data, we do not expect to estimate the parameter *exactly* (unless we are very lucky), that is, estimation error is almost certain even when using an unbiased estimator. Hence there is some uncertainty in our estimation, so it would be advisable to communicate the level of uncertainty (or imprecision) in conjunction with the point estimate.

The standard error (the square root of the variance, i.e. the standard deviation, of an estimator) acts as a measure of estimation (im)precision, and is used in the construction of the confidence intervals covered in this chapter. Informally, you can think of (most) confidence intervals as representing our 'best guess plus or minus a bit', where the magnitude of this 'bit' is dependent on the:

- confidence level
- sample size
- amount of variation in the population/sample.

This method of expressing the accuracy of an estimate is easily understood and requires no statistical sophistication for interpretation.

More formally, an $x\%$ confidence interval *covers* the unknown parameter with $x\%$ probability *over repeated samples*. A visual illustration is provided in Figure 9.2. The red and blue lines each represent a confidence interval (each confidence interval is obtained from a different sample). In total there are 10 lines (8 blue, 2 red) reflecting 10 independent random samples drawn from the same population. In this example, 80% of the time (8 out of the 10 confidence intervals) happen to cover μ (whose true value is indicated by the green arrow). If this 80% figure was the long-run percentage (i.e. over *many* repeated samples), then such confidence intervals would have an 80% *coverage probability*. Hence 80% of the time we would obtain a confidence interval for μ which *covers* (or *spans*, or *includes*) μ. In practice, though, we may only have one sample, hence one confidence interval. With respect to Figure 9.2 there is a 20% risk that it is a 'red' interval. If it was the left red confidence interval, this would lead us to think μ is smaller than it actually is; if it was the right red confidence interval, this would lead us to think μ is larger than it actually is.

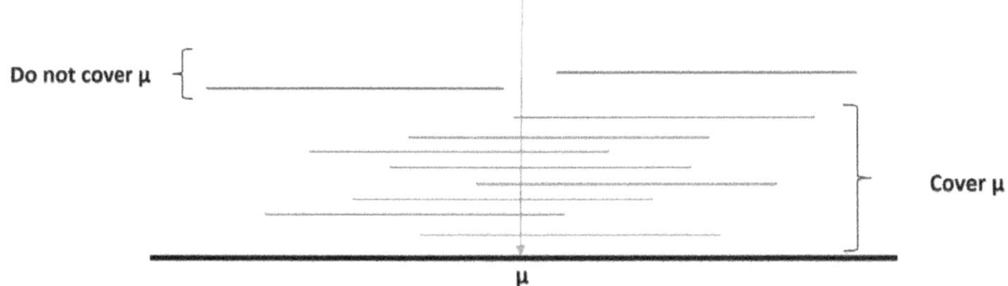

Figure 9.2 Coverage (in blue) and non-coverage (in red) of μ for several confidence intervals (one confidence interval per sample).

It is important to distinguish *point estimation* (using sample data to obtain a numerical estimate of an unknown population parameter) from a *confidence interval* (an interval estimate of the parameter whose width indicates how reliable the point estimate is).

At this point, make sure you are clear about the distinction between *statistics* (such as point and interval estimators presented in this chapter) and *parameters* (population characteristics, e.g. the parameters of various probability distributions presented in Chapter 5).

Clearly, a very wide confidence interval would show that our estimate was not very reliable, as we could not be sure that its value was close to the true parameter value, whereas a narrow confidence interval would correspond to a more reliable estimate. The degree of confidence which we have in our confidence interval can be expressed numerically. An ideal situation is a narrow interval with a high *coverage probability* (typically greater than the 80% achieved in Figure 9.2). With these points in mind we now show how such intervals can be computed from sample data in some basic situations.

9.5 GENERAL FORMULAE FOR NORMALLY DISTRIBUTED STATISTICS

Chapter 7 introduced the sampling distribution of $\bar{X}$. We will now draw on this sampling theory.

9.5.1 Variance known (σ^2 known)

Suppose a random sample of size n is drawn from $N(\mu, \sigma^2)$, with σ^2 known. Let $\bar{X}$ be our chosen estimator of μ such that its sampling distribution is

$$\bar{X} \sim N\left(\mu, \frac{\sigma^2}{n}\right).$$

We require a confidence interval defined by a pair of values (the 'endpoints' of the confidence interval) such that the probability the interval *covers* μ (the coverage probability) is high.

Since $\bar{X}$ is normally distributed it follows that, upon standardising $\bar{X}$, we have

$$Z = \frac{\bar{X} - \mu}{\sigma / \sqrt{n}} \sim N(0,1). \tag{9.4}$$

Therefore, assuming a 95% coverage probability,

$$P\left(-1.96 < \frac{\bar{X} - \mu}{\sigma / \sqrt{n}} < 1.96\right) = 0.95.$$

This means that the central 95% of the $N(0, 1)$ curve is between –1.96 and 1.96 (also recall Section 5.15.3). This can be verified in Excel using `=NORM.S.DIST(1.96,1)-NORM.S.DIST(-1.96,1)`. Since $\sigma / \sqrt{n} > 0$ (a standard error is always strictly positive), we have

$$\begin{aligned}
0.95 &= P\left(-1.96 < \frac{\bar{X} - \mu}{\sigma / \sqrt{n}} < 1.96\right) && \text{(from above)} \\
&= P\left(-1.96 \times \frac{\sigma}{\sqrt{n}} < \bar{X} - \mu < 1.96 \times \frac{\sigma}{\sqrt{n}}\right) && \text{(multiply through by } \sigma / \sqrt{n}\text{)} \\
&= P\left(-1.96 \times \frac{\sigma}{\sqrt{n}} < \mu - \bar{X} < 1.96 \times \frac{\sigma}{\sqrt{n}}\right) && \text{(multiply through by } -1\text{)} \\
&= P\left(\bar{X} - 1.96 \times \frac{\sigma}{\sqrt{n}} < \mu < \bar{X} + 1.96 \times \frac{\sigma}{\sqrt{n}}\right) && \text{(et voilà!)}
\end{aligned}$$

Endpoints for a 95% confidence interval for μ (variance known)

When sampling from a normal distribution, a 95% confidence interval for μ has endpoints $\bar{X} \pm 1.96 \times \sigma / \sqrt{n}$. Hence the reported confidence interval would be

$$\left(\bar{X} - 1.96 \times \frac{\sigma}{\sqrt{n}}, \bar{X} + 1.96 \times \frac{\sigma}{\sqrt{n}}\right).$$

This is a simple, but very important, result. As we shall see, it can be applied to give confidence intervals in many different situations such as for the estimation of a mean, a proportion, a difference between means and a difference between proportions.

The above derivation was for a 95% confidence interval (i.e. with a 95% coverage probability), which is a generally accepted confidence requirement. Of course, it is possible to have different levels of confidence, say 90% or 99% (the 80% demonstrated in Figure 9.2 is much less common). Fortunately, we can use the same argument as above. However, a different multiplier coefficient drawn from the standard normal distribution is required (i.e. not 1.96). For convenience, key values are given below, where z_α denotes the z-value which cuts off $100\alpha\%$ probability in the upper tail of the standard normal distribution.

For 90% confidence, use the multiplier $z_{0.05} = 1.645$.

For 95% confidence, use the multiplier $z_{0.025} = 1.96$.

For 99% confidence, use the multiplier $z_{0.005} = 2.576$.

Unfortunately, the method used so far in this section is limited by the assumption that σ^2 is *known*. This means, in effect, that we need to know the true population variance, but we do not know the population mean – since this is what we are trying to estimate. This seems implausible. Why would you know σ^2, but not know μ?

In such cases it will be necessary to *estimate the standard error* from the data. This requires a modification both of the approach and, in particular, of the general formula for the endpoints of a confidence interval.

9.5.2 Variance unknown (σ^2 unknown)

Here we consider the case where the standard error of $\bar{X}$ is estimated: taking the sample standard deviation, S, we use $S / \sqrt{n}$ to estimate the true standard error, $\sigma / \sqrt{n}$. It may be tempting to think, given (9.4), that simply substituting $\sigma / \sqrt{n}$ with $S / \sqrt{n}$ also results in

$$\frac{\bar{X} - \mu}{S / \sqrt{n}} \sim N(0,1)$$

that is, that the distribution remains the standard normal distribution, *but* because of the additional sampling variability of the estimated standard error, this new, transformed function of the data will have a more dispersed distribution than the standard normal – the Student's *t* distribution. Hence we have that

$$\frac{\bar{X}-\mu}{S/\sqrt{n}} \sim t_{n-1}.$$

9.5.3 Student's *t* distribution

'Student' was the pen name of William S. Gosset (1876–1937) who is credited with developing this distribution.

Sidenote

Curious readers may wonder why Gosset was not vain enough to call it Gosset's *t* distribution - after all, who wouldn't want to achieve such statistical immortality? In fact the reason for the pen name was the refusal of Guinness (his employer when he discovered this distribution) to allow its researchers to publish papers, fearing leaks of trade secrets, forcing Gosset to publish anonymously as 'Student'. Poor Gosset.

You should be familiar with its generic shape, which resembles the standard normal (i.e. bell-shaped and symmetric about 0) but with 'fatter' tails. We get different versions of the *t* distribution for different degrees of freedom, ν, the parameter of the distribution. Graphical examples of the *t* distribution for various degrees of freedom are given in Figure 9.3, but note that as $\nu \to \infty$ (in words, 'as the degrees of freedom tend to infinity'), we approach the standard normal distribution; that is, $t_\nu \to N(0, 1)$ as $\nu \to \infty$.

For our purposes, we will use this distribution whenever we are performing statistical inference for population means when population variances are *unknown*, and hence are estimated from the data. The correct degrees of freedom will depend on the degrees of freedom used to estimate the variance.

Assuming a 95% coverage probability, for a given ν we can find $t_{0.025,n-1}$ such that:

$$P\left(-t_{0.025,n-1} < \frac{\bar{X}-\mu}{S/\sqrt{n}} < t_{0.025,n-1}\right) = 0.95$$

where $t_{0.025,n-1}$ cuts off 2.5% probability in the upper tail of the *t* distribution with $n-1$ degrees of freedom. On rearranging the inequality within the brackets we get

$$P\left(\bar{X} - t_{0.025,n-1} \times \frac{S}{\sqrt{n}} < \mu < \bar{X} + t_{0.025,n-1} \times \frac{S}{\sqrt{n}}\right) = 0.95.$$

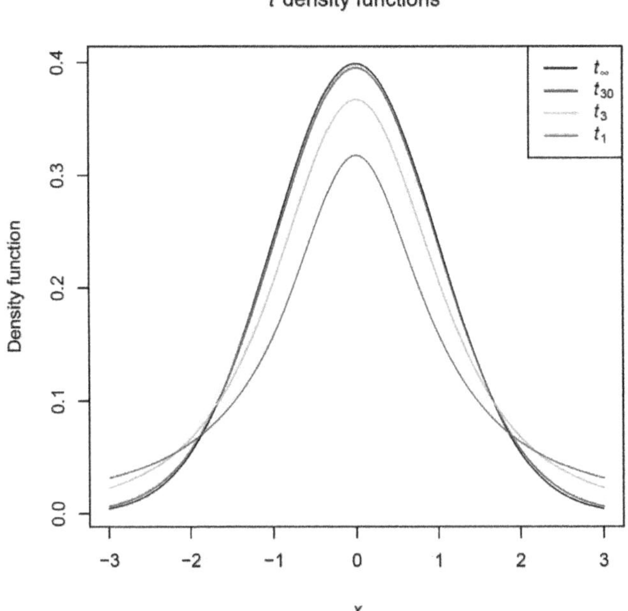

Figure 9.3 Student's *t* distribution for various degrees of freedom as indicated.

Endpoints for a 95% confidence interval for μ (variance unknown)

A 95% confidence interval for μ has endpoints $\bar{X} \pm t_{0.025,n-1} \times S/\sqrt{n}$, leading to a reported confidence interval of the form:

$$\left(\bar{X} - t_{0.025,n-1} \times \frac{S}{\sqrt{n}}, \bar{X} + t_{0.025,n-1} \times \frac{S}{\sqrt{n}}\right),$$

where $t_{0.025,n-1}$ is the *t*-value which cuts off 2.5% probability in the upper tail of the *t* distribution with $n-1$ degrees of freedom.

The *t*-values can be obtained in Excel using the `T.INV` function.

Excel function: `T.INV`

`=T.INV(probability, deg_freedom)` returns the inverse of the left-tailed probability of the Student's *t* distribution, where:

- `probability` is the probability associated with the Student's *t* distribution
- `deg_freedom` is the number of degrees of freedom with which to characterise the distribution.

Important note

In the following applications, whenever the t distribution is used and we have *large* sample size(s) (hence large degrees of freedom), it is acceptable to use standard normal values as approximations due to the tendency of the t distribution to the standard normal distribution as the degrees of freedom approach infinity. What constitutes a 'large' sample size is rather subjective. However, as a rule of thumb, treat anything over 30 as 'large'.

9.5.4 Confidence interval for a single mean (σ^2 known)

Given observed sample values $x_1, x_2, \ldots, x_n$, the point estimate of μ is $\bar{x} = \sum_{i=1}^{n} x_i / n$. Assuming the (population) variance, σ^2, is known, the standard error of $\bar{x}$ is $\sigma / \sqrt{n}$ (and hence also known).

Confidence interval endpoints for a single mean (σ^2 known)

In such instances, we use the standard normal distribution when constructing a $100(1-\alpha)\%$ confidence interval with endpoints

$$\bar{x} \pm z_{\alpha/2} \times \frac{\sigma}{\sqrt{n}} \quad \Rightarrow \quad \left(\bar{x} - z_{\alpha/2} \times \frac{\sigma}{\sqrt{n}}, \bar{x} + z_{\alpha/2} \times \frac{\sigma}{\sqrt{n}}\right)$$

where $z_{\alpha/2}$ is the z-value which cuts off $100\alpha/2\%$ probability in the upper tail of the standard normal distribution to ensure a $100(1-\alpha)\%$ confidence interval.

For example, for $\alpha = 0.05$, we have a $100(1 - 0.05)\% = 95\%$ confidence interval, and we require the z-value which cuts off $\alpha/2 = 0.025$ (i.e. 2.5%) probability in the upper tail of the standard normal distribution, which is 1.96, and can be obtained using `=NORM.S.INV(0.975)`.

Example 9.5

Measurements of the diameter of a random sample of 200 ball bearings produced by a machine gave a sample mean of $\bar{x} = 0.824$. The population standard deviation, σ, is 0.042.

We compute 95% and 99% confidence intervals for the true mean value of the diameter of the ball bearings.

Since we are told that $\sigma = 0.042$, a 95% confidence interval, where $\alpha = 0.05$, has endpoints

$$\bar{x} \pm 1.96 \times \frac{\sigma}{\sqrt{n}} = 0.824 \pm 1.96 \times \frac{0.042}{\sqrt{200}} = 0.824 \pm 0.006$$

where $z_{0.025} = 1.96$ is the z-value which cuts off $100\alpha/2\% = 2.5\%$ probability in the upper tail of the standard normal distribution obtained using `=NORM.S.INV(0.975)`. In other words, the interval is (0.818, 0.830), which *covers* the true mean with a probability of 95%.

(Continued)

To compute a 99% confidence interval (where $\alpha = 0.01$), since σ^2 is known we require $z_{\alpha/2} = z_{0.005}$, that is, the z-value which cuts off 0.5% probability in the upper tail of the standard normal distribution.

We have that $z_{0.005} = 2.576$, obtained using `=NORM.S.INV(0.995)`, so a 99% confidence interval has endpoints:

$$\bar{x} \pm 2.576 \times \frac{\sigma}{\sqrt{n}} = 0.824 \pm 2.576 \times \frac{0.042}{\sqrt{200}} = 0.824 \pm 0.008.$$

In other words, the interval is (0.816, 0.832). Note the higher level of confidence has resulted in a *wider* confidence interval, as expected since *ceteris paribus* the 'price' of the benefit of a higher confidence level is the cost of a wider confidence interval.

9.5.5 Confidence interval for a single mean (σ^2 unknown)

In practice it is unusual for σ^2 to be known. (Why would we know σ^2, but not μ?) However, we can estimate σ^2 with the sample variance, that is, use the estimator

$$S^2 = \frac{1}{n-1}\sum_{i=1}^{n}\left(X_i - \bar{X}\right)^2.$$

This is because S^2 is an unbiased estimator of σ^2, as noted in Section 9.3. (Recall that an unbiased estimator means the point estimate is correct *on average*, over repeated samples.) The degrees of freedom associated with this estimator are $n - 1$, where n is the sample size.

Confidence interval endpoints for a single mean (σ^2 unknown)

In such instances, we use the t distribution when constructing a $100(1 - \alpha)\%$ confidence interval with endpoints

$$\bar{x} \pm t_{\alpha/2,n-1} \times \frac{s}{\sqrt{n}} \quad \Rightarrow \quad \left(\bar{x} - t_{\alpha/2,n-1} \times \frac{s}{\sqrt{n}}, \bar{x} + t_{\alpha/2,n-1} \times \frac{s}{\sqrt{n}}\right)$$

where $t_{\alpha/2,\,n-1}$ is the t-value which cuts off $100\alpha/2\%$ probability in the upper tail of the t distribution with $n - 1$ degrees of freedom, obtained from `T.INV`.

Example 9.6

A company producing designer label jeans carries out a sampling exercise in order to estimate the average price which retailers are charging for the jeans. A random sample of 12 retailers gives the following descriptive statistics (in pounds):

$\bar{x} = 41.625$, $s = 7.840$.

We seek a 95% confidence interval for μ, the mean price of the jeans for all retailers. The estimated standard error of the sample mean is

$$\frac{s}{\sqrt{n}} = \frac{7.840}{\sqrt{12}} = 2.2632$$

on $n - 1 = 11$ degrees of freedom. Hence a 95% confidence interval for μ has endpoints

$$41.625 \pm 2.201 \times 2.2632$$

that is, the confidence interval is

(£36.64, £46.61).

Two important points are the following.

- Make sure you see where the 2.201 comes from. It is $t_{0.025,11}$, that is, the t-value above which lies 2.5% probability for a Student's t distribution with 11 degrees of freedom. In Excel, this is obtained using `=T.INV(0.975,11)`.
- Make sure you report confidence intervals in the form (£36.64, £46.61). That is, you *must* compute the actual endpoints and report these as an *interval*, as that is what a confidence *interval* is! Note the lower endpoint should be given first.

9.6 CONFIDENCE INTERVAL FOR A SINGLE PROPORTION

We often want to estimate a (population) proportion, such as in surveys of consumer attitudes. In Chapter 7 we gave the sampling distribution of the sample proportion as follows.

Sampling distribution of the sample proportion, P

The sampling distribution of the sample proportion, P, (estimator of the population proportion, π) is approximately

$$P \sim \mathrm{N}\left(\pi, \frac{\pi(1-\pi)}{n}\right).$$

This result is a consequence of the central limit theorem applied to the proportion of successes for a binomial distribution, or equivalently the parameter of a Bernoulli distribution.

Hence $\mathrm{Var}(P) = \pi(1 - \pi)/n$, so the standard error is $\mathrm{S.E.}(P) = \sqrt{\pi(1-\pi)/n}$. Unfortunately, this depends on π, precisely what we are trying to estimate, hence the true standard error is unknown, so must itself be estimated. As π is unknown, the best we can do is replace it with our point estimate of it, $p = r/n$, hence the *estimated standard error* is

$$\mathrm{E.S.E.}(p) = \sqrt{\frac{p(1-p)}{n}} = \sqrt{\frac{r/n(1-r/n)}{n}}.$$

Confidence interval endpoints for a single proportion

An *approximate* 100(1 – α)% confidence interval for a single proportion has endpoints

$$p \pm z_{\alpha/2} \times \sqrt{\frac{p(1-p)}{n}} \quad \Rightarrow \quad \left(p - z_{\alpha/2} \times \sqrt{\frac{p(1-p)}{n}}, p + z_{\alpha/2} \times \sqrt{\frac{p(1-p)}{n}}\right)$$

where $z_{\alpha/2}$ is the *z*-value which cuts off 100α/2% probability in the upper tail of the standard normal distribution, obtained using `NORM.S.INV`.

Note that although we are estimating a variance, for proportions we do *not* use the *t* distribution for the following two reasons.

- The standard error has not been estimated by S^2.
- The sample size n has to be large for the central limit theorem normal approximation to hold, and so the standard normal distribution is appropriate in this case.

Example 9.7

A survey is conducted by a bank to estimate the proportion of its customers who would be interested in using a proposed new mobile telephone banking service.

If we denote the population proportion of customers who are interested in this proposal by π, and it is found that 68 out of 150 customers are in favour, then we would estimate π by $p = 68/150 = 0.453$. Hence a 95% confidence interval for π has endpoints

$$0.453 \pm 1.96 \times \sqrt{\frac{0.453(1-0.453)}{150}} \quad \Rightarrow \quad (0.37, 0.53).$$

Note that, for a 95% confidence interval, $\alpha = 0.05$ and so we use $z_{0.025} = 1.96$ in the computation of this 95% confidence interval.

9.7 SAMPLE SIZE DETERMINATION

The question 'How large a sample do I need?' is a common one when sampling. The answer to this depends on the *quality of inference* which the researcher requires from the data. In the estimation context, this can be expressed in terms of the accuracy of estimation. If the researcher requires that there should be a 95% chance that the estimation error should be no larger than e units (we refer to e as the tolerance on the estimation error), then this is equivalent to having a 95% confidence interval of width $2e$. Note here e represents the *half-width* of the confidence interval since the point estimate is, by construction, at the centre of the confidence interval.

Sample size determination for a single mean

To estimate μ to within e units with $100(1-\alpha)\%$ confidence, we require a sample of size

$$n \geq \frac{(z_{\alpha/2})^2 \sigma^2}{e^2} \tag{9.5}$$

where $z_{\alpha/2}$ is the z-value which cuts off $100\alpha/2\%$ probability in the upper tail of the standard normal distribution, obtained using `NORM.S.INV`.

Sample size determination for a single proportion

To estimate π to within e units with $100(1-\alpha)\%$ confidence, we require a sample of size

$$n \geq \frac{(z_{\alpha/2})^2 p(1-p)}{e^2} \tag{9.6}$$

where $z_{\alpha/2}$ is the z-value which cuts off $100\alpha/2\%$ probability in the upper tail of the standard normal distribution, obtained using `NORM.S.INV`.

In (9.6), p should be an approximate value of π, perhaps obtained from a pilot study, or alternatively we make an assumption of this value based on judgement and/or experience. If a pilot study is not feasible and a value cannot be assumed, then set $p = 0.50$ in (9.6) as a 'conservative' choice, as this value gives the maximum possible standard error (this can be shown using calculus).

Example 9.8

A simple random sample of 50 households is taken from a large population of households in a city. The sample mean and standard deviation of weekly expenditure on non-alcoholic beverages are £18 and £4, respectively. How many *more* observations are required to estimate μ to within 1 unit with 99% confidence?

Here, $e = 1$, and we can assume $\sigma = 4$ since the initial sample with $n = 50$ is 'large' and hence we would expect $s \approx \sigma$. For 99% confidence, we use $z_{0.005} = 2.576$. Hence, using (9.5), we have

$$n \geq \frac{(2.576)^2 \times 4^2}{1^2} = 106.17.$$

Remembering that n must be an integer; the smallest n satisfying this is 107. (Note that we round *up*, otherwise had we rounded down it would lead to less precision.) So, 107 – 50 = 57 *more* observations are required.

Example 9.9

The reaction time of a patient to a certain stimulus is known to have a standard deviation of 0.05 seconds. How large a sample of measurements must a psychologist take in order to be 95% confident and 99% confident, respectively, that the error in the estimate of the mean reaction time will not exceed 0.01 seconds?

For 95% confidence, we use $z_{0.025} = 1.96$. So, using (9.5), n is to be chosen such that

$$n \geq \frac{1.96^2 \times 0.05^2}{0.01^2}.$$

Hence we find that $n \geq 96.04$. Since n must be an integer, 97 observations are required to achieve an error of 0.01 or less with 95% confidence.

For 99% confidence, we use $z_{0.005} = 2.576$. So, using (9.5), n is to be chosen such that:

$$n \geq \frac{2.576^2 \times 0.05^2}{0.01^2}.$$

Hence we find that $n \geq 165.89$. Since n must be an integer, 166 observations are required to achieve an error of 0.01 or less with 99% confidence.

Note that a higher level of confidence requires a larger sample size as more information (sample data) is required to achieve a higher level of confidence for a given tolerance, e.

Example 9.10

A pilot study estimates a proportion to be 0.50. If we wish to be 95% confident of estimating the true population proportion with an error no greater than 0.03, how large a sample is required?

Here $e = 0.03$, and we have an initial estimate of $p = 0.50$. For 95% confidence, we use $z_{0.025} = 1.96$. Hence, using (9.6), we have

$$n \geq \frac{1.96^2 \times 0.50 \times (1 - 0.50)}{0.03^2} = 1067.11.$$

So, rounding up, we require a sample size of 1068.

The result in Example 9.10 explains why opinion polls often have sample sizes of approximately 1000. This is because a 3 percentage point half-width (i.e. $e = 0.03$ expressed as a proportion) is often an acceptable tolerance, and a 95% confidence level is the most widely used.

9.8 DIFFERENCE BETWEEN TWO POPULATION PROPORTIONS

The correct approach to the comparison of two population proportions, π_1 and π_2, is via the *difference* between the population proportions, $\pi_1 - \pi_2$. The sample proportions P_1 and P_2 are, by the central limit theorem for large sample sizes n_1 and n_2, respectively, (approximately) normally distributed as

$$P_1 \sim N\left(\pi_1, \frac{\pi_1(1-\pi_1)}{n_1}\right) \quad \text{and} \quad P_2 \sim N\left(\pi_2, \frac{\pi_2(1-\pi_2)}{n_2}\right).$$

When *independent* random samples are drawn from two separate populations, then these distributions are statistically independent. Therefore, the difference between P_1 and P_2 is also (approximately) normally distributed such that

$$P_1 - P_2 \sim N\left(\pi_1 - \pi_2, \frac{\pi_1(1-\pi_1)}{n_1} + \frac{\pi_2(1-\pi_2)}{n_2}\right).$$

Clearly, $\text{Var}(P_1 - P_2)$, and hence $\text{S.E.}(P_1 - P_2) = \sqrt{\text{Var}(P_1 - P_2)}$, depend on the *unknown* parameters π_1 and π_2. So we must resort to the *estimated standard error*:

$$\text{E.S.E.}(P_1 - P_2) = \sqrt{\frac{P_1(1-P_1)}{n_1} + \frac{P_2(1-P_2)}{n_2}}.$$

Confidence interval endpoints for the difference between two proportions

With point estimates for π_1 and π_2 of $p_1 = r_1/n_1$ and $p_2 = r_2/n_2$, respectively, an *approximate* $100(1 - \alpha)\%$ confidence interval for the difference between two population proportions has endpoints:

$$p_1 - p_2 \pm z_{\alpha/2} \times \sqrt{\frac{p_1(1-p_1)}{n_1} + \frac{p_2(1-p_2)}{n_2}} \qquad (9.7)$$

where $z_{\alpha/2}$ is the z-value which cuts off $100\alpha/2\%$ probability in the upper tail of the standard normal distribution, obtained using `NORM.S.INV`.

Example 9.11

We use (9.7) to calculate 95% and 90% confidence intervals for the difference between the population proportions of the general public who are aware of a particular retailed product before and after an advertising campaign. Two surveys were conducted and the results of the two random samples were:

	Sample size	Number aware
Before campaign	150	68
After campaign	120	65

(Continued)

To avoid working with negative differences whenever possible (to keep notation simpler by working with positive values), let $p_1 = r_1/n_1 = 65/120 = 0.5417$ and $p_2 = r_2/n_2 = 68/150 = 0.4533$. Hence our point estimate of the difference is

'After' – 'Before' = $p_1 - p_2 = 0.5417 - 0.4533 = 0.0884$.

A 95% confidence interval for the difference between population proportions, $\pi_1 - \pi_2$, therefore has endpoints

$$0.0884 \pm 1.96 \times \sqrt{\frac{0.4533(1-0.4533)}{150} + \frac{0.5417(1-0.5417)}{120}}$$

which can be expressed as (–0.031, 0.208).

A 90% confidence interval has endpoints

$$0.0884 \pm 1.645 \times \sqrt{\frac{0.4533(1-0.4533)}{150} + \frac{0.5417(1-0.5417)}{120}}$$

which can be expressed as (–0.012, 0.189).

Note that both confidence intervals *include zero* (since they both have a negative lower bound and a positive upper bound). This suggests there is no significant difference in public awareness. This idea has close parallels with hypothesis testing, introduced in Chapter 10.

9.9 DIFFERENCE BETWEEN TWO POPULATION MEANS

In this section we are primarily interested in the difference between two population means, $\mu_1 - \mu_2$. There are four cases to be considered, depending on whether variances are known or unknown, in which case we can assume they are either equal or unequal, and the case of paired datasets.

9.9.1 Unpaired samples - variances known

Suppose we have random samples of size n_1 and n_2 from two normal populations, $N(\mu_1,\sigma_1^2)$ and $N(\mu_2,\sigma_2^2)$. Hence the sampling distributions of $\bar{X}_1$ and $\bar{X}_2$ are

$$\bar{X}_1 \sim N\left(\mu_1, \frac{\sigma_1^2}{n_1}\right) \quad \text{and} \quad \bar{X}_2 \sim N\left(\mu_2, \frac{\sigma_2^2}{n_2}\right).$$

A natural estimator of $\mu_1 - \mu_2$ is $\bar{X}_1 - \bar{X}_2$. For *independent* random samples drawn from two separate populations, $\bar{X}_1$ and $\bar{X}_2$ are independent. Therefore, the sampling distribution of their difference is

$$\bar{X}_1 - \bar{X}_2 \sim N\left(\mu_1 - \mu_2, \frac{\sigma_1^2}{n_1} + \frac{\sigma_2^2}{n_2}\right). \tag{9.8}$$

Confidence interval endpoints for the difference between two population means (variances known)

If the population variances σ_1^2 and σ_2^2 are known, a $100(1-\alpha)\%$ confidence interval for $\mu_1 - \mu_2$ has endpoints

$$\bar{x}_1 - \bar{x}_2 \pm z_{\alpha/2} \times \sqrt{\frac{\sigma_1^2}{n_1} + \frac{\sigma_2^2}{n_2}} \quad (9.9)$$

where $z_{\alpha/2}$ is the z-value which cuts off $100\alpha/2\%$ probability in the upper tail of the standard normal distribution, obtained using `NORM.S.INV`.

9.9.2 Unpaired samples - variances unknown and unequal

We have the same set-up as above, with the same sampling distribution for $\bar{X}_1 - \bar{X}_2$ in (9.8), but now the population variances σ_1^2 and σ_2^2 are *unknown*. Assuming *large* sample sizes, say greater than 30, we can replace these unknown parameters with the respective sample variances s_1^2 and s_2^2 and continue to use standard normal values when determining confidence interval endpoints. The justification is that since the sample sizes are large, we would expect reasonably accurate estimates of the population variances, such that $s_1^2 \approx \sigma_1^2$ and $s_2^2 \approx \sigma_2^2$.

Confidence interval endpoints for the difference between two population means (variances unknown, large sample sizes)

If the population variances σ_1^2 and σ_2^2 are unknown, provided the sample sizes n_1 and n_2 are large (greater than 30), an *approximate* $100(1-\alpha)\%$ confidence interval for $\mu_1 - \mu_2$ has endpoints

$$\bar{x}_1 - \bar{x}_2 \pm z_{\alpha/2} \times \sqrt{\frac{s_1^2}{n_1} + \frac{s_2^2}{n_2}}$$

where $z_{\alpha/2}$ is the z-value which cuts off $100\alpha/2\%$ probability in the upper tail of the standard normal distribution, obtained using `NORM.S.INV`.

9.9.3 Unpaired samples - variances unknown and equal

In some circumstances we may be able to justify the assumption that the two populations being sampled are of *equal variability*. In which case, suppose we have random samples of size n_1 and n_2 from two normal populations, $N(\mu_1, \sigma^2)$ and $N(\mu_2, \sigma^2)$, that is, the populations have a *common variance*, σ^2, which is unknown. (If the population variances were known, then we would know their true values. Hence no assumptions would be necessary and we could use (9.9).) Therefore, the sampling distributions of $\bar{X}_1$ and $\bar{X}_2$ are

$$\bar{X}_1 \sim N\left(\mu_1, \frac{\sigma^2}{n_1}\right) \quad \text{and} \quad \bar{X}_2 \sim N\left(\mu_2, \frac{\sigma^2}{n_2}\right).$$

A natural estimator of $\mu_1 - \mu_2$ is still $\bar{X}_1 - \bar{X}_2$. Since we have *independent* (unpaired) samples, $\bar{X}_1$ and $\bar{X}_2$ are independent, hence the sampling distribution of their difference is

$$\bar{X}_1 - \bar{X}_2 \sim N\left(\mu_1 - \mu_2, \sigma^2\left(\frac{1}{n_1} + \frac{1}{n_2}\right)\right).$$

The problem is that this common variance σ^2 is unknown, so needs to be estimated. Should we use S_1^2 or S_2^2 as an estimator of σ^2? Answer: use both, by *pooling* the two sample variances, since both contain useful information about σ^2.

Pooled variance estimator

The **pooled variance estimator**, where S_1^2 and S_2^2 are sample variances from samples of size n_1 and n_2, respectively, is

$$S_p^2 = \frac{(n_1 - 1)S_1^2 + (n_2 - 1)S_2^2}{n_1 + n_2 - 2} \tag{9.10}$$

on $n_1 + n_2 - 2$ degrees of freedom, where the subscript '*p*' denotes 'pooled'.

Hence S_p^2 is the weighted average of the sample variances S_1^2 and S_2^2, where the weights are

$$\frac{n_1 - 1}{n_1 + n_2 - 2} \quad \text{and} \quad \frac{n_2 - 1}{n_1 + n_2 - 2},$$

respectively. So if $n_1 = n_2$, then we give the sample variances *equal weight*. Intuitively, this should make sense. As the sample size increases, a sample variance provides a more accurate estimate of σ^2. Hence if $n_1 \neq n_2$, the sample variance calculated from the larger sample is more reliable, so is given greater weight in the pooled variance estimator. Of course, if $n_1 = n_2$, then the variances are equally reliable, hence they are given equal weight.

Confidence interval endpoints for the difference between two population means (variances unknown, assumed equal)

If the population variances σ_1^2 and σ_2^2 are unknown but assumed equal, a $100(1 - \alpha)\%$ confidence interval for $\mu_1 - \mu_2$ has endpoints

$$\bar{x}_1 - \bar{x}_2 \pm t_{\alpha/2, n_1+n_2-2} \times \sqrt{s_p^2\left(\frac{1}{n_1} + \frac{1}{n_2}\right)} \tag{9.11}$$

where s_p^2 is the estimate from the pooled variance estimator (9.10), and where $t_{\alpha/2, n_1+n_2-2}$ is the t-value which cuts off $100\alpha/2\%$ probability in the upper tail of the Student's t distribution with $n_1 + n_2 - 2$ degrees of freedom, obtained using `T.INV`.

An obvious problem is how to decide whether to assume the unknown variances are equal or unequal. Consider the following points.

- If $\sigma_1^2 = \sigma_2^2$, then we would expect approximately equal sample variances, i.e. $s_1^2 \approx s_s^2$, since both sample variances would be estimating the same (common) variance. If the sample variances are very different, then this would suggest $\sigma_1^2 \neq \sigma_2^2$. Note that a formal 'hypothesis test' (discussed in Chapter 10) of $H_0 : \sigma_1^2 = \sigma_2^2$ could be performed.
- If we are sampling from two 'similar' populations (e.g. companies in the same industry) then an *assumption* of equal variability in these 'similar' populations would be reasonable.

Example 9.12

Two companies supplying a similar service are compared for their reaction times (in days) to complaints. Random samples of recent complaints to these companies produced the following table:

	Sample size	Sample mean	Sample std. dev.
Company A	12	8.5	3.6
Company B	10	4.8	2.1

We compute a 95% confidence interval for the true difference in mean reaction times and use this interval to decide if one company is faster than the other, on average, in reacting to complaints.

Because the markets are 'similar', it is reasonable to assume (although it is only an assumption!) that the two population variances are equal. Under this assumption, using (9.10), we have

$$s_p^2 = \frac{(12-1)\times 3.6^2 + (10-1)\times 2.1^2}{12+10-2} = 9.1125$$

on $n_1 + n_2 - 2 = 12 + 10 - 2 = 20$ degrees of freedom. So the estimated standard error of the difference in sample means is

$$\sqrt{s_p^2\left(\frac{1}{n_1}+\frac{1}{n_2}\right)} = \sqrt{9.1125\times\left(\frac{1}{12}+\frac{1}{10}\right)} = \sqrt{9.1125\times 0.1833} = 1.2925.$$

Hence a 95% confidence interval for the difference in means, using (9.11), is

$$8.5 - 4.8 \pm 2.086 \times 1.2925 \Rightarrow (1.01, 6.39)$$

where $t_{0.025,\,20} = 2.086$ (we have estimated the common variance, so we use the *t* distribution, here with 20 degrees of freedom, obtained in Excel using `=T.INV(0.975,20)`).

As zero does *not* lie in this interval, we conclude that the data suggest that company B is faster, on average, than company A in reacting to complaints. Since the variable is reaction time, so a *lower* sample mean suggests a *faster* average reaction time.

9.9.4 Paired (dependent) samples

Paired-sample methods are used in special cases when the two samples are not statistically independent. For our purposes, such paired data are likely to involve observations on the *same* individuals in two different states – such as 'before' and 'after' some intervening event. A paired-sample experimental design is advantageous since it allows researchers to determine whether or not significant changes have occurred as a result of the intervening event free of bias from other factors, since these have been *controlled for* by observing the same individuals.

A necessary, but not sufficient, condition for the presence of paired-sample data is that $n_1 = n_2$, in order to have 'pairs' of data values. Common sense needs to be exercised to determine whether or not we have paired data. An example of such a dataset would be observations of the *same* individuals at two different points in time, typically 'before' and 'after' some event, such as 'analytical skill' before and after reading this book. One hopes, of course, that this would result in a mean increase, or at the very least no decrease, in 'analytical skill'!

This scenario is easy to analyse as the paired data can simply be reduced to a 'one-sample' analysis by working with *differenced data*. That is, suppose two samples generated sample values $x_1, x_2, \ldots, x_n$ and $y_1, y_2, \ldots, y_n$, respectively (note the same number of observations, n, in each sample). To compute the differences we have

$$d_1 = x_1 - y_1,\ d_2 = x_2 - y_2,\ \ldots,\ d_n = x_n - y_n.$$

It follows that $\bar{x}_d = \bar{x} - \bar{y}$, so that by using the differences to compute a confidence interval for $\mu_d = \mu_X - \mu_Y$, we get the required confidence interval for $\mu_X - \mu_Y$. Therefore, the technique follows that in Section 9.5.5.

Example 9.13

The table below shows the before and after weights (in pounds) of 8 adults after a new advertised diet. We determine a 95% confidence interval for the mean loss of weight due to the diet. Based on this, we can then judge whether we are convinced that the diet reduces weight, on average.

Before	After	Before	After
127	122	150	144
130	120	147	138
114	116	167	155
139	132	153	152

The differences (calculated as 'Before – After') are

5, 10, −2, 7, 6, 9, 12, 1.

Hence $n = 8$, $\bar{x}_d = 6$ and $s_d = 4.66$ on $n - 1 = 7$ degrees of freedom. The estimated standard error of the sample mean is $s/\sqrt{n} = 4.66/\sqrt{8} = 1.65$. Using the t distribution on 7 degrees of freedom, for 95% confidence we use $t_{0.025,\,7} = 2.365$, obtained in Excel using `=T.INV(0.975,7)`.

So a 95% confidence interval for the mean difference in weight before and after the diet is $\bar{x}_d \pm t_{0.025,n-1} \times s_d / \sqrt{n}$, that is,

$$6 \pm 2.365 \times 1.65 \Rightarrow (2.1, 9.9).$$

Since zero is not included in this confidence interval, we conclude that the diet *does* appear to reduce weight, that is, the average weight loss appears to be positive.

9.10 SUMMARY OF COMMON EXCEL FUNCTIONS

Appendix A summarises common Excel functions for constructing confidence intervals.

9.11 CHAPTER OVERVIEW

This chapter has examined the desirable properties of estimators. The mean squared error criterion was discussed as a way of choosing between competing estimators, taking into account the bias and variance of an estimator. The concepts of estimation are obviously extremely important for a manager who wants to collect a reasonable amount of data so as to make a good judgement of the overall situation. Point estimates are our 'best guesses' of unknown parameter values, but due to the risk of estimation error it is necessary to attach error bounds to point estimates, and we have seen several cases of confidence interval construction.

9.12 KEY VOCABULARY

Bias
Bias-variance trade-off
Confidence interval
Degrees of freedom
Estimation error
Mean squared error
Minimum variance unbiased estimator
Negatively biased estimator
(Point) estimate
(Point) estimation
(Point) estimator
Pooled variance estimator
Positively biased estimator
Student's *t* distribution
Tolerance on the estimation error
Unbiased estimator
Variance

9.13 EXERCISES

9.13.1 Test your understanding

1 What is the difference between a point estimate and a point estimator?
2 How is the bias of an estimator defined?

3 If $\hat{\theta}$ is an estimator of θ, provide an expression involving $E(\hat{\theta})$ and θ such that $\hat{\theta}$ is:

(a) a positively biased estimator of θ
(b) an unbiased estimator of θ
(c) a negatively biased estimator of θ.

4 Would you prefer the variance of an estimator to be large or small? Briefly justify your view.
5 What is meant by the bias–variance trade-off when evaluating the performance of estimators?
6 Provide a formula for the mean squared error of an estimator, and explain the purpose of the mean squared error.
7 Is unbiasedness a variant or an invariant property? Briefly explain why.
8 What is meant by the 'coverage probability' of an interval estimator?
9 When sampling from a normal distribution, how are the endpoints of a 95% confidence interval for μ calculated:

(a) when σ^2 is known?
(b) when σ^2 is unknown?

10 What is the best confidence level to use in interval estimation? 'Well, James, it depends' may feature in your answer, but explain what it depends on!
11 Discuss any similarities and any differences between the standard normal distribution and the Student's *t* distribution.
12 How are the endpoints of a $100(1 - \alpha)\%$ confidence interval for a single population proportion calculated?
13 What three factors affect the minimum required sample size when estimating:

(a) a single population mean?
(b) a single population proportion?

14 How are the endpoints of a $100(1 - \alpha)\%$ confidence interval for the difference between two population proportions calculated?
15 What is the purpose of the pooled variance estimator? How is it calculated?
16 How are the endpoints of a $100(1 - \alpha)\%$ confidence interval for the difference between two population means calculated:

(a) when σ_1^2 and σ_2^2 are known?
(b) when σ_1^2 and σ_2^2 unknown?
(c) when working with paired (dependent) samples?

17 A business requires an inexpensive check on the value of stock in its warehouse. In order to do this, a random sample of 50 items is taken and valued. The average value of these is computed to be £320.41, with a (sample) standard deviation of £40.60. It is known that there are 9875 items in the total stock.

(a) Estimate the total value of the stock to the nearest £10,000.
(b) Calculate a 95% confidence interval for the mean value of all items and hence determine a 95% confidence interval for the total value of the stock.
(c) You are told this confidence interval is too wide for decision purposes. Assess how many more items would need to be sampled to obtain an interval with the same degree of confidence, but with half the width.

18 Two advertising companies each give quotations for nine different campaigns. Their quotations (in thousands of pounds) are shown in the following table. Calculate a 95% confidence interval for the true difference between average quotations. Can you deduce from this interval if one company is more expensive on average than the other?

Company	1	2	3	4	5	6	7	8	9
A	39	24	36	42	45	30	38	32	39
B	46	26	32	39	51	34	37	41	44

19 In order to assess the impact of an advertising campaign, a restaurateur monitors his daily revenue before and after the campaign. The table below shows some sample statistics of daily sales calculated over a period of 60 days prior to the campaign, and 45 days after the campaign. Determine a 95% confidence interval for the increase in average daily sales due to the campaign. Is there strong evidence that the campaign has increased sales?

	Before campaign	After campaign
Number of days	60	45
Mean daily sales	£503	£559
Standard deviation	£21	£29

20 In a market research study to compare two chocolate bar wrappings, 30 out of 50 children preferred a gold wrapping to a silver wrapping, whereas 25 out of 40 adults preferred the silver wrapping. Compute a 95% confidence interval for the difference in the true proportions in favour of gold wrapping between the two groups.

It is decided to take further samples of children and adults so that we finally sample the same number of adults and children such that the final estimator of the difference between proportions is within 0.06 of the true difference (with 95% confidence). How many more adults and children need to be sampled?

21 A factory has 1000 workers. A simple random sample of 100 of these had weekly salaries with a (sample) mean of £315 and a (sample) standard deviation of £20.

(a) Calculate a 90% confidence interval for the mean weekly salary of all workers in the factory.

(b) How many more workers should be sampled if it is required that the estimate is to be within £3 of the true average (again, with 90% confidence)?

Note that this means a tolerance of £3 – equivalent to a confidence interval width of £6.

22 A company recently redesigned its website to increase its appeal to younger consumers (those aged under 30). Random samples of younger consumers were surveyed before and after the redesign to see if they had a positive opinion of the website. The results were as follows:

	Sample size	Respondents with a positive opinion
Before redesign	125	75
After redesign	150	111

(a) Compute a 98% confidence interval for the difference between the proportions of younger consumers with a positive view before and after the website redesign. Briefly interpret your confidence interval.

(b) Briefly discuss any concerns had the sample sizes been 25 and 30, instead of 125 and 150, respectively.

23 A pharmaceutical company has developed a new vaccine to immunise against Covid-19 and needs to determine the vaccine's efficacy. A randomised experiment was conducted to address this question. The study randomly allocated 200 people to either a group where the vaccine was administered, or a group where a placebo was given. These people were monitored and the numbers of those who did not go on to contract Covid-19 (and those who did) were recorded. The results are summarised below:

	Developed Covid-19	Did not develop Covid-19
Vaccine group	21	79
Placebo group	48	52

(a) Provide a 90% confidence interval for the difference in the proportions of those who did *not* develop Covid-19 between those who took the vaccine and the placebo group.

(b) Explain, with reasons, whether 200 people in this study are a sufficient number.

24 A random sample is drawn from a normal distribution, $N(\mu, 36)$. You are told that a 90% confidence interval for the population mean is (6.78, 8.22). What was the size of the sample?

25 Based on the central limit theorem, you are told that a 99% confidence interval for a population proportion is (0.5782, 0.7018). What was the size of the sample used?

26 Suppose a coin is to be tossed n times for the purpose of estimating π, where $\pi = P(\text{heads})$.

(a) State the approximate sampling distribution of P, the sample proportion, and briefly state the condition on n which should be satisfied for the approximation to be reasonable.

(b) How large must n be to guarantee that the *width* of the 99% confidence interval for π will be less than 0.02?

27 A company wishes to investigate whether average brand awareness varies between older and younger people. Random samples of 15 adults over the age of 60 and 14 adults aged between 18 and 30 scored their brand awareness on a scale from 1 to 100. Summaries of these scores are presented below.

	Sample size	Sample mean	Sample variance
Over 60s	15	68.7	15.4
18-30s	14	74.3	18.2

(a) Construct a 99% confidence interval for the difference between mean brand awareness scores and explain in *one sentence* how the confidence interval should be interpreted.

(b) Is it possible that there is no difference between older and younger adults in terms of their average brand awareness? Briefly justify your view.

28 Two market research companies each take random samples to assess the public's attitude towards a particular clothing brand. If n represents the sample size and r the number of people with a positive view, the results of these independent surveys are as follows:

	n	r
Company 1	400	160
Company 2	900	324

(a) If π is the population proportion with a positive view of the clothing brand, determine a 95% confidence interval to comment on the compatibility of the two companies' results.

(b) An observer decides to estimate π using both datasets and uses the estimator

$$a\left(\frac{R_1}{n_1}\right)+b\left(\frac{R_2}{n_2}\right),$$

where a and b are constants. Show that we must have $b = 1 - a$ for this estimator to be unbiased and, subject to this, find a value of a which will make this estimator the most efficient (i.e. with the minimum standard error).

29 Twelve independent observations are sampled from a population known to be normal, $N(\mu_X, 9\sigma^2)$. For these, the sample mean is 12.6 and the sample standard deviation is 1.1.

Sixteen independent observations are sampled from a population known to be normal, $N(\mu_Y, 8\sigma^2)$. For these, the sample mean is 10.1 and the sample standard deviation is 1.8.

Determine a 95% confidence interval for $\mu_X - \mu_Y$.

30 Ten independent observations are sampled from a normal population, $N(\mu_X, 4\sigma^2)$. For these, the sample mean is 12.3 and the sample standard deviation is 1.2.

Fourteen independent observations are sampled from a normal population, $N(\mu_Y, 8\sigma^2)$. For these, the sample mean is 10.1 and the sample standard deviation is 1.9.

Determine a 95% confidence interval for $\mu_X - \mu_Y$.

9.13.2 Practice with Excel

Head over to the companion website for Excel examples and screencasts!

9.14 PROOF

This proof is not essential to review (or master), but is included for the interested reader. A black square, ■, simply denotes the end of the proof. Enjoy.

The mean squared error (MSE) of an estimator is the average squared error. Formally, this is defined as

$$\text{MSE}(\hat{\theta}) = \text{E}((\hat{\theta}-\theta)^2) = \text{Var}(\hat{\theta}) + (\text{Bias}(\hat{\theta}))^2. \tag{9.12}$$

It is possible to decompose this into components involving both the bias and the variance of an estimator. Recall that

$$\mathrm{Var}(X) = \mathrm{E}(X^2) - (\mathrm{E}(X))^2 \Rightarrow \mathrm{E}(X^2) = \mathrm{Var}(X) + (\mathrm{E}(X))^2.$$

Also, note that for any constant k, $\mathrm{Var}(X \pm k) = \mathrm{Var}(X)$, hence adding or subtracting a constant has no effect on the variance of a random variable. Noting that the true parameter θ is some (unknown) constant (even though θ is an unknown constant, it is known to be a constant), it immediately follows, by setting $X = (\hat{\theta} - \theta)$, that

$$\begin{aligned} \mathrm{MSE}(\hat{\theta}) &= \mathrm{E}((\hat{\theta} - \hat{\theta})^2) \\ &= \mathrm{Var}(\hat{\theta} - \theta) + (\mathrm{E}(\hat{\theta} - \theta))^2 \\ &= \mathrm{Var}(\hat{\theta}) + (\mathrm{Bias}(\hat{\theta}))^2. \end{aligned} \tag{9.13}$$

It is the form of the MSE given by (9.13), rather than (9.12), which we tend to use in practice. ■

10

HYPOTHESIS TESTING

Chapter contents

Chapter level: *Intermediate*

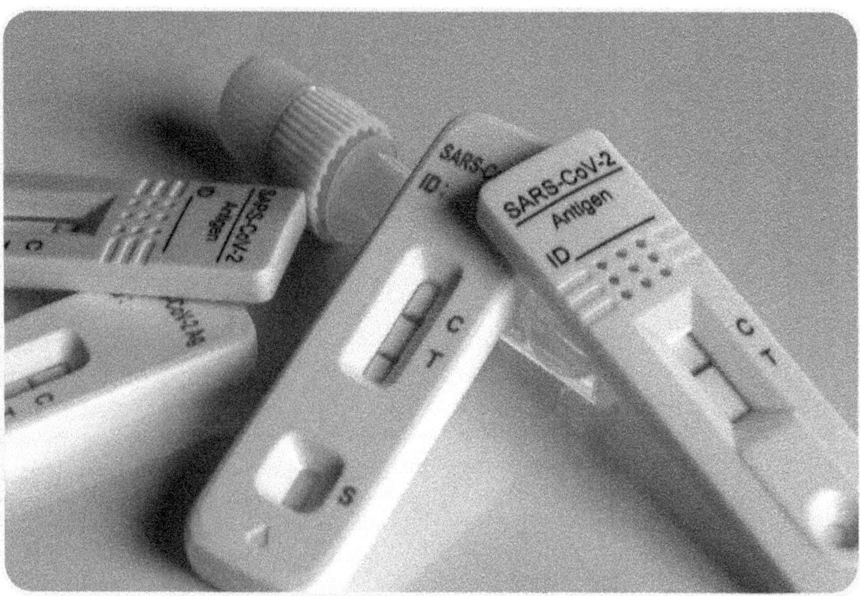

Source: Photo by Alexandra_Koch via Pixabay.

Key concepts

- Statistical significance
- *p*-values
- Power

Chapter value

We interrogate data to search for evidence to support/refute theories, claims and hypotheses.

Key takeaway

Any significant result could be a false positive.
Any non-significant result could be a false negative.

Chapter outline

Hypothesis testing concerns the pursuit of *evidence* in defence of, or to refute, statements or claims made about a population. In most contexts considered here, these statements will be framed in terms of the *parameters of distributions*, such as a mean or a proportion. Depending on our objective, we could use hypothesis testing in one of two ways:

- A claim has been made by a person or company about which we are suspicious (e.g. advertised product specifications not being adhered to), and we seek to refute the claim by demonstrating a 'significant' deviation from the claim observed in our data.
- We wish to make a claim (e.g. that our new product is better than those of competitors), and we seek 'evidence' to justify and defend our claim to make it credible.

Learning outcomes

After completing this chapter, you should be able to:

- set up the null and alternative hypotheses for a problem and state whether the latter is one-sided or two-sided, leading to a one-tailed or two-tailed test, respectively
- define and apply the terminology of hypothesis testing
- define and explain the types of errors which can be made in hypothesis testing
- perform hypothesis tests on means and proportions.

Motivational case: Manufacturer loses its fizz, business goes flat

Aquafizz is a manufacturer of bottles of carbonated water. Each bottle is sold with contents of 500 millilitres advertised on the label. A regular customer of Aquafizz noticed that the most recent batch they had purchased seemed to have 'significantly' less than 500 millilitres of product per bottle, based on the water line appearing to be much lower than usual.

Feeling slightly aggrieved, the customer is considering formally complaining to Aquafizz that they have systematically underfilled their bottles below the advertised contents of 500 millilitres.

How should the customer go about making a valid case with evidence to support their suspicion?

10.1 INTRODUCTION

This chapter considers **hypothesis testing**, that is, decision theory whereby we make a *binary decision* between two competing hypotheses, denoted by H_0 and H_1, where:

- H_0 is the null hypothesis
- H_1 is the alternative hypothesis.

Our binary decision is whether to 'reject' H_0 or 'not reject' H_0, and this decision is data-driven. However, before we consider statistical tests we begin with a legal analogy – the decision of a jury in a court trial.

10.2 STATISTICAL JURIES

In a criminal court, defendants are put on trial because the police suspect (rightly or wrongly) that they are guilty of a crime. Cases could be tried for various offences, ranging from breach of the peace to murder. To take a business example, directors of a company may be prosecuted for fraudulent accounting. When it comes to determining whether or not the suspect is guilty, the police are not impartial due to their *a priori* suspicion of guilt – they would have arrested the suspect with reason – so determination of whether or not a defendant is guilty is undertaken by an independent (and hopefully objective!) jury. (In complicated fraud trials, the outcome may actually be decided only by a panel of judges rather than by jurors formed of members of the public. However, we could think of the judges as being the jury!)

The jury has to decide between the two competing hypotheses,

H_0: not guilty and H_1: guilty,

which in the accounting fraud trial example would equate to

H_0: no fraud committed and H_1: fraud committed.

Note that these hypotheses are mutually exclusive and collectively exhaustive (MECE again!), in that the defendant either did, or did not, commit the alleged crime. While the defendant would be aware of the truth, the decision-makers (i.e. the jury) are not. For example, if the defendant pleaded 'not guilty', this is either an honest plea (they are innocent) or a lie (they are guilty but are trying to escape conviction). Even if the defendant pleaded 'guilty', this may not be truthful (they may be incentivised to 'take the rap' in return for their loved ones being looked after – or saved from harm – by more powerful figures, such as in organised crime circles).

In most jury-based legal systems around the world there is the *presumption of innocence until proven guilty*. This equates to the jury initially assuming H_0 (not guilty, no fraud committed, etc.) to be true, which is the working hypothesis. A jury must continue to believe in the null hypothesis until they feel the evidence presented to the court proves guilt *beyond a reasonable doubt*, which represents the burden of proof required to establish guilt. In our statistical world of hypothesis testing, this will be known as the significance level, the threshold of evidence needed to reject H_0.

The jury uses the following (qualitative) decision rule to make a judgement. If the evidence is:

- *inconsistent* with the defendant being not guilty, then reject the null hypothesis (i.e. convict, find guilty) such that the defendant is found guilty beyond a reasonable doubt.

- *consistent* with the defendant being not guilty, then do not reject the null hypothesis (i.e. acquit, find not guilty).

Note that the jury is *not* testing whether the defendant is guilty, rather the jury is testing the null hypothesis of 'not guilty'. Failure to reject H_0 does not prove innocence, rather the jury concludes the evidence is *not sufficiently inconsistent* with H_0 to indicate guilt beyond a reasonable doubt (the case made by the prosecution is not considered to be strong enough). Admittedly, what constitutes a 'reasonable doubt' is subjective, which is why juries do not always reach a unanimous verdict – hearing the same prosecution and defence arguments in court, not all jurors may be convinced of the defendant's guilt, even though they have observed the same 'data'!

Statistical hypothesis testing follows this same logical path.

10.2.1 Miscarriages of justice

In a perfect world juries would always convict the guilty and acquit the innocent. Sadly, it is not a perfect world and so sometimes juries reach incorrect decisions, convicting the innocent and acquitting the guilty. In mitigation of the jury system, one hopes at least that juries *get it right far more often than they get it wrong*, but this is an important reminder that miscarriages of justice do occur from time to time, demonstrating that the jury system is not infallible! (I will leave you to judge(!) whether there is a better system to use.)

Statistical hypothesis testing also risks making mistakes which we will formally define as Type I errors and Type II errors, also known as *false positives* and *false negatives*, respectively.

10.3 TYPE I AND TYPE II ERRORS

In any hypothesis test there are two types of *inferential decision error* which could be committed. Clearly, we would like to reduce the *probabilities* of these errors as much as possible. These two types of error are called Type I error and Type II error, defined as follows.

- **Type I error**: rejecting H_0 when it is true. This can be thought of as a 'false positive'. Denote the *probability* of this type of error by α. The value of α is *under our control*.
- **Type II error**: failing to reject H_0 when it is false. This can be thought of as a 'false negative'. Denote the *probability* of this type of error by β. The value of β is *not under our (direct) control*.

Ideally, we would like $\alpha = 0$ (i.e. the probability of a Type I error to be zero) and $\beta = 0$ (i.e. the probability of a Type II error to be zero as well), such that our decisions ('reject H_0' and 'do not reject H_0') are always correct. This, though, is not realistic. Instead, we would like α and β to be as small as possible while being mindful that the risks of false positives and false negatives will not be zero.

Which is worse, a Type I error or a Type II error? Well, James, it depends! While both errors are undesirable, depending on the context of the hypothesis test it could be argued either way about which one is worse. However, on balance, a Type I error is usually considered to be more problematic.

Example 10.1

In terms of trials by jury, conventional wisdom is that it is better to let 100 guilty people walk free than to convict a single innocent person. While you are welcome to disagree, this view is consistent with Type I errors being more problematic!

Example 10.2

An exceptional case when we would consider a Type II error to be worse would be in testing for an infectious disease. Readers will no doubt remember taking several tests during the Covid-19 pandemic. A false positive (a Type I error) means you self-isolate needlessly thinking you have the virus, while a false negative (a Type II error) means you do not self-isolate but are infectious, risking becoming a 'superspreader' infecting many others, which is *much* worse.

The possible decision space can be presented as shown in Table 10.1.

Table 10.1 Decision space in hypothesis testing.

		Decision made	
		H_0 not rejected	H_0 rejected
True state of nature	**H_0 true**	Correct decision	Type I error
	H_1 true	Type II error	Correct decision

Example 10.3

If H_0 represents 'not guilty' and H_1 represents 'guilty', a Type I error would be finding an innocent person guilty (bad for them), while a Type II error would be finding a guilty person innocent (bad for the victim/society, but admittedly good for them!).

The *complement* of a Type II error probability, that is $1 - \beta$, is called the power of the test – the probability that the test will reject a false null hypothesis. Hence power measures the ability of the test to reject a false H_0, and so we seek the *most powerful test* for any testing situation. Hence by seeking the 'best' test, we mean the best in the 'most powerful' sense.

Example 10.4

During the pandemic, there was a choice of tests (rapid antigen, PCR, etc.). Ideally, you would want to use the best test, wouldn't you? What is 'best' though? It could be in terms of speed and/or convenience (such as the rapid antigen test), or in terms of Covid detection accuracy (such as the PCR test). In terms of *power* alone, we would opt for PCR over rapid antigen. In statistical testing, we would choose the best test in terms of power alone, but we should be mindful that on occasions we may accept the use of a less powerful test for the sake of expediency (analogous to the use of rapid antigen tests).

Unlike α, we do *not* control test power (as we do not control β). However, we can increase test power by *increasing the sample size, n*. A larger sample size will inevitably improve the accuracy of our hypothesis test decision-making. However, there is a trade-off in that a larger n means greater data collection costs.

Example 10.5

In the rush to develop Covid-19 vaccines (who wants to be locked down forever?), health authorities in each country would need to license and approve each vaccine for use. In matters of life and death, to obtain approval would require very 'powerful' evidence to justify rapid rollouts. As such, each candidate vaccine would have to undergo a series of *clinical trials*, with the number of test patients increasing at each stage. For example:

- Phase 1: $n_1 \approx 20$–100, checking for *safety* of the vaccine on a small scale, while monitoring for any side-effects.
- Phase 2: $n_2 \approx 500$–1000, checking for *effectiveness* of the vaccine, and appropriate size/number of doses (conditional on Phase 1 being successful).
- Phase 3: $n_3 \approx 10{,}000$–50,000, testing the vaccine on heterogeneous subjects (gender, age, ethnicities, etc.) to 'prove' it should be approved for use in the general population (conditional on Phase 2 being successful).

While different countries may prescribe different numerical values for each of n_1, n_2 and n_3 (perhaps due to different clinical opinions on these requirements), note that $n_1 < n_2 \ll n_3$, where $\ll$ means 'much less than'.

These concepts can be summarised as *conditional probabilities*, as shown in Table 10.2.

Table 10.2 Conditional probabilities in hypothesis testing.

	Decision	
	H_0 not rejected	H_0 rejected
H_0 true	$1-\alpha$	P(Type I error) = α
H_1 true	P(Type II error) = β	Power = $1-\beta$

We have

$$P(\text{H}_0 \text{ not rejected} \mid \text{H}_0 \text{ is true}) = 1 - \alpha \text{ and } P(\text{H}_0 \text{ rejected} \mid \text{H}_0 \text{ is true}) = \alpha$$

such that, by design,

$$P(\text{H}_0 \text{ not rejected} \mid \text{H}_0 \text{ is true}) + P(\text{H}_0 \text{ rejected} \mid \text{H}_0 \text{ is true}) = 1,$$

and

$$P(\text{H}_0 \text{ not rejected} \mid \text{H}_1 \text{ is true}) = \beta \text{ and } P(\text{H}_0 \text{ rejected} \mid \text{H}_1 \text{ is true}) = 1 - \beta$$

such that

$$P(\text{H}_0 \text{ not rejected} \mid \text{H}_1 \text{ is true}) + P(\text{H}_0 \text{ rejected} \mid \text{H}_1 \text{ is true}) = 1.$$

Ceteris paribus, if you decrease α you increase β and vice versa. Hence there is a *trade-off*. However, treating Type I errors as being more serious, this is why we control the value of α through the significance level and then we seek the most powerful test to minimise β, or equivalently to maximise $1 - \beta$.

10.3.1 Significance level

Since we control for the probability of a Type I error, α, what value should this be?

Well, in general we test at the $100\alpha\%$ significance level, for $\alpha \in [0,1]$. The default choice is $\alpha = 0.05$, that is, we test 'at the 5% significance level'. This means that, on average, 1 in every 20 *true* null hypotheses are incorrectly rejected. Of course, this value of α is *subjective*, and a different significance level may be chosen. The *severity* of a Type I error in the context of a specific hypothesis test might, for example, justify a more conservative or liberal choice for α. Could you tolerate a 1 in 20 error rate when H_0 is true? Would 1 in 10 (a 10% significance level) be acceptable? Perhaps 1 in 100 (a 1% significance level)? Ultimately, it is a judgement call.

In fact, noting our look at confidence intervals in the context of estimation in Chapter 9, we could view the *significance level in testing as the complement of the confidence level in estimation* (strictly speaking, this would apply to so-called 'two-tailed' hypothesis tests, discussed later). For example:

- a 90% confidence level in estimation has parallels with a 10% significance level in testing ($\alpha = 0.10$)
- a 95% confidence level in estimation has parallels with a 5% significance level in testing ($\alpha = 0.05$)
- a 99% confidence level in estimation has parallels with a 1% significance level in testing ($\alpha = 0.01$).

The most common significance levels are 10%, 5% and 1%, such that:

- rejecting H_0 at the 10% significance level (but not lower) reflects a *weakly significant* result, with *weak evidence*
- rejecting H_0 at the 5% significance level (but not lower) reflects a *moderately significant* result, with *moderate evidence*
- rejecting H_0 at the 1% significance level reflects a *highly significant* result, with *strong evidence.*

Recall that a jury's threshold to deliver a verdict of 'guilty' is 'beyond a reasonable doubt'. Well, in hypothesis testing our choice of α plays the role of this reasonable doubt goalpost. We are free to move this goalpost as we deem appropriate, albeit this should be decided before performing the hypothesis test. The more serious a Type I error is, the smaller we may set α to minimise the risk of a Type I error occurring, that is, reduce the risk of incorrectly rejecting a true null hypothesis.

What is reasonable for reasonable doubt?

While criminal trials require guilt to be proven 'beyond a reasonable doubt', in civil trials (such as when party A sues party B for breach of contract), given imprisonment and loss of liberty are not at stake (any punishment would be monetary, in the form of damages) a Type I error is less severe. This is reflected (in some jurisdictions) as deciding the case based on the 'balance of probabilities'. This can be thought of as a significance level of 50%!

Once this goalpost has been set, how do we actually use α to decide whether or not to reject H_0? For that, we use *p-values*.

10.4 P-VALUES, EFFECT SIZE AND SAMPLE SIZE INFLUENCES

Our principal tool for deciding whether or not to reject H_0 is the *p*-value.

Definition: *p*-value

A **p-value** is the probability of the event that the 'test statistic' (a known function of our data) takes the observed value or more extreme (i.e. more unlikely) values under H_0. It is a measure of the discrepancy between the null hypothesis, H_0, and the data evidence.

- A 'small' *p*-value indicates that the data are *inconsistent* with H_0.
- A 'large' *p*-value indicates that the data are *consistent* with H_0.

So, *p*-values may be seen as a measure of how compatible our data are with the null hypothesis, such that as the *p*-value gets closer to 1 the data evidence becomes more compatible with H_0

(i.e. H_0 seems more credible), while as the *p*-value gets closer to 0 the data evidence becomes less compatible with H_0 (i.e. H_0 seems more incredible).

Example 10.6

Consider two business directors on trial for accounting fraud. The jury tests

H_0: not guilty versus H_1: guilty.

Consider the following two scenarios.

a Auditors are called as expert witnesses and they clearly explain the fraud they uncovered, including email records between the two directors referencing their fraudulent activities. The directors are unable to provide a credible defence. In this case the evidence appears clear-cut, that is, the evidence presented is (highly) inconsistent with H_0 and hence H_0 is rejected. This can be thought of as the *p*-value being sufficiently small. The directors are found guilty beyond a reasonable doubt.

b The only evidence of accounting fraud is circumstantial. The directors' defence lawyers provide robust arguments casting doubt on whether fraud had actually occurred. While not proof of innocence, the evidence is too weak to justify finding the directors guilty, beyond a reasonable doubt. This can be thought of as the *p*-value being sufficiently large.

Example 10.7

Suppose we are interested in evaluating the mean income (in thousands of pounds) of a community. Suppose income in the population is modelled as $N(\mu, 25)$ (income is not normally distributed, but heavily positively skewed - we ignore this fact here for simplicity). A random sample of $n = 25$ observations is taken, yielding a sample mean of 17 (i.e. $\bar{X} = 17$).

Independently of the data, three expert economists give their own opinions as follows.

- Dr A claims the population mean income is $\mu = 16$.
- Ms B claims the population mean income is $\mu = 15$.
- Mr C claims the population mean income is $\mu = 14$.

How can we assess these experts' contradictory statements? (At most one expert is correct, and they could all be incorrect.)

Here, the sampling distribution of the sample mean is

$$\bar{X} \sim N\left(\mu, \frac{\sigma^2}{n}\right) = N\left(\mu, \frac{25}{25}\right) = N(\mu, 1)$$

since $\sigma^2 = 25$ and $n = 25$. We assess the statements of the three expert economists based on this sampling distribution, with a standard error of $\sigma / \sqrt{n} = 1$.

If Dr A's claim is correct, then $\bar{X} \sim N(16, 1)$. The observed value $\bar{x} = 17$ is *one standard error away from* μ (since $\bar{x} - \mu = 17 - 16 = 1$, and $\sigma/\sqrt{n} = 1$), and may be regarded as a typical observation from the distribution (i.e. nothing out of the ordinary). Hence there is *little inconsistency* between the claim and the data evidence. This one standard error difference between the claim that $\mu = 16$ and the estimate of μ given by $\bar{x} = 17$ can reasonably be attributed to sampling error. This is shown in Figure 10.1.

If Ms B's claim is correct, then $\bar{X} \sim N(15, 1)$. The observed value $\bar{x} = 17$ begins to look a bit 'extreme', as it is *two standard errors away from* μ (since $17 - 15 = 2$). Hence there is *some inconsistency* between the claim and the data evidence (we are somewhat surprised to obtain a point estimate of μ as far away as two standard errors from the claimed value). This two standard error difference between the claim that $\mu = 15$ and the estimate of μ given by $\bar{x} = 17$ is less likely to be attributable to sampling error, casting some doubt on Ms B's claim. This is shown in Figure 10.2.

If Mr C's claim is correct, then $\bar{X} \sim N(14, 1)$. The observed value $\bar{x} = 17$ is very extreme, as it is *three standard errors away from* μ (since $17 - 14 = 3$). Hence there is *strong inconsistency* between the claim and the data evidence. This three standard error difference between the claim that $\mu = 14$ and the estimate of μ given by $\bar{x} = 17$ is very unlikely to be attributable to sampling error, casting significant doubt on Mr C's claim. This is shown in Figure 10.3.

We can actually calculate the *conditional probability* of observing a sample mean at least one, two and three standard errors, respectively, beyond the claims of each expert economist. This simply involves standardisation of $\bar{X}$ conditioning on the claimed value of μ in each case.

- Under H_0: $\mu = 16$ (Dr A's claim), the probability of being at least one standard error *above or below* 16 is

  $P(\bar{X} \geq 17) + P(\bar{X} \leq 15) = P(|\bar{X} - 16| \geq 1) = 0.3173.$

- Under H_0: $\mu = 15$ (Ms B's claim), the probability of being at least two standard errors *above or below* 15 is

  $P(\bar{X} \geq 17) + P(\bar{X} \leq 13) = P(|\bar{X} - 15| \geq 2) = 0.0455.$

- Under H_0: $\mu = 14$ (Mr C's claim), the probability of being at least three standard errors *above or below* 14 is

  $P(\bar{X} \geq 17) + P(\bar{X} \leq 11) = P(|\bar{X} - 14| \geq 3) = 0.0027.$

These conditional probabilities are the *p*-values for the respective sets of hypotheses,

$$H_0: \mu = \mu_0 \text{ versus } H_1: \mu \neq \mu_0,$$

where μ_0 is the economist's claimed value of μ. Note that

$$0.0027 < 0.0455 < 0.3173$$

such that the *greater the difference* (the greater the incompatibility) between the data evidence and the claim (in the null hypothesis), the *smaller* the *p*-value.

In summary, of the three claims the one we would be most willing to *reject* would be the claim that $\mu = 14$, because if the hypothesis $\mu = 14$ is true, the probability of observing $\bar{x} = 17$, or more extreme values (i.e. $\bar{x} \geq 17$ or $\bar{x} \leq 11$), would be as small as 0.0027. We are comfortable with this decision, as *such a small-probability event would be very unlikely to occur in a single experiment*.

On the other hand, we would be far less comfortable rejecting the claim that $\mu = 16$, because if the hypothesis $\mu = 16$ is true, the probability of observing $\bar{x} = 17$, or more extreme values (i.e. $\bar{x} \geq 17$ or $\bar{x} \leq 15$) is much larger at 0.3173. However, this does not imply that Dr A's claim is necessarily true.

Finally, note that we have been careful to talk about 'not rejecting' H_0, rather than 'accepting' H_0. Always remember that a statistical test is incapable of 'accepting' a hypothesis!

10.4.1 Interpretation of *p*-values

In practice the statistical analysis of data is performed by computers using statistical or econometric software packages. Some simple common hypothesis tests may be performed in Excel. Regardless of the specific hypothesis being tested, the execution of a hypothesis test by a computer returns a *p*-value. Fortunately, regardless of the test being conducted, there is a ***universal decision rule*** for *p*-values.

We have explained that we control for the probability of a Type I error through our choice of significance level, α, where $\alpha \in [0, 1]$. Since *p*-values are also probabilities, that's what the *p* stands for, we simply compare *p*-values with our chosen benchmark significance level, α.

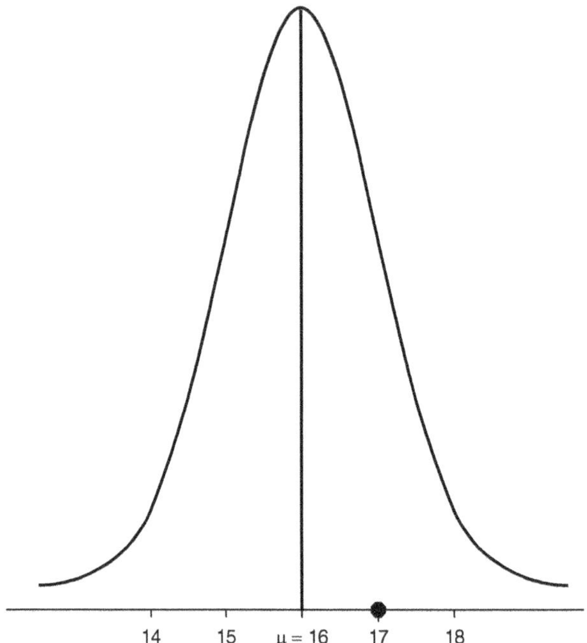

Figure 10.1 How $\bar{x} = 17$ if Dr A's claim is correct that $\mu = 16$ in Example 10.7.

Decision rule using *p*-values

When testing at the $100\alpha\%$ significance level, for $\alpha \in [0, 1]$,

$$\text{if the } p\text{-value} \begin{cases} \leq \alpha & \text{then reject } H_0 \\ > \alpha & \text{then do not reject } H_0. \end{cases}$$

The *p-value decision rule* is shown in Figure 10.4 for $\alpha = 0.05$.

Clearly, the magnitude of the *p*-value (compared with α) determines whether or not H_0 is rejected. Therefore, it is important to consider *two key influences* on the magnitude of the *p*-value: the *effect size* and the *sample size*.

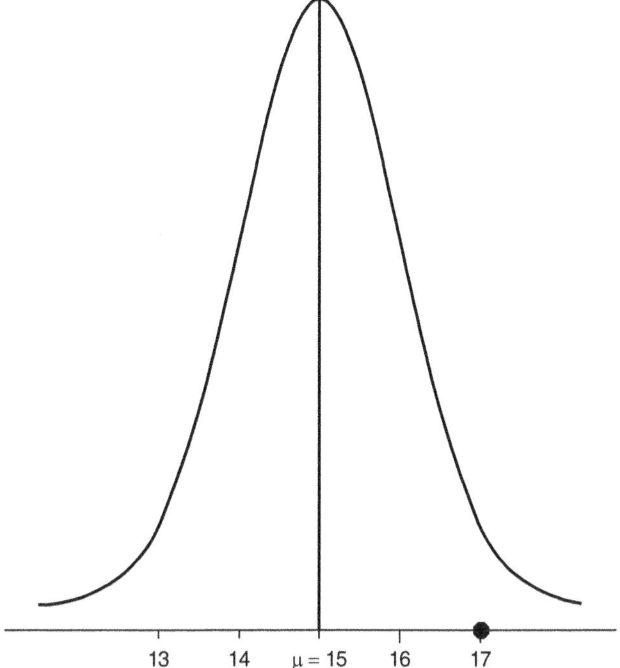

Figure 10.2 How $\bar{x}$ = 17 if Ms B's claim is correct that μ = 15 in Example 10.7.

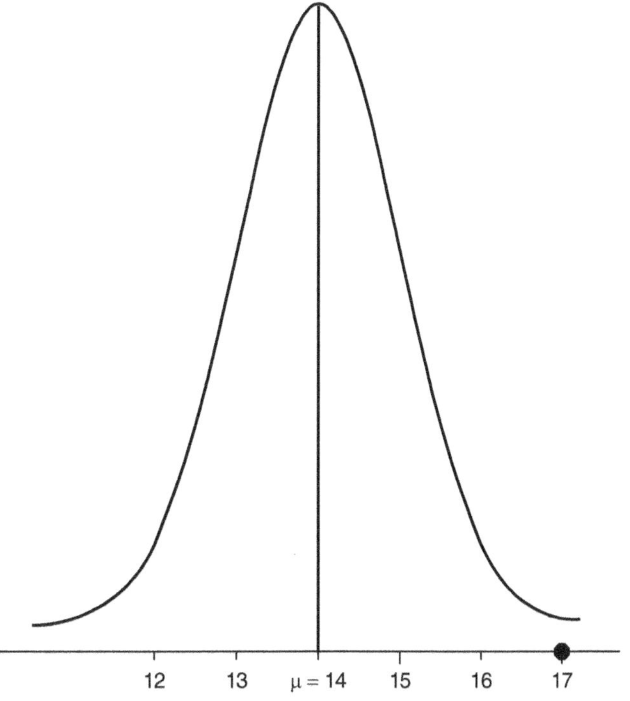

Figure 10.3 How $\bar{x}$ = 17 if Mr C's claim is correct that μ = 14 in Example 10.7.

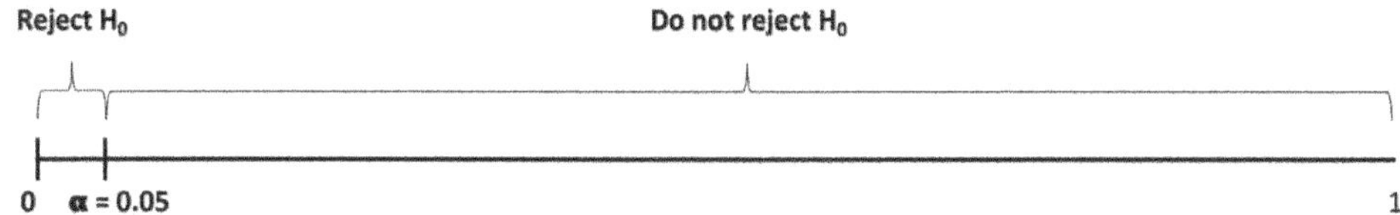

Figure 10.4 Hypothesis testing decision rule using *p*-values with a 5% significance level.

10.4.2 Effect size influence

The (unstandardised) effect size reflects the difference between what you would *expect* to observe if the null hypothesis is true and what is *actually* observed in a random experiment. Equality between our expectation and observation would equate to a zero effect size, which (while not proof that H_0 is true) provides the most convincing evidence in favour of H_0 – for example, if $\bar{x} = \mu_0$. As the difference between our expectation and observation increases, the data evidence becomes increasingly inconsistent with H_0, making us more likely to reject H_0. Hence *as the effect size gets larger, the p-value gets smaller* (and so is more likely to be below α, which would result in rejection of H_0).

To illustrate this idea, consider the experiment of tossing a coin 100 times and observing the number of heads. Quite rightly, you would not doubt the coin is fair (i.e. unbiased) if you observed *exactly* 50 heads as this is what you would expect from a fair coin (50% of tosses would be expected to be heads, and the other 50% tails). However, it is possible that you are:

- somewhat sceptical that the coin is fair if you observe 40 or 60 heads, say
- even more sceptical that the coin is fair if you observe 35 or 65 heads, say
- highly sceptical that the coin is fair if you observe 30 or 70 heads, say.

In this situation, the greater the difference between the number of heads and tails, the more evidence you have that the coin is not fair. In fact, if we test

$$H_0: \pi = 0.50 \text{ versus } H_1: \pi \neq 0.50,$$

where $\pi = P(\text{heads})$, for $n = 100$ tosses of the coin we would expect 50 heads and 50 tails. It can be shown that *for this fixed sample size* (of $n = 100$) the *p*-value is sensitive to the effect size (the difference between the observed sample proportion of heads and the expected proportion of 0.50) as follows:

Observation	Expectation	Effect size	*p*-value	Decision if $\alpha = 0.05$
50 heads & 50 tails	50 heads & 50 tails	0.50 – 0.50 = 0.00	1	H_0 is not rejected
55 heads & 45 tails	50 heads & 50 tails	0.55 – 0.50 = 0.05	0.3682	H_0 is not rejected
60 heads & 40 tails	50 heads & 50 tails	0.60 – 0.50 = 0.10	0.0569	H_0 is not rejected
70 heads & 30 tails	50 heads & 50 tails	0.70 – 0.50 = 0.20	< 0.0001	H_0 is rejected
80 heads & 20 tails	50 heads & 50 tails	0.80 – 0.50 = 0.30	≈ 0.0000	H_0 is rejected

So, we clearly see the *inverse relationship* between the effect size and the *p*-value.

The above is an example of a *sensitivity analysis* where we consider the pure influence of the effect size on the *p*-value while *controlling for* (fixing) the sample size. We now proceed to control for the effect size to examine the sample size influence.

10.4.3 Sample size influence

Ceteris paribus, a larger sample size should lead to a more *representative* sample and the characteristics of the sample should more closely resemble those of the population distribution from which the sample is drawn.

In the context of the coin toss, this would mean the observed sample proportion of heads should converge to the true probability of heads, π, as $n \to \infty$.

As such, we consider the sample size influence on the *p*-value. For a non-zero effect size *the p-value decreases as the sample size increases*. (A zero effect size would result in non-rejection of H_0, regardless of n.)

Continuing the coin toss example, let us fix the (absolute) effect size at 0.10, i.e. in each of the following examples the observed sample proportion of heads differs by a fixed proportion of 0.10 (= 10%).

Observation	Expectation	Sample size	*p*-value	Decision if $\alpha = 0.05$
6 heads & 4 tails	5 heads & 5 tails	$n = 10$	0.7539	H_0 is not rejected
12 heads & 8 tails	10 heads & 10 tails	$n = 20$	0.5034	H_0 is not rejected
18 heads & 12 tails	15 heads & 15 tails	$n = 30$	0.3616	H_0 is not rejected
60 heads & 40 tails	50 heads & 50 tails	$n = 100$	0.0569	H_0 is not rejected
150 heads & 100 tails	125 heads & 125 tails	$n = 250$	0.0019	H_0 is rejected

So, we clearly see the *inverse relationship* between the sample size and the *p*-value.

We defined the *power* of the test as the probability that the test will reject a false null hypothesis. In order to reject the null hypothesis it is necessary to have a sufficiently small *p*-value (less than α), hence we see that we can immediately increase the power of a test by increasing the sample size. Of course, the trade-off would be the increase in data collection costs!

Example 10.8

Let $\{X_1, X_2, ..., X_{20}\}$, taking values either 1 or 0, be the outcomes of an experiment of tossing a coin 20 times, where

$$P(X_i = 1) = \pi = 1 - P(X_i = 0), \text{ for } \pi \in (0, 1).$$

We are interested in testing

$$H_0: \pi = 0.50 \text{ versus } H_1: \pi \neq 0.50.$$

(Continued)

Suppose there are 17 X_is taking the value 1, and 3 X_is taking the value 0. Will you reject the null hypothesis at the 1% significance level?

Let $T = X_1 + X_2 + \cdots + X_{20}$. Therefore, $T \sim \text{Bin}(20, \pi)$, since the sum of independent and identically distributed Bernoulli trials has a binomial distribution (see Section 5.4). We use T as the test statistic, that is, a known function of the data - here, the total number of heads. With the given sample, we observe $t = 17$. What are the more extreme values of T if H_0 is true?

Under H_0, $E(T \mid H_0) = E(T \mid \pi = 0.50) = n\pi = 20 \times 0.50 = 10$, that is, we would expect 10 heads (and 10 tails) in $n = 20$ tosses of a fair coin. Hence 3 is as extreme as 17 (relative to the expectation of 10), and the more extreme values (again, relative to the expectation of 10) are:

0, 1, 2, 18, 19, 20.

Therefore, the p-value is

$$\left(\sum_{i=0}^{3} + \sum_{i=17}^{20}\right) P_{H_0}(T = i) = \left(\sum_{i=0}^{3} + \sum_{i=17}^{20}\right) \frac{20!}{i!(20-i)!}(0.50)^i (1-0.50)^{20-i} \qquad \text{(binomial probabilities)}$$

$$= 2 \times 0.50^{20} \sum_{i=0}^{3} \frac{20!}{i!(20-i)!} \qquad \text{(noting the symmetry when } \pi = 0.50\text{)}$$

$$= 2 \times 0.50^{20} \times \left(1 + 20 + 20 \times \frac{19}{2!} + \frac{20 \times 19 \times 18}{3!}\right) \qquad \text{(evaluating)}$$

$$= 0.0026. \qquad \text{(et voilà!)}$$

So we reject the null hypothesis of a fair coin at the 1% significance level, since $0.0026 < 0.01$.

10.4.4 Practical significance versus statistical significance

It has been stated that statistically significant results are those which produce sufficiently small p-values. In other words, statistically significant results are those which provide strong evidence against H_0 in favour of H_1. Such results are not necessarily significant in terms of being of *practical importance*. They might be significant *only in the statistical sense*. This is the case when your response to the results of the study is 'who cares?' or 'so what?'.

There is always a *possibility of statistical significance but not practical significance* with large sample sizes. In contrast, with smaller samples, results may not be statistically significant even if they represent the truth about the population(s).

10.5 TESTING A POPULATION MEAN CLAIM

We consider the hypothesis test of a population mean in the context of the customer's concern over the carbonated water bottles of Aquafizz.

Inevitably, the amount of water in the purchased bottles will exhibit slight variations attributable to the bottle-filling machine at the factory not putting in *identical* quantities of water in each bottle. The labels on each bottle may state '500 ml', but this equates to a claim about the *average* contents of *all* bottles produced (in the population of bottles).

Let X denote the quantity of water in a bottle. It would seem reasonable to assume a normal distribution for X (as an approximating model) such that $X \sim N(\mu, \sigma^2)$, and we wish to test

$$H_0: \mu = 500 \text{ ml versus } H_1: \mu < 500 \text{ ml}.$$

For the customer to make a valid complaint of systematically underfilled bottles, sample data will be required. Suppose a random sample of $n = 100$ bottles is taken, and let us assume that $\sigma = 10$ ml. We know that

$$\bar{X} \sim N\left(\mu, \frac{\sigma^2}{n}\right) = N\left(\mu, \frac{10^2}{25}\right) = N(\mu, 1).$$

Further, suppose that the sample mean in our random sample of 100 is $\bar{x} = 497$ ml. Clearly, we see that

$$\bar{x} = 497 \neq 500 = \mu,$$

where 500 is the claimed value of μ being tested in H_0.

The question is whether we judge the difference between $\bar{x} = 497$ and the claim $\mu = 500$ to be

a *small, and hence attributable to sampling error* (so we think H_0 is true)
b *large, and hence classified as statistically significant* (so we think H_1 is true).

Determination of the p-value will allow us to choose between explanations (a) and (b). We proceed by *standardising* $\bar{X}$ such that

$$Z = \frac{\bar{X} - \mu}{\sigma / \sqrt{n}} \sim N(0,1)$$

acts as our test statistic. Note the test statistic includes the effect size, $\bar{X} - \mu$, as well as the sample size, n.

Using our sample data, we now obtain the *test statistic value* (noting the *influence of both the effect size and the sample size,* and hence ultimately the influence on the p-value):

$$\frac{497 - 500}{10 / \sqrt{100}} = -3.$$

The p-value is the probability of our test statistic value or a more extreme value conditional on H_0. Noting that H_1: $\mu < 500$, 'more extreme' here means a z-value ≤ -3. This can be expressed as:

$$p\text{-value} = P(Z \leq -3) = 0.00135.$$

Note that this value can easily be obtained using Microsoft Excel, say, as

=NORM.S.DIST(–3,1)

where the function `NORM.S.DIST(z,1)` returns the *cumulative* probability $P(Z \leq z)$ for $Z \sim N(0, 1)$. It is shown in Figure 10.5.

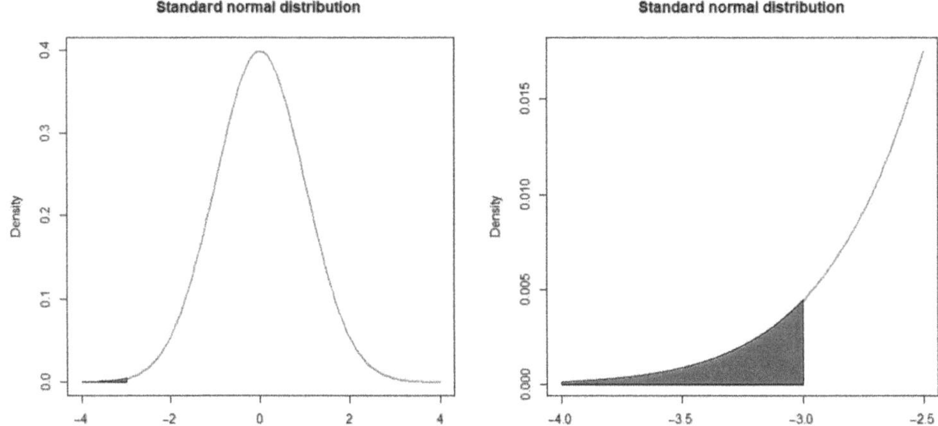

Figure 10.5 The standard normal distribution, indicating the *p*-value of 0.00135 in red. Note that the right-hand plot is a zoomed-in version of the left-hand tail of the left-hand plot.

We now apply the *p*-value decision rule, shown in Figure 10.4. Since $0.00135 < 0.05$ we reject H_0 and conclude that the result is 'statistically significant' at the 5% significance level (and also, of course, at the 1% significance level, since $0.00135 < 0.01$). Hence this is a *highly significant* result, with *strong evidence* that $\mu < 500$. The customer has a (statistically valid) case.

Finally, recall the possible decision space in Table 10.1. As we have rejected H_0 this means one of two things:

- *either* we have correctly rejected H_0
- *or* we have committed a Type I error.

Although the *p*-value is very small, indicating it is *highly unlikely* that this is a Type I error, unfortunately we cannot be *certain* which outcome has actually occurred!

Activity 10.1

Determine to what extent the customer would have evidence of Aquafizz's bottles being systematically underfilled if:

a the effect size is fixed, but the sample size varies:
   (i) $\bar{x} = 497$ with $n = 10$
   (ii) $\bar{x} = 497$ with $n = 20$
   (iii) $\bar{x} = 497$ with $n = 50$.

b the sample size is fixed, but the effect size varies:
   (i) $\bar{x} = 500$ with $n = 100$
   (ii) $\bar{x} = 499$ with $n = 100$
   (iii) $\bar{x} = 498$ with $n = 100$.

c How is the *p*-value affected by the effect size and sample size?

10.6 HYPOTHESIS TEST FOR A SINGLE MEAN (σ^2 KNOWN)

We consider the test of a single population mean when the population variance, σ^2, is *known*. To test H_0: $\mu = \mu_0$ when sampling from $N(\mu, \sigma^2)$ we use the following test statistic.

z test for a single mean (σ^2 known)

In this case, the test statistic is

$$Z = \frac{\bar{X} - \mu_0}{\sigma / \sqrt{n}} \sim N(0,1). \qquad (10.1)$$

Hence *p*-values are obtained from the standard normal distribution, using the `NORM.S.DIST` function in Excel.

Example 10.9

The mean lifetime of 100 components in a sample is 1570 hours and their standard deviation is known to be 120 hours. μ is the mean lifetime of all the components produced. Is it likely that the sample comes from a population whose mean is 1600 hours?

We perform a two-tailed test since we are testing whether or not μ is equal to 1600 hours. (Common sense might lead us to perform a lower-tailed test since 1570 < 1600, suggesting that if μ is not equal to 1600 hours, then it is likely to be less than 1600 hours. However, since this is framed as a two-tailed test, a justification for performing a lower-tailed test would be required, should you decide to opt for a lower-tailed test. Indeed, in principle the alternative hypothesis should be determined *before* data is collected, to avoid the data biasing our choice of alternative hypothesis!)

Hence we test

H_0: $\mu = 1600$ versus H_1: $\mu \neq 1600$.

Since σ (and hence σ^2) is known, we use (10.1) to calculate the test statistic value, which is

$$z = \frac{\bar{x} - \mu_0}{\sigma / \sqrt{n}} = \frac{1570 - 1600}{120 / \sqrt{100}} = -2.50.$$

For this two-tailed test the *p*-value is

$p\text{-value} = 2 \times P(Z > |-2.5|) = 2 \times P(Z \geq 2.5) = 2 \times 0.0062 = 0.0124,$

computed using `=2*NORM.S.DIST(-2.5,1)`. It is shown in Figure 10.6.

Since 0.01 < 0.0124 < 0.05, we conclude using the *p*-value that the test is significant at the 5% significance level, but not at the 1% significance level. Hence the test is *moderately significant*, with *moderate evidence* to suggest that the mean lifetime of components, μ, is not equal to 1600 hours.

(Continued)

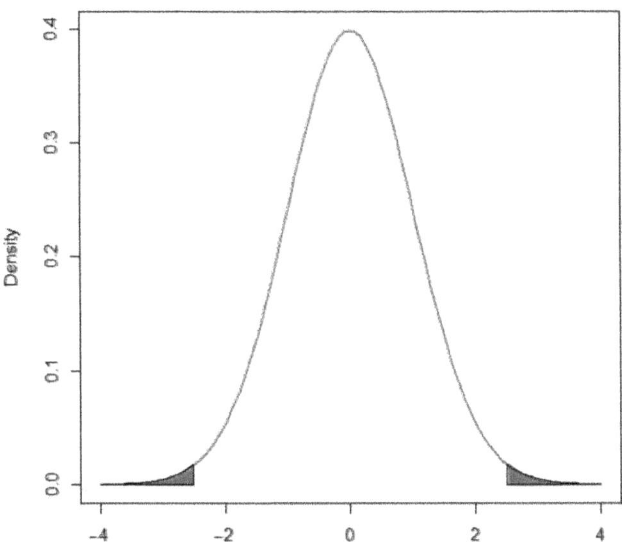

Figure 10.6 The standard normal distribution, indicating the *p*-value of 0.0124 in red.

10.7 HYPOTHESIS TEST FOR A SINGLE MEAN (σ^2 UNKNOWN)

Here the only difference from the previous case is that σ^2 is *unknown*. In which case it is estimated with the estimator S^2, the sample variance. To test H_0: $\mu = \mu_0$ when sampling from $N(\mu, \sigma^2)$ we use the following test statistic.

t test for a single mean (σ^2 unknown)

In this case, the test statistic is

$$T = \frac{\bar{X} - \mu_0}{S / \sqrt{n}} \sim t_{n-1}. \tag{10.2}$$

Hence *p*-values are obtained from the Student's *t* distribution with $n - 1$ degrees of freedom, using the `T.DIST` function in Excel.

Excel function: `T.DIST`

`=T.DIST(x, deg_freedom, cumulative)` returns the Student's left-tailed *t* distribution, where:

- `x` is the numeric value at which to evaluate the distribution
- `deg_freedom` is an integer indicating the number of degrees of freedom

- `cumulative` is a logical value: for the cumulative distribution function, use 1 or `TRUE`; for the probability density function, use 0 or `FALSE`.

The determination of the *p*-value will depend on whether the test is a *lower-tailed, upper-tailed* or *two-tailed* test. In the examples below, suppose the test statistic value is `x` with `df` degrees of freedom.

- If H_1: $\mu < \mu_0$, the *p*-value would be `=T.DIST(x,df,1)`.
- If H_1: $\mu > \mu_0$, the *p*-value would be `=1-T.DIST(x,df,1)`.
- If H_1: $\mu \neq \mu_0$, the *p*-value would be `=2-2*T.DIST(ABS(x),df,1)`, where the `ABS` function returns the absolute value of `x`.

Example 10.10

A study on the impact of comprehensive planning on financial performance reported that the average annual return on investment for American banks was 10.2%, and suggested that banks which exercised comprehensive planning would do better than this. A random sample of 26 such banks gave the following percentage returns on investment. Do these data support the claim?

10.00, 11.90, 9.90, 10.09, 10.31, 9.96, 10.34, 10.30, 10.50,
10.23, 10.72, 11.54, 10.81, 10.15, 9.04, 11.55, 10.81, 8.69,
10.74, 10.31, 10.76, 10.92, 11.26, 11.21, 10.20, 10.76.

We test

H_0: $\mu = 10.2$ versus H_1: $\mu > 10.2$.

Note that the alternative hypothesis is one-sided as this is the region of interest (we hypothesise that banks exercising comprehensive planning perform *better* than 10.2%). This implies that an upper-tailed test is required.

The summary statistics are $n = 26$, $\bar{x} = 10.5$ and $s = 0.714$. Hence, using (10.2), the test statistic value is

$$t = \frac{\bar{x} - \mu_0}{s/\sqrt{n}} = \frac{10.5 - 10.2}{0.714/\sqrt{26}} = 2.14.$$

For this upper-tailed test the *p*-value is

p-value $= P(T > 2.14) = 0.0212$,

computed using `=1-T.DIST(2.14,25,1)`. It is shown in Figure 10.7.

We see that $0.01 < 0.0212 < 0.05$, hence the test is significant at the 5% significance level. Note that we can view the *p*-value as the smallest value of α such that we would reject the null hypothesis. We conclude that the test is *moderately significant* with *moderate evidence* against the null hypothesis and that comprehensive planning does improve the average annual return on investment.

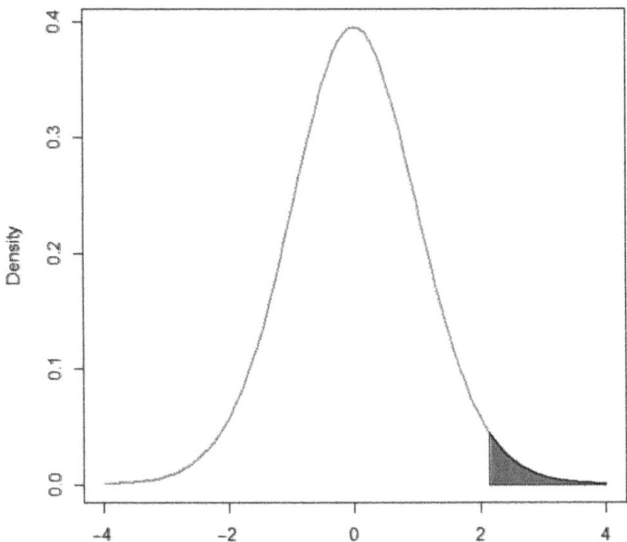

Figure 10.7 The Student's *t* distribution with 25 degrees of freedom, indicating the *p*-value of 0.0212 in red.

10.8 HYPOTHESIS TEST FOR A SINGLE PROPORTION

We now consider the hypothesis test for a single proportion. Recall from Chapter 9 that by the central limit theorem, the (approximate) sampling distribution of the estimator P (i.e. the sample proportion) is

$$P \sim N\left(\pi, \frac{\pi(1-\pi)}{n}\right),$$

with the standard error of the sample proportion being

$$\text{S.E.}(P) = \sqrt{\frac{\pi(1-\pi)}{n}}.$$

When testing

$$H_0: \pi = \pi_0$$

where π_0 is the claimed value of the population proportion under H_0, the standard error is

$$\sqrt{\frac{\pi_0(1-\pi_0)}{n}},$$

leading to the following test statistic, achieved by standardising the sample proportion, P.

z test for a single proportion

In this case, the test statistic is:

$$Z = \frac{P - \pi_0}{\sqrt{\pi_0(1-\pi_0)/n}} \sim N(0,1) \quad \text{(approximately, for large } n\text{).} \qquad (10.3)$$

Validity requires $n\pi_0 > 5$ and $n(1 - \pi_0) > 5$. Hence *p*-values are obtained from the standard normal distribution, using the `NORM.S.DIST` function in Excel.

Suppose the test statistic value is `x`.

- If H_1: $\pi < \pi_0$, the *p*-value would be `=NORM.S.DIST(x,1)`.
- If H_1: $\pi > \pi_0$, the *p*-value would be `=1-NORM.S.DIST(x,1)`.
- If H_1: $\pi \neq \pi_0$, the *p*-value would be `=2-2*NORM.S.DIST(ABS(x),1)`.

Example 10.11

To illustrate this, let us extend Example 9.7 where we consider a survey conducted by a bank to estimate the proportion of its customers who would be interested in using a proposed new mobile telephone banking service. If we denote the population proportion of customers who are interested in this proposal by π, and it is found that 68 out of a random sample of 150 customers are in favour, then we would estimate π as $p = 68/150 = 0.453$.

Suppose that other surveys have shown that 40% of the public are interested in mobile telephone banking and it is proposed to test whether or not the above survey agrees with this figure, that is, we conduct a two-tailed test:

H_0: $\pi = 0.40$ versus H_1: $\pi \neq 0.40$.

The test statistic value is, using (10.3),

$$z = \frac{p - \pi_0}{\sqrt{\pi_0(1-\pi_0)/n}} = \frac{0.453 - 0.40}{\sqrt{0.40 \times 0.60/150}} = 1.325.$$

For this two-tailed test the *p*-value is

p-value = $P(Z > |1.325|) = 0.1852$,

computed using `=2-2*NORM.S.DIST(ABS(1.325),1)`. It is shown in Figure 10.8.

Since $0.1852 > 0.10$, the *p*-value exceeds the 10% significance level, hence we do not reject H_0 - the test result is *not* statistically significant. There is *insufficient evidence* to justify rejecting H_0.

(Continued)

We conclude that the data are consistent with the null hypothesis and that the level of interest shown among the bank's customers for the proposed new mobile telephone banking service may well be 40%.

Note that if we had an *a priori* reason to believe that interest would be *greater* than 40% (without being influenced by the sample proportion being greater than 0.40), we would conduct an upper-tailed test of

$$H_0: \pi = 0.40 \text{ versus } H_1: \pi > 0.40.$$

The test statistic value would remain at 1.325, but now the *p*-value would be halved, since `=1-NORM.S.DIST(1.325,1)` returns 0.0926, and since $0.0926 < 0.10$ we would reject H_0 at the 10% significance level. The test is now *weakly significant*, with *weak evidence* that more than 40% are interested in the proposed new mobile telephone banking service. Note the *p*-value of 0.0926 is the red area in the right tail *only* in Figure 10.8.

While this is a different decision than the two-tailed test, it is *not inconsistent* since

$$\text{not reject } H_0 \neq \text{accept } H_0.$$

The *power* of the test has increased with the adoption of an upper-tailed H_1 because the effect of halving the two-tailed *p*-value makes it easier to reject H_0 by increasing the chance that the *p*-value falls below the chosen significance level.

10.9 DIFFERENCE BETWEEN TWO POPULATION PROPORTIONS

As with confidence intervals in Section 9.8, the correct approach for the comparison of two population proportions, π_1 and π_2, is to consider the *difference* between them, $\pi_1 - \pi_2$. When testing for equal proportions (i.e. a zero difference), the null hypothesis is

$$H_0: \pi_1 - \pi_2 = 0, \text{ or equivalently } H_0: \pi_1 = \pi_2.$$

We derive the test statistic by standardising the (approximate, by the central limit theorem) sampling distribution of the difference between two independent sample proportions, $P_1 - P_2$, given by

$$P_1 - P_2 \sim N\left(\pi_1 - \pi_2, \frac{\pi_1(1-\pi_1)}{n_1} + \frac{\pi_2(1-\pi_2)}{n_2}\right),$$

leading to the proposed test statistic (via standardisation) of

$$\frac{P_1 - P_2 - (\pi_1 - \pi_2)}{\sqrt{\pi_1(1-\pi_1)/n_1 + \pi_2(1-\pi_2)/n_2}} \sim N(0,1)$$

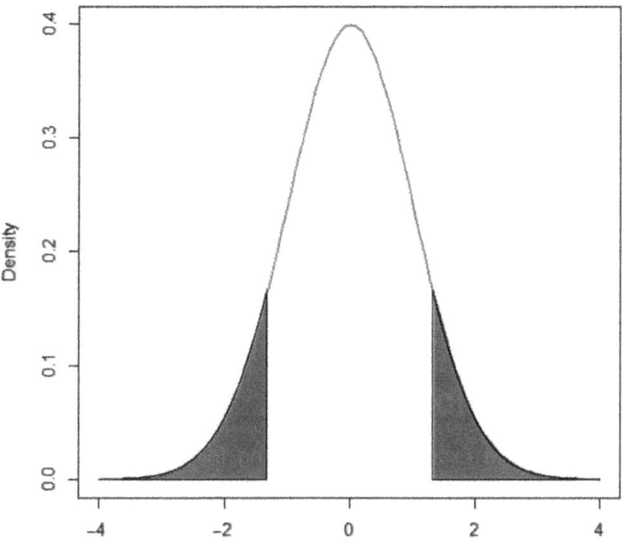

Figure 10.8 The standard normal distribution, indicating the *p*-value of 0.1852 in red.

approximately, for large n_1 and n_2. However, when evaluating this test statistic, which values do we use for π_1 and π_2? In the test of a single proportion, we had H_0: $\pi = \pi_0$, where π_0 is the tested (known) value.

When comparing two proportions, under H_0 no value is given for π_1 and π_2, only that they are equal, that is,

$$\pi_1 = \pi_2 = \pi,$$

where π is the *common proportion* whose value, of course, is still unknown! Hence we need to *estimate* π from the sample data using the *pooled proportion estimator*.

Pooled proportion estimator

If R_1 and R_2 represent the number of 'favourable' responses from two independent random samples with sample sizes of n_1 and n_2, respectively, then the **pooled proportion estimator** is

$$P = \frac{R_1 + R_2}{n_1 + n_2}. \tag{10.4}$$

This leads to the following revised test statistic.

z test for the difference between two proportions

In this case, the test statistic is

$$Z = \frac{P_1 - P_2 - (\pi_1 - \pi_2)}{\sqrt{P(1-P)(1/n_1 + 1/n_2)}} \sim N(0,1) \quad \text{(approximately, for large } n_1 \text{ and } n_2\text{).} \qquad (10.5)$$

Hence *p*-values are obtained from the standard normal distribution, using the `NORM.S.DIST` function in Excel.

Example 10.12

To illustrate this, let us extend Example 9.11 by testing for a difference between the population proportions of the general public who are aware of a particular retailed product before and after an advertising campaign. Two surveys were conducted and the results of the two random samples were as follows:

	Sample size	Number aware
Before campaign	150	68
After campaign	120	65

If π_1 and π_2 are the true population proportions aware before and after the campaign, respectively, then we wish to test

H_0: $\pi_1 = \pi_2$ versus H_1: $\pi_1 < \pi_2$.

Note that we use a one-sided alternative hypothesis on the assumption that the campaign would not *decrease* awareness - an example of the importance of using common sense in determining the alternative hypothesis!

After checking that this way round the value we get is positive (avoiding negative differences wherever possible to keep the notation as 'light' as possible), we estimate the difference in the population proportions as

$$\text{'After'} - \text{'Before'} = p_2 - p_1 = \frac{65}{120} - \frac{68}{150} = 0.0884.$$

On the assumption that H_0 is true, we estimate the common proportion, π, using (10.4), to be

$$\frac{68+65}{150+120} = 0.4926.$$

So our test statistic value, using (10.5), is

$$z = \frac{0.0884}{\sqrt{0.4926 \times (1-0.4926) \times (1/150 + 1/120)}} = 1.44.$$

The *p*-value for this upper-tailed test is

$$P(Z > 1.44) = 0.0749,$$

using `=1-NORM.S.DIST(1.44,1)`. It is shown in Figure 10.9. Since 0.0749 > 0.05, we are unable to reject H_0 for any significance level $\alpha < 0.0749$, such as at the 5% significance level. However, the test is significant at the 10% significance level (because 0.0749 < 0.10). Hence the test is *weakly significant*, as there is *weak evidence* that the campaign has increased awareness.

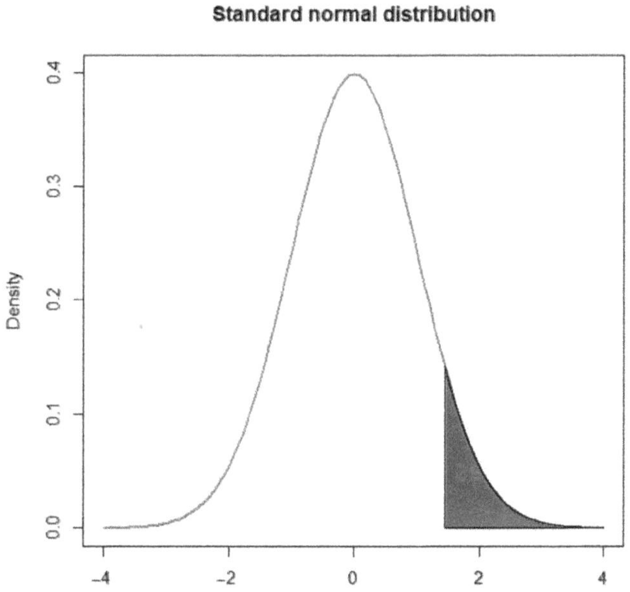

Standard normal distribution

Density

0.0 0.1 0.2 0.3 0.4

-4 -2 0 2 4

Figure 10.9 The standard normal distribution, indicating the *p*-value of 0.0749 in red.

10.10 DIFFERENCE BETWEEN TWO POPULATION MEANS

In this section we are primarily interested in the difference between two population means, $\mu_1 - \mu_2$. There are four cases to consider.

10.10.1 Unpaired samples - variances known

Suppose we have two random samples of size n_1 and n_2, respectively, drawn from $N(\mu_1, \sigma_1^2)$ and $N(\mu_2, \sigma_2^2)$, where σ_1^2 and σ_2^2 are *known*. Testing for the equality of means gives the null hypothesis

$$H_0: \mu_1 = \mu_2 \text{ or, in terms of their difference, } H_0: \mu_1 - \mu_2 = 0.$$

The sampling distribution of $\bar{X}_1 - \bar{X}_2$ is

$$\bar{X}_1 - \bar{X}_2 \sim N\left(\mu_1 - \mu_2, \frac{\sigma_1^2}{n_1} + \frac{\sigma_2^2}{n_2}\right)$$

which, when standardised, gives the test statistic.

z test for the difference between two means (variances known)

In this case, the test statistic is

$$Z = \frac{\bar{X}_1 - \bar{X}_2 - (\mu_1 - \mu_2)}{\sqrt{\sigma_1^2 / n_1 + \sigma_2^2 / n_2}} \sim N(0,1). \qquad (10.6)$$

Hence *p*-values are obtained from the standard normal distribution, using `NORM.S.DIST` in Excel.

Note that if testing for the equality of means, then $\mu_1 - \mu_2 = 0$ under H_0. Hence, in (10.6), we set the term $\mu_1 - \mu_2$ equal to 0.

10.10.2 Unpaired samples - variances unknown and unequal

We have the same set-up as above, with the same sampling distribution of $\bar{X}_1 - \bar{X}_2$, but now the population variances σ_1^2 and σ_2^2 are *unknown*. Assuming *large* sample sizes, we can replace these unknown parameters with the sample variance estimators S_1^2 and S_2^2, respectively, to obtain the test statistic.

z test for the difference between two means (variances unknown)

If the population variances σ_1^2 and σ_2^2 are unknown, provided sample sizes n_1 and n_2 are large (greater than 30),

$$Z = \frac{\bar{X}_1 - \bar{X}_2 - (\mu_1 - \mu_2)}{\sqrt{S_1^2 / n_1 + S_2^2 / n_2}} \sim N(0,1) \quad \text{(approximately, for large } n_1 \text{ and } n_2\text{)}. \qquad (10.7)$$

Hence *p*-values are obtained from the standard normal distribution, using `NORM.S.DIST` in Excel.

Note that if testing for the equality of means, then $\mu_1 - \mu_2 = 0$ under H_0. Hence, in (10.7), we set the term $\mu_1 - \mu_2$ equal to 0.

10.10.3 Unpaired samples - variances unknown and equal

Although still unknown, if we assume the population variances are equal to some common variance (i.e. $\sigma_1^2 = \sigma_2^2 = \sigma^2$), then we only have one (common) unknown variance to estimate. As with confidence intervals in Section 9.9.3, we utilise the pooled variance estimator, given by

$$S_p^2 = \frac{(n_1 - 1)S_1^2 + (n_2 - 1)S_2^2}{n_1 + n_2 - 2}.$$

t test for the difference between two means (variances unknown)

If the population variances σ_1^2 and σ_2^2 are unknown but assumed equal, then

$$T = \frac{\bar{X}_1 - \bar{X}_2 - (\mu_1 - \mu_2)}{\sqrt{S_p^2(1/n_1 + 1/n_2)}} \sim t_{n_1+n_2-2}, \qquad (10.8)$$

where S_p^2 is the pooled variance estimator. Hence *p*-values are obtained from the Student's *t* distribution with $n_1 + n_2 - 2$ degrees of freedom, using `T.DIST` in Excel.

Note that if testing for the equality of means, then $\mu_1 - \mu_2 = 0$ under H_0. Hence, in (10.8), we set the term $\mu_1 - \mu_2$ equal to 0.

Example 10.13

To illustrate this, let us extend Example 9.12 and consider two companies supplying a similar service being compared for their mean reaction times (in days) to complaints. Random samples of recent complaints to these companies gave the following statistics:

	Sample size	Sample mean	Sample std. dev.
Company A	12	8.5	3.6
Company B	10	4.8	2.1

We want to test for a difference between mean reaction times, that is, we test

H_0: $\mu_A = \mu_B$ versus H_1: $\mu_A \neq \mu_B$.

Because the markets are 'similar', it is reasonable to assume (although it is only an assumption!) that the two population variances are equal. Under this assumption, the estimate of the common variance is

$$s_p^2 = \frac{(12-1) \times 3.6^2 + (10-1) \times 2.1^2}{12 + 10 - 2} = 9.1125.$$

(Continued)

Therefore, the test statistic value, using (10.8), is

$$t = \frac{8.5 - 4.8}{\sqrt{9.1125 \times (1/12 + 1/10)}} = 2.87.$$

There are 12 + 10 – 2 = 20 degrees of freedom, hence we obtain the *p*-value from the t_{20} distribution. The *p*-value is returned by `2-2*T.DIST(ABS(2.87),20,1)` which gives 0.0095. It is shown in Figure 10.10. Since 0.0095 < 0.01 (just!), we reject H_0 at the 1% significance level. On this basis, we have a *highly significant* result, and we conclude that there is *strong evidence* that the mean reaction times are different. Indeed, it appears that company B reacts faster, on average, than company A.

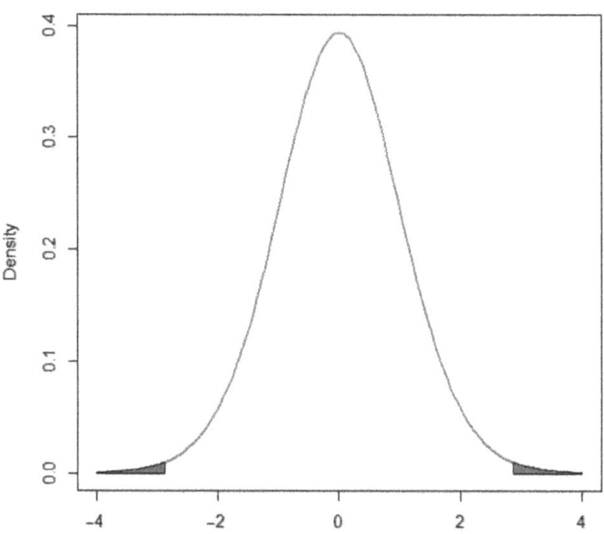

Figure 10.10 The Student's *t* distribution with 20 degrees of freedom, indicating the *p*-value of 0.0095 in red.

10.10.4 Paired (dependent) samples

Recall from Section 9.9.4 that for paired (dependent) samples we work with *differenced data* to reduce matters to a one-sample analysis. As before, we compute the differenced data as

$$d_1 = x_1 - y_1,\ d_2 = x_2 - y_2,\ \ldots,\ d_n = x_n - y_n,$$

reducing the two-sample problem to a one-sample problem. The test is then analogous to the hypothesis test of a single mean with σ^2 unknown.

t test for the difference in means in paired samples

Using the sample mean and sample standard deviation of differenced data,

$$T = \frac{\bar{X}_d - \mu_d}{S_d / \sqrt{n}} \sim t_{n-1}. \tag{10.9}$$

Hence *p*-values are obtained from the Student's *t* distribution with $n - 1$ degrees of freedom, using `T.DIST` in Excel.

Example 10.14

The table below shows the before and after weights (in pounds) of eight adults after a diet. Test whether there is evidence that the diet is effective.

Before	After	Before	After
127	122	150	144
130	120	147	138
114	116	167	155
139	132	153	152

We want to test

$H_0: \mu_1 = \mu_2$ versus $H_1: \mu_1 > \mu_2$,

which is equivalent to testing

$H_0: \mu_d = 0$ versus $H_1: \mu_d > 0$,

where we choose a one-tailed test because we are looking for a reduction (if there is any change, we would expect weight *loss* from a diet!) and we define $\mu_d = \mu_1 - \mu_2$ since we anticipate that this way round the values will (more likely) be positive.

The differences (calculated as 'Before – After') are:

5, 10, –2, 7, 6, 9, 12, 1.

Hence $n = 8$, $\bar{x}_d = 6$ and $s_d = 4.66$ on $n - 1 = 7$ degrees of freedom. Using (10.9), the test statistic value is

$$t = \frac{6 - 0}{4.66 / \sqrt{8}} = 3.64.$$

(Continued)

The p-value is returned by `1-T.DIST(3.64,7,1)`, which gives 0.0041. It is shown in Figure 10.11. Since $0.0041 < 0.01$, we reject H_0 at the 1% significance level. On this basis, we have a *highly significant* result, and we conclude that there is *strong evidence* that the diet reduces weight, on average.

10.11 SUMMARY OF COMMON EXCEL FUNCTIONS

Appendix A summarises common Excel functions for conducting hypothesis testing.

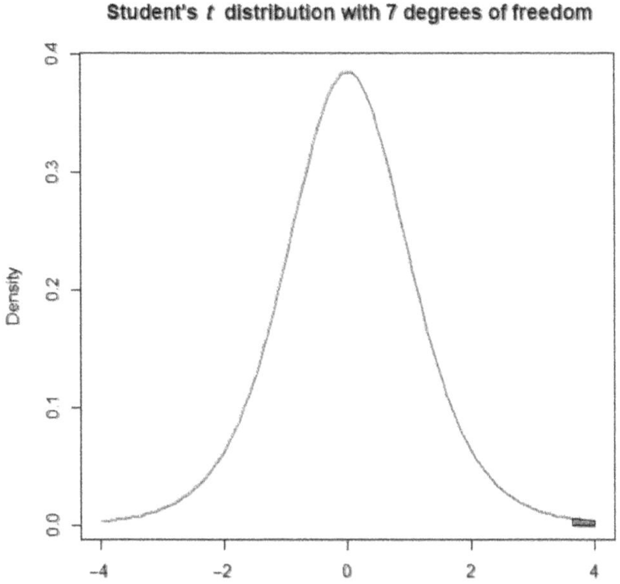

Figure 10.11 The Student's t distribution with 7 degrees of freedom, indicating the p-value of 0.0041 in red.

10.12 CHAPTER OVERVIEW

This chapter has considered the mechanics of hypothesis testing, whereby a claim about a population is tested by examining the data evidence and seeing to what extent the data support or refute the claim. In each hypothesis test we make a binary decision whether or not to reject the null hypothesis. As we make a binary decision, there are two types of errors which could occur: Type I errors and Type II errors, known as false positives and false negatives, respectively. Statistically, a test statistic is used to process the data conditional on the null hypothesis being true which produces a test statistic with a known probability distribution. Based on this distribution and the test statistic value (derived from our observed data) a p-value can be computed, which acts as our measure of statistical significance. By controlling for the probability of a Type I error through the significance level, we compare the p-value with the significance level to judge the extent of statistical significance.

10.13 KEY VOCABULARY

Alternative hypothesis
Decision rule
Decision space
Effect size
Hypothesis testing
Null hypothesis
p-value
Pooled proportion estimator
Power
Sample size influence
Significance level
Test statistic
Type I error
Type II error

10.14 EXERCISES

10.4.1 Test your understanding

1 What is the difference between a null hypothesis and an alternative hypothesis?
2 In hypothesis testing, we make a binary decision. What are the two possible decisions?
3 If you served on a jury, how would you decide whether to find the defendant guilty or not guilty?
4 What is a Type I error? What is a Type II error?
5 Which is worse, a Type I error or a Type II error? 'Well, James, it depends' may feature in your answer, but explain what it depends on!
6 In a hypothesis testing context, what is α and what is β?
7 What is 'power' in a hypothesis testing context and is it desirable?
8 Write out, in matrix form, the decision space in hypothesis testing.
9 What are common values for the significance level in hypothesis testing, and how do these affect the reported strength of evidence?
10 Define the p-value.
11 Can we ever 'accept' a hypothesis? Briefly justify your view.
12 What is the hypothesis testing decision rule using p-values?
13 What is an effect size and how does it influence the p-value?
14 What is the sample size's influence on the p-value?
15 Does statistical significance imply practical significance?
16 When sampling from $N(\mu, \sigma^2)$, what is the procedure for performing a hypothesis test for μ when:
   (a) σ^2 is known?
   (b) σ^2 is unknown?
17 What is the procedure for performing a hypothesis test for a single proportion, π?
18 What is the procedure for performing a hypothesis test for the difference between:
   (a) two proportions?
   (b) two means? (Report all cases.)
19 Can a hypothesis test which is not significant at the 5% significance level be significant at the 10% significance level?

20 When testing H_0: $\mu = 4$ versus H_1: $\mu > 4$, explain why an observed sample mean of $\bar{x} = 3$ would *not* result in the rejection of H_0. (Answer without conducting a full hypothesis test.)

21 A random sample of size $n = 8$ is drawn from a normal distribution with an unknown mean μ and an unknown variance $\sigma^2 < \infty$. It is desired to test

H_0: $\mu = -3$ versus H_1: $\mu \neq -3$.

Suppose that the sample data are such that

$\bar{x} = -4.74$ and $s^2 = 2.69$.

Conduct the hypothesis test by calculating the *p*-value.

22 Suppose H_0: $\mu = 240$ is tested against H_1: $\mu < 240$ at the 1% significance level using a random sample of $n = 25$ observations from $N(\mu, 50^2)$. What is the probability of a Type II error if $\mu = 220$?

23 A paired-difference experiment under two conditions used a random sample of $n = 61$ adults and reported a sample mean difference of 2.326 and a standard deviation of 7.6 for the differences. The researchers reported a *t* statistic value of 2.390, when testing whether the means of the two conditions are the same.

(a) Show how the researchers obtained the *t* statistic value of 2.390.

(b) Calculate the *p*-value of the test and use the *p*-value to draw a conclusion about the significance of the test. Use a 5% significance level.

24 Consider the test of H_0: $\mu = 60$ versus H_1: $\mu \neq 60$ using a 5% significance level. If the data consist of a random sample of size 16 from a normal distribution having $\sigma = 4$, determine the power of the test when:

(a) $\mu = 57$

(b) $\mu = 61$.

Recall that the power of a test is the probability that the test will reject a false null hypothesis.

25 In a wire-based nail manufacturing process the target length for cut wire is 22 cm. It is known that widths vary with a standard deviation equal to 0.08 cm. In order to monitor this process, a random sample of 50 separate wires is accurately measured and the process is regarded as operating satisfactorily (the null hypothesis) if the sample mean width lies between 21.97 cm and 22.03 cm, so that this is the decision procedure used (i.e. if the sample mean falls within this range then the null hypothesis is not rejected, otherwise the null hypothesis is rejected).

(a) Determine the probability of a Type I error for this test.

(b) Determine the probability of making a Type II error when the process is actually cutting to a length of 22.05 cm.

(c) Find the probability of rejecting the null hypothesis when the true cutting length is 22.01 cm. (This is the power of the test when the true mean is 22.01 cm.)

26 An accounting firm wishes to test whether 6% of a large number of transactions contain errors against an alternative hypothesis that there are more than 6% errors. In order to test this claim, they examine a random sample of 200 transactions and find that exactly 18 of these are in error. Calculate the *p*-value for the appropriate hypothesis test and comment on this value.

27 In a particular city it is known, from past surveys, that 25% of households regularly use a washing powder named 'Snolite'. After an advertising campaign, a survey of 300 randomly selected households showed that 100 had recently purchased Snolite. Is there evidence that the campaign has been successful? Use a 1% significance level.

28 A museum conducts a survey of its visitors in order to assess the popularity of a device which is used to provide information on the museum exhibits. The device will be withdrawn if fewer than 30% of all of the museum's visitors make use of it. Of a random sample of 80 visitors, 20 chose to use the device.

(a) Carry out a test at the 5% significance level to see if the device should be withdrawn and state your conclusions.

(b) What is the power of this test if the actual percentage of all visitors who would use this device is only 20%? (Remember that power is the complement of the Type II error probability.)

29 A company recently redesigned its website to increase its appeal to younger consumers (those aged under 30). Random samples of younger consumers were surveyed before and after the redesign to see if they had a positive opinion of the website. The results were as follows:

	Sample size	Respondents with a positive opinion
Before redesign	125	75
After redesign	150	111

(a) Do the survey results indicate the redesign has been effective? Conduct a suitable hypothesis test, reporting the p-value and comment on your results. State any assumptions that you make.

(b) Briefly discuss any concerns had the sample sizes been 25 and 30, instead of 125 and 150, respectively.

30 A consumer report examined potential differences between two brands of tyres. The mean lifespan of the tyres is of primary concern. The available data, measured in thousands of miles, is provided below.

	Sample size	Sample mean	Sample standard deviation
Brand X	14	23.6	1.9
Brand Y	15	24.8	1.6

(a) Use an appropriate hypothesis test to determine whether there is evidence of a difference in the mean lifespans of the two brands. Comment on your findings.

(b) State clearly any assumptions you made in part (a).

(c) Repeat the procedure in part (a) to determine whether the mean lifespan of the tyres of brand Y is greater than that of the brand X tyres.

(d) Based on your test conclusion in part (c), explain which type of error may have been committed, and what the practical consequences of the error would be.

31 A pharmaceutical company has developed a new vaccine to immunise against Covid-19 and needs to determine the vaccine's efficacy. A randomised experiment was conducted to address this question. The study randomly allocated 200 people to either a group where the vaccine was administered, or a group where a placebo was given. These people were monitored and the numbers of those who did not go on to contract Covid-19 (and those who did) were recorded. The results are summarised below:

	Developed Covid-19	Did not develop Covid-19
Vaccine group	21	79
Placebo group	48	52

(a) Carry out an appropriate hypothesis test at the 1% significance level to determine whether the proportion of people who did *not* develop Covid-19 is higher in the vaccine group than in the placebo group. State the test hypotheses, and specify your test statistic and its distribution under the null hypothesis. Comment on your findings and clearly state any assumptions you make.

(b) Explain, with reasons, whether it is sufficient to have 200 people in this study.

32 A company wishes to investigate whether its average brand awareness varies between older and younger people. Random samples of 15 adults over the age of 60 and 14 adults aged between 18 and 30 scored their brand awareness on a scale from 1 to 100. Summaries of these scores are presented below.

	Sample size	Sample mean	Sample variance
Over 60s	15	68.7	15.4
18-30s	14	74.3	18.2

(a) Use an appropriate hypothesis test to determine whether the mean brand awareness score is higher for the younger age group. State clearly the hypotheses, the test statistic and its distribution under the null hypothesis. Comment on your findings and clearly state any assumptions you make.

(b) Is it possible that there is no difference between older and younger adults in terms of their average brand awareness? Briefly discuss.

33 A survey is conducted to compare customer satisfaction in two branches of a bank. Various customers visiting the two branches were selected randomly, and asked if they were satisfied with the services provided by the branch. The results of this survey are shown in the following table.

	Sample size	Number satisfied
Branch A	153	115
Branch B	188	120

You are asked to consider an appropriate hypothesis test to determine whether there is a difference between the two bank branches regarding the proportion of satisfied customers. Perform a suitable test and comment on your findings. Specify the test statistic you use and its distribution under the null hypothesis.

34 A market research company has conducted a survey of adults in two large towns, either side of an international border, in order to judge attitudes towards a controversial internationally broadcast celebrity television programme. The following table shows some of the information obtained by the survey:

	Town A	Town B
Sample size	50	50
Sample number approving of the programme	26	22

(a) Conduct an appropriate hypothesis test, at the 5% significance level, of the claim that the population proportions approving the programme in the two towns are equal.
(b) Would your conclusion be the same if, in both towns, the sample sizes had been 100 (with the same sample proportions of approvals)?

35 The data in the following table show the numbers of daily parking offences in two areas of a city. The day identifications are unknown and the recordings were not necessarily made on the same days. Is there evidence that the areas experience different numbers of offences?

Area A	Area B
38	32
38	38
29	22
45	30
42	34
33	28
27	32
32	34
32	24
34	

10.14.2 Practice with Excel

Head over to the companion website for Excel examples and screencasts!

11

BIVARIATE ANALYSIS

Chapter contents

Chapter level: ***Beginner***

Source: Photo by Charles Gao via Unsplash.

Key concepts

- Association
- Correlation
- Relationship strength

Chapter value

Variables may be related. We explore different types of bivariate relationships, including their strength.

Key takeaway

Correlation is not causation, and beware spurious correlations – always perform a sense check!

Chapter outline

Use of the prefix 'bi-' means two of something. *Bi*cycle means two wheels, *bi*lingual means knowledge of two languages, and hence *bi*variate analysis means analysing two variables. In a bivariate setting we care about exploring *relationships* between variables. This can be done visually with tables or plots. Such visual inspection is a helpful starting point as a form of exploratory analysis to discover and identify patterns in data, after which we seek to quantify any apparent relationships.

Depending on the levels of measurement of the variables, we can refer to *associations* and *correlations*. Attaching numeric values to these provides simple metrics for us to assess the *strength* of observed relationships. However, we need to be cautious about declaring a *causal* relationship - as the saying goes, 'correlation does not imply causation'! Confirming a cause-and-effect relationship, outside of a laboratory where 'other things' can be strictly controlled for, is extremely challenging in practice.

In an era of big data in particular, when we can examine countless combinations of variables, inevitably 'spurious' relationships will emerge. To mitigate the risk of committing a causal fallacy, we should at a minimum be able to offer theoretical arguments or rationales about why changes in one variable should *cause* changes in another - basically, a (common) sense check!

Learning outcomes

After completing this chapter, you should be able to:

- perform exploratory data analysis with cross-tabulations and scatter plots
- compute statistics for cross-tabulations to assess statistical significance of associations and measure their strength
- calculate the sample correlation coefficient, r, and test its significance
- explain the meaning of a particular value of r.

Motivational case: Tricks for clicks

GameStart is a new start-up e-retailer of second-hand computer games and assorted electronics. Its founder and CEO wants to maximise sales of those visiting its website.

Aware of the success of e-commerce giants like Amazon and Alibaba in recommending products for people to buy ('Customers who bought this also bought ...'), GameStart would like to implement its own product recommendation tool by placing suggested other products to buy on each individual product page to drive sales volume.

How should GameStart go about developing a recommendation system to maximise its cross-selling?

11.1 INTRODUCTION

Consider two variables, X and Y. They might be *independent* (one has no effect on the other) or they may exhibit a relationship (they 'move' together in some sense). Our goal in this chapter is to detect relationships and determine their nature.

Every variable has a level of measurement – either categorical (nominal or ordinal) or measurable (discrete or continuous; the latter interval or ratio). In a bivariate analysis, we have two variables, so there are three possible combinations:

(i) Two categorical variables, which can be arranged in a **contingency table** or **cross-tabulation** (synonyms).
(ii) One categorical and one measurable variable, which can be arranged using side-by-side box plots.
(iii) Two measurable variables, which can be arranged in a scatter plot.

11.2 CROSS-TABULATION ANALYSIS

If we suspect that two categorical variables (sometimes referred to as factors) may be related, we can refer to a possible *association* between them. Data can be presented in a cross-tabulation comprising a row variable with r levels and a column variable with c levels. *Frequency counts* are then reported in the cells corresponding to each 'contingency' (combination of levels). We sample a certain number of units (such as customers) and classify them according to the two factors of interest.

Example 11.1

Consider Tableau's sample Superstore dataset. We can create a simple cross-tabulation as shown in Figure 11.1.

Note how the highlighted table on the right provides a better visual sense of the *relative frequencies* across combinations of product category (the row variable, with r = 3 levels) and delivery mode (the column variable, with c = 4 levels).

Cross-tabulation of Product Category and Delivery Mode

Category	Delivery Mode: First Class	Same Day	Second Class	Standard Class
Furniture	205	89	306	901
Office Supplies	995	347	1,318	3,929
Technology	254	80	352	1,224

Cross-tabulation of Product Category and Delivery Mode

Category	Delivery Mode: First Class	Same Day	Second Class	Standard Class
Furniture	205	89	306	901
Office Supplies	995	347	1,318	3,929
Technology	254	80	352	1,224

Figure 11.1 Cross-tabulation and highlighted table of Product category and Delivery mode.

In this section we will introduce a test procedure for establishing whether there is statistical evidence of an association between two categorical variables (i.e. factors or attributes).

In this test framework the null hypothesis, H_0, is that the two factors are *not* associated, while the alternative hypothesis, H_1, is that they *are* associated. Note that H_1 does not specify the *nature* of the association, just that there *is* an association (which we would need to investigate further if we end up rejecting H_0). Each data unit we sample has one level of each factor.

Example 11.2

An insurance company wishes to investigate whether an association exists between the area of a city and the reason for an insurance claim. If so, then the insurer could *price-discriminate*, setting the value of an insurance policy premium to reflect the risk of a claim being made - the greater the risk of a claim would mean a larger premium charged to compensate the insurer for the greater risk exposure.

Three areas of a city (A, B and C) were considered, along with three types of insurance claim (burglary, fire damage and car theft). Data on $n = 150$ insurance claims was collected, noting the area and type of claim, as shown in the following contingency table:

		Type of insurance claim			
		Burglary	Fire damage	Car theft	Total
Area	**A**	30	19	6	**55**
	B	12	23	14	**49**
	C	8	18	20	**46**
Total		**50**	**60**	**40**	**150**

The cell frequencies are known as *observed frequencies* and show how the data is spread across the different combinations of factor levels. We can denote these by O_{ij}, which represents the observed frequency in the ith row and jth column. For example, $O_{12} = 19$ and $O_{31} = 8$.
The first step in any analysis is to complete the row and column totals (as already done in this table).

11.2.1 Expected frequencies

We proceed by computing a corresponding set of *expected frequencies*, conditional on the null hypothesis of no association between the factors (i.e. that the factors are *independent*).

Now suppose that you are only given the row and column totals for the frequencies. If the factors were assumed to be independent (as they are under H_0), consider how you would calculate the expected frequencies. Recall from Chapter 4 that if A and B are two independent events, then

$$P(A \cap B) = P(A)P(B).$$

We now apply this idea.

Example 11.3

For the data in Example 11.2, if a claim was selected at random from the 150 claims then we can determine the following probabilities:

(Continued)

- *P*(an insurance claim is for a burglary) = 50/150
- *P*(an insurance claim is in area A) = 55/150.

Hence, under H_0, we have

$$P(\text{an insurance claim is for a burglary in area A}) = \frac{50}{150} \times \frac{55}{150},$$

and so the *expected number* of insurance claims for burglaries in area A is *n* times this joint probability,

$$150 \times \frac{50}{150} \times \frac{55}{150}.$$

So the expected frequency is obtained by multiplying the product of the 'marginal' probabilities by *n*, the total number of observations. This can be generalised as follows.

Expected frequencies in cross-tabulations

The **expected frequency**, E_{ij}, for the cell in row *i* and column *j* of a cross-tabulation with *r* rows and *c* columns, is

$$E_{ij} = \frac{\text{row } i \text{ total} \times \text{column } j \text{ total}}{\text{total number of observations}} = \frac{\text{row } i \text{ total} \times \text{column } j \text{ total}}{n}$$

where $i = 1, 2, ..., r$ and $j = 1, 2, ..., c$.

Example 11.4

The completed expected frequency table for the data in Example 11.2 is (rounding to 2 decimal places (dp)) as follows:

		Type of insurance claim			
		Burglary	Fire damage	Car theft	Total
Area	**A**	18.33	22.00	14.67	**55**
	B	16.33	19.60	13.07	**49**
	C	15.33	18.40	12.27	**46**
Total		**50**	**60**	**40**	**150**

11.2.2 Test statistic

In order to perform a hypothesis test, we need a *test statistic* and to know its (approximate) distribution under H_0 to calculate the *p*-value. To motivate our choice of test statistic, if H_0 is true then we would expect to observe *small* differences between the observed and expected frequencies (i.e. *small effect sizes*), while *large* differences (i.e. *large effect sizes*) would suggest that H_1 is true. This is because the expected frequencies have been calculated conditional on the null hypothesis of independence (i.e. no association). Hence, if H_0 is actually true, what we actually observe (the observed frequencies) should be (approximately) equal to what we expect to observe (the expected frequencies), that is, $O_{ij} \approx E_{ij}$ for all *i*, *j*.

χ^2 test of association

Let the cross-tabulation have *r* rows and *c* columns. Then formally the **test statistic** used for tests of association is

$$\sum_{i=1}^{r}\sum_{j=1}^{c}\frac{(O_{ij}-E_{ij})^2}{E_{ij}} \sim \chi^2_{(r-1)(c-1)}. \tag{11.1}$$

Hence *p*-values are obtained from the χ^2 distribution with (*r* - 1)(*c* - 1) degrees of freedom, in Excel using

```
=CHISQ.DIST.RT(test_statistic_value, degrees_of_freedom).
```

This test statistic was first used by the statistician Karl Pearson, hence it is often referred to as 'Pearson's chi-squared statistic'.

Note that the 'double summation' in (11.1) just means summing over all rows and all columns. This test statistic follows an (approximate) *chi-squared distribution* with (r – 1)(c – 1) degrees of freedom, where *r* and *c* denote the number of rows and columns, respectively, in the contingency table. The approximation is reasonable provided all the expected frequencies are *at least 5*. For large enough *n*, this condition is likely to be satisfied, since expected frequencies are calculated by multiplying the joint probabilities (under independence) by *n*.

The χ^2 (chi-squared) distribution

A χ^2 **(chi-squared) distribution** is only defined over positive values. The precise shape of the distribution is dependent on the degrees of freedom, which is the parameter of the distribution. Figure 11.2 illustrates the chi-squared distribution for a selection of degrees of freedom.

Although the shape of the distribution does change quite significantly for different degrees of freedom, note that the distribution is always positively skewed.

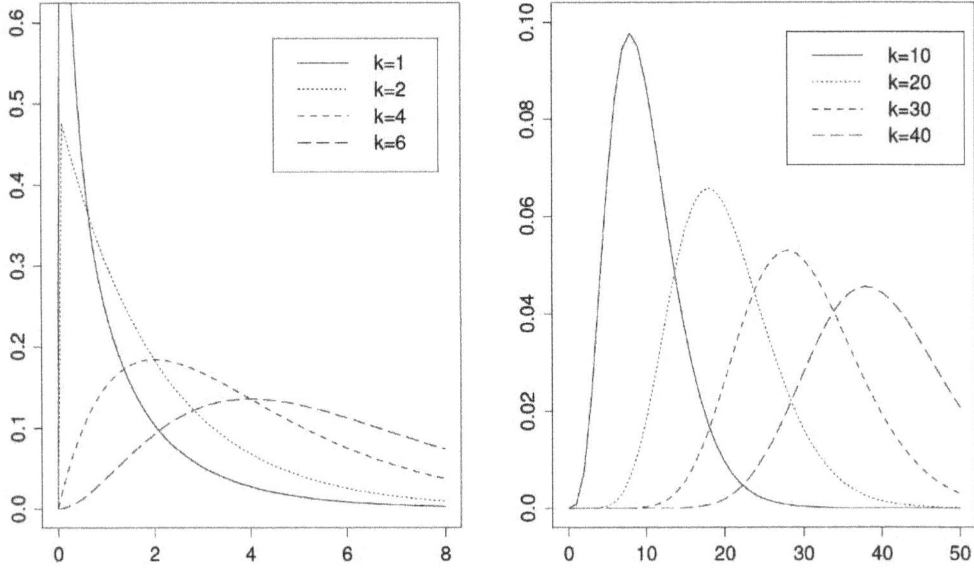

Figure 11.2 The chi-squared distribution for various degrees of freedom, *k*.

Can I have the bill, please?

Using data is not 'free'. Every time we use the data to calculate something, we must 'pay'. Payments are in the 'currency' of degrees of freedom, such that the price we are charged is *one degree of freedom for each use of the data*.

The general expression for the number of degrees of freedom in tests for association is:

(number of cells) – (number of times data are used to calculate the E_{ij} values).

For an $r \times c$ cross-tabulation, we begin with rc cells. We lose one degree of freedom for needing to use the total number of observations to compute the expected frequencies. However, we also use the row and column totals in these calculations, but we only need $r - 1$ row totals and $c - 1$ column totals, as the final one in each case can be deduced using the total number of observations. Hence we only 'lose' $r - 1$ degrees of freedom to calculate $r - 1$ row totals (all row totals are constrained to sum to n). Similarly, we use the data $c - 1$ times to calculate $c - 1$ column totals (costing us $c - 1$ degrees of freedom) all of which must sum to n. Hence the overall degrees of freedom we have left are:

$$rc - (r - 1) - (c - 1) - 1 = (r - 1)(c - 1).$$

11.2.3 Performing the test

As discussed in Chapter 10, we choose a significance level at which to conduct the test, by specifying α, against which we compare the p-value. However, are we performing a one-tailed test or a two-tailed test? Eagle-eyed readers may have spotted it is an *upper-tailed test* from the use of the Excel function `CHISQ.DIST.RT` underneath (11.1)!

To verify this, we need to consider what sort of test statistic values would be considered extreme under H_0. As seen in Figure 11.2, the chi-squared distribution only takes positive values. The squared term in the numerator of the test statistic in (11.1) ensures the test statistic value will be positive (the E_{ij} values in the denominator are clearly positive too as they are (expected) frequencies). If H_0 is true, then the observed and expected frequencies should be quite similar, since the expected frequencies are computed conditional on the null hypothesis of independence. This means that the *differences* $O_{ij} - E_{ij}$ should be quite small for all cells. In contrast, if H_0 is not true, then we would expect comparatively large values for the differences $O_{ij} - E_{ij}$ due to large differences between the two sets of frequencies. Therefore, upon squaring to give the $(O_{ij} - E_{ij})^2$ values, sufficiently *large* test statistic values suggest that we should reject H_0. Hence tests of association are always *upper-tailed tests*.

Example 11.5

Using the data in Example 11.2, we proceed with the hypothesis test. Below, the calculations are presented as an extended cross-tabulation where the three rows in each cell correspond to the observed frequencies, the expected frequencies and the test statistic contributors, respectively. Note all expected frequencies are greater than 5. Lucky us.

			Burglary	Fire damage	Car theft	Total
		O_1	30	19	6	**55**
	A	E_1	18.33	22.00	14.67	
		$(O_1 - E_1)^2/E_1$	7.48	0.41	5.15	
		O_2	12	23	14	**49**
Area	**B**	E_2	16.33	19.60	13.07	
		$(O_2 - E_2)^2/E_2$	1.13	0.59	0.06	
		O_3	8	18	20	**46**
	C	E_3	15.33	18.40	12.27	
		$(O_3 - E_3)^2/E_3$	3.48	0.01	4.82	
Total			**50**	**60**	**40**	**150**

Using (11.1), we obtain a test statistic value of

$$\sum_{i=1}^{3}\sum_{j=1}^{3}\frac{(O_{ij} - E_{ij})^2}{E_{ij}} = 7.48 + 0.41 + \cdots + 4.82 = 23.13.$$

Since $r = c = 3$, we have $(r - 1)(c - 1) = (3 - 1)(3 - 1) = 4$ degrees of freedom. The p-value is

(Continued)

$P(X \geq 23.13) = 0.000119$

where $X \sim \chi_4^2$. We can obtain this *p*-value in Excel using:

```
=CHISQ.DIST.RT(23.13,4)
```

Hence the test is *highly significant* (since 0.000119 < 0.01) and we conclude that there is *strong evidence* of an association between the factors. The *p*-value is shown in Figure 11.3.

Looking again at the cross-tabulation, comparing the observed and expected frequencies, the *nature* of this association becomes clear - burglary claims are more prevalent in area A whereas car theft claims are more prevalent in area C. We can deduce this by looking at the cells with large test statistic contributors (large values of $(O_{ij} - E_{ij})^2/E_{ij}$, which are a consequence of large differences between the observed and expected frequencies.

From the insurance company's perspective this is a valuable insight. When a prospective customer wishes to take out an insurance policy, the customer's address (and hence area of the city) is useful information to assess the risk that they will make an insurance claim (i.e. the insurer would have to pay out the redress amount, hitting profitability). For example, the cost of a policy to insure against burglary would be much higher for residents of area A than of area C; the cost of a policy to insure against car theft would be much higher for residents of area C than of area A.

In practice risk will depend on multiple factors, not just area. We will explore *multivariate* models in later chapters.

The conclusions in Example 11.5 are fairly obvious, given the small dimensions of the contingency table. However, for data involving more factors, and more factor levels, this type of analysis can be very insightful. Cells which make a large contribution to the test statistic value (i.e. which have large values of $(O_{ij} - E_{ij})^2/E_{ij}$) should be studied carefully when determining the nature of an association. This is because, in cases where H_0 has been rejected, rather than simply concluding that there *is* an association between two categorical variables, it is helpful to describe the *nature* of the association.

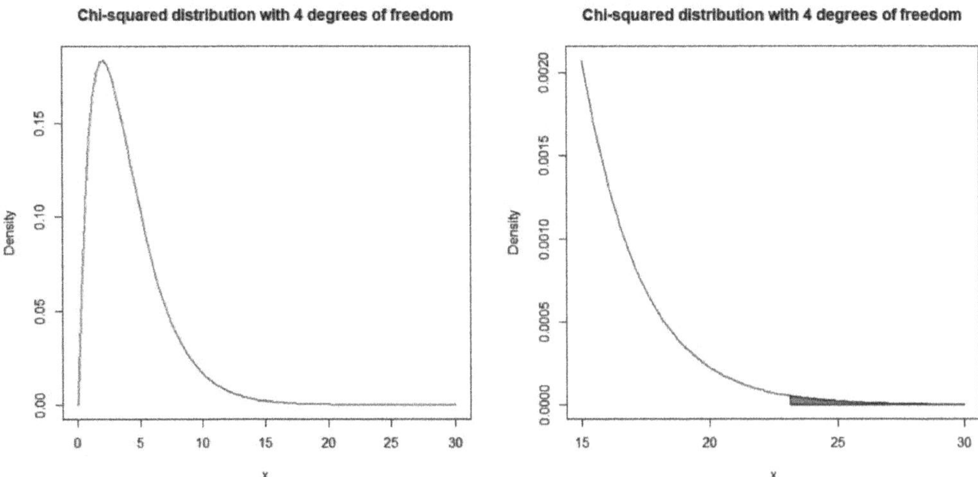

Figure 11.3 The chi-squared distribution with 4 degrees of freedom, indicating the *p*-value of 0.000119 in red. Note the right-hand plot is a zoomed-in version of the right-hand tail of the left-hand plot.

If we had a 2 × 2 contingency table, then there are two ways of testing an equivalent hypothesis: (i) a χ^2 test as outlined above, and (ii) a test of the difference between proportions as detailed in Section 10.9.

Example 11.6

Let us revisit the dataset in Example 11.1 to check whether there is statistical evidence of an association between product category and delivery mode. We test

H_0: No association between product category and delivery mode

versus

H_1: Association between product category and delivery mode.

The Excel tables below show the observed frequencies (O_{ij}, as presented in Example 11.1), expected frequencies (E_{ij}), and $(O_{ij} - E_{ij})^2/E_{ij}$ values, respectively.

	A	B	C	D	E	F
1	**Observed**	First Class	Same Day	Second Class	Standard Class	Total
2	Furniture	205	89	306	901	1501
3	Office Supplies	995	347	1318	3929	6589
4	Technology	254	80	352	1224	1910
5	Total	1454	516	1976	6054	10000
6						
7	**Expected**	First Class	Same Day	Second Class	Standard Class	
8	Furniture	218.2454	77.4516	296.5976	908.7054	1501
9	Office Supplies	958.0406	339.9924	1301.9864	3988.9806	6589
10	Technology	277.714	98.556	377.416	1156.314	1910
11	Total	1454	516	1976	6054	10000
12						
13	**(O – E)^2/E**	First Class	Same Day	Second Class	Standard Class	
14	Furniture	0.803868586	1.721921078	0.298064198	0.065338215	2.889192
15	Office Supplies	1.425823966	0.144433987	0.196957038	0.901902701	2.669118
16	Technology	2.024938592	3.493700394	1.711567755	3.962067912	11.19227
17	Total	4.254631144	5.360055458	2.206588992	4.929308828	**16.75058**

The test statistic value, shown in bold, is 16.75 (rounded). Here we have $r = 3$ and $c = 4$, hence $(r - 1)(c - 1) = 6$ degrees of freedom. The p-value is 0.0102, obtained from Excel using

```
=CHISQ.DIST.RT(16.75,6)
```

which is greater than $\alpha = 0.01$, say, hence we do not reject H_0 and conclude that this is a *non-significant* test at the 1% significance level such that there is *no* statistical evidence of an association between the two factors (of course, it is significant at the 5% significance level since $0.0102 < 0.05$). The p-value is shown in Figure 11.4.

Note that relative to the insurance data from Example 11.2 where $n = 150$, here we have $n = 10{,}000$ which is far larger. From Chapter 10 we know that test *power* increases with sample size so, *ceteris paribus*,

(Continued)

with such a large sample size we might have expected to find very strong evidence of an association. However, the *p*-value being greater than 0.01 indicates otherwise. So the (small) effect size influence dominates the large sample size influence. While it is possible that we may have committed a Type II error (a false negative), we would expect the test power to be high given the large *n*, so the probability of a Type II error is small, so our conclusion is likely to be correct - a *true negative* of no association!

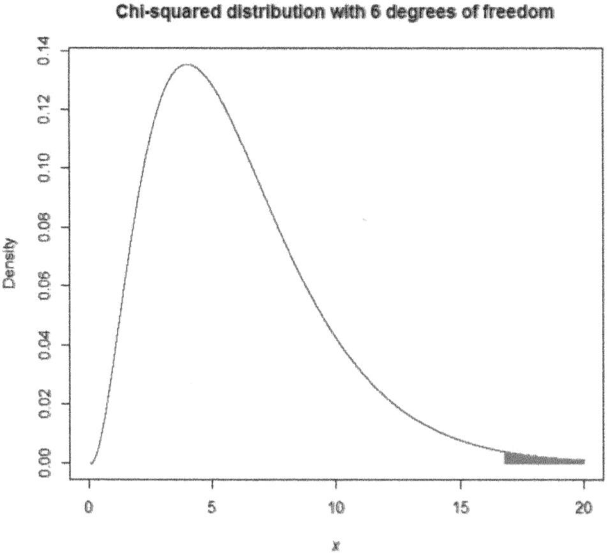

Figure 11.4 The chi-squared distribution with 6 degrees of freedom, indicating the *p*-value of 0.0102 in red.

11.2.4 Strength of association

So far we have used the chi-squared test to check whether there is statistical evidence of an association between two factors. When there is, such as in Example 11.5, it does not tell us *how strong* the association is, merely the strength of evidence of an association (of whatever strength). However, when there is no such evidence, such as in Example 11.6 then, of course, there is no such strength of association to investigate!

We now introduce two useful statistics for quantifying the *strength of association*. There are others, but for brevity we restrict attention to the following two.

Phi coefficient

If we have a 2 × 2 cross-tabulation (i.e. when $r = c = 2$), then the **phi coefficient** is

$$\phi = \sqrt{\frac{\chi^2}{n}}$$

where χ^2 is the test statistic value computed using (11.1) and n is the total number of observations, as before.

The phi coefficient takes values in the unit interval, $\phi \in [0, 1]$. When $\phi = 0$ (which is only when $\chi^2 = 0$), there is no association. The stronger the association between the two factors, the higher the value of ϕ.

(Note that this special 2 × 2 case will arise in Example 11.15 and also in Chapter 16 in the context of a 'confusion matrix' when we construct predictive classification models.)

Contingency coefficient

The **contingency coefficient** is a more general version of the phi coefficient, applicable to cross-tabulations of any dimension. It is calculated as

$$C = \sqrt{\frac{\chi^2}{\chi^2 + n}}$$

where χ^2 is the test statistic value computed using (11.1) and n is the total number of observations, as before.

The contingency coefficient takes values in the unit interval, $C \in [0, 1]$. When $C = 0$ (which is only when $\chi^2 = 0$), there is no association. As $C \rightarrow 1$, the stronger the association between the two factors, the higher the value of C.

However, C does not always reach its maximum possible value of 1. The maximum value depends on the dimensions of the cross-tabulation. As such, comparison of C values across multiple cross-tabulations is only advisable if the cross-tabulations are all of the same size.

11.3 SIDE-BY-SIDE BOX PLOTS

A bivariate analysis involving one categorical and one measurable variable is best visualised with **side-by-side box plots**. Since a measurable variable is quantitative, conventional measures of central tendency and dispersion are meaningful and can be compared across factor levels. Box plots, however, offer a quick view of the distributions by factor levels to visually identify any interesting features.

Example 11.7

Again, using Tableau's sample Superstore dataset, suppose we are interested in checking for any relationship between quantity sold and technology products, by customer ID. Side-by-side box plots are shown in Figure 11.5.

(Continued)

Accessories and Phones have very similar distributions, both with some large outliers indicating some customers ordered large quantities. In contrast, Copiers and Machines have similar distributions but with less variation in quantities sold than Accessories and Phones.

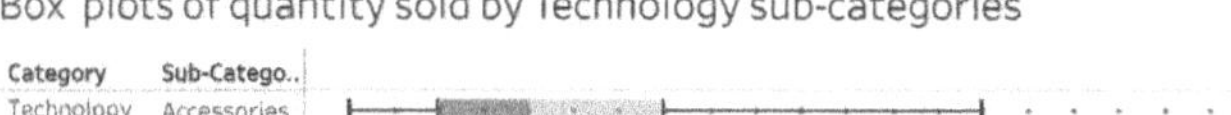

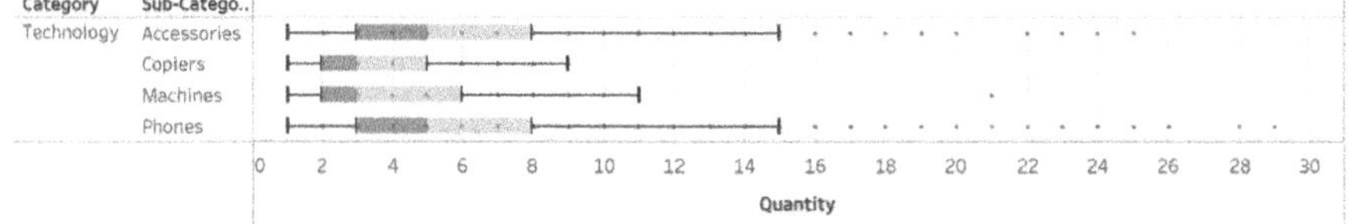

Figure 11.5 Example of side-by-side box plots.

11.4 CORRELATION (IS NOT CAUSATION!)

Perhaps the most interesting (dare I say exciting) type of relationship is that of **correlation** between two measurable (quantitative) variables. While our focus in this chapter is the *bivariate* setting (i.e. two variables), we may wish to look at the relationship between many variables (i.e. *multivariate* analysis). *Linear regression* (Chapters 13 and 14), *discriminant analysis* (Chapter 16), *factor analysis* (Chapter 17), and some kinds of *cluster analysis* (Chapter 18) all use related ideas and techniques, so it is important to have a good understanding of correlation.

Let us assume that we have some data in *paired form*: (x_i, y_i), for $i = 1, 2, \ldots, n$. When dealing with paired data, the first action is to construct a **scatter plot** (or *scatter diagram*) of the data, and visually inspect it for any apparent relationship between the two variables.

Example 11.8

In a university town, the sales, *y* (in thousands of pounds), of 10 coffee shops are closely related to the student population, *x* (in thousands), in their neighbourhoods.

Student population, *x*	2	6	8	8	12	16	20	20	22	26
Sales, *y*	58	105	88	118	117	137	157	169	149	202

We plot *y* against *x*, and draw a straight line through the middle of the data points, as shown in Figure 11.6.

A fairly *strong, positive, linear* relationship is seen. This means that *x* and *y* are correlated. If we assumed *x* caused *y* (just an assumption!) then it seems students enjoy coffee! As do I.

If we are thinking of opening a new coffee shop (perhaps a franchise of a well-known chain), the scatter plot suggests we should target opening in an area with a large student population if we want to achieve a high level of sales, and why wouldn't we?!

Data showing a general 'upward shape' as in Figure 11.6 is said to be *positively correlated*, and we shall see how to quantify this correlation. We now consider other possible scatter patterns.

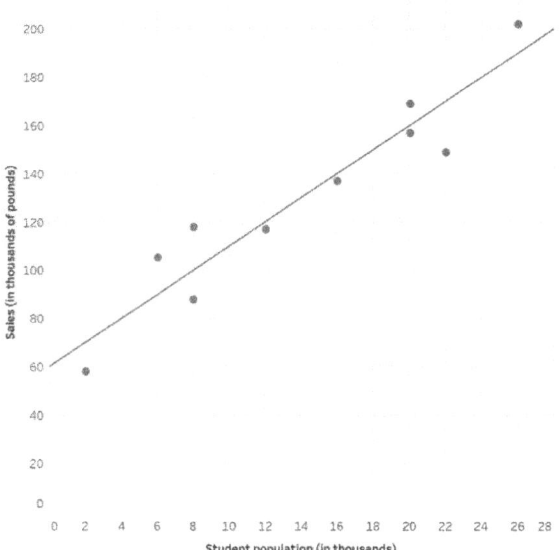

Figure 11.6 Scatter plot of coffee sales against student population for Example 11.8.

Example 11.9

Figure 11.7 shows different examples of scatter plots of observations of X and Y, and different values of the sample correlation, r, defined later. The line shown in each plot is the *best-fitting* (least-squares) line for the scatter plot, which will be introduced in Chapter 13.

- In (a), X and Y are perfectly linearly related, and $r = 1$.
- Plots (b), (c) and (e) show relationships of different strengths.
- In (c), the variables are negatively correlated.
- In (d), there is no linear relationship, and $r = 0$.
- Plot (f) shows that r can be 0 even if two variables are clearly related, if that relationship is not *linear*.

11.4.1 Causal and non-causal relationships

When two variables are correlated, an interesting question which arises is whether the correlation indicates a *causal* relationship. In Example 11.8, we observed that student population and coffee shop sales are positively correlated. It is reasonable to assume that more (coffee-loving) students result in more coffee shop sales. In this case, the relationship is (logically) causal.

Now consider ice cream sales and sun cream sales. A positive correlation is expected, but the relationship is *not* causal. It is not the selling of ice cream which causes sun cream sales to rise, nor vice versa. Rather both sales respond to warm weather and so these sales are seasonal, with both rising and falling together in response to other variables such as temperature and/or sunshine hours.

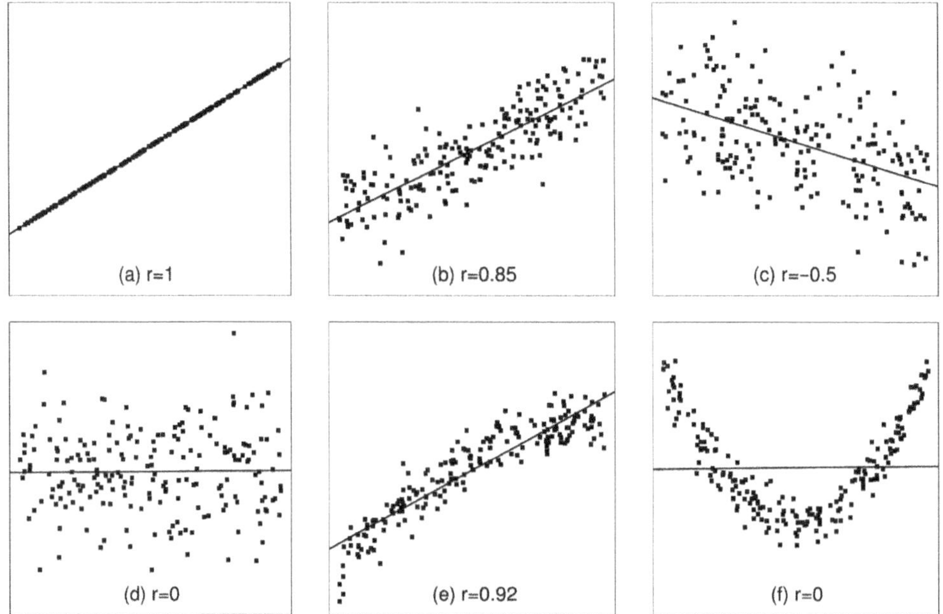

Figure 11.7 Scatter plots depicting various sample correlations as discussed in Example 11.9.

It should be clear from this that care needs to be taken in interpreting correlated relationships. Remember: *correlation is not causation!*

11.4.2 Correlation coefficient

The *strength* of a linear relationship between two random variables is given by the **correlation coefficient**. For random variables X and Y, the *population* correlation coefficient, a *parameter* denoted by ρ, is defined as

$$\rho = \frac{\mathrm{E}((X - \mathrm{E}(X))(Y - \mathrm{E}(Y)))}{\sqrt{\mathrm{Var}(X)\mathrm{Var}(Y)}} = \frac{\mathrm{E}(XY) - \mathrm{E}(X)\mathrm{E}(Y)}{\sqrt{\mathrm{Var}(X)\mathrm{Var}(Y)}},$$

and some people may refer to this as the 'product-moment correlation coefficient'. Technically, ρ can only be determined if we have perfect knowledge of the bivariate distribution function of X and Y, $F_{X,Y}$. In practice $F_{X,Y}$ is unknown so we will need to *estimate* ρ, using the *sample correlation coefficient*, from a random sample of observations of X and Y, that is, using sample paired data (x_i, y_i), for $i = 1, 2, \ldots, n$.

Sample correlation coefficient

The **sample correlation coefficient**, denoted by r, is

$$r = \frac{\sum_{i=1}^{n} x_i y_i - n\bar{x}\bar{y}}{\sqrt{\left(\sum_{i=1}^{n} x_i^2 - n\bar{x}^2\right)\left(\sum_{i=1}^{n} y_i^2 - n\bar{y}^2\right)}} \tag{11.2}$$

and can be computed in Excel using the `=CORREL(array1,array2)` function, where:

- `array1` is a range of cell values (the x_i values, say)
- `array2` is a second range of cell values (the y_i values, say).

As correlation is symmetric, the order of the two arrays does not matter.

The **sample correlation coefficient** *measures* how closely the points in a scatter plot lie around (or 'coalesce') a straight line, and the *sign* of r tells us the direction of this line (i.e. upward-sloping or downward-sloping, for positive and negative r, respectively). It does *not* tell us the *gradient* of this line – this is what we will determine with linear regression (see Chapter 13).

Properties of the correlation coefficient

Both correlation coefficients (the parameter ρ, and its estimator r) have the following properties. They:

- are independent of the *scale* of measurement
- are independent of the *origin* of measurement
- are *symmetric*, that is, the correlation of X and Y is the same as the correlation of Y and X
- can only take values between -1 and +1, that is,

  $$-1 \leq \rho \leq 1 \quad \text{and} \quad -1 \leq r \leq 1,$$

  or, to put it another way, $|\rho| \leq 1$ and $|r| \leq 1$, that is, correlation coefficients always have an absolute value less than or equal to 1.

Correlation coefficients are *scale-invariant*, meaning the numeric values of ρ and r have interpretable meanings.

Covariance (for the interested reader)

Technically, correlation is *scaled covariance*, where 'covariance' is a measure of how two variables move together, that is, how they 'co-vary'. However, covariance is *scale-variant*, so

(Continued)

while its sign tells us the direction of any co-movement, its magnitude depends on the units of measurement. This is why we prefer the *scale-invariant* population correlation coefficient,

$$\rho = \frac{\mathrm{Cov}(X,Y)}{\sqrt{\mathrm{Var}(X)\ \mathrm{Var}(Y)}} = \frac{\mathrm{E}(X,Y) - \mathrm{E}(X)\mathrm{E}(Y)}{\sqrt{\mathrm{Var}(X)\ \mathrm{Var}(Y)}} = \frac{\gamma}{\sigma_X \sigma_Y},$$

where Cov(X, Y) = γ is the population covariance, and the *scale-invariant* sample correlation coefficient,

$$r = \frac{\text{Sample covariance}}{\sqrt{\text{Sample covariance of } X \times \text{Sample covariance of } Y}}$$

$$= \frac{\left(\sum_{i=1}^{n} x_i y_i - n\bar{x}\bar{y}\right)/(n-1)}{\sqrt{\left(\sum_{i=1}^{n} x_i^2 - n\bar{x}^2\right)/(n-1) \times \left(\sum_{i=1}^{n} y_i^2 - n\bar{y}^2\right)/(n-1)}}$$

$$= \frac{\sum_{i=1}^{n} x_i y_i - n\bar{x}\bar{y}}{\sqrt{\left(\sum_{i=1}^{n} x_i^2 - n\bar{x}^2\right)\left(\sum_{i=1}^{n} y_i^2 - n\bar{y}^2\right)}}$$

where the $n-1$ terms cancel.

Having defined the correlation coefficient, it is important to remember the following when interpreting r (or ρ):

- An r (or ρ) near the top of this range (i.e. near 1) indicates a *strong, positive linear* relationship between X and Y.
- An r (or ρ) near the bottom of this range (i.e. near –1) indicates a *strong, negative linear* relationship between X and Y.
- Zero correlation indicates that X and Y are not linearly related, that is, the variables are *uncorrelated*.

Figure 11.8 shows how we may describe correlation coefficients in words: 'positive' or 'negative' (depending on sign), and 'strong', 'moderate' or 'weak' (depending on magnitude).

Example 11.10

For the dataset in Example 11.8, we have $n = 10$, $\bar{x} = 14$, $\bar{y} = 130$, and

$$\sum_{i=1}^{10} x_i^2 = 2528, \quad \sum_{i=1}^{10} y_i^2 = 184{,}730 \quad \text{and} \quad \sum_{i=1}^{10} x_i y_i = 21{,}040.$$

Hence the sample correlation coefficient, using (11.2), is

$$r = \frac{21{,}040 - 10 \times 14 \times 130}{\sqrt{(2528 - 10 \times 14^2)(184{,}730 - 10 \times 130^2)}} = 0.9501$$

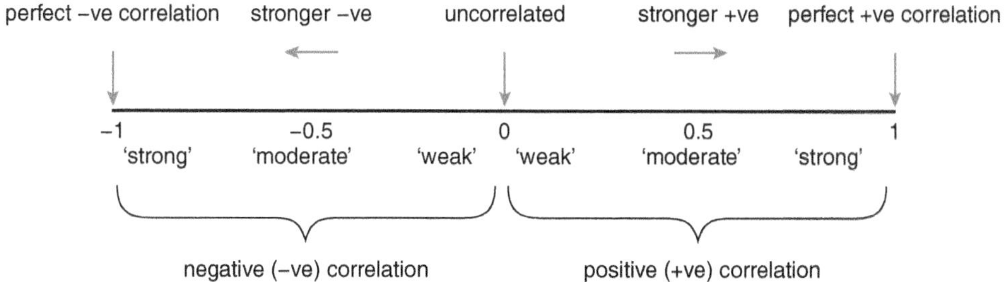

Figure 11.8 Values of correlation coefficients on the continuum [–1, 1].

or, more efficiently, using Excel's `CORREL` function:

	A	B	C	D
1	Student population	Sales		
2	2	58		
3	6	105		
4	8	88		
5	8	118		
6	12	117		
7	16	137		
8	20	157		
9	20	169		
10	22	149		
11	26	202		
12				
13	=CORREL(A2:A11,B2:B11)			
14	0.950122955	<- value returned by CORREL function		

Leveraging Figure 11.8, we can therefore describe the relationship between student population and coffee sales as a *strong, positive* correlation. We also note that the value of r agrees with the scatter plot shown in Figure 11.6 where the points tightly coalesce around the line of best fit.

Example 11.11

To emphasise, correlation assesses the strength of *linear* relationships between variables only. If $\rho = 0$ (or $r = 0$) this does *not* imply that X and Y are independent, since the variables could have a nonlinear relationship. For example, if

$$y = x(1 - x), \quad \text{for } 0 \leq x \leq 1,$$

then the correlation is zero (as they are not *linearly* related), but, clearly, there is a well-defined relationship between the two variables, so they are certainly not independent. Since $y = x - x^2$ (multiplying out the bracket term) we can see that x and y have a *quadratic* relationship. Figure 11.9

(Continued)

demonstrates this point for simulated sample data, where we see a clear relationship between x and y, but it is obviously not a linear relationship. In fact, these data are scattered around a parabola with (approximate) equation $y = 2(x - 15)(85 - x)$. Data of this kind would have a sample correlation near zero (here, $r = 0.148$), which can be described as a weak, positive, linear relationship. However, the scatter plot clearly showcases the nonlinear relationship between the variables.

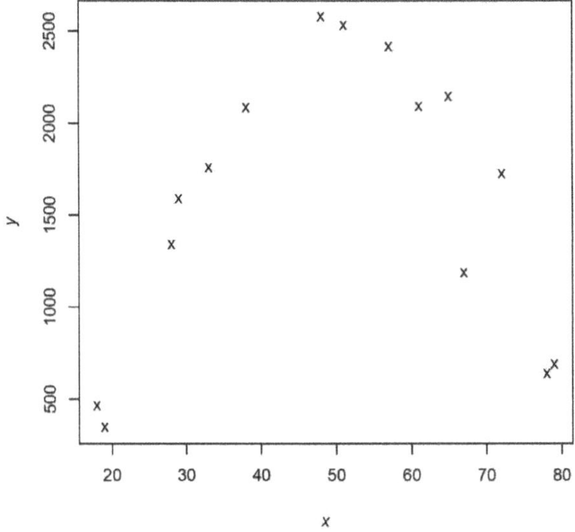

Figure 11.9 Scatter plot showing a nonlinear relationship as described in Example 11.11.

Example 11.12

Here we present the famous example of Anscombe's quartet. Consider the following four paired datasets:

Dataset 1		Dataset 2		Dataset 3		Dataset 4	
X_1	Y_1	X_2	Y_2	X_3	Y_3	X_4	Y_4
10.0	8.04	10.0	9.14	10.0	7.46	8.0	6.58
8.0	6.95	8.0	8.14	8.0	6.77	8.0	5.76
13.0	7.58	13.0	8.74	13.0	12.74	8.0	7.71
9.0	8.81	9.0	8.77	9.0	7.11	8.0	8.84
11.0	8.33	11.0	9.26	11.0	7.81	8.0	8.47
14.0	9.96	14.0	8.10	14.0	8.84	8.0	7.04
6.0	7.24	6.0	6.13	6.0	6.08	8.0	5.25
4.0	4.26	4.0	3.10	4.0	5.39	19.0	12.50
12.0	10.84	12.0	9.13	12.0	8.15	8.0	5.56
7.0	4.82	7.0	7.26	7.0	6.42	8.0	7.91
5.0	5.68	5.0	4.74	5.0	5.73	8.0	6.89

Quickly eyeballing the raw data, are there any interesting features?

Your answer will depend on how eagle-eyed you are! On close inspection, you might notice that $X_1 = X_2 = X_3$, and that the X_4 values are almost all 8s.

Let's dig deeper. First, let's consider simple descriptive statistics of each variable, summarised below:

	A	B	C	D	E	F	G	H
1	*X1*		*Y1*		*X2*		*Y2*	
2								
3	Mean	9	Mean	7.500909	Mean	9	Mean	7.500909
4	Standard Error	1	Standard Error	0.612541	Standard Error	1	Standard Error	0.612568
5	Standard Deviation	3.316625	Standard Deviation	2.031568	Standard Deviation	3.316625	Standard Deviation	2.031657
6	Sample Variance	11	Sample Variance	4.127269	Sample Variance	11	Sample Variance	4.127629
7	Sum	99	Sum	82.51	Sum	99	Sum	82.51
8	Count	11	Count	11	Count	11	Count	11
9								
10	*X3*		*Y3*		*X4*		*Y4*	
11								
12	Mean	9	Mean	7.5	Mean	9	Mean	7.500909
13	Standard Error	1	Standard Error	0.612196	Standard Error	1	Standard Error	0.612242
14	Standard Deviation	3.316625	Standard Deviation	2.030424	Standard Deviation	3.316625	Standard Deviation	2.030579
15	Sample Variance	11	Sample Variance	4.12262	Sample Variance	11	Sample Variance	4.123249
16	Sum	99	Sum	82.5	Sum	99	Sum	82.51
17	Count	11	Count	11	Count	11	Count	11

Amazing! The sample means (and hence sums, given $n = 11$) and the sample standard deviations (and hence sample variances) of the X and Y variables, respectively, are the same (well, at least to a few decimal places):

$$\bar{x}_1 = \bar{x}_2 = \bar{x}_3 = \bar{x}_4 = 9, \quad s_{x_1} = s_{x_2} = s_{x_3} = s_{x_4} = 3.316625$$

and

$$\bar{y}_1 = \bar{y}_2 = \bar{y}_3 = \bar{y}_4 = 7.50 \text{ (to 2 dp)}, \quad s_{y_1} = s_{y_2} = s_{y_3} = s_{y_4} = 2.03 \text{ (to 2 dp)}.$$

Next, we compute the correlation between each paired dataset using the `CORREL` Excel function. This returns (to 4 dp)

$$r_{X_1,Y_1} = 0.8164, \quad r_{X_2,Y_2} = 0.8162, \quad r_{X_3,Y_3} = 0.8163 \text{ and } r_{X_4,Y_4} = 0.8165.$$

So, based on the sample correlation coefficient, the strength of the linear relationship between each pair of variables is for practical purposes the same - a *strong, positive, linear* relationship.

So far, based on these computed statistics, the datasets appear indistinguishable. Yet, looking at the raw data they are clearly different!

What about if we *visualise* each dataset? Since we have two quantitative variables, the appropriate data visualisation tool is a simple scatter plot. A dashboard comprising scatter plots of all four datasets is shown in Figure 11.10, with 'lines of best fit' (covered in Chapter 13) superimposed.

Now we can clearly see the value added from data visualisation. We can conclude the following:

- Dataset 1: The empirical correlation is most appropriate since this exhibits the most 'natural' (positive) linear relationship. As X_1 increases, Y_1 increases, approximately linearly. Note, though, that we have no evidence that X_1 *causes* Y_1, nor vice versa.

(Continued)

- Dataset 2: X_2 and Y_2 are clearly related, but in a *nonlinear* way. A parabola would be a more appropriate way to model the relationship between these variables. Note that a strong correlation coefficient (here of $r_{X_2,Y_2} = 0.8162$) does not guarantee that a *linear* relationship is the most suitable!
- Dataset 3: If we exclude the outlier, then X_3 and Y_3 are perfectly (positively) correlated. While $r_{X_3,Y_3} = 0.8163$ does indeed indicate a strong positive correlation, the outlier is a highly 'influential' point preventing the correlation being computed to be $r_{X_3,Y_3} = 1$. There is no single right answer about what to actually *do* with outliers - it is a judgement call. Rather we should identify and then investigate them - perhaps this outlier might be the result of 'fat finger syndrome' (a data entry error) which, upon correction, would make it fall into line (quite literally!); or perhaps it is a genuine outlier, in which case we would need to consider whether its distortionary effect justifies its exclusion.
- Dataset 4: Again, an obvious outlier results in $r_{X_4,Y_4} = 0.8165$. Excluding the point would produce $r_{X_4,Y_4} = 0$, since there would then be no variation in the X_4 data! While the points would be vertically aligned, they would *not* be correlated, as X_4 would just be a constant (of 8.0).

The moral of the story? Always visualise your data first, so that you don't miss something obvious. Elephants and rooms spring to mind!

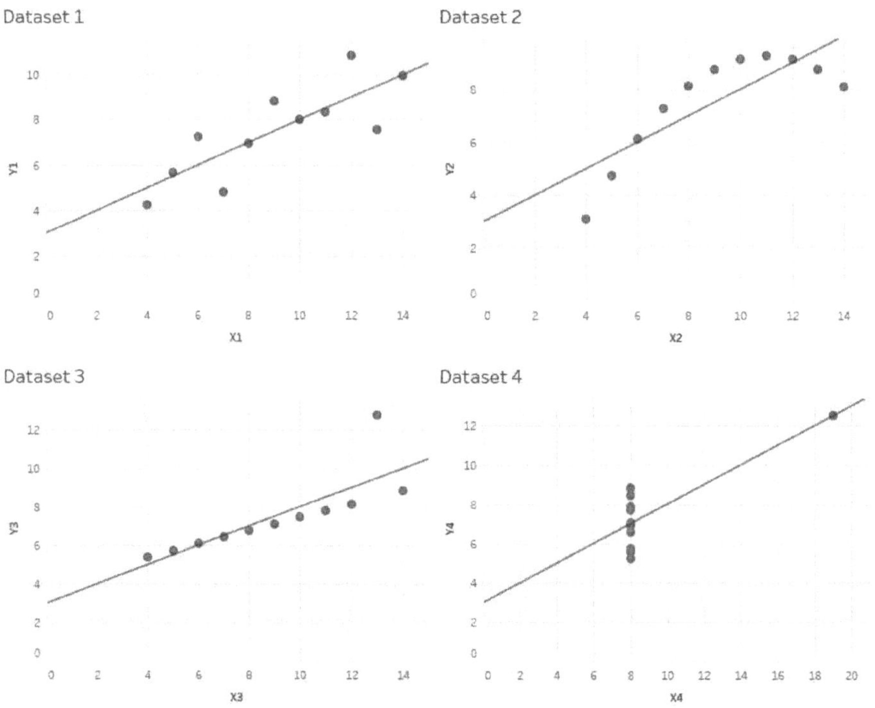

Figure 11.10 Scatter plots and lines of best fit for each dataset in Example 11.12.

11.4.3 Spearman rank correlation

As we saw in Chapter 2, we can use the median and interquartile range as measures of location and dispersion, respectively, instead of the mean and standard deviation (or variance). Similarly, we have an alternative to r, the ***Spearman rank correlation***, r_s.

To compute r_s we *rank* the x_i and y_i values in ascending order and use the *ranks* of the x_i and y_i values, rather than their actual values. Of course, it may be that we *only* have the ranks, in which case we would have to use this method.

Spearman rank correlation

If there are no tied rankings of x_i and y_i, the **Spearman rank correlation** is

$$r_s = 1 - \frac{6\sum_{i=1}^{n} d_i^2}{n(n^2-1)} \tag{11.3}$$

where the d_i values are the *differences in the ranks* between each x_i and y_i.

As with other order statistics, such as the median and quartiles, it is helpful to use the Spearman rank correlation if you are worried about the effect of extreme observations (outliers) in your sample. The possible values of r_s are the same as for r: $-1 \le r_s \le 1$, or equivalently $|r_s| \le 1$.

Example 11.13

An aptitude test has been designed to examine a prospective salesperson's ability to sell. Ten current staff sit the test. Instead of putting achieved scores in the computer, a research assistant ranks the individuals in ascending order in terms of the test as well as productivity. The ranked data are as follows:

Staff member	A	B	C	D	E	F	G	H	I	J
Rank order in test	2	3	5	1	4	9	10	6	7	8
Rank order in productivity	1	2	3	4	5	6	7	8	9	10

Does it look as if the test is a good predictor of sales ability?

We first compute the differences in the ranks:

Staff member	A	B	C	D	E	F	G	H	I	J
d_i	1	1	2	−3	−1	3	3	−2	−2	−2
d_i^2	1	1	4	9	1	9	9	4	4	4

Summing the squared values gives

$$\sum_{i=1}^{10} d_i^2 = 46.$$

Hence, using (11.3), we have

$$r_s = 1 - \frac{6 \times 46}{10 \times (10^2 - 1)} = 0.7212$$

which is quite strong, indicating that the test is a reasonably good predictor of sales ability.

11.4.4 Test for correlation coefficients

Given sample data from two populations, we want to use the observations to make a judgement as to whether or not the variables are correlated in the population. There exists a simple formal test for the existence of a non-zero correlation between two variables, and this is now described and demonstrated.

If ρ represents the population correlation coefficient between X and Y, then we might want to test the possibility that ρ had a specific value ρ_0, say, such that $-1 \leq \rho_0 \leq 1$ (remembering that a correlation coefficient must lie between –1 and 1). That is, we might wish to test

$$H_0: \rho = \rho_0 \text{ versus } H_1: \rho \neq \rho_0.$$

However, we are almost always interested in the question of whether or not two population variables are correlated at all versus them being uncorrelated. That is to say, the situation of most interest is when the 'target' value ρ_0 is zero (which means uncorrelated variables), hence we perform the *two-tailed test* of

$$H_0 : \rho = 0 \text{ versus } H_1 : \rho \neq 0 \tag{11.4}$$

if we have no *a priori* rationale about the sign of any correlation (we think the correlation could be positive or negative). However, often for real-world variables, we could likely anticipate the sign (common sense – which we know is not common! – would likely argue why any correlation between X and Y should be positive or negative) in which case we should conduct an appropriate one-sided test to *maximise the power* of the test – an upper-tailed test if we suspect positive correlation; a lower-tailed test if we suspect negative correlation.

Test for a correlation coefficient

Under H_0, the **test statistic** for testing (11.4) is

$$T = \frac{r\sqrt{n-2}}{\sqrt{1-r^2}} \sim t_{n-2}. \tag{11.5}$$

Hence p-values are obtained from the Student's t distribution with $n - 2$ degrees of freedom, using `T.DIST` in Excel.

Note that the (absolute) value of (11.5) is (i) increasing in r (the stronger the sample correlation coefficient, the larger the test statistic value, *ceteris paribus*), and (ii) increasing in n (the larger the sample size, the larger the test statistic value, *ceteris paribus*). Remark (i) reflects the *effect size influence*, and remark (ii) reflects the *sample size influence*. Note that n also affects the degrees of freedom of the t_{n-2} distribution, hence how fat/thin-tailed the test statistic distribution is, with implications for the magnitude of the p-value.

Example 11.14

For the dataset in Example 11.8, we test

$H_0: \rho = 0$ versus $H_1: \rho > 0.$

Note that we perform an upper-tailed test since, sensibly, if the student population size and coffee shop sales are correlated, they should be *positively* correlated - it is implausible that more students would result in lower coffee shop sales!

The test statistic value is

$$t = \frac{r\sqrt{n-2}}{\sqrt{1-r^2}} = \frac{0.9501 \times \sqrt{10-2}}{\sqrt{1-0.9501^2}} = 8.615.$$

The p-value is

$P(T > 8.615) = 0.00001276$

where $T \sim t_8$ (there are $n - 2 = 10 - 2 = 8$ degrees of freedom), calculated in Excel using `=T.DIST.RT(8.615,8)` which returns `1.276E-05` which is 1.276×10^{-5}. The p-value is shown in Figure 11.11.

The test result is *extremely(!) significant*, and so we conclude that student population and coffee shop sales are positively correlated, based on *very strong evidence*. Since the p-value is so small, the risk of a false positive (Type I error) is negligible, so we are effectively convinced of the existence of a positive correlation between these two variables.

In passing, from our knowledge of the Student's t distribution, we should immediately recognise that a t-value of the order of 8.615 is a very extreme value, so we should not be surprised to obtain such a small p-value. Digging deeper, recall that there are two influences on the p-value (from Chapter 10):

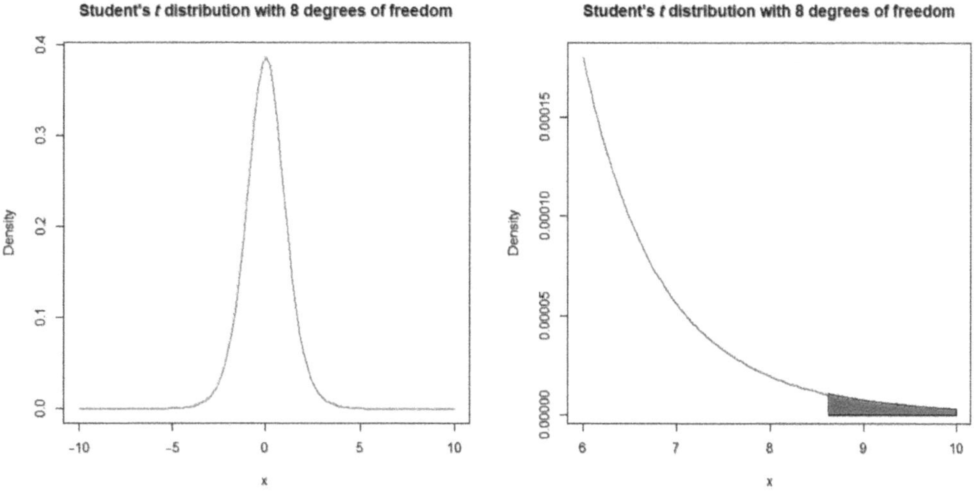

Figure 11.11 The Student's t distribution with 8 degrees of freedom, indicating the p-value of 1.276×10^{-5} in red. Note the right-hand plot is a zoomed-in version of the right-hand tail of the left-hand plot.

(Continued)

- The effect size: here this is r, which is the deviation from $\rho_0 = 0$ in the null hypothesis. As $r = 0.9501$ this is a (very) strong positive correlation, so the effect size is very large. If $\rho = 0$, then it is unlikely we would observe such a strong sample correlation coefficient. The fact that we did here should result in us rejecting H_0, *ceteris paribus*.
- The sample size: here $n = 10$ is small, and a small sample size indicates low test power making it more difficult to reject H_0, again *ceteris paribus*.

Overall, we have a large effect size (which works to decrease the p-value) and a small sample size (which works to increase the p-value). Since the p-value here is tiny, we can attribute the strong statistical significance to the effect size!

Example 11.15

Recall that GameStart wants to develop a recommendation system on its website to maximise cross-selling. As a new e-retailer selling second-hand computer games and assorted electronics, it has amassed initial transaction records of who bought what from its early customers.

We wish to apply correlation analysis to see which products tend to be purchased together (by the same customers) such that new visitors to the website will see an Amazon-style 'Customers who bought this also bought ...' banner displayed, raising their awareness of other products which GameStart expects will appeal to them, and hopefully that they then purchase.

When the website launched, suppose only seven products were on sale (which we will call A, B, ..., G), all of which could be shown on the landing page of GameStart. Hence each visitor could see all seven products displayed, so were aware of every possible item for purchase and could decide whether or not to buy it. (Okay, seven seems a very small number, but this is just to keep the example small for illustrative purposes.) As the e-retailer grows it will probably offer many thousands of products, say, hence these would not all be immediately visible to each visitor, so to raise awareness it will be necessary to promote those items that GameStart *thinks* a customer is most likely to buy based on the purchasing behaviour of previous customers.

In this instance we have binary data: 1 if a customer bought the product, and 0 otherwise (i.e. they did not buy the product). We will assume that all purchases were of a single quantity.

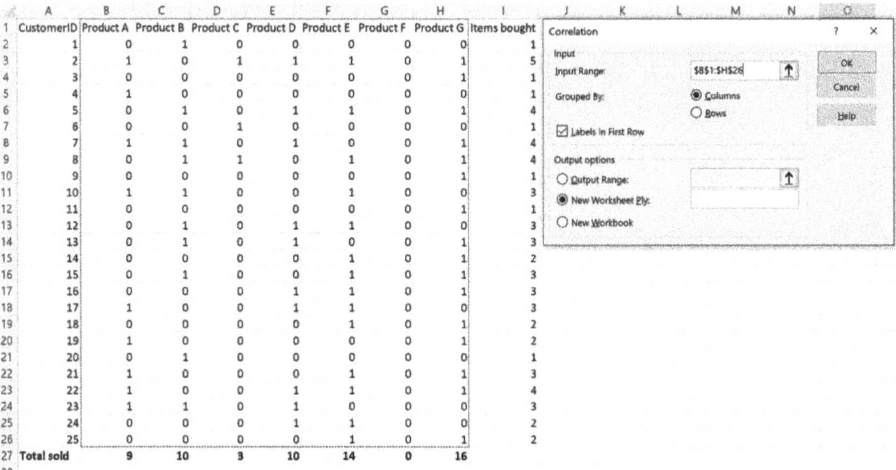

CustomerID	Product A	Product B	Product C	Product D	Product E	Product F	Product G	Items bought
1	0	1	0	0	0	0	0	1
2	1	0	1	1	1	0	1	5
3	0	0	0	0	0	0	1	1
4	1	0	0	0	0	0	0	1
5	0	1	0	1	1	0	1	4
6	0	0	1	0	0	0	0	1
7	1	1	0	1	0	0	1	4
8	0	1	1	0	1	0	1	4
9	0	0	0	0	0	0	1	1
10	1	1	0	0	1	0	0	3
11	0	0	0	0	0	0	1	1
12	0	1	0	1	1	0	0	3
13	0	1	0	1	0	0	1	3
14	0	0	0	0	1	0	1	2
15	0	1	0	0	1	0	1	3
16	0	0	0	1	1	0	1	3
17	1	0	0	1	1	0	0	3
18	0	0	0	0	1	0	1	2
19	1	0	0	0	0	0	1	2
20	0	1	0	0	0	0	0	1
21	1	0	0	0	1	0	1	3
22	1	0	0	1	1	0	1	4
23	1	1	0	1	0	0	0	3
24	0	0	0	1	1	0	0	2
25	0	0	0	0	1	0	1	2
Total sold	9	10	3	10	14	0	16	

We can see that the most popular product is G, with 16 of the first 25 customers purchasing it. However, product F has achieved no sales - perhaps it is priced too high, or maybe it is just an unpopular product (if the former, GameStart may choose to reduce the price; if the latter, GameStart may wish to withdraw it from sale). Customer 2 is the most prolific customer, with five purchases - perhaps a loyalty/reward scheme could be introduced as a customer retention initiative to encourage them to continue shopping with GameStart, especially if they buy high profit margin products!

Next we can analyse a **correlation matrix**, which returns all possible pairwise correlations between products: $r_{A,B}$, $r_{A,C}$, etc. This can be computed using the `Correlation` option in the Data Analysis add-in, with dialog box as shown above. Note the input range of the data, also that we have labels in the first row, and that product sales records are grouped by columns (columns B to H; we have no desire to use the customer IDs to compute correlations).

In general, for n products there will be

$$\frac{n^2 - n}{2}$$

paired comparisons. To see this, we have a correlation matrix of $n \times n = n^2$ elements, but the n elements on the leading diagonal will be 1s since these represent correlations of a variable with itself (and a variable is always perfectly correlated with itself), so these can be ignored. Subtracting, we now have $n^2 - n$ elements. Since the correlation matrix is symmetric (i.e. $r_{i,j} = r_{j,i}$), half of the remaining elements are duplicates so we can also ignore these. This results in $(n^2 - n)/2$ 'unique' pairwise correlations of interest (recall paired-comparison scaling in Section 8.4.1). Here we have $n = 7$, so there are $(7^2 - 7)/2 = 21$ paired-sample correlations.

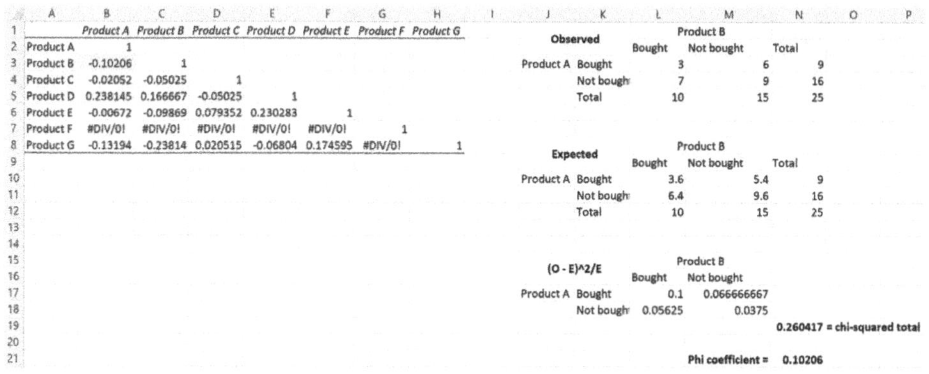

	Product A	Product B	Product C	Product D	Product E	Product F	Product G
Product A	1						
Product B	-0.10206	1					
Product C	-0.02052	-0.05025	1				
Product D	0.238145	0.166667	-0.05025	1			
Product E	-0.00672	-0.09869	0.079352	0.230283	1		
Product F	#DIV/0!	#DIV/0!	#DIV/0!	#DIV/0!	#DIV/0!	1	
Product G	-0.13194	-0.23814	0.020515	-0.06804	0.174595	#DIV/0!	1

Observed		Product B		
		Bought	Not bought	Total
Product A	Bought	3	6	9
	Not bough	7	9	16
	Total	10	15	25

Expected		Product B		
		Bought	Not bought	Total
Product A	Bought	3.6	5.4	9
	Not bough	6.4	9.6	16
	Total	10	15	25

(O - E)^2/E		Product B	
		Bought	Not bought
Product A	Bought	0.1	0.066666667
	Not bough	0.05625	0.0375

0.260417 = chi-squared total

Phi coefficient = 0.10206

These pairwise correlations are shown below the 1s on the leading diagonal in the correlation matrix above on the left. Note that since product F achieved no sales, all data values for product F were zero, hence there was no variation in sales for this product across customers. As such, with no variation, the correlation is undefined for all pairs involving product F (the `#DIV/0!` results).

Note how the sample correlation coefficients correspond to the *phi coefficient* introduced earlier, which you will recall is a measure of the strength of association for 2 × 2 cross-tabulations. Given the binary nature of the data, it is possible to construct cross-tabulations for pairs of products. An example is shown for products A and B above on the right. The observed frequencies correspond to the incidence of bought/not bought for this pair of products. For example, three of the 25 customers bought A

(Continued)

and B (customer IDs 7, 10 and 23). The expected frequencies are calculated in the table below it, after which the $(O_{ij} - E_{ij})^2/E_{ij}$ values are reported, which total 0.260417, producing a phi coefficient of $\sqrt{0.260417/10} = 0.10206$. However, the correlation coefficient helpfully provides the sign/direction of association ($r_{A,B} = -0.10206$, highlighted in yellow), unlike the phi coefficient.

We can see that the strongest correlation is $r_{A,D} = 0.238145$. So if a website visitor looked at product A (product D), then it makes sense to recommend product D (product A) in a 'Customers who bought this also bought ...' banner. Similarly for products D and E (the second largest correlation, $r_{D,E} = 0.230283$). Why stop there? How about offering *bundles* of products? Let's have a deal to purchase A, D and E together for a (charm) price of £29.99 - now that's cross-selling!

Example 11.15 provides an introduction to the field of *market basket analysis*. What else might we like to know beyond simple correlations? How about *probabilities* of purchase? Fear not, we will explore this theme in Chapter 16. Stay tuned!

We end this chapter with a cautionary tale of the dangers of **spurious correlations**. Beware fallacious conclusions – the world is not always as it seems...

Beware spurious correlations!

In a world of automation and data mining, countless pairs of variables can be quickly checked for significant correlations. Inevitably, some *spurious correlations* (i.e. false positives) will emerge. So, it is essential to perform a (common) sense check to avoid falling into the trap of thinking you have found an extremely strong relationship with inferred predictive power! While countless examples exist, tylervigen.com has assembled an entertaining selection of spurious correlations. My personal favourite is shown in Figure 11.12.

If you were a cheese manufacturer you might be looking for *leading indicators*, that is, variables with some predictive power such that your variable (here cheese sales) *lags* these leading indicators. Based on Figure 11.12, rushing to the morgues to see the latest bedsheet casualties could help you with your sales forecasts! Clearly nonsense. A classic spurious result since even the most open-minded individual would struggle to make a case for why these should be genuinely related. Unless somehow cheese consumption turns you wild in bed with fatal results!

Spurious results aside, what I find surprising is how deadly bedsheets can be. If you ever needed an excuse *not* to make your bed, you now have it! Depending on the circumstances, the victims may be possible contenders for the Darwin Awards (darwinawards.com).

Also, recently a strong correlation emerged between Covid cases in the USA and the price of the cryptocurrencies Bitcoin and Ethereum, prompting the *Financial Times* to ask: 'Is there a correlation between US Covid cases and crypto prices?' (https://www.ft.com/content/aef6cba4-1c94-4b9a-a4b3-329077b72dea). Note in passing that this is an excellent example of 'Betteridge's law of headlines', which states that any headline that ends in a question mark can be answered by the word '*no*!'.

Per capita cheese consumption (in pounds) and Deaths by being tangled in bedsheets (number of deaths)

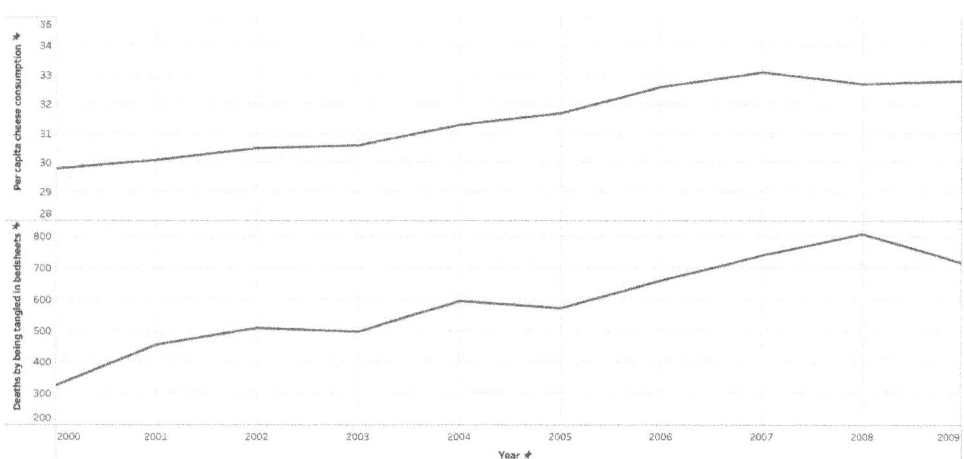

Figure 11.12 The above two time-series variables have a sample correlation of r = 0.9471, but are completed unrelated variables, hence the correlation is spurious.

11.5 CHAPTER OVERVIEW

This chapter has exposed us to the fascinating world of relationships – between variables, that is, not people! In a bivariate world of two variables we begin with exploratory data analysis – cross-tabulations, side-by-side box plots and scatter plots being useful displays. We have also sought statistical evidence of associations and correlations by deploying appropriate hypothesis tests, as well as quantifying the strength of any discovered relationships. However, we must remember the old adage that 'correlation is not causation'. Of course, causal relationships are of great interest, and we will proceed to study these in the following chapters.

11.6 KEY VOCABULARY

- Causation (≠ correlation!)
- Chi-squared distribution
- Chi-squared test (of association)
- Contingency coefficient
- Contingency table/cross-tabulation
- Correlation (≠ causation!)
- Correlation coefficient
- Correlation matrix
- Expected frequency
- Phi coefficient
- Sample correlation coefficient
- Scatter plot
- Side-by-side box plots
- Spearman rank correlation
- Spurious correlation

11.7 EXERCISES

11.7.1 Test your understanding

1 What type of exploratory analysis would you propose for:

(a) two categorical variables?

(b) one categorical variable and one measurable variable?

(c) two measurable variables?

2 In a hypothesis test of association, what are H_0 and H_1?
3 How are expected frequencies calculated in cross-tabulations, and why are they calculated in this way?
4 What condition is required on the expected frequencies so that the chi-squared distribution may be used when testing for association?
5 State the test statistic for a test of association and its distribution under H_0.
6 Which Excel function can be used to calculate *p*-values for a test of association? Include the function's arguments.
7 Name two ways of quantifying the strength of association between two categorical variables. When can each be used?
8 Are correlation and causation the same? Briefly justify your view.
9 What are the properties of the correlation coefficient?
10 What values of a correlation coefficient would you say constitute:
   (a) strong correlation?
   (b) moderate correlation?
   (c) weak correlation?
11 What is the Spearman rank correlation? How is it calculated, and when is it used?
12 When testing a correlation coefficient with H_0: $\rho = 0$, state the test statistic, its distribution under H_0 and how the test statistic value is affected by the:
   (a) effect size
   (b) sample size.
13 What is a 'spurious correlation'? Provide an example.
14 'Uncorrelated variables imply independent variables'. Do you agree? Briefly justify your view.
15 A 5 × 3 contingency table results in a test statistic value of 17.55. What is the corresponding *p*-value?
16 The following table shows the numbers of car accidents in an urban area over a period of time. These are classified by severity and by type of vehicle. Carry out a test for association on these data and draw conclusions.

	Severity of accident		
	Minor	Medium	Major
Saloon	29	39	16
Van	15	24	12
Sports car	7	20	12

17 'Footfall' is the daily number of customers per unit sales area of a shop, and 'Ticket price' is the average sale price of an item in the shop's offer. Shops are classified as offering low-, medium- or high-price items and, during any sales period, as having low, medium or high footfall. An analyst studies a sample of shops and obtains the following frequency data:

	Low price	Medium price	High price
Low footfall	28	42	46
Medium footfall	38	86	54
High footfall	64	75	35

Perform an appropriate hypothesis test to check whether there is evidence of an association between footfall and ticket price. What do you conclude?

18 A survey was conducted to investigate the relationship between hotels and the primary reason for not returning. The following table shows the results of this survey:

	Primary reason for not returning			
	Price of room	Hotel location	Room quality	Total
Hotel A	23	37	40	100
Hotel B	35	16	49	100
Hotel C	46	42	12	100
Total	104	95	101	300

(a) Based on the data in the table, and *without conducting a significance test*, would you say there is an association between the hotel and the primary reason for not returning?
(b) Perform an appropriate hypothesis test to check whether there is evidence of an association between the hotel and the primary reason for not returning. What do you conclude?

19 The following table shows the number of salespeople employed by a company and the corresponding values of sales (in thousands of pounds).

Salespeople (x)	210	209	219	225	232	221	220	233	200	215	205	227
Sales (y)	206	200	204	215	222	216	210	218	201	212	204	212

Compute the sample correlation coefficient for these data and carry out a formal test for a relationship between the number of salespeople and sales.

20 For 15 paired observations, the sample correlation coefficient is calculated to be $r = -0.6172$.

(a) Test H_0: $\rho = 0$ versus H_1: $\rho < 0$ at the 1% significance level.
(b) Following the test in part (a), briefly explain whether it is worthwhile to test H_0: $\rho = 0$ versus H_1: $\rho \neq 0$ at the 1% significance level.

11.7.2 Practice with Excel

Head over to the companion website for Excel examples and screencasts!

12

ANALYSIS OF VARIANCE

Chapter contents

Chapter level: ***Intermediate***

Source: Photo by Hal Gatewood via Unsplash

Key concepts

- Analysing variation
- Explanatory factors
- Interactions

Chapter value

A dependent variable's variation is decomposed to identify what factors drive the variation.

Key takeaway

Analysts seek to understand the causes of things, which equates to analysing variation.

Chapter outline

Variety is the spice of life. In our analytics world, 'variety' equates to *variation*. Variation is all around us. Customers have different attitudes, tastes, preferences and lifetime values. Websites have different churn rates. Companies' stocks have different volatilities. Once we recognise variation exists, we then seek to *explain* the cause(s) of that variation.

Analysis of variance - as the name suggests - analyses the variation in a 'dependent' variable and seeks to attribute it to one or more 'independent' variables. This notion of 'dependence' will extend to the following chapters on linear regression. The distinction? Analysis of variance requires *categorical* independent variables (known as 'factors'), while linear regression makes use of (mainly) *quantitative* independent variables. If we have at least two independent variables, it is possible (and of great interest) to investigate whether there exists an *interaction* between them, whereby the influence of one factor on the dependent variable itself depends on another factor! Exciting stuff.

Learning outcomes

After completing this chapter, you should be able to:

- explain the purpose of analysis of variance (ANOVA)
- conduct examples of one-way and two-way ANOVA in Excel
- perform hypothesis tests and construct confidence intervals for one-way and two-way ANOVA
- describe one-way and two-way ANOVA, including decomposition of the total variation, explanatory power, hypothesis testing and interpretation of results
- interpret results, including the relative importance of factors and interaction effects.

Motivational case: Stop the press – ink-redible revenues

Newspapers realise revenue from (i) advertising and (ii) sales. If it's a 'free' newspaper, then only from (i)! *News Daily* is one such 'free' newspaper, but it is in a financially precarious position, with declining print circulation forcing it to improve its digital offering. In keeping with its mission to make its news accessible to everyone it has decided to make its website free to access, instead of hiding behind a 'paywall' (restricting access to readers who pay a subscription). As such, advertising is the sole revenue stream so it is essential to maximise this (sole) income source.

News Daily's proprietor is interested in researching how effective paid-for advertising is on its website. The proprietor suspects that the number of customer enquiries generated from advertisements depends on two key factors: the day of the week (Monday to Friday, ignoring weekends), and the section of the website where the advertisement appears (news, business and sports).

How could News Daily develop a differential pricing strategy for paid-for advertisements on its website to maximise revenue?

12.1 INTRODUCTION

The motto of my *alma mater*, the London School of Economics and Political Science, is *rerum cognoscere causas*. This phrase can be traced back to the Latin poet Virgil: '*Felix qui potuit rerum cognoscere causas*' (Fortunate is he, who is able to know the causes of things). In statistics we strive to *understand* the *causes* of *variation* in a variable of interest (the 'thing'). Recall the flow chart in Figure 1.1 which distinguished between independent variables (causes) and dependent variables (effects)? Well, our mission here is to formally analyse and quantify the extent to which the variation we observe in a dependent variable (such as a customer's intention to purchase) can be attributed to one or more independent variables (such as our marketing mix variables, the 4Ps). Our goal is literally to 'understand the causes of things', where our dependent variables are the things we seek to understand.

12.2 TESTING FOR EQUALITY OF THREE POPULATION MEANS

We begin with an illustrative example to test the hypothesis that *three* population means are equal.

Example 12.1

To assess the effectiveness of different advertising strategies (digital, newspaper and billboard), a random sample of 6 weeks' sales figures was obtained from each of the three strategies (we assume the strategies were geo-specific so any sale is attributable to only one strategy). The units sold (in thousands) resulting from each advertising strategy are listed in the table below.

Strategy 1 (digital)	Strategy 2 (newspaper)	Strategy 3 (billboard)
85	71	59
75	75	64
82	73	62
76	74	69
71	69	75
85	82	67

Can we infer from these data that there is evidence of a difference in effectiveness among the advertising strategies?

Suppose units sold from strategy j follow the distribution $N(\mu_j, \sigma^2)$, for $j = 1, 2, 3$. So we assume units sold are normally distributed with the *same variance* for each strategy, σ^2, but *possibly different means* (i.e. μ_1, μ_2 and μ_3 may, or may not, be equal).

We need to test the null hypothesis that the population means are *all equal*:

$$H_0: \mu_1 = \mu_2 = \mu_3.$$

If H_0 is true, and since a normal distribution is uniquely defined by its mean and variance (see Chapter 5), then the distribution of units sold would be the *same* normal distribution, $N(\mu, \sigma^2)$, regardless of advertising strategy, since the means would be equal *and* the variances would be equal. This would indicate that units sold are *not* sensitive to the type of advertising strategy. The left-hand plot of Figure 12.1 illustrates an example of $\mu_1 = \mu_2 = \mu_3$.

If H_0 is not true, then *at least one* μ_j is different from the other two. Note that the alternative hypothesis, H_1, is a *composite* hypothesis as there are many ways in which H_0 is not true - for example, all three means are different ($\mu_1 \neq \mu_2 \neq \mu_3$) or only two means are the same (such as $\mu_1 = \mu_2 \neq \mu_3$, etc.). The right-hand plot of Figure 12.1 illustrates a case where $\mu_1 > \mu_2 > \mu_3$.

The raw sales data form a 6 × 3 array. Denote the data point of units sold at the (i, j)th position by X_{ij}. For example, $X_{41} = 76$ since this references the fourth observation ($i = 4$) in the first group ($j = 1$). Similarly, $X_{63} = 67$. We compute the column sample means first where the jth column sample mean is:

$$\overline{X}_{\cdot j} = \frac{X_{1j} + X_{2j} + \cdots + X_{n_j j}}{n_j}$$

where n_j is the sample size of group j (here $n_j = 6$ for all $j = 1, 2, 3$). Note that the group sample sizes do *not* need to be the same, although they happen to be equal here.

This leads to $\bar{x}_{\cdot 1} = 79$, $\bar{x}_{\cdot 2} = 74$ and $\bar{x}_{\cdot 3} = 66$. Transposing the table (to enhance readability), we get:

	Observation						
	1	2	3	4	5	6	Mean
Strategy 1 (digital)	85	75	82	76	71	85	79
Strategy 2 (newspaper)	71	75	73	74	69	82	74
Strategy 3 (billboard)	59	64	62	69	75	67	66

Note that, in general, we are not restricted to testing only *three* groups. This will be generalised later to k groups. For now, we set $k = 3$ (i.e. digital, newspaper and billboard).

Now, if H_0 is true then $\mu_1 = \mu_2 = \mu_3 = \mu$, where μ is the (common) population mean. In effect, we can ignore the subscript j. In which case the three observed sample means $\bar{x}_{\cdot 1}$, $\bar{x}_{\cdot 2}$ and $\bar{x}_{\cdot 3}$ should be *very close to each other* as they represent three (independent) point estimates of the same parameter, μ. Hence all of them should be close to the 'overall' sample mean, $\bar{x}$, which is

$$\bar{x} = \frac{\bar{x}_{\cdot 1} + \bar{x}_{\cdot 2} + \bar{x}_{\cdot 3}}{3} = \frac{79 + 74 + 66}{3} = 73,$$

that is, the mean value of all 18 observations. (Since $n_1 = n_2 = n_3 = 6$, we may simply take the arithmetic mean of the group sample means (i.e. attach equal weights). For different group sample sizes, the group sample means would need to be weighted accordingly with weights of n_j/(overall sample size). We will see such a case in Example 12.4.)

So, under H_0, we have four point estimates of μ, namely $\bar{x}_{\cdot 1}$, $\bar{x}_{\cdot 2}$, $\bar{x}_{\cdot 3}$ and $\bar{x}$. Of these, $\bar{x}$ should be the *most accurate* since it is based on (all) 18 observations, rather than just 6 observations for each group sample mean (recall that precision of estimation should increase with sample size, *ceteris*

(Continued)

paribus). However, these four point estimates are all different: 79, 74, 66 and 73, for $\bar{x}_{\cdot 1}$, $\bar{x}_{\cdot 2}$, $\bar{x}_{\cdot 3}$ and $\bar{x}$, respectively. Specifically, we observe *variation* in these estimates. The obvious question arises - what is the *cause* of this variation? Advertising strategy, or chance? Or perhaps a mixture of the two, but then is it more due to advertising strategy or more due to chance?

So, we wish to perform a hypothesis test based on the *variation in the sample means* such that the greater the variation, the more likely we are to reject H_0 and conclude that the choice of advertising strategy *does* affect units sold. One possible measure for the variation in the sample means, $\bar{X}_{\cdot j}$, about the overall sample mean, $\bar{x}$, for $j = 1, 2, 3$, is the *sum of squared deviations* (motivated by the sample variance introduced in Chapter 2):

$$\sum_{j=1}^{3}(\bar{X}_{\cdot j} - \bar{X})^2. \tag{12.1}$$

However, (12.1) is *not scale-invariant*, so it would be difficult to judge whether the realised value is large enough to warrant rejection of H_0 due to the magnitude being dependent on the units of measurement of the data. For example, what would constitute a 'large' value for (12.1)? Would 82 be considered large, say? Well, James, it depends! Specifically, whether measurements are in 'units' or 'thousands of units' would affect the order of magnitude (82,000 versus 82, say). So, we seek a *scale-invariant test statistic* such that large values can be easily identified as such.

Just as we may scale the covariance between two quantitative variables to give the scale-invariant correlation coefficient (as seen in Chapter 11), so we can similarly scale (12.1) to give the following possible test statistic:

$$T = \frac{\sum_{j=1}^{3}(\bar{X}_{\cdot j} - \bar{X})^2}{\text{sum of the three sample variances}}.$$

Hence we would reject H_0 for large values of (the random variable) T. Note the observed value $t = 0$ if $\bar{x}_{\cdot 1} = \bar{x}_{\cdot 2} = \bar{x}_{\cdot 3}$, which would mean that there is *no variation at all* between the sample means. In this case all the sample means would equal $\bar{x}$, and common sense would tell us that if we observed absolutely zero variation in the sample means, then we have absolutely no evidence of any difference in the population means!

It remains to determine the *distribution* of T under H_0.

Problems similar to those in Example 12.1 arise in many other practical business situations. For example:

- comparing the *returns* of stocks in three different *sectors* (such as consumer staples, industrials, financials)
- comparing the *effectiveness* of three Covid-19 *vaccines* (such as Oxford AstraZeneca, Moderna and Pfizer)
- comparing *confectionery sales* using three different *chocolate types* (such as dark, milk and white chocolate)
- comparing *brand awareness* among different *consumer segments* (such as young, middle-aged and old).

We now proceed to formally introduce the *one-way analysis of variance* model.

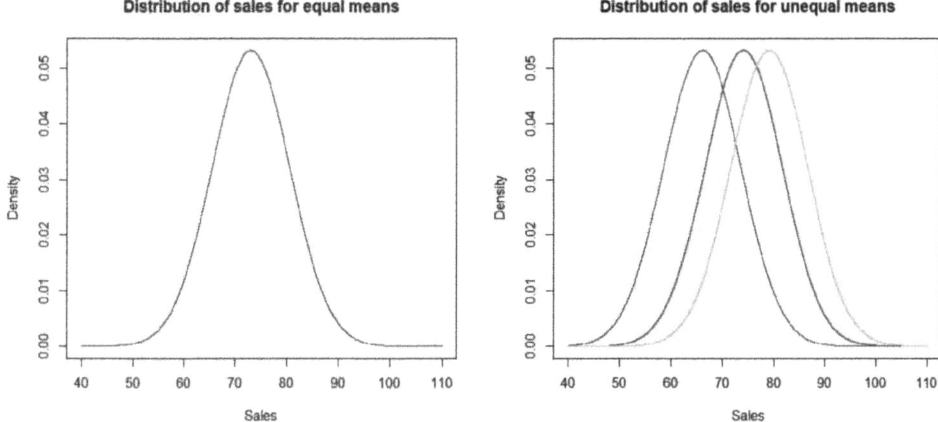

Figure 12.1 Left-hand plot shows the same distribution of units sold, where H_0 is true (i.e. $\mu_1 = \mu_2 = \mu_3$). Here the distribution is centred on 73. Right-hand plot shows one possibility (of several) where H_0 is not true - in this instance $\mu_1 = 79$ (green), $\mu_2 = 74$ (red) and $\mu_3 = 66$ (blue), such that $\mu_1 > \mu_2 > \mu_3$. Note that the distributions have the same variance, σ^2 (an assumption of our model).

Case study: Asset class performance

Investors have a wide range of asset classes to choose between when deciding what to do with their money. Bonds, equities, gold, and even cryptocurrency!

Admittedly, investors will have different risk appetites and objectives - some merely seek to preserve their wealth, while others seek to grow it. Financial markets can be benign and at other times highly volatile. In any given year does performance, in terms of investment returns, vary significantly by asset class? Let's look at the '(asset) class of 2021':

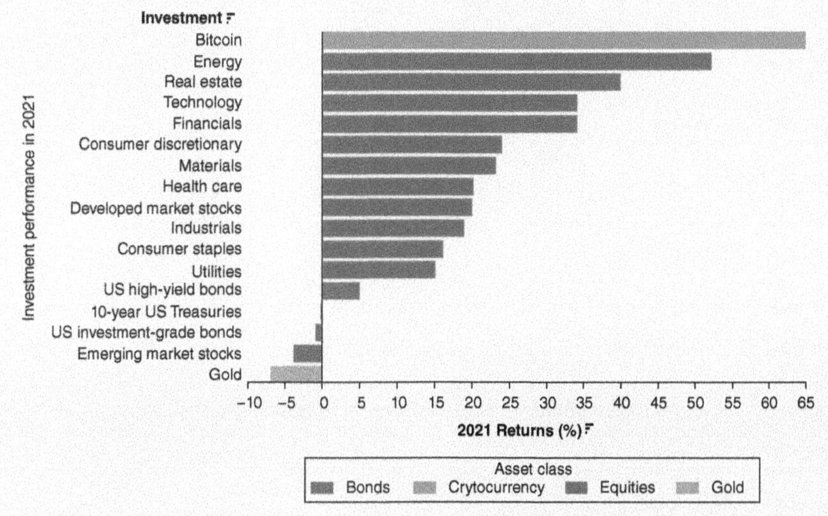

Source: FT calculations (https://www.ft.com/content/64980671-f086-42c0-91dc-17aa1fc93ee0).

(Continued)

We immediately see the *variation in returns*, with Bitcoin leading the way. Bitcoin cheerleaders view the cryptocurrency as 'digital gold' and, in 2021 at least, Bitcoin's fortunes dramatically contrasted with those of its non-digital peers, with gold being the worst performer among the investments considered.

Note how this simple chart gives a visual sense about how a factor (here, asset class) could help explain variation in a quantitative dependent variable (here, percentage return). We have conducted (informally) our first analysis of variance!

Spoiler alert! What goes up, can go down. The year 2021 was soon followed by the *crypto winter* of 2022, brought about by bearish market sentiment accelerated with the collapse of FTX. OMG.

12.3 ONE-WAY ANALYSIS OF VARIANCE

We now extend Example 12.1 to consider a general setting where there are k independent random samples available from k normal distributions $N(\mu_j, \sigma^2)$, for $j = 1, 2, \ldots, k$. (Example 12.1 corresponds to $k = 3$.) Remember, we assume a constant variance, σ^2, for each $j = 1, 2, \ldots, k$.

Denote by $X_{1j}, X_{2j}, \ldots, X_{n_j j}$ the random sample with sample size n_j from $N(\mu_j, \sigma^2)$, for $j = 1, 2, \ldots, k$. Our goal is to test

$$H_0: \mu_1 = \mu_2 = \ldots = \mu_k \text{ versus } H_1: \text{not all } \mu_j \text{ are equal.}$$

One-way analysis of variance (one-way ANOVA) involves a continuous dependent variable and *one* categorical independent variable (sometimes called a *factor* or *treatment*), where the k different *levels* of the categorical variable are the k different groups.

We now introduce statistics associated with one-way ANOVA.

Statistics associated with one-way ANOVA (for interested readers)

The jth sample mean is

$$\overline{X}_{\cdot j} = \frac{1}{n_j}\sum_{i=1}^{n_j} X_{ij}.$$

The overall sample mean is

$$\overline{X} = \frac{1}{n}\sum_{j=1}^{k}\sum_{i=1}^{n_j} X_{ij} = \frac{1}{n}\sum_{j=1}^{k} n_j \overline{X}_{\cdot j}$$

where $n = \sum_{j=1}^{k} n_j$ is the total number of observations across all k groups.

The total variation is

$$SS_X = \sum_{j=1}^{k}\sum_{i=1}^{n_j}(X_{ij} - \overline{X})^2$$

with $n - 1$ degrees of freedom.

The between-groups variation is

$$B = \sum_{j=1}^{k} n_j (\bar{X}_{\cdot j} - \bar{X})^2$$

with $k - 1$ degrees of freedom.

The within-groups variation is

$$W = \sum_{j=1}^{k} \sum_{i=1}^{n_j} (X_{ij} - \bar{X}_{\cdot j})^2$$

with $n - k = \sum_{j=1}^{k} (n_j - 1)$ degrees of freedom.

The ANOVA decomposition is

$$\sum_{j=1}^{k} \sum_{i=1}^{n_j} (X_{ij} - \bar{X})^2 = \sum_{j=1}^{k} n_j (\bar{X}_{\cdot j} - \bar{X})^2 + \sum_{j=1}^{k} \sum_{i=1}^{n_j} (X_{ij} - \bar{X}_{\cdot j})^2 \quad \Leftrightarrow \quad SS_X = B + W.$$

We have already discussed the *j*th sample mean and overall sample mean. The **total variation**,

$$SS_X = \sum_{j=1}^{k} \sum_{i=1}^{n_j} (X_{ij} - \bar{X})^2,$$

is a measure of the overall (total) variability in the data from all *k* groups about the overall sample mean, $\bar{X}$. The 'double summation operator, $\Sigma\Sigma$ (already seen in Section 11.2.2), simply means adding up the squared deviations from the mean across all observations ($i = 1, 2, \ldots, n_j$) across all groups ($j = 1, 2, \ldots, k$). Note that *SS* stands for 'sum of squares'.

ANOVA decomposition

The **ANOVA decomposition** splits this total variation, SS_X, up into two components: the **between-groups variation**, *B* (which is attributable to the factor level, such as advertising strategy type), and the **within-groups variation**, *W* (which is attributable to the variation *within* each group, and this is assumed to be the same σ^2 for each group - think of this as the naturally occurring variation), that is, we have

$$SS_X = B + W.$$

Provided there is at least some variation in the dependent variable (i.e. not all observations are equal), then $SS_X > 0$ (i.e. it is strictly positive). *B* and *W* are sums of squares, so are non-negative (i.e. $B \geq 0$ and $W \geq 0$).

If all observations were equal, that is, if all $x_{ij} = \bar{x}$, then $SS_X = 0$ and hence there is (literally) no variation to explain. In which case, find something else to analyse!

Informally, we can think of B as representing the *explained variation*, that is, the amount of the variation in the dependent variable which can be attributed to the factor level, and we can think of W as representing the *unexplained variation*, that is, the leftover or 'residual' variation which cannot be attributed to the factor level. Again, informally,

total variation = explained variation + unexplained variation.

12.3.1 Explanatory power

It is helpful to have a simple metric to quantify how 'good' a model is. In this setting, we would benefit from a measure of the *effect size* – namely a measure of the **explanatory power** of the factor. η^2 (eta-squared) serves this purpose. It is very straightforward, and there is always beauty in simplicity.

η^2 (eta-squared)

η^2 (eta-squared) is the proportion of the variation in the dependent variable explained by an ANOVA model. For one-way ANOVA, it is

$$\eta^2 = \frac{B}{SS_X} = \frac{\text{explained variation}}{\text{total variation}}$$

provided $SS_X > 0$ - that is, for the definition to hold we must have at least *some* variation in the dependent variable.

Since $0 \le B \le SS_X$ (because $B \ge 0$ and $W = SS_X - B \ge 0$), it must be that $\eta^2 \in [0, 1]$, that is, its value lies between 0 and 1. The better the explanatory power of the factor, the closer η^2 gets to 1. This is a good thing as we seek *rerum cognoscere causas*!

12.3.2 Putting it all together

While we can (and will) use Excel to perform the calculations for the data in Example 12.1, for illustrative purposes let us see the calculations performed manually and verify that we get the same values in the Excel output. While, of course, we would *not* perform manual calculations in practice, to develop a proper sense of what the numbers in Excel output mean and how they are calculated, we note the following useful formulae for manual computations.

- The total number of observations is $n = \sum_{j=1}^{k} n_j$.
- The group and overall sample means are $\bar{X}_{\cdot j} = \sum_{i=1}^{n_j} X_{ij} / n_j$ and $\bar{X} = \sum_{j=1}^{k} n_j \bar{X}_{\cdot j} / n$, respectively.
- The total variation is $SS_X = B + W = \sum_{j=1}^{k} \sum_{i=1}^{n_j} X_{ij}^2 - n\bar{X}^2$.
- The between-groups variation is $B = \sum_{j=1}^{k} n_j \bar{X}_{\cdot j}^2 - n\bar{X}^2$.

- The within-groups variation is $W = \sum_{j=1}^{k}\sum_{i=1}^{n_j} X_{ij}^2 - \sum_{j=1}^{k} n_j \overline{X}_{\cdot j}^2 = \sum_{j=1}^{k}(n_j - 1)S_j^2$ where S_j^2 is the jth sample variance.

In order to test H_0: $\mu_1 = \mu_2 = \cdots = \mu_k$, we define the following test statistic:

$$F = \frac{\sum_{j=1}^{k} n_j(\overline{X}_{\cdot j} - \overline{X})^2 / (k-1)}{\sum_{j=1}^{k}\sum_{i=1}^{n_j}(X_{ij} - \overline{X}_{\cdot j})^2 / (n-k)} = \frac{B/(k-1)}{W/(n-k)}. \tag{12.2}$$

Under H_0, $F \sim F_{k-1,\ n-k}$, which follows an F distribution. We omit technical details about *why* expression (12.2) has an F distribution.

The *F* distribution

The **F distribution** is a family of continuous distributions, with non-zero probabilities for $x > 0$. Each member of the F family is defined by a pair of degrees of freedom, df_1 and df_2, called the *degrees of freedom in the numerator and denominator*, respectively. The general shape of its pdf is shown in Figure 12.2.

For $F \sim F_{df_1, df_2}$, the expected value, (i.e. the mean), is

$$E(F) = \frac{df_2}{df_2 - 2} \quad \text{for } df_2 > 2.$$

If $F \sim F_{df_1, df_2}$, then $1/F \sim F_{df_2, df_1}$, that is, the inverse of F is also F-distributed, but with the degrees of freedom reversed.

If $T \sim t_k$, then $T^2 \sim F_{1,k}$. This result means that if you square a t_k-distributed variable, you obtain an $F_{1,k}$-distributed variable. This means that t tests can be performed as F tests upon squaring. We will see an example of this in Chapter 13.

For which values of the test statistic should we reject H_0? Well, the greater B is relative to W, the better the factor is at explaining the variation in the dependent variable ($\eta^2 \to 1$). Since the test statistic is increasing in B (because B is in the numerator), the one-way ANOVA F test is an *upper-tailed test*, such that for sufficiently large test statistic values we would reject H_0.

In Excel, the statistical significance will be determined by the p-value, which is the area under the $F_{k-1,n-k}$ distribution to the *right* of the test statistic value – that is, the p-value of the test is

$$p\text{-value} = P(F > f),$$

as shown in Figure 12.3 assuming $f = 4$ and $F \sim F_{10,10}$. Note that the *larger* the value of f, the *smaller* the p-value (the smaller the area to the right of f). The test statistic value and p-value are inversely related.

The results of a one-way ANOVA are typically reported in a *one-way ANOVA table* which we can think of as an 'audit trail' of how the p-value is ultimately obtained.

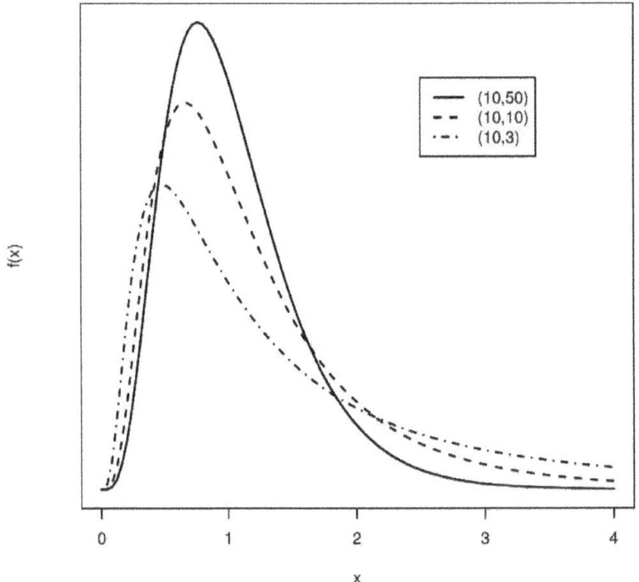

Figure 12.2 *F* distributions for various degrees of freedom.

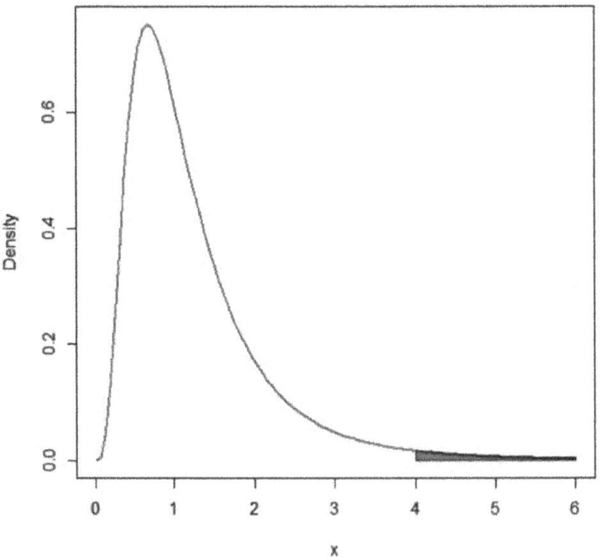

Figure 12.3 The red shaded area corresponds to the *p*-value for a one-way ANOVA *F* test, assuming $f = 4$ is the test statistic value, drawn from $F_{10,10}$ under H_0. As usual, reject H_0 if the *p*-value is less than α.

One-way ANOVA table

It is common for results to be presented in a **one-way ANOVA table** as follows:

Source of variation	SS	df	MS	F	p-value
Between groups	B	$k-1$	$B/(k-1)$	$\frac{B/(k-1)}{W/(n-k)}$	p
Within groups	W	$n-k$	$W/(n-k)$		
Total	SS_x	$n-1$			

From this, the *p*-value is sufficient to establish whether there is evidence of a difference between the population means (i.e. if $p < \alpha$). The rest of the table is just explaining how this *p*-value is determined. For reference the:

- *SS* column is the ANOVA decomposition, reporting the values of B, W and $SS_x = B + W$
- *df* column reports the degrees of freedom of the test statistic's *F* distribution: $k - 1 = df_1$ and $n - k = df_2$, totalling $n - 1$
- *MS* column is the 'mean sum of squares', calculated as the respective row's *SS*/*df*
- *F* is the test statistic value, being the ratio of the between groups and within groups *MS*. You can see why $k - 1 = df_1$ is the degrees of freedom in the *numerator*, and why $n - k = df_2$ is the degrees of freedom in the *denominator*.

Example 12.2

Continuing with Example 12.1, for the given data, $k = 3$, $n_1 = n_2 = n_3 = 6$, $n = n_1 + n_2 + n_3 = 18$, $\bar{x}_{\cdot 1} = 79$, $\bar{x}_{\cdot 2} = 74$, $\bar{x}_{\cdot 3} = 66$ and $\bar{x} = 73$. The sample variances are calculated to be $s_1^2 = 34$, $s_2^2 = 20$ and $s_3^2 = 32$. Therefore

$$b = \sum_{j=1}^{3} 6(\bar{x}_{\cdot j} - \bar{x})^2 = 6 \times ((79-73)^2 + (74-73)^2 + (66-73)^2) = 516$$

and

$$\begin{aligned} w &= \sum_{j=1}^{3}\sum_{i=1}^{6}(x_{ij} - \bar{x}_{\cdot j})^2 = \sum_{j=1}^{3}\sum_{i=1}^{6} x_{ij}^2 - 6\sum_{j=1}^{3}\bar{x}_{\cdot j}^2 \\ &= \sum_{j=1}^{3} 5s_j^2 \\ &= 5 \times (34 + 20 + 32) \\ &= 430. \end{aligned}$$

Hence

$$f = \frac{b/(k-1)}{w/(n-k)} = \frac{516/2}{430/15} = 9.$$

(Continued)

Under H_0: $\mu_1 = \mu_2 = \mu_3$, $F \sim F_{k-1,n-k} = F_{2,15}$. The *p*-value (using `=F.DIST.RT(9,2,15)` in Excel) is:

$$P(F > 9) = 0.0027 < 0.01.$$

Hence we can reject H_0 at the 1% significance level and conclude that there is strong evidence of a difference in the effectiveness of advertising strategy on units sold. The *p*-value is shown in Figure 12.4.

The one-way ANOVA table is as follows:

Source of variation	SS	df	MS	F	p-value
Between groups	516	2	258	9	0.0027
Within groups	430	15	28.667		
Total	946	17			

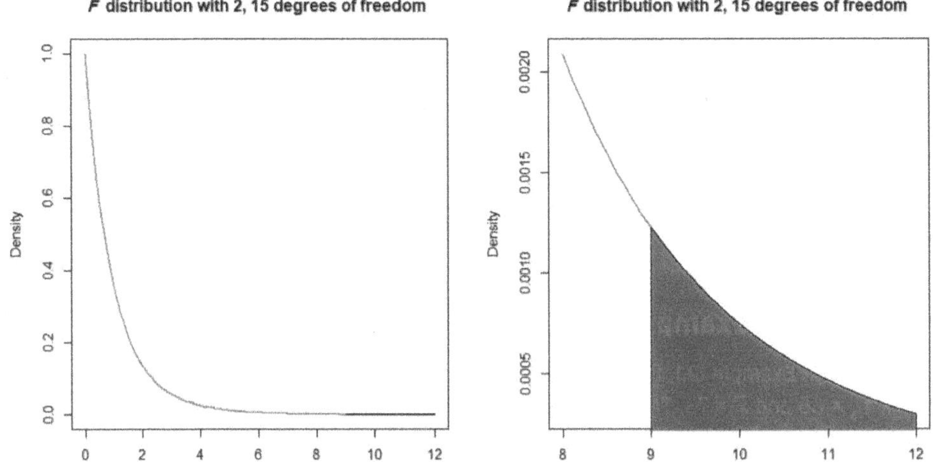

Figure 12.4 The *F* distribution with 2, 15 degrees of freedom, indicating the *p*-value of 0.0027 in red. Note the right-hand plot is a zoomed-in version of the right-hand tail of the left-hand plot.

12.3.3 One-way ANOVA in Excel

Clearly, manual calculations are extremely tedious. Fortunately, using the Data Analysis Excel add-in, we can conduct one-way ANOVA tests with ease in Excel.

To do so, we must prepare the data accordingly in spreadsheet form, preferably with the observations arranged columnwise by group. From the Data Analysis add-in we select `Anova: Single Factor`, as shown in Figure 12.5.

In the Anova: Single Factor dialog box, shown in Figure 12.6, we need to specify the range of the input data – here the cell range `$A$1:$C$7`, which is grouped in columns ('Digital' in column A, etc.) and since row 1 contains the strategy types (as opposed to observations) we must check the `Labels in First Row` option. The default significance level `Alpha` to be used for the F test is 0.05. Although this may be changed, it is somewhat redundant since we know we simply compare the p-value with whichever α we deem appropriate. We can specify the output location. Let's stick with the default of `New Worksheet`.

Upon clicking `OK` we obtain the output as shown in Figure 12.7. Note how the ANOVA table agrees with our manual calculations (phew!). The `F crit` is redundant for our purposes (it specifies the smallest F value such that we would reject H_0 at the specified significance level, in this case 5% as we kept the default alpha of 0.05). The p-value is sufficient to deduce the strength of the statistical significance, and is arguably more informative on its own. In this case the p-value is 0.0027 (rounded), which is well below 0.01, hence this is a *highly significant* result with *strong evidence* of a difference in the population means.

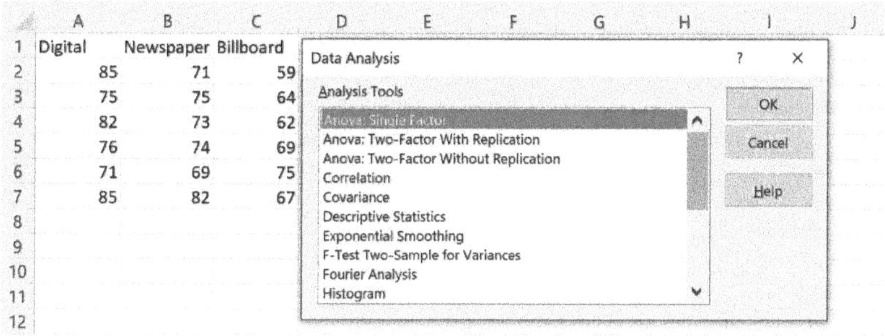

	A	B	C
1	Digital	Newspaper	Billboard
2	85	71	59
3	75	75	64
4	82	73	62
5	76	74	69
6	71	69	75
7	85	82	67

Data Analysis
Analysis Tools
Anova: Single Factor
Anova: Two-Factor With Replication
Anova: Two-Factor Without Replication
Correlation
Covariance
Descriptive Statistics
Exponential Smoothing
F-Test Two-Sample for Variances
Fourier Analysis
Histogram
OK
Cancel
Help

Figure 12.5 Data from Example 12.1 in Excel with the Data Analysis option box.

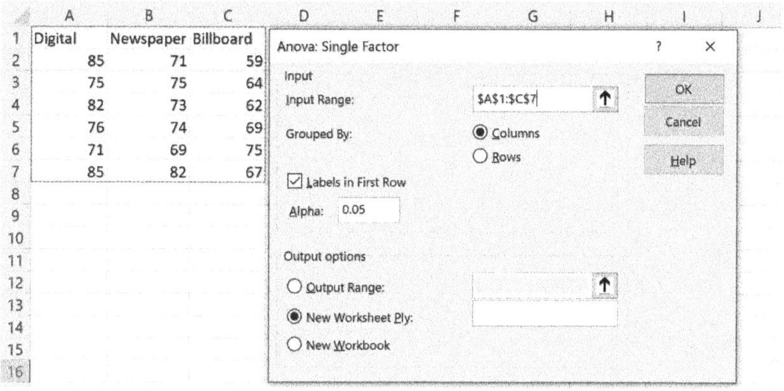

	A	B	C
1	Digital	Newspaper	Billboard
2	85	71	59
3	75	75	64
4	82	73	62
5	76	74	69
6	71	69	75
7	85	82	67

Anova: Single Factor
Input
Input Range: $A$1:$C$7
Grouped By: Columns / Rows
Labels in First Row
Alpha: 0.05
Output options
Output Range:
New Worksheet Ply:
New Workbook
OK
Cancel
Help

Figure 12.6 Data from Example 12.1 and Anova: Single Factor dialog box.

However, we have previously said that H_1 is a composite hypothesis, which states that μ_1, μ_2 and μ_3 are not all equal. It does *not* specify in *what way* they are not all equal. For this, we leverage the summary descriptive statistics box at the top of Figure 12.7. It seems that digital advertising is most effective, on average resulting in 79,000 units sold (figures are in thousands), followed by newspaper advertising (74,000) and then billboard advertising (66,000). We should also consider the *relative costs* of these respective strategies (units sold represent the benefit, but the greatest benefit may not be optimal if the associated costs are prohibitive), although this information is not provided.

The moral of the story? Never focus only on the benefits; a cost–benefit analysis is always prudent!

In passing, we note that there is some variation in the sample variances: $s_1^2 = 34$, $s_2^2 = 20$ and $s_3^2 = 32$.

Our model assumes *equal* variances across all groups of σ^2. The seemingly smaller variance of the newspaper group suggests a possible violation of the equal-variance assumption, although with $n_1 = n_2 = n_3 = 6$, the sample sizes are very small so imprecise variance estimates should not be surprising. We note in passing that a test called *Levene's test* can be deployed to assess the equal-variance assumption, although we shall not consider it in this text.

	A	B	C	D	E	F	G
1	Anova: Single Factor						
2							
3	SUMMARY						
4	*Groups*	*Count*	*Sum*	*Average*	*Variance*		
5	Digital	6	474	79	34		
6	Newspaper	6	444	74	20		
7	Billboard	6	396	66	32		
8							
9							
10	ANOVA						
11	*Source of Variation*	*SS*	*df*	*MS*	*F*	*P-value*	*F crit*
12	Between Groups	516	2	258	9	0.002703	3.68232
13	Within Groups	430	15	28.66667			
14							
15	Total	946	17				

Figure 12.7 Results for the one-way ANOVA for the data from Example 12.1.

In addition to a one-way ANOVA table, we can also obtain the following:

- An *estimator* of σ (i.e. the square root of the common variance, σ^2) is

$$\hat{\sigma} = S = \sqrt{\frac{W}{n-k}},$$

which is a pooled estimate, making use of all $n = \sum_{j=1}^{k} n_j$ observations.

- 95% confidence intervals for μ_j are given by

$$\bar{X}_{\cdot j} \pm t_{0.025,\, n-k} \times \frac{S}{\sqrt{n_j}} \quad \text{for } j = 1, 2, \ldots, k$$

where $t_{0.025,\, n-k}$ is the top 2.5th percentile of the Student's t_{n-k} distribution, which can be obtained in Excel using `=T.INV.2T(0.05,degrees_of_freedom)`. While this is similar to the construction of confidence intervals for a population mean with unknown variance in Chapter 9, note here the 'improved' estimate of σ exploiting all n observations, not just those in the jth group. Our equal-variance assumption across groups allows us to obtain a better estimate of σ rather than only using s_j.

Example 12.3

Continuing Example 12.2, assuming a common variance for each group, we see that

$$\hat{\sigma} = s = \sqrt{\frac{430}{15}} = \sqrt{28.667} = 5.3541.$$

Since $t_{0.025,15}$ = 2.1314, in Excel using `=T.INV.2T(0.05,15)`, we obtain the following 95% confidence intervals for μ_1, μ_2 and μ_3, respectively:

$$j=1: \quad 79 \pm 2.1314 \times \frac{5.3541}{\sqrt{6}} \quad \Rightarrow \quad (74.34, 83.66)$$

$$j=2: \quad 74 \pm 2.1314 \times \frac{5.3541}{\sqrt{6}} \quad \Rightarrow \quad (69.34, 78.66)$$

$$j=3: \quad 66 \pm 2.1314 \times \frac{5.3541}{\sqrt{6}} \quad \Rightarrow \quad (61.34, 70.66).$$

Note, for example, that the 95% confidence intervals for digital (j = 1) and billboard (j = 3) do *not* overlap (the lower bound of the former, 74.34, is above the upper bound of the latter, 70.66), which is consistent with our earlier rejection of the null hypothesis that all population means are equal.

Example 12.4

In early 2020, with the Covid-19 pandemic emerging, many companies were laying off workers. A poll conducted during March 2020 asked a random sample of workers how long (in months) it would be before they faced significant financial hardship if they lost their jobs. They are classified into four income groups: Over \$50,000, \$30,000-\$50,000, \$20,000-\$30,000 and under \$20,000. We use the Data Analysis add-in to prepare descriptive statistics of the classified data, as shown below.

Can we infer that income group has a significant impact on the mean length of time before facing financial hardship? (The thesis being that, *ceteris paribus*, higher-income groups are able to save more, and can draw down these savings for longer in the event of becoming unemployed.) The first few observations of each income group are:

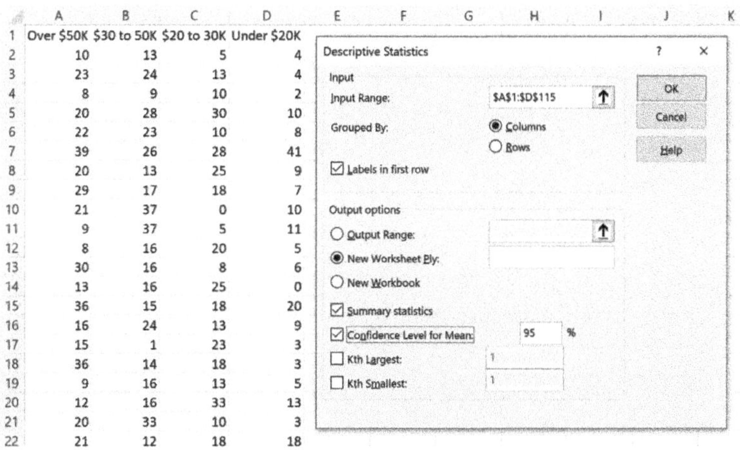

	A	B	C	D
1	Over \$50K	\$30 to 50K	\$20 to 30K	Under \$20K
2	10	13	5	4
3	23	24	13	4
4	8	9	10	2
5	20	28	30	10
6	22	23	10	8
7	39	26	28	41
8	20	13	25	9
9	29	17	18	7
10	21	37	0	10
11	9	37	5	11
12	8	16	20	5
13	30	16	8	6
14	13	16	25	0
15	36	15	18	20
16	16	24	13	9
17	15	1	23	3
18	36	14	18	3
19	9	16	13	5
20	12	16	33	13
21	20	33	10	3
22	21	12	18	18

(Continued)

The descriptive statistics are as follows:

	A	B	C	D	E	F	G	H
1	*Over $50K*		*$30 to 50K*		*$20 to 30K*		*Under $20K*	
2								
3	Mean	22.20512821	Mean	18.45614035	Mean	15.49382716	Mean	9.313433
4	Standard Error	1.766069267	Standard Error	0.890455554	Standard Error	1.025917755	Standard Error	0.98799
5	Median	20	Median	17.5	Median	13	Median	7
6	Mode	20	Mode	20	Mode	13	Mode	3
7	Standard Deviation	11.02909904	Standard Deviation	9.507463627	Standard Deviation	9.233259794	Standard Deviation	8.087043
8	Sample Variance	121.6410256	Sample Variance	90.39186462	Sample Variance	85.25308642	Sample Variance	65.40027
9	Kurtosis	-0.03684242	Kurtosis	0.27345479	Kurtosis	0.466415095	Kurtosis	2.600071
10	Skewness	0.586426254	Skewness	0.608645308	Skewness	0.751831882	Skewness	1.451709
11	Range	48	Range	44	Range	45	Range	41
12	Minimum	2	Minimum	1	Minimum	0	Minimum	0
13	Maximum	50	Maximum	45	Maximum	45	Maximum	41
14	Sum	866	Sum	2104	Sum	1255	Sum	624
15	Count	39	Count	114	Count	81	Count	67
16	Confidence Level(95.0%)	3.575220318	Confidence Level(95.0%)	1.764153054	Confidence Level(95.0%)	2.041641397	Confidence Level(95.0%)	1.972585

Inspection of the sample means (highlighted in yellow) suggests that there is a difference between income groups (lower-income groups, on average, appear to experience financial hardship sooner), but we need to conduct a one-way ANOVA test to see whether the differences are *statistically significant*.

We apply one-way ANOVA to test whether the means in the k = 4 groups are equal, that is, we test H_0: $\mu_1 = \mu_2 = \mu_3 = \mu_4$, from highest to lowest income groups.

We have n_1 = 39, n_2 = 114, n_3 = 81 and n_4 = 67 (obtained from the highlighted 'Count' row). Note that, unlike Example 12.1, the sample sizes are *different*. The overall sample size is

$$n = \sum_{j=1}^{k} n_j = 39 + 114 + 81 + 67 = 301.$$

Also $\bar{x}_{\cdot 1}$ = 22.205, $\bar{x}_{\cdot 2}$ = 18.456, $\bar{x}_{\cdot 3}$ = 15.494, $\bar{x}_{\cdot 4}$ = 9.313 (rounded) and

$$\begin{aligned}\bar{x} &= \frac{1}{n}\sum_{j=1}^{k} n_j \bar{x}_{\cdot j}\\ &= \frac{39 \times 22.205 + 114 \times 18.456 + 81 \times 15.494 + 67 \times 9.313}{301}\\ &= 16.110.\end{aligned}$$

Note how $\bar{x}$ is not a simple arithmetic mean of the $\bar{x}_{\cdot j}$ values due to unequal sample sizes. We have *weighted* them accordingly with weights of n_j/n. Now, the between-groups variation is

$$\begin{aligned}b &= \sum_{j=1}^{k} n_j(\bar{x}_{\cdot j} - \bar{x})^2\\ &= 39 \times (22.205 - 16.110)^2 + 114 \times (18.456 - 16.110)^2\\ &\quad + 81 \times (15.494 - 16.110)^2 + 67 \times (9.313 - 16.110)^2\\ &= 5202.078.\end{aligned}$$

We have s_1^2 = 11.029² = 121.641, s_2^2 = 9.507² = 90.392, s_3^2 = 9.233² = 85.253 and s_4^2 = 8.087² = 65.400 (all highlighted), hence the within-groups variation is

$$\begin{aligned}w = \sum_{j=1}^{k}\sum_{i=1}^{n_j}(x_{ij} - \bar{x}_{\cdot j})^2 &= \sum_{j=1}^{k}(n_j - 1)s_j^2\\ &= 38 \times 121.641 + 113 \times 90.392 + 80 \times 85.253 + 66 \times 65.400\\ &= 25{,}973.305.\end{aligned}$$

We can now compute η^2, the explanatory power of the income group factor. We have

$$\eta^2 = \frac{B}{SS_X} = \frac{\text{explained variation}}{\text{total variation}} = \frac{5202.078}{5202.078 + 25{,}973.305} = 0.1669,$$

indicating that 16.69% of the variation in months before financial hardship is experienced can be explained by income group. Of course, this suggests there is 83.31% unexplained variation, which would be explained by variables other than income group. We should not be too disappointed with a seemingly high unexplained variation component - remember it is a complex world, and realistically *many* variables will impact the speed of experiencing financial hardship!

We proceed to perform our hypothesis test. The test statistic value is

$$f = \frac{b/(k-1)}{w/(n-k)} = \frac{5202.078/3}{25{,}973.305/(301-4)} = 19.828.$$

Under H_0, $F \sim F_{k-1,n-k} = F_{3,297}$. Hence the *p*-value is

$$P(F > 19.828) = 9.64 \times 10^{-12} \approx 0.000,$$

using `=F.DIST.RT(19.828,3,297)` in Excel. We reject H_0 at the 1% (or even 0.01%) significance level, i.e. there is *(very!) strong evidence* that income group has a significant impact on the mean length of time before facing financial hardship.

Instead of the above manual calculations, we may simply (and much prefer to!) use Excel:

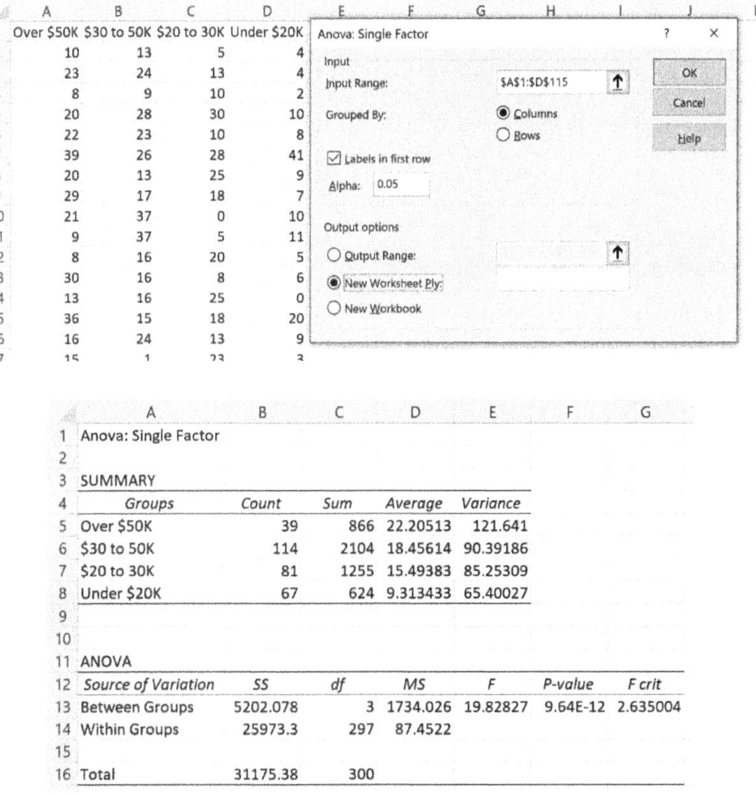

	A	B	C	D
1	Over $50K	$30 to 50K	$20 to 30K	Under $20K
2	10	13	5	4
3	23	24	13	4
4	8	9	10	2
5	20	28	30	10
6	22	23	10	8
7	39	26	28	41
8	20	13	25	9
9	29	17	18	7
10	21	37	0	10
11	9	37	5	11
12	8	16	20	5
13	30	16	8	6
14	13	16	25	0
15	36	15	18	20
16	16	24	13	9

Anova: Single Factor

SUMMARY

Groups	Count	Sum	Average	Variance
Over $50K	39	866	22.20513	121.641
$30 to 50K	114	2104	18.45614	90.39186
$20 to 30K	81	1255	15.49383	85.25309
Under $20K	67	624	9.313433	65.40027

ANOVA

Source of Variation	SS	df	MS	F	P-value	F crit
Between Groups	5202.078	3	1734.026	19.82827	9.64E-12	2.635004
Within Groups	25973.3	297	87.4522			
Total	31175.38	300				

(Continued)

Note that the *p*-value is tiny! It is just 9.64×10^{-12}, denoted in Excel as '`9.64E-12`'. Recall that the `F crit` value (for the default $\alpha = 0.05$) means that there is a 5% probability of an $F_{3,\ 297}$ distribution being above 2.635004 (the red shaded area below). The *p*-value is the area to the right of the *F* test statistic value of 19.828, which is clearly tiny.

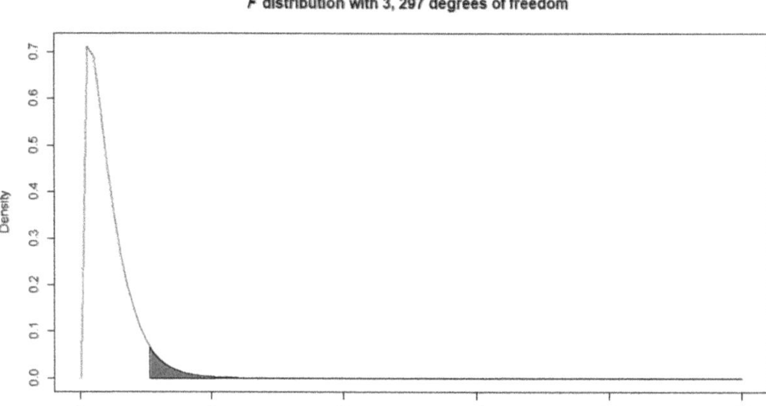

The pooled estimate of σ is

$$s = \sqrt{\frac{w}{n-k}} = \sqrt{\frac{25{,}973.305}{301-4}} = \sqrt{87.4522} = 9.352.$$

Note that the *MS* within groups, 87.4522, is the estimate of the common variance, σ^2, reported in the one-way ANOVA table.

A 95% confidence interval for μ_j is (using `=T.INV.2T(0.05,297)`)

$$\bar{x}_{\cdot j} \pm t_{0.025,\,297} \times \frac{s}{\sqrt{n_j}} = \bar{x}_{\cdot j} \pm 1.968 \times \frac{9.352}{\sqrt{n_j}} = \bar{x}_{\cdot j} \pm \frac{18.405}{\sqrt{n_j}}.$$

Hence, for example, a 95% confidence interval for μ_1 is

$$22.205 \pm \frac{18.405}{\sqrt{39}} \quad \Rightarrow \quad (19.258,\ 25.152),$$

and a 95% confidence interval for μ_4 is

$$9.313 \pm \frac{18.405}{\sqrt{67}} \quad \Rightarrow \quad (7.064,\ 11.562).$$

Notice that these two confidence intervals do *not* overlap, which is consistent with our conclusion that there is a difference between the group means. Clearly, and unsurprisingly, higher-income groups can survive longer before experiencing financial hardship due to a higher buffer of savings. Problem solved, right? Well, only in part. Recall that $\eta^2 = 0.1669$, and so while income group may be *a* significant independent variable, it is *not the only one*. It is likely to be just one of several, and more research would be required to identify, and to understand, the *other* causes of things!

Note that any minor differences between manual calculations and Excel values are due to rounding errors in intermediate calculations.

12.4 FROM ONE-WAY TO TWO-WAY ANOVA

One-way ANOVA: a review

We have independent observations $X_{ij} \sim N(\mu_j, \sigma^2)$ for $i = 1, 2, ..., n_j$ and $j = 1, 2, ..., k$. We are interested in testing

$$H_0: \mu_1 = \mu_2 = \cdots = \mu_k.$$

The variation of the X_{ij} values is (possibly) driven by a factor at different levels $\mu_1, \mu_2, ..., \mu_k$, and certainly (possibly in addition) to random fluctuations (i.e. *random errors*). We test whether such a factor effect exists or not. We can *reparameterise* (great word!) our model in a one-way ANOVA problem as follows:

$$X_{ij} = \mu + \beta_j + \varepsilon_{ij} \text{ for } i = 1, 2, ..., n_j \text{ and } j = 1, 2, ..., k$$

where $\varepsilon_{ij} \sim N(0, \sigma^2)$ and the ε_{ij} are independent. μ is the *average effect* and β_j is the *factor effect* (equivalently, treatment effect) at the jth level. Note that $\sum_{j=1}^{k} \beta_j = 0$ for the parameters in the model to be 'identifiable'. (To learn about parameter identification, I recommend taking an econometrics course.) The null hypothesis (i.e. that the group means are all equal) can also be expressed as

$$H_0: \beta_1 = \beta_2 = \cdots = \beta_k = 0.$$

If H_0 is true, then we can simply write

$$X_{ij} = \mu + \varepsilon_{ij},$$

that is, that the factor has *no effect*, with all variation in the X_{ij} driven by the random error term, ε_{ij}. Why bother with this reparameterisation? Well, writing $X_{ij} = \mu + \beta_j + \varepsilon_{ij}$ decomposes each observation of our dependent variable into three parts:

- the average effect, μ
- the factor effect (if it exists), β_j
- the 'noise', ε_{ij}

where the noise can be viewed as natural variation, or if you like, a 'catch-all' variable representing 'everything else' which *creates* or *generates* each X_{ij}. This error term (sometimes referred to as white noise) will be especially useful in regression analysis, introduced in Chapter 13. Note the use of the *normal distribution* to model this noise process, with a zero mean - another important use of the normal distribution, here as a distributional assumption in ANOVA. It is normal to see the normal used!

12.5 TWO-WAY ANALYSIS OF VARIANCE

While one-way ANOVA has got us up and running, it is perhaps wishful thinking (even naïve) to suppose that only *one* factor will lead us to nirvana by demystifying all variation in our dependent variable! So, let's keep ourselves grounded, but extend our model framework to accommodate *two* factors, giving rise to **two-way analysis of variance**. However, once we include two factors we will be interested in any possible **interaction** effect between them – the situation where the level of one factor influences the effect of the level of the other factor on the dependent variable.

Example 12.5

Consider the following cases of potential interest.

(a) To what extent are sales influenced by price level (classified as low, medium and high) *and/or* advertising expenditure (also classified as low, medium and high)?
(b) Does brand perception vary by consumer age group (classified as, say, under 30, 30–49 and 50+) *and/or* gender (classified as male, female and non-binary)?
(c) Is the effectiveness of paid-for advertising in a newspaper affected by day of the week (Monday to Friday) *and/or* where the advertisement appears (news, business and sports sections)?*

*Looks suspiciously reminiscent of our start-of-chapter motivational case!

With an eye on our transition to linear regression in Chapter 13, we will adapt our notation slightly as follows:

- Y will denote the dependent variable (which is quantitative)
- X_1 will denote factor 1 (which is categorical), with k_1 distinct levels
- X_2 will denote factor 2 (which is categorical), with k_2 distinct levels
- X_1X_2 will denote the interaction of the two factors.

As the dependent variable is still quantitative it will exhibit variation, now denoted by SS_Y, and explaining this variation remains our objective. In a two-way ANOVA, we decompose this total variation as follows:

$$SS_Y = SS_{X_1} + SS_{X_2} + SS_{X_1X_2} + SS_W$$

where

- SS_{X_1} and SS_{X_2} are the components of SS_Y attributable to factors 1 and 2, respectively
- $SS_{X_1X_2}$ is the component due to the interaction of X_1 and X_2
- SS_W is the within-groups variation (i.e. the naturally occurring, or 'residual', variation).

The explanatory power of a two-way ANOVA model is the proportion of variation in Y attributable to one or other factors, and is still referred to as η^2, which in this context is

$$\eta^2 = \frac{SS_{X_1} + SS_{X_2} + SS_{X_1X_2}}{SS_Y}$$

and continues to be between 0 and 1 due to the sums of squares all being non-negative (with $SS_Y > 0$ to be defined).

When checking for statistical significance we will need to perform separate tests for each factor and the interaction as follows.

Hypothesis testing in two-way ANOVA

1 To test for the significance of *factor 1*, the test statistic is

$$F = \frac{SS_{X_1} / (k_1 - 1)}{SS_W / (n - k_1 k_2)} = \frac{MS_{X_1}}{MS_W} \sim F_{k_1 - 1, n - k_1 k_2}$$

under the null hypothesis of *no factor 1 effect*. Excel returns the corresponding *p*-value.

2 To test for the significance of *factor 2*, the test statistic is

$$F = \frac{SS_{X_2} / (k_2 - 1)}{SS_W / (n - k_1 k_2)} = \frac{MS_{X_2}}{MS_W} \sim F_{k_2 - 1, n - k_1 k_2}$$

under the null hypothesis of *no factor 2 effect*. Excel returns the corresponding *p*-value.

3 To test for the significance of the *interaction* between factors 1 and 2, the test statistic is

$$F = \frac{SS_{X_1 X_2} / (k_1 - 1)(k_2 - 1)}{SS_W / (n - k_1 k_2)} = \frac{MS_{X_1 X_2}}{MS_W} \sim F_{(k_1 - 1)(k_2 - 1), n - k_1 k_2}$$

under the null hypothesis of *no interaction effect*. Excel returns the corresponding *p*-value.

Example 12.6

News Daily has collated data on the number of enquiries (to the nearest thousand) generated by advertisements appearing on its website (obtained by monitoring the number of click-throughs). To run the two-way ANOVA routine, we use the `Anova: Two-Factor With Replication` option via the Data Analysis add-in.

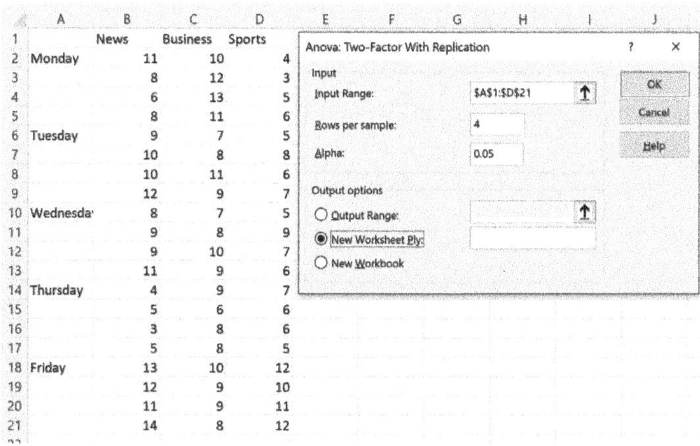

	A	B	C	D
1		News	Business	Sports
2	Monday	11	10	4
3		8	12	3
4		6	13	5
5		8	11	6
6	Tuesday	9	7	5
7		10	8	8
8		10	11	6
9		12	9	7
10	Wednesda	8	7	5
11		9	8	9
12		9	10	7
13		11	9	6
14	Thursday	4	9	7
15		5	6	6
16		3	8	6
17		5	8	5
18	Friday	13	10	12
19		12	9	10
20		11	9	11
21		14	8	12

(Continued)

`Rows per sample` is set equal to 4 because there are four observations per day of the week, consistent with data collected over a month (there are four weeks, approximately, in a month!). Note here $k_1 = 5$ (five days of the week), $k_2 = 3$ (three sections of the website) and $n = 60$ (the total number of observations).

We focus on the two-way ANOVA table produced:

ANOVA						
Source of Variation	*SS*	*df*	*MS*	*F*	*P-value*	*F crit*
Sample	146.8333	4	36.70833	20.90981	8.52E-10	2.578739
Columns	53.73333	2	26.86667	15.3038	8.5E-06	3.204317
Interaction	135.7667	8	16.97083	9.66693	1.12E-07	2.152133
Within	79	45	1.755556			
Total	415.3333	59				

The overall explanatory power of the model is calculated to be

$$\eta^2 = \frac{SS_{X_1} + SS_{X_2} + SS_{X_1X_2}}{SS_Y} = \frac{146.8333 + 53.73333 + 135.7667}{415.3333} = 0.8098$$

indicating that just over 80% of the variation in advertisement click-throughs can be attributed to the day of the week and/or the section where the advertisement is placed. Quite impressive!

We now need to do some detective work to judge the significance of each factor and their interaction. The `Sample` row corresponds to the day of the week. We test

H_0: Day of the week does not affect number of generated enquiries

versus the alternative hypothesis that there is some effect (note there are multiple possible types of effect - this is a composite hypothesis). The test statistic value is

$$\frac{SS_{X_1} / (k_1 - 1)}{SS_W / (n - k_1k_2)} = \frac{146.8333 / 4}{79 / 45} = \frac{MS_{X_1}}{MS_W} = \frac{36.70833}{1.755556} = 20.90981.$$

The *p*-value is

$P(F > 20.90981) = 8.52 \times 10^{-10}$

where $F \sim F_{4,45}$. Hence there is *(very!) strong evidence* that the day of the week impacts enquiries (as measured by click-throughs).

The `Columns` row corresponds to the section of the website where advertisements are placed. We test:

H_0: Section of the website does not affect number of generated enquiries

versus the alternative hypothesis that there is some effect (again, a composite hypothesis). The test statistic value is

$$\frac{SS_{X_2} / (k_2 - 1)}{SS_W / (n - k_1k_2)} = \frac{53.7333 / 2}{79 / 45} = \frac{MS_{X_2}}{MS_W} = \frac{26.86667}{1.755556} = 15.3038.$$

The *p*-value is

$$P(F > 15.3038) = 8.5 \times 10^{-6}$$

where $F \sim F_{2,\,45}$. Hence there is, again, *(very!) strong evidence* that the section of the website impacts enquiries (click-throughs).

The `Interaction` row corresponds to the interaction effect. We test:

H_0: There is no interaction effect on the number of generated enquiries

versus the alternative hypothesis that there is some interaction effect (there are many possible types of interactions - we will consider these shortly). The test statistic value is:

$$\frac{SS_{X_1X_2} / (k_1 - 1)(k_2 - 1)}{SS_W / (n - k_1k_2)} = \frac{135.7667 / 8}{79 / 45} = \frac{MS_{X_1X_2}}{MS_W} = \frac{16.97083}{1.755556} = 9.66693.$$

The *p*-value is

$$P(F > 9.66693) = 1.12 \times 10^{-7}$$

where $F \sim F_{8,45}$. Hence there is, yet again, *(very!) strong evidence* of an interaction effect on enquiries (click-throughs).

The results of Example 12.6 may well be pleasing, but there are still some unanswered questions:

1. While both factors may be statistically significant, what is their *relative importance*, that is, is one factor more influential than another and, if so, by how much?
2. When there is evidence of an interaction, what is the *nature* of the interaction?

We proceed to address both of these issues.

12.5.1 Relative importance of factors

We can use ω^2 (omega-squared) to measure the proportion of the variation in the dependent variable which is related to a factor. The *relative contribution* of factor X_i is calculated as

$$\omega^2_{X_i} = \frac{SS_{X_i} - ((k_i - 1) \times MS_W)}{SS_Y + MS_W}.$$

The $\omega^2_{X_i}$ values can be compared across factors to judge their **relative importance**.

12.5.2 Interaction effects

There are different possible 'patterns' of interaction effects. These are best assessed visually using a **means plot** whereby the mean (average) value of the dependent variable is plotted for each combination of factor levels.

Suppose our dependent variable, Y, is sales. We have two potential explanatory factors. X_1 is age group with four levels as follows:

- X_{11} = those aged 18–29
- X_{12} = those aged 30–39
- X_{13} = those aged 40–49
- X_{14} = those aged 50+

that is, X_{11} denotes the first level of the first factor. X_2 is gender with two levels (assume all self-identified as either male or female) as follows:

- X_{21} = male
- X_{22} = female

that is, X_{21} denotes the first level of the second factor.

No interaction

The phrase 'no interaction' means that knowledge of the level of one factor has no effect on the other factor's level effect on the dependent variable. An example of a means plot showing no interaction is shown in Figure 12.8.

Note that the two lines are *parallel*, with equal distances between means for each level of age group. Regardless of age group, sales for female consumers are, on average, always above those of male consumers by the *same* amount (in this case the difference is 1 unit). Regardless of gender, older customers on average spend more than younger customers, due to the means getting progressively higher as we move rightwards from 18–29 (the youngest age group) to 50+ (the oldest age group). This suggests that the product being sold appeals more to older consumers, with slightly greater popularity among females.

Ordinal interaction

An ordinal interaction means that *order* is sustained such that the means of Y strictly increase (or decrease) as we pass through the factor levels in order. An example of a means plot showing ordinal interaction is shown in Figure 12.9.

Note that the two lines are now *not* parallel, but one still lies above (or below!) the other. Regardless of age group, sales for male consumers are, on average, always above those of female consumers, but by varying amounts. The biggest difference is for the 18–29 age group. Regardless of gender, younger consumers on average spend more than older consumers, due to the means getting progressively higher as we move leftwards from 50+ (the oldest age group) to 18–29 (the youngest age group). This suggests the product being sold appeals more to younger consumers, and seems to appeal especially to young male consumers. Hence there is an ordinal interaction – the effect of age group on sales depends on gender, with the interaction being most prominent among the 18–29 age group.

Disordinal interaction without crossover

A disordinal interaction means that order is *not* sustained such that the means of Y do not strictly increase (or decrease) as we pass through the factor levels in order of all factors. 'Without crossover' means that the lines do not cross. An example of such a means plot is shown in Figure 12.10.

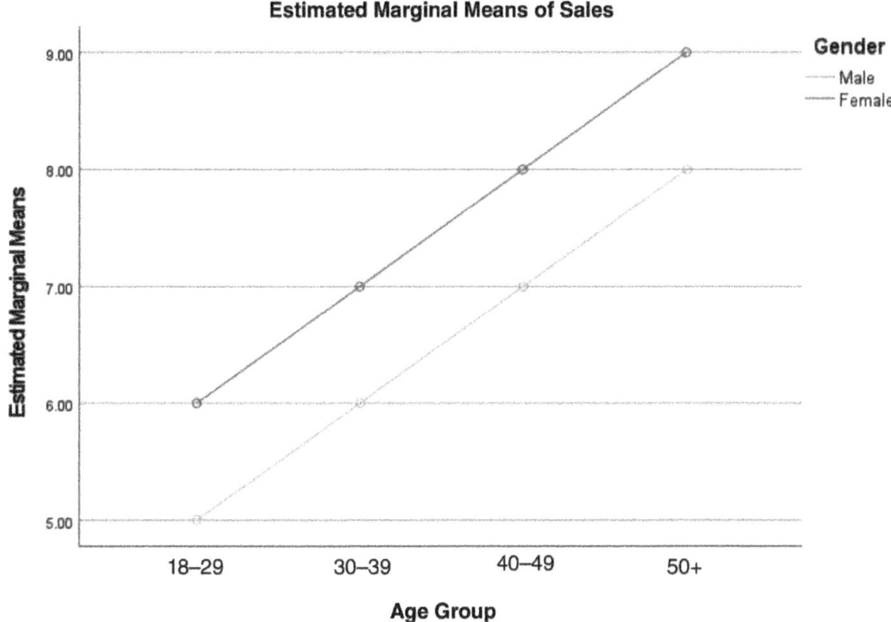

Figure 12.8 Example of no interaction between age group and gender, indicated by parallel lines.

Note that here there is no crossover, as one line still lies above (or below!) the other. Regardless of age group, sales for male consumers are, on average, always above those of female consumers, but by varying amounts with the difference increasing from the 18–29 to the 30–39 age groups, then reducing from the 30–39 to 40–49 age groups, then increasing again from the 40–49 to 50+ age groups. The biggest difference is for the 30–39 age group. It seems that the product is tailored more towards males than females, gradually appealing more to older consumers. However, among those 40–49 the gender effect is minimal for some reason. What is the reason? Impossible to deduce from the information provided – some further market research would be required – perhaps some qualitative research via focus groups of this demographic.

Disordinal interaction with crossover

The other type of disordinal interaction is *with* crossover, i.e. the lines *do* cross. An example of such a means plot is shown in Figure 12.11.

Now it is *not* the case that male/female consumers have sales strictly above their female/male counterparts – now it depends on the age group! For those under 40 (the 18–29 and 30–39 age groups) females spend more, while it is the reverse for the older age groups. Also, *within* an age group the difference between average sales among males and females varies by age group, with the largest differences among the 18–29 and 30–39 age groups. It seems this product's appeal is quite sensitive to the consumer's age and gender. Try to think what the product might be!

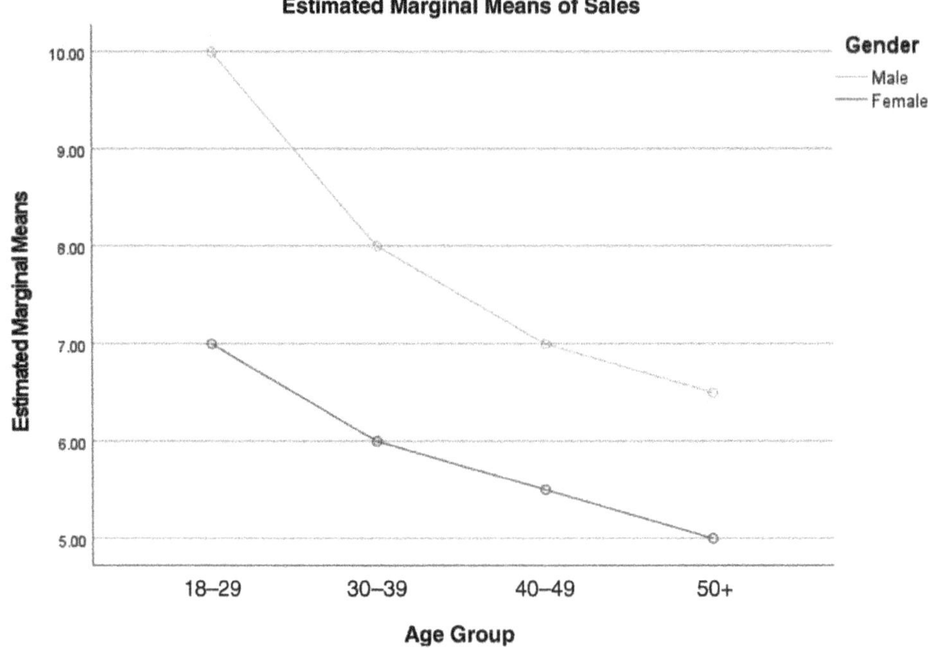

Figure 12.9 Example of an ordinal interaction between age group and gender, indicated by non-parallel lines.

Example 12.7

Continuing Example 12.6, we first determine the relative importance of day of the week and section where the advertisement is displayed by calculating ω^2 for each factor. We have

$$\omega_{X_1}^2 = \frac{SS_{X_1} - ((k_1 - 1) \times MS_W)}{SS_Y + MS_W} = \frac{146.8333 - ((5-1) \times 1.755556)}{415.3333 + 1.755556} = 0.335$$

for the day of the week factor, and

$$\omega_{X_2}^2 = \frac{SS_{X_2} - ((k_2 - 1) \times MS_W)}{SS_Y + MS_W} = \frac{53.7333 - ((3-1) \times 1.755556)}{415.3333 + 1.755556} = 0.120$$

for the section of the newspaper factor. We have that

$$\frac{\omega_{X_1}^2}{\omega_{X_2}^2} = \frac{0.335}{0.120} = 2.79 \approx 3,$$

hence day of the week is nearly three times as influential on click-throughs as section of the newspaper.

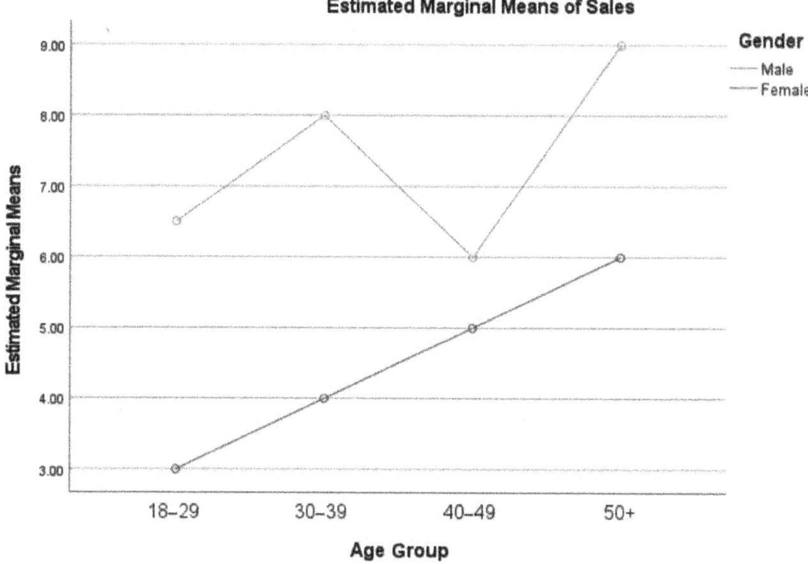

Figure 12.10 Example of a disordinal interaction between age group and gender.

We now examine the nature of the interaction by way of a means plot:

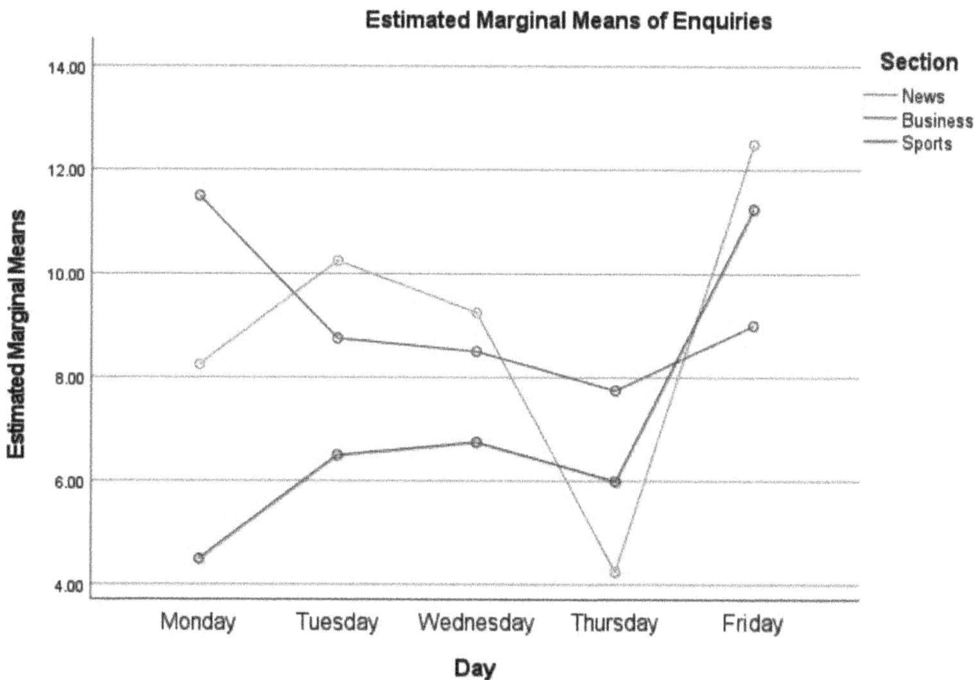

(Continued)

Most strikingly, we observe that advertisements displayed in the sports section tend to be least effective in the early part of the week, although a large number of enquiries are generated from the sports section on a Friday. This would likely be due to sports fans browsing the sports section on a Friday to read up on the sports fixtures scheduled for that weekend.

The effectiveness of advertisements in the business section peaks on a Monday (perhaps business people briefing themselves on business news at the start of the week) and gradually tails off as the week progresses (perhaps due to fatigue from working hard), with a slight uptick on Friday.

Placement in the news section seems to suffer a sharp fall on Thursdays. It does not seem immediately clear why that may be the case, so it would be prudent to investigate further.

Recall the original business problem of News Daily - to develop a differential pricing strategy for paid-for advertisements on its website to maximise revenue. Well, it is clear that the effectiveness of advertisements is dependent on *when* and *where* they appear (with the *when* being nearly three times as influential as the *where*). As such, News Daily can indeed set differential prices reflecting the expected number of enquiries the client can anticipate. For example, it should be quite cheap to advertise in the sports section on a Monday (it would achieve a relatively lower number of click-throughs), with the highest prices reserved for Friday placements in the news and business sections (lots of click-throughs, and hence hopefully lots of sales). The greater the perceived benefit to the client from advertising, the greater the cost they would be willing to pay. News Daily can now look forward to revenue maximisation by setting placement prices optimally!

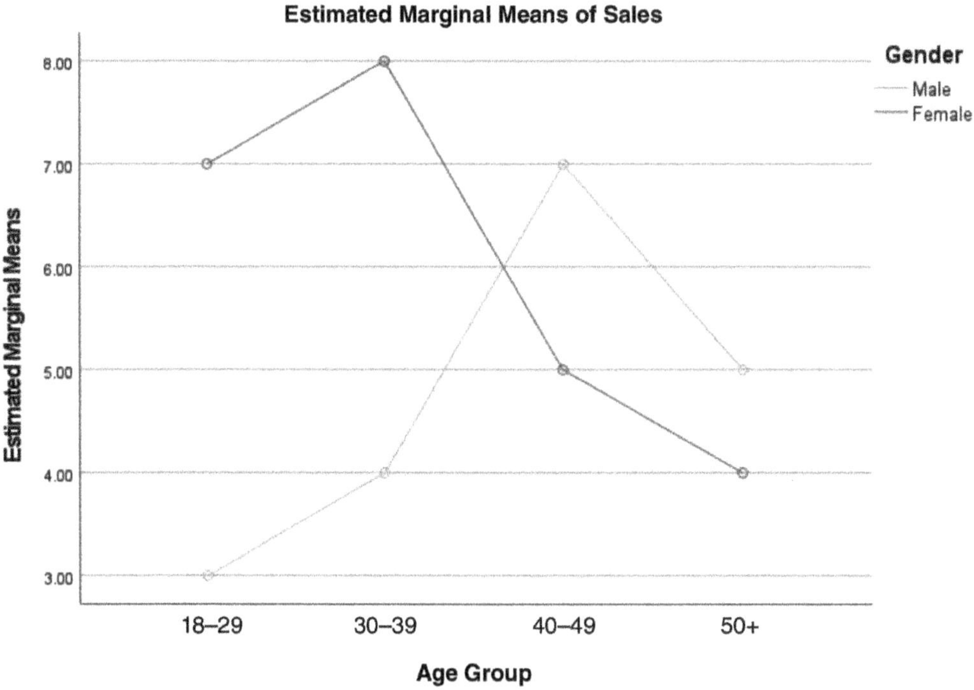

Figure 12.11 Example of a disordinal interaction between age group and gender.

12.6 CHAPTER OVERVIEW

This chapter's main objective has been to understand the causes of things – *rerum cognoscere causas* – through the analysis of variance (ANOVA) model. Specifically, we have sought to use categorical variables (factors, such as age group and gender) to explain the variation in a quantitative dependent variable (such as sales or customer enquiries). Explanatory power has been introduced to offer a simple summary metric to judge overall how good an ANOVA model is at explaining this variation. Starting with one factor, we progressed to two factors, for which it is necessary to assess the relative importance of the factors, as well as to investigate whether any interaction between the factors exists, including its nature.

12.7 KEY VOCABULARY

ANOVA decomposition	Interaction	Relative importance, ω^2
Between-groups variation	Means plot	Total variation
Explanatory power, η^2	One-way ANOVA	Two-way ANOVA
F distribution	One-way ANOVA table	Within-groups variation

12.8 EXERCISES

12.8.1 Test your understanding

1. In an analytical sense, what do we mean by 'understanding the causes of things'?
2. Think of some examples of measurable dependent variables that a manager may be interested in understanding. For each, list possible categorical variables you believe may exert a causal influence, briefly justifying your view in each case.
3. In a one-way ANOVA model, what assumptions are made about the observations of the dependent variable?
4. What are the null and alternative hypotheses in a one-way ANOVA?
5. Explain the ANOVA decomposition (a) in words, and (b) using formulae.
6. How is explanatory power measured in a one-way ANOVA and how is the statistic used interpreted?
7. ANOVA tests are performed using upper-tailed *F* tests.
   (a) Given a test statistic value, *f*, which Excel function could be used to calculate the *p*-value?
   (b) Using an appropriate sketch, illustrate the *p*-value graphically.
8. What information is provided in a one-way ANOVA table? What do the different entries represent?
9. If you wanted to compute a 95% confidence interval for μ_j in a one-way ANOVA context, how would you proceed?
10. An alternative parameterisation of the one-way ANOVA model is

    $X_{ij} = \mu + \beta_j + \varepsilon_{ij}$ for $i = 1, 2, \ldots, n_j$ and $j = 1, 2, \ldots, k$.

    Explain each of the terms μ, β_j and ε_{ij}.

11 How does a two-way ANOVA differ from a one-way ANOVA?

12 What are the possible hypothesis tests which could be conducted in a two-way ANOVA?

13 In a two-way ANOVA how could you determine the relative importance of the two factors?

14 Explain the different types of interaction which could feature in a two-way ANOVA. You may find it helpful to sketch these, but also describe the nature of each interaction.

15 Three trainee salespeople were working on a trial basis. Salesperson A was tried for 5 days and made a total of 440 sales. Salesperson B was tried for 7 days and made a total of 630 sales. Salesperson C was tried for 10 days and made a total of 690 sales. Note that these figures are total sales, not daily averages. The sum of the squares of all 22 daily sales ($\sum x_i^2$) is 146,840.

(a) Construct a one-way analysis of variance table.

(b) Would you say there is a difference between the mean daily sales of the three salespeople? Justify your answer.

(c) Construct a 95% confidence interval for the mean difference between salesperson B and salesperson C. Would you say there is a difference?

16 An executive of a prepared frozen meals company is interested in the amounts of money spent on such products by families in different income ranges. The table below lists the monthly expenditures (in dollars) on prepared frozen meals from 15 randomly selected families divided into three groups according to their incomes.

Under $15,000	$15,000-$30,000	Over $30,000
45.2	53.2	52.7
60.1	56.6	73.6
52.8	68.7	63.3
31.7	51.8	51.8
33.6	54.2	
39.4		

(a) Based on these data, can we infer at the 5% significance level that the population mean expenditures on prepared frozen meals are the same for the three different income groups?

(b) Report the one-way ANOVA table.

(c) Construct 95% confidence intervals for the mean expenditures of the first (under $15,000) and the third (over $30,000) income groups.

17 Does the level of success of publicly traded companies affect the way their board members are paid? The annual payments (in $000s) of randomly selected publicly traded companies to their board members were recorded. The companies were divided into four quarters according to the returns in their stocks, and the payments from each quarter were grouped together. Some summary statistics are provided below.

Quarter	Sample size	Sample mean	Sample standard deviation
Q1	30	74.10	15.81
Q2	30	75.67	13.57
Q3	30	78.50	15.28
Q4	30	81.30	15.59

(a) Can we infer that the amount of payment differs significantly across the four groups of companies?

(b) Construct 95% confidence intervals for the mean payment of the first-quarter companies and the fourth-quarter companies.

18 Do the following data appear to violate the assumptions underlying one-way analysis of variance? Explain why or why not.

Treatment			
A	B	C	D
1.78	8.41	0.57	9.45
8.26	5.61	3.04	8.47
3.57	3.90	2.67	7.69
4.69	3.77	1.66	8.53
2.13	1.08	2.09	10.04

19 An indicator of the value of a stock relative to its earnings is its *price–earnings ratio*: the average of a given year's high and low selling prices divided by its annual earnings. The following table provides the price–earnings ratios for a sample of 30 stocks, ten each from the financial, industrial and utility sectors of the New York Stock Exchange. Test at the 1% significance level whether the true mean price–earnings ratios for the three market sectors are the same. Use the ANOVA table format to summarise your results.

Financial	Industrial	Utility
11.4	9.4	15.4
12.3	18.4	16.3
10.8	15.9	10.9
9.8	21.6	19.3
14.3	17.1	15.1
16.1	20.2	12.7
11.9	18.6	16.8
12.4	22.9	14.3
13.1	18.6	13.8
14.6	19.9	15.0

20 The following table shows monthly percentage audience shares of three major networks' evening news broadcasts in five major cities over three months. Perform a two-way ANOVA. Is either factor statistically significant at the 5% significance level? Is there an interaction? If so, what is its nature?

City	BBC	ITV	Sky
A	21.3	17.8	20.2
	21.8	18.4	21.0
	21.5	17.7	20.9
B	20.6	17.5	20.1
	20.2	17.9	19.7
	20.9	17.4	19.8
C	24.1	16.1	19.4
	25.2	15.4	19.1
	24.6	16.2	19.8
D	23.6	18.3	20.8
	23.8	18.5	21.2
	23.5	18.6	21.3
E	21.8	17.0	28.7
	21.5	17.3	28.3
	21.4	17.5	29.2

12.8.2 Practice with Excel

Head over to the companion website for Excel examples and screencasts!

13

LINEAR REGRESSION

Chapter contents

Chapter level: ***Intermediate***

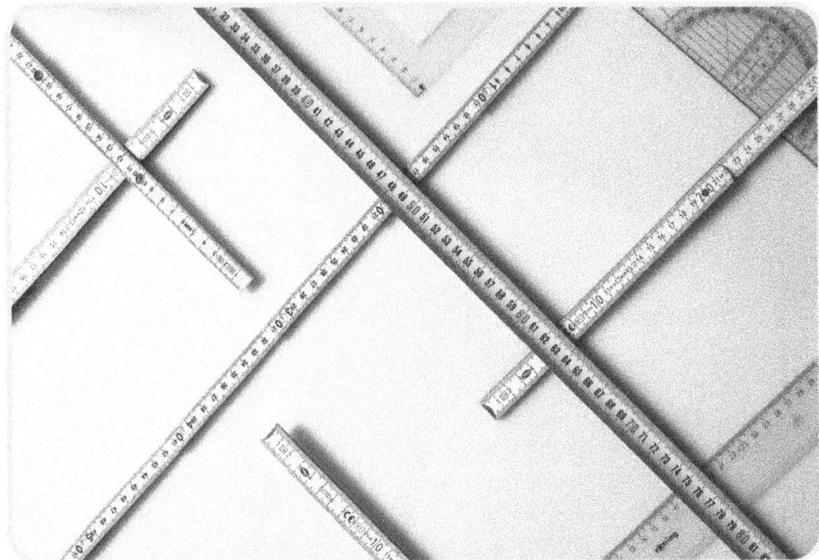

Source: Photo by Bru-nO via Pixabay.

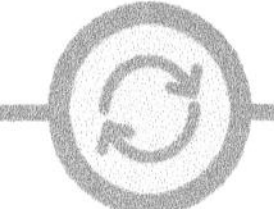

Key concepts

- Least-squares estimation
- R^2
- Elasticities

Chapter value

Regression is a popular technique to quantify and test how sensitive y is to unit changes in x.

Key takeaway

R^2 provides a simple measure of the explanatory power of a linear regression to assess how good the model is.

Chapter outline

Is the world *linear*? No. Is the world *approximately* linear? Sometimes. Is it easier to deal with *linear* relationships than *nonlinear* relationships? Absolutely, yes! Linear regression assumes an approximate linear relationship between a quantitative dependent variable and one or more (usually quantitative) independent variables. Analogous to ANOVA in Chapter 12, regression analysis seeks to explain the variation in the dependent variable. In situations where we can control the independent variable(s), we can then predict the dependent variable - with some uncertainty, of course!

Learning outcomes

After completing this chapter, you should be able to:

- conduct a simple linear regression analysis in Excel
- interpret the least-squares estimates of regression coefficients and test their significance
- analyse the analysis of variance table in Excel regression output
- comment on the explanatory power of the model
- visually examine the residuals
- estimate price elasticities of demand using logarithmic transformations
- assess the risk of a stock based on its beta.

Motivational case: Hunger games

6-Twelve is a chain of convenience stores selling a selection of food, beverages and essential everyday items. Open 6am to midnight, 365 days a year, 6-Twelve is well known for offering convenience to its customers. Convenience, though, comes at a price. Staffing the store at unsociable hours requires greater worker remuneration; locating stores in high-footfall areas means high rental payments for prime location sites. As such, 6-Twelve's business needs to be sufficiently cash-generative to cover its operating costs, so it needs to price its products optimally.

Aware that its customers have relatively inelastic demand (they are willing to pay a 'convenience premium'), how could 6-Twelve decide how best to set its prices?

13.1 INTRODUCTION

Regression analysis is one of the most frequently used statistical techniques. It aims to model an explicit relationship between one **dependent variable** (also called a response variable – the variable we are trying to explain), often denoted as y, and one or more **independent variables** (also called covariates, regressors or explanatory variables – the variable(s) we think influence y), often denoted as $x_1, x_2, \ldots, x_k$, where k is the number of independent variables. Figure 1.1 gave several examples of *causes* (examples of y) and *effects* (examples of $x_1, x_2, ..., x_k$), some of which are under our control (the marketing mix variables – the 4 Ps) while others are uncontrollable (the situational factors).

The goal of regression analysis is to ***understand*** how y depends on $x_1, x_2, ..., x_k$ and to predict or control the unobserved y based on the observed or chosen $x_1, x_2, ..., x_k$. This chapter considers the case when $k = 1$, also known as *simple* linear regression. Chapter 14 considers *multiple* linear regression, when $k \geq 2$.

In high school mathematics classes, you would likely have encountered the equation of a line. Depending on your teacher's preference, you probably saw this written algebraically as:

$$y = a + bx \quad \text{or} \quad y = mx + c.$$

In either case, these represent one variable, y, as a *linear* function of another variable, x. The *coefficient* of x (b in the first representation; m in the second) is the *slope* or *gradient*, representing the *sensitivity* of y to a *unit change* in x. (For readers familiar with calculus, we have that $dy/dx = b = m$, the rate of change in y for a unit change in x.) The constants a and c represent the y-intercept, that is, the value of y when $x = 0$.

Together, a and b (or m and c, but let's stick with the $y = a + bx$ specification) represent the parameters of the line. If we specify numerical values for a and b then we know which *specific* line we are dealing with.

Example 13.1

If we set $a = 3$ and $b = 2$, then the line $y = 3 + 2x$ has a y-intercept (when $x = 0$) of 3, since $3 + 2 \times 0 = 3$, and an x-intercept (when $y = 0$) of –1.5, since $0 = 3 + 2x$ solves for $x = -1.5$. We can plot this as follows:

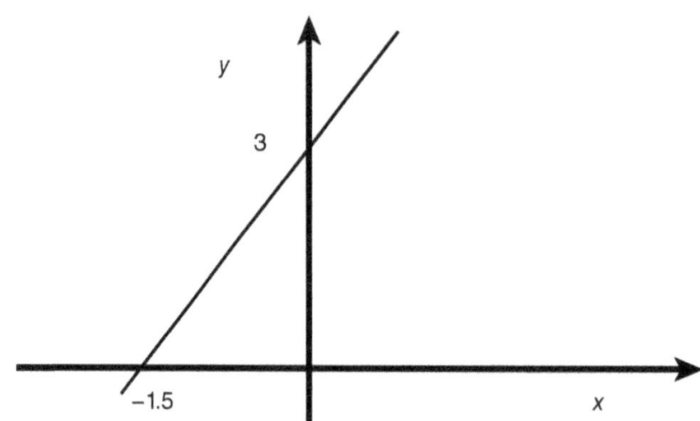

If we set $a = 2$ and $b = -1$, then the line $y = 2 - x$ has a y-intercept (when $x = 0$) of 2, since $2 - 0 = 2$, and an x-intercept (when $y = 0$) of 2, since $0 = 2 - x$ solves for $x = 2$. We can plot this as follows:

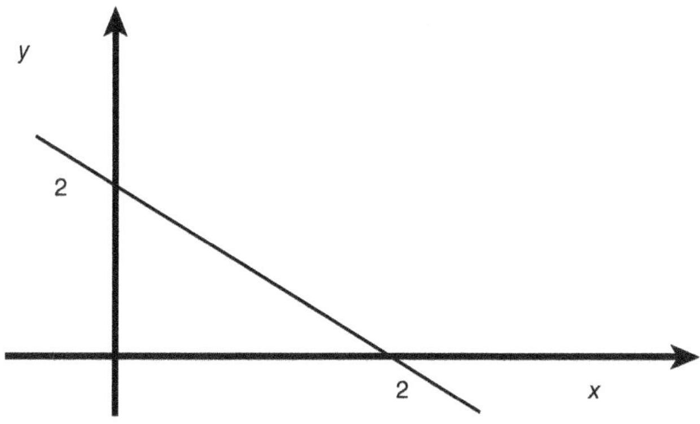

So what? This seems somewhat abstract, right? Well, the two linear equations in Example 13.1 are examples of *deterministic* relationships. That is, if you know x, you *know* y with certainty. If $y = 3 + 2x$, then if $x = 6$ then $y = 15$, and if $x = 7$ then $y = 17$. You give me an x, then I can give you the y with certainty. Note here that the *change* in y when x increased by one unit from 6 to 7 is $17 - 15 = 2$, which, unsurprisingly, is the slope coefficient in $y = 3 + 2x$.

We will now change our notation slightly, letting $\beta_0 = a$ and $\beta_1 = b$, hence the mathematical (deterministic) linear model is

$$y = \beta_0 + \beta_1 x. \tag{13.1}$$

In practice the real world tends *not* to be perfectly linear, but some quantitative variables may exhibit an imperfect linear relationship, that is, they may be *correlated* with a correlation coefficient, r, close to +1 or close to −1, as discussed in Chapter 11.

So how do we modify (13.1) to account for this 'deviation' from perfect linearity? We do so with an error term, denoted by ε, where ε is a random variable and assumed (in a standard regression model) to follow a *normal distribution* with zero mean and constant variance, σ^2 (i.e. $\varepsilon \sim N(0, \sigma^2)$). We can think of ε as a sort of 'catch-all' variable capturing the 'residual' effect on y which is *not* explained by x. Therefore, we have

$$y = \beta_0 + \beta_1 x + \varepsilon.$$

We proceed with some simple illustrative examples.

Example 13.2

Continuing Example 11.8, in a university town, the sales, y (in thousands of pounds), of 10 coffee shops were found to be strongly positively correlated with the student population, x (in thousands), in their neighbourhoods. We plot y against x, and draw a straight line through the middle of the data points, as shown in Figure 11.6, and reproduced below.

(Continued)

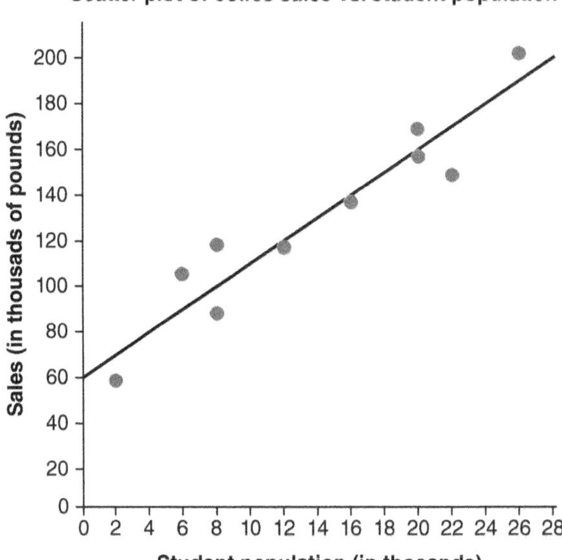

Visual inspection of the scatter plot clearly reveals an *approximate*, but not perfect, linear relationship between y and x. We would expect y (sales) to depend on x (student population) and not vice versa (more students buy more coffee, not the other way round), so we can model the relationship as

$$y = \beta_0 + \beta_1 x + \varepsilon$$

where β_0 is the y-intercept, β_1 is the slope of the straight line, and ε stands for the random error term such that $\varepsilon \sim N(0, \sigma^2)$, modelling the imperfect nature of the linear relationship. In the scatter plot of Figure 11.6, the points lie close to the drawn line, but they do not lie *on* the line itself.

For a given student population, x, the predicted sales, denoted $\hat{y}$, would be $\hat{y} = \beta_0 + \beta_1 x$ *if* we knew the true values of β_0 and β_1, noting that the expected value of the error term is zero (i.e. $E(\varepsilon) = 0$). In practice, the values of β_0 and β_1 are *unknown*, and will need to be *estimated* using our sample data. Fear not, Excel will come to the rescue!

Example 13.3

Consider the heights, x, and weights, y, of 69 students in a class. We plot y against x, and draw a straight line through the middle of the data cloud:

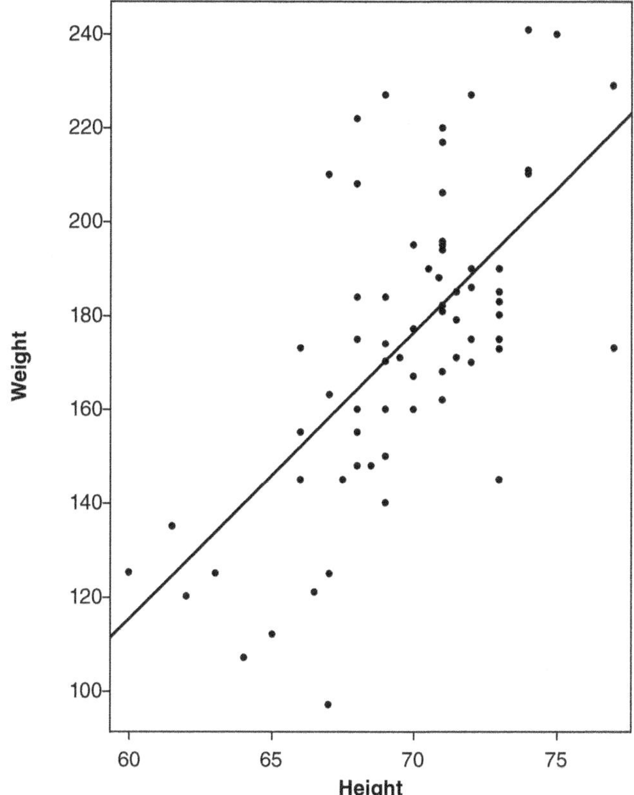

Visual inspection of the scatter plot again clearly reveals an *approximate*, but not perfect, linear relationship between y and x. We would expect y (weight) to depend on x (height) and not vice versa (your height determines your weight, not the other way round), so we can model the relationship as

$$y = \beta_0 + \beta_1 x + \varepsilon$$

where β_0 is the y-intercept, β_1 is the slope of the straight line, and ε stands for the random error term such that $\varepsilon \sim N(0, \sigma^2)$, again modelling the imperfect nature of the linear relationship. In the scatter plot, the points do not lie *on* the line itself but are scattered around it, broadly revealing a positive correlation.

For a given height, x, the predicted value $\hat{y} = \beta_0 + \beta_1 x$ may be viewed as a kind of 'standard weight'.

Example 13.4

Some other possible examples of y and x are shown in the following table.

y variable (dependent)	x variable (independent)	Rationale
Sales	Price	Price goes up (down), sales go down (up) as per the law of demand, negative correlation expected
Weight	Calories in diet	Calories consumed up (down), weight goes up (down), positive correlation expected
Salary	Tenure	As tenure increases, salary increases, longer tenure expected to lead to higher-paid positions
Present FTSE 100 index value	Past FTSE 100 index value	Past can affect the present, present cannot affect the past, clear time order (x occurs before y)
Consumption	Income	If your income goes up (down), you consume more (less), marginal propensity to consume is positive

In most cases, there are several x variables involved. We will consider such situations in Chapter 14, where $k \geq 2$.

Note that in the case of 'Consumption' and 'Income', identifying which variable is x and which is y may not be so straightforward. Students of macroeconomics will know the 'national income identity' of $Y = C + I + G + NX$, which says that national income (Y), is the sum of consumption (C), investment (I), government spending (G) and net exports (NX). This suggests that (national) income is the *dependent* variable, driven by consumption - spend your way to economic recovery! This is an example of *endogeneity* which, roughly, is an extension of linear regression to a system of equations in which dependent and independent variables can swap roles in other equations within the system.

Sound interesting? Then I recommend taking an econometrics course.

Some questions to consider are the following:

- How to draw a line through data clouds, that is, how to *estimate* β_0 and β_1?
- How *accurate* is the fitted line?
- What is the error in *predicting* (a future) y?

So our objectives in regression analysis include estimating unknown parameters and assessing the precision of their estimates, as well as testing the adequacy of the proposed model and the relevance of the explanatory variable.

13.2 PARAMETER ESTIMATION

For given paired-sample data, (x_i, y_i) for $i = 1, 2, ..., n$, we could first produce a scatter plot from which any linear relationship would be visible, as seen in Examples 13.2 and 13.3. When the data indicate a correlation (whether positive or negative), it suggests we should perform a (simple) linear regression, provided that a *causal* relationship seems reasonable. So, we need to estimate the *population* regression line using the *sample* data, that is, we need to estimate β_0 and β_1. This estimated line is often called the **line of best fit**.

How do we choose this line, that is, how do we obtain values of β_0 and β_1? We require a formal criterion for determining the line of *best* fit. Note that whenever you want the 'best' of something you need to clarify in what sense it is considered 'best'. Geometrically, the best-fitting line is that which *most closely goes through the data cloud*. Look again at the best-fitting lines shown in the scatter plots for Examples 13.2 and 13.3. Any other line would be sub-optimal (and therefore not 'best'). Clearly hand-drawing such lines by eye is prone to error, so we turn to an optimisation technique called **least-squares estimation**. Specifically, we seek to minimise the sum of the squared error terms:

$$\min_{\beta_0,\beta_1} \sum_{i=1}^{n} \varepsilon_1^2 = \min_{\beta_0,\beta_1} \sum_{i=1}^{n} (y_i - \beta_0 - \beta_1 x_i)^2.$$

In words, we seek the values of β_0 and β_1 which *minimise* (the 'min') the above sum of *squares* function, hence the term 'least squares'.

We see that the error terms are used to estimate the parameters (*intercept* and *slope*) of the model. The intercept tells us the value of the dependent variable when the independent variable is zero. The slope tells us by how much y changes when x increases by one unit.

Least-squares estimators and line of best fit

The least-squares estimator of β_1 is

$$\hat{\beta}_1 = \frac{\sum_{i=1}^{n} x_i y_i - n\bar{x}\bar{y}}{\sum_{i=1}^{n} x_i^2 - n\bar{x}^2}.$$

The least-squares estimator of β_0 is

$$\hat{\beta}_0 = \bar{y} + \hat{\beta}_1 \bar{x}.$$

Hence the line of best fit has the equation

$$\hat{y} = \hat{\beta}_0 + \hat{\beta}_1 x$$

where $\hat{y}$ is our estimate of y based on the line of best fit for a given x.

Example 13.5

Continuing Example 13.2, we have

$$\sum_{i=1}^{10} x_i = 140, \quad \sum_{i=1}^{10} x_i^2 = 2528, \quad \sum_{i=1}^{10} y_i = 1300, \quad \sum_{i=1}^{10} y_i^2 = 184{,}730 \quad \text{and} \quad \sum_{i=1}^{10} x_i y_i = 21{,}040.$$

Since n = 10, we have $\bar{x}$ = 140/10 = 14 and $\bar{y}$ = 1300/10 = 130, hence

$$\hat{\beta}_1 = \frac{\sum_{i=1}^{10} x_i y_i - n\bar{x}\bar{y}}{\sum_{i=1}^{10} x_i^2 - n\bar{x}^2} = \frac{21{,}040 - (10 \times 14 \times 130)}{2528 - (10 \times 14^2)} = 5.0.$$

We then estimate the intercept to be

$$\hat{\beta}_0 = \bar{y} + \hat{\beta}_1 \bar{x} = 130 - 0.5803 \times 14 = 60.0.$$

Hence the least-squares regression line is:

$\hat{y}$ = 60.0 + 5.0x.

In practice, we will use Excel to perform the calculations for us. Just take note that the values returned by the regression procedure have formulae behind them - the values returned are not the result of magic!

13.2.1 Simple linear regression in Excel

To perform a simple linear regression in Excel, select `Regression` from the Data Analysis add-in as shown in Figure 13.1.

Input the cell range containing the y and x data, respectively, ensuring `Labels` is checked if the first row contains the variable names – as in this case. Calling the residual and line fit plots will allow us to visually examine the residuals, essentially estimates of ε_i. Figure 13.2 shows the specifications.

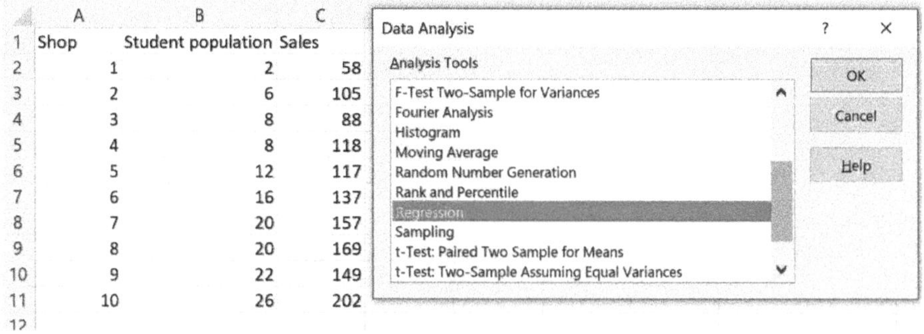

	A	B	C
1	Shop	Student population	Sales
2	1	2	58
3	2	6	105
4	3	8	88
5	4	8	118
6	5	12	117
7	6	16	137
8	7	20	157
9	8	20	169
10	9	22	149
11	10	26	202
12			

Data Analysis ? ×
Analysis Tools
F-Test Two-Sample for Variances
Fourier Analysis
Histogram
Moving Average
Random Number Generation
Rank and Percentile
Regression
Sampling
t-Test: Paired Two Sample for Means
t-Test: Two-Sample Assuming Equal Variances
OK
Cancel
Help

Figure 13.1 Selecting `Regression` from the Data Analysis add-in in Excel.

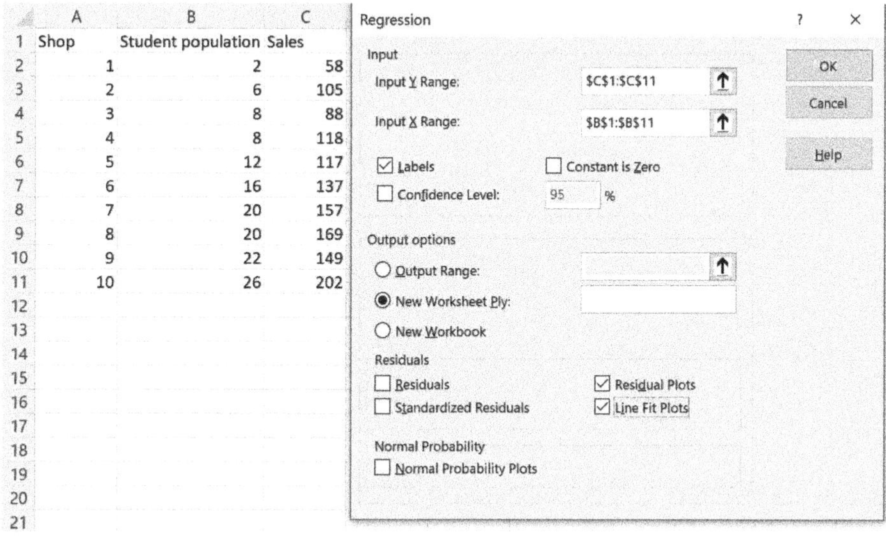

Figure 13.2 Specifying simple linear regression requirements in Excel.

Note that Excel offers the option to suppress β_0 (set it to zero) by checking the `Constant is Zero` box. Setting the intercept to zero forces the line of 'best' fit through the origin, but imposing this constraint would result in a 'non-best' line if $\beta_0 \neq 0$! In most cases, when $x = 0$ it is unlikely that $y = 0$, but that is precisely what $\beta_0 = 0$ would imply (e.g. with no work experience, your salary would still be strictly positive). So, use this check box with care.

We obtain the output as shown in Figure 13.3. For now, let's focus on the parameter estimates, $\hat{\beta}_0 = 60$ and $\hat{\beta}_1 = 5$, highlighted in yellow, from which we obtain the best-fitting line equation $\hat{y} = 60 + 5x$. We can see that 5 is the coefficient of x, but in what sense is 60 a coefficient? It doesn't appear to be multiplied by anything. Well, it *is* a coefficient – of 1! We could have written our regression model as

$$y = \beta_0 \times 1 + \beta_1 \times x + \varepsilon,$$

which makes clear how β_0 and β_1 are the coefficients of 1 and x, respectively. Indeed, we can think of '1' as an independent variable which is in fact a constant. However, this overcomplicates our notation so we simply write $y = \beta_0 + \beta_1 x + \varepsilon$.

We will discuss (some of) the other values in the output later. For now, the 'student population residual plot' is a plot of the *residuals*, $e_i = \hat{\varepsilon}_i$ (i.e. estimates of the unobserved error terms ε_i), computed as the difference between the observed value y_i and its predicted value from the regression model, $\hat{y}_i$, that is,

$$e_i = y_i - \hat{y}_i = y_i - \hat{\beta}_0 - \hat{\beta}_1 x = y_i - 60 - 5x.$$

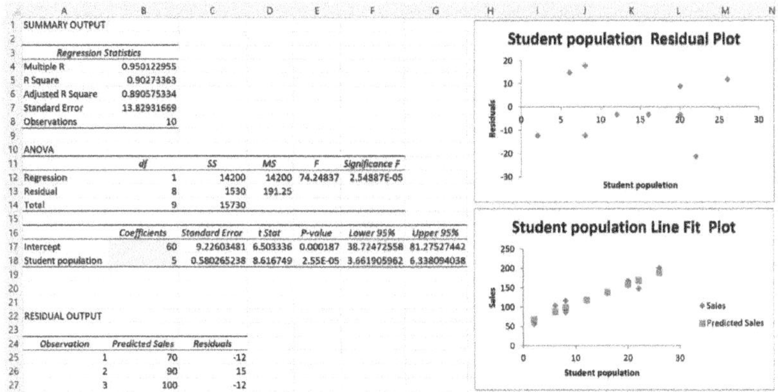

SUMMARY OUTPUT

Regression Statistics	
Multiple R	0.950122955
R Square	0.90273363
Adjusted R Square	0.890575334
Standard Error	13.82931669
Observations	10

ANOVA

	df	SS	MS	F	Significance F
Regression	1	14200	14200	74.24837	2.54887E-05
Residual	8	1530	191.25		
Total	9	15730			

	Coefficients	Standard Error	t Stat	P-value	Lower 95%	Upper 95%
Intercept	60	9.22603481	6.503336	0.000187	38.72472558	81.27527442
Student population	5	0.580265238	8.616749	2.55E-05	3.661905962	6.338094038

RESIDUAL OUTPUT

Observation	Predicted Sales	Residuals
1	70	-12
2	90	15
3	100	-12

Figure 13.3 Excel output for a simple linear regression.

For example, the first three residuals are shown in cells `C25:C27`, such that

$$e_1 = y_1 - \hat{y}_1 = 58 - 60 - 5 \times 2 = -12,$$

$$e_2 = y_2 - \hat{y}_2 = 105 - 60 - 5 \times 6 = 15,$$

$$e_3 = y_3 - \hat{y}_3 = 88 - 60 - 5 \times 8 = -12.$$

Recall our assumption that $\varepsilon_i \sim N(0, \sigma^2)$ for all $i = 1, 2, ..., n$? Well, if true, then a plot of the residuals should reveal 'random scatter', with no obvious pattern and with only a few 'large' residuals, which is the case here. If there *was* a clear pattern, then we could improve the regression model by incorporating whatever factor(s) explain the residuals, but this would then lead to a multiple linear regression (see Chapter 14).

13.3 ANALYSIS OF VARIANCE - REGRESSION STYLE

Our overall objective is to explain the response variable, y, which is a random variable. Specifically, we are trying to explain the *variation* in the response variable, as we did in Chapter 12 using one or two categorical variables (one-way and two-way ANOVA, respectively). When employing simple linear regression, we attempt to do this using a single quantitative explanatory variable. We have seen above how estimation of the regression model parameters, β_0 and β_1, is carried out using paired-sample data (x_i, y_i), for $i = 1, 2, ..., n$.

But how 'good' is a particular regression model? Is our choice of the x variable appropriate? Casually looking at a scatter plot gives us a rough idea, but we would prefer a simple measure to judge the overall *explanatory power* of the model. In short, we seek the equivalent of η^2 introduced in Chapter 12.

We proceed to *decompose the variation* in y into its explained and unexplained components. In Chapter 12 we discussed ANOVA, whereby we decomposed the total variation of a continuous dependent variable. In a similar way we can decompose the total variation of y in the simple linear regression model.

Regression ANOVA decomposition

It can be shown that the **regression ANOVA decomposition** is

$$\sum_{i=1}^{n}(y_i-\bar{y})^2=\sum_{i=1}^{n}\hat{\beta}_1^2(x_i-\bar{x})^2+\sum_{i=1}^{n}\left(y_i-\hat{\beta}_0-\hat{\beta}_1x_i\right)^2$$

or, in words (where 'SS' stands for 'sum of squares'),

Total SS = Regression SS + Residual SS.

Given that our objective is to explain as much of the Total SS as possible, we see that we can decompose the Total SS into two components – the amount we are able to explain using the hypothesised model, called the *Regression SS*, and the remaining variation which we are unable to explain with the model, called the *Residual SS*.

A convenient, and conventional, way of presenting variation results is via an *analysis of variance* (ANOVA) table for regression. This has the following format (for simple linear regression):

Analysis of variance (ANOVA) table for regression

The standard format of an **ANOVA regression table** is as follows:

Source of variation	Degrees of freedom	Sum of squares	Mean sum of squares	F statistic	p-value
Regression	1	$\sum_{i=1}^{n}\hat{\beta}_1^2(x_i-\bar{x})^2$	(Regression SS)/1	f	$P(F_{1,\,n-2}>f)$
Residual	$n-2$	$\sum_{i=1}^{n}\left(y_i-\hat{\beta}_0-\hat{\beta}_1x_i\right)^2$	(Residual SS)/$(n-2)$		
Total	$n-1$	$\sum_{i=1}^{n}(y_i-\bar{y})^2$			

where f = Regression MS/Residual MS, that is, the ratio of the regression and residual mean sums of squares, respectively.

Some important points to note about this table are as follows:

- There is only one degree of freedom for regression due to the presence of only one explanatory variable in the model (recall that $k = 1$).
- The 'mean sum of squares' is the 'sum of squares' divided by the 'degrees of freedom'.
- (Residual SS)/$(n-2)$ is the *residual variance* and is the estimate of σ^2, that is, the variance of the error term (recall that $\varepsilon_i \sim N(0, \sigma^2)$).
- f is a test statistic value for testing H_0: $\beta_1^2=0$ (discussed later).

13.3.1 Coefficient of determination

A popular method of measuring the overall fit of the regression model is to express the *proportion of the total variability in the response variable which is explained by the model*. This statistic is known as the coefficient of determination, denoted by R^2, and is defined as:

$$R^2 = \frac{\text{Regression SS}}{\text{Total SS}} = \frac{\sum_{i=1}^{n} \widehat{\beta}_1^2 (x_i - \bar{x})^2}{\sum_{i=1}^{n} (y_i - \bar{y})^2}.$$

Clearly, $0 \leq R^2 \leq 1$ (since $0 \leq$ Regression SS $\leq$ Total SS) and the closer R^2 is to 1, the better the explanatory power of the model. In order to interpret R^2 in words, we could say that the R^2 value gives the proportion of the total variation in the response variable which is explained by the regression model. If $R^2 = 1$, then we would have a perfect fit, with all the data points lying exactly along a straight line. Obviously, this is *highly unlikely* to happen in practice!

Note that $R^2 = r^2$, where r is the sample correlation coefficient between the x and y variables. However, this is *only* true in the case of simple linear regression. In multiple linear regression (Chapter 14) it does not hold because the response variable is linked to several different explanatory variables, and hence the situation is more complicated.

	A	B	C	D	E	F
1	SUMMARY OUTPUT					
2						
3	*Regression Statistics*					
4	Multiple R	0.950122955				
5	R Square	0.90273363				
6	Adjusted R Square	0.890575334				
7	Standard Error	13.82931669				
8	Observations	10				
9						
10	ANOVA					
11		*df*	*SS*	*MS*	*F*	*Significance F*
12	Regression	1	14200	14200	74.24837	2.54887E-05
13	Residual	8	1530	191.25		
14	Total	9	15730			

Figure 13.4 The regression statistics and ANOVA regression table in Excel output.

Continuing with the Excel output, we now focus on the regression statistics and ANOVA regression table, shown in Figure 13.4. In the ANOVA table we see the regression ANOVA decomposition

$$\text{Total SS} = \text{Regression SS} + \text{Residual SS} \Leftrightarrow 15{,}730 = 14{,}200 + 1530$$

from which we obtain the R^2 value (called `R Square`)

$$R^2 = \frac{\text{Regression SS}}{\text{Total SS}} = \frac{14{,}200}{15{,}730} = 0.9027,$$

so we conclude that 90.27% of the variation in coffee shop sales can be attributed to the student population. This is a really good regression model!

We can also see that R^2 is the square of the sample correlation coefficient, r, which we calculated separately in Example 11.10 using the `CORREL` Excel function. Conveniently, it is returned as part of the `Regression Statistics` table in the regression output (called `Multiple R`):

$$R^2 = r^2 \Leftrightarrow 0.9027 = 0.9501^2.$$

In case you are wondering, `Adjusted R Square` will be discussed in Chapter 14, since this is relevant when comparing regression models with different numbers of explanatory variables. In this chapter, we only consider *one* explanatory variable, so such comparisons are not possible.

Note also the estimate of the error term variance, $\hat{\sigma}^2$, which is the `Residual MS`, hence $\hat{\sigma}^2 = 191.25$. Its square root is reported as the `Standard Error` in the `Regression Statistics` table: $\hat{\sigma} = \sqrt{191.25} = 13.83$.

13.4 A GENERAL TEST FOR THE EFFECT OF A VARIABLE

As well as providing the means to calculate R^2 (using the Regression SS and Total SS) and an estimate of σ^2 (the Residual MS), the regression ANOVA table gives a quick-and-easy statistical test of the significance of the model, that is, whether the model contributes at all towards the explanation of the total variability of the response variable. If, as here, we are dealing with simple linear regression (i.e. a single explanatory variable), then this is equivalent to *testing for the effect of the explanatory variable*. In particular, it is equivalent to testing whether $\beta_1 = 0$, which, if true, would mean changes in x have *no effect* on y, against $\beta_1 \neq 0$, meaning x exerts *some effect* (whether positive or negative) on y.

In linear regression analysis, there is a probability distribution which plays a major part, the F distribution, as introduced in Chapter 12. In fact, it is usual to test H_0: $\beta_1^2 = 0$ against H_1: $\beta_1^2 > 0$, because $\beta_1 \neq 0$ means $\beta_1^2 > 0$, and this remark is closely related to the fact that $F_{1,k} = (t_k)^2$ – that is, an F distribution with 1 degree of freedom in the numerator is the square of a Student's t distribution. In discussing multiple linear regression, the same type of test can be used to *jointly test the effects of all variables*, and even of groups of variables. Therefore, it is a valuable test in *model selection*, as will be seen in Chapter 14.

F test for regression ANOVA

The test statistic for testing H_0: $\beta_1 = 0$ against H_1: $\beta_1 \neq 0$ (which is equivalent to testing H_0: $\beta_1^2 = 0$ against H_1: $\beta_1^2 > 0$) is the ratio of the regression mean sum of squares to the residual mean sum of squares (i.e. the residual variance), as given in the regression ANOVA table. Under H_0: $\beta_1^2 = 0$, we have

$$F = \frac{\text{Regression MS}}{(\text{Residual SS})/(n-2)} \sim F_{1,n-2}.$$

(Continued)

Hence p-values are obtained from the F distribution with 1 degree of freedom in the numerator and $n - 2$ degrees of freedom in the denominator, called `Significance F` in the Excel regression ANOVA table.

If H_1: $\beta_1^2 > 0$ is true, it can be shown that $E(F) > 1$, and for this reason this is always an *upper-tailed test.*

Continuing with the Excel output, we now focus on the F test components of the regression ANOVA table, as shown in Figure 13.5.

We test

$$H_0: \beta_1 = 0 \quad \text{versus} \quad H_1: \beta_1 \neq 0,$$

or equivalently

$$H_0: \beta_1^2 = 0 \quad \text{versus} \quad H_1: \beta_1^2 > 0\ .$$

ANOVA					
	df	*SS*	*MS*	*F*	*Significance F*
Regression	1	14200	14200	74.24837	2.54887E-05
Residual	8	1530	191.25		
Total	9	15730			

Figure 13.5 *F* test results for simple linear regression in Excel.

The test statistic value is (as given in the ANOVA table)

$$f = \frac{\text{Regression MS}}{(\text{Residual SS})/(n-2)} = \frac{14{,}200}{1530/8} = \frac{14{,}200}{191.25} = 74.24837.$$

The p-value is

$$P(F > 74.24837) = 2.54887 \times 10^{-5}$$

where $F \sim F_{1,\,8}$, which is (much!) smaller than any reasonable significance level, so we reject H_0 and conclude that there is *(very) strong evidence* that student population affects coffee shop sales.

If the coffee shop chain wanted to open a new branch, it would be wise to open in an area with a large student population. Perhaps this result is not too surprising given the strong correlation, and hence large R^2 value. However, we should perhaps be slightly cautious – our model does not explicitly take into account other variables which may be relevant, such as the amount of competition in a particular area.

We now proceed to perform statistical inference (hypothesis tests and confidence intervals) on β_0 and β_1 directly. Of these two parameters, it is β_1 that is of greater importance, since the relationship between y and x hinges on this parameter value, while β_0 just corresponds to the value of y when $x = 0$. Often, it is unlikely we would encounter situations in practice with $x = 0$. For example, considering Example 13.2, are there really any ***university*** towns with no students?!

13.5 HYPOTHESIS TESTING AND CONFIDENCE INTERVALS FOR REGRESSION MODEL PARAMETERS

We now consider statistical inference of the parameters in the simple linear regression model. This will involve performing hypothesis testing and constructing confidence intervals.

In each case the test statistic value will take the general form

$$\frac{\text{point estimate} - \text{hypothesised value under H}_0}{\text{standard error}}.$$

Technically, the denominator is the *estimated* standard error, since σ^2 is unknown. However, Excel regression output refers to this as the 'standard error' so, for consistency, this term will be used.

In each case the $100(1 - \alpha)\%$ confidence interval endpoints will take the general form

$$\text{point estimate} \pm t_{\alpha/2,\, n-2} \times \text{standard error}.$$

Hypothesis test of β_1

For some constant, c, we test

$$H_0: \beta_1 = c \text{ versus } H_1: \beta_1 \neq c.$$

Under H_0, the test statistic is

$$T = \frac{\hat{\beta}_1 - c}{\text{standard error of } \hat{\beta}_1} \sim t_{n-2}.$$

Hence p-values are obtained from the Student's t distribution with $n - 2$ degrees of freedom, and are conveniently returned in Excel regression output.

A very special case is when $c = 0$, since if this is true then there is *no linear relationship* between x and y.

Hypothesis test of β_0

For some constant, c, we test:

H_0: $\beta_0 = c$ versus H_1: $\beta_0 \neq c$.

Under H_0, the test statistic is

$$T = \frac{\hat{\beta}_0 - c}{\text{standard error of } \hat{\beta}_0} \sim t_{n-2}.$$

Hence p-values are obtained from the Student's t distribution with $n - 2$ degrees of freedom, and are also conveniently returned in Excel regression output.

A very special case is when $c = 0$, since if this is true then the intercept equals zero so that the (true) line *passes through the origin*. However, this would be rare in practice.

Confidence interval for β_1

A $100(1 - \alpha)\%$ confidence interval for β_1 has the general form:

$$\hat{\beta}_1 \pm t_{\alpha/2,n-2} \times \text{standard error of } \hat{\beta}_1$$

where $t_{\alpha/2,\, v-2}$ is the t-value which cuts off $100\alpha/2\%$ probability in the upper tail of the Student's t distribution with $n - 2$ degrees of freedom. Conveniently, endpoints for a 95% confidence interval are returned in the Excel regression output, and we have the option to change the confidence level if we wish by checking the `Confidence Level` box and specifying our choice of confidence level (the default is 95%) as shown in Figure 13.2.

Confidence interval for β_0

A $100(1 - \alpha)\%$ confidence interval for β_0 has the general form:

$$\hat{\beta}_0 \pm t_{\alpha/2,n-2} \times \text{standard error of } \hat{\beta}_0$$

where $t_{\alpha/2,\, v-2}$ is the t-value which cuts off $100\alpha/2\%$ probability in the upper tail of the Student's t distribution with $n - 2$ degrees of freedom. Conveniently, endpoints for a 95% confidence interval are also returned in the Excel regression output, and we have the option to change the confidence level if we wish, as above.

Continuing with the Excel output, we now focus on testing the significance of the student population variable and reporting a 95% confidence interval for β_1 by focusing on Figure 13.6.

	Coefficients	*Standard Error*	*t Stat*	*P-value*	*Lower 95%*	*Upper 95%*
Intercept	60	9.22603481	6.503336	0.000187	38.72472558	81.27527442
Student population	5	0.580265238	8.616749	2.55E-05	3.661905962	6.338094038

Figure 13.6 Hypothesis tests and confidence intervals returned in Excel regression output.

We test

$$H_0: \beta_1 = 0 \text{ versus } H_1: \beta_1 \neq 0.$$

The test statistic value is (rounding highlighted values in Figure 13.6)

$$t = \frac{\hat{\beta}_1}{\text{standard error of } \hat{\beta}_1} = \frac{5}{0.5803} = 8.6167.$$

The p-value is

$$2 \times P(T > 8.6167) = 2.55 \times 10^{-5}$$

where $T \sim t_8$, which is (much!) smaller than any reasonable significance level, so we reject H_0 and conclude that there is *(very!) strong evidence* that student population affects coffee shop sales. Note the '2 ×' in the p-value calculation is due to it being a *two-tailed test*, since $H_1: \beta_1 \neq 0$.

Note how Excel defaults to a two-tailed test. In this regression model, *a priori* (i.e. before we observed the data) we would have expected any effect of student population on coffee shop sales to be *positive* (more students, more coffee sold), so really we should have conducted an *upper-tailed test*, i.e. we should test:

$$H_0: \beta_1 = 0 \text{ versus } H_1: \beta_1 > 0.$$

As H_0 is unchanged, the test statistic value is not affected (it is computed conditional on H_0), so only the p-value is affected. Since $\hat{\beta}_1 > 0$, a positive coefficient, consistent with $\beta_1 > 0$, the upper-tailed test p-value is just the Excel reported p-value *divided* by 2. Hence

$$P(T > 8.6167) = \frac{2.55 \times 10^{-5}}{2} = 1.27 \times 10^{-5}$$

where $T \sim t_8$, as before. Clearly, in this instance this does not affect the test conclusion, which remains *highly significant.*

A 95% confidence interval for β_1 is

$$\hat{\beta}_1 \pm t_{0.025,\,8} \times \text{standard error of } \hat{\beta}_1 \Leftrightarrow 5 \pm 2.306 \times 0.5803$$

which gives the interval (3.66, 6.34). This means we are 95% confident that β_1 is between 3.66 and 6.34. Crucially, this confidence interval *excludes zero,* indicating a positive effect of student population on coffee shop sales. By construction, this is the same inference as for the *two-tailed* t test above at the 5% significance level.

Note that 2.306 is obtained using `=T.INV(0.975,8)` or `=T.INV.2T(0.05,8)`, that is, $P(T > 2.306) = 0.025$.

Hang on a minute. The two-tailed t test of H_0: $\beta_1 = 0$ seems suspiciously like the F test of H_0: $\beta_1^2 = 0$, and also it seems reminiscent of the test of the correlation coefficient in Example 11.14. Is this a coincidence? No! These are in fact *three equivalent tests.* A case not just of double vision, but triple vision.

Three equivalent tests

There is more than one way to test for the significance of the explanatory variable, x, in explaining y for a simple linear regression model. To summarise, the following are three equivalent tests:

1. Test H_0: $\beta_1 = 0$ versus H_1: $\beta_1 \neq 0$ using the test statistic

$$\frac{\hat{\beta}_1}{\text{standard error of } \hat{\beta}_1} \sim t_{n-2}.$$

2. Test H_0: $\beta_1^2 = 0$ versus H_1: $\beta_1^2 > 0$ using the test statistic

$$\frac{\text{Regression MS}}{(\text{Residual SS})/(n-2)} \sim F_{1,n-2}.$$

3. Test H_0: $\rho = 0$ versus H_1: $\rho \neq 0$ using the test statistic

$$\frac{r\sqrt{n-2}}{\sqrt{1-r^2}} \sim t_{n-2}.$$

In fact it can be shown that

$$\frac{\hat{\beta}_1}{\text{standard error of } \hat{\beta}_1} = \sqrt{\frac{\text{Regression MS}}{(\text{Residual SS})/(n-2)}} = \frac{r\sqrt{n-2}}{\sqrt{1-r^2}}$$

and

$$t_{n-2} = \sqrt{F_{1,n-2}},$$

which demonstrates that these three tests are equivalent (although we omit a technical verification in this text).

So, what was the point of learning three different ways of doing the same thing? Well, remember that *correlation does not imply causation*. If we suspected a correlation, but not a causal effect, between x and y, then we should frame our test as that of a correlation coefficient. If we could argue for a causal effect (x affects y), then we could conduct either a t test or an F test of β_1.

If we were unsure about whether $\beta_1 > 0$ or $\beta_1 < 0$ (i.e. if we were unsure whether the linear effect of x on y was positive or negative), then we would conduct a two-tailed t test, which is the default p-value returned by Excel, and which is equivalent to the F test. However, if we wanted to conduct a one-tailed test, because we anticipated the sign of the effect of x on y, then we could 'override' the default two-tailed t test, as we did above. But note that if we have more than one explanatory variable, then the F test and t test are *not* equivalent. This will be discussed in Chapter 14.

13.6 PREDICTION

Apart from trying to understand which variable affects y, an important application is to be able to *predict* the value of the dependent variable for a given value of the independent variable. Based on the observations (x_i, y_i), for $i = 1, 2, \ldots, n$, we fit a regression model:

$$\hat{y} = \hat{\beta}_0 + \hat{\beta}_1 x.$$

Our goal is to predict the *unobserved* y corresponding to a *known* x.

For the analysis to be more informative, we would like to have some 'error bars' for our prediction. We introduce two methods as follows:

- a confidence interval for $E(y \mid x) = \beta_0 + \beta_1 x$, that is, for the expectation of y for a given value of x
- a prediction interval for $y \mid x$, that is, for y for a given value of x.

A confidence interval is an *interval estimator* of an unknown parameter (i.e. for a constant), while a prediction interval is for a *random variable*. They are different and serve different purposes.

For multiple occurrences of a given value of x it's likely that there would be *variation* in the corresponding y values.

Example 13.6

In the dataset shown in Figure 13.2, shops 3 and 4 both had x values of 8, but different corresponding y values (88 and 118, respectively). Also, shops 7 and 8 both had x values of 20, but different corresponding y values (157 and 169, respectively). So multiple occurrences of a given x typically do not all result in the same value of y.

We should compute a confidence interval if we want to estimate the *expected value* of y for a given x – that is, due to the anticipated variation in y values for multiple occurrences of a given value of x, we estimate the *average* value of y. We have that

$$E(y \mid x) = E(\beta_0 + \beta_1 x + \varepsilon) = E(\beta_0) + E(\beta_1 x) + E(\varepsilon) = \beta_0 + \beta_1 x$$

since $E(\varepsilon) = 0$ by assumption. $\beta_0 + \beta_1 x$ is a constant, with unknown β_0 and β_1 (but known x, chosen by us). The corresponding (point) estimator of $E(y \mid x)$ is:

$$\widehat{E(y \mid x)} = \hat{\beta}_0 + \hat{\beta}_1 x.$$

If our interest is in predicting y for a *single* instance of x (rather than an average value over multiple occurrences), then since

$$y \mid x = \beta_0 + \beta_1 x + \varepsilon$$

this requires us to predict a *random variable* due to y being a function of the random variable ε. The point prediction is

$$\hat{y} \mid x = \hat{\beta}_0 + \hat{\beta}_1 x.$$

Although $\widehat{E(y \mid x)} = \hat{y} \mid x$ (i.e. the point estimate and the point prediction for a given x are the same), there is *greater uncertainty* in predicting the random variable $y \mid x$ than there is in estimating the constant $E(y \mid x)$. Intuitively, it is more challenging to predict a random variable as there is variability in the values it can take. This is reflected in the corresponding *error bars*, in that the prediction interval is *wider* than the corresponding confidence interval.

Confidence interval for E(y | x)

A 100(1 − α)% *confidence interval* for E(y | x) is

$$\hat{\beta}_0 + \hat{\beta}_1 x \pm t_{\alpha/2,n-2} \times \sqrt{\hat{\sigma}^2 \times \frac{\sum_{i=1}^{n}(x_i - x)^2}{n\sum_{j=1}^{n}(x_j - \bar{x})^2}}. \tag{13.2}$$

Such a confidence interval contains the true expectation E(y) with probability 1 − α *over repeated samples*. It does *not* cover y with probability 1 − α.

Prediction interval for y | x

A 100(1 − α)% *prediction interval* covering y | x with probability 1 − α is

$$\hat{\beta}_0 + \hat{\beta}_1 x \pm t_{\alpha/2,n-2} \times \sqrt{\hat{\sigma}^2 \times \left(1 + \frac{\sum_{i=1}^{n}(x_i - x)^2}{n\sum_{j=1}^{n}(x_j - \bar{x})^2}\right)}. \tag{13.3}$$

Such a prediction interval is an interval which contains y with probability 1 − α.

We may assume that the y to be predicted is *independent* of $y_1, y_2, \ldots, y_n$ used in the estimation of the linear regression model.

The prediction interval for $y \mid x$ is *wider* than the confidence interval for $E(y \mid x)$, due to the '1+' term which increases the (estimated) standard error, that is, the square root term. The prediction interval contains the unobserved *random variable* $y \mid x$ with probability $1 - \alpha$, while the confidence interval contains the unknown *constant* $E(y \mid x)$ with probability $1 - \alpha$ over repeated samples.

Notice how the (estimated) standard error in each interval increases substantially as the distance of x from the sample mean, $\bar{x}$, increases, that is, the quadratic term

$$\sum_{i=1}^{n}(x_i - x)^2 \text{ becomes ever larger than } \sum_{j=1}^{n}(x_j - \bar{x})^2$$

as x gets further away from $\bar{x}$ (in either direction). This reflects the loss of confidence in prediction as we move further away from the mean of the observed x variable values.

Provided we are predicting y for an x value which is *within* the available x data, then we can be fairly confident in our prediction. This is what we call **interpolation**. However, if we base our prediction on an x value *outside* the available x data, then we should view the prediction with caution. This would be an example of **extrapolation**, which is risky since the relationship between x and y may change for such out-of-sample values of x. The relationship may not continue to be linear; it may be nonlinear, trend-changing or it may plateau. The thing to remember about extrapolation is that there are two types of people in the world – those who can extrapolate and...

Example 13.7

Suppose the coffee shop chain has identified several potential sites for new branches. Each site would serve an area with a student population of 18,000 (hence $x = 18$ as the data used in Example 13.2 is in thousands). Before deciding whether to proceed to open in these locations, senior management would like to:

(a) determine the expected sales across these multiple sites
(b) predict sales for any one of these sites to gauge sales turnover if only one new site was opened.

For task (a), a confidence interval is appropriate, as we need to estimate $E(y \mid x = 18)$. For task (b), we require a prediction interval for $y \mid x = 18$.

The point estimate of $E(y \mid x = 18)$ and point prediction of $y \mid x = 18$ are both

$$\widehat{\beta}_0 + \widehat{\beta}_1 \times 18 \Rightarrow 60 + 5 \times 18 = 150.$$

From the previous regression ANOVA table (Figure 13.5) we know that $\sigma^2 = 191.25$. We desire 95% confidence and prediction intervals, so since $n = 10$ we use $t_{0.025,\ 8} = 2.306$ (obtained using `=T.INV(0.975,8)` or `=T.INV.2T(0.05,8)`). From the raw x data, we can compute the following descriptive statistics:

$$\bar{x} = 14$$

and

$$s_x^2 = \frac{1}{n-1}\sum_{i=1}^{n}(x_i - \bar{x})^2 = 63.11 \quad \Rightarrow \quad \sum_{i=1}^{n}(x_i - \bar{x})^2 = 567.99$$

Note that

$$\sum_{i=1}^{n}(x_i - x)^2 = \sum_{i=1}^{n}\left(x_i - 2xx_i + x^2\right) = \sum_{i=1}^{n}x_i^2 - 2x\sum_{i=1}^{n}x_i + nx^2$$

and so here, given that $\sum_{i=1}^{10} x_i = 140$ and $\sum_{i=1}^{10} x_i^2 = 2528$, we have

$$\sum_{i=1}^{10}(x_i - 18)^2 = \sum_{i=1}^{10} x_i^2 - 36\sum_{i=1}^{10} x_i + 10 \times 18^2 = 2528 - 36 \times 140 + 3240 = 728.$$

Hence a 95% confidence interval for $E(y \mid x = 18)$ using (13.2) is

$$150 \pm 2.306 \times \sqrt{191.25 \times \frac{728}{10 \times 567.99}} \quad \Rightarrow \quad (138.58,\ 161.42)$$

so we are 95% confident that the average sales across multiple sites with student populations of 18,000 are between £138,580 and £161,420.

A 95% prediction interval for $y \mid x = 18$ using (13.3) is

$$150 \pm 2.306 \times \sqrt{191.25 \times \left(1 + \frac{728}{10 \times 567.99}\right)} \quad \Rightarrow \quad (116.13,\ 183.87)$$

so there is a 95% probability that the sales from a single site with a student population of 18,000 are between £116,130 and £183,870. Note how the prediction interval is wider, reflecting the greater uncertainty in predicting for a single site.

Example 13.8

Since the range of the raw x data spanned from $x_1 = 2$ to $x_{10} = 26$, Example 13.7 is an example of *interpolation*, since $x = 18$ fell in this range. We repeat the exercise of computing confidence and prediction intervals, but now for prospective sites with (very!) large student populations of $x = 50$, which is considerably beyond the x data maximum of 26 (as can be seen from Figure 13.1). This is an example of *extrapolation*. Since $x = 50$ is very far from $\bar{x} = 14$, we would expect very wide intervals to result.

The point estimate of $E(y \mid x = 50)$ and point prediction of $y \mid x = 50$ are both

$$\widehat{\beta}_0 + \widehat{\beta}_1 \times 50 \Rightarrow 60 + 5 \times 50 = 310.$$

Also

$$\sum_{i=1}^{10}(x_i - 50)^2 = \sum_{i=1}^{10} x_i^2 - 100\sum_{i=1}^{n} x_i + 10 \times 50^2 = 2528 - 100 \times 140 + 25{,}000 = 13{,}528.$$

(Continued)

Hence a 95% confidence interval for E(y | x = 50) using (13.2) is

$$310 \pm 2.306 \times \sqrt{191.25 \times \frac{13{,}528}{10 \times 567.99}} \quad \Rightarrow \quad (260.78,\ 359.22).$$

A 95% prediction interval for y | x = 50 using (13.3) is

$$310 \pm 2.306 \times \sqrt{191.25 \times \left(1 + \frac{13{,}528}{10 \times 567.99}\right)} \quad \Rightarrow \quad (251.36,\ 368.64).$$

By construction, of course, the prediction interval is wider than the confidence interval (due to the '1+' term), but notice how these intervals are much wider than the corresponding intervals in Example 13.7. We pay a price for this extreme extrapolation due to our ignorance of the relationship between y and x for such a large value of x. Given the higher expected operational costs (staffing, retail area, etc.) it makes the decision whether to open in these very large student areas more difficult - if the realised E(y | x = 50) and y | x = 50 happened to be at the lower bounds of these intervals (if we are unlucky), these might be loss-making coffee shops. Of course, realised outcomes may be at the upper bounds (if we are lucky), potentially making them highly profitable. We conclude that the decision whether or not to open is much *riskier* than when x = 18.

13.7 ELASTICITIES

Elasticities are extremely useful to firms when determining their optimal pricing strategies. By knowing how people will *react* to price changes, they can *predict* (and, therefore, maximise) their future revenues, and hence profits (ignoring costs). Firms can also use estimates of *cross-price elasticities* to find out the extent of other firms' behaviour which will influence their products. For example, if company A's close competitor drastically decreases its prices, company A will most probably also have to cut its own prices in response, otherwise it may risk losing many customers – let the price war commence! Moreover, by knowing the *income elasticity of demand*, firms can adjust their stock decisions to current and expected economic growth rates, and hence households' income growth rates. You would encounter elasticities in great theoretical detail in a microeconomics course; however, we can use linear regression to estimate the *values* which can assist price-setting decisions in practice.

Price elasticity of demand - an economic excursion

The **price elasticity of demand** (PED) is the responsiveness of quantity demanded to changes in the price of a good. Given the law of demand, for most goods and services we would expect the PED to be negative because when the price *increases*, the quantity demanded *decreases* (customers would always wish to pay less), and vice versa. Therefore, the two variables move in *opposite* directions.[1]

[1]On the other hand, the PED for *Giffen* goods (these are inferior goods where people consume more as the price increases) or *Veblen* goods (luxury goods – think conspicuous consumption) would be *positive* because when the price of a Giffen or Veblen good increases, the quantity demanded increases as well. The two variables move in the *same* direction.

We define the PED as follows, where P denotes price and Q_d denotes the quantity demanded:

$$\text{PED} = \frac{\text{percentage change in quantity demanded}}{\text{percentage change in price}} = \frac{\Delta Q_d / Q_d}{\Delta P / P} = \frac{\Delta Q_d}{\Delta P} \times \frac{P}{Q_d}.$$

Note that Δ (the Greek capital letter 'delta') in the above formula denotes 'change'.

- The demand for goods is said to be *elastic* if the percentage change in quantity demanded is *greater* than the percentage change in the price. In this case the PED (ignoring the sign, i.e. in absolute terms) is greater than 1. A 1% increase in price leads to a reduction in quantity demanded of *more* than 1%.
- The demand for goods is said to be *inelastic* if the percentage change in quantity demanded is *less* than the percentage change in the price. In this case the PED (again, in absolute terms) is less than 1. A 1% increase in price leads to a reduction in quantity demanded of less than 1%.
- The demand for goods is said to be *unitary elastic* if the percentage change in quantity demanded is equal to the percentage change in price. In this case the PED (again, in absolute terms) is equal to 1. Therefore a 1% increase in price leads to a reduction in quantity demanded of 1% (the effects offset each other).

So what? Well, we can summarise the relationship between price changes, PED and total revenue as shown in Figure 13.7. Note that in the case of elastic and inelastic demand, there is a dominant effect on total revenue from either P or Q.

So, there is also a close relationship between price elasticity of demand and firms' revenues. The total amount that people spend is exactly the same as the total sales revenue that firms receive. As a result, the formula for price elasticity of demand could be stated in terms of percentage changes in firms' sales revenue rather than in terms of percentage changes in demand.

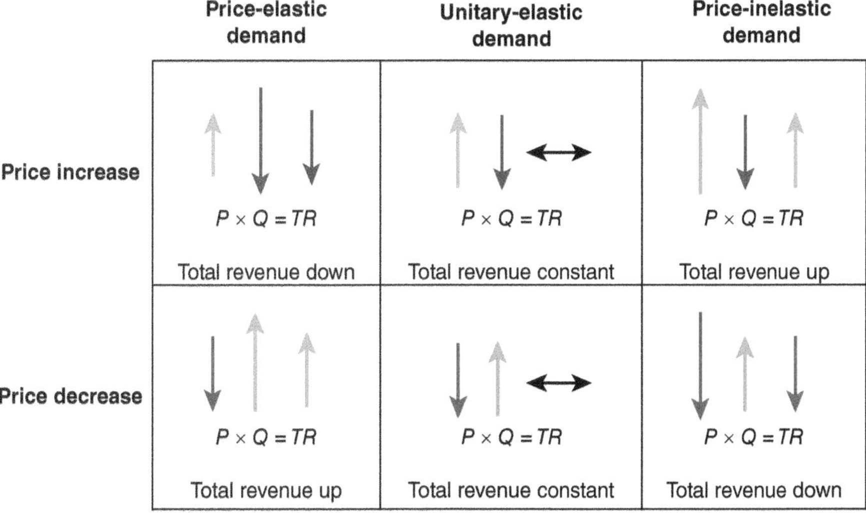

Figure 13.7 The effect of price elasticity of demand on total revenue (TR) when prices change, where $TR = P \times Q$ (total revenue equals price times quantity). Arrow size reflects magnitude of change.

Example 13.9

Recall the convenience store chain 6-Twelve. Given the expectation that consumers are willing to pay a 'convenience premium', that is, higher prices than when purchasing equivalent products at less convenient locations (requiring a time cost to reach and shop there), 6-Twelve could experiment with different prices across its network of stores and monitor how sensitive sales turn out to be.

Having collected data on prices and sales, a simple linear regression could be run to quantify the PED. If a particular product proved to be price inelastic, a price increase could be considered, as the positive effect this would have on total revenue would dominate (exceed) the negative effect from the reduced quantity sold, as per Figure 13.7.

Suppose 6-Twelve experimented with prices on its range of sandwiches. Assume the same price regardless of sandwich filling within a store. Also, assume that the experiment was conducted across 11 'similar' stores - 'similar' in the sense of number of customers, footfall etc. - such that we can reasonably assume to have controlled for all other factors which might affect demand other than price. (Perhaps this is naïvely optimistic, but let's go with the flow!) The price of sandwiches is set at £0.10 price increments ranging from £2.99 to £3.99, i.e. all sandwiches are priced at £2.99 in one store, all are priced £3.09 in another store etc.[2] Since price elasticities deal with *percentage* changes, we should *not* run a regression of the form

$$\text{quantity sold} = \beta_0 + \beta_1 \text{price} + \varepsilon$$

as the estimate of β_1 represents the change in quantity sold for a unit change in price, which is not what we want. Instead, we should take *logarithms* of 'quantity sold' and 'price' and run the regression:

$$\log(\text{quantity sold}) = \beta_0 + \beta_1 \log(\text{price}) + \varepsilon.$$

In this 'log-log' model, the interpretation of β_1 is now the *percentage* change in quantity for a 1 *percentage point* increase in price (i.e. *this* is the PED).

Below are the data and plots of 'quantity sold' against 'price' and 'log(quantity sold)' against 'log(price)', obtained using the `=LN()` Excel function, working with the natural logarithm - which you likely covered in high school mathematics, albeit you may not have appreciated its practical use back then!

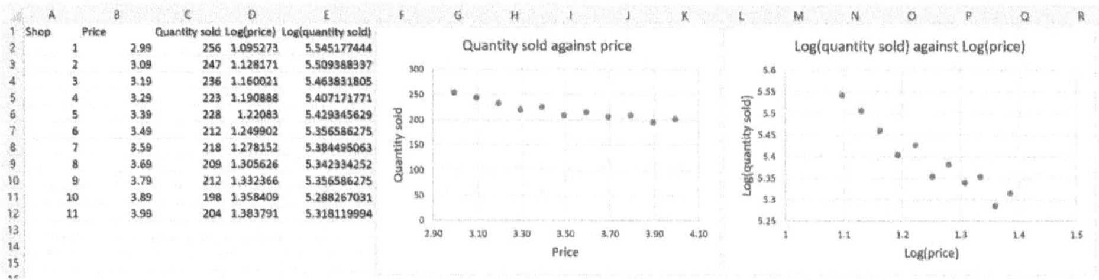

Shop	Price	Quantity sold	Log(price)	Log(quantity sold)
1	2.99	256	1.095273	5.545177444
2	3.09	247	1.128171	5.509388337
3	3.19	236	1.160021	5.463831805
4	3.29	223	1.190888	5.407171771
5	3.39	228	1.22083	5.429345629
6	3.49	212	1.249902	5.356586275
7	3.59	218	1.278152	5.384495063
8	3.69	209	1.305626	5.342334252
9	3.79	212	1.332366	5.356586275
10	3.89	198	1.358409	5.288267031
11	3.99	204	1.383791	5.318119994

If you have ever studied 'Economics 101', you surely would have worked with basic 'supply and demand curves' (or probably *lines*!), for which it is customary to have 'price' on the *y*-axis and 'quantity' on the *x*-axis, *but* this is the wrong way round! Consider demand - consumers choose quantity based (in part)

[2]Note the psychological use of *charm prices*. By setting a price ending in '9' or '99', say, consumers think the price is much lower than it actually is. £2.99 is only £0.01 cheaper than £3.00, but seeing the '2' first (reading left to right) gives an impression of a much cheaper product than seeing a '3' – of course, this is just an illusion!

on the price; they do not choose the price based on the quantity (bartering aside). The dependent variable is quantity and the independent variable is price. By convention we plot the dependent variable on the *y*-axis and the independent variable on the *x*-axis. Unfortunately, (some of) the early economists got muddled between cause and effect (or were simply contrarian), and put price on the *y*-axis and ended up showing 'inverse demand/supply functions' (price as a function of quantity). The above scatter plots show the demand function (we ignore supply in this problem). (For those interested, I recommend S. Gordon (1982). Why did Marshall transpose the axes? *Eastern Economic Journal*, 8(1), 31-45. http://www.jstor.org/stable/40324797)

Running the log-log model regression in Excel returns the following output:

	A	B	C	D	E	F	G
1	SUMMARY OUTPUT						
2							
3	*Regression Statistics*						
4	Multiple R	0.951808364					
5	R Square	0.905939162					
6	Adjusted R Square	0.895487957					
7	Standard Error	0.025974168					
8	Observations	11					
9							
10	ANOVA						
11		*df*	*SS*	*MS*	*F*	*Significance F*	
12	Regression	1	0.058481163	0.058481163	86.68275327	6.46468E-06	
13	Residual	9	0.006071917	0.000674657			
14	Total	10	0.06455308				
15							
16		*Coefficients*	*Standard Error*	*t Stat*	*P-value*	*Lower 95%*	*Upper 95%*
17	Intercept	6.396875083	0.107344954	59.59176336	5.31738E-13	6.154043927	6.639706239
18	Log(price)	-0.800115175	0.085938181	-9.310357311	6.46468E-06	-0.994520847	-0.605709502

The estimated model is

$$\widehat{\log(\text{quantity sold})} = 6.39 - 0.80\log(\text{price}),$$

so we estimate the price elasticity of demand to be 0.80 (we usually express elasticities in terms of absolute value). So, a 1% *increase* in the price of sandwiches results in a 0.8% *decrease* in demand for sandwiches. Since the PED is less than 1 (in absolute value), sandwiches have *inelastic demand*. As such, 6-Twelve could consider increasing the price of its sandwiches as the price effect on total revenue will be greater than the effect from a reduction in demand (see Figure 13.7).

6-Twelve could consider researching demand elasticities for other products, and could even explore cross-price elasticites of demand for substitute and complementary products. We will explore this using multiple regression in Chapter 14.

In passing, note that $R^2 = 0.9059$, hence this is a very good explanatory model, indicating that demand for sandwiches is almost exclusively determined by price. The PED estimate is highly significant, with a *p*-value of 6.46×10^{-6}; although as we would expect β_1 to be negative by the law of demand (sandwiches are neither a Giffen nor Veblen good), we could have performed a lower-tailed test. Since $\beta_1 < 0$ this means we would divide the *p*-value by 2, but this makes no practical difference in this instance (3.23×10^{-6} is also *(very!) highly significant*).

Now, let's apply regression analysis to the world of finance. ('Greed is good'. Discuss.)

Example 13.10

We apply the simple linear regression model to study the relationship between two series of financial returns. This regression model is an example of the *capital asset pricing model*, which is a simple asset pricing model commonly used in finance given by:

$$y_t = \alpha + \beta x_t + \varepsilon_t,$$

where y_t is a stock return and x_t is a market return at time t, for $t = 1, 2, ..., T$ (note the use of t for 'time', given the time-series nature of returns, with T being the time-series equivalent of n). Here we are using the *finance-specific parameters* α and β in place of our usual β_0 and β_1. The 'market return' should be that of the relevant benchmark market index, typically the stock index on which the specific stock is listed. For example, Lloyds Bank PLC (one of the UK's largest banking groups, and a *bellwether stock* of the health of the UK economy) is a constituent of the FTSE 100 index, while Tesla Inc. is part of the S&P 500 (at the time of writing!).

The total risk of the stock is

$$\frac{1}{T}\sum_{t=1}^{T}(y_t - \bar{y})^2 = \frac{1}{T}\sum_{t=1}^{T}(\hat{y}_t - \bar{y})^2 + \frac{1}{T}\sum_{t=1}^{T}(y_t - \hat{y}_t)^2.$$

The market-related (or systematic) risk is

$$\frac{1}{T}\sum_{t=1}^{T}(\hat{y}_t - \bar{y})^2 = \frac{1}{T}\hat{\beta}^2\sum_{t=1}^{T}(x_t - \bar{x})^2.$$

The firm-specific risk is

$$\frac{1}{T}\sum_{t=1}^{T}(y_t - \hat{y}_t)^2.$$

Note the following observations:

(i) β measures the market-related (or systematic) risk of the stock.
(ii) Market-related risk is unavoidable, while firm-specific risk may be 'diversified away' through *hedging*.
(iii) Variance is a simple measure (and one of the most frequently used) of risk in finance.

So, knowing the beta of a stock helps investors judge how *risky* it is and whether they wish to add it to their portfolio. Managers of publicly listed companies might also keep a close eye on their own company's beta to judge how risky the market perceives the company to be, and whether that is a fair reflection of their stewardship of the company!

Daily prices are definitely *not* independent as they exhibit *serial correlation* - high (low) prices tend to follow high (low) prices. This is problematic from a regression model assumption perspective (take an econometrics course to better understand why). However, daily *returns* may be thought of as a sequence of uncorrelated random variables. Stock returns are defined as

$$\text{return} = \frac{\text{current price} - \text{previous price}}{\text{previous price}} \approx \ln\left(\frac{\text{current price}}{\text{previous price}}\right)$$

when the difference between the two prices is small.

Once we have a sufficient history of returns data of the specific stock of interest and the appropriate market benchmark, we can simply regress the stock's returns on the market's returns, and the estimate of the slope coefficient, β, is the beta of the stock!

By definition, the beta of the market is 1 (regressing *x* on *x*, i.e. regressing *x* on itself, inevitably produces a perfect positive correlation with a slope of 1), so a stock's risk relative to the market should be with respect to 1. Hence:

- if $\beta < 1$, this is a *defensive stock* - for example, if $\beta = 0.5$ then if the underlying market index went up by 1%, the stock would go up by only 0.5% (not great!) but if the market went down by 1% (which it can!), this is muted as a fall of only 0.5% in the stock (phew!) - hence defensive.
- if $\beta > 1$, this is a *risky stock* - for example, if $\beta = 2$ then if the underlying market index went up by 1%, the stock would go up 2% (great) but if the market went down by 1%, this is amplified as a fall of 2% in the stock (ouch!) - hence risky.

Let's consider two FTSE 100 stocks: Lloyds Bank PLC (traded with ticker symbol LLOY) and GlaxoSmithKline PLC, a global health-care company (traded with ticker symbol GSK). We use daily returns throughout 2021 and regress these against the contemporaneous FTSE 100 daily returns (i.e. with corresponding matching dates). A subset of data on prices and returns for LLOY, GSK and the FTSE 100 is as follows:

	A	B	C	D	E	F	G
1	Date	LLOY	GSK	FTSE 100	LLOY return	GSK return	FTSE 100 return
2	04/01/2021	34.84	1376.00	6571.88	0.010619948	-0.000436029	0.006142839
3	05/01/2021	35.21	1375.40	6612.25	0.055382024	0.02399302	0.034724942
4	06/01/2021	37.16	1408.40	6841.86	-0.007265904	-0.007384283	0.002207002
5	07/01/2021	36.89	1398.00	6856.96	-0.00162643	0.007439216	0.002377147
6	08/01/2021	36.83	1408.40	6873.26	-0.018191692	-0.009514359	-0.010879844
7	11/01/2021	36.16	1395.00	6798.48	0.016039823	-0.020071685	-0.006526459
8	12/01/2021	36.74	1367.00	6754.11	-0.013609145	0.004096544	-0.001271818
9	13/01/2021	36.24	1372.60	6745.52	0.005794702	0.015153758	0.008367035
10	14/01/2021	36.45	1393.40	6801.96	-0.01399177	0.014496879	-0.00973984
11	15/01/2021	35.94	1413.60	6735.71	0.006399555	-0.009620809	-0.002235844

Note that to run the regressions in Excel including the row names (the 'labels') the returns data should be immediately below the row names. Therefore, the returns actually correspond to the date in the row *below*. For example, the return on LLOY on 05/01/2021 is

$$\frac{35.21 - 34.84}{34.84} = 0.010619948.$$

(Continued)

We first calculate the beta of LLOY:

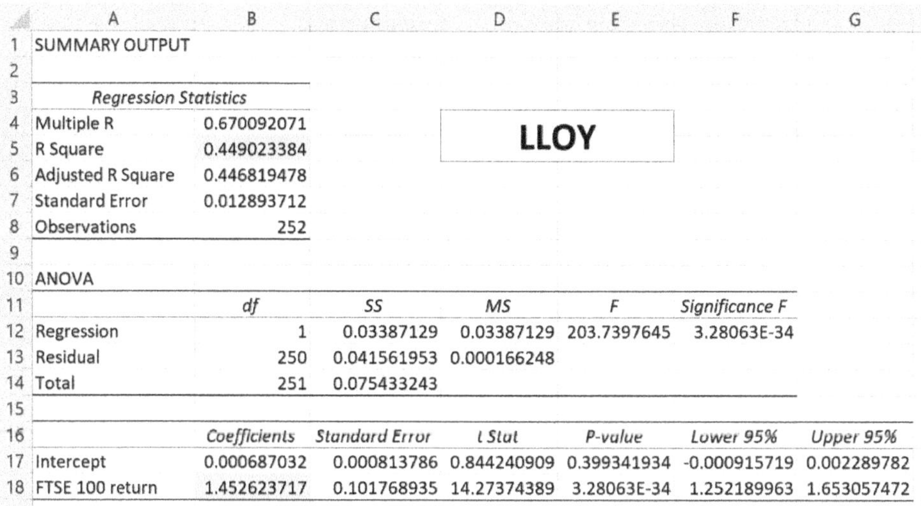

	A	B	C	D	E	F	G
1	SUMMARY OUTPUT						
2							
3	*Regression Statistics*						
4	Multiple R	0.670092071		LLOY			
5	R Square	0.449023384					
6	Adjusted R Square	0.446819478					
7	Standard Error	0.012893712					
8	Observations	252					
9							
10	ANOVA						
11		*df*	*SS*	*MS*	*F*	*Significance F*	
12	Regression	1	0.03387129	0.03387129	203.7397645	3.28063E-34	
13	Residual	250	0.041561953	0.000166248			
14	Total	251	0.075433243				
15							
16		*Coefficients*	*Standard Error*	*t Stat*	*P-value*	*Lower 95%*	*Upper 95%*
17	Intercept	0.000687032	0.000813786	0.844240909	0.399341934	-0.000915719	0.002289782
18	FTSE 100 return	1.452623717	0.101768935	14.27374389	3.28063E-34	1.252189963	1.653057472

From the regression output the beta is 1.45, indicating that this is quite a risky stock (relative to the market benchmark of 1). Note that $R^2 = 0.4490$, indicating that just over half the variation in LLOY returns is *not* explained by FTSE 100 returns. This should not be surprising - bank stocks are likely to be affected by many factors, in particular interest rates. (In March 2023, financial markets were rocked with the bank failures/takeovers of Silicon Valley Bank (SVB) and Credit Suisse. In particular, SVB's failure can be attributed to a 'maturity mismatch', itself exacerbated by a period of sustained rising interest rates.)

Turning to GSK:

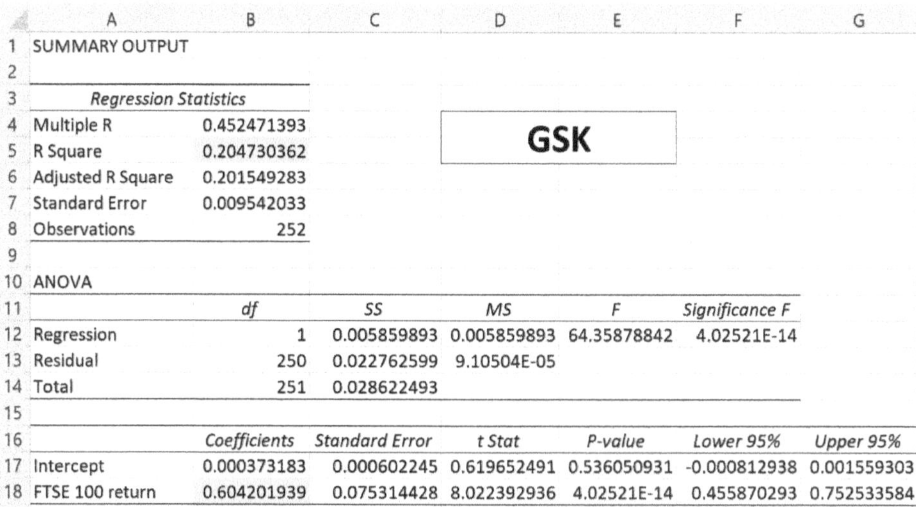

	A	B	C	D	E	F	G
1	SUMMARY OUTPUT						
2							
3	*Regression Statistics*						
4	Multiple R	0.452471393		GSK			
5	R Square	0.204730362					
6	Adjusted R Square	0.201549283					
7	Standard Error	0.009542033					
8	Observations	252					
9							
10	ANOVA						
11		*df*	*SS*	*MS*	*F*	*Significance F*	
12	Regression	1	0.005859893	0.005859893	64.35878842	4.02521E-14	
13	Residual	250	0.022762599	9.10504E-05			
14	Total	251	0.028622493				
15							
16		*Coefficients*	*Standard Error*	*t Stat*	*P-value*	*Lower 95%*	*Upper 95%*
17	Intercept	0.000373183	0.000602245	0.619652491	0.536050931	-0.000812938	0.001559303
18	FTSE 100 return	0.604201939	0.075314428	8.022392936	4.02521E-14	0.455870293	0.752533584

From the regression output the beta is 0.60, indicating that this is quite a defensive stock (again, relative to the market benchmark of 1). Note that R^2 = 0.2047, indicating that nearly 80% of the variation in GSK returns is *not* explained by FTSE 100 returns. This should not be surprising either - think about the variables which the returns of a global health-care company would be sensitive to.

In practice, we would expect the beta of a stock to change over time, reflecting its variable level of risk. Also, the computed beta would be sensitive to the time horizon of the dataset (we could have used 5 years, say, instead of 1 year) and the frequency of the returns (we could have used quarterly, monthly or weekly periods, say, instead of daily).

13.8 TESTS OF ASSUMPTIONS AND ROBUSTNESS

13.8.1 Outliers

A natural move in the analysis of any dataset would be to look at the residuals, that is, the differences between what we observe (the y_i values) and what our model predicts (the $\hat{y}_i$ values, i.e. the values of $\hat{\beta}_0 + \hat{\beta}_1 x_i$). So, for $i = 1, 2, \ldots, n$, the ith residual is defined to be

$$e_i = y_i - \hat{y}_i = y_i - \hat{\beta}_0 - \hat{\beta}_1 x_i.$$

Plots of these residuals may reveal further relationships in the data and the presence of 'wild' values may suggest deleting specific observations, that is, excluding selected observations as *outliers* or *anomalous points*.

One method of detecting outliers is to compute the *standardised residual* for each data point. This is the ratio of e_i to its (estimated) standard error. Standardised residuals greater than 2 would be regarded as suspicious, and values greater than 3 would strongly suggest an outlier. This links to the 'empirical rules' of the normal distribution, outlined in Section 5.15.3.

More appropriate residuals may also be calculated using 'dropped case' techniques, such that a residual does not relate to a regression in which its own data are used. This is a simple example of a technique known as *cross-validation analysis*.

13.8.2 Influential points

Dropping points from the regression and watching the changes in $\hat{\beta}_0$, $\hat{\beta}_1$ and $\hat{\sigma}^2$ gives information about the influence of a point.

13.8.3 Robust regression

Dropping 'wild' and 'influential' points may, with care, produce a more *robust* result – a result less liable to perturbations than using all of the data. Trimming the x-values may lead to the same result.

13.8.4 Precision weighting (weighted least squares)

When we are certain that Var(ε_i) changes with values of x in a systematic way – contrary to one of our model assumptions – then we have to write Var(ε_i) = σ_i^2 , since it can differ for different values of the subscript i. In this case, all the regression formulae are as before, but *all* data summations are replaced by *weighted* sums using $1/\sigma_i^2$ as the weighting. For example,

$$\sum_{i=1}^{n} x_i \text{ is replaced by } \sum_{i=1}^{n} \frac{x_i}{\sigma_i^2},$$

$$\sum_{i=1}^{n} x_i^2 \text{ is replaced by } \sum_{i=1}^{n} \frac{x_i^2}{\sigma_i^2}$$

and

$$n \text{ is replaced by } \sum_{i=1}^{n} \frac{1}{\sigma_i^2}.$$

However, although we mention these potential complications to the topics so far discussed, we shall not pursue them any further. Just be aware that the simple linear regression model presented is the most basic form of linear regression analysis. Enter stage left an econometrics course!

13.9 CHAPTER OVERVIEW

This chapter has introduced the simple linear regression model – a powerful tool for explaining the variation in a dependent variable, y, of interest. Our focus has been on the 'simple' model as we have restricted y to depend on only one variable – this will be relaxed in Chapter 14. We have seen how to estimate the regression model parameters, assess the significance of the explanatory variable, quantify the explanatory power of the model, and use the model for prediction purposes.

13.10 KEY VOCABULARY

ANOVA regression table
Coefficient of determination, R^2
Confidence interval
Dependent (response) variable
Elasticity
Error term
Extrapolation
Independent (explanatory) variable
Interpolation
Least-squares estimation
Line of best fit
Parameters
Prediction interval
Price elasticity of demand
Regression ANOVA decomposition
Residual

13.11 EXERCISES

13.11.1 Test your understanding

1. What is the difference between a dependent variable and an independent variable?
2. In a simple linear regression model, what do β_0 and β_1 represent?
3. Why do we include an error term in a regression model? Does it have any assumptions?
4. Which optimisation technique is used to estimate β_0 and β_1?
5. Does it make sense to suppress β_0 to be equal to zero? Justify your view.
6. What is a residual?
7. Explain the regression ANOVA decomposition.
8. What useful information does an ANOVA regression table provide?
9. Explain how the coefficient of determination is calculated, and how it should be interpreted.
10. Outline the F test for regression ANOVA.
11. Outline the t tests for β_0 and β_1, respectively.
12. Outline how to construct confidence intervals for β_0 and β_1, respectively.
13. Three equivalent tests were presented. When would you argue to use one over another?
14. For a given x, what is the difference between a confidence interval for $E(y \mid x)$ and a prediction interval for $y \mid x$? Why is the prediction interval wider?
15. Which is riskier, interpolation or extrapolation? Justify your view.
16. How can a simple linear regression model be used to estimate an elasticity?
17. In a simple linear regression model of the form $y = \beta_0 + \beta_1 x + \varepsilon$, where the dependent variable is income (in dollars) and the independent variable is age (in years), the value of β_0 was estimated to be –203.56.

    (a) Interpret this estimate of β_0.
    (b) Explain why such an estimate could occur if you are told that age and income are highly correlated in the sample data used to run the regression.

18. A car insurance company would like to examine the relationship between driving experience and insurance premium. For this reason, a random sample of ten drivers is taken and their years of driving experience (x) and monthly insurance premium (y, in pounds) is recorded. The data are shown in the table below.

Driver	1	2	3	4	5	6	7	8	9	10
Driving experience (x)	6	3	11	10	15	6	25	16	15	20
Insurance premium (y)	66	88	51	70	44	56	42	60	45	40

    (a) Determine the sample correlation coefficient and interpret its value.
    (b) Determine the least-squares line of y on x.
    (c) Based on the regression equation in part (b), what will be the predicted monthly insurance premium for a driver with 12 years of experience? Will you trust this value? Justify your answer.

19 The data below show the yearly expenditure (in thousands of pounds) by a cosmetics company on advertising a particular brand of perfume.

Year (x)	1	2	3	4	5	6	7	8
Expenditure (y)	170	170	275	340	435	510	740	832

(a) Fit a regression line to the data and report a 95% confidence interval for its slope.
(b) Perform an F test using the ANOVA table and use this to compute the R^2 statistic for the fit. Comment on the goodness of fit of the linear regression model.
(c) Predict the expenditure for year 9 and calculate a 95% prediction interval for the actual expenditure.

20 A company would like to predict how its trainees in sales will perform based on the results of an aptitude test that is given to them at the beginning of the training. The table below contains the test scores (x) and the values of the sales (y, in hundreds of dollars) for nine randomly selected trainees during the first month of working at the company.

Trainee	A	B	C	D	E	F	G	H	I
x	1.8	2.6	2.8	3.4	3.6	4.2	4.8	5.2	5.4
y	5.4	6.4	6.0	6.2	6.8	7.0	7.6	7.3	7.6

(a) Produce a scatter diagram of these data.
(b) Determine the sample correlation coefficient. Interpret its value.
(c) Report the least-squares line of y on x.
(d) Based on the regression model above, what amount of sales during the first month would you expect from someone who scored 4 in this aptitude test? Would you trust this value? Justify your answer.

21 The director of a local tourism authority would like to know whether a family's annual expenditure on recreation (y), measured in thousands of dollars, is related to their annual income (x), also measured in thousands of dollars. In order to explore this potential relationship, the variables x and y were recorded for 10 randomly selected families who visited the area last year. The results were as follows:

Family	1	2	3	4	5	6	7	8	9	10
x	41.2	50.1	52.0	62.0	44.5	37.7	73.5	37.5	56.7	65.2
y	2.4	2.7	2.8	8.0	3.1	2.1	12.1	2.0	3.9	8.9

(a) Draw a scatter diagram of these data.
(b) Determine the sample correlation coefficient. Interpret your findings.
(c) Determine the least-squares line of y on x.
(d) Do you find the analyses in parts (b) and (c) appropriate? Justify your answer and suggest any alternative ways to model the relationship between x and y.

22 The yearly profits (in thousands of pounds) made by a company over a period of eight consecutive years are shown below.

Year	1	2	3	4	5	6	7	8
Profit	18	21	34	31	44	46	60	75

(a) Fit a straight line to these data and compute a 95% confidence interval for the 'true' yearly increase in profits.
(b) The company accountant forecasts the profits for year 9 to be £90,000. Is this forecast reasonable if it is based on the above data?

23 The manager of a store selling shoes is looking into the association between daily sales (in hundreds of dollars) in the store, y, and the number of customers who visited the store in that day, x. For this reason, in 10 days selected at random the variables x and y were recorded. They appear in the table below:

Days	1	2	3	4	5	6	7	8	9	10
Number of customers (x)	90	92	50	74	78	88	87	51	53	42
Sales (y)	11.2	11.1	6.8	9.2	9.4	10.1	9.4	7.7	8.2	6.1

(a) Draw a scatter diagram of these data.
(b) Determine the sample correlation coefficient. Interpret your findings.
(c) Determine the least-squares line of y on x.
(d) Suppose that you observe more data and when you draw the corresponding scatter diagram a nonlinear association is revealed. Discuss how this can be interpreted in the context of the problem.

24 A study into used cars examined whether there is a relationship between their prices (in thousands of dollars) and their mileages (in thousands of miles) when they were sold at auction. A random sample of $n = 20$ sales was collected and a linear regression was run.

An analyst summarised Excel output for the linear regression model as below.

Predictor	Coefficient	Standard error	*t* statistic	*p*-value
Constant	17.000	0.3437	49.4606	1.10×10^{-20}
Mileage	−0.055	0.0093	−5.9792	1.18×10^{-5}

Residual MS = 0.3192 R-sq = 66.51%.

(a) Calculate and interpret the sample correlation coefficient.
(b) Write down the equation of the estimated regression line.
(c) What conclusion can you draw about the connection between the two variables?
(d) A used car which has been driven for 35,000 miles will soon be sold at auction. What is its expected selling price to the nearest dollar?

13.11.2 Practice with Excel

Head over to the companion website for Excel examples and screencasts!

14

MULTIPLE REGRESSION

Chapter contents

Chapter level: ***Intermediate***

Source: Photo by 652234 via Pixabay.

Key concepts

- Adjusted R^2
- Omitted-variable bias
- Dummy variables

Chapter value

Aspects of multiple regression model building are set out, including modelling challenges.

Key takeaway

We face trade-offs between model complexity and explanatory power, as well as redundant and omitted variables.

Chapter outline

What drives sales? Price? Marketing spend? Brand image? All of the above, and more? Whether it's sales, market share, customer perception or any other *y* of interest, we would expect it to have several determinants, that is, we need to consider several, or *multiple*, independent variables. Our work in Chapter 13 has provided a great base on which to build, and we now incorporate multiple *regressors* into our model, each of which is expected to exert some influence on *y*.

With *multiple regression* we can accommodate quantitative *and* categorical regressors, and even model interactions between them - for example, the effectiveness of marketing spend may depend on the media channel used. Fortunately, there are economies of scale having studied simple linear regression (such as R^2 and assessing statistical significance), but also some new challenges related to multiple regression model building. So, on your marks, get set, regress!

Learning outcomes

After completing this chapter, you should be able to:

- summarise the linear regression model with several explanatory variables, and explain the interpretation of estimated coefficients
- perform statistical inference on estimated regression models
- report explanatory power using R^2, and use adjusted R^2 to compare the relative performance of regression models of different complexities
- consider analytical issues of variable misspecification, including omitted-variable bias
- construct interaction variables and dummy variables
- be aware of the consequences of multicollinearity
- explain the basic mechanisms of model selection techniques.

Motivational case: Mind the (pay) gap

Human resources (HR) at a blue chip company received concerns raised by some employees about gender discrimination in pay. Given the risk of aggrieved employees seeking an employment tribunal to air their grievances, HR staff want to undertake some analysis now to see whether there is a basis to claims of pay discrimination based on gender. They realise that there will inevitably be variation in salaries of staff, but they expect many factors would likely explain this variation, such as tenure (length of service) with the company, and hence seniority of role, as well as qualifications. However, pay should not be determined based on gender.

If the company were found to be guilty of such discrimination, management are concerned about negative publicity from an employment tribunal and the inevitable risk of reputational damage to the company name. How should HR investigate to see whether there is any evidence of such pay discrimination?

14.1 INTRODUCTION

During our study of analysis of variance in Chapter 12, we began with one-way ANOVA whereby one factor (a categorical variable, such as 'advertising strategy' in Example 12.1) could be used to explain variation in a quantitative dependent variable (such as 'quantity sold'). We then extended this to the two-way ANOVA model to allow for two factors (categorical variables, such as 'section of a website' and 'day of advertisement' in Example 12.6) to explain variation in a quantitative dependent variable (such as 'number of enquiries generated by advertising'). More generally, we could consider an *n*-way ANOVA, with *n* factors.

Simple linear regression (in Chapter 13) is analogous to one-way ANOVA except that the independent variable has to be quantitative. Multiple regression is analogous to *n*-way ANOVA, where we may consider a mixture of quantitative and categorical regressors. This is summarised in Table 14.1.

Table 14.1 Comparison of ANOVA and regression techniques.

	One-way ANOVA	*n*-way ANOVA	Simple linear regression	Multiple regression
Number of dependent variables and type	1 quantitative	1 quantitative	1 quantitative	1 quantitative
Number of independent variable(s) and type	1 categorical	≥ 2 categorical	1 quantitative	≥ 2 all quantitative or mix of quantitative and categorical

As can be seen, common to all these analyses is a single quantitative dependent variable – such as sales. This variable exhibits variation (e.g. sales will fluctuate in practice), and we seek to understand the driving factors which explain this variation (such as advertising spend and amount of discounting). The approaches simply vary in terms of the *number* and *type* of these independent (i.e. explanatory) variables.

14.2 VISUALISING RELATIONSHIPS BETWEEN THREE VARIABLES

Consider first a multiple regression model with *two* quantitative independent variables, x_1 and x_2, since this can be visualised in three dimensions, that is, using a system of three coordinates in (x_1, x_2, y) space, while more variables require higher-order dimensions that we cannot visualise. For a three-variable model, the relationship between the three variables (three dimensions) is modelled using a *plane* (two dimensions; think of it like a sheet of paper held in the air) rather than a *line*. However, we still refer to such a model as a *linear* model.

Our model is

$$y = \beta_0 + \beta_1 x_1 + \beta_2 x_2 + \varepsilon, \tag{14.1}$$

where we continue to assume $\varepsilon \sim N(0, \sigma^2)$ as in Chapter 13 (i.e. the error term is a normal random variable with zero mean and constant variance). In (14.1), we have the following quantities:

- β_0 is the intercept, that is, the expected value of y when $x_1 = 0$ and $x_2 = 0$ (note that the intercept is often of no interest since it is rare for $x_1 = 0$ and $x_2 = 0$ in practice)
- β_1 is the change in y when x_1 is changed by one unit, *while controlling for* x_2 (i.e. with x_2 held constant)
- β_2 is the change in y when x_2 is changed by one unit, *while controlling for* x_1 (i.e. with x_1 held constant).

Figure 14.1 shows an example of *no relationship* between y, and x_1 and x_2. In this (extreme) case, the model is simply a horizontal plane (like a sheet of paper, remember) which passes through the point ($x_1 = 0, x_2 = 0, y = \beta_0$).

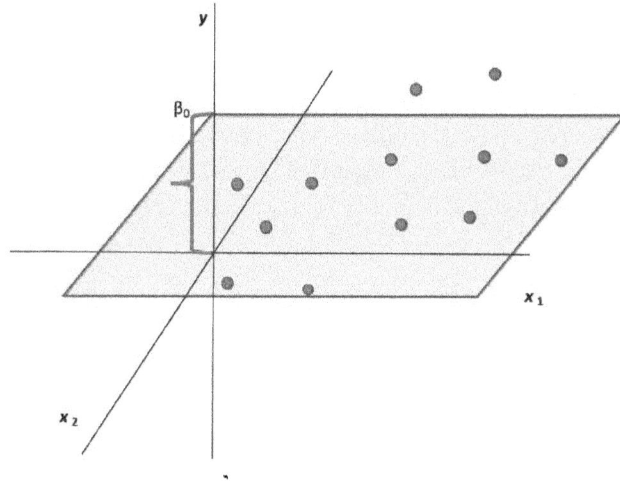

Figure 14.1 No relationship between y, x_1 and x_2.

Of course, in practice we would look to choose variables for x_1 and x_2 that would plausibly be related with y!

Example 14.1

If y = *sales*, then we may suppose y is influenced by x_1 = advertising spend and x_2 = discount amount. The model

sales = $\beta_0 + \beta_1$advertising spend + $\beta_2$discount amount + ε

(Continued)

is then a sloping plane (like a sloping sheet of paper), as shown in Figure 14.2, which passes through the points:

- $(x_1 = 0, x_2 = 0, y = \beta_0)$, that is, y represents expected sales when there is no advertising spend, and no discount
- $(x_1 = 1, x_2 = 0, y = \beta_0 + \beta_1)$, that is, y represents sales when there is 1 unit of advertising spend, and no discount.
- $(x_1 = 0, x_2 = 1, y = \beta_0 + \beta_2)$, that is, y sales when there is no advertising spend, and 1 unit of discount.

Let's now dive straight in to running an empirical regression analysis in Excel.

14.2.1 Three-variable regression in Excel

We will now demonstrate how to run a three-variable regression in Excel to illustrate the effects of different marketing instruments on the weekly sales volume of a certain food product in a supermarket over a two-year period, hence n = 104 (i.e. two 52-week years). There are observations on the following variables: *lsales* = logarithm of weekly sales, *price* = promotion price and *advertising* = advertising spend.

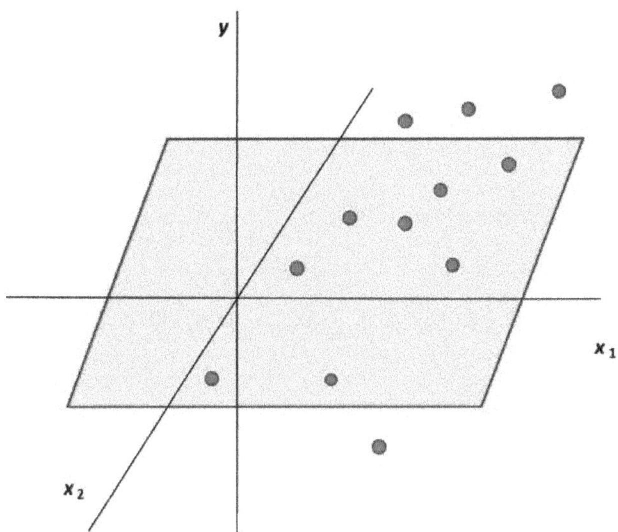

Figure 14.2 A (linear) relationship between y, and x_1 and x_2.

We first show scatter plots between *lsales* and each of the proposed independent variables in Figure 14.3. What can we observe from these pairwise plots?

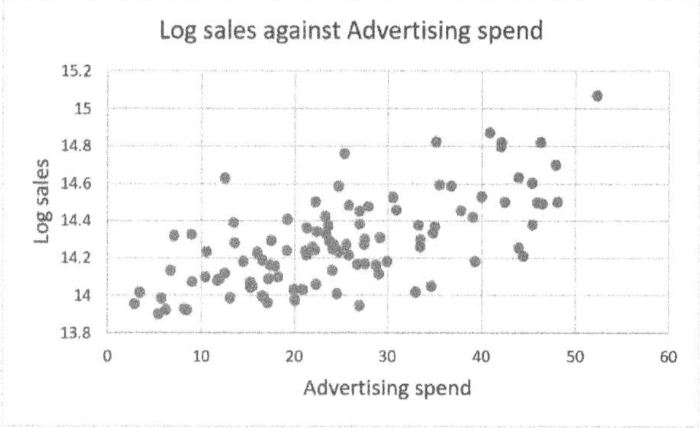

Figure 14.3 Scatter plots of log sales against promotion price (top) and log sales against advertising spend (bottom).

- There is a *negative correlation* between log sales and promotion price, as we might expect by the law of demand – price up, sales down.
- There is a *positive correlation* between log sales and advertising spend, also as we might expect – more advertising spend, higher sales.

Why use the *logarithm* of weekly sales, instead of just weekly sales? *Nonlinear transformations* can be useful if there is evidence of curvature in bivariate scatter plots. Examples of nonlinear transformations are taking the *logarithm* (e.g. $\log(y)$) and taking the *square root* (e.g. $\sqrt{y}$). These may be applied to the dependent and/or independent variables, exercising judgement as appropriate.

The linear nature of the relationships seen in Figure 14.3 justifies our applying the logarithmic transformation to sales. For comparison, an (admittedly subtle) curvature can be seen when we consider sales, rather than log sales, especially with respect to promotion price as shown in Figure 14.4.

We now regress *lsales* on *price* and *advertising*. Our regression model is:

$$lsales = \beta_0 + \beta_1 price + \beta_2 advertising + \varepsilon.$$

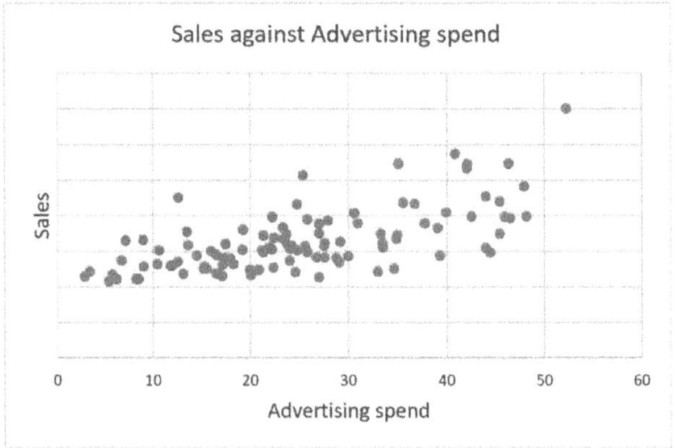

Figure 14.4 Scatter plots of sales against promotion price (top) and sales against advertising spend (bottom).

Note that in terms of data arrangement, when conducting multiple regression in Excel, all data of the independent variables must be in *adjacent* columns such that the ranges for these can be expressed using a data array in the `Input X Range` item of the dialog box, as shown in Figure 14.5 with the array reference `$A$1:$B$105`.

The regression output returned is shown in Figure 14.6.

The estimated regression model makes use of the estimated coefficients, returned in cell range `B17:B19` in Figure 14.6. We have, to three decimal places (with standard errors of the respective parameter estimates in parentheses):

$$\widehat{lsales} = \underset{(0.291)}{17.047} - \underset{(0.081)}{0.870} \times price + \underset{(0.001)}{0.010} \times advertising.$$

We note that $\hat{\beta}_1 = -0.870 < 0$, consistent with the negative correlation seen between *lsales* and *price* in Figure 14.3. Similarly, $\hat{\beta}_2 = 0.010 > 0$, consistent with the positive correlation seen between *lsales* and *advertising*.

We proceed by performing a *joint test of significance* by testing

$$H_0 : \beta_1 = \beta_2 = 0 \text{ versus } H_1 : \beta_1 \neq 0 \text{ and/or } \beta_2 \neq 0$$

that is, if H_0 is true, then changes in *price* and *advertising* have no effect on *lsales* (the model is essentially useless), while if we can reject H_0 then at least one of *price* and *advertising* is significant in explaining *lsales*.

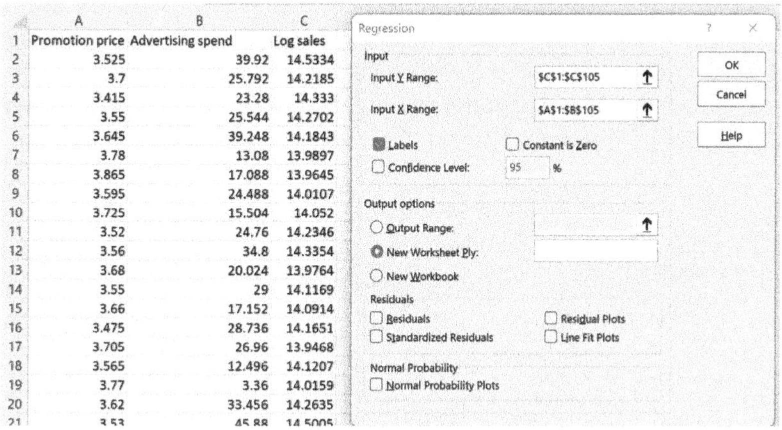

	A	B	C
1	Promotion price	Advertising spend	Log sales
2	3.525	39.92	14.5334
3	3.7	25.792	14.2185
4	3.415	23.28	14.333
5	3.55	25.544	14.2702
6	3.645	39.248	14.1843
7	3.78	13.08	13.9897
8	3.865	17.088	13.9645
9	3.595	24.488	14.0107
10	3.725	15.504	14.052
11	3.52	24.76	14.2346
12	3.56	34.8	14.3354
13	3.68	20.024	13.9764
14	3.55	29	14.1169
15	3.66	17.152	14.0914
16	3.475	28.736	14.1651
17	3.705	26.96	13.9468
18	3.565	12.496	14.1207
19	3.77	3.36	14.0159
20	3.62	33.456	14.2635

Figure 14.5 Excel regression dialog box for a multiple regression. Note that the independent variables are in the adjacent columns A and B, respectively.

The test statistic value of this *F* test (the test statistic follows an *F* distribution under H_0) is given in the regression ANOVA table in cell `E12` as 145.518, with a corresponding *p*-value of 1.80×10^{-30}, which is tiny! Hence H_0 is rejected at any reasonable significance level and so we have *(very!) strong evidence* that at least one of β_1 and β_2 is not equal to zero. Given the scatter plots in Figure 14.3 we are perhaps not that surprised by this result!

Clearly, knowing that 'at least one of β_1 and β_2 is not equal to zero' does not tell us whether it is one of them or both of them. We need to investigate further. So next we consider individual *t* tests of

$$H_0 : \beta_1 = 0 \text{ versus } H_1 : \beta_1 \neq 0$$

and

$$H_0 : \beta_2 = 0 \text{ versus } H_1 : \beta_2 \neq 0$$

to look for statistical evidence for the significance of *price* and *advertising*, respectively. The respective test statistic values (i.e. *t* values) are

$$\frac{\hat{\beta}_1}{\text{standard error of } \hat{\beta}_1} = \frac{-0.870}{0.081} = -10.715$$

$$\frac{\hat{\beta}_2}{\text{standard error of } \hat{\beta}_2} = \frac{0.010}{0.001} = 9.081$$

(cells D18:D19) with (tiny!) p-values of 2.395×10^{-18} and 9.473×10^{-15} (cells E18:E19), respectively, indicating that both slope coefficients are non-zero.

Technically, since we would have expected $\beta_1 < 0$ and $\beta_2 > 0$ *a priori* (i.e. before looking at the data *lsales* and *price* would be expected to have a negative relationship; *lsales* and *advertising* a positive relationship), these t tests could have been conducted as *lower-tailed* and *upper-tailed* tests, respectively. Since $\hat{\beta}_1 < 0$ and $\hat{\beta}_2 > 0$ (i.e. the estimated coefficients have the expected signs), to perform these as one-tailed tests the p-values in cells E18:E19 can simply be divided by 2. However, it is clear that this makes no practical difference to the statistical significance of the tests as the two-tailed p-values are already so tiny!

	A	B	C	D	E	F	G
1	SUMMARY OUTPUT						
2							
3	*Regression Statistics*						
4	Multiple R	0.861608991					
5	R Square	0.742370053					
6	Adjusted R Square	0.73726847					
7	Standard Error	0.125200468					
8	Observations	104					
9							
10	ANOVA						
11		*df*	*SS*	*MS*	*F*	*Significance F*	
12	Regression	2	4.562022068	2.281011034	145.5175849	1.80018E-30	
13	Residual	101	1.583190888	0.015675157			
14	Total	103	6.145212955				
15							
16		*Coefficients*	*Standard Error*	*t Stat*	*P-value*	*Lower 95%*	*Upper 95%*
17	Intercept	17.046928	0.290993165	58.5818845	8.76729E-80	16.46967584	17.62418017
18	Promotion price	-0.870229784	0.081214997	-10.71513661	2.395E-18	-1.031338491	-0.709121077
19	Advertising spend	0.009937297	0.001094312	9.080861417	9.47269E-15	0.007766476	0.012108118

Figure 14.6 Result of the multiple regression of log sales on promotion price and advertising spend.

Turning to the estimated coefficients, $\hat{\beta}_1 = -0.870$ indicates that a 1-unit increase in the promotion price *decreases* weekly sales by 87%, *controlling for advertising spend*; clearly weekly sales at this supermarket are price-sensitive! Also, $\hat{\beta}_2 = 0.010$ indicates that a 1-unit increase in advertising spend *increases* weekly sales by 1%, *controlling for promotion price*. Note that our interpretation cites the *percentage* change in weekly sales; this is due to the use of the *logarithm* of weekly sales, rather than simply weekly sales.

We could also compute 95% confidence intervals for the regression coefficients (which are conveniently returned in the Excel output in cell range F17:G19 for β_0, β_1 and β_2) given by the formula

$$\hat{\beta}_i \pm t_{0.025,n-3} \times \text{standard error of } \hat{\beta}_i.$$

Since $n - 3 = 104 - 3 = 101$, then $t_{0.025,101} = 1.984$ (obtained using `=T.INV.2T(0.05,101)`). Hence for β_1 we have

$$-0.870 \pm 1.984 \times 0.081 \Rightarrow (-1.031, -0.709)$$

and for β_2 we have

$$0.010 \pm 1.984 \times 0.001 \Rightarrow (0.008, 0.012).$$

In each case we are 95% confident that the true value of β_i falls between the lower and upper endpoints of the respective interval. Note how both of these 95% confidence intervals *exclude* zero, which is consistent with the significant t tests above, indicating that the true coefficients are non-zero. In short, promotion price *and* advertising spend affect (the logarithm of) weekly sales!

How good is this regression model? We may well have statistical significance of *price* and *advertising* , but jointly how much of *lsales* do they explain? To answer this, we need to look at R^2. Here $R^2 = 0.742$ (cell `B5`). Therefore, 74.2% of the variation of *lsales* can be explained (jointly) with *price* and *advertising*. Not bad!

14.3 THE MULTIPLE LINEAR REGRESSION MODEL

In general, we model the dependent variable, y, as a linear function of k independent variables, the x_i variables:

$$\begin{aligned} y &= \beta_0 + \beta_1 x_1 + \cdots + \beta_k x_k + \varepsilon \\ &= \beta_0 + \sum_{i=1}^{k} \beta_i x_i + \varepsilon, \end{aligned} \tag{14.2}$$

with the usual assumptions on the error term applied. Note that the regression equation has $k + 1$ coefficients (the β_i terms), including the intercept, β_0.

Of interest is the relationship between y and the k independent variables. The great thing about the multiple general linear model is that we are not restricted to analysing relationships that are 'planar' (recall the plane shown in Figure 14.2). It is possible to use higher-order terms – for example, quadratic powers of an x_i (e.g. x_1^2) or even cross-products of independent variables (e.g. x_1x_2 if we suspected an *interaction* between x_1 and x_2).

The assumptions for multiple linear regression can be summarised as follows.

- y is accurately modelled as a linear combination of the x_i variables.
- The random error term, ε, is assumed to have a normal distribution with a mean of zero and a constant variance, σ^2.
- The error terms, ε, are independent.
- The x_i variables and error terms are uncorrelated.

A theoretical summary of multiple regression can be found at the end of this chapter.

As in Chapter 13, our objectives in multiple regression analysis include estimating unknown parameters and assessing the precision of their estimates, as well as testing the adequacy of the proposed model and the relevance of the explanatory variables.

Case study: Multi-factor models

While there are numerous applications of linear regression, one example is in finance using so-called *multi-factor models*. These seek to explain the variation of individual securities, or even portfolios of securities. Two or more factors are analysed to quantify the relationships between variables and security performance.

In essence, multi-factor models are a natural extension of the capital asset pricing model, introduced in Example 13.10. The multi-factor model is a finance application of (14.2). A famous example is the *Fama-French three-factor model*, named after Eugene Fama and Kenneth French. Their three-factor model is

$$r_i = r_f + \beta_1(r_m - r_f) + \beta_2 SMB_i + \beta_3 HML_i + \varepsilon_i,$$

where

- r_i is security *i*'s expected return
- r_f is the risk-free rate
- $r_m - r_f$ is the market risk premium
- β_1, β_2 and β_3 are the factor 'loadings'
- *SMB* is the 'small minus big' factor, that is, the excess returns of companies with a small market capitalisation ('market cap') over those with a large market cap
- *HML* is the 'high minus low' factor, that is, the excess returns of value stocks over growth stocks.

Of interest is the estimation of β_1, β_2 and β_3 which represent the sensitivities of the expected return to the respective factors.

We continue to use least-squares estimation to estimate all the β_i coefficients. In the three-dimensional case, we can think of this as placing a sheet of paper such that it most closely goes through the three-dimensional scatter plot of points, as illustrated in Figure 14.2.

14.3.1 Model hypothesis test

Consider the general linear model in (14.2). Of particular interest is the following hypothesis test:

$$H_0 : \beta_1 = \beta_2 = \cdots = \beta_k = 0 \text{ versus } H_1 : \text{at least one of the } \beta_i \text{ coefficients is not zero.}$$

Under H_0, *none* of the independent variables affects y, whereas if we reject H_0 then there is statistical evidence that *at least one* of the independent variables *does* affect y. As such, this test of whether all the regression coefficients are equal to zero is known as a joint test of significance and can be used to test the overall significance of the regression model. Provided that $\varepsilon_i \sim N(0,\sigma^2)$, then under H_0 the test statistic is

$$F = \frac{(\text{Regression SS})/k}{(\text{Residual SS})/(n-k-1)} \sim F_{k,n-k-1}.$$

We reject H_0 at the $100\alpha\%$ significance level if $P(F > f) < \alpha$, where $F \sim F_{k,\, n-k-1}$, that is, if the *p*-value is less than α.

In practice, if we have chosen sensible independent variables to include in the regression, then almost certainly this F test will be significant. However, the test does not tell us *which* of the independent variables is/are significant, just that *at least one* is. Therefore, we need to conduct t tests of individual slope coefficients. In the unlikely event that we fail to reject H_0 in the above F test, this would render the model useless and hence the model would not warrant any further statistical investigation.

Regression ANOVA decomposition and R^2

As we have a single dependent variable, y, then just as with the simple linear regression model in Chapter 13, we can decompose the total variation of y such that

$$\sum_{i=1}^{n}(y_i - \bar{y})^2 = \sum_{i=1}^{n}(\hat{y}_i - \bar{y})^2 + \sum_{i=1}^{n}\hat{\varepsilon}_i^2$$

or, in words,

Total SS = Regression SS + Residual SS.

The **coefficient of determination, R^2**, continues to be

$$R^2 = \frac{\text{Regression SS}}{\text{Total SS}}$$

and measures the explanatory power of the model, arguably the single best statistic for demonstrating how 'good' the regression model is such that it is advisable to report R^2 when summarising a model to convey how much of y the independent variables jointly explain.

14.3.2 Adjusted R^2

Ceteris paribus, the larger the value of R^2 the better. Therefore, it may be tempting to turn to multiple regression and simply add an almost unlimited number of x variables. By doing so, the Regression SS would increase (and hence the Residual SS would decrease by the same amount, since the Total SS would not change when more x variables are added), and so R^2 would increase. So as k increases,

$$\underset{\leftrightarrow}{\text{Total SS}} = \underset{\uparrow}{\text{Regression SS}} + \underset{\downarrow}{\text{Residual SS}} \quad \Rightarrow \quad R^2 \uparrow.$$

So, it seems a no-brainer to simply add in every x variable we can think of! But wait a moment. More x variables mean more regression coefficients to be estimated, which increases the *complexity* of the model. For a set of n observations, we force them to 'work harder' by making them estimate more model parameters. As such, we face a trade-off:

- *ceteris paribus*, as k increases, R^2 increases (good)
- *ceteris paribus*, as k increases, the model complexity increases (bad).

Hence we need a way to resolve this trade-off. Fear not, adjusted R^2 comes to the rescue!

Adjusted R^2 is a modification of R^2 which *adjusts* (hence the name) for the number of independent variables, k, in the linear regression model. You have probably noticed it before when analysing regression output (e.g. cell `B6` in Figure 14.6), and wondered what it is!

Adjusted R^2 increases only if the addition of an extra independent variable improves the model by more than would be expected by chance. It can be used to choose between competing regression models of the same y with different numbers of independent variables.

Adjusted R^2

Adjusted R^2 literally adjusts R^2 to take into account the number of independent variables in the linear regression model. It is defined as

$$R^2_{adj} = 1 - \frac{(n-i)(1-R^2)}{n-k},$$

where

- $i = 1$ if there is an intercept (which is usually the case), and 0 otherwise (if the intercept is suppressed to be zero, i.e. if $\beta_0 = 0$)
- n = the number of observations used to fit the model
- k = the number of β_i parameters in the model.

How to use R^2 and adjusted R^2? Let's consider an example.

Example 14.2

Given two possible independent variables, x_1 = *price* and x_2 = *advertising*, to help explain y = *lsales*, we could just include one of these using a simple linear regression. So we could consider either of the following simple linear regression models:

Model A: $lsales = \beta_0 + \beta_1 price + \varepsilon$

or

Model B: $lsales = \beta_0 + \beta_1 advertising + \varepsilon$

and choose the model with the higher R^2, since this would do a better job at explaining y. Alternatively, we could include *both* independent variables and work with:

Model C: $lsales = \beta_0 + \beta_1 price + \beta_2 advertising + \varepsilon.$

A model is *nested* when all of its independent variables are included in a larger model. Here models A and B are both nested in model C, since model C includes *price* (so model A is nested) and *advertising* (so model B is nested too). By construction, it *must* be the case that R_C^2 (the R^2 of model C) is greater than R_A^2 and R_B^2. However, model C is more complex due to an additional coefficient to estimate, which is β_2.

Comparing the adjusted R^2 values across the three models provides a way for us to choose the best one. However, suppose only one of *price* and *advertising* was a genuine independent variable (let's assume it's *price*); then model C would suffer from larger standard errors of the parameter estimates (a problem that can occur when irrelevant independent variables are included), and so would be inefficient relative to the 'true' model A.

Let's revisit the supermarket example in Section 14.2.1. The estimated regression results are (with standard errors in parentheses)

$$\widehat{lsales} = \underset{(0.356)}{18.122} - \underset{(0.103)}{1.109} \times price \qquad R^2 = 0.532, \qquad R^2_{adj} = 0.527 \qquad \text{(model A)}$$

$$\widehat{lsales} = \underset{(0.042)}{13.944} + \underset{(0.002)}{0.014} \times advertising \qquad R^2 = 0.450, \qquad R^2_{adj} = 0.441 \qquad \text{(model B)}$$

$$\widehat{lsales} = \underset{(0.291)}{17.047} + \underset{(0.081)}{0.870} \times price + \underset{(0.001)}{0.010} \times advertising \qquad R^2 = 0.742, \qquad R^2_{adj} = 0.737 \qquad \text{(model C)}$$

from which we can see that model A is superior to model B because $R_A^2 > R_B^2$ (0.532 > 0.450). Note that since these models are equally simple (one independent variable each) there is no need to consult adjusted R^2 since complexity is automatically controlled for (they each have $k = 1$).

Having eliminated model B, we are left with a choice between model A and model C, which differ in terms of complexity ($k = 1$ independent variable versus $k = 2$). Since $R^2_{adj,A} < R^2_{adj,C}$ (0.527 < 0.737), we prefer model C. (Note that $R_A^2 < R_C^2$ is guaranteed by construction since model A is nested in model C, which is why we shift focus to comparing the adjusted R^2s.)

Notice also that the standard errors in model C for $\hat{\beta}_1$ and $\hat{\beta}_2$ are *smaller* than their respective counterparts in models A and B, suggesting that both *price* and *advertising* are important independent variables (as confirmed in Section 14.2.1).

14.4 TO INCLUDE, OR NOT TO INCLUDE? THE PERILS OF VARIABLE MISSPECIFICATION

Recall the flow chart in Figure 1.1 whereby numerous controllable and uncontrollable independent variables were depicted as influencing a selection of dependent variables. So, for any y variable of interest, which x variables should we include in our regression model? Is it better to have many, or only a few? How many would be too many? How few would be too few?

As usual we face a trade-off. On the one hand, we value simplicity over complexity, suggesting less is more. On the other hand, we wouldn't want to exclude any important independent variables. We now consider some possible implications of the 'to include, or not to include' decision!

14.4.1 Occam's razor

Attributed to William of Ockham from the Middle Ages, Occam's razor is the *principle of parsimony*. In terms of modelling, this principle favours models with as few parameters as possible. In a linear regression context, this means having as few β_i coefficients as possible, and hence as few independent variables as possible.

If we were to add *irrelevant* independent variables, then such variables are effectively redundant, or superfluous – they serve no purpose in terms of explaining y, but add to model complexity with more coefficient parameters to estimate. While parameter estimates are *unbiased* (meaning on average correct, as discussed in Chapter 9) in the presence of superfluous independent variables (good), their standard errors tend to be large, and hence *inefficient* (bad). Larger standard errors indicate less precise parameter estimates, and can lower the statistical power of t tests of regression coefficients. Recall that $t = \hat{\beta}_i$ /(standard error of $\hat{\beta}_i$), so the larger the denominator, the smaller t is and hence the larger the p-value is, and so it is less likely to be significant.

14.4.2 Omitted-variable bias

We can think of the error term in a regression model, ε, as a 'catch-all' variable which captures everything else which explains y except for the independent variables that have been explicitly included. Ideally, this error term should be *uncorrelated* with the independent variables. Provided we have included all relevant explanatory variables in the model (i.e. as x variables), then this should be satisfied. However, if we omit important variables that explain y, then this can cause omitted-variable bias.

In what sense do we mean 'bias'? Well, the erroneous omission of important explanatory variables can bias (up or down) the coefficient estimates of the independent variables actually included in a regression model, resulting in misleading inference. In the extreme, omitted-variable bias can result in coefficient estimates with illogical signs. This is best seen by way of example.

Example 14.3

An analyst in the aviation sector wants to examine how the level of competitiveness on different routes affects airfares. The expectation is that the more competitive the route (i.e. with more airlines operating flights), competitive forces would make airfares lower as consumers can shop around for the cheapest fare.

The analyst examined n = 100 routes, and calculated the logarithm of airfares, *logfare* (to measure prices) and calculated the amount of competition, *competition*, as the inverse of the market share of the largest carrier on the route, such that

$$competition = \frac{1}{\text{largest market share of an airline on the route}} \times 100\%.$$

Hence a monopoly (i.e. a route served by a single carrier) results in *competition* = 1 (since the largest market share is 100%), while more competitive routes with less concentration of carriers produce larger values of *competition* (e.g. *competition* = 2 if the most dominant airline has 50% market share). The simple linear regression model is then

$$logfare = \beta_0 + \beta_1 competition + \varepsilon,$$

where we expect $\beta_1 < 0$, that is, *more* competition produces *lower* prices. The estimated regression line is (with standard errors in parentheses)

$$\widehat{logfare} = \underset{(0.157)}{4.253} + \underset{(0.038)}{0.133} \times competition.$$

The t statistic for $\hat{\beta}_1$ is $t = \hat{\beta}_1$/(standard error of $\hat{\beta}_1$) = 0.133/0.038 = 3.50, which is *highly significant* (the p-value is *less than* 0.001). The analyst concludes that the *greater* the amount of competition on a route, the *higher* the ticket price - this defies commercial logic! Competition regulators (who seek to regulate the concentration of firms in an industry) the world over would despair!

What's gone wrong? Well, this is a classic example of *omitted-variable bias.* Clearly, the amount of competition cannot be the *only* determinant of airfares, with important omitted variables being captured in the error term, and this would mean that *competition* and ε would be correlated, creating omitted-variable bias.

What might be an example of an omitted variable here? Well, presumably the duration of the flight would be relevant, with longer flights being associated with higher prices. The analyst decides to incorporate flight duration by using the logarithm of the distance between departure and arrival airports, *logdistance*. The model now becomes

$$logfare = \beta_0 + \beta_1 competition + \beta_2 logdistance + \varepsilon,$$

resulting in the estimated regression line (with standard errors in parentheses)

$$\widehat{logfare} = \underset{(1.267)}{-0.536} - \underset{(0.101)}{0.228} \times competition + \underset{(0.242)}{0.922} \times logdistance.$$

Now the coefficient of *competition* has the correct (negative) sign, and *logdistance* has the correct (positive) sign. Our interpretation is:

- a 1-unit increase in *competition* decreases airfares by 22.8% (since the dependent variable is in logarithmic form), *controlling for logdistance*
- a 1% increase in flight distance increases airfares by 0.922%, *controlling for competition.*

This example has shown that omitted-variable bias can be serious. The analyst's initial failure to control for flight distance resulted in a *positive bias* in the estimation of β_1. The bias was so large that the estimated coefficient ended up being positive (0.133) rather than negative (-0.228, after controlling for *logdistance*)!

Example 14.3 provides a cautionary tale about being paranoid over Occam's razor. The tendency to keep a regression model as 'small' as possible, that is, with minimal independent variables, risks important variables being excluded, and hence omitted-variable bias could occur!

14.4.3 Consequences of variable misspecification in regression models

For simplicity, let's consider the possible scenarios when we have available the variables y, x_1 and x_2. These are summarised in Table 14.2.

Table 14.2 Consequences of variable misspecification in regression models.

	True relationship	
Estimated model	$y = \beta_0 + \beta_1 x_1 + \varepsilon$	$y = \beta_0 + \beta_1 x_1 + \beta_2 x_2 + \varepsilon$
$\hat{y} = \hat{\beta}_0 + \hat{\beta}_1 x_1$	Specification is correct, so no issues arise	Omitted-variable bias risk with invalid standard errors (induced by Occam's razor)
$\hat{y} = \hat{\beta}_0 + \hat{\beta}_1 x_1 + \hat{\beta}_2 x_2$	Unbiased coefficients (good), but standard errors are inefficient (i.e. large), lowering precision (can occur when fear of omitted-variable bias)	Specification is correct, so no issues arise

We now consider two further types of independent variables which may be included in multiple linear regression models – *interactions* and *dummy variables*.

14.5 INTERACTIONS

The concept of an interaction was introduced in Chapter 12, whereby the effect of one factor level on the dependent variable itself depended on the level of a second factor. We simply extend this idea to two quantitative variables, such as x_1 and x_2, by taking the *product* such that an interaction variable is formed as x_1x_2. We could then consider the multiple regression model

$$y = \beta_0 + \beta_1 x_1 + \beta_2 x_2 + \beta_3 x_1 x_2 + \varepsilon.$$

Example 14.4

Extending Example 14.2, let's model an interaction between promotion price and advertising spend for the (logarithm of) weekly sales of a supermarket. Our model is:

$$lsales = \beta_0 + \beta_1 price + \beta_2 advertising + \beta_3(price \times advertising) + \varepsilon.$$

What is the effect of a unit change in *price* on *lsales*? Without the interaction, the effect is given by β_1; however, with the interaction the *price* effect depends on *advertising*. For readers familiar with calculus, we calculate

$$\frac{\partial\, lsales}{\partial\, price} = \beta_1 + \beta_3\, advertising.$$

So, the effect of *price* on *lsales* is formed of two components: a *fixed effect*, β_1, and a *variable effect*, β_3, which depends on the amount of *advertising* . If $\beta_3 = 0$, then there is no interaction and *price* only affects *lsales* through β_1. Therefore, we are interested in performing a *t* test of significance on β_3.

Similarly, what is the effect of a unit change in *advertising* on *lsales*? Without the interaction, the effect is given by β_2; however, with the interaction the *advertising* effect depends on *price*. We calculate

$$\frac{\partial \, lsales}{\partial \, advertising} = \beta_2 + \beta_3 \; price.$$

So, the effect of *advertising* on *lsales* is formed of two components: a *fixed effect*, β_2, and a *variable effect*, β_3, which depends on the amount of *price*. If $\beta_3 = 0$, then there is no interaction and *advertising* only affects *lsales* through β_2. Either way, we are interested in performing a *t* test of significance on β_3.

The regression results are as follows:

	A	B	C	D	E	F	G
1	SUMMARY OUTPUT						
2							
3	*Regression Statistics*						
4	Multiple R	0.868773515					
5	R Square	0.75476742					
6	Adjusted R Square	0.747410443					
7	Standard Error	0.12276019					
8	Observations	104					
9							
10	ANOVA						
11		*df*	*SS*	*MS*	*F*	*Significance F*	
12	Regression	3	4.63820653	1.546068843	102.5920539	2.11041E-30	
13	Residual	100	1.507006425	0.015070064			
14	Total	103	6.145212955				
15							
16		*Coefficients*	*Standard Error*	*t Stat*	*P-value*	*Lower 95%*	*Upper 95%*
17	Intercept	15.83645731	0.609300915	25.99119241	2.81796E-46	14.62762165	17.04529297
18	Promotion price	-0.521077009	0.174516019	-2.985840567	0.003555971	-0.867311821	-0.174842198
19	Advertising spend	0.055390821	0.0202443	2.736119313	0.007357385	0.015226706	0.095554936
20	Interaction	-0.013202048	0.005871724	-2.248410741	0.026744617	-0.024851382	-0.001552714

So the estimated model is (with standard errors in parentheses)

$$\widehat{lsales} = \underset{(0.609)}{15.836} - \underset{(0.175)}{0.521}\, price + \underset{(0.020)}{0.055}\, advertising - \underset{(0.006)}{0.013}\,(price \times advertising).$$

Examining the *p*-values in the cell range `E18:E20`, we see that *price*, *advertising* and their interaction are all either *moderately or highly significant*, and so we conclude that the effect on *lsales* of each independent variable depends on the other variable. Specifically:

- a 1-unit increase in *price* decreases *lsales* by $0.521 + 0.013 \times advertising$
- a 1-unit increase in *advertising* increases *lsales* by $0.055 - 0.013 \times price$; so if $price > 4.231$ (which is 0.055/0.013) then this would actually *decrease lsales*!

14.6 DUMMY VARIABLES

Often we may want to include *categorical* independent variables in a regression model, such as gender or age group. Of course, we have seen how to work with *only* categorical independent variables in our work on ANOVA in Chapter 12; but now we want to combine quantitative and categorical independent variables. To do so, we use dummy variables, which take only two values, 0 and 1, such that

$$x = \begin{cases} 1 & \text{if case possesses a particular attribute} \\ 0 & \text{otherwise,} \end{cases}$$

with the '0' case being the reference category.

Dummy variables can be included in a regression alongside quantitative independent variables, although the interpretation of the coefficients is different. We cannot talk about a one-unit increase in a dummy variable; rather, the coefficient gives the *expected difference* in the dependent variable of cases in the '1' category relative to the reference category. t tests of significance are as before.

Given the binary nature of dummy variables, if our categorical variable of interest has k levels, then we require $k - 1$ dummy variables to unambiguously distinguish the k levels. For example, if the categorical variable is binary (i.e. $k = 2$), then we only need *one* dummy variable since it is equal to 1 for one of the two factor levels, and 0 for the other; so knowing the value of a single dummy variable is sufficient to know the level unambiguously.

Example 14.5

Suppose we conduct a survey of our customers and we ask individuals to report their satisfaction with our product using a 10-point Likert scale (as discussed in Chapter 8), along with their gender (a categorical variable) and age (a quantitative variable). If every respondent self-identified as either male or female, then we could model gender with a single dummy variable, *gender*. The choice of reference category is *arbitrary*, so we could have either

$$genderm = \begin{cases} 1 & \text{if respondent identifies as male} \\ 0 & \text{otherwise (i.e. the respondent identifies as female)} \end{cases}$$

or

$$genderf = \begin{cases} 1 & \text{if respondent identifies as female} \\ 0 & \text{otherwise (i.e. the respondent identifies as male),} \end{cases}$$

and suppose we decided to create the regression model

$$satisfaction = \beta_0 + \beta_1 age + \beta_2 genderm + \varepsilon \tag{14.3}$$

or

$$satisfaction = \beta_0 + \beta_1 age + \beta_2 genderf + \varepsilon. \tag{14.4}$$

Note that our inference about the relationship between customer satisfaction and their demographics is *not* affected by whether we use the representation in (14.3) or (14.4). However, the interpretation of β_2 in (14.3) is the expected difference in customer satisfaction *between a male and a female*, controlling for age; whereas β_2 in (14.4) is the expected difference in customer satisfaction *between a female and a male*, controlling for age. The same comparison is made, albeit from different perspectives. (Think of 'glass half full' versus 'glass half empty'.)

Suppose the estimated regressions are (with standard errors in parentheses)

$$\widehat{satisfaction} = \underset{(1.490)}{0.357} + \underset{(0.032)}{0.081} \times age + \underset{(0.742)}{1.748} \times genderm \tag{14.5}$$

and

$$\widehat{satisfaction} = \underset{(1.613)}{2.105} + \underset{(0.032)}{0.081} \times age - \underset{(0.742)}{1.748} \times genderf. \tag{14.6}$$

Note that the estimated coefficients of *genderm* and *genderf* just have opposite signs. Saying that males have satisfaction levels 1.748 units *higher* than females (controlling for age) is equivalent to saying that females have satisfaction levels 1.748 units *lower* than males (again, controlling for age). Hence it does not matter which gender is chosen to be the reference category.

Does the fact that the intercepts are different matter? No! Suppose we wanted to predict customer satisfaction for a 36-year-old female. Using (14.5) with *genderm* = 0 for a female, the prediction is

$$0.357 + 0.081 \times 36 + 1.748 \times 0 = 3.273,$$

while using (14.6) with *genderf* = 1 for a female, the prediction is

$$2.105 + 0.081 \times 36 - 1.748 \times 1 = 3.273.$$

What if we included *genderm* and *genderf* in the regression? Well, if we tried to estimate the regression

$$satisfaction = \beta_0 + \beta_1 age + \beta_2 genderm + \beta_3 genderf + \varepsilon$$

in Excel, it would 'override' our regression model specification, effectively deciding to ignore one of the two dummy variables, because otherwise it would be impossible to distinguish the effect of *genderm* on *satisfaction* from that of *genderf*. The table of regression coefficients would be:

	Coefficients	Standard Error	t Stat	P-value	Lower 95%	Upper 95%
Intercept	2.104574224	1.613329269	1.304491441	0.203076713	-1.205704005	5.414852452
age	0.080687761	0.0320452	2.517935956	0.018040078	0.014936442	0.146439079
genderm	0	0	65535	#NUM!	0	0
genderf	-1.747538577	0.742438094	-2.353783557	#NUM!	-3.270895714	-0.22418144

Why does this happen? It is because *genderm* and *genderf* have *perfect* negative correlation, since

$$genderm = 1 \text{ when } genderf = 0 \quad \text{and} \quad genderm = 0 \text{ when } genderf = 1.$$

This causes a problem called *multicollinearity*, which is discussed briefly later. Note, though, that we could include *genderm* and *genderf* provided we suppress the intercept to be zero, that is, force $\beta_0 = 0$, and consider the model

$$satisfaction = \beta_1 age + \beta_2 genderm + \beta_3 genderf + \varepsilon.$$

(Continued)

In the Excel regression dialog box, we can in fact force $\beta_0 = 0$ by checking the `Constant is Zero` box. (This is a special case of when it can be desirable to suppress the intercept to be zero.) Doing so returns:

	Coefficients	*Standard Error*	*t Stat*	*P-value*	*Lower 95%*	*Upper 95%*
Intercept	0	#N/A	#N/A	#N/A	#N/A	#N/A
age	0.080687761	0.0320452	2.517935956	0.018040078	0.014936442	0.146439079
genderm	2.104574224	1.613329269	1.304491441	0.203076713	-1.205704005	5.414852452
genderf	0.357035647	1.490033191	0.239615902	0.812437788	-2.700259925	3.414331218

Example 14.6

Suppose we wanted to investigate whether the degree of product usage affected customer satisfaction, where we classify product usage into one of four types: (i) heavy users, (ii) medium users, (iii) light users and (iv) non-users. So, this categorical variable has $k = 4$ levels, which requires us to define $k - 1 = 4 - 1 = 3$ dummy variables. While the choice of reference category is arbitrary, when the levels are *ordinal* (i.e. when they are in a ranked order, as in this case), it seems reasonable to use the 'lowest' level as the reference category - in this instance, this would be 'non-users'. The three dummy variables would then be:

$$x_1 = \begin{cases} 1 & \text{if a heavy user} \\ 0 & \text{otherwise,} \end{cases} \quad x_2 = \begin{cases} 1 & \text{if a medium user} \\ 0 & \text{otherwise} \end{cases} \quad \text{and} \quad x_3 = \begin{cases} 1 & \text{if a light user} \\ 0 & \text{otherwise,} \end{cases}$$

such that knowing the values of x_1, x_2 and x_3 will allow us to unambiguously determine the user level:

Product usage category	x_1	x_2	x_3
Heavy users	1	0	0
Medium users	0	1	0
Light users	0	0	1
Non-users	0	0	0

Suppose we considered the multiple linear regression model

$$y = \beta_0 + \beta_1 x_1 + \beta_2 x_2 + \beta_3 x_3 + \sum_{i=4}^{k} \beta_i x_i + \varepsilon,$$

where x_4, x_5, ..., x_k are other independent variables of interest, resulting in an estimated equation

$$\hat{y} = \hat{\beta}_0 + \hat{\beta}_1 x_1 + \hat{\beta}_2 x_2 + \hat{\beta}_3 x_3 + \sum_{i=4}^{k} \hat{\beta}_i x_i.$$

In this case, controlling for all other variables:

- $\hat{\beta}_1$ is the estimated difference in y of heavy users compared with non-users (i.e. the comparison is with respect to the *reference category*).
- $\hat{\beta}_2$ is the estimated difference in y of medium users compared with non-users
- $\hat{\beta}_3$ is the estimated difference in y of light users compared with non-users.

What if we wanted to compare, say, heavy and medium users? We can! The estimated difference in *y* between these two types would be:

$$\hat{\beta}_1 - \hat{\beta}_2$$

Similarly, $\hat{\beta}_3 - \hat{\beta}_1$ would tell us the estimated difference in *y* between light users and heavy users. So, we can make any pairwise comparisons we like! Cool.

14.7 MULTICOLLINEARITY

'Independent' variables in a regression should ideally be *statistically independent* (i.e. the variables should not be related to each other, and should only be related to *y*). However, it is not an ideal world. In practice, we would expect some *correlation* between the 'independent' variables. While this would mean the variables are not independent, provided the correlation is only mild it is not too problematic. Multicollinearity may be an issue when at least two independent variables are highly correlated.

Recall how to interpret correlation coefficients as introduced in Chapter 11 and reproduced in Figure 14.7 for convenience.

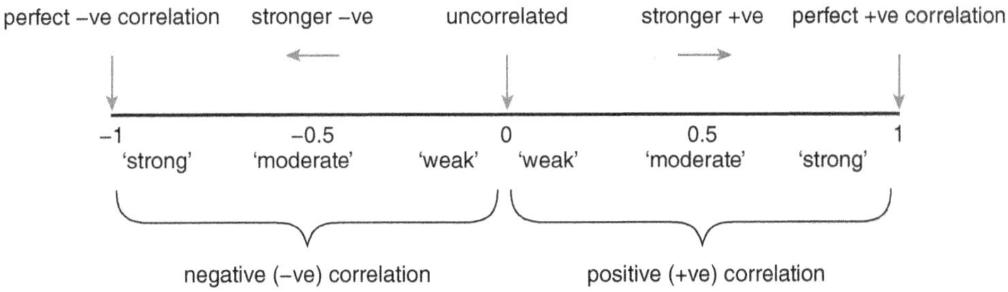

Figure 14.7 Values of correlation coefficients on the continuum [–1, 1].

If some independent variables are strongly correlated, then it becomes very difficult to distinguish the effects of these individually on the dependent variable, since movements in one are 'shadowed' by movements in the other. In the extreme, if there is *perfect* correlation between two independent variables, then the regression model fails.

We saw an example of this in Example 14.5 when we attempted to use two dummy variables for a binary variable (without suppressing the intercept to be zero). *genderm* and *genderf* were noted to have a perfect negative correlation, so Excel decided to 'ignore' *genderm*. This is an example of the so-called *dummy-variable trap* which occurs when *k* dummy variables are used for a categorical variable with *k* levels. The reason we use *k* – 1 dummy variables is to circumvent this problem.

What are the implications of strongly (but not perfectly) correlated variables in a multiple regression? Such multicollinearity makes for unstable estimation of the regression coefficients and can result in variables being non-significant. As usual, this is best seen by way of example!

Example 14.7

Continuing Example 14.5, let's incorporate an interaction between *age* and *genderm*. Recall that we create an interaction variable as the *product* of two variables. Our regression model is:

$$satisfaction = \beta_0 + \beta_1 age + \beta_2 genderm + \beta_3 age \times genderm + \varepsilon,$$

with the following results:

	A	B	C	D	E	F	G
1	SUMMARY OUTPUT						
2							
3	*Regression Statistics*						
4	Multiple R	0.602192912					
5	R Square	0.362636304					
6	Adjusted R Square	0.289094339					
7	Standard Error	1.977160591					
8	Observations	30					
9							
10	ANOVA						
11		*df*	*SS*	*MS*	*F*	*Significance F*	
12	Regression	3	57.82840259	19.2761342	4.931011894	0.007647989	
13	Residual	26	101.6382641	3.909164003			
14	Total	29	159.4666667				
15							
16		*Coefficients*	*Standard Error*	*t Stat*	*P-value*	*Lower 95%*	*Upper 95%*
17	Intercept	0.722135008	2.50377925	0.288418002	0.775313676	-4.424456949	5.868726965
18	age	0.072213501	0.056584689	1.27620213	0.213166921	-0.044097994	0.188524995
19	genderm	1.178529497	3.194613949	0.368911398	0.715180979	-5.388093521	7.745152515
20	genderm*age	0.012697936	0.069265125	0.183323663	0.855966208	-0.129678566	0.155074439

Despite the non-negligible R^2 (36.26% of satisfaction is explained by the model) and the highly significant F test of

$$H_0 : \beta_1 = \beta_2 = \beta_3 = 0,$$

indicating that at least one coefficient of the three independent variables is non-zero, the t tests of all three variables are *non-significant* (see the *p*-values in cells `E18:E20`). How can we explain this seemingly paradoxical situation? Well, let's examine the correlation matrix between these variables:

	A	B	C	D
1		*age*	*genderm*	*genderm*age*
2	age	1		
3	genderm	0.224203	1	
4	genderm*age	0.493578	0.934142	1

Aha! We can see that the sample correlation between *genderm* and the interaction is 0.934, which is very strong, indicating a likely case of multicollinearity. This explains the *imprecise estimates* of the regression coefficients (the large standard errors in cells `C18:C20`), which result in small t statistics (since $t = \hat{\beta}_i$ /(standard error of $\hat{\beta}_i$), so a large standard error in the denominator makes t small), and hence large (and so non-significant) *p*-values.

14.8 MODEL SELECTION TECHNIQUES

Once we have decided which dependent variable, y, interests us, it can be challenging to decide on which is the *best* model to explain it, especially if we have data on many candidate independent variables. One option is to begin with all these variables and then eliminate the least significant ones, based on p-values for the t tests of each variable. For a dataset with a 'small' number of variables, a final model can be obtained reasonably quickly. If you start with a 'large' model, however, eliminating one variable at a time can potentially be a time-consuming process. You would have to continue this process until only variables with p-values lower than some threshold value, such as 0.10 or 0.05, remain. So, removing one variable at a time manually for:

- small datasets is a reasonable approach
- large datasets can take too long.

In more advanced texts you may get to study several possible model selection techniques. Just an overview is provided here to put these on your radar.

- *Forward selection*. This first selects the best single independent variable, then it selects the next best variable among those yet to be selected, which is then added to the first selected variable. Forward selection continues this process, but stops when it reaches the point where no additional variables have a p-value below a threshold level, such as 0.05.
- *Backward elimination*. This starts with the full model. Next, the independent variable which is the least significant, given the other variables, is removed from the model. Backward elimination continues this process until all of the remaining variables have a p-value below a threshold level, such as 0.05.
- *Stepwise selection*. This works as a combination of forward selection and backward elimination, with default 'entry' p-values, such as 0.05, and default 'stay' p-values, such as 0.10.

14.8.1 Forward selection

Forward selection starts with an empty, or 'null', model:

$$y = \beta_0 + \varepsilon.$$

The method computes an F statistic for each independent variable not in the model and examines the largest of these statistics. If it is significant at a specified significance level, then the corresponding independent variable is added to the model. Once a variable has entered it is retained in the model until the procedure stops. The process is repeated until none of the remaining variables meets the specified entry threshold. This process is illustrated in Figure 14.8.

14.8.2 Backward elimination

Backward elimination starts off with the full model of all k candidate variables:

$$y = \beta_0 + \beta_1 x_1 + \beta_2 x_2 + \cdots + \beta_k x_k + \varepsilon.$$

Results of F tests for each individual parameter estimate are examined, and the *least* significant variable which falls *above* the specified significance level is removed. Once a variable has been removed from the model, it remains excluded until the procedure stops. The process is repeated until no more variables in the model meet the specified significance level for removal. This process is illustrated in Figure 14.9.

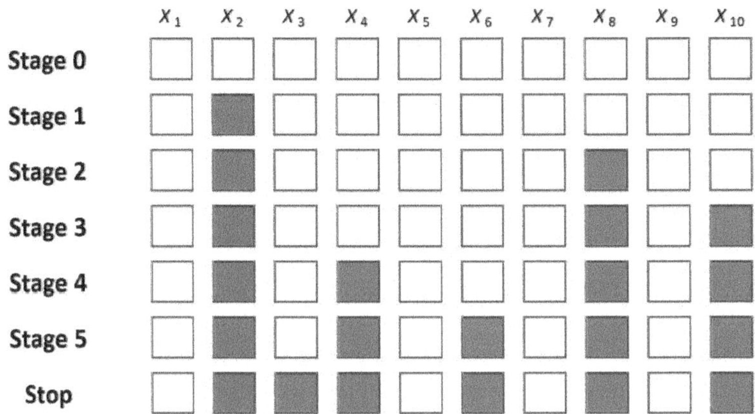

Figure 14.8 Illustration of the forward selection method. Variables enter in the following order: X_2, X_8, X_{10}, X_4, X_6, X_3.

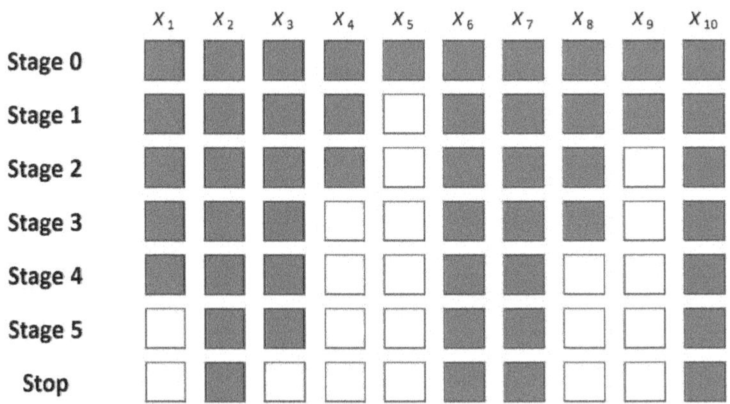

Figure 14.9 Illustration of the backward elimination method. Variables are removed in the following order: X_5, X_9, X_4, X_8, X_1, X_3.

14.8.3 Stepwise selection

Stepwise selection is similar to forward selection in that it starts with the empty (null) model:

$$y = \beta_0 + \varepsilon.$$

Then in incremental steps it updates the model one variable at a time. However, the method differs from forward selection in that variables already in the model do not necessarily remain in the model. The backward component of the method removes variables from the model which do not meet the significance criteria specified to remain in the model. The stepwise selection process ends when no more variables can be added to the model or if the most recent variable added to the model is the only variable removed in the subsequent backward elimination. This process is illustrated in Figure 14.10.

It is suggested to use variable selection techniques to short-list several candidate models, and then use judgement and expertise to select the variables which result in the best model within the business context of the problem. In this light, these methods should be viewed as tools to *assist* with model building, rather than returning 'definitive' models.

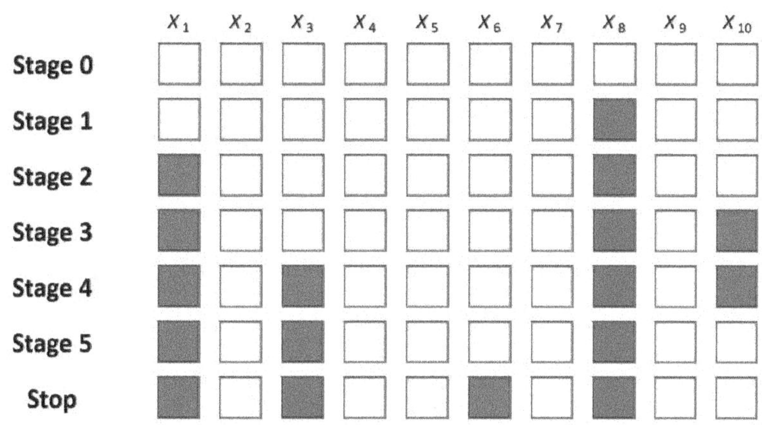

Figure 14.10 Illustration of the stepwise selection method. Variables enter/exit in the following order: X_8 (enter), X_1 (enter), X_{10} (enter), X_3 (enter), X_{10} (exit), X_6 (enter).

14.9 CASE STUDY: GENDER DISCRIMINATION IN PAY

We end this chapter with an application of multiple linear regression to address the claims of gender discrimination in pay as discussed in the chapter's opening motivational case.

Recall that staff in the HR department of a blue chip company want to investigate whether there is any substance to claims of pay discrimination based on gender before matters get escalated to an employment tribunal and the inevitable negative publicity that this would attract.

They have access to internal payroll data of 100 employees and so it is decided to use multiple linear regression to explain the variation of staff salaries on the payroll. Data on the following variables for each employee are available:

- annual salary, *salary*
- age, *age*
- gender, *gender*

- tenure with the company, *tenure*
- years of education (excluding primary education), *education*.

All 100 employees self-identified as either male or female, so it was decided to code the *gender* variable as

$$gender = \begin{cases} 1 \text{ if male} \\ 0 \text{ if female} \end{cases}$$

and to see whether there is an interaction between *age* and *gender*. The following regression model is formed:

$$salary = \beta_0 + \beta_1 age + \beta_2 gender + \beta_3 tenure + \beta_4 education + \beta_5 age \times gender + \varepsilon.$$

The following regression results were obtained:

	A	B	C	D	E	F	G
1	SUMMARY OUTPUT						
2							
3	*Regression Statistics*						
4	Multiple R	0.880768784					
5	R Square	0.77575365					
6	Adjusted R Square	0.763825653					
7	Standard Error	15584.66285					
8	Observations	100					
9							
10	ANOVA						
11		*df*	*SS*	*MS*	*F*	*Significance F*	
12	Regression	5	78980726167	15796145233	65.03637027	5.29896E-29	
13	Residual	94	22830881333	242881716.3			
14	Total	99	1.01812E+11				
15							
16		*Coefficients*	*Standard Error*	*t Stat*	*P-value*	*Lower 95%*	*Upper 95%*
17	Intercept	-12796.98721	8616.952352	-1.485094345	0.140864788	-29906.1481	4312.173687
18	Age	666.3455387	225.7902221	2.951170926	0.003996548	218.0337598	1114.657318
19	Gender	16278.76509	11494.78106	1.416187486	0.16002584	-6544.392167	39101.92236
20	Tenure	3010.319507	279.1379551	10.78434319	4.00524E-18	2456.084553	3564.55446
21	Education	8018.201829	918.7966462	8.726851434	9.33956E-14	6193.90955	9842.494109
22	Age*Gender	-499.5395021	278.4154922	-1.794223081	0.075992415	-1052.339988	53.26098418

The estimated model is (with standard errors in parentheses)

$$\widehat{salary} = \underset{(8616.95)}{-12{,}796} - \underset{(225.79)}{666.35}\, age + \underset{(11{,}494.78)}{16{,}278.77}\, gender + \underset{(279.14)}{3{,}010.32}\, tenure + \underset{(918.80)}{8{,}018}\, education$$
$$- \underset{(278.42)}{499.54}\, age \times gender.$$

$R^2 = 0.7758$ indicates that 77.58% of the variation in annual salary is explained by the model, indicating that these independent variables have captured most of the variation in salaries, and the joint test of significance is *highly significant*, as seen by the tiny *p*-value in cell F12, meaning we clearly reject

$$H_0 : \beta_1 = \beta_2 = \beta_3 = \beta_4 = \beta_5 = 0.$$

Of course, it is of interest whether there is any evidence of pay discrimination based on gender. Given the suspicion that males may be paid more on average than females, and noting how the dummy variable *gender* has been defined, we could test

$$H_0 : \beta_2 = 0 \text{ versus } H_1 : \beta_2 > 0.$$

The *t* statistic is t = 16,278.77/11,494.78 = 1.416 (cell D19) and since $\hat{\beta}_2 > 0$ (i.e. the sign is positive and so it is in the expected direction under H_1) the *p*-value is *half* of the two-tailed test *p*-value in cell E19, that is, 0.160/2 = 0.080 which is *not* significant at the 5% significance level (but offers *weak evidence* at the 10% significance level). So, although $\hat{\beta}_2$ = 16,278.77 may seem a large (and positive) coefficient, due to the large standard error, this is *not* significantly different from zero (assuming a 5% significance level).

However, *gender* also features in our model as part of the interaction term. So we also need to test

$$H_0 : \beta_5 = 0 \text{ versus } H_1 : \beta_5 \neq 0,$$

assuming a two-tailed test. The *t* statistic is t = –499.54/278.42 = –1.794 (cell D22) which, again, is non-significant at the 5% significance level since the *p*-value in cell E22 is 0.076 > 0.05.

In conclusion, based on the regression model, there does *not* seem to be (sufficient) evidence of gender discrimination in pay at this blue chip company, so in the event of an employment tribunal, the company could offer up this analysis in their defence.

Case closed? Not necessarily. This is a somewhat superficial analysis, with more investigation required. For example:

- does the model suffer from *multicollinearity*? Well, the correlation matrix is

	A	B	C	D	E	F
1		*Age*	*Gender*	*Tenure*	*Education*	*Age*Gender*
2	Age	1				
3	Gender	0.106338175	1			
4	Tenure	0.468541207	-0.082232181	1		
5	Education	0.215433597	-0.049257931	0.100387326	1	
6	Age*Gender	0.371194822	0.926600961	0.028281269	0.003418398	1

  and it is clear that *gender* and the interaction term are highly correlated, with a very strong correlation of 0.9266. So, it is possible that the collinear nature of these two variables has resulted in imprecise estimates, that is, large standard errors, small(ish) *t*-values, and large(ish) *p*-values. Perhaps the presence of multicollinearity is 'hiding' true gender discrimination.

- does the model suffer from *omitted-variable bias*? Perhaps. Although $R^2 = 0.7758$, there could be at least one important independent variable which has been omitted from the model. If so, then there could be an omitted-variable bias problem, with the estimated coefficients β_2 and β_5 potentially biased upwards or downwards.

In conclusion, 'proving' gender discrimination in pay beyond a reasonable doubt is not so straightforward. Admittedly, civil cases are decided 'on the balance of probabilities', while in criminal cases the bar is set at the higher level of 'beyond a reasonable doubt'.

Mind the (pay) gap

In 2018 there was a well-publicised example of suspected pay discrimination against female employees at the British Broadcasting Corporation (BBC). High-profile female journalists at the BBC alleged they were not paid the same as male colleagues for equal work.

This resulted in an inquiry by the Equality and Human Rights Commission. In the end several male BBC presenters agreed to take a pay cut, to narrow the identified pay gap. Interestingly, an alternative solution to narrow the gap would have been to increase the pay of female presenters (rather than to cut the pay of male presenters).

14.10 CHAPTER OVERVIEW

This chapter has extended the previous simple linear regression model by incorporating more than one explanatory variable, which is more realistic given that the real world is very complex and variables of interest (such as sales) will inevitably be affected by several factors. A joint test of significance can be used to simultaneously test whether at least one of the independent variables is significant, and then separate t tests may be conducted to assess the significance of each independent variable individually.

R^2 continues to be used as a measure of explanatory power, while adjusted R^2 allows us to choose between regression models of different sizes by helping to resolve the trade-off between R^2 and model complexity. Variable misspecification was also discussed, in particular the perils of omitted-variable bias. The modelling of interactions, dummy variables, multicollinearity and model selection techniques concluded the chapter.

14.11 KEY VOCABULARY

Adjusted R^2
Coefficient of determination, R^2
Dummy variable
Interaction
Joint test of significance
Least-squares estimation
Model selection techniques
Multicollinearity
Occam's razor
Omitted-variable bias
Reference category

14.12 EXERCISES

14.12.1 Test your understanding

1 Provide a comparison of ANOVA and regression techniques in terms of their dependent and independent variables.

2 In the multiple linear regression model

$$y = \beta_0 + \beta_1 x_1 + \beta_2 x_2 + \varepsilon,$$

provide brief interpretations of the parameters β_0, β_1 and β_2.

3 List the assumptions of the multiple linear regression model.

4 Outline details of the joint test of significance in a multiple linear regression with k independent variables.

5 Is there any difference in (a) the regression ANOVA decomposition, and (b) R^2 between the simple and multiple linear regression models?

6 What is adjusted R^2 used for and how is it calculated?

7 What is Occam's razor?

8 Explain the concept of omitted-variable bias.

9 What are the two types of variable misspecification in regression models, and what are their respective consequences?

10 What are interactions and how are they constructed?

11 In the multiple regression model

$$y = \beta_0 + \beta_1 x_1 + \beta_2 x_2 + \beta_3 x_1 x_2 + \varepsilon,$$

what is the effect of x_1 on y?

12 What is the purpose of a dummy variable and how is it defined? Does the choice of reference category matter?

13 If an independent variable is categorical with $k = 3$ levels, how would this be modelled in a multiple linear regression, and why?

14 If an independent variable is categorical with $k = 3$ levels, explain how you would determine the estimated differences between all possible pairwise comparisons.

15 Explain what multicollinearity is, and why it is problematic.

16 Distinguish between the following model selection techniques:

(a) forward selection
(b) backward elimination
(c) stepwise selection.

17 A credit card company wants to understand the variation in credit card charges accrued by its customers. While the company profits from these charges, it is concerned that customers with very high charges may be at greater risk of default – a bad outcome for both the customer and the company. It was decided to perform a multiple linear regression. A random sample of $n = 1000$ current credit card customers was obtained, with information on the following variables:

- Annual charges, in pounds
- Annual income, in thousands of pounds
- Age

- Household size
- Gender (1 = female, 0 = male)
- Exceeded credit limit in past 12 months? (1 = yes, 0 = no).

A multiple linear regression was run and the results were:

	A	B	C	D	E	F	G
1	SUMMARY OUTPUT						
2							
3	*Regression Statistics*						
4	Multiple R	0.568422364					
5	R Square	0.323103984					
6	Adjusted R Square	0.319699075					
7	Standard Error	4985.118884					
8	Observations	1000					
9							
10	ANOVA						
11		*df*	*SS*	*MS*	*F*	*Significance F*	
12	Regression	5	11791193853	2358238771	94.89355909	9.09282E-82	
13	Residual	994	24702301826	24851410.29			
14	Total	999	36493495678				
15							
16		*Coefficients*	*Standard Error*	*t Stat*	*P-value*	*Lower 95%*	*Upper 95%*
17	Intercept	1995.758284	978.928241	2.038717651	0.041742395	74.75508843	3916.76148
18	Annual income	115.9058592	5.622354426	20.61518191	6.79015E-79	104.8728127	126.9389057
19	Age	-21.0604831	14.84221185	-1.41895853	0.156224587	-50.18614849	8.065182298
20	Household size	512.0991509	73.81656182	6.937456016	7.18653E-12	367.2449673	656.9533345
21	Gender	-107.1666067	316.1912136	-0.338929743	0.734734243	-727.6455208	513.3123073
22	Exceeded credit limit	391.5493926	553.9528941	0.706827957	0.479839057	-695.5019717	1478.600757

(a) Write out the full regression model, including any assumptions, and the estimated model.
(b) Interpret each estimated coefficient.
(c) Perform a joint test of significance and test each independent variable separately.
(d) Briefly discuss any changes you would recommend making to the model.

14.12.2 Practice with Excel

Head over to the companion website for Excel examples and screencasts!

14.13 OPTIONAL MATERIAL ON MULTIPLE LINEAR REGRESSION MODEL STATISTICAL INFERENCE

Digging deeper - theoretical summary of multiple regression (for the interested reader)

Let $(y_i, x_{i1}, x_{i2}, \ldots, x_{ik})$, for $i = 1, 2, \ldots, n$, be observations from the model

$$y_i = \beta_0 + \beta_1 x_{i1} + \beta_2 x_{i2} + \cdots + \beta_k x_{ik} + \varepsilon_i$$

where

$E(\varepsilon_i) = 0$, $\mathrm{Var}(\varepsilon_i) = \sigma^2 > 0$ and $\mathrm{Cov}(\varepsilon_i, \varepsilon_j) = 0$ for all $i \neq j$.

The multiple linear regression model is a natural extension of the simple linear regression model, just with more parameters: $\beta_0, \beta_1, \beta_2, \ldots, \beta_k$ and σ^2.
Treating all of the x_{ij} values as constants as before, we have

$E(y_i) = \beta_0 + \beta_1 x_{i1} + \beta_2 x_{i2} + \cdots + \beta_k x_{ik}$ and $\mathrm{Var}(y_i) = \sigma^2$.

$y_1, y_2, \ldots, y_n$ are uncorrelated with each other, again as before. If in addition $\varepsilon_i \sim N(0, \sigma^2)$, then

$$y_i \sim N\left(\beta_0 + \sum_{j=1}^{k} \beta_j x_{ij}, \sigma^2\right).$$

Estimation of the intercept and slope parameters is still performed using least-squares estimation. The least-squares estimators $\hat{\beta}_0, \hat{\beta}_1, \hat{\beta}_2, \ldots, \hat{\beta}_k$ are obtained by minimising

$$\sum_{i=1}^{n} \varepsilon_i^2 = \sum_{i=1}^{n} \left(y_i - \beta_0 - \sum_{j=1}^{k} \beta_j x_{ij} \right)^2$$

leading to the fitted regression model

$$\hat{y} = \hat{\beta}_0 + \hat{\beta}_1 x_1 + \hat{\beta}_2 x_2 + \cdots + \hat{\beta}_k x_k.$$

The residuals are expressed as:

$$\hat{\varepsilon}_i = y_i - \hat{\beta}_0 - \sum_{j=1}^{k} \hat{\beta}_j x_{ij}.$$

Just as with the simple linear regression model, we can decompose the total variation of y such that:

$$\sum_{i=1}^{n} (y_i - \bar{y})^2 = \sum_{i=1}^{n} (\hat{y}_i - \bar{y})^2 + \sum_{i=1}^{n} \hat{\varepsilon}_i^2$$

or, in words,

Total SS = Regression SS + Residual SS.

An unbiased estimator of σ^2 is

$$\hat{\sigma}^2 = \frac{1}{n-k-1} \sum_{i=1}^{n} \left(y_i - \hat{\beta}_0 - \sum_{j=1}^{k} \hat{\beta}_j x_{ij} \right)^2 = \frac{\text{Residual SS}}{n-k-1}.$$

(Continued)

We can test a single slope coefficient by testing

$$H_0 : \beta_i = 0 \text{ versus } H_1 : \beta_i \neq 0.$$

Under H_0, the test statistic is

$$T = \frac{\hat{\beta}_i}{\text{standard error of } \hat{\beta}_i} \sim t_{n-k-1}$$

and we reject H_0 if the p-value is less than α. However, note the slight difference in the interpretation of the slope coefficient β_j. In the multiple regression setting, β_j is the effect of x_j on y, *holding all other independent variables constant* - this is, unfortunately, not always practical.

It is also possible to test whether all the regression coefficients are equal to zero. This is known as a *joint test of significance* and can be used to test the overall significance of the regression model, that is, whether there is at least one significant explanatory (independent) variable, by testing

$$H_0 : \beta_1 = \beta_2 = \cdots = \beta_k = 0 \text{ versus } H_1 : \text{at least one } \beta_i \neq 0.$$

Indeed, it is preferable to perform this joint test of significance *before* conducting t tests of individual slope coefficients. Failure to reject H_0 would render the model useless and hence the model would not warrant any further statistical investigation. Provided $\varepsilon \sim N(0, \sigma^2)$, under $H_0 : \beta_1 = \beta_2 = \cdots = \beta_k = 0$, the test statistic is

$$F = \frac{(\text{Regression SS}) / k}{(\text{Residual SS}) / (n-k-1)} \sim F_{k,n-k-1}.$$

We reject H_0 if the p-value is less than α.

It may be shown that

$$\text{Regression SS} = \sum_{i=1}^{n} (\hat{y}_i - \bar{y})^2 = \sum_{i=1}^{n} \left(\hat{\beta}_1 (x_{i1} - \bar{x}_1) + \hat{\beta}_2 (x_{i2} - \bar{x}_2) + \cdots + \hat{\beta}_k (x_{ik} - \bar{x}_k) \right)^2.$$

Hence, under H_0, f (the test statistic value) should be (very) small.

15

TIME-SERIES ANALYSIS AND FORECASTING

Chapter contents

Chapter level: ***Intermediate***

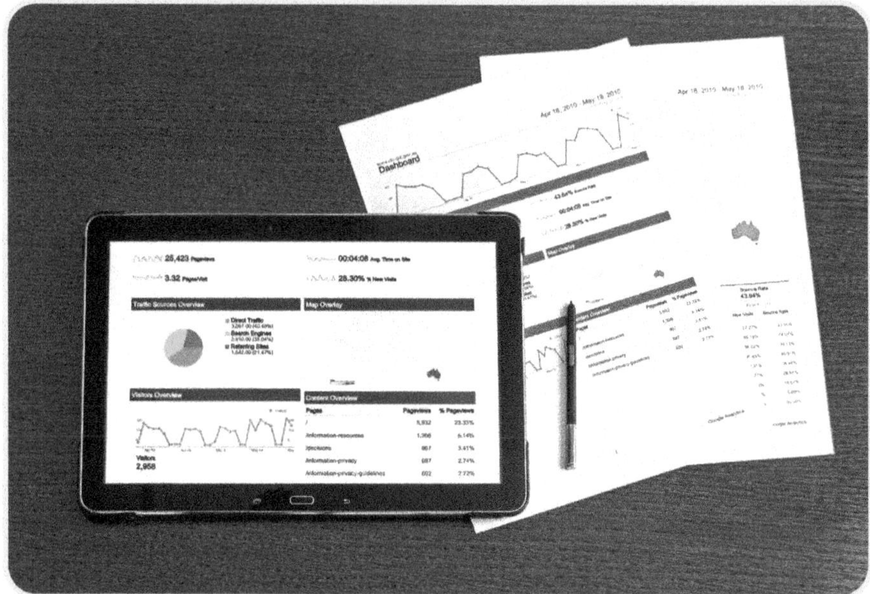

Source: Photo by Pexels via Pixabay.

Key concepts

- Trend and seasonality
- Exponential smoothing
- Predictive accuracy

Chapter value

Extrapolative forecasting models allow trend and seasonality to be used to form forecasts.

Key takeaway

Future-revealing crystal balls do not exist, but forecasting is preferable to doing nothing!

Chapter outline

Time. Allegedly it equals money, it continually advances, it flies. Variables change over time. Sales, earnings, sentiment, market share, etc. are all prone to fluctuations over time. Decisions are made in the present, informed by the past, based on expectations of the future. Our expectations of the future are comprised of *forecasts*. In this chapter we consider possible ways of forecasting the future, to assist decision-making in the present, making use of data from the past. *Trends* and *seasonality* often appear in time-series data, and we consider how to model these to generate forecasts. As expected, all forecasts are uncertain, so we need to assess how 'good' forecasts are by judging *predictive accuracy* in a retrospective manner.

Learning outcomes

After completing this chapter, you should be able to:

- recall the terminology of forecasting
- classify different forecasting models
- decompose a time-series variable into its trend and seasonal components
- build simple forecasting models using moving averages and exponential smoothing
- quantify predictive accuracy using common metrics, such as root mean squared error.

Motivational case: Scoophecy of a cool future

Nice-cream is a manufacturer of luxury ice cream. With flavours galore, it is a popular brand with approximately 10% market share thanks to celebrity endorsements and a competitive pricing strategy, despite its products being positioned at the luxury end of the ice cream market.

Having traded for some time, management have noticed a year-on-year increase in sales, but (unsurprisingly) have witnessed a spike in sales during the warm summer months, and a dip in sales during the cold, dark winter months. Pandemic-affected sales were evident in 2020.

To ensure supply meets demand, management would like to forecast sales volumes for the coming year. How might they go about this?

Source: Photo by Lama Roscu via Unsplash.

'Past is experience. Present is experiment. Future is expectation.' Anon.

Forecasting in action

The early 2020s witnessed a surge in inflation around the world due to various demand and supply factors, prompting many central banks to raise interest rates. However, uncertainty about the future path of inflation makes interest rate setting - and hence business investment decisions - challenging. It is thought it can take around 18 months for interest rate changes to fully work their way through an economy, so setting interest rates is based on *expectations* of the world 18 months into the future!

Macroeconomic forecasts are frequently published. For example, the Bank of England (BoE) publishes a quarterly *Monetary Policy Report* which features forecasts on various economic indicators. You are encouraged to (skim) read the various forecasts the BoE (or other central bank of your choice) makes, and pay close attention to the various assumptions on which their forecasts are based. Often, forecasts are presented as a *fan chart* that widens as the forecasts are projected further into the future, reflecting the greater uncertainty as the 'lead time' increases (it is easier to forecast the near future than the distant future).

Clearly, the BoE does not have a monopoly over forecasting, and to its credit it also publishes the results of surveys of external forecasters demonstrating how there is no single 'right' forecast, with actual forecasts varying based on the forecasting models and assumptions used.

15.1 INTRODUCTION

A **forecast** is an estimate of a variable's value at some time period in the future. Our focus will be on *quantitative forecasting*, specifically estimating:

- the *expected value* of a variable at some future time point
- the *error* associated with the forecast.

Definition

A **time series** is a sequence of realised observations of a variable, X, recorded at *equidistant points* in time, denoted by

$$\{x_1, x_2, \ldots, x_{t-1}, x_t, x_{t+1}, \ldots\}$$

that is, the time series starts in period 1.

By 'equidistant' we mean the observations must occur with the same **frequency**, such as daily, weekly, monthly, annually, etc.

Example 15.1

If we have *daily* frequency data, such as *daily* sales turnover, starting on Monday, then

x_1 = Monday sales, x_2 = Tuesday sales, . . . , x_5 = Friday sales.

If we have *monthly* frequency data, such as *monthly* sales turnover, starting with January, then

x_1 = January sales, x_2 = February sales, . . . , x_{12} = December sales.

Note that the observations must be equidistant in time, that is, all observations in the time series must have the same frequency.

15.1.1 Why forecast?

Forecasting helps decision-makers reach better-informed decisions. Examples include inventory management, production and capacity planning. There are two types of problems:

1. *Forecasting when an event occurs.* Event timings, such as a recession or surge in consumer demand, are important for managers to pre-empt.
2. *Forecasting a time series.* Business examples include sales revenues, stock price and product demand.

We will proceed with (2), since (1) may be incorporated into it.

Example 15.2

We consider some examples of forecasting problems.

Variable type	Who forecasts?	Uses of forecasts
Business (sales, retention, acquisition, demand)	Firms Competitors Equity analysts	Inventory control Sales targets Performance

(Continued)

Variable type	Who forecasts?	Uses of forecasts
Macroeconomic (inflation, unemployment, GDP, interest rates)	Central banks Analysts	Economic policy Investment decisions
Financial (foreign exchange rates, share prices, commodity prices)	Financial institutions Companies Traders/speculators	Risk management Supply chain management Speculation

15.1.2 Forecasting versus prediction

People may often use the terms *forecasting* and *prediction* interchangeably. However, they are not synonymous and have subtle differences.

Forecasting uses past data to effectively extrapolate into the future. Using time-series analysis, regression and other statistical methods, quantitative estimates of the future can be calculated. Forecasting techniques are scientific, based on data analysis and calculations.

Example 15.3

'Extrapolating the linear trend seen in past sales, I forecast Q1 sales growth to be 4.6%, rising to 5.2% in Q2.'

Prediction can be done by anyone such that predictions are forward-looking statements about what may happen based on judgement, gut instinct or other arbitrary methods, with or without the use of data. Predictions are prone to *bias*.

Example 15.4

'I predict sales of our new electric flying car will really take off! Who wouldn't want their own private air transport? The sky's the limit for sales growth next year, perhaps 100% or more!'

If you think about the weather, we consult weather *forecasts* rather than weather *predictions*, as these will be based on meteorological study of satellite data. Over the years, weather forecasts have become more accurate due to the collection of more data and more sophisticated modelling techniques.

15.2 CLASSIFYING FORECASTS

Classification of forecasting approaches is based on two criteria: (i) the *lead time*, and (ii) the *information used*.

15.2.1 Lead time

Lead time refers to the amount of time between when the forecast is made and the future time period which is being forecast.

Example 15.5

A forecast made in January 2025 for sales in January 2027 has a lead time of 2 years.

Lead times can easily be classified into the *short run, medium run* and *long run*, representing different time horizons. Short-term forecasting occurs when there is no expectation of a material change in the data-generating process (the process which results in the evolution of the time series) throughout the duration of the lead time. This means that the past may be extrapolated into the future. Of course, things change over time, including data-generating processes. If a material change is expected during the lead time, then we would be undertaking medium-run forecasting. If we have minimal or no information about the data-generating process towards the end of the lead time then this would constitute long-run forecasting, which ventures into prediction territory as there will need to be a lot of expert opinion incorporated with whatever limited data are available.

Example 15.6

The duration of short-run, medium-run and long-run forecasts depends on the nature of the variable being forecasted (which will affect the stability of the data-generating process) and their corresponding lead times. Consider the following examples with approximate lead times:

	Associated forecast lead times		
Variable	**Short-run**	**Medium-run**	**Long-run**
Staple food sales	< 1 year	1 to 4 years	> 4 years
Specific apparel item sales	< 6 months	6 to 12 months	–
Car sales	< 2 years	2 to ≈ 8 years	$>\approx 8$ years
Foreign exchange rates	< 30 days	20 days to 1 year	> 1 year
Procurement of airliners	–	5 to 20 years	> 20 years

Note that fashion is a fast-moving industry - especially fast-fashion retailers (clue is in the name!) - so long-run forecasts for specific garments are not necessary. In contrast, an airline seeking to expand its fleet cannot have same-day delivery of a new airliner - waiting times for new aircraft can be several years, so forecasting passenger numbers (and hence required capacity) in the short run is pointless.

Example 15.7

Demand for electric vehicles (EVs) is expected to grow significantly over the next decade, and probably beyond - a long-run prediction! A critical component of any EV is its battery, which is not your typical AA size used in a remote control. Rather, lithium is a key metal used in the production of EV batteries. Unsurprisingly, global demand for lithium has been forecast to grow year-on-year.

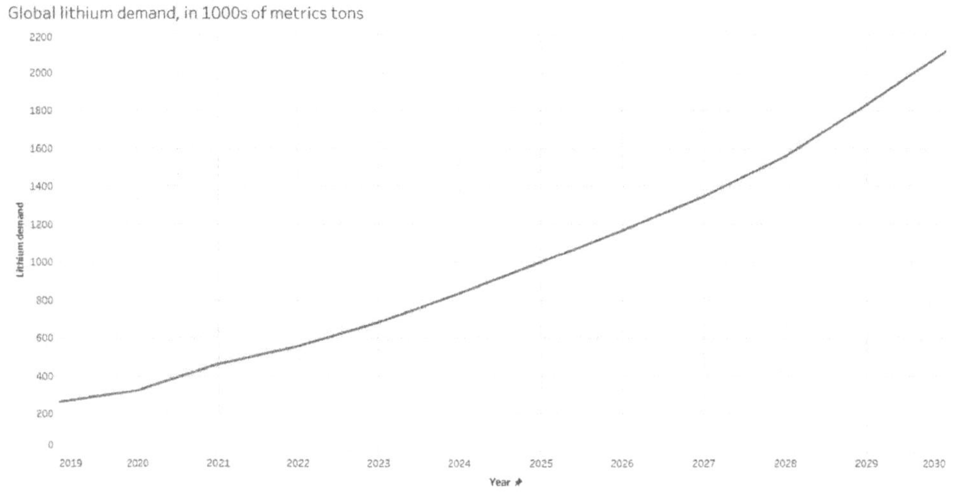

Source: https://www.statista.com/chart/28000/lithium-demand-forecast/

Note although the annual forecasts are strictly increasing, these are not simply a constant multiple of the previous year (where Δ means 'change'):

Year	2019	2020	2021	2022	2023	2024	2025	2026	2027	2028	2029	2030
Δ Year-on-year (in thousands of tonnes)	-	64	138	94	126	153	16	166	180	211	271	283
Δ Year-on-year(in %)	-	24.3	42.2	20.2	22.5	22.3	19.7	16.6	15.4	15.6	17.4	15.5

The forecasts would have been determined using an appropriate forecasting model, that is, adopting a scientific approach.

15.2.2 Information used

Forecasts are expectations of the future based on past and present data. Which data? Well, James, it depends! We distinguish between *extrapolative* models, that is, univariate models which seek to exploit patterns in the data of the variable being forecast, and *causal* models, that is, multivariate models which draw on one or more explanatory variables to form the forecast. Our focus in the remainder of the chapter will be on extrapolative models.

Extrapolative forecasting models

Recall that a time series is a sequence of realised observations, equidistant in time, of a random variable X, denoted by

$$\{x_1, x_2, \ldots, x_{t-1}, x_t, x_{t+1}, \ldots\}.$$

Suppose we wish to make a forecast of X at time t with lead time $j > 0$, that is, we seek to forecast X_{t+j}. In an extrapolative model we are basing the forecast on the *history of the time series*, namely the past and present values of X, that is, $x_1, x_2, \ldots, x_{t-1}$ (the past values) and x_t (the present value). The forecast itself is the conditional expectation of X_{t+j}, that is, conditional on the past and present data, denoted by

$$\mathrm{E}_t(X_{t+j} \mid X_1, X_2, \ldots, X_t).$$

For example, suppose we had daily frequency data. If $j = 1$, then $\mathrm{E}_t(X_{t+1} \mid X_1, X_2, \ldots, X_t)$ would represent the forecast made *today* (the t subscript on E) of the variable's value *tomorrow* based on the series history up to and including today's current value.

Extrapolative forecasting is a very convenient approach, since it requires no information beyond the historic series. While in practice X may be influenced by many other variables, no information on these other variables is incorporated into the forecasting methodology. We are simply seeking to *extrapolate* historic characteristics of the series, such as *trends* and *seasonality*, expecting them to continue into the future – which, of course, is not guaranteed. Investment advertisements, for example, often have the obligatory small print declaring 'past investment performance is no guarantee of future investment returns' – an effective disclaimer of responsibility for future losses!

Due to their simplicity, extrapolative-based forecasts provide an easy way to get an up-and-running forecasting model. Once its predictive accuracy has been determined, we then have a benchmark case against which to judge more sophisticated forecasting models.

Causal forecasting models

Plausibly we would expect X to be affected by other variables such as Y, Z, etc. For example, product sales (X) may be influenced by consumer confidence (Y) and marketing spend (Z). We may hypothesise that both Y and Z may affect X, possibly with a lag in the case of advertising spend. As in the extrapolative case, the forecast is a *conditional expectation*. For a forecast made at time t with lead time j, we have

$$\mathrm{E}_t(X_{t+j} \mid X_1, X_2, \ldots, X_t, Y_1, Y_2, \ldots, Y_t, Z_1, Z_2, \ldots, Z_t).$$

Note that we are not limited to two explanatory variables. We may include as many as we wish, although the marginal benefit of each additional explanatory variable is likely to diminish (i.e. diminishing marginal returns).

By explicitly modelling explanatory variables into a forecast, various scenarios may be modelled. For example, if consumer confidence increased by, say, 5% and marketing spend increased by, say, 10%, we could forecast sales in period $t + j$.

Trade-offs

As with any form of model building, we face choices. To end up with the 'best' model we need to balance the costs and benefits. *Costs* associated with forecasting are:

- data collection costs
- software costs
- development costs
- forecast error costs.

Benefits associated with forecasting are:

- better decisions from accurate forecasts
- robust models (insensitive to changing conditions, which therefore give models long lifespans)
- automated models, which are desirable.

Weighing up the costs and benefits can be subjective. Nonetheless, it is important to appreciate the trade-offs involved. Schematically, we can summarise the trade-offs between costs and amount of forecasting effort as shown in Figure 15.1. We, of course, seek the 'sweet spot'.

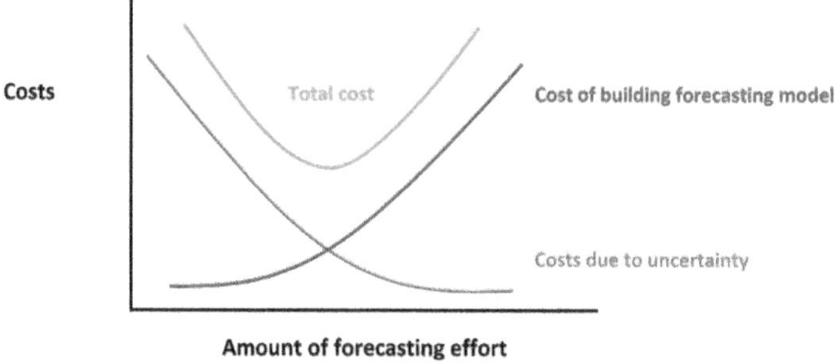

Figure 15.1 Trade-offs involved in developing forecasts.

15.3 DECOMPOSING A TIME SERIES

Time-series variables can be decomposed into four constituent parts.

1. Trend. This is the *long-run direction* of the time series. Trends can be *linear* or *nonlinear,* such as exponential, and it is possible to use a regression-based model.

2. Seasonal effects. For quarterly data these could relate to the traditional 'seasons' of spring, summer, autumn and winter (e.g. for electricity demand) or perhaps proxied by Q1, Q2, Q3 and Q4, but a 'season' would depend on the data frequency. For example, daily data may have a day-of-the-week effect (e.g. a supermarket may experience higher sales on Saturdays).

3 Cycles. The long-run (business) cycles which are distinct from seasonal effects. Think economic booms and recessions.
4 Random noise. The random fluctuations which inevitably occur, as well as 'blips' and market crashes, etc.

Items 1–3 in the above list are the systematic components. By estimating these components, a forecast can be obtained by reconstituting them using the decomposition. Given that cycle lengths are irregular (each economic boom and recession can have different lengths), our focus will be on modelling the trend and seasonal components.

Figure 15.2 shows some time-series examples of sales using Tableau. Note how for each division (Consumer, Corporate and Home Office) sales are gradually increasing over time, with the dashed lines indicating the linear trends of each series. The plotted trend lines have postive slopes, reflecting the gradual increase in sales (if sales had been declining over time, the trend line would have had a negative slope).

Clearly, these three time series do not follow a perfect line, with the deviations from the lines being due to a combination of seasonal effects, cycles and random noise.

Forecasts are also visible, surrounded by error bars (the shaded areas). Notice how historic patterns in each series are extrapolated into the future. These forecasts are calculated by adjusting the trend estimate accordingly.

15.3.1 Trend

Time series may exhibit trends. The simplest type is a linear trend (i.e. a straight line). As seen in Figure 15.2, trend lines can be extrapolated into the future to assist with obtaining the numerical forecasts. Forecasts can be fine-tuned with seasonal and cyclical adjustments.

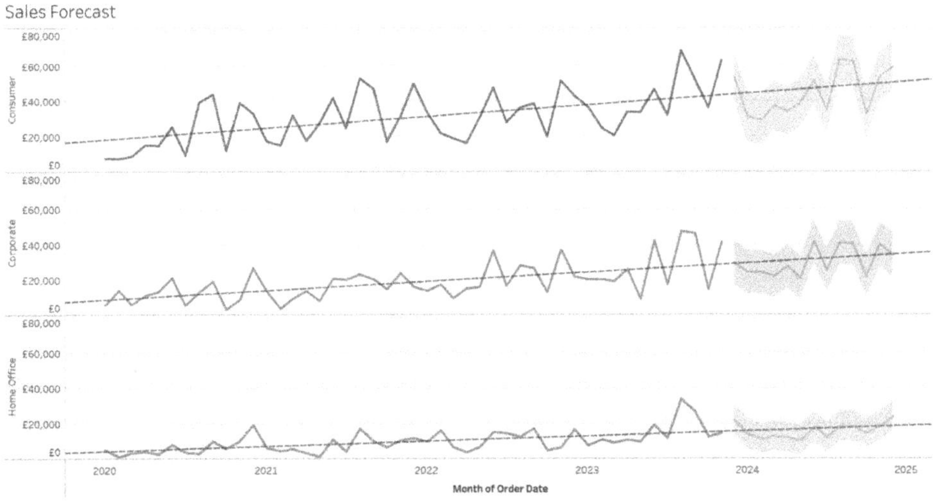

Figure 15.2 Examples of time series, including sales forecasts.

How to find the trend? A process of *smoothing* helps to remove seasonal, cyclical and random noise components. Smoothing is achieved by averaging time-series observations over a specific number of values. Smoothing may be achieved using:

- (unweighted) moving averages
- weighted moving averages.

Note that unweighted moving averages are special cases of weighted moving averages, where the weights are equal. For weighted moving averages the choice of weights can be subjective.

Let the trend at time period t be denoted T_t. This is calculated using

$$T_t = \frac{1}{N} \sum_{i=-(N-1)/2}^{(N-1)/2} X_{t+i} \tag{15.1}$$

where N is an odd integer. As N increases, so does the smoothing effect due to the averaging over a greater number of values.

Example 15.8

For $N = 3$ we have a three-point moving average:

$$T_t = \frac{1}{3}\sum_{i=-1}^{1} X_{t+i} = \frac{X_{t-1} + X_t + X_{t+1}}{3}.$$

Note that T_t is based on the average of the current value, X_t, and the values immediately before, X_{t-1}, and after, X_{t+1}.

For $N = 5$ we have a five-point moving average:

$$T_t = \frac{1}{5}\sum_{i=-2}^{2} X_{t+i} = \frac{X_{t-2} + X_{t-1} + X_t + X_{t+1} + X_{t+2}}{5}.$$

Note that T_t is based on the average of the current value, X_t, and the two values immediately before, X_{t-1}, X_{t-2}, and after, X_{t+1}, X_{t+2}.

Example 15.9

Financial time-series data can be very noisy. Moving averages can be effective at smoothing the series. Consider the FTSE 100 closing prices from January 2020 to August 2022. Applying five-point (spanning a week) and 25-point (spanning just over a month) moving averages allows us to achieve various degrees of smoothing. Note the steep decline in early 2020 as the financial markets woke up to Covid-19 - just a one-third wipe-out of FTSE 100 market capitalisation then!

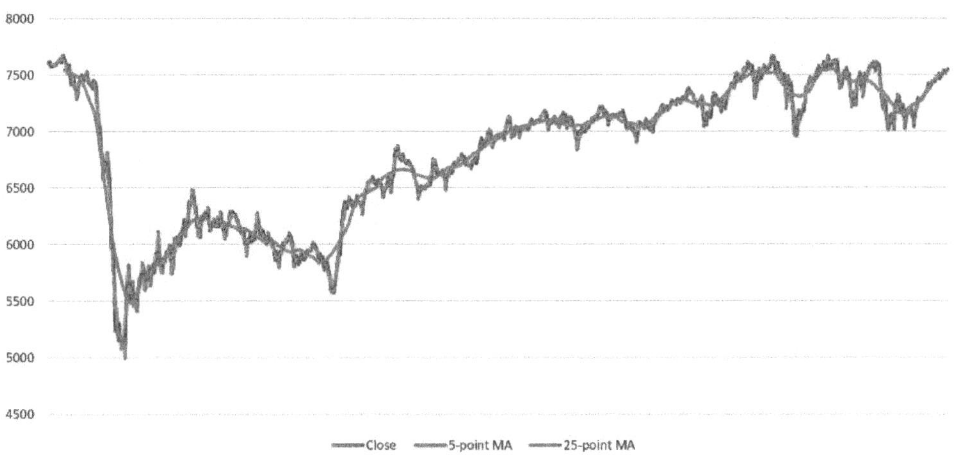

Example 15.10

Weighted moving averages can be used if we wanted to attach greater weight to observations close to (in a temporal sense) the period we are smoothing for. Weights must sum to 1. Let w_i be the weight attached to X_{t+i}, for $i = -(N-1)/2, \ldots, (N-1)/2$. If $N = 5$, we could have

$$w_{-2} = w_2 = 0.10,\ w_{-1} = w_1 = 0.20,\ w_0 = 0.40,$$

such that

$$\sum_{i=-2}^{2} w_i = 0.10 + 0.20 + 0.40 + 0.20 + 0.10 = 1.$$

The five-point moving averages would then be calculated as

$$T_t = \frac{1}{5}\sum_{i=-2}^{2} w_i X_{t+i} = \frac{X_{t-2} + 2X_{t-1} + 4X_t + 2X_{t+1} + X_{t+2}}{10}.$$

Note that the choice of the weights is subjective.

15.3.2 Seasonality

Seasonal effects impact time-series variables in specific periods when observations occur. Seasonal weather patterns, for example, would affect ice cream sales, as well as demand for air conditioning and heating. Known events such as the end of the tax year and public holidays are other examples.

When present, seasonal effects can contribute a significant amount of the variation seen in time-series data. As such, we seek to isolate and quantify seasonal effects. Having done so, we can then *seasonally adjust* trend forecasts to improve forecast accuracy by adjusting to take account of the season for which the forecast is made.

First, we need to isolate the underlying trend, that is, the series value which would have been expected in the absence of any other time-series component (seasonal, cyclical and noise). If there are N periods per year, and N is even, then we require a centred moving average, since there is no midpoint. For example, for weekly data $N = 52$ (even), for monthly data $N = 12$ (even), and for quarterly data $N = 4$ (even). The (non-centred) moving average formula (15.1) required the number of observations to be averaged over to be odd. For even N, centering is necessary to ensure an averaged value matches the period of an observation as opposed to falling inbetween two observations.

To proceed, we effectively take an average of moving averages, that is, *smooth the smoothed observations*. The trend estimate for an even number of periods per year is

$$T_t^c = \frac{T_t + T_{t+1}}{2},$$

where 'c' indicates a centred moving average and where

$$T_t = \frac{1}{N}\sum_{i=-N/2}^{N/2-1} X_{t+i}.$$

Example 15.11

For quarterly data, $N = 4$, we hence have

$$T_t^c = \frac{T_t + T_{t+1}}{2} = \frac{(X_{t-2} + X_{t-1} + X_t + X_{t+1})/4 + (X_{t-1} + X_t + X_{t+1} + X_{t+2})/4}{2}$$
$$= \frac{X_{t-2} + 2(X_{t-1} + X_t + X_{t+1}) + X_{t+2}}{8}.$$

For monthly data, $N = 12$, we have

$$T_t^c = \frac{T_t + T_{t+1}}{2} = \frac{(X_{t-6} + X_{t-5} + \cdots + X_{t+5})/12 + (X_{t-5} + X_{t-4} + \cdots + X_{t+6})/12}{2}$$
$$= \frac{X_{t-6} + 2(X_{t-5} + \cdots + X_{t+5}) + X_{t+6}}{24}.$$

Having isolated the trend, the seasonal patterns need to be quantified. To assist, we adopt the following notation:

$$X_t = X_{i,j},$$

where $X_{i,j}$ is the jth period in year i. It follows that $t = iN + j$, where N is the number of periods per year.

Example 15.12

For quarterly data, starting in Q1 of 2020, $N = 4$ (four quarters per year) and so $X_{3,2}$ denotes Q2 of year 3, that is, Q2 of 2022.

For monthly data, starting in January of 2020, $N = 12$ (twelve months per year) and so $X_{5,7}$ denotes month 7 of year 5, that is. July 2024.

Seasonality may be modelled in different ways, such as with an *additive* model or *multiplicative* model. We will focus on the multiplicative model, since this takes into account that for later time points there is often extra variation. A multiplicative model accounts for this, whereas an additive model simply adds seasonality to linearity as a fixed effect.

Multiplicative model of trend and seasonality

The time-series observation $X_{i,j}$ is modelled as

$$X_{i,j} = T_{i,j} S_j + \varepsilon_{i,j}$$

for $j = 1, 2, \ldots, N$, where $S_1, S_2, \ldots, S_N$ are the seasonal effects such that

$$\sum_{j=1}^{N} S_j = N$$

and $\varepsilon_{i,j}$ is the noise component. By assumption, $E(\varepsilon_{i,j}) = 0$ for all i, j.

In the *absence* of seasonality, then $S_1 = S_2 = \cdots = S_N = 1$, and the time-series observation is just assumed to exhibit trend plus noise, that is, we have

$$X_{i,j} = T_{i,j} + \varepsilon_{i,j}.$$

15.3.3 Forecasting using a multiplicative model of trend and seasonality

If we assume a linear trend, then we can run a simple linear regression of the *deseasonalised* data, $D_t = D_{i,j}$, as the dependent variable, on a time index, t, as the independent variable, where

$$D_t = D_{i,j} = \frac{X_{i,j}}{\hat{S}_j},$$

that is, we run the regression

$$D_t = \beta_0 + \beta_1 t + \varepsilon_t.$$

With a sample size of T observations (not to be confused with the $T_{i,j}$ notation indicating a trend!), i.e. $t = 1, 2, \ldots, T$, we can then make forecasts with a lead time of j, using the formula

$$\hat{X}_{T+j} = \underbrace{\left(\hat{\beta}_0 + \hat{\beta}_1 \times (T+j)\right)}_{\text{estimate of the trend}} \times \underbrace{\hat{S}_j}_{\text{seasonal adjustment of trend}}.$$

Example 15.13

Recall Nice-cream, the purveyor of luxury ice cream. The company has the following monthly sales volumes (in thousands of litres) for the last five years of trading:

Year	Jan	Feb	Mar	Apr	May	Jun	Jul	Aug	Sep	Oct	Nov	Dec
2018	121.4	148.6	173.9	246.3	271.4	394.1	468.3	491.0	321.4	221.7	173.8	124.5
2019	127.9	1567	182.6	259.4	285.7	413.8	492.7	516.4	338.4	232.0	180.3	126.4
2020	135.7	163.4	101.3	154.6	224.3	397.6	415.9	463.8	350.5	241.9	186.7	141.2
2021	142.7	171.3	201.2	285.6	313.9	455.3	538.6	563.7	371.2	256.1	197.5	142.6
2022	148.3	177.4	208.6	297.4	331.2	479.5	572.1	612.2	389.6	267.5	211.4	152.6

We begin by plotting the data to visually inspect for any signs of a trend and/or seasonality:

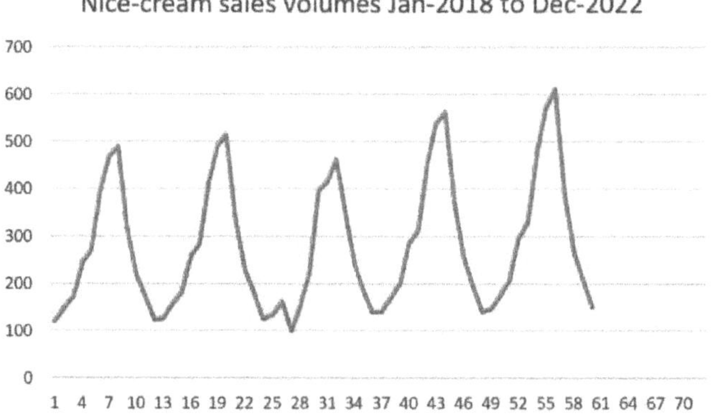

Seasonality is clearly evident, with sales peaking in the summer months (in the northern hemisphere!), with a slight increasing trend over time. Note that in 2020 there seemed to be lower sales - especially in March and April 2020, likely to be attributable to Covid lockdowns with demand for Nice-cream hit - not nice!

To obtain the seasonally adjusted monthly forecasts for sales volumes in 2023 we proceed as follows. Note that the steps make reference to the following Excel spreadsheet.

Month	t	X_t	T_t	S_j	Seasonal index	Deseasonalised series	Forecasts
Jan-18	1	121.4			0.498	243.9	123.4
Feb-18	2	148.6			0.597	249.0	148.6
Mar-18	3	173.9			0.603	288.4	150.8
Apr-18	4	246.3			0.865	284.9	217.3
May-18	5	271.4			1.007	269.6	254.1
Jun-18	6	394.1			1.528	257.9	387.6
Jul-18	7	468.3	263.3	1.779	1.755	266.8	447.1
Aug-18	8	491.0	263.9	1.860	1.863	263.6	476.7
Sep-18	9	321.4	264.6	1.215	1.265	254.1	325.1
Oct-18	10	221.7	265.5	0.835	0.867	255.6	224.0
Nov-18	11	173.8	266.7	0.652	0.670	259.3	173.8
Dec-18	12	124.5	268.1	0.464	0.483	258.0	125.7
Jan-19	13	127.9	269.9	0.474	0.498	256.9	130.3
Feb-19	14	156.7	272.0	0.576	0.597	262.6	156.8
Mar-19	15	182.6	273.8	0.667	0.603	302.8	159.2
Apr-19	16	259.4	274.9	0.944	0.865	300.0	229.2
May-19	17	285.7	275.6	1.037	1.007	283.8	268.0
Jun-19	18	413.8	275.9	1.500	1.528	270.7	408.7
Jul-19	19	492.7	276.4	1.783	1.755	280.7	471.3
Aug-19	20	516.4	277.0	1.865	1.863	277.2	502.5
Sep-19	21	338.4	273.8	1.236	1.265	267.6	342.6
Oct-19	22	232.0	266.1	0.872	0.867	267.5	235.9
Nov-19	23	180.3	259.2	0.696	0.670	269.0	183.1
Dec-19	24	126.4	255.9	0.494	0.483	261.9	132.4
Jan-20	25	135.7	252.1	0.538	0.498	272.6	137.1
Feb-20	26	163.4	246.7	0.662	0.597	273.8	165.1
Mar-20	27	101.3	245.0	0.414	0.603	168.0	167.5
Apr-20	28	154.6	245.9	0.629	0.865	178.8	241.2
May-20	29	224.3	246.6	0.910	1.007	222.8	281.9
Jun-20	30	397.6	247.5	1.607	1.528	260.1	429.8
Jul-20	31	415.9	248.4	1.675	1.755	237.0	495.6
Aug-20	32	463.8	249.0	1.863	1.863	249.0	528.2
Sep-20	33	350.5	253.5	1.383	1.265	277.1	360.0

	Sjs	Sjs	Sjs	Sjs	Sjs	Average	Normalised
January		0.47385	0.538367	0.499046	0.477252	0.497129	0.497810796
February		0.576121	0.662432	0.580244	0.564691	0.595872	0.596689503
March		0.667012	0.413505	0.670118	0.658165	0.6022	0.60302606
April		0.94363	0.628722	0.946636	0.934681	0.863417	0.864601897
May		1.036663	0.909662	1.036858	1.037472	1.005164	1.006542994
June		1.49957	1.606735	1.501401	1.497346	1.526263	1.528357241
July	1.778551	1.782884	1.67454	1.774386		1.75259	1.754995176
August	1.860465	1.864568	1.862744	1.854098		1.860469	1.863021852
September	1.214606	1.235732	1.382757	1.218681		1.262944	1.264676795
October	0.834963	0.87188	0.919422	0.838595		0.866215	0.86740363
November	0.65176	0.695691	0.685662	0.644153		0.669317	0.670234983
December	0.464415	0.493879	0.507131	0.462486		0.481978	0.482639074
					Sum =	11.98356	12

SUMMARY OUTPUT

Regression Statistics	
Multiple R	0.593208
R Square	0.351896
Adjusted R Square	0.340722
Standard Error	27.50709
Observations	60

ANOVA

	df	*SS*	*MS*	*F*	*gnificance F*
Regression	1	23827.99	23827.99	31.49184	5.89E-07
Residual	58	43885.13	756.6402		
Total	59	67713.12			

	Coefficients	*tandard Err*	*t Stat*	*P-value*	*Lower 95%*	*Upper 95%*
Intercept	246.6953	7.192018	34.30127	3.26E-40	232.299	261.0917
t	1.150715	0.205054	5.611759	5.89E-07	0.740254	1.561176

- The time period t is shown in column B, and the raw data X_t in column C (truncated in the screenshot).
- Since these are monthly data (i.e. an even number of months per year), we should use a 12-point centred moving average to smooth the data. We compute

$$T_t^c = T_{i,j}^c = \frac{X_{t-6} + 2(X_{t-5} + \cdots + X_{t+5}) + X_{t+6}}{24}$$

  and the values are shown in column D. Note there are no entries in cell range `D2:D7` due to insufficient past data for smoothing.
- Next, we isolate the seasonal effect by dividing the original (raw) data, $X_{i,j}$, by the smoothed series, $T_{i,j}^c$. Hence our *preliminary* estimates of S_j are derived by rearranging the multiplicative model (ignoring the noise component):

$$X_{i,j} = T_{i,j}^c S_j \quad \Rightarrow \quad S_j = \frac{X_{i,j}}{T_{i,j}^c}$$

  shown in column E.
- We then compute the *seasonal averages*. To do this, we take all the S_j figures for each month (in cell range `K2:O13`) and take the *average* of these for each month (in cell range `P2:P13`). Note that the sum of the seasonal averages is 11.98356 (cell `P14`). Ideally, this should be 12, such that the average seasonal average is 1. (No seasonal effects would mean that all the S_j values are 1, while any $S_j > 0$ would indicate an above-trend sales volume, and any $S_j < 0$ would indicate a below-trend sales volume. In all cases, the S_j should average to 1.)
- We now *normalise* the seasonal averages so that they do sum to 12 (equivalently average to 1). To do this we use the formula:

$$\text{seasonal index} = \frac{\text{seasonal average}}{\text{sum of averages}} \times 12.$$

(Continued)

These seasonal indices are shown in cells `Q2:Q13` (highlighted), with confirmation that they sum to 12 in cell `Q14`. Plotting these by month yields the following graph:

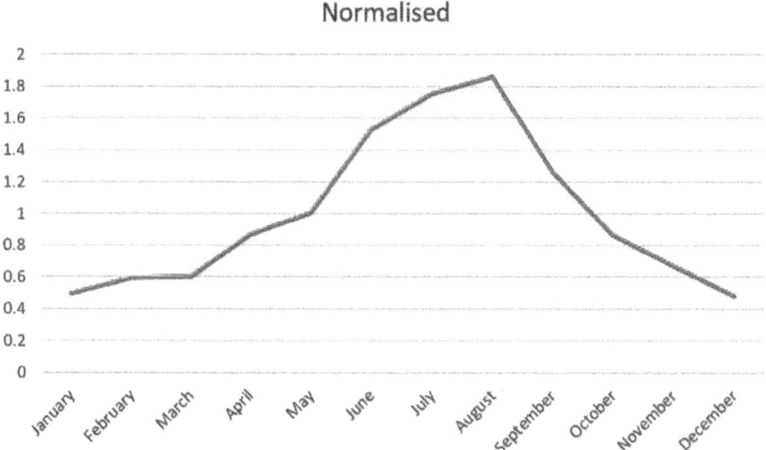

Notice that seasonal averages above 1 (like the maximum of 1.863 in August) indicate sales above trend, as we would expect for ice cream in the summer months, while seasonal averages below 1 (like the minimum of 0.483 in December) indicate sales below trend. If there were no seasonality at all, each seasonal average would be equal to 1, which when multiplied by the trend value would result in zero seasonal adjustment.

- The seasonal indices are entered in column F such that we have one (common) index value for each month. These can be applied to all months, regardless of whether a centred moving average was obtainable or not.
- We then *deseasonalise* the data by dividing the original data by the respective seasonal index ($D_{i,j} = X_{i,j}/S_j$) which appears in column G. A plot of the deseasonalised data (with trend line) is as follows:

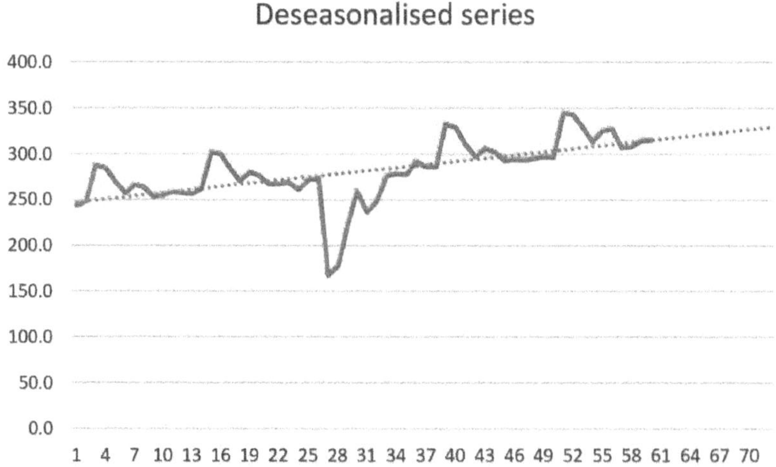

The Covid pandemic impact of 2020 is clearly evident. Without the pandemic we would not have expected the significant fall in sales volume around the time of the first lockdowns.

- Having obtained the deseasonalised series, we run a simple linear regression with the *deseasonalised data* as the dependent variable, $D_{i,j}$, and the *month number* as the independent variable, t. The regression results appear on the bottom right-hand side of the spreadsheet. All we care about are the coefficients (highlighted). This allows us to write the estimated trend line as

  $$\hat{D}_{i,j} = 246.695 + 1.151t$$

  which is shown plotted above. Note the (statistically significant) positive slope which suggests that demand for Nice-cream is gradually increasing over time. In passing we note that $R^2 = 0.352$, that is, 35.2% of the deseasonalised series can be explained by 'time' (the trend). Clearly, this value is somewhat deflated due to the Covid effects on sales volumes in 2020, so we should not be too concerned. Indeed, one could argue that 2020 was not representative of normal trading conditions, such that the 2020 data could have been adjusted/cleaned to reflect what might have been *without* Covid, producing a stronger linear trend. Interested readers: have a go!

- Finally, to obtain forecasts, we substitute suitable values for t into the estimated trend line expression. For example, to forecast for January 2023 ($t = 60$) the *trend estimate* is

  $$246.695 + (1.151 \times 60) = 315.8.$$

  However, this forecast needs to be *seasonally adjusted* - ice cream sales will be below trend in wintry January - so we multiply it by the appropriate seasonal index, that is, we multiply it by the January index of 0.49781, giving our forecast of 157.2. (Since $0.49781 < 1$, the seasonal adjustment is downward, i.e. below trend.)

The following plot shows X_t (in blue) and the forecasts (in orange). Note how the historic series patterns are extrapolated into 2023, forming the basis of our forecasts.

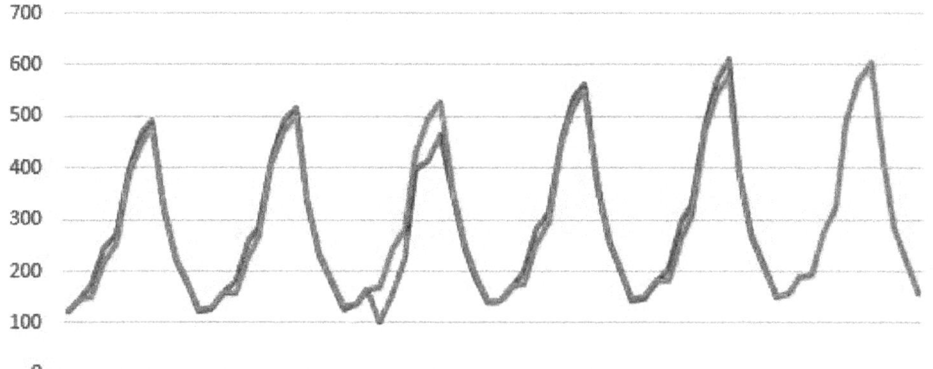

Not bad! Okay, 2020 forecasts failed to pre-empt the pandemic, but who in 2019 expected the world to lock down a few months later, let alone who anticipated the impact on the ice cream market?

15.4 ASSESSING FORECAST ACCURACY

The future is uncertain, and so by extension any forecasts of the future are also uncertain. While the forecasts of Nice-cream 2023 sales volumes in Example 15.13 *seem* plausible, are they the 'best' forecasts? Should production capacity decisions be made based on this extrapolative model? What we have derived is *one* set of forecasts, but clearly there are many other possible sets based on other forecasting models. We need a way to assess *forecast accuracy*.

But how? If the future hasn't happened yet, how can we possibly judge whether our forecasts are reliable? To answer this, we need to engage in a spot of time travel through a process called *backtesting*.

Back to the future

Children (and adults) of the 1980s will recall the time-travelling exploits of Marty McFly in the *Back to the Future* movie franchise. Firing up the DeLorean time machine allowed Marty and Doc to travel through time, backwards or forwards, depending on the film. Simply input your desired date into the dashboard, hit the magic 88 miles per hour, then welcome to the past/ future.

We adapt this idea to assessing forecast accuracy. While the future hasn't happened yet, the past has! So, we can look 'back in time' to judge the performance of a forecasting model by seeing how well it performed in predicting past observations.

Looking at the actual sales volumes and forecasted sales volumes in Example 15.13, we see visually that the forecasts tracked the past X_t values very closely, with the exception of 2020, but I think we can be charitable and forgive our simple extrapolative model from failing to anticipate a global pandemic! Hindsight and all that.

15.4.1 Forecast accuracy metrics

In matters of forecasting, there are clearly many possible forecasting models we *could* construct to forecast X_{t+j}. How should we choose among them? Well, the accuracy of forecasts can be judged based on the forecast errors by comparing the actual history of X_t values with the same-period forecasts, X_t, to see how such *retrospective forecasting* performed. Hence the forecast error in period t is

$$X_t - \hat{X}_t.$$

There are several possible quality metrics we could employ. We review some of the most common. Assume throughout that there are T known forecast errors, that is, we have $X_t - \hat{X}_t$ for $t = 1, 2, \ldots, T$.

Root mean squared error

The **root mean squared error** (RMSE) is calculated by taking the (positive) square root of the average (mean) squared error (hence the name). The formula is

$$\text{RMSE} = \sqrt{\frac{1}{T}\sum_{t=1}^{T}\left(X_t - \hat{X}_t\right)^2}.$$

Due to the squaring, large forecast errors are penalised heavily: when our model is wrong by a wide margin, we wish to 'punish' the model for such big mistakes. The smaller the RMSE, the better.

Mean absolute error

The **mean absolute error** (MAE) is calculated by taking the average (mean) of the absolute errors, that is, ignoring the forecast error sign (overestimates and underestimates are not distinguished). The formula is

$$\text{MAE} = \frac{1}{T}\sum_{t=1}^{T}\left|X_t - \hat{X}_t\right|.$$

Without any squaring, the MAE does not punish large forecast errors as heavily as RMSE. The smaller the MAE, the better.

Intuitively, the MAE is perhaps a more appropriate measure for judging forecast accuracy. However, it is technically less convenient since the function $g(x) = |x|$ is not differentiable at $x = 0$. So what? Well, if we are trying to analytically find the *minimum* MAE model, we run into optimisation (calculus) problems. As such, the RMSE is used more often.

Mean absolute scaled error

The **mean absolute scaled error** (MASE) is a normalised metric which takes the form of a ratio comparing model forecast errors with the naïve forecasts which are simply the previous value of the variable. Hence $\hat{X}_t = X_{t-1}$, that is, naïve forecasts assume no change between the current period and the next period - simple, but naïve! So, a naïve forecast model has a MASE of 1, with superior forecasting models having a MASE less than 1. The formula is

$$\text{MASE} = \frac{\frac{1}{T}\sum_{t=1}^{T}\left|X_t - \hat{X}_t\right|}{\frac{1}{T-1}\sum_{t=2}^{T}\left|X_t - X_{t-1}\right|}.$$

The smaller the MASE, the better.

Mean absolute percentage error

The **mean absolute percentage error** (MAPE) considers the magnitude of the forecast error with respect to X_t in terms of a percentage. It is undefined if $X_t = 0$ in any period - a problem not encountered with MASE. The formula is

$$\text{MAPE} = 100 \times \frac{1}{T}\sum_{t=1}^{T}\left|\frac{X_t - \hat{X}_t}{X_t}\right|.$$

The smaller the MAPE, the better.

Akaike information criterion

The **Akaike information criterion** (AIC) works a bit like adjusted R^2 in regression, in that we have to pay a 'complexity penalty' such that the more parameters the forecasting model has, the bigger the estimation price we have to pay. The formula is

$$\text{AIC} = T \times \ln\left(\frac{\sum_{t=1}^{T}\left(X_t - \hat{X}_{t-1}\right)^2}{T}\right) + 2(k+1),$$

where k is the number of model parameters. The smaller the AIC, the better.

15.5 TREND-BASED TIME-SERIES MODELS

Having seen how we may decompose a time series into its trend, seasonality, cyclical and noise components, we consider other possible trend-based forecasting models.

The most basic model would be that of a time-series variable at time t, X_t, exhibiting natural variation about a trend also at time t, denoted T_t. We have the simple additive model

$$X_t = T_t + \varepsilon_t,$$

where the noise component (independent of the trend) is assumed to be normally distributed, with a zero mean and a constant variance, σ_ε^2, i.e. $\varepsilon_t \sim N(0, \sigma_\varepsilon^2)$.

Suppose we subject the trend to a small amount of variation from period to period, such that

$$T_t = T_{t-1} + a_t$$

where $a_t \sim N(0, \sigma_a^2)$. This means the *expected* change in the series each period, ΔX_t, is zero, since by independence and the zero-mean variables a_t and ε_t we have

$$\begin{aligned}E(\Delta X_t) = E(X_t - X_{t-1}) &= E(T_t + \varepsilon_t - T_{t-1} - \varepsilon_{t-1})\\ &= E(T_t - T_{t-1}) + E(\varepsilon_t) - E(\varepsilon_{t-1})\\ &= E(a_t) + E(\varepsilon_t) - E(\varepsilon_{t-1})\\ &= 0.\end{aligned}$$

In any time period t we would like the noise variation to be much greater than the trend disturbance term. As such we assume that

$$\sigma_\varepsilon^2 \gg \sigma_a^2,$$

where $\gg$ means 'much greater than'. So X_t is a process with a 'level' T_t which is itself subject to a small (low-variance) random change each period, a_t, and a period-specific 'shock' of ε_t, which will likely be larger in magnitude due to the much larger variance of σ_ε^2.

When determining a forecast, our objective is to come up with our best possible estimate of T_t (the level) because this will be the optimal forecast at time t for X_{t+j}, that is, a forecast with a lead time of $j > 0$.

Now let's marginally increase the complexity of the model slightly by introducing an *incremental trend*, b_t, which allows us to model the systematic change in the series level at time period t. To make it more realistic, let this term also be subject to some random variation, denoted c_t. The model is still additive,

$$X_t = T_t + \varepsilon_t,$$

but now we have

$$T_t = T_{t-1} + a_t + b_t \text{ and } b_t = b_{t-1} + c_t$$

where $c_t \sim N(0, \sigma_c^2)$ and $\sigma_\varepsilon^2 \gg \sigma_c^2$.

15.5.1 Estimating the model

Previously we have used moving averages to smooth time-series processes. We have seen different ways of doing this, depending on how many periods, N, are being averaged – a simple moving average for an odd number of periods; a centred moving average for an even number of periods (such as with monthly or quarterly data with seasonality).

While moving averages allow trend estimation, there is a *truncation* of the series. For example, to compute a five-point moving average for period t, we need 'future' observations up to period $t + 2$ to compute the trend estimate. As such, if the present period is t, then the moving average value is only computable two periods into the future (i.e. with a lag), which can be problematic.

15.5.2 Exponential smoothing

To circumvent the 'insufficient data' problem which stems from moving averages, we may instead use an exponential smoothing model (also known as an *exponential weighted moving average* model). The estimate of the one-period-ahead trend, T_{t+1}, based on the observed series data up to the present period t, is given by

$$\hat{T}_{t+1} = \alpha X_t + \alpha^2 X_{t-1} + \alpha^3 X_{t-2} + \cdots \quad (15.2)$$

where α is a smoothing constant/parameter, which takes values between 0 and 1. For any $0 < \alpha < 1$, we have that

$$\alpha > \alpha^2 > \alpha^3 > \cdots,$$

such that *less weight is placed on more historic data*. Effectively, as data becomes 'older' it is deemed less valuable and so it is essentially 'discounted' more heavily. By recursive substitution, it can be shown that (15.2) may be written as

$$\hat{T}_{t+1} = \alpha X_t + (1-\alpha)\hat{T}_t,$$

or equivalently

$$\hat{T}_{t+1} = \hat{T}_t + a(X_t - \hat{T}_t).$$

In practice, this means that the estimate of the level at time $t + 1$ (made in period t) equals the previous estimate $\hat{T}_t$ (i.e. the estimate of the trend at time t made at time $t - 1$) plus α times the previous forecast error, $X_t - \hat{T}_t$ (i.e. the difference between the realised observation in period t and its forecasted value made in the previous period).

We can represent this basic 'updating equation' as

new estimate = old estimate + smoothing parameter × (outcome − old estimate).

How do we estimate the smoothing parameter α?

The smoothing parameter α can take any value between 0 and 1. Naturally, the question arises: which value? Remember, whenever we have a choice, we always want the 'best', but we need to clarify in what sense something is considered 'best' or 'optimal'.

Given that our goal is to forecast, it seems reasonable to form an *optimisation problem*, whereby we set an *objective function* (the function to be optimised in some sense). Suppose we choose the RMSE as our preferred quality metric. Since we would wish the RMSE to be as small as possible (errors are bad, after all!), this means we have a *minimisation* problem. Specifically,

$$\min_{0 \le \alpha \le 1} \frac{1}{T}\sum_{t=2}^{T}(T_t - \hat{T}_t)^2,$$

where

$$\hat{T}_t = \alpha X_{t-1} + (1-\alpha)\hat{T}_{t-1}.$$

There is not an analytical solution for finding α, rather it is found by a so-called *grid search method*. We may use Excel Solver to solve this optimisation problem.

Example 15.14

A retailer wishes to estimate its sales next week based on a time series of weekly sales for the previous quarter (i.e. 13 weeks of data). Weekly sales (in thousands of units) have been as follows:

Week #	1	2	3	4	5	6	7	8	9	10	11	12	13
Sales (in 000s)	45	52	48	58	53	61	55	64	70	67	74	77	75

We will use exponential smoothing to forecast sales in week 14, that is, a one-period-ahead forecast. Plotting the data, a trend is evident:

The one-period forecast will be

$$\hat{T}_{14} = \alpha X_{13} + (1-\alpha)\hat{T}_{13}.$$

We need to find the value of α, for $0 \leq \alpha \leq 1$, which will minimise the RMSE. A spreadsheet model is set up as follows:

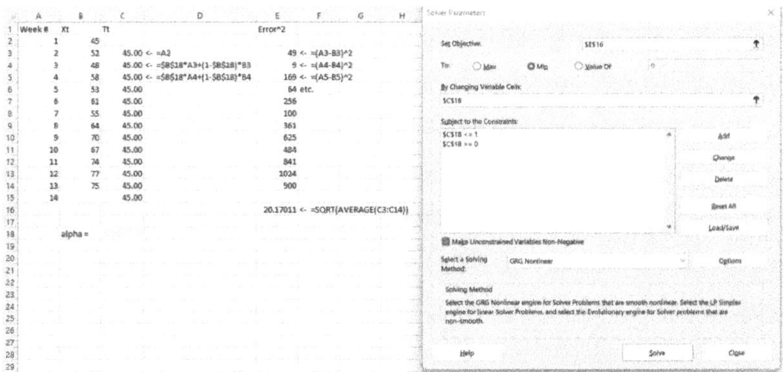

(Continued)

Invoking Excel's Solver (from the Data pane, select `Solver`) we set the objective to be the value in cell `E16` which is the RMSE, by having Excel experiment with different values of α in cell `C18` (highlighted) subject to the constraints that $\alpha \leq 1$ and $\alpha \geq 0$. Solver works using a grid search method (think of it a bit like iterative trial and error) rather than solving for α analytically.

We require a starting point for the process, which is

$$\hat{T}_2 = X_1 = 45$$

as shown in cell `C3`. Thereafter, the cell range `C4:C15` returns

$$\hat{T}_t = \alpha X_{t-1} + (1 - \alpha)\,\hat{T}_{t-1}\,, \text{ for } t = 3, 4, \ldots, 14,$$

such that the one-period-ahead forecast appears in cell `C15`. The screenshot above has cell `C18` blank, which is equivalent to $\alpha = 0$, which is why $\hat{T}_2 = \hat{T}_3 = \cdots = \hat{T}_{14} = 45$.

Pressing `Solve` returns the RMSE-minimising smoothing parameter, that is, we set $\alpha = 0.7404261$, which returns an RMSE value of 5.899325 (compare this with the null $\alpha = 0$ model RMSE of 20.17011). Since we have used Solver it is *impossible* to find a different α which returns a *lower* RMSE.

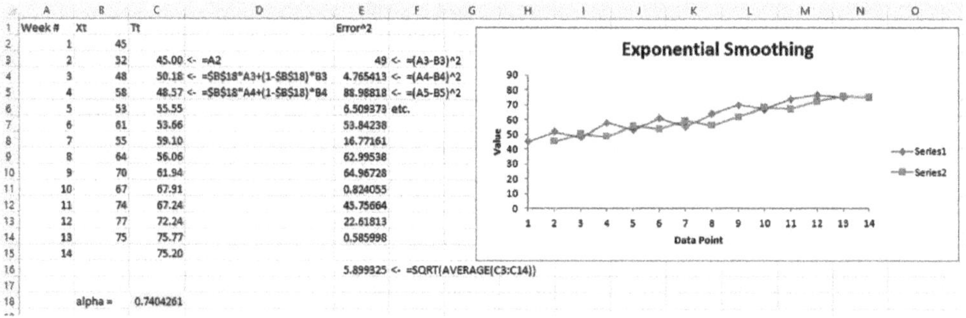

	A	B	C	D	E	F
1	Week #	Xt	Tt		Error^2	
2	1	45				
3	2	52	45.00 <- =A2		49 <- =(A3-B3)^2	
4	3	48	50.18 <- =$B$18*A3+(1-$B$18)*B3		4.765413 <- =(A4-B4)^2	
5	4	58	48.57 <- =$B$18*A4+(1-$B$18)*B4		88.98818 <- =(A5-B5)^2	
6	5	53	55.55		6.509373 etc.	
7	6	61	53.66		53.84238	
8	7	55	59.10		16.77161	
9	8	64	56.06		62.99538	
10	9	70	61.94		64.96728	
11	10	67	67.91		0.824055	
12	11	74	67.24		45.75664	
13	12	77	72.24		22.61813	
14	13	75	75.77		0.585998	
15	14		75.20			
16					5.899325 <- =SQRT(AVERAGE(C3:C14))	
17						
18		alpha =	0.7404261			

The forecast for week 14 sales is 75,200 units (recall that the X_t values are in thousands).

Clearly, we could have used a different objective function, but the RMSE works well. If we developed alternative forecasting models to solve this problem, we could compare the RMSEs across them all to determine their relative forecast accuracies.

15.6 FORECASTING IN TABLEAU

Up to this point, we have built various univariate forecasting models in Excel. As expected, Tableau provides some ready-made forecasting capabilities, allowing the user to experiment with different kinds of additive and multiplicative forecasting models featuring a trend and/or seasonality.

Figure 15.3 shows a Tableau worked example of sales forecasts. Right-clicking on any of the forecasts in the visualisations allows the `Forecast Options` dialog box to be accessed.

A few worthwhile comments are as follows:

- For the forecast length, this refers to the lead time. We would likely not wish to forecast beyond the medium run – perhaps 2 years maximum in this instance.
- For the source data there is the option to exclude the last period's observation. If the last period is still 'active' or subject to revision or reconciliation, it may be advisable to omit the last value in the presence of uncertainty over its true value.

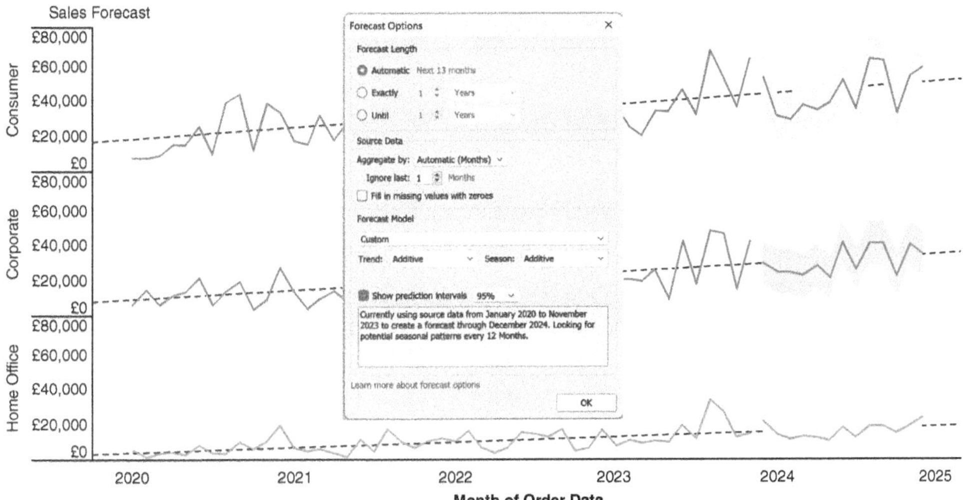

Figure 15.3 Sales forecasts example in Tableau.

- The forecast model may be additive or multiplicative, with the option of excluding a trend and/or seasonality.
- Uncertainties associated with forecasts can be visualised by plotting 90%, 95% and 99% prediction intervals. This produces fan charts which become wider with increased lead times, reflecting the greater uncertainty of forecasting greater lead times.

As shown in Figure 15.4, Tableau provides forecast model summaries, which for these series are heavily influenced by seasonal effects rather than a trend. Note in the final column how forecasts can be classified in terms of their quality. The categories are 'Good', 'Ok' and 'Poor' and are judged relative to the naïve forecast based on the current observation only (you may wish to review the MASE). Relative to the naïve forecast:

- 'Good' means that the forecast has less than half as much error
- 'Ok' means that the forecast is likely to have less error
- 'Poor' means the forecast has more error.

Note that Tableau derives its forecasts based on exponential smoothing – what a coincidence, we've already covered it! – and each forecasting model is returned with several quality metrics: RMSE, MAE, MASE, MAPE and AIC, also previously covered. These metrics are useful as benchmarks against which to compare any other forecasting models.

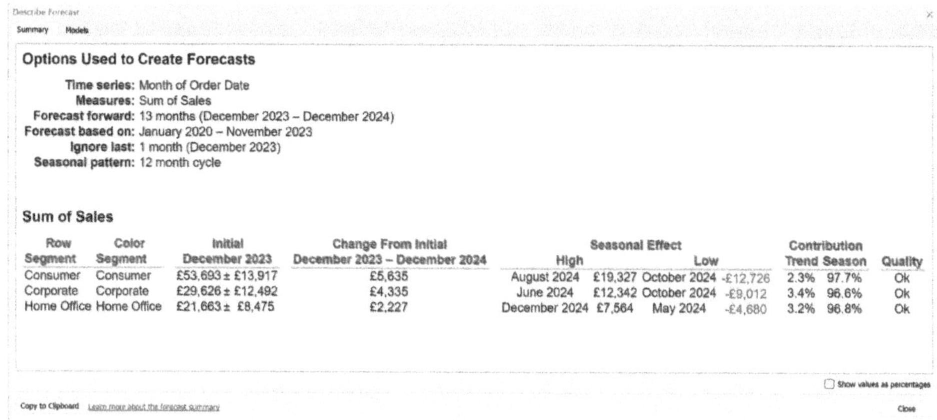

Describe Forecast

Summary Models

Options Used to Create Forecasts

Time series: Month of Order Date
Measures: Sum of Sales
Forecast forward: 13 months (December 2023 – December 2024)
Forecast based on: January 2020 – November 2023
Ignore last: 1 month (December 2023)
Seasonal pattern: 12 month cycle

Sum of Sales

Row Segment	Color Segment	Initial December 2023	Change From Initial December 2023 – December 2024	Seasonal Effect High		Seasonal Effect Low		Contribution Trend	Contribution Season	Quality
Consumer	Consumer	£53,693 ± £13,917	£5,635	August 2024	£19,327	October 2024	-£12,726	2.3%	97.7%	Ok
Corporate	Corporate	£29,626 ± £12,492	£4,335	June 2024	£12,342	October 2024	-£9,012	3.4%	96.6%	Ok
Home Office	Home Office	£21,663 ± £8,475	£2,227	December 2024	£7,564	May 2024	-£4,680	3.2%	96.8%	Ok

Show values as percentages

Copy to Clipboard Learn more about the forecast summary Close

Figure 15.4 Forecast model summaries in Tableau.

Smoothing coefficients (parameters) are also reported, as shown in Figure 15.5, calculated based on optimisation:

- α is the *level* smoothing coefficient
- β is the *trend* smoothing coefficient
- γ is the *seasonal* smoothing coefficient.

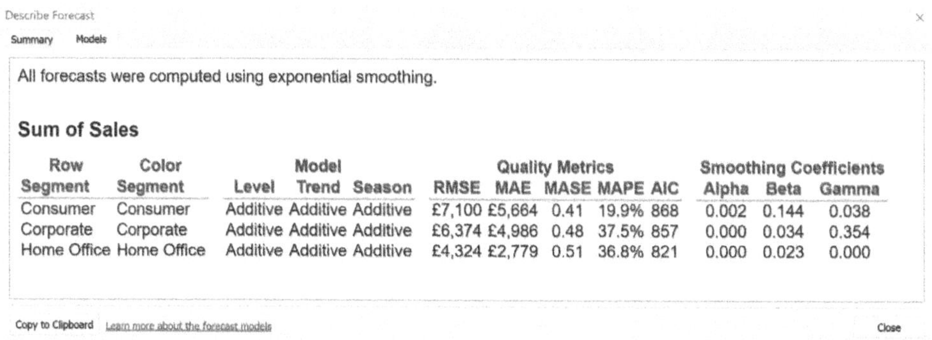

Describe Forecast

Summary Models

All forecasts were computed using exponential smoothing.

Sum of Sales

Row Segment	Color Segment	Model Level	Model Trend	Model Season	RMSE	MAE	MASE	MAPE	AIC	Alpha	Beta	Gamma
Consumer	Consumer	Additive	Additive	Additive	£7,100	£5,664	0.41	19.9%	868	0.002	0.144	0.038
Corporate	Corporate	Additive	Additive	Additive	£6,374	£4,986	0.48	37.5%	857	0.000	0.034	0.354
Home Office	Home Office	Additive	Additive	Additive	£4,324	£2,779	0.51	36.8%	821	0.000	0.023	0.000

Copy to Clipboard Learn more about the forecast models Close

Figure 15.5 Optimal smoothing coefficients reported in Tableau.

15.7 CHAPTER OVERVIEW

This chapter has looked at how time-series variables can be decomposed into the constituent parts of trend, seasonality, cyclicality and noise. Trends and seasonal effects are the easiest components to model, and we have reviewed a selection of univariate (extrapolative) time-series models which allow forecasts of the future to be computed. Forecasting is obviously an uncertain occupation, so various quality metrics have been introduced as a way to compare performance across different forecasting models. While bespoke models can be created in Excel, Tableau features some easy-to-use extrapolative forecasting techniques, with clear performance summaries. In closing, I forecast that you will forecast in the future!

15.8 KEY VOCABULARY

Akaike information criterion (AIC)
Centred moving average
Conditional expectation
Cycles
Exponential smoothing
Forecast
Forecasting
Forecast error
Frequency
Lead time
Mean absolute error (MAE)
Mean absolute percentage error (MAPE)
Mean absolute scaled error (MASE)
Prediction
Random noise
Root mean squared error (RMSE)
Seasonal effects
Smoothing constant/ parameter
Systematic components
Time series
Trend

15.9 EXERCISES

15.9.1 Test your understanding

1 Why forecast?
2 What is a time series?
3 Provide examples of the possible frequencies of time-series data you would expect to encounter in business.
4 What is the difference between forecasting and prediction?
5 What is a lead time? Explain what distinguishes whether a lead time is classified as:
   (a) short-run
   (b) medium-run
   (c) long-run.
6 Outline the features of:
   (a) extrapolative forecasting models
   (b) causal forecasting models.
7 Which is better, an extrapolative or a causal forecasting model? 'Well, James, it depends' may feature in your answer, but explain what it depends on!
8 Summarise the trade-offs involved in developing forecasts.
9 Describe each of the following four constituent parts of a time series. For each, provide a real-world example of a time series that you would expect would feature it, briefly justifying why.
   (a) Trend
   (b) Seasonal effects
   (c) Cycles
   (d) Random noise.
10 What is the purpose of a moving average?

11 Explain how a five-point unweighted moving average is calculated. If instead you wanted to use a five-point weighted moving average, how would you choose the weights to use? Briefly justify your view.

12 What is a centred moving average? If you had quarterly data, explain how the centred moving average would be calculated.

13 Why could it be argued that a multiplicative model is preferable to an additive model?

14 Write out the multiplicative model featuring trend and seasonality.

15 What is meant by deseasonalised data and how can a simple linear regression be run using it?

16 How can we assess forecast accuracy today when forecasts are of the future which hasn't yet happened?

17 Define a forecast error.

18 Explain how each of the following forecast accuracy measures is calculated and mention a distinctive feature of each.

(a) Root mean squared error
(b) Mean absolute error
(c) Mean absolute scaled error
(d) Mean absolute percentage error
(e) Akaike information criterion.

Which is your favourite, and why?

19 Outline how exponential smoothing works.

20 How would you choose the value of the smoothing parameter, α, in exponential smoothing? Briefly justify your view.

21 What inbuilt forecast options does Tableau have?

22 How does Tableau classify forecasts as being 'Good', 'Ok' or 'Poor'?

23 Suggest, with reasons, your recommended time-series model for forecasting:

(a) gas demand
(b) a stock market index.

24 Your manager has provided you with the following history of quarterly sales (in millions of pounds) over the past four years.

	Quarter 1	Quarter 2	Quarter 3	Quarter 4
Year 1	23.16	22.99	23.37	22.19
Year 2	23.41	23.87	24.19	23.55
Year 3	24.04	24.90	24.27	22.97
Year 4	24.88	25.64	25.46	24.83

(a) Create sales forecasts for each quarter in years 5 and 6 using a multiplicative model featuring trend and seasonality.
(b) Prepare a short memo for your manager explaining your approach and briefly discuss how reliable you expect the forecasts to be.

25 A wholesaler wants to use exponential smoothing to predict monthly sales. At the end of January, the wholesaler's forecast for March sales was 11,000. In February, 15,000 units were sold, and during March 19,000 units were sold.

(a) At the end of March, what is the wholesaler's forecast for the total number of units which will be sold during the following May and June? Use a smoothing constant of 0.25.

(b) If the value of 0.25 for the smoothing constant could be changed, briefly explain how a different value could be determined.

26 Source any time series of your choice online, and create forecasts for it!

15.9.2 Practice with Excel

Head over to the companion website for Excel examples and screencasts!

16

DISCRIMINANT ANALYSIS

Chapter contents

Chapter level: ***Advanced***

Source: Photo by Republica via Pixabay.

Key concepts

- Discriminant score
- Classification
- Centroids

Chapter value

A set of predictor variables can be used to classify cases, while assessing relative importance.

Key takeaway

Misclassifications can have asymmetric consequences, so examine rates of false positives and false negatives.

Chapter outline

Discrimination, bad; discriminant analysis, good. This chapter demonstrates how to classify cases (such as consumers or job applicants) into distinct groups, by distinguishing cases, literally discriminating between them, based on a set of observed predictor variables. In essence, we seek a *characteristic profile*, that is, a sense of what a typical, or representative, group member looks like - 'looks' not in the sense of physical attributes (that is bad discrimination), but in terms of the chosen predictor variables, such as income or previous customer interactions.

This technique has some parallels with multiple linear regression (Chapter 14), in that we seek a linear combination of significant predictor variables, although here we use these to derive discriminant 'scores' upon which individuals are *classified* to be of a particular group based on a suitable decision rule. However, classification models are never perfect, so we need to consider not just the percentage of (in)correct classifications, but that *misclassification errors* are not necessarily all equally bad - some may be more serious than others!

Learning outcomes

After completing this chapter, you should be able to:

- explain the principles and purpose of discriminant analysis, and relate them to practical business cases
- describe the process for conducting discriminant analysis, such as problem formulation, estimating and assessing the significance of discriminant function coefficients, and quantifying classification accuracy using a confusion matrix
- distinguish between the different types of misclassification and judge the suitability of model adoption based on different error rates.

Motivational case: Got the X factor? Y? Z?

Headhunters is a large recruitment agency. It has decided to investigate whether different job classifications appeal to different personality types. Three job classifications were considered and indexed as follows: (1) front-of-house/customer-facing, (2) back office and (3) remote roles requiring people to work on their own. Psychometric tests were conducted on 100 candidates previously placed into these different roles, measuring their interest in outdoor activities, attitude towards social events and how reserved they consider themselves to be.

Given the level of competition among recruitment agencies, how could Headhunters use the psychometric test results to ensure optimal placement of job prospects to vacancy types, thus ensuring repeat business from clients?

To buy, or not to buy?

Elon Musk, the somewhat outspoken tech entrepreneur, spent much of 2022 debating whether or not to buy Twitter, now rebranded as X. Following an initial bid of a hefty $44 billion, within a few weeks Musk queried the valuation by suggesting the proportion of non-authentic accounts significantly exceeded Twitter's own estimates that less than 5% were spam or fake accounts.

So, what was the truth? 5%, 20%, more? How to quantify this? Enter *Botometer* (https://botometer.osome.iu.edu/) with its scoring model approach. In essence, each Twitter account is assigned a score on a 0-5 scale, based on the extent to which its activity is human-like (a score of 0) or bot-like (a score of 5).

More human-like | Uncertain | More bot-like

0 1 2 3 4 5

For accounts which are thought to be Twitter bots, these are then further classified into one of several types, such as 'echo-chamber', 'fake follower' and 'spammer'. Discriminant analysis works in this way - identifying a set of predictor variables that allows objects (here Twitter accounts) to be scored and subsequently classified with an acceptable (hopefully!) degree of accuracy. Sold.

16.1 INTRODUCTION

Discriminant analysis is a form of classification, whereby cases (such as customers, individuals or any well-defined 'objects') are placed into distinct categories/groups based on some *numeric score*.

Arguably the most widely known example of such a predictive classification model is that of *credit scores*, which can be used by prospective lenders to assess the creditworthiness of prospective borrowers, with the credit score acting as an indicator of credit risk, and hence of default risk. Once relevant predictor variables are identified (salary, amount of outstanding loans, number of financial dependents, etc.), acquiring this information, say through a loan application form, can be useful to determine the degree of loan eligibility. The bank can then answer the question 'to lend, or not to lend?'.

Inevitably, the lending decision is made under uncertainty as those deemed creditworthy may yet end up defaulting, while those rejected may have nonetheless repaid the loan. The risk of *misclassification*!

Example 16.1

Prospective borrowers are one of two types: those who will repay the loan, and those who will default (whether partially or in full). Prospective lenders need to judge who is who when making their lending decisions. Suppose the bank develops a classification model which predicts whether the loan applicant is a 'defaulter' or a 'non-defaulter'. The possible outcomes are shown in the matrix below:

		Predicted type	
		Defaulter (negative, refuse loan)	Non-defaulter (positive, advance loan)
Actual type	Defaulter	Correct prediction (true negative)	Incorrect prediction (false positive)
	Non-defaulter	Incorrect prediction (false negative)	Correct prediction (true positive)

So, we see that there are two types of correct predictions: classifying defaulters correctly (*true negatives*) and non-defaulters correctly (*true positives*), correctly refusing loans to defaulters, and advancing loans to non-defaulters, respectively. However, there are two distinct misclassifications: advancing a loan to a defaulter (a *false positive*) and refusing a loan to a non-defaulter (a *false negative*).

Which of these two misclassifications is worse? Well, James, it depends! It is arguably subjective. While the bank would incur a bad debt in the case of false positives (a realised loss), the bank would have unrealised profits from the false negatives - since these are genuine non-defaulters, the bank's profits on the loan are unrealised, as no loan is made! We could even speculate that those refused a loan might not choose to do business again with the bank, and hence the bank would have lost the full *customer lifetime value* of such non-defaulters, resulting in an opportunity cost potentially far in excess of the losses incurred on the false positives.

For now, we appreciate that classification models can be wrong in more than one way, with the (monetary or practical) consequences often *asymmetric in terms of severity*. When assessing the predictive accuracy of classification models, it is important to look beyond the headline overall predictive accuracy to consider the different error rate types. More on this later.

To run a discriminant analysis, our population of interest must be divisible into *mutually exclusive groups*, with a minimum requirement of two groups. (If the population is homogeneous then everyone is of the same type, hence no discrimination is required if there is only one group!) We then require information on a set of assumed *predictor variables* to distinguish – that is, to *discriminate* – between each distinct group. Such information could come from observations, or active data collection such as through surveys. A discriminant analysis model is then developed to *score each case*, and then an optimal *decision rule* is determined to facilitate the classification. Once formulated, the scoring model and decision rule are applied to new cases (out-of-sample predictions).

Example 16.2

Some examples of discriminant analysis applications and their likely associated predictor variables are as follows:

(Continued)

Distinct groups	Likely predictor variables
Loan defaulters and non-defaulters	Income, age, household size, outstanding loans
Churners and loyal customers	Length of custom/patronage, education attainment, expenditure level, whether a loyalty scheme member
Customers quick to trade up (e.g. smartphones) and sclerotic customers	Income, age, past brand-switching behaviour
Graduate school applicants who would complete programme and those who would withdraw	Examination scores, class attendance, financial means

In finance applications, common accounting predictor variables could be used to classify companies according to their bankruptcy risk. In market research applications, survey responses could be used to classify 'influencers', that is, prime targets to attract to promote or endorse new products. In recruitment, aptitude tests, such as verbal reasoning and numeracy marks, could be used to screen candidates for interview or hiring decisions. Wannabe investment bankers often have to navigate such pre-hire tests to make it onto competitive internships or graduate entry programmes.

16.2 DISCRIMINANT ANALYSIS MODEL

When constructing a discriminant analysis model, we need at least one *discriminant function*, which is a *linear combination of predictor variables*. The number of discriminant functions depends on:

- the number of groups to be classified, which we will denote by g
- the number of predictor variables used in the model, which we will denote by k.

The number of discriminant functions will be $\min(g - 1, k)$, the smaller of the two values $g - 1$ and k. We will consider examples where $g = 2$ (two-group discriminant analysis) and $g = 3$ (three-group discriminant analysis), usually with $k \leq 5$ or 6 predictor variables.

Example 16.3

For $g = 2$, for example for classifying defaulters and non-defaulters with $k = 5$ predictor variables, then we will have

$$\min(2 - 1, 5) = \min(1, 5) = 1 \text{ discriminant function.}$$

For $g = 3$, for example for Headhunters classifying three job types with $k = 3$ predictor variables, then we will have

$$\min(3 - 1, 3) = \min(2, 3) = 2 \text{ discriminant functions.}$$

For now, we consider $g = 2$, that is, a two-group discriminant analysis. Suppose a telecoms firm is concerned about a high level of *churn* recently (i.e. losing its customers to its competitors). The company has decided to use discriminant analysis to construct a model capable of predicting which existing customers may churn. To do so, we will need one discriminant function which transforms a set of multivariate observations into discriminant scores which are then used to discriminate between both groups (denoted G_1 = the churners, and G_2 = the non-churners, i.e. loyal customers).

Discriminant function

The **discriminant function** can be represented as

$$D_j = \beta_0 + \beta_1 X_{1,j} + \beta_2 X_{2,j} + \cdots + \beta_k X_{k,j},$$

where

- D_j is the **discriminant score** of the jth case (out of n cases), hence for $j = 1, 2, \ldots, n$
- $X_1, X_2, \ldots, X_k$ are the k predictor variables used to discriminate the groups
- β_i, for $i = 0, 1, 2, \ldots, k$, are the discriminant function's **unstandardised coefficients**, that is, the weights attached to each predictor variable (plus the constant β_0) to determine the discriminant score.

This is sometimes called (Fisher's) linear discriminant function.

Further, suppose we choose the following $k = 5$ predictor variables for churn:

- months with service, X_1
- age in years, X_2
- years at current address, X_3
- household income in thousands, X_4
- number of people in household, X_5.

In vector notation, for brevity, the unstandardised coefficients can be represented by the vector $\mathbf{B}$, and the multivariate observation for individual j can be represented by the vector $\mathbf{X}_j$, where

$$\mathbf{B} = \begin{pmatrix} \beta_0 \\ \beta_1 \\ \beta_2 \\ \beta_3 \\ \beta_4 \\ \beta_5 \end{pmatrix} \quad \text{and} \quad \mathbf{X}_j = \begin{pmatrix} 1 \\ X_{1,j} \\ X_{2,j} \\ X_{3,j} \\ X_{4,j} \\ X_{5,j} \end{pmatrix}.$$

The univariate discriminant score (a single number) can then be expressed, using vector multiplication as

$$D_j = \mathbf{B}'\mathbf{X}_j = \beta_0 + \beta_1 X_{1,j} + \beta_2 X_{2,j} + \cdots + \beta_5 X_{5,j}.$$

Note that the values in the vector $\mathbf{X}_j$ will vary across the j cases, but the vector of unstandardised coefficients, **B**, is *fixed* across j. For reference only, a simplifying assumption is that the 'covariance matrix', $\boldsymbol{\Omega}$, is assumed to be equal across the two groups.

How to compute **B**, the vector of unstandardised coefficients? We seek the best possible discrimination, but, as usual, what do we mean by 'best'? Our objective is to *maximise the homogeneity* within each group, that is, we choose **B** to *minimise the within-group discriminant score variance*, while *maximising the distance between the groups*. We avoid technical details, as software will take care of all the number-crunching for us! What a relief.

Once **B** is obtained, how to choose the decision rule? The centroids are the *averages* (means) of the discriminant scores for all cases in each group. When $g = 2$, we simply use the average of the two centroids ($\bar{D}_{G_1}$ and $\bar{D}_{G_2}$, one per group) as the cut-off point, c, where

$$c = \frac{\bar{D}_{G_1} + \bar{D}_{G_2}}{2}.$$

For any new case, say the $(n + 1)$th case, we compute the discriminant score

$$D_{n+1} = \mathbf{B}'\mathbf{X}_{n+1}$$

and classify this case to the nearest centroid by comparison to c.

16.2.1 Assessing predictive accuracy

A popular way to assess the performance of any classification method is by using a confusion matrix. The good news is that it is not particularly confusing to understand, despite the name! Recall the matrix shown in Example 16.1 regarding the different kinds of correct and incorrect classifications. A confusion matrix is essentially this, but where the frequencies of each outcome are presented. For example, when $g = 2$, suppose we label these groups as 'negative' and 'positive' such that:

	Predicted group		
Actual group	**Negative**	**Positive**	**Total**
Negative	n_{11}	n_{12}	$n_{1\cdot}$
Positive	n_{21}	n_{22}	$n_{2\cdot}$
Total	$n_{\cdot 1}$	$n_{\cdot 2}$	n

where

- n_{11} is the number of correct classifications of negative cases (*true negatives*)
- n_{12} is the number of incorrect classifications of negative cases (*false positives*)

- n_{21} is the number of incorrect classifications of positive cases (*false negatives*)
- n_{22} is the number of correct classifications of positive cases (*true positives*)
- $n_{1.} = n_{11} + n_{12}$ is the total number of negative cases
- $n_{2.} = n_{21} + n_{22}$ is the total number of positive cases
- $n_{.1} = n_{11} + n_{21}$ is the total number of negative predictions
- $n_{.2} = n_{12} + n_{22}$ is the total number of positive predictions
- $n = n_{1.} + n_{2.} = n_{.1} + n_{.2}$ is the total number of cases (and hence also the number of predictions).

From this confusion matrix, we can derive various *performance measures*. The following are some of the simplest and most helpful. Note that each is a proportion (between 0 and 1), and can simply be multiplied by 100 to be expressed as a percentage.

- The overall predictive accuracy,

$$\text{OPA} = \frac{n_{11} + n_{22}}{n},$$

returns the *proportion of correctly classified cases*. (The larger, the better!)

- The true positive rate,

$$\text{TPR} = \frac{n_{22}}{n_{21} + n_{22}} = \frac{n_{22}}{n_{2.}},$$

returns the *proportion of correctly classified positive cases*. (The larger, the better!)

- The true negative rate,

$$\text{TNR} = \frac{n_{11}}{n_{11} + n_{12}} = \frac{n_{11}}{n_{1.}},$$

returns the *proportion of correctly classified negative cases*. (The larger, the better!)

- The false positive rate,

$$\text{FPR} = \frac{n_{12}}{n_{12} + n_{22}} = \frac{n_{12}}{n_{.2}},$$

returns the *proportion of incorrect positively classified cases*. (The smaller, the better!)

- The false negative rate,

$$\text{FNR} = \frac{n_{21}}{n_{11} + n_{21}} = \frac{n_{21}}{n_{.1}},$$

returns the *proportion of incorrect negatively classified cases*. (The smaller, the better!)

16.2.2 Training and test datasets

In practice, we 'split' the available dataset into two parts: the training data (used for parameter estimation, i.e. to 'train' the model) and the test data, used to assess out-of-sample model performance. Software can usually apply leave-one-out cross-validation (LOOCV) whereby each case has a turn playing the role of the test data, with the iterated remaining $n - 1$ cases forming the training data.

If there is no separate test dataset, that is, all cases are used for training, then the overall predictive accuracy measure risks suffering from overfitting, in that when assessing predictive performance we should not be too surprised if the model correctly classifies cases which themselves were used to estimate the model! Overfitting results in inflated measures of model performance, providing an overly optimistic assessment of how good the classification model is. As such, the OPA measure (indeed, all the above performance measures) should be computed for the cross-validated setting, to offer a more *objective* view of model performance. While OPA will be lower, it will be more realistic!

16.2.3 Another perspective

An alternative way of viewing the classification problem is using *conditional probability*. Specifically, given a multivariate observation $\mathbf{X}_j$, what is the probability that the case belongs to group i, g_i, for $i = 1, 2$? To answer this, we simply use *Bayes' theorem*:

$$P(g_i \mid \mathbf{X}_j) = \frac{P(\mathbf{X}_j \mid g_i)\, P(g_i)}{P(\mathbf{X}_j \mid g_1)\, P(g_1) + P(\mathbf{X}_j \mid g_2)\, P(g_2)}.$$

Then:

- if $P(g_i \mid \mathrm{X}_j) > 0.50$, classify the case as g_i
- if $P(g_i \mid \mathrm{X}_j) < 0.50$, do not classify the case as g_i.

For the *prior probabilities*, $P(g_i)$, it is simplest to use 1/(number of groups), although if a better estimate can be justified then this may be used instead.

16.3 TWO-GROUP DISCRIMINANT ANALYSIS: EMPIRICAL EXAMPLE

While Excel has previously been our software tool of choice, here we will use SPSS (Statistical Package for the Social Sciences, available at https://www.ibm.com/uk-en/products/spss-statistics) as this is a very user-friendly platform for conducting discriminant analysis, as well as other multivariate techniques covered in Chapters 17 and 18.

In Section 16.2 we introduced a telecoms firm concerned about a high level of churn which has decided to use discriminant analysis to construct a model capable of predicting which existing customers may churn. We will:

- state the theoretical and estimated discriminant analysis models
- comment on the relative importance of the predictor variables
- determine the predictive accuracy of the model.

To do so, we will make use of the sample dataset `telco.sav` which comes with a standard SPSS installation, and reflects a hypothetical telecoms company with various usage and demographic variables. The file extension `.sav` indicates an SPSS datafile. Upon opening the file, it launches in SPSS and the `Data View` is visible, as shown in Figure 16.1. Resembling an Excel spreadsheet, the usual principles of data management apply: variables are shown columnwise, and observations (in this case customers) are shown rowwise. A critical difference with Excel is that the variable names are *not* in row 1, but above it, unlike Excel where it is customary for variable names ('data labels') to be in the first row.

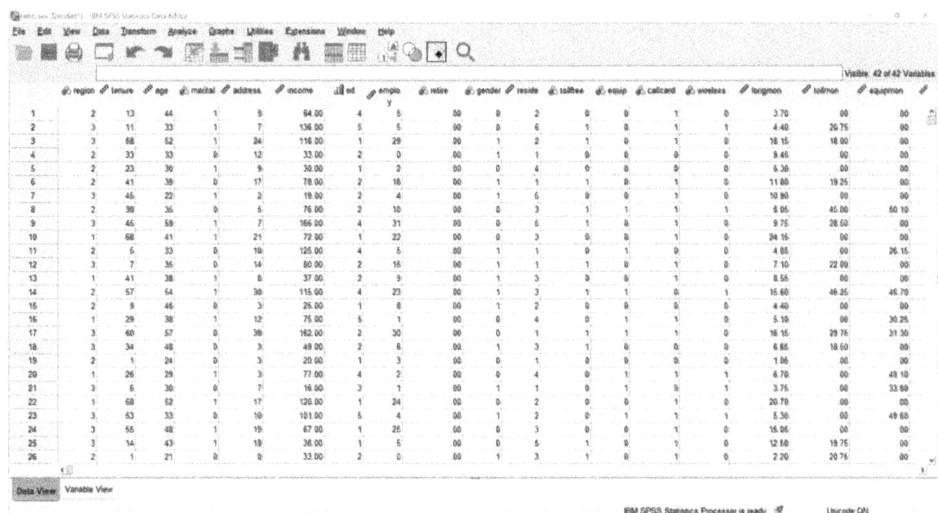

	region	tenure	age	marital	address	income	ed	employ	retire	gender	reside	tollfree	equip	callcard	wireless	longmon	tollmon	equipmon
1	2	13	44	1	9	64.00	4	5	.00	0	2	0	0	1	0	3.70	.00	.00
2	3	11	33	1	7	136.00	5	5	.00	0	6	1	0	1	1	4.40	20.75	.00
3	3	68	52	1	24	116.00	1	29	.00	1	2	1	0	1	0	18.15	18.00	.00
4	2	33	33	0	12	33.00	2	0	.00	1	1	0	0	0	0	9.45	.00	.00
5	2	23	30	1	9	30.00	1	2	.00	0	4	0	0	0	0	6.30	.00	.00
6	2	41	39	0	17	78.00	2	16	.00	1	1	1	0	1	0	11.80	19.25	.00
7	3	45	22	1	2	19.00	2	4	.00	1	5	0	0	1	0	10.90	.00	.00
8	2	38	35	0	5	76.00	2	10	.00	0	3	1	1	1	1	6.05	45.00	50.10
9	3	45	59	1	7	166.00	4	31	.00	0	5	1	0	1	0	9.75	28.50	.00
10	1	68	41	1	21	72.00	1	22	.00	0	3	0	0	1	0	24.15	.00	.00
11	2	5	33	0	10	125.00	4	5	.00	1	1	0	1	0	0	4.85	.00	26.15
12	3	7	35	0	14	80.00	2	15	.00	1	1	1	0	1	0	7.10	22.00	.00
13	1	41	38	1	8	37.00	2	9	.00	1	3	0	0	1	0	8.55	.00	.00
14	2	57	54	1	30	115.00	4	23	.00	1	3	1	1	0	1	15.60	46.25	46.70
15	2	9	46	0	3	25.00	1	8	.00	1	2	0	0	0	0	4.40	.00	.00
16	1	29	38	1	12	75.00	5	1	.00	0	4	0	1	1	0	5.10	.00	30.25
17	3	60	57	0	38	162.00	2	30	.00	0	1	1	1	1	0	16.15	29.75	31.30
18	3	34	48	0	3	49.00	2	6	.00	1	3	1	0	0	0	6.65	18.50	.00
19	2	1	24	0	3	20.00	1	3	.00	0	1	0	0	0	0	1.05	.00	.00
20	1	26	29	1	3	77.00	4	2	.00	0	4	0	1	1	1	6.70	.00	48.10
21	3	6	30	0	7	16.00	3	1	.00	1	1	0	1	0	1	3.75	.00	33.60
22	1	68	52	1	17	120.00	1	24	.00	0	2	0	0	1	0	20.70	.00	.00
23	3	53	33	0	10	101.00	5	4	.00	1	2	0	1	1	1	5.30	.00	49.60
24	3	55	48	1	19	67.00	1	25	.00	0	3	0	0	1	0	15.05	.00	.00
25	3	14	43	1	18	36.00	1	5	.00	0	5	1	0	1	0	12.50	19.75	.00
26	2	1	21	0	0	33.00	2	0	.00	1	3	1	0	1	0	2.20	20.75	.00

Figure 16.1 Data View of the dataset `telco.sav` in SPSS.

	Name	Type	Width	Decimals	Label	Values	Missing	Columns	Align	Measure	Role
1	region	Numeric	4	0	Geographic indicator	{1, Zone 1}...	None	6	Right	Nominal	Input
2	tenure	Numeric	4	0	Months with service	None	None	6	Right	Scale	Input
3	age	Numeric	4	0	Age in years	None	None	6	Right	Scale	Input
4	marital	Numeric	4	0	Marital status	{0, Unmarried}...	None	7	Right	Nominal	Input
5	address	Numeric	4	0	Years at current address	None	None	7	Right	Scale	Input
6	income	Numeric	8	2	Household income in thousands	None	None	10	Right	Scale	Input
7	ed	Numeric	4	0	Level of education	{1, Did not complete high school}...	None	6	Right	Ordinal	Input
8	employ	Numeric	4	0	Years with current employer	None	None	6	Right	Scale	Input
9	retire	Numeric	8	2	Retired	{.00, No}...	None	10	Right	Nominal	Input
10	gender	Numeric	4	0	Gender	{0, Male}...	None	6	Right	Nominal	Input
11	reside	Numeric	4	0	Number of people in household	None	None	6	Right	Scale	Input
12	tollfree	Numeric	4	0	Toll free service	{0, No}...	None	8	Right	Nominal	Input
13	equip	Numeric	4	0	Equipment rental	{0, No}...	None	6	Right	Nominal	Input
14	callcard	Numeric	4	0	Calling card service	{0, No}...	None	8	Right	Nominal	Input
15	wireless	Numeric	4	0	Wireless service	{0, No}...	None	8	Right	Nominal	Input
16	longmon	Numeric	8	2	Long distance last month	None	None	10	Right	Scale	Input
17	tollmon	Numeric	8	2	Toll free last month	None	None	10	Right	Scale	Input
18	equipmon	Numeric	8	2	Equipment last month	None	None	10	Right	Scale	Input
19	cardmon	Numeric	8	2	Calling card last month	None	None	10	Right	Scale	Input
20	wiremon	Numeric	8	2	Wireless last month	None	None	10	Right	Scale	Input
21	longten	Numeric	8	2	Long distance over tenure	None	None	10	Right	Scale	Input
22	tollten	Numeric	8	2	Toll free over tenure	None	None	10	Right	Scale	Input
23	equipten	Numeric	8	2	Equipment over tenure	None	None	10	Right	Scale	Input
24	cardten	Numeric	8	2	Calling card over tenure	None	None	10	Right	Scale	Input
25	wireten	Numeric	8	2	Wireless over tenure	None	None	10	Right	Scale	Input
26	multline	Numeric	4	0	Multiple lines	{0, No}...	None	8	Right	Nominal	Input
27	voice	Numeric	4	0	Voice mail	{0, No}...	None	6	Right	Nominal	Input
28	pager	Numeric	4	0	Paging service	{0, No}...	None	6	Right	Nominal	Input

Figure 16.2 Variable View of the dataset `telco.sav` in SPSS.

For this dataset there are 42 variables, and records for n = 1000 customers. Navigating to the `Variable View` tab (bottom left of the screen) provides a summary of each variable: each *row* in the Variable View corresponds to a *column* in the Data View. This is shown in Figure 16.2.

Of particular note are the following variable attributes:

- `Name` corresponds to the variable name displayed in the Data View.
- `Label` can provide a more detailed description of what the variable is than simply its name. For example, 'tenure' is ambiguous, but the label 'Months with service' is much clearer.
- `Values` indicates the categories associated with each numeric code for categorical variables.
- `Missing` can be used to inform SPSS of values which are missing (such as item non-response in surveys) and hence should be excluded from calculations, albeit there are no such instances in this dataset.
- `Measure` records the level of measurement of the variable. In SPSS there are three levels: 'nominal', 'ordinal' and 'scale' (measurable).

To perform discriminant analysis in SPSS, proceed as follows using the drop-down menus at the top of the screen.

- **Analyze > Classify > Discriminant....**
- Move the relevant categorical (dependent) variable into the `Grouping Variable` box, in this case 'Churn within last month' (bottom of the list).
- Click on `Define Range...`. In the pop-up window, enter appropriate values for `Minimum` and `Maximum` (in this case 0 and 1, for 'No', did not churn and, 'Yes', did churn, respectively). Click on `Continue`.
- Move the relevant predictor variables into the `Independents` box. Select `Enter independents together` (default option), which forces all independent variables to be included – stepwise may be selected to perform stepwise selection, as described in Chapter 14). Here we will use 'Months with service' (X_1), 'Age in years' (X_2), 'Years at current address' (X_3), 'Household income in thousands' (X_4) and 'Number of people in household' (X_5).
- Click on `Statistics...`. In the pop-up window, in the `Descriptives` box select `Means` and `Univariate ANOVAs`. In the `Matrices` box, check `Within-groups correlation`. In the `Function Coefficients` box, check `Unstandardized`. Click on `Continue`.
- Click on `Classify...`. In the `Prior probabilities` box check `All groups equal` (default). In the `Display` box check `Summary table` and `Leave-one-out classification` (so LOOCV training and test datasets are used). In the `Use Covariance Matrix` box check `Within-groups` (default). Click on `Continue`.
- Click on `Save...`. In the dialog box check all three options `Predicted group membership`, `Discriminant scores` and `Probabilities of group membership`. Click on `Continue`.
- Click `OK`.

Let us jump to the updated Data View to see what SPSS has calculated.

The first seven cases are shown in Figure 16.3. The `churn` column shows the true group memberships (0 = did not churn, 1 = did churn). The adjacent columns to the right show the following:

- `Dis_1` shows the predicted group membership (0 for does not churn, 1 for churn)
- `Dis1_1` reports the case's respective discriminant score, D_i

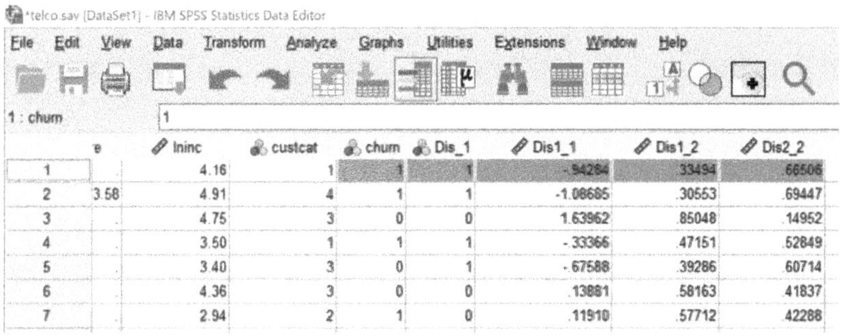

*telco.sav [DataSet1] - IBM SPSS Statistics Data Editor

File Edit View Data Transform Analyze Graphs Utilities Extensions Window Help

1 : churn 1

	e	lninc	custcat	churn	Dis_1	Dis1_1	Dis1_2	Dis2_2
1	.	4.16	1	1	1	-.94284	.33494	.66506
2	3.58	4.91	4	1	1	-1.08685	.30553	.69447
3	.	4.75	3	0	0	1.63962	.85048	.14952
4	.	3.50	1	1	1	-.33366	.47151	.52849
5	.	3.40	3	0	1	-.67588	.39286	.60714
6	.	4.36	3	0	0	.13881	.58163	.41837
7	.	2.94	2	1	0	.11910	.57712	.42288

Figure 16.3 Updated Data View after discriminant analysis has been run.

- `Dis1_2` reports the posterior probability of the case belonging to group 1 (non-churners), $P(g_1 \mid \mathbf{X}_j)$
- `Dis2_2` reports the posterior probability of the case belonging to group 2 (churners), $P(g_2 \mid \mathbf{X}_j)$.

For example, the highlighted case in Figure 16.3, $j = 1$ (a churner), has a discriminant score of –0.94284, with a 33.494% chance of belonging to group 1, and a 66.506% chance of belonging to group 2, hence this has been classified as belonging to group 2. (Note that 33.494% + 66.506% = 100%, since the case *must* be assigned to one of the two MECE groups.) This is an example of a correct classification – well done to the model!

For another example, case $j = 5$ (a non-churner) has a discriminant score of –0.67588, with a 39.286% chance of belonging to group 1, and a 60.714% chance of belonging to group 2, hence this has been classified as belonging to group 2. This is an example of an incorrect classification – what a useless model! (Note that case $j = 7$ is another misclassification, whereby a churner has been classified as a non-churner. Oh dear.)

Our attention now shifts to the SPSS output returned in the separate *output window*. Many results tables are presented. While each table (and every value in each table) means something, some tables are of greater interest than others, hence our focus will be on the most salient parts of the overall output to assist our interpretation and evaluation of the model.

A good place to start is with a *simple exploratory analysis*, looking at descriptive statistics by group, and all cases pooled together, as shown in Figure 16.4.

'Good' predictor variables should have *very different means* across the two groups, combined with *small standard deviations*. From a practical perspective, 'Months with service' looks promising: churners, on average, had been with the telecoms firm for 22.43 months, while non-churners amassed average custom lengths of 40.47 months – nearly double! In contrast, the means of 'Number of people in household' are very similar (2.3223 ≈ 2.3540). This is somewhat anecdotal evidence – we need a more rigorous analysis, which we will see below. However, initially we suspect longer-tenured customers are less likely to churn – they seem to like the service if they stay with the firm, so have no real need to leave, unless they are too lazy or sclerotic to leave!

Since we are discriminating between $g = 2$ groups using $k = 5$ predictor variables, we require only one discriminant function (see Example 16.3). The *theoretical model* is

$$D_j = \beta_0 + \beta_1 X_{1,j} + \beta_2 X_{2,j} + \beta_3 X_{3,j} + \beta_4 X_{4,j} + \beta_5 X_{5,j}$$

Group Statistics

Churn within last month		Mean	Std. Deviation	Valid N (listwise) Unweighted	Weighted
No	Months with service	40.4683	20.56515	726	726.000
	Age in years	43.6336	12.71819	726	726.000
	Years at current address	13.0565	10.55107	726	726.000
	Household income in thousands	83.5386	119.40447	726	726.000
	Number of people in household	2.3223	1.43001	726	726.000
Yes	Months with service	22.4307	17.58737	274	274.000
	Age in years	36.5182	10.52198	274	274.000
	Years at current address	7.5620	7.39355	274	274.000
	Household income in thousands	61.6277	60.97078	274	274.000
	Number of people in household	2.3540	1.45338	274	274.000
Total	Months with service	35.5260	21.35981	1000	1000.000
	Age in years	41.6840	12.55882	1000	1000.000
	Years at current address	11.5510	10.08668	1000	1000.000
	Household income in thousands	77.5350	107.04416	1000	1000.000
	Number of people in household	2.3310	1.43579	1000	1000.000

Figure 16.4 Descriptive statistics by group, and all cases pooled together.

Canonical Discriminant Function Coefficients

	Function 1
Months with service	.043
Age in years	.021
Years at current address	.006
Household income in thousands	-.001
Number of people in household	.055
(Constant)	-2.537

Unstandardized coefficients

Figure 16.5 Unstandardised coefficients for a discriminant analysis.

with the estimated model derived from the output table with the *unstandardised* coefficients, shown in Figure 16.5. Hence in vector notation we have

$$\mathbf{B} = \begin{pmatrix} -2.537 \\ 0.043 \\ 0.021 \\ 0.006 \\ -0.001 \\ 0.055 \end{pmatrix} \quad \text{and} \quad \mathbf{X}_j = \begin{pmatrix} 1 \\ X_{1,j} \\ X_{2,j} \\ X_{3,j} \\ X_{4,j} \\ X_{5,j} \end{pmatrix},$$

and so the estimated model, using vector multiplication (where **B**' is the transpose of the column vector **B**), is

$$D_j = \mathbf{B}'\mathbf{X}_j = -2.537 + 0.043X_{1,j} + 0.021X_{2,j} + 0.006X_{3,j} - 0.001X_{4,j} + 0.055X_{5,j}.$$

Analogous to the joint significance F test for multiple linear regression models, we seek an equivalent test to determine the statistical significance of our discriminant function. Fortunately, SPSS provides this. The test is based on *Wilks' lambda'*, λ, expressed as

$$\text{Wilks'}\lambda = \frac{\text{Within groups sum of squares}}{\text{Total sum of squares}}.$$

As Wilks' $\lambda \to 1$, the *smaller* the difference between the means of the discriminant scores in each group (bad!). As Wilks' $\lambda \to 0$, the *larger* the difference between the mean discriminant scores in each group (good!). The hypothesis test is conducted using a test statistic which is a chi-squared transformation of Wilks' λ, with degrees of freedom equal to the number of predictor variables. The result is shown in Figure 16.6.

Wilks' Lambda

Test of Function(s)	Wilks' Lambda	Chi-square	df	Sig.
1	.851	161.094	5	<.001

Figure 16.6 Wilks' lambda and associated hypothesis test components.

Hence in this case the *p*-value is $P(X > 161.094) < 0.001$, where $X \sim \chi^2_5$, so this is a *highly significant* result and so we have *strong evidence* of (the good type of) discrimination.

Somewhat analogous to the individual *t* tests in multiple linear regression, SPSS conducts one-way ANOVA *F* tests (see Chapter 12) for each predictor variable to assess their statistical significance. In these univariate (one-way) ANOVA tests, the predictor variable serves as the dependent variable, with the groups serving as the independent variable. Figure 16.7 shows the results.

Tests of Equality of Group Means

	Wilks' Lambda	F	df1	df2	Sig.
Months with service	.858	165.170	1	998	<.001
Age in years	.936	68.145	1	998	<.001
Years at current address	.941	62.669	1	998	<.001
Household income in thousands	.992	8.396	1	998	.004
Number of people in household	1.000	.097	1	998	.756

Figure 16.7 Results of univariate (one-way) ANOVA tests in a discriminant analysis.

All variables are highly significant, except 'Number of people in household' (p-value of 0.756) which could be a candidate for removal from the model. However, are all the other predictor variables *equally* influential in discriminating between the groups? Unlikely.

Note that it would be *wrong* to just compare the unstandardised coefficients to judge relative importance, since $X_1, X_2, ..., X_5$ are measured on very different scales. We consider simple descriptive statistics of the predictor variables, shown in Figure 16.8.

The variation in ranges (minimum to maximum values), means and standard deviations across these five variables is clear to see, such that the unstandardised coefficients do not take these into account, so we should not look at the β_i values directly to determine relative importance – a small (large) unstandardised coefficient may be multiplied by a large (small) predictor variable value. Instead, we should look at the standardised coefficients which, helpfully, are provided in the SPSS output, shown in Figure 16.9.

From these it is clear that 'Months with service' is (by some margin) the most important predictor variable, followed by 'Age in years', with the other three variables being fairly inconsequential, with standardised coefficients close to zero. We are now even more persuaded that customer loyalty is related to churn (the longer a customer has been with the service, the more loyal they have been). However, it is not clear from the coefficient whether customer loyalty tends to *increase* or *decrease* the likelihood of churn.

Descriptive Statistics

	N	Minimum	Maximum	Mean	Std. Deviation
Months with service	1000	1	72	35.53	21.360
Age in years	1000	18	77	41.68	12.559
Years at current address	1000	0	55	11.55	10.087
Household income in thousands	1000	9.00	1668.00	77.5350	107.04416
Number of people in household	1000	1	8	2.33	1.436
Valid N (listwise)	1000				

Figure 16.8 Descriptive statistics of the predictor variables.

Standardized Canonical Discriminant Function Coefficients

	Function
	1
Months with service	.847
Age in years	.251
Years at current address	.059
Household income in thousands	-.057
Number of people in household	.079

Figure 16.9 Standardised coefficients from a discriminant analysis.

In passing, we should also note the possibility of *multicollinearity*, which poses a risk in discriminant analysis similar to that posed in multiple linear regression. Strong correlations between predictor variables 'cloud' our interpretation of the true effects, so it is wise to examine the correlation matrix, shown in Figure 16.10.

Pooled Within-Groups Matrices

		Months with service	Age in years	Years at current address	Household income in thousands	Number of people in household
Correlation	Months with service	1.000	.441	.480	.226	-.035
	Age in years	.441	1.000	.638	.316	-.261
	Years at current address	.480	.638	1.000	.212	-.205
	Household income in thousands	.226	.316	.212	1.000	-.097
	Number of people in household	-.035	-.261	-.205	-.097	1.000

Figure 16.10 Correlation matrix of the predictor variables.

Eyeballing the correlation matrix, no particularly strong correlations are evident (the strongest correlation is between 'Age in years' and 'Years at current address' ($r = 0.638$) which is hardly surprising since the longer you live somewhere the older you become!), suggesting any multicollinearity is likely to be mild. While somewhat subjective, this will suffice for our purposes.

A table complementary to that of the standardised coefficients to assist with judging the relative importance of predictor variables is that of the structure correlations. These are the correlation coefficients between the predictor variables and the discriminant function, reported in descending order in Figure 16.11.

Structure Matrix

	Function 1
Months with service	.971
Age in years	.623
Years at current address	.598
Household income in thousands	.219
Number of people in household	-.024

Pooled within-groups correlations between discriminating variables and standardized canonical discriminant functions
Variables ordered by absolute size of correlation within function.

Figure 16.11 Structure correlations from a discriminant analysis.

This matrix corroborates with our earlier deduction that 'Months with service' is the most important predictor variable, followed by 'Age in years'.

We have already seen the results of the classification for the first seven cases in the Data View (Figure 16.3). However, exactly how have the discriminant scores been calculated and how has the classification of each case been made?

To answer the first question, SPSS simply computes $D_j = \mathbf{B}'\mathbf{X}_j$. For example, for the first case ($j = 1$), we have (using vector multiplication)

$$D_1 = \mathbf{B}'\mathbf{X}_1 = \begin{pmatrix} -2.537 & 0.043 & 0.021 & 0.006 & -0.001 & 0.055 \end{pmatrix} \begin{pmatrix} 1 \\ 13 \\ 44 \\ 9 \\ 64 \\ 2 \end{pmatrix}$$

$$= -2.537 \times 1 + 0.043 \times 13 + 0.021 \times 44 + 0.006 \times 9 - 0.001 \times 64 + 0.055 \times 2$$
$$= -0.94284.$$

Note that the values in **B** are rounded, which explains the small difference if you compute manually.

SPSS tabulates the *group centroids*, that is, the average discriminant scores for each group, reported in Figure 16.12.

Functions at Group Centroids

	Function
Churn within last month	1
No	.257
Yes	-.682

Unstandardized canonical discriminant functions evaluated at group means

Figure 16.12 Group centroids from a discriminant analysis.

Looking at the group centroids, *on average* those who did not churn in the dataset had an average discriminant score of 0.257, versus −0.682 for those who did churn. Hence the classification rule can be obtained from computing the *midpoint* of these centroids:

$$c = \frac{\bar{D}_{G_1} + \bar{D}_{G_2}}{2} = \frac{0.257 + (-0.682)}{2} = -0.2125$$

such that

$$\text{for } D_j \begin{cases} < -0.2125 & \text{classify as 'churn'} \\ > -0.2125 & \text{classify as 'not churn'} \\ = -0.2125 & \text{equally likely to churn or not churn.} \end{cases}$$

This explains why SPSS classified the first seven cases as shown. For example, $D_1 = -0.94284 < -0.2125$, hence the first case was classified as a churner (correctly!), while $D_3 = 1.63962 > -0.2125$ was classified as a non-churner (also correctly!).

Of interest is a comparison of the *distribution* of discriminant scores across the two groups, shown in Figure 16.13. We see that churners tend to have low (negative) discriminant scores with a heavily skewed distribution. In contrast, the non-churners have a more symmetric distribution of their discriminant scores (centred around 0.257, shown rounded as 0.26 in the legend). Hence we anticipate a significant problem of *false positives* (non-churners with negative discriminant scores being mistaken for churners).

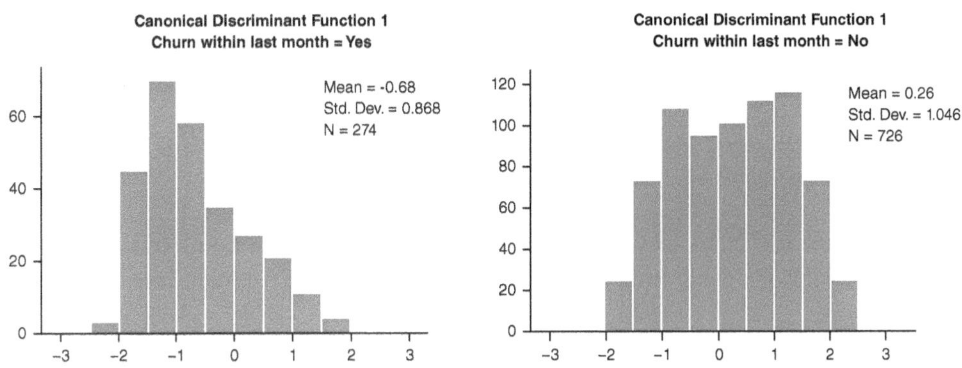

Figure 16.13 Distribution of discriminant scores across two groups.

Armed with knowledge of the centroids, we can now draw a conclusion about the nature of the effects of each predictor variable on the risk of churning by looking at the *signs* of the unstandardised coefficients. We see that the higher (lower) the discriminant score, the more likely a customer will be classified as a non-churner (churner). Hence, *ceteris paribus*:

- since $\hat{\beta}_1 = 0.043 > 0$, the *greater* the number of months with service a customer has, the *less* likely they are to churn
- since $\hat{\beta}_2 = 0.021 > 0$, the *older* a customer is, the *less* likely they are to churn
- since $\hat{\beta}_3 = 0.006 > 0$, the *longer* a customer has resided at their current address, the *less* likely they are to churn
- since $\hat{\beta}_4 = -0.001 < 0$, the *higher* a customer's income is, the *more* likely they are to churn
- since $\hat{\beta}_5 = 0.055 > 0$, the *larger* the household size, the *less* likely they are to churn.

However, we had a total of $n = 1000$ cases, which would be too tedious to examine case by case. Fear not, using Figure 16.14 we now consult the *confusion matrix*.

The overall predictive accuracy of the model can be calculated using the *cross-validated cases* (obtained using LOOCV). The proportion of correctly classified cases is (looking at the leading diagonal count entries for the cross-validated part of the table):

$$\text{OPA} = \frac{457 + 198}{1000} = 0.655,$$

Classification Results[a,c]

		Churn within last month	Predicted Group Membership No	Predicted Group Membership Yes	Total
Original	Count	No	458	268	726
		Yes	76	198	274
	%	No	63.1	36.9	100.0
		Yes	27.7	72.3	100.0
Cross-validated[b]	Count	No	457	269	726
		Yes	76	198	274
	%	No	62.9	37.1	100.0
		Yes	27.7	72.3	100.0

a. 65.6% of original grouped cases correctly classified.

b. Cross validation is done only for those cases in the analysis. In cross validation, each case is classified by the functions derived from all cases other than that case.

c. 65.5% of cross-validated grouped cases correctly classified.

Figure 16.14 Confusion matrix for a discriminant analysis.

hence the model has 65.5% overall predictive accuracy (as reported in Figure 16.14 under footnote 'c.'). Note the (marginally inflated) OPA using the original cases (without cross-validation) of

$$\text{OPA} = \frac{458+198}{1000} = 0.656$$

or 65.6% (as reported in Figure 16.14 under footnote 'a.'). Here the effect of *overfitting* is very minor, but in other situations it may be more dramatic.

Using the cross-validated cases, we can also compute other performance measures. The true positive and true negative rates are, respectively,

$$\text{TPR} = \frac{198}{76+198} = 72.3\%, \quad \text{TNR} = \frac{457}{457+269} = 62.9\%,$$

while the false positive and false negative rates are, respectively:

$$\text{FPR} = \frac{269}{269+198} = 57.6\%, \quad \text{FNR} = \frac{76}{457+76} = 14.3\%.$$

We noted above our concern about excessive amounts of false positives (from a comparison of the discriminant score distributions in Figure 16.13), and this is confirmed by the very high FPR of 57.6%.

So, in conclusion, do we like this model? Well, James, it depends! What is good enough for the telecoms firm? Overall, the classifications are correct about two-thirds of the time. Could we do better with another model (with a different set of predictor variables)? Perhaps. We should also consider the error rates. Which is worse in this setting, a false positive or a false negative? Let us consider the implications.

- A *false positive* means we think someone will churn when they will not. If we suspect a risk of churn, presumably there will be some proactive (and pre-emptive) attempt to prevent churn – for example, offering a discount to incentivise customer retention. This would needlessly eat into the profit margin from such a customer, as without the discount they would have stayed anyway! The high FPR of 57.6% is bad news in this respect.

- A *false negative* means we think someone will not churn when in fact they will. If we suspect no (or minimal) risk of churn, there would be no such proactive intervention, but this customer would then be lost. Had there been a sweetener such as a discount offered, such a customer *may* have been persuaded to stay (depending on how sweet the sweetener was, and how smooth-talking the giver was) with presumably some strictly positive customer lifetime value to the firm, which is otherwise lost. The FNR is 'only' 14.3%, so even if we consider false negatives to be worse in this setting, they are much less likely than false positives.

Therefore, depending on the perceived relative severity of false positives versus false negatives, a judgement needs to be made about what would be an acceptable FPR and/or FNR. Ultimately, it is a judgement call – *your* judgement call!

Given that 'Months with service' and 'Age in years' are the most important predictor variables, it is evident that loyal, older customers are most desirable as they seem 'locked in' as retained customers. On the flip side, newer, younger customers are the high-risk churners. As a business strategy, the firm should do everything possible to interact with its newest and youngest customers to make them feel valued. Such customer retention costs would be offset by the reduced likelihood of churn in the long run!

16.4 THREE-GROUP DISCRIMINANT ANALYSIS: EMPIRICAL EXAMPLE

We conclude this chapter with an example of three-group discriminant analysis. Here we address Headhunters' problem outlined at the beginning of this chapter.

Recall that Headhunters is a large recruitment agency. It has decided to investigate whether different job classifications appeal to different personality types. Three job classifications were considered and indexed as follows: (1) front-of-house/customer-facing, (2) back office and (3) remote roles requiring people to work on their own. Psychometric tests were conducted on 100 candidates previously placed into these different roles, giving rise to three possible predictor variables:

- 'Interest in outdoor activities', X_1
- 'Attitude towards social events', X_2
- 'Reserved score', X_3.

As there are $g = 3$ groups and $k = 3$ predictor variables, we can estimate:

$$\min(g - 1, k) = \min(3 - 1, 3) = \min(2, 3) = 2 \text{ discriminant functions.}$$

The theoretical model is

$$D_{1,j} = \mathbf{A}'\mathbf{X}_j = \alpha_0 + \alpha_1 X_{1,j} + \alpha_2 X_{2,j} + \alpha_3 X_{3,j},$$
$$D_{2,j} = \mathbf{B}'\mathbf{X}_j = \beta_0 + \beta_1 X_{1,j} + \beta_2 X_{2,j} + \beta_3 X_{3,j}.$$

Note that we will obtain *two sets* of unstandardised coefficients, one for each discriminant function. We use the vector notations **A** and **B** to distinguish them. To be clear, the same set of predictor variables is used in each discriminant function, but since $\mathbf{A} \neq \mathbf{B}$ these will give rise to different discriminant scores for each case, denoted by $D_{1,j}$ and $D_{2,j}$, respectively.

A quick look at the Data and Variable Views is provided in Figure 16.15.

Figure 16.15 Data and Variables Views of the Headhunters dataset.

	Outdoor	Social	Reserved	Role	Dis_1	Dis1_1	Dis2_1	Dis1_2	Dis2_2	Dis3_2
1	10	22	5	1	1	1.50282	-.25691	.82700	.16178	.01122
2	14	17	6	1	2	.09815	.30195	.21029	.61935	.17036
3	19	33	7	1	1	2.81875	1.66148	.82025	.17952	.00024
4	14	29	12	1	1	1.59437	-.10620	.82558	.16585	.00857
5	14	25	7	1	1	1.54456	.40375	.72015	.27125	.00860
6	20	25	12	1	2	.41010	1.01811	.18720	.75212	.06068
7	6	18	4	1	1	1.11194	-1.07062	.84180	.12222	.03597

Figure 16.16 Updated Data View after discriminant analysis has been run.

Upon running a three-group discriminant analysis in SPSS, let's examine the updated Data View in Figure 16.16. The first seven cases are shown. The `Role` column shows the true group memberships (1 = Front-of-house, 2 = Back office, 3 = Remote role). The adjacent columns to the right show the following:

- `Dis_1` shows the predicted group membership (1, 2 or 3)
- `Dis1_1` reports the case's respective score for the first discriminant function, $D_{1,j}$
- `Dis2_1` reports the case's respective score for the second discriminant function, $D_{2,j}$
- `Dis1_2` reports the posterior probability of the case belonging to group 1 (front-of-office), $P(g_1 \mid \mathbf{X}_j)$
- `Dis2_2` reports the posterior probability of the case belonging to group 2 (back office), $P(g_2 \mid \mathbf{X}_j)$
- `Dis3_2` reports the posterior probability of the case belonging to group 3 (remote role), $P(g_3 \mid \mathbf{X}_j)$.

For example, the $j = 1$ case (front-of-office), its first discriminant function score is 1.50282, and its second discriminant function score is −0.25691, with an 82.700% chance of belonging to group 1, a 16.178% chance of belonging to group 2, and just a 1.122% chance of belonging to group 3, hence this has been classified as belonging to group 1. (Note that 82.700% + 16.178% + 1.122% = 100%, since the case *must* be assigned to one of the three groups.) This is an example of a correct classification. In contrast, for case $j = 2$ (also front-of-office), this has been incorrectly classified as belonging to group 2, due to the largest posterior probability of 61.935%.

Group Statistics

Role type		Mean	Std. Deviation	Valid N (listwise) Unweighted	Weighted
Front-of-house	Interest in outdoor activities	11.61	5.309	33	33.000
	Attitude towards social events	25.64	4.386	33	33.000
	Reserved score	9.27	2.908	33	33.000
Back office	Interest in outdoor activities	18.00	4.070	33	33.000
	Attitude towards social events	20.76	5.013	33	33.000
	Reserved score	10.03	3.137	33	33.000
Remote role	Interest in outdoor activities	15.44	3.871	34	34.000
	Attitude towards social events	15.32	3.400	34	34.000
	Reserved score	13.35	3.692	34	34.000
Total	Interest in outdoor activities	15.02	5.135	100	100.000
	Attitude towards social events	20.52	6.018	100	100.000
	Reserved score	10.91	3.696	100	100.000

Figure 16.17 Descriptive statistics by group, and all cases pooled together.

We proceed with a simple exploratory analysis, looking at descriptive statistics by group, and all cases pooled together, shown in Figure 16.17. Remember that 'good' predictor variables should have *very different means* across the three groups, combined with *small standard deviations*. The three job types would likely require different personality types, especially front-of-house/customer-facing versus remote roles – the former requiring rather outgoing personalities, the latter much less so. We see that the means of 'Attitude towards social events' ranges from 15.32 (remote role) to 25.64 (front-of-house), suggesting this could be a good predictor: more sociable people may be better suited to customer-facing roles which require strong interpersonal and communication skills.

Since we are discriminating between $g = 3$ groups, using $k = 3$ predictor variables, we require two discriminant functions. Recall that the *theoretical model* is

$$D_{1,j} = \mathbf{A}'\mathbf{X}_j = \alpha_0 + \alpha_1 X_{1,j} + \alpha_2 X_{2,j} + \alpha_3 X_{3,j},$$
$$D_{2,j} = \mathbf{B}'\mathbf{X}_j = \beta_0 + \beta_1 X_{1,j} + \beta_2 X_{2,j} + \beta_3 X_{3,j},$$

with the estimated model derived from the output table with the unstandardised coefficients, shown in Figure 16.18. Hence in vector notation we have

Canonical Discriminant Function Coefficients

	Function	
	1	2
Interest in outdoor activities	-.064	.206
Attitude towards social events	.200	.028
Reserved score	-.150	-.125
(Constant)	-1.494	-2.319

Unstandardized coefficients

Figure 16.18 Unstandardised coefficients for a discriminant analysis.

$$\mathbf{A} = \begin{pmatrix} -1.494 \\ -0.064 \\ 0.200 \\ -0.150 \end{pmatrix}, \quad \mathbf{B} = \begin{pmatrix} -2.319 \\ 0.206 \\ 0.028 \\ -0.125 \end{pmatrix} \quad \text{and} \quad \mathbf{X}_j = \begin{pmatrix} 1 \\ X_{1j} \\ X_{2j} \\ X_{3j} \end{pmatrix}$$

and so the estimated discriminant functions are

$$D_{1,j} = \mathbf{A}'\mathbf{X}_j = -1.494 - 0.064X_{1,j} + 0.200X_{2,j} - 0.150X_{3,j},$$
$$D_{2,j} = \mathbf{B}'\mathbf{X}_j = -2.319 + 0.206X_{1,j} + 0.028X_{2,j} - 0.125X_{3,j}.$$

We assess the statistical significance of each discriminant function based on Wilks' λ, shown in Figure 16.19. With two discriminant functions, the first is superior, with a smaller associated Wilks' λ. We conclude that both discriminant functions are statistically significant, with the first offering better discrimination, but using *both* discriminant functions will help us in borderline cases when otherwise using only $D_{1,j}$ may be inconclusive.

Wilks' Lambda

Test of Function(s)	Wilks' Lambda	Chi-square	df	Sig.
1 through 2	.319	109.736	6	<.001
2	.787	23.048	2	<.001

Figure 16.19 Wilks' lambda and associated hypothesis test components.

Looking at the one-way ANOVA F test results in Figure 16.20, we see that all three predictor variables are highly significant. However, are they all *equally* influential in discriminating between the groups? Not necessarily. Consulting simple descriptive statistics of the predictor variables in Figure 16.21, we see that there is no dramatic difference in the scales of measurement (similar ranges); nevertheless we would not expect the three predictors to be equally important.

We proceed to look at the standardised coefficients in Figure 16.22. Given that the first discriminant function is more influential, our focus is on comparing the standardised coefficients just for this function. Clearly, we see that 'Attitude towards social events' seems the most important, about

0.860/|–0.489| = 1.76 times as important as (76% more important than) 'Reserved score', which in turn seems to be about |–0.489|/|–0.287| = 1.70 times as important as (70% more important than) 'Interest in outdoor activities'. (Note that 'Attitude towards social events' is about 0.860/|–0.287| = 3 times as important as 'Interest in outdoor activities'.)

Tests of Equality of Group Means

	Wilks' Lambda	F	df1	df2	Sig.
Interest in outdoor activities	.738	17.214	2	97	<.001
Attitude towards social events	.502	48.034	2	97	<.001
Reserved score	.766	14.846	2	97	<.001

Figure 16.20 Results of univariate (one-way) ANOVA tests in a discriminant analysis.

Descriptive Statistics

	N	Minimum	Maximum	Mean	Std. Deviation
Interest in outdoor activities	100	0	28	15.02	5.135
Attitude towards social events	100	8	35	20.52	6.018
Reserved score	100	1	20	10.91	3.696
Valid N (listwise)	100				

Figure 16.21 Descriptive statistics of the predictor variables.

We reach the same conclusion about relative importance by consulting the structure correlations, shown in Figure 16.23.

Multicollinearity is of no concern whatsoever, with negligible bivariate correlations between the predictor variables, as seen from the correlation matrix in Figure 16.24.

To see how the discriminant scores are computed, recall that $D_{1,j} = \mathbf{A}'\mathbf{X}_j$ and $D_{2,j} = \mathbf{B}'\mathbf{X}_j$. For example, for the first case (j = 1), we have (using vector multiplication)

$$D_{1,1} = \mathbf{A}'\mathbf{X}_1 = \begin{pmatrix} -1.494 & -0.064 & 0.200 & -0.150 \end{pmatrix} \begin{pmatrix} 1 \\ 10 \\ 22 \\ 5 \end{pmatrix}$$
$$= -1.494 \times 1 - 0.064 \times 10 + 0.200 \times 22 - 0.150 \times 5$$
$$= 1.50282$$

and

$$D_{2,1} = \mathbf{B}'\mathbf{X}_1 = \begin{pmatrix} -2.319 & 0.206 & 0.028 & -0.125 \end{pmatrix} \begin{pmatrix} 1 \\ 10 \\ 22 \\ 5 \end{pmatrix}$$
$$= -2.319 \times 1 + 0.206 \times 10 + 0.028 \times 22 - 0.125 \times 5$$
$$= -0.25691.$$

Note that the values in **A** and **B** are rounded, which explains the small differences if you compute manually. SPSS tabulates the *group centroids*, that is, the average discriminant scores for each group, in Figure 16.25.

Standardized Canonical Discriminant Function Coefficients

	Function	
	1	2
Interest in outdoor activities	-.287	.919
Attitude towards social events	.860	.122
Reserved score	-.489	-.407

Figure 16.22 Standardised coefficients from a discriminant analysis.

Structure Matrix

	Function	
	1	2
Attitude towards social events	.821*	.090
Reserved score	-.427*	-.376
Interest in outdoor activities	-.298	.910*

Pooled within-groups correlations between discriminating variables and standardized canonical discriminant functions
Variables ordered by absolute size of correlation within function.

*. Largest absolute correlation between each variable and any discriminant function

Figure 16.23 Structure correlations from a discriminant analysis.

With two discriminant functions, we can view the centroids as coordinates in two-dimensional space. As such we can plot them along with the pairs of discriminant scores for all cases in the dataset, as shown in Figure 16.26. The centroids are indicated by squares, with the colour-coded circles the discriminant score pairs for each case, that is, $(D_{1,j}, D_{2,j})$ for $j = 1, 2, ..., 100$ (since we have data on 100 people).

For the decision rule to enable classification, each case's group prediction is to the role type whose centroid it is nearest geometrically. Notice how in Figure 16.26 the blue circles (front-of-office roles) tend to be clustered to the right of the plot, with discriminant function 1 scores (the x coordinates) roughly in the interval [0, 4], and discriminant function 2 scores (the y coordinates) roughly in the interval [–3, 2]. Next, the green circles (back office) are quite dispersed, with x coordinates in the interval [–4, 3] and y coordinates in the interval [–1, 3]. Finally, the red circles (remote role) tend to be clustered to the left of the plot, with x coordinates tending to range from [–3, 0] and y coordinates in the interval [–3, 2].

This plot shows that we should expect some misclassifications when we examine the confusion matrix. For example, some green (back office) circles are clearly nearer the front-of-house centroid, while others are nearer the remote role centroid.

Focusing on the first discriminant function, we can see that the higher (lower) the first discriminant score is, the more likely the individual would be in a front-of-house role (remote role). Hence, *ceteris paribus*:

- since $\hat{\alpha}_1 = -0.064 < 0$, the *greater* the individual's interest in outdoor activities is, the *more* likely they are to be in a remote role (perhaps easier to pop outdoors for fresh air when not supervised!)
- since $\hat{\alpha}_2 = 0.200 > 0$, the *greater* the individual's attitude towards social events is, the *more* likely they are to be in a front-of-house role (perhaps a greater desire to be around people, hence preference for a front-of-house role)
- since $\hat{\alpha}_3 = -0.150 < 0$, the *greater* the individual's reserved score is, the *more* likely they are to be in a remote role (perhaps a tendency to avoid being around people, hence a preference for remote work).

Pooled Within-Groups Matrices

		Interest in outdoor activities	Attitude towards social events	Reserved score
Correlation	Interest in outdoor activities	1.000	.000	.024
	Attitude towards social events	.000	1.000	.080
	Reserved score	.024	.080	1.000

Figure 16.24 Correlation matrix of the predictor variables.

Functions at Group Centroids

	Function	
Role type	1	2
Front-of-house	1.486	-.355
Back office	-.013	.731
Remote role	-1.429	-.365

Unstandardized canonical discriminant functions evaluated at group means

Figure 16.25 Group centroids from a discriminant analysis.

We now consult the confusion matrix in Figure 16.27. The overall predictive accuracy of the model can be calculated using the *cross-validated cases* (obtained using LOOCV). The proportion of correctly classified cases is (looking at the leading diagonal count entries for the cross-validated part of the confusion matrix)

$$\text{OPA} = \frac{23+22+29}{100} = 0.740,$$

hence the model has 74.0% overall predictive accuracy (as reported in Figure 16.27 under footnote 'c.'). Note the (marginally inflated) OPA using the original cases (without cross-validation) of

$$\text{OPA} = \frac{26+23+29}{100} = 0.780$$

or 78.0% (as reported under footnote 'a.'). Here the effect of *overfitting* is 4 percentage points. The off-leading diagonal entries show the misclassifications:

- 9 front-of-house cases were incorrectly classified as back office
- 1 front-of-house case was incorrectly classified as remote role
- 7 back office cases were incorrectly classified as front-of-house
- 4 back office cases were incorrectly classified as remote role
- 0 remote role cases were incorrectly classified as front-of-house (success!)
- 5 remote role cases were incorrectly classified as back office.

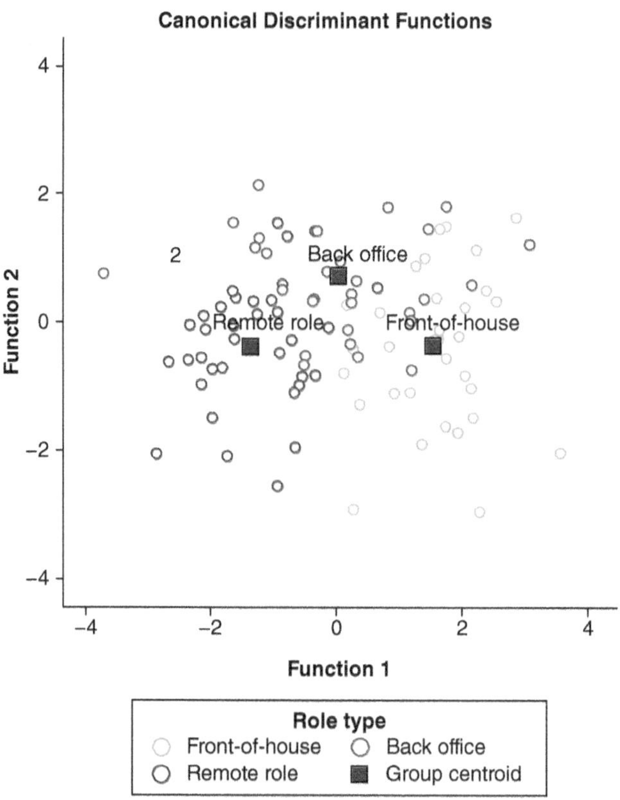

Figure 16.26 Plot of pairs of discriminant scores for each case and group centroids.

Since there are $g = 3$ groups, it does not make sense to refer to true/false positive/negative rates, because 'positive' and 'negative' are only meaningful in binary settings.

So, can Headhunters use the psychometric scores to better place job applicants? Well, James, as with the two-group case, it depends! Is the overall predictive accuracy at 74% satisfactory? We have only used three predictor variables, and it would be reasonable to speculate that other factors such as age, mobility, caring responsibilities, etc. may be influential, especially for remote roles. On the positive side, Headhunters at least has a working model against which to benchmark any other models. Also, thought should be given to the relative severity of the different kinds of misclassifications. For example, placing an extreme introvert into a front-of-house role may be highly anxiety-inducing, whereas placing an extreme extrovert in a remote role may lead to boredom, which might be considered less serious than anxiety affecting mental health.

As ever, such decisions are judgement calls – remember, *your* judgement call!

16.5 CHAPTER OVERVIEW

This chapter has introduced classification models using discriminant analysis. Based on a set of predictor variables, discriminant scores for each case are computed. Classification to a group is then made based on the nearest centroid, whereby a centroid acts as a characteristic profile of a typical group member. The relative importance of predictor variables in discriminant analysis models has been explored, based on standardised coefficients and structure correlations. Assessing predictive accuracy is achieved by consulting the confusion matrix – a tabulated tally of cases and whether or not they have been correctly classified. Reference to leave-one-out cross-validation ensures we do not fall into the trap of model overfitting, that is, thinking a model has better overall predictive accuracy than it actually does, achieved by dividing observations into training and test datasets. We have also considered the possible asymmetry of different types of misclassification. Ultimately, value judgements need to be made about whether a model is adequate enough to be used in practice!

Classification Results[a,c]

			Predicted Group Membership			
		Role type	Front-of-house	Back office	Remote role	Total
Original	Count	Front-of-house	26	7	0	33
		Back office	7	23	3	33
		Remote role	0	5	29	34
	%	Front-of-house	78.8	21.2	.0	100.0
		Back office	21.2	69.7	9.1	100.0
		Remote role	.0	14.7	85.3	100.0
Cross-validated[b]	Count	Front-of-house	23	9	1	33
		Back office	7	22	4	33
		Remote role	0	5	29	34
	%	Front-of-house	69.7	27.3	3.0	100.0
		Back office	21.2	66.7	12.1	100.0
		Remote role	.0	14.7	85.3	100.0

a. 78.0% of original grouped cases correctly classified.

b. Cross validation is done only for those cases in the analysis. In cross validation, each case is classified by the functions derived from all cases other than that case.

c. 74.0% of cross-validated grouped cases correctly classified.

Figure 16.27 Confusion matrix for a discriminant analysis.

16.6 KEY VOCABULARY

Centroid
Classification
Confusion matrix
Discriminant analysis
Discriminant function
Discriminant score
False negative rate (FNR)
False positive rate (FPR)
Leave-one-out cross-validation (LOOCV)
Overall predictive accuracy (OPA)
Overfitting
SPSS
Standardised coefficients
Structure correlations
Test data
Training data
True negative rate (TNR)
True positive rate (TPR)
Unstandardised coefficients

16.7 EXERCISES

16.7.1 Test your understanding

1 In a binary classification context, what are the four possible types of classification?
2 In discriminant analysis which is worse, a false positive or a false negative? 'Well, James, it depends' may feature in your answer, but explain what it depends on!
3 Can an object/case belong to more than one group in a discriminant analysis? Explain why or why not.
4 If you wanted to build a model to discriminate between defaulters and non-defaulters of a loan, which predictor variables would you recommend including in the model? Briefly justify your view.
5 For g groups and k predictor variables, how many discriminant functions will there be?
6 What is a 'good' value of k, the number of predictor variables? Briefly justify your view.
7 For the discriminant function

$$D_j = \beta_0 + \beta_1 X_{1,j} + \beta_2 X_{2,j} + \cdots + \beta_k X_{k,j}$$

define all terms.

8 For $g = 2$ groups, how can a classification decision rule be developed based on the centroids?
9 What is the purpose of a confusion matrix?
10 Consider the following confusion matrix for a two-group classification problem:

	Predicted group		
Actual group	Negative	Positive	Total
Negative	n_{11}	n_{12}	$n_{1\cdot}$
Positive	n_{21}	n_{22}	$n_{2\cdot}$
Total	$n_{\cdot 1}$	$n_{\cdot 2}$	n

Describe in words what each n value represents.

11 With respect to the confusion matrix in Question 10, explain how to calculate each of the following:

(a) the overall predictive accuracy
(b) the true positive rate

(c) the true negative rate
(d) the false positive rate
(e) the false negative rate.

12 At a high level, how does leave-one-out cross-validation work? You should refer to training and test data in your response.
13 What is meant by 'overfitting' in a discriminant analysis context?
14 When trying to identify 'good' predictor variables for discriminant analysis only using descriptive statistics, what would we be looking out for?
15. What is the difference between unstandardised coefficients and standardised coefficients? For what purpose is each type useful?
16 How would you check whether multicollinearity may be a concern in a discriminant analysis model?
17 What are the group centroids, and what purpose do they serve?
18 Explain how discriminant scores would be calculated:

(a) for a model discriminating between $g = 2$ groups
(b) for a model discriminating between $g = 3$ groups.

19 Would you expect the overall predictive accuracy to be higher or lower when based on cross-validated cases compared to original cases? Briefly justify your view.
20 If you had confusion matrices for several different discriminant analysis models (trying to classify the same distinct groups), how would you propose to compare the performances across the models?

16.7.2 Practice with SPSS

Head over to the companion website for SPSS examples and screencasts!

17

FACTOR ANALYSIS

Chapter contents

Chapter level: ***Advanced***

Source: Photo by Brett Jordan via Unsplash.

Key concepts

- Data reduction
- Underlying factors
- Surrogate variables

Chapter value

Factor analysis is a form of data reduction such that we can streamline the number of variables.

Key takeaway

Factors are hidden constructs correlated with things we observe. We quantify what we don't directly see.

Chapter outline

Style. Extraversion. Price-consciousness. Each is an example of a *factor* or *construct*. None is tangible. None is directly observed. What does it mean to be stylish? Extraverted? Price-conscious? Factors are in practice often 'fuzzy' and hard to directly quantify. While you could look up a dictionary definition, this is *qualitative*, but we seek a *quantitative* variable. However, there are observable variables which we would expect to be (highly) correlated with each factor. For example, brands bought or amount spent on clothing would reflect attitude to fashion and hence style; social diary activity or number of parties attended would reflect how extraverted someone is; actively seeking out discounts or 'trading down' would reflect price-conscious behaviour. *Factor analysis* provides a way to quantify hidden, or 'latent', factors, and also permits *data reduction* - an in-demand requirement in an era of big data - by reducing the number of variables (reducing the 'dimensionality' of a dataset).

Learning outcomes

After completing this chapter, you should be able to:

- explain the purpose of factor analysis in terms of data reduction and summarisation
- conduct a factor analysis in SPSS and interpret output, addressing the correlation matrix, deciding the appropriate number of factors and computing factor scores
- interpret extracted factors by using factor rotation
- judge the performance of factor analysis by way of a residual analysis.

Motivational case: The key to home sweet home

Righthome is a new estate agency (real estate) chain and is aggressively recruiting a team of sales negotiators for its new head office. Working in this sector is not for the faint-hearted, and only those with strong, assertive personalities are considered likely to be successful in the role. To help screen the large number of job applications, Righthome requires applicants to complete a short online questionnaire asking them to rate themselves on various personal attributes such as ambition and drive.

How can Righthome use the questionnaire results to determine which candidates are most suitable to be short-listed for interview (in addition to them having a strong résumé)?

17.1 INTRODUCTION

Modern businesses often are not short of data. Large datasets are common, but pose the challenge of being *too* large to handle and make sense of. Market research surveys, social media posts, high-frequency financial data, geolocation data of where customers live, to name but a few. Managers aspire to *understand* what the data is telling us by *extracting the most useful information* in it in order to make better and more effective business decisions. Recall the DIKW pyramid in Figure 1.2.

We have seen datasets arranged in tabular form – a data array with variables columnwise and observations rowwise. In this chapter we look at how to *reduce the number of columns*, that is, reduce the number of variables to a more manageable number of 'factors' by exploiting correlations which exist among the original variables, while in Chapter 18 we look at how to *reduce the number of rows*, that is, reduce the number of observations to a more manageable number, by looking for 'similar' cases and grouping them together into 'clusters' (think market segmentation).

Suppose our original dataset is arranged as follows in spreadsheet form:

	Variable 1	...	Variable k
Observation 1	X_{11}	...	X_{1k}
⋮	⋮	⋮	⋮
Observation n	X_{n1}	...	X_{nk}

That is, we have n observations on each of k variables. Let X_{ij} denote the ith value in the jth column, for $i = 1, 2,..., n$ and $j = 1, 2,..., k$. Each observation, for example, could be a survey respondent, with each variable representing the response to a question (in such cases we might expect multiple instances of *item non-response*, that is, a lot of empty cells reflecting unanswered questions, posing a challenge about how to deal with such missing values – *imputation* by substituting the mean is one possible solution). Alternatively, each row could be a customer transaction, with the variables being details of the order and the customer (billing information, delivery address, etc.). Tableau's sample Superstore dataset, seen in Chapter 3, is an excellent example.

Whatever the nature of the dataset, each row is multivariate, with multiple variables required to describe it. Each multivariate observation is viewed as a (multivariate) random variable, susceptible to random behaviour according to some (multivariate) probability distribution. Because of this, in the event of a missing value, knowledge of the other $k - 1$ variables for a case may help us *improve* our prediction of the missing value, although we could not say with certainty what the true value is as there will always be a random component preventing us from making a perfect prediction.

A *multivariate random variable* is a natural extension of its univariate counterpart. Univariate random variables reflect single quantities (see Chapter 5), with their behaviour represented by a probability distribution – either discrete (e.g. the binomial) or continuous (e.g. the normal). A multivariate random variable (such as a set of responses to a market research survey) is characterised by a *multivariate probability distribution*. Consider the following bivariate (two-variable) example, which is the simplest multivariate case.

Example 17.1

Suppose, for a randomly selected customer of a clothing retailer, we let

X = their height (in centimetres) and Y = their weight (in kilograms).

Suppose further that the *univariate* (marginal) distributions of X and Y are approximately normal, such that

$X \sim N(174.9, 7.39^2)$ and $Y \sim N(84.2, 15.63^2)$

and the bivariate (joint) distribution of (X, Y) is a bivariate normal distribution.

Plots of the univariate and bivariate probability density functions are shown in Figures 17.1, 17.2 and 17.3.

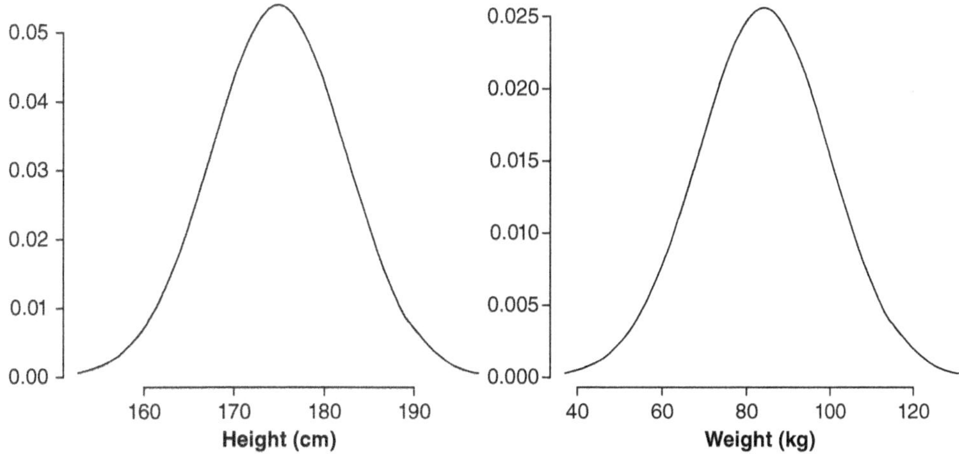

Figure 17.1 Univariate marginal probability density functions for Example 17.1.

We have already considered some multivariate modelling techniques, such as analysis of variance (Chapter 12) and multiple linear regression (Chapter 14). In both cases we clearly distinguished between *dependent* and *independent* variables, with our main objective being to explain as much of the variation in the dependent variable as possible.

In this chapter, we do *not* distinguish between dependent and independent variables. Our objective is different. Instead, we wish to leverage the *interdependencies* - the correlations - between multiple observed variables in order to extract the underlying core constructs which adequately summarise the observed variables.

Example 17.2

Suppose a consumer questionnaire about shampoo preferences collected data on $k = 20$ questions, thus giving rise to responses on 20 variables. In practice, we might expect people to buy shampoo based on just a handful of 'factors' - underlying constructs such as:

- value for money
- desired hair effect (shiny, volume, anti-dandruff)
- suitability for hair types (damaged, dyed, dry)
- usage attributes (ease of rinsing, irritation-free)
- bottle design (shape, colour, whether recyclable).

The actual questions asked will have been designed with the intention of gaining insights into consumers' actual perceptions of these constructs. With data on 20 variables, with perhaps five underlying factors (as listed above), our objective is **data reduction**. By this we mean reducing the *dimensionality* of the dataset columnwise, such that the underlying factors are 'recovered' from the larger number of observed variables.

(Continued)

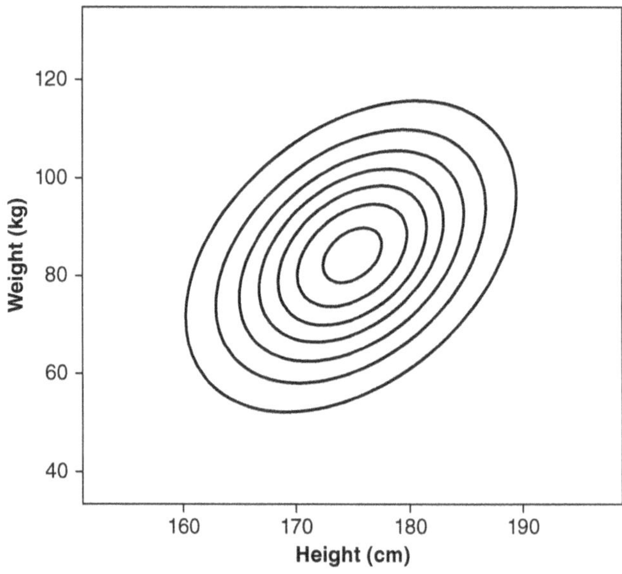

Figure 17.2 Bivariate joint probability density function (a 'contour plot') for Example 17.1.

For example, with several related questions about shampoo prices and perceived quality, it would likely be possible to extract a value-for-money factor due to the expected correlations between price- and quality-related questions. Note that 'value for money' does not equate to 'cheap', rather it concerns whether someone considers the price paid to be commensurate with the perceived product or service quality. (Dare I ask whether this book is good value for money? Well, James, it depends!)

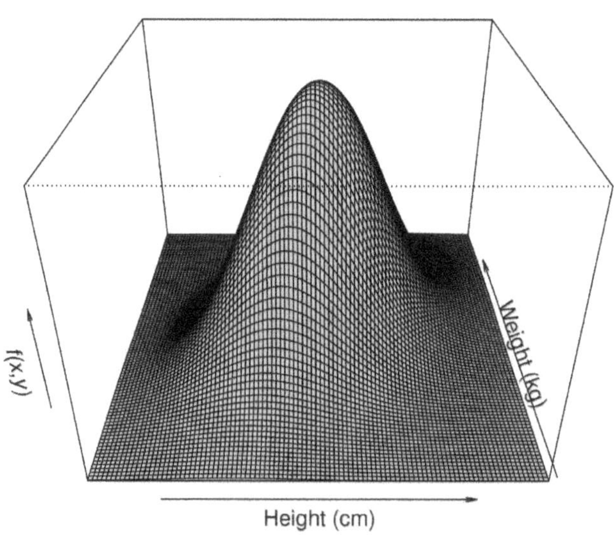

Figure 17.3 Bivariate joint probability density function for Example 17.1.

Factor analysis enables us to reduce k observed variables to a smaller number, m, of factors (i.e. $m < k$). This is what is meant by data reduction in a columnwise sense (rowwise data reduction, using cluster analysis, will be covered in Chapter 18). Since factors can be 'fuzzy', it is important that any extracted factors are straightforward to interpret so that we can easily name them, albeit perhaps subjectively. Once factors have been identified, each case (row) can be *scored* for each factor, creating a set of quantitative measurements of each factor, which can then be used in further analysis.

Myers-Briggs personality types

What is your personality type? *Myers-Briggs* is a well-known way of classifying people's personalities based on responses to a series of questions. (Like any methodology, it is open to criticism, but let's go with it regardless!)

Strictly speaking, this is a combination of *factor analysis* and *classification*. The 'factors' are personality traits, and people are scored based on each of these. There are four categories, each with two 'poles':

- extraverts (E) versus introverts (I)
- intuitives (N) versus sensors (S)
- feelers (F) versus thinkers (T)
- judgers (J) versus perceivers (P)

and a personality type reported by four letters - for example, ENFP (a campaigner) or ISTJ (a logistician). If you think these terms are somewhat vague, I agree! (What does it really mean to be a 'feeler'?) Remember that factors are not directly observed and are often fuzzy in their definition.

By completing a series of relevant questions, such as

- 'Do you enjoy participating in group activities?' (indicative of E or I)
- 'On entering, can you "read a room"?' (indicative of N or S)
- 'Do you always go with your gut feeling?' (indicative of F or T)
- 'Are you a very organised person?' (indicative of J or P)

factor scores can be determined. These scores are then used for classification into one of $2^4 = 16$ personality types (there are two poles for each of four factors).

Since some job roles may be better suited to particular personalities, if managers know the personality types of employees then forming teams, whether to ensure a suitable mix of different personalities (perhaps to foster innovation by bouncing ideas off each other) or to ensure good team chemistry (by avoiding conflict-inducing personality clashes), would likely be easier.

There are many free personality test questionnaires online which, if you answer honestly, will tell you your personality type. Presumably, you know yourself better than anyone, so judge how accurate you think the classification is! Full disclosure: I'm an ESTJ (executive), apparently.

17.2 FACTOR ANALYSIS MODEL

Based on a set of k *correlated* observed variables, we seek to uncover the m underlying dimensions (where $m < k$), known as factors, which these reflect. However, it may not be obvious what the value of m is, so we will need to exercise some judgement to determine the appropriate number of factors, that is, to determine the true dimensionality of the data.

Since we expect the k observed variables to be correlated, using them directly in a regression, say, may result in *multicollinearity* – recall that in Section 14.7 we noted this problem of strong correlations between independent variables in a multiple linear regression model (it is also a potential concern in discriminant analysis, as seen in Chapter 16). Fortunately, we can apply factor analysis to extract factors which are *uncorrelated* with each other. Hence if we wanted to use the m factors as independent variables in a regression (or as predictor variables in a discriminant analysis), then we could eliminate the problem of multicollinearity altogether, and we would have the benefit of having a simpler model (since $m < k$), satisfying Occam's razor (Section 14.4.1) by shaving off the number of independent variables. This seems like a win–win situation, but any benefit always comes at a cost, and the downside is that the m factors may be hard to adequately profile, and data reduction is likely to come at the expense of some loss of information.

Chapter 11 discussed correlation – the *strength* of the linear relationship between two (measurable) variables. Scatter plots allow us to get a visual sense of whether any linear relationship exists, while the (sample) correlation coefficient, r, quantifies its strength, given for variables x and y by

$$r = \frac{\text{Sample covariance}}{\sqrt{(\text{Sample covariance of } X) \times (\text{Sample covariance of } Y)}} = \frac{\sum_{i=1}^{n} x_i y_i - n\bar{x}\bar{y}}{\sqrt{\left(\sum_{i=1}^{n} x_i^2 - n\bar{x}^2\right)\left(\sum_{i=1}^{n} y_i^2 - n\bar{y}^2\right)}}.$$

When we have more than two variables, the bivariate correlations between each pair can be reported in a correlation matrix (as discussed in Example 11.15).

Factor analysis uses the correlation matrix as its input, which is then 'decomposed' to identify the key underlying factors, or *principal components*. The factors are extracted to ensure they are uncorrelated (highly desirable if we intend to use factor scores in a multiple regression or a discriminant analysis). Also, the factors are conveniently derived in *rank order* in terms of how much variation among the original variables has been explained.

Computationally, factor analysis works with *standardised* variables. Each observed variable, X_j, for $j = 1, 2, \ldots, k$, is standardised, denoted below as X_j', by subtracting its (sample) mean, $\bar{X}_j$, and dividing by its (sample) standard deviation, S_j,

$$X_j' = \frac{X_j - \bar{X}_j}{S_j},$$

and then each standardised variable is subsequently modelled as a *linear combination* of the underlying common factors, F_i, for $i = 1, 2, \ldots, m$, and a variable-specific factor, V_j, which represents the random variation specific to X_j', such that

$$X_1' = \alpha_{11}F_1 + \alpha_{21}F_2 + \cdots + \alpha_{m1}F_m + V_1,$$

$$X_2' = \alpha_{12}F_1 + \alpha_{22}F_2 + \cdots + \alpha_{m2}F_m + V_2,$$

$$\vdots$$

$$X_j' = \alpha_{1j}F_1 + \alpha_{2j}F_2 + \cdots + \alpha_{mj}F_m + V_j,$$

$$\vdots$$

$$X_k' = \alpha_{1k}F_1 + \alpha_{2k}F_2 + \cdots + \alpha_{mk}F_m + V_k.$$

Since we do not expect the m common factors to explain *all* of the variation in the X_j' values, we need to include the V_j factor. The coefficients on the F_i factors are known as the factor loadings. As we might expect, the factor model has some assumptions attached to it. These are as follows:

- The expected value of each factor is zero, $\mathrm{E}(F_i) = 0$, for $i = 1, 2, \ldots, m$.
- The variance of each factor is 1, $\mathrm{Var}(F_i) = 1$, for $i = 1, 2, \ldots, m$.
- The factors are uncorrelated with each other (equivalently, have zero covariance), $\mathrm{Cov}(F_i, F_j) = 0$ for all $i \neq j$. (When $i = j$ then $\mathrm{Cov}(F_i, F_i) = \mathrm{Var}(F_i) = 1$.)
- The expected value of the random variation term is zero, $\mathrm{E}(V_j) = 0$, for $j = 1, 2, \ldots, k$.
- The random variation terms are uncorrelated with each other, $\mathrm{Cov}(V_i, V_j) = 0$ for all $i \neq j$.
- The factors and random variation terms are uncorrelated with each other, $\mathrm{Cov}(F_i, V_j) = 0$ for all $i = 1, 2, \ldots, m$ and $j = 1, 2, \ldots, k$.

In summary, by making the above assumptions, the factor loadings can be determined. The variance of each standardised variable, X_j' (which is 1, due to the standardisation), can be written as

$$1 = \mathrm{Var}(X_j') = \underbrace{\alpha_{1j}^2 + \alpha_{2j}^2 + \cdots + \alpha_{mj}^2}_{\text{communality}} + \mathrm{Var}(V_j).$$

As indicated, the sum of the squared factor loadings is called the communality of X_j' and represents the variation of X_j' explained by the common factors collectively. $\mathrm{Var}(V_j)$ is the specific variance of X_j'. Ideally, we would like the communalities to be *as large as possible* (as close to 1 as possible, with $\mathrm{Var}(V_j)$ as close to 0 as possible).

Note that the F_i (and the V_j) factors are *not* observed. We only have data on the X_j (and hence the X_j'). However, due to the F_i being common to all of the X_j, we may write each common factor as a linear combination of the (standardised) observed variables, that is,

$$F_1 = \beta_{11}X_1' + \beta_{21}X_2' + \cdots + \beta_{k1}X_k',$$

$$F_2 = \beta_{12}X_1' + \beta_{22}X_2' + \cdots + \beta_{k2}X_k',$$

$$\vdots$$

$$F_i = \beta_{1i}X_1' + \beta_{2i}X_2' + \cdots + \beta_{ki}X_k',$$

$$\vdots$$

$$F_m = \beta_{1m}X_1' + \beta_{2m}X_2' + \cdots + \beta_{km}X_k'.$$

Our task is to transform the observed variables into a set of uncorrelated linear combinations of these (standardised) variables.

We can think of our objective as a two-stage process. First, we convert the original k correlated variables into k uncorrelated variables, known as *principal components analysis*. Second, we reduce the k uncorrelated components into m uncorrelated factors (where $m < k$), known as *factor analysis*.

17.3 FACTOR ANALYSIS: FULL EMPIRICAL WORKTHROUGH

Suppose a retailer recently conducted a customer satisfaction survey, with $n = 150$ respondents, to determine satisfaction levels across the following attributes:

- price satisfaction, X_1
- product range satisfaction, X_2
- packaging satisfaction, X_3
- customer service satisfaction, X_4
- product quality satisfaction, X_5.

Each attribute was scored on a five-point Likert scale (see Chapter 8), ranging from 1 = strongly negative to 5 = strongly positive. The retailer wanted to identify the underlying dimensions which explain the correlations among responses to the above five attributes, so decided to undertake a factor analysis.

We proceed to conduct a factor analysis of the data using SPSS. We begin by eyeballing the observed variables (the first 10 cases), shown in Figure 17.4. Variation in the responses is evident.

To perform factor analysis in SPSS, proceed as follows.

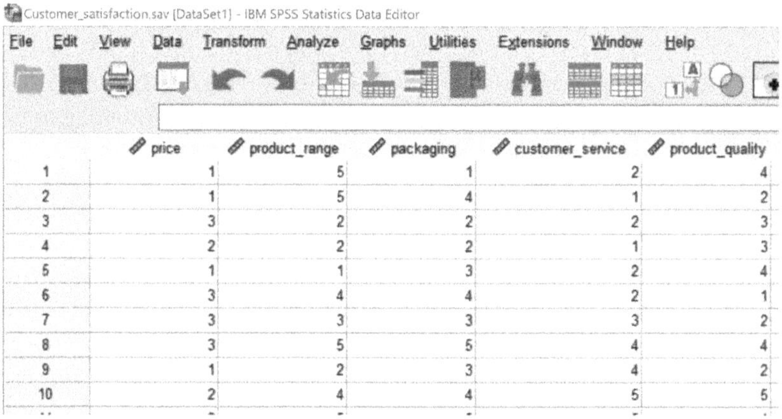

Customer_satisfaction.sav [DataSet1] - IBM SPSS Statistics Data Editor

File Edit View Data Transform Analyze Graphs Utilities Extensions Window Help

	price	product_range	packaging	customer_service	product_quality
1	1	5	1	2	4
2	1	5	4	1	2
3	3	2	2	2	3
4	2	2	2	1	3
5	1	1	3	2	4
6	3	4	4	2	1
7	3	3	3	3	2
8	3	5	5	4	4
9	1	2	3	4	2
10	2	4	4	5	5

Figure 17.4 The first 10 responses to the customer satisfaction survey.

- **Analyze > Dimension Reduction > Factor...** (since our objective is to reduce the dimensionality of the data).
- Move the relevant factors into the `Variables` box (in this case all five satisfaction variables). Note that there is no distinction between dependent and independent variables, since we are only concerned with the interdependencies between these observed variables.
- Click on `Descriptives...`. In the pop-up window, in the `Statistics` box check `Initial solution` (default). In the `Correlation Matrix` box check `Coefficients`, `Significance levels`, `Reproduced`, and also check `KMO and Bartlett's test of sphericity`. Click on `Continue`.
- Click on `Extraction...`. In the pop-up window, for `Method` select `Principal components` (default). In the `Analyze` box, check `Correlation matrix`. In the `Extract` box, check

`Based on Eigenvalue` for values greater than 1 (default). In the `Display` box check `Unrotated factor solution` (default) and `Scree plot`. Click on `Continue`. (There are several methods for estimating factor loadings. We will use the popular 'principal components' approach such that we ignore components which explain only a small amount of variation. Maximum likelihood estimation is an alternative to principal components, especially if we are willing to assume a multivariate normal distribution for the original variables. It is recommended to experiment with different methods, that is, conduct a *sensitivity analysis*, and if similar conclusions are reached regardless of approach, then we may consider the results to be robust.)

- Click on `Rotation...`. In the `Method` box check `Varimax`. In the `Display` box check `Rotated solution` (default) and `Loading plot(s)`. Click on `Continue`.
- Click on `Scores...`. In the pop-up window, check `Save as variables` and `Display factor score coefficient matrix`. Click on `Continue`.
- Click on `OK`.

As with discriminant analysis in Chapter 16, many results tables are presented. While each table (and every value in each table) means something, some tables are of greater interest than others, hence our focus will be on the most salient parts of the overall output to assist our interpretation and evaluation of the model.

*Customer_satisfaction.sav [DataSet1] - IBM SPSS Statistics Data Editor

File Edit View Data Transform Analyze Graphs Utilities Extensions Window Help

	price	product_range	packaging	customer_service	product_quality	FAC1_1	FAC2_1
1	1	5	1	2	4	.16683	-1.52951
2	1	5	4	1	2	-.29571	-.79491
3	3	2	2	2	3	-.96597	.95233
4	2	2	2	1	3	-1.21051	-.23821
5	1	1	3	2	4	-.79476	-1.27363
6	3	4	4	2	1	-.65991	1.60926
7	3	3	3	3	2	-.52513	1.33107
8	3	5	5	4	4	1.13127	1.61770
9	1	2	3	4	2	-.45057	-.93100
10	2	4	4	5	5	1.30934	.19923

Figure 17.5 Updated Data View showing two sets of factor scores.

The Data View in Figure 17.5 shows what SPSS has calculated. Factor scores of *two* extracted factors can be seen in the columns adjacent to the original variables $X_1, X_2, \ldots, X_5$. This tells us that SPSS has managed to reduce $k = 5$ variables into $m = 2$ underlying factors. For now, these are technically named `FAC1_1` and `FAC2_1`, somewhat meaningless. It will be up to us to come up with more useful names, and we shall in due course. For now, note the variation in the factor scores for the 10 cases shown. For example, the factor 1 scores of cases 4 and 10 are −1.21051 and 1.30934, respectively, which are the minimum and maximum factor 1 scores shown in Figure 17.5. If we look at the multivariate observations for these two cases, that is, the response values in rows 4 and 10, respectively, we have in row vector form

$$\mathbf{X}_4 = (2 \;\; 2 \;\; 2 \;\; 1 \;\; 3) \quad \text{and} \quad \mathbf{X}_{10} = (2 \;\; 4 \;\; 4 \;\; 5 \;\; 5),$$

indicating some differences in their survey responses, especially for customer service satisfaction, X_4 (1 and 5, very dissatisfied and very satisfied customers, respectively!). We will see later how the factor scores have been computed.

Correlation Matrix

		Price satisfaction	Product range satisfaction	Packaging satisfaction	Customer service satisfaction	Product quality satisfaction
Correlation	Price satisfaction	1.000	.021	.020	-.014	-.113
	Product range satisfaction	.021	1.000	.082	.596	.537
	Packaging satisfaction	.020	.082	1.000	.206	.198
	Customer service satisfaction	-.014	.596	.206	1.000	.431
	Product quality satisfaction	-.113	.537	.198	.431	1.000
Sig. (1-tailed)	Price satisfaction		.398	.404	.433	.084
	Product range satisfaction	.398		.160	.000	.000
	Packaging satisfaction	.404	.160		.006	.008
	Customer service satisfaction	.433	.000	.006		.000
	Product quality satisfaction	.084	.000	.008	.000	

Figure 17.6 Correlation matrix for the input variables of a factor analysis.

We next consider the correlation matrix for these five observed variables, shown in Figure 17.6. We observe some sample correlation coefficients which are highly significant (those with p-values less than 0.01). Recall (Section 11.4.4) that the test of H_0: $\rho = 0$ versus H_1: $\rho \neq 0$ uses the test statistic

$$\frac{r\sqrt{n-2}}{\sqrt{1-r^2}} \sim t_{n-2}.$$

Note that SPSS has taken the liberty of conducting one-tailed tests, that is, if the sample correlation r_{ij}, for $i = 1, 2,\ldots, 5$, $j = 1, 2,\ldots, 5$ and $i \neq j$, is positive then H_1: $\rho_{ij} > 0$, and if it is negative then H_1: $\rho_{ij} < 0$. The sample correlation coefficients are reported in the top half of the correlation matrix, with the p-values for all the pairwise correlation tests in the bottom half. There are significant correlations between the following pairs of variables:

- X_1 and X_5 (at the 10% significance level, since the p-value = 0.084)
- X_2 and X_4 (at the 0.1% significance level, since the p-value < 0.001)
- X_2 and X_5 (at the 0.1% significance level, since the p-value < 0.001)
- X_3 and X_4 (at the 1% significance level, since the p-value = 0.006)
- X_3 and X_5 (at the 1% significance level, since the p-value = 0.008)
- X_4 and X_5 (at the 0.1% significance level, since the p-value < 0.001).

Therefore, it seems some of the variables are correlated, suggesting that factor analysis may be appropriate. However, this should be confirmed using the Kaiser–Meyer–Olkin (KMO) statistic and/or Bartlett's test of sphericity. The KMO and Bartlett's test table in Figure 17.7 provide two 'appropriateness tests' to judge whether factor analysis is worthwhile to perform on the observed variables.

KMO and Bartlett's Test

Kaiser-Meyer-Olkin Measure of Sampling Adequacy.		.641
Bartlett's Test of Sphericity	Approx. Chi-Square	132.152
	df	10
	Sig.	<.001

Figure 17.7 Kaiser-Meyer-Olkin statistic and Bartlett's test of sphericity results.

Omitting technical details of computation, a Kaiser–Meyer–Olkin (KMO) measure of sampling adequacy of at least 0.5 is desirable (the larger the better, up to 1.0). Bartlett's test of sphericity tests (for $k = 5$)

$$H_0: \begin{pmatrix} \rho_{11} & \rho_{12} & \rho_{13} & \rho_{14} & \rho_{15} \\ \rho_{21} & \rho_{22} & \rho_{23} & \rho_{24} & \rho_{25} \\ \rho_{31} & \rho_{32} & \rho_{33} & \rho_{34} & \rho_{35} \\ \rho_{41} & \rho_{42} & \rho_{43} & \rho_{44} & \rho_{45} \\ \rho_{51} & \rho_{52} & \rho_{53} & \rho_{54} & \rho_{55} \end{pmatrix} = \begin{pmatrix} 1 & 0 & 0 & 0 & 0 \\ 0 & 1 & 0 & 0 & 0 \\ 0 & 0 & 1 & 0 & 0 \\ 0 & 0 & 0 & 1 & 0 \\ 0 & 0 & 0 & 0 & 1 \end{pmatrix}$$

that is, that the true correlation matrix for the population is the 'identity matrix' with 0s off the leading diagonal (and 1s along the leading diagonal), which would correspond to uncorrelated observed variables in the population, against H_1 that the true correlation matrix is *not* the identity matrix, meaning that at least *some* of the observed variables are truly correlated (whether positively or negatively). Again omitting technical details of computation, Bartlett's test is based on a test statistic which is approximately chi-squared distributed (hence its *p*-value is derived from this distribution). Here, we have a test statistic value of 132.152 on 10 degrees of freedom. The *p*-value is less than 0.001, that is, it is a *highly significant* test statistic value, hence we reject the null hypothesis that in the population the correlation matrix is an identity matrix. Therefore, we proceed with factor analysis as we have *(very!) strong evidence* that there are some correlated variables among $X_1, X_2, \ldots, X_5$.

Communalities

	Initial	Extraction
Price satisfaction	1.000	.925
Product range satisfaction	1.000	.705
Packaging satisfaction	1.000	.196
Customer service satisfaction	1.000	.672
Product quality satisfaction	1.000	.643

Extraction Method: Principal Component Analysis.

Figure 17.8 Communalities for a factor analysis.

Next, we look at the *communalities table*, shown in Figure 17.8. After standardising the variables, each X_j' then has a variance of 1.0. Recall that the *communalities* represent the proportion of variance explained by the (to be determined) common factors, that is, the amount of variance a variable shares with all the other variables being considered. We see that, with the exception of packaging satisfaction, all the variables have 'high' communalities (above 0.6, say).

Total Variance Explained

Component	Initial Eigenvalues			Extraction Sums of Squared Loadings			Rotation Sums of Squared Loadings		
	Total	% of Variance	Cumulative %	Total	% of Variance	Cumulative %	Total	% of Variance	Cumulative %
1	2.117	42.340	42.340	2.117	42.340	42.340	2.117	42.339	42.339
2	1.024	20.471	62.810	1.024	20.471	62.810	1.024	20.471	62.810
3	.947	18.931	81.742						
4	.559	11.182	92.924						
5	.354	7.076	100.000						

Extraction Method: Principal Component Analysis.

Figure 17.9 Breakdown of the variance explained by each component.

We now see why SPSS extracted two factors by examining Figure 17.9. With k variables, we can identify a maximum of k principal components (here $k = 5$), referred to as 'components' in Figure 17.9. However, not all components are necessarily useful. To determine the number of factors (components) we can look at a variety of methods – hopefully we decide on the same number of factors using each approach.

First, we consider the *eigenvalues* for each factor – these are, in descending order, 2.117, 1.024, 0.947, 0.559 and 0.354. Given that the standardised variables have a variance of 1.0, only factors with eigenvalues greater than 1 should be used (such factors are deemed superior to an original (standardised) variable). In passing, recall that in the `Extraction...` dialog box when setting up the factor analysis in SPSS we instructed it to extract factors 'based on eigenvalues greater than 1' (default), as shown in Figure 17.10. Therefore, here we can extract two common factors.

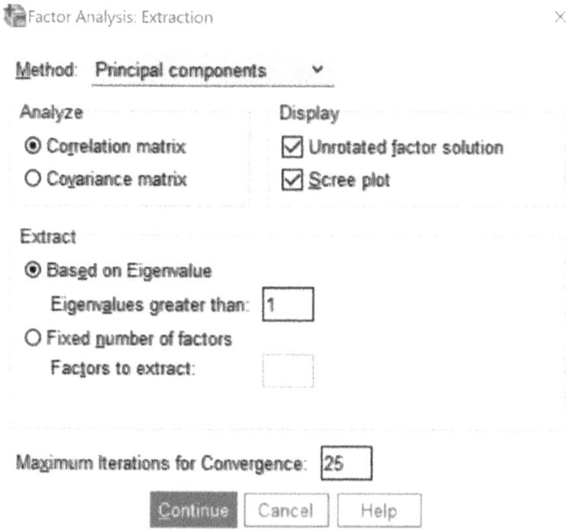

Factor Analysis: Extraction

Method: Principal components

Analyze
- ◉ Correlation matrix
- ○ Covariance matrix

Display
- ☑ Unrotated factor solution
- ☑ Scree plot

Extract
- ◉ Based on Eigenvalue
  - Eigenvalues greater than: 1
- ○ Fixed number of factors
  - Factors to extract:

Maximum Iterations for Convergence: 25

Continue | Cancel | Help

Figure 17.10 Dialog box specifying how factors should be extracted.

Second, we seek common factors which cumulatively account for a large percentage of the total variance (typically at least 60%). We see the first factor accounts for 42.340%, while the second factor accounts for 20.471%, so the first two factors combined account for a cumulative percentage of:

$$42.340\% + 20.471\% = 62.810\%$$

of the total variance. Subsequent factors (each with eigenvalues less than 1) add little to this cumulative percentage so, again, two factors seem appropriate. So, we have achieved data reduction from $k = 5$ observed variables to $m = 2$ common factors (still to be named). The price we pay is a loss of information, the

$$100\% - 62.810\% = 37.190\%$$

variance discarded. Does the benefit justify the cost? Well, James, it depends! Cost–benefit analyses are always subjective, but if we can give meaningful names to the two factors, then arguably 'yes'!

We now examine the scree plot in Figure 17.11. Meant to resemble a cliff face ('scree' is the name given to the rocks which gather at the base of a cliff), a scree plot is a plot of the eigenvalues against the number of factors in the order of extraction. This is just a visualisation of the relative magnitudes of the eigenvalues for each factor (component). We continue to treat factors as 'good' if their eigenvalues exceed 1, and 'bad' otherwise. Any sharp drop visible in a scree plot can be used to indicate the 'right' number of factors so, again, two factors seem reasonable, provided they are meaningful in practice. However, it is a fair critique that the second and third extracted factors have very similar eigenvalues, albeit either side of 1 (1.024 and 0.947), so only the first of these two is retained but has similar variation to the other. In this case, the scree is harder to discern visually.

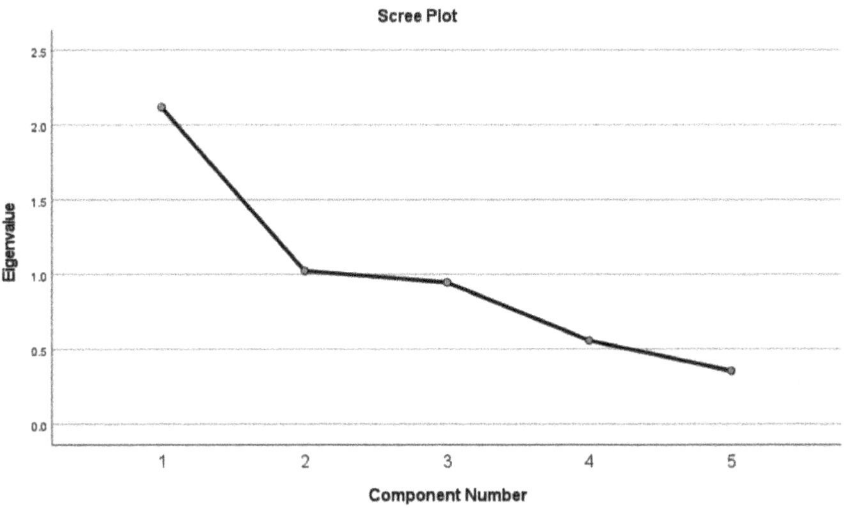

Figure 17.11 Scree plot in a factor analysis.

Component Matrix[a]

	Component	
	1	2
Price satisfaction	-.067	.960
Product range satisfaction	.839	.041
Packaging satisfaction	.351	.271
Customer service satisfaction	.817	.067
Product quality satisfaction	.787	-.152

Extraction Method: Principal Component Analysis.
a. 2 components extracted.

Figure 17.12 Component matrix of factor loadings (correlations) between input variables and extracted factors.

We now turn to the *component matrix* in Figure 17.12. The component matrix reports the factor loadings (which are simple correlations) between each variable and each factor (component). Although it *seems* that X_2, X_4 and X_5 load highly on factor 1 (with correlations of 0.839, 0.817 and 0.787, respectively), and X_1 loads highly on factor 2 (with a correlation of 0.960), we can 'rotate' this matrix to ease the interpretability.

Factor rotation

For each extracted factor, an analyst needs to be able to attach a meaningful name so it can be of practical use. In order to understand which of the original variables correlate most with each extracted factor, we can examine the *component matrix*. However, sometimes observed variables may not have sufficiently strong correlations with the factors, making it difficult to name them. Often, especially when *k* is very large, the initial factors may suffer from being difficult to interpret.

A clever aspect of factor analysis stems from noting that once we have chosen the number of factors, *m*, the factor definitions are not unique. Without losing any explanatory power, we can use the process of **factor rotation** such that we end up in the position of having each observed variable either correlate strongly (indicating relevance in naming the factor) or weakly (indicating irrelevance, so we can ignore) with each of the extracted factors.

There are different approaches to rotation, such as:

- *Varimax*, which seeks to minimise how many variables correlate highly with each factor (the most common)
- *Quartimax*, which seeks to minimise how many factors are required to explain a variable
- *Equamax*, which is a combination of varimax and quartimax.

We will use the varimax procedure, which uses as its objective function the variance of the squared loadings on the rotated factors. The varimax algorithm rotates the axes until maximisation of the objective function is achieved. Omitting technical details, the result is strong correlations (whether positive or negative) between the factors and *some* of the variables, with very weak correlations with the other variables, meaning there is little ambiguity about how to name the factors. Trust me, this is great!

Rotated Component Matrix[a]

	Component	
	1	2
Price satisfaction	-.071	.959
Product range satisfaction	.838	.045
Packaging satisfaction	.349	.272
Customer service satisfaction	.816	.071
Product quality satisfaction	.788	-.149

Extraction Method: Principal Component Analysis.
Rotation Method: Varimax with Kaiser Normalization.

a. Rotation converged in 3 iterations.

Figure 17.13 Rotated component matrix of factor loadings (correlations) between input variables and extracted factors.

We now check the *rotated component matrix* in Figure 17.13. Using the varimax rotation procedure to obtain the simplest structure of the factor matrix, we obtain factor loadings which more clearly load highly on *one, and only one,* common factor. Our previous suspicions that X_2, X_4 and X_5 load highly on factor 1 and that X_1 loads highly on factor 2 are confirmed by this rotated factor matrix (correlations of 0.838, 0.816 and 0.788 for factor 1, and 0.959 for factor 2). Note that although here the original component matrix was quite clear, in other situations there can be *much less ambiguity* about which variables load highly on a factor using the rotated component matrix.

We can also look at the factor loading plot in Figure 17.14. This is a plot of the input variables using the factor loadings (based on the rotated component matrix) as *coordinates*. Since we only have two factors, we can plot the factor loadings in two-dimensional space, that is, with factor 1 loadings on the *x*-axis and factor 2 loadings on the *y*-axis. Remember the factor loadings are just correlation coefficients, so the axes of the factor loading plot span from –1 to +1. This plot allows us to easily visualise which variables load highly onto which factors.

Again, X_2 (product range satisfaction), X_4 (customer service satisfaction) and X_5 (product quality satisfaction) load highly on factor 1 (at the right end of the horizontal axis), and X_1 (price

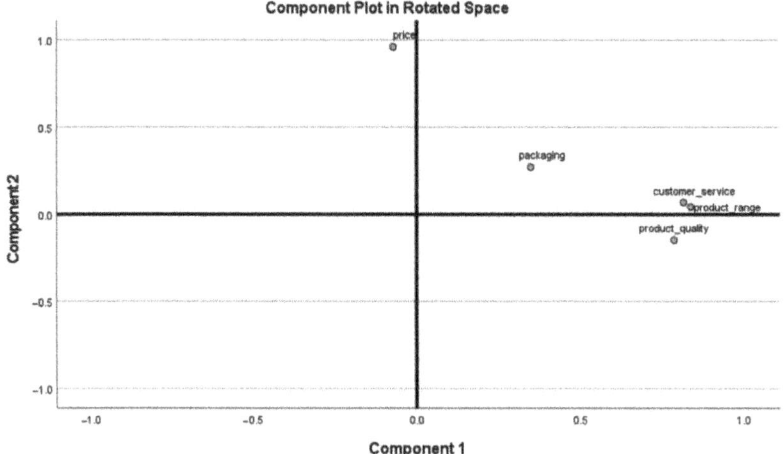

Figure 17.14 Factor loading plot based on the rotated component matrix.

satisfaction) loads highly on factor 2 (at the top of the vertical axis). Note that X_3 (packaging satisfaction) does not load highly on either factor. We can now interpret the two common factors, having determined which of the input variables are highly correlated with which factor.

It is clear that X_2 and X_5 are both product-related (range and quality), which when combined with X_4 (customer service) may be thought of as being the *customer experience* factor, based on their experience with the product and customer service. Note that this is just a suggestion – any alternative name which suitably summarises and captures the joint essence of X_2, X_4 and X_5 would suffice. Since only X_1 correlates with factor 2, then factor 2 is the *price* factor, with little room for debate over the name here!

We now turn to the *component score coefficient matrix*, shown in Figure 17.15. It is now possible to calculate factor scores for each customer satisfaction survey respondent, that is, the 'customer experience' score and the 'price' score. These are returned in SPSS as new columns in the original data matrix (as seen in Figure 17.5) and are calculated using

$$F_i = \beta_{1i}X'_1 + \beta_{2i}X'_2 + \cdots + \beta_{5i}X'_5$$

for $i = 1, 2$, since we have two factors. Specifically,

$$\text{Customer experience} = F_1 = -0.036X'_1 + 0.396X'_2 + 0.165X'_3 + 0.386X'_4 + 0.372X'_5$$

and

$$\text{Price} = F_2 = 0.937X'_1 + 0.042X'_2 + 0.265X'_3 + 0.067X'_4 + 0.147X'_5.$$

Remember that the X'_j are standardised variables (not the original values in our data matrix), such that

$$X'_j = \frac{X_j - \bar{X}_j}{S_j}.$$

Component Score Coefficient Matrix

	Component	
	1	2
Price satisfaction	-.036	.937
Product range satisfaction	.396	.042
Packaging satisfaction	.165	.265
Customer service satisfaction	.386	.067
Product quality satisfaction	.372	-.147

Extraction Method: Principal Component Analysis.
Rotation Method: Varimax with Kaiser Normalization.
Component Scores.

Figure 17.15 Component score coefficient matrix for a factor analysis.

Descriptive Statistics

	N	Minimum	Maximum	Mean	Std. Deviation
Price satisfaction	150	1	3	1.91	.822
Product range satisfaction	150	1	5	3.25	1.321
Packaging satisfaction	150	1	5	3.10	1.384
Customer service satisfaction	150	1	5	3.27	1.339
Product quality satisfaction	150	1	5	3.19	1.402
Valid N (listwise)	150				

Figure 17.16 Descriptive statistics of the input variables.

In passing, we note the sample means and sample standard deviations of $X_1, X_2, \ldots, X_5$ shown in Figure 17.16. So, we have that the standardised variables are computed as

$$X_1' = \frac{X_1 - 1.91}{0.822}, \quad X_2' = \frac{X_2 - 3.25}{1.321}, \quad X_3' = \frac{X_3 - 3.10}{1.384}, \quad X_4' = \frac{X_4 - 3.27}{1.339}, \quad X_5' = \frac{X_5 - 3.19}{1.402}.$$

Using the previous examples of cases 4 and 10, given by

$$\mathbf{X}_4 = (2 \quad 2 \quad 2 \quad 1 \quad 3) \quad \text{and} \quad \mathbf{X}_{10} = (2 \quad 4 \quad 4 \quad 5 \quad 5),$$

we can calculate the corresponding standardised values to be

$$
\mathbf{X}_4' = \begin{pmatrix} \dfrac{2-1.91}{0.822} \\ \dfrac{2-3.25}{1.321} \\ \dfrac{2-3.10}{1.384} \\ \dfrac{1-3.27}{1.339} \\ \dfrac{3-3.19}{1.402} \end{pmatrix} = \begin{pmatrix} 0.11353 \\ -0.94398 \\ -0.79466 \\ -1.69221 \\ -0.13317 \end{pmatrix} \quad \text{and} \quad \mathbf{X}_{10}' = \begin{pmatrix} \dfrac{2-1.91}{0.822} \\ \dfrac{4-3.25}{1.321} \\ \dfrac{4-3.10}{1.384} \\ \dfrac{5-3.27}{1.339} \\ \dfrac{5-3.19}{1.402} \end{pmatrix} = \begin{pmatrix} 0.11353 \\ 0.57043 \\ 0.65018 \\ 1.29404 \\ 1.29361 \end{pmatrix}.
$$

Note that if you try to replicate these calculations manually, any slight differences will be due to rounding of the reported sample means and sample standard deviations to two decimal places in Figure 17.16.

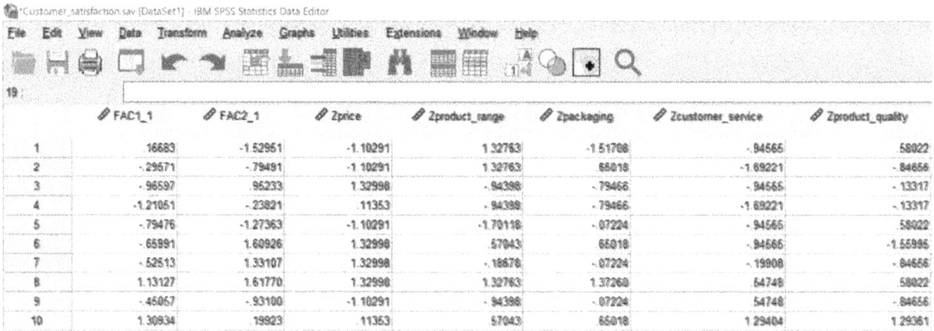

*Customer_satisfaction.sav [DataSet1] - IBM SPSS Statistics Data Editor

File Edit View Data Transform Analyze Graphs Utilities Extensions Window Help

	FAC1_1	FAC2_1	Zprice	Zproduct_range	Zpackaging	Zcustomer_service	Zproduct_quality
1	.16683	-1.52951	-1.10291	1.32763	-1.51708	-.94565	.58022
2	-.29571	-.79491	-1.10291	1.32763	.65018	-1.69221	-.84656
3	-.96597	.95233	1.32998	-.94398	-.79466	-.94565	-.13317
4	-1.21051	-.23821	.11353	-.94398	-.79466	-1.69221	-.13317
5	-.79476	-1.27363	-1.10291	-1.70118	-.07224	-.94565	.58022
6	-.65991	1.60926	1.32998	.57043	.65018	-.94565	-1.55995
7	-.52513	1.33107	1.32998	-.18678	-.07224	-.19908	-.84656
8	1.13127	1.61770	1.32998	1.32763	1.37260	.54748	.58022
9	-.45067	-.93100	-1.10291	-.94398	-.07224	.54748	-.84656
10	1.30934	.19923	.11353	.57043	.65018	1.29404	1.29361

Figure 17.17 Standardised values, X'_j, used to compute the factor scores F_1 and F_2.

We can now see how the factor scores are determined by examining Figure 17.17, which shows the standardised X_j values (i.e. X_j'), denoted by `Zprice` etc. It is not necessary to show these explicitly; SPSS can simply return the factor scores (the standardised values are only shown here for illustrative purposes). So, for example, the factor 1 and factor 2 scores for respondent (row) 4 are

$$
\begin{aligned}
F_{1,4} &= -0.036\times 0.11353 + 0.396\times(-0.94398) + 0.165\times(-0.79466) + 0.386\times(-1.69221) + 0.372\times(-0.13317) \\
&= -1.21051, \\
F_{2,4} &= 0.937\times 0.11353 + 0.042\times(-0.94398) + 0.265\times(-0.79466) + 0.067\times(-1.69221) - 0.147\times(-0.13317) \\
&= -0.23821,
\end{aligned}
$$

while the factor 1 and factor 2 scores for respondent (row) 10 are

$$
\begin{aligned}
F_{1,10} &= -0.036\times 0.11353 + 0.396\times 0.57043 + 0.165\times 0.65018 + 0.386\times 1.29404 + 0.372\times 1.29361 \\
&= 1.30934, \\
F_{2,10} &= 0.937\times 0.11353 + 0.042\times 0.57043 + 0.265\times 0.65018 + 0.067\times 1.29404 - 0.147\times 1.29361 \\
&= 0.19923.
\end{aligned}
$$

Note that if you try to replicate these calculations manually, any slight differences will be due to rounding of the values reported in the *component score coefficient matrix* to three decimal places in Figure 17.15.

The factor scores could be used to construct satisfaction-based indices. These $m = 2$ factor scores can now be used instead of the original $k = 5$ variables in subsequent multivariate analyses (such as a multiple linear regression or a discriminant analysis). By construction, since we used the varimax rotation procedure, these factor scores are *uncorrelated* and hence there is absolutely no chance of multicollinearity if these served as independent variables! Note that we can check that these are uncorrelated by producing a correlation matrix of the factor scores, shown in Figure 17.18.

Correlations

		REGR factor score 1 for analysis 1	REGR factor score 2 for analysis 1
REGR factor score 1 for analysis 1	Pearson Correlation	1	.000
	Sig. (2-tailed)		1.000
	N	150	150
REGR factor score 2 for analysis 1	Pearson Correlation	.000	1
	Sig. (2-tailed)	1.000	
	N	150	150

Figure 17.18 Correlation matrix of factor scores from a factor analysis.

Alternatively, if we would rather not use the factor scores (as they are a synthetic creation and not directly observable, with possible issues around the practical interpretation of extracted factors) we could instead use so-called surrogate variables. A surrogate variable is one of the original observed variables which is used as a *proxy* for a common factor. We choose the original variable which loads most highly with an extracted factor (remember a factor loading is just a correlation, so we seek the original variable which is most highly correlated with a factor). Looking at the rotated component matrix (Figure 17.13), we see that X_2 (product range satisfaction) would be the surrogate variable for common factor 1 (a factor loading of 0.838), and X_1 (price satisfaction) would be the surrogate variable for common factor 2 (a factor loading of 0.959).

After all this analysis, how 'good' has the factor analysis been? For each multivariate technique considered previously we had a simple metric to judge overall model performance. For example, for analysis of variance this was η^2 (Chapter 12), for linear regression it was R^2 (Chapters 13 and 14), and for discriminant analysis it was overall predictive accuracy, OPA (Chapter 16). For factor analysis, model fit can be assessed by seeing how well the extracted factors can 'reproduce' the original correlations, as per the correlation matrix. Since each observed variable is assumed to have some random variation specific to X_j, we would not expect perfect reproduction of the original correlation matrix, but if the communalities are large enough (recall that the communalities represent the variation explained by the common factors) then the reproduced correlations should be 'close' to the original correlations. If the factor model reflects the original data structure well, then the reconstructed correlation matrix from the factors should approximate well the original correlation matrix.

For our customer satisfaction survey dataset, the *reproduced correlation matrix* is shown in Figure 17.19. The top half of this matrix table shows the values of the reproduced correlations. Note that on the leading diagonal these are simply the communalities (seen previously in Figure 17.8): 0.925, 0.705, 0.196, 0.672 and 0.643. The bottom half shows the residuals. These represent the *differences* between the original correlations (the r_{ij}) and the reproduced correlations (the $\tilde{r}_{ij}$) such that (due to symmetry of the correlation matrix)

Reproduced Correlations

		Price satisfaction	Product range satisfaction	Packaging satisfaction	Customer service satisfaction	Product quality satisfaction
Reproduced Correlation	Price satisfaction	.925[a]	-.017	.236	.010	-.199
	Product range satisfaction	-.017	.705[a]	.305	.688	.654
	Packaging satisfaction	.236	.305	.196[a]	.304	.235
	Customer service satisfaction	.010	.688	.304	.672[a]	.632
	Product quality satisfaction	-.199	.654	.235	.632	.643[a]
Residual[b]	Price satisfaction		.038	-.216	-.023	.086
	Product range satisfaction	.038		-.223	-.092	-.117
	Packaging satisfaction	-.216	-.223		-.098	-.037
	Customer service satisfaction	-.023	-.092	-.098		-.202
	Product quality satisfaction	.086	-.117	-.037	-.202	

Extraction Method: Principal Component Analysis.

a. Reproduced communalities.

b. Residuals are computed between observed and reproduced correlations. There are 7 (70.0%) non-redundant residuals with absolute values greater than 0.05.

Figure 17.19 Reproduced correlation matrix for a factor analysis.

$$\text{residual}_{ij} = r_{ij} - \tilde{r}_{ij} = r_{ji} - \tilde{r}_{ji} = \text{residual}_{ji}.$$

For example, the original correlation between price satisfaction and product range satisfaction was $r_{12} = r_{21} = 0.021$ with a reproduced correlation of $\tilde{r}_{12} = \tilde{r}_{21} = -0.017$. Hence the residual is

$$\text{residual}_{12} = r_{12} - \tilde{r}_{12} = r_{21} - \tilde{r}_{21} = 0.021 - (-0.017) = 0.038.$$

So, for what values would we be willing to classify a residual as 'good' versus 'bad'? To answer this, let's first consider the range of possible residual values. Since correlation coefficients always take values in [−1, 1], the minimum possible value of a residual is when

$$\text{residual}_{ij} = r_{ij} - \tilde{r}_{ij} = -1 - (+1) = -2$$

and the maximum possible value of a residual is when:

$$\text{residual}_{ij} = r_{ij} - \tilde{r}_{ij} = 1 - (-1) = 2.$$

A 'perfect' residual would be when

$$\text{residual}_{ij} = r_{ij} - \tilde{r}_{ij} = 0 \quad \Leftrightarrow \quad r_{ij} = \tilde{r}_{ij}.$$

SPSS adjudicates that a 'good' residual is one with an *absolute* value less than or equal to 0.05, and a 'bad' residual is one with an *absolute* value greater than 0.05, which we can visualise as shown in Figure 17.20. This seems a very narrow range of tolerance for 'good' residuals, so we may wish to be a bit more flexible and accommodating in practice.

As seen in the footnote to the reproduced correlations table in Figure 17.19, 7 out of 10 (70%) of the residuals exceed SPSS's (absolute value) threshold of 0.05. We note these are:

$$\text{residual}_{13} = -0.216,\ \text{residual}_{15} = 0.086,\ \text{residual}_{23} = -0.223,\ \text{residual}_{24} = -0.092,$$

$$\text{residual}_{25} = -0.117,\ \text{residual}_{34} = -0.098,\ \text{residual}_{45} = -0.202.$$

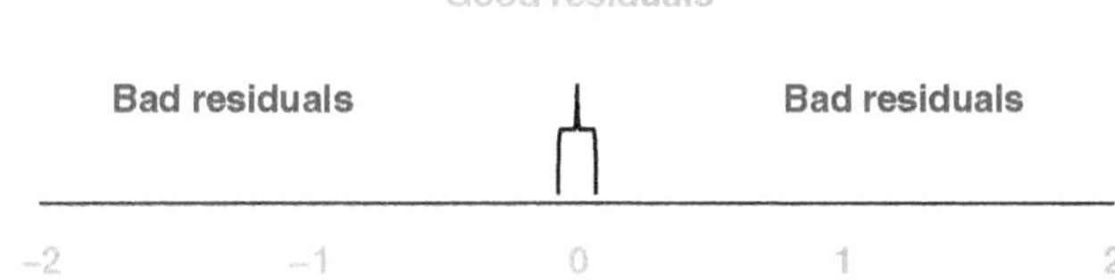

Figure 17.20 Classification of residuals in a factor analysis as 'good' and 'bad'.

While classifying any (absolute) residual above 0.05 as bad/non-redundant is a simple classification rule, such simplicity suffers from the 'edge-of-the-cliff' effect (a lot of physical geography with all this talk of screes and cliffs!). Residuals of 0.051 and 1.999, say, would both be classified as 'bad', but they differ significantly in terms of magnitude. As such, it is advisable to take a more holistic view of the residuals, such as by plotting them, as shown in Figure 17.21. Subjectively, the residuals do not seem 'too' large (none being far from zero) such that overall the model fit is pleasing and we should feel happy to use the results of this factor analysis. Phew!

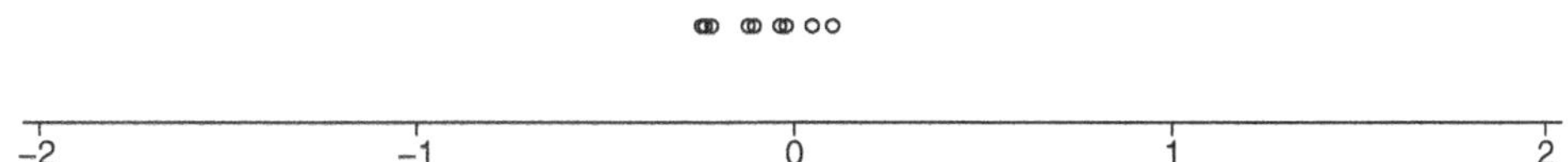

Figure 17.21 Plot of the residuals from a factor analysis.

We now consider one more example of factor analysis, applied to the chapter's opening motivational case.

17.4 FACTOR ANALYSIS: FURTHER EXAMPLE

Recall from the beginning of this chapter that Righthome is a new estate agency chain seeking to recruit sales negotiators for its new head office. After advertising the positions, it has received a total of 48 applications, and only those with strong, assertive personalities will be deemed worthwhile to interview. Each applicant has completed an online questionnaire where they had to score themselves, from 0 (not at all) to 10 (completely), on the extent to which they consider themselves to possess the following characteristics:

- Ambition, X_1
- Drive, X_2
- Experience, X_3
- Grasp, X_4
- Honesty, X_5
- Likeability, X_6
- Lucidity, X_7
- Potential, X_8
- Salesmanship, X_9
- Self-confidence, X_{10}
- Suitability, X_{11}.

Our goal is to see whether these $k = 11$ observed variables can be reduced to a smaller number of useful factors. In particular, Righthome would benefit from a factor reflecting assertiveness, given the nature of the role of a sales negotiator.

Let's begin by eyeballing the data (the first 10 applicants) as shown in Figure 17.22. We see variation in the questionnaire scores, with quite a few 10s evident – clearly a lot of confident applicants!

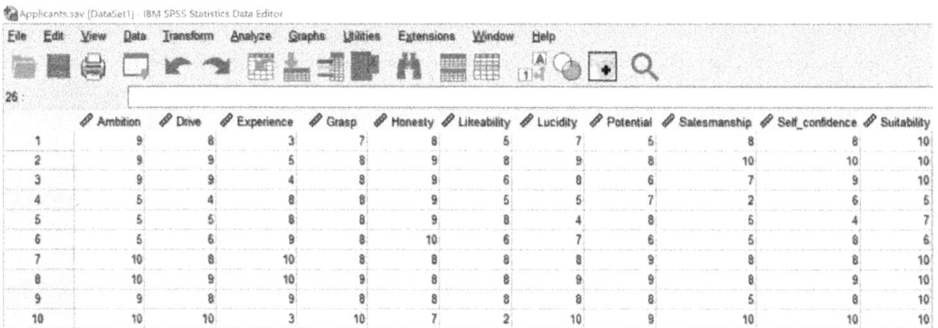

	Ambition	Drive	Experience	Grasp	Honesty	Likeability	Lucidity	Potential	Salesmanship	Self_confidence	Suitability
1	9	8	3	7	8	5	7	5	8	8	10
2	9	9	5	8	9	8	9	8	10	10	10
3	9	9	4	8	9	6	8	6	7	9	10
4	5	4	8	8	9	5	5	7	2	6	5
5	5	5	8	8	9	8	4	8	5	4	7
6	5	6	9	8	10	6	7	6	5	8	6
7	10	8	10	8	8	8	8	9	8	8	10
8	10	9	10	9	8	8	9	9	8	9	10
9	9	8	9	8	8	8	8	8	5	8	10
10	10	10	3	10	7	2	10	9	10	10	10

Figure 17.22 Online questionnaire responses of the first 10 applicants.

	esty	Likeability	Lucidity	Potential	Salesmanship	Self_confidence	Suitability	FAC1_1	FAC2_1	FAC3_1
1	8	5	7	5	8	8	10	.80176	.15862	-.60802
2	9	8	9	8	10	10	10	1.11464	.44504	.17081
3	9	6	8	6	7	9	10	.87771	.26562	-.15452
4	9	5	5	7	2	6	5	-.50858	.55909	.26288
5	9	8	4	8	5	4	7	-.74991	1.21163	.84888
6	10	6	7	6	5	8	6	-.06508	.62246	.40482
7	8	8	8	9	8	8	10	.60228	1.49809	.08264
8	8	8	9	9	8	9	10	.86023	1.42038	.04673
9	8	8	8	8	5	8	10	.35037	1.34149	.21105
10	7	2	10	9	10	10	10	1.92940	.01349	-1.42516

Figure 17.23 Updated Data View showing three sets of factor scores.

The Data View in Figure 17.23 shows what SPSS has calculated. Factor scores of three factors can be seen in the columns adjacent to the input variables $X_1, X_2, \ldots, X_{11}$. This tells us that SPSS has managed to reduce the $k = 11$ variables to $m = 3$ underlying factors. For now, these are technically named `FAC1_1`, `FAC2_1` and `FAC3_1`. We will aim to name these later.

We next consider the correlation matrix for these eleven variables, shown in Figure 17.24. Fortunately, and as we might have expected, we see a large number of strong, highly significant correlations. Interestingly, the only negative correlation is that between experience and honesty – so it seems that those who have been in the trade for longer are less honest! (To paraphrase Hollywood, all data are fictitious, and any inferences resembling real-life stereotypes of the estate agency profession are purely coincidental!)

We confirm the appropriateness of factor analysis using the KMO statistic and/or Bartlett's test of sphericity, by checking Figure 17.25. The KMO measure of sampling adequacy is 0.794 (well in excess of our minimum desirable value of 0.5), and Bartlett's test of sphericity tests (for $k = 11$)

$$H_0 : \mathbf{P}_{11} = \mathbf{I}_{11},$$

Correlation Matrix

		Ambition	Drive	Experience	Grasp	Honesty	Likeability	Lucidity	Potential	Salesmanship	Self-confidence	Suitability
Correlation	Ambition	1.000	.780	.195	.784	.215	.347	.758	.769	.860	.842	.435
	Drive	.780	1.000	.337	.714	.280	.393	.698	.788	.815	.704	.623
	Experience	.195	.337	1.000	.299	-.156	.141	.147	.348	.255	.015	.693
	Grasp	.784	.714	.299	1.000	.386	.503	.883	.876	.782	.721	.528
	Honesty	.215	.280	-.156	.386	1.000	.645	.356	.416	.240	.410	.003
	Likeability	.347	.393	.141	.503	.645	1.000	.483	.606	.362	.302	.327
	Lucidity	.758	.698	.147	.883	.356	.483	1.000	.777	.818	.808	.416
	Potential	.769	.788	.348	.876	.416	.606	.777	1.000	.754	.672	.574
	Salesmanship	.860	.815	.255	.782	.240	.362	.818	.754	1.000	.800	.558
	Self-confidence	.842	.704	.015	.721	.410	.302	.808	.672	.800	1.000	.250
	Suitability	.435	.623	.693	.528	.003	.327	.416	.574	.558	.250	1.000
Sig. (1-tailed)	Ambition		<.001	.092	<.001	.071	.008	<.001	<.001	<.001	<.001	.001
	Drive	.000		.010	.000	.027	.003	.000	.000	.000	.000	.000
	Experience	.092	.010		.019	.145	.170	.159	.008	.040	.459	.000
	Grasp	.000	.000	.019		.003	.000	.000	.000	.000	.000	.000
	Honesty	.071	.027	.145	.003		.000	.007	.002	.050	.002	.493
	Likeability	.008	.003	.170	.000	.000		.000	.000	.006	.018	.012
	Lucidity	.000	.000	.159	.000	.007	.000		.000	.000	.000	.002
	Potential	.000	.000	.008	.000	.002	.000	.000		.000	.000	.000
	Salesmanship	.000	.000	.040	.000	.050	.006	.000	.000		.000	.000
	Self-confidence	.000	.000	.459	.000	.002	.018	.000	.000	.000		.043
	Suitability	.001	.000	.000	.000	.493	.012	.002	.000	.000	.043	

Figure 17.24 Correlation matrix for the input variables of a factor analysis.

where $\mathbf{P}_{11}$ is the population correlation matrix for 11 variables, and $\mathbf{I}_{11}$ is the 11 × 11 identity matrix. Here we have a test statistic value of 510.313, which is from an approximate χ^2 distribution with 55 degrees of freedom. The p-value is less than 0.001, that is, it is a *highly significant* test statistic value, hence we reject the null hypothesis that in the population the correlation matrix is an identity matrix. Therefore, we proceed with factor analysis as we have *(very!) strong evidence* that there are some correlated variables among $X_1, X_2, \ldots, X_{11}$.

KMO and Bartlett's Test

Kaiser-Meyer-Olkin Measure of Sampling Adequacy.		.794
Bartlett's Test of Sphericity	Approx. Chi-Square	510.313
	df	55
	Sig.	<.001

Figure 17.25 Kaiser-Meyer-Olkin statistic and Bartlett's test of sphericity results.

Next, we look at the communalities table in Figure 17.26. After standardising the variables, each X_j' has a variance of 1.0. Recall that the *communalities* represent the proportion of variance explained by the (to be determined) common factors, that is, the amount of variance a variable shares with all the other variables being considered. We see that all the variables have 'high' communalities (all well above 0.75, which is excellent).

We now see why SPSS extracted three factors, by examining Figure 17.27. Using the principal components extraction method, with $k = 11$ variables we can identify 11 components. Given that the standardised variables have a variance of 1.0, only factors with eigenvalues greater than 1 should be used. Therefore, here we can extract (the first) three common factors. We note that combined these account for

$$59.539\% + 15.150\% + 10.829\% = 85.518\%$$

Communalities

	Initial	Extraction
Ambition	1.000	.878
Drive	1.000	.793
Experience	1.000	.849
Grasp	1.000	.845
Honesty	1.000	.851
Likeability	1.000	.863
Lucidity	1.000	.837
Potential	1.000	.866
Salesmanship	1.000	.882
Self-confidence	1.000	.888
Suitability	1.000	.856

Extraction Method: Principal Component Analysis.

Figure 17.26 Communalities for a factor analysis.

of the total variance. Subsequent factors (each with eigenvalues less than 1) add little to this cumulative percentage so, again, three factors seem appropriate. So, we have achieved data reduction from $k = 11$ observed variables to $m = 3$ common factors (still to be named). The price we pay is a loss of information, the:

$$100\% - 85.518\% = 14.482\%$$

variance discarded. Here the loss of information seems minimal for a significant amount of data reduction ($11 \rightarrow 3$).

Total Variance Explained

Component	Initial Eigenvalues			Extraction Sums of Squared Loadings			Rotation Sums of Squared Loadings		
	Total	% of Variance	Cumulative %	Total	% of Variance	Cumulative %	Total	% of Variance	Cumulative %
1	6.549	59.539	59.539	6.549	59.539	59.539	5.286	48.054	48.054
2	1.667	15.150	74.689	1.667	15.150	74.689	2.118	19.257	67.311
3	1.191	10.829	85.518	1.191	10.829	85.518	2.003	18.208	85.518
4	.384	3.488	89.006						
5	.331	3.010	92.016						
6	.255	2.315	94.331						
7	.221	2.010	96.341						
8	.159	1.442	97.783						
9	.116	1.059	98.842						
10	.086	.784	99.626						
11	.041	.374	100.000						

Extraction Method: Principal Component Analysis.

Figure 17.27 Breakdown of the variance explained by each component.

We now examine the scree plot in Figure 17.28. The scree plot flattens out from the fourth factor, suggesting three factors are reasonable, provided they are meaningful in practice.

Now look at the component matrix in Figure 17.29. Recall that the component matrix reports the factor loadings (which are simple correlations) between each variable and each factor. It appears that X_1, X_2, X_4, X_7, X_8, X_9 and X_{10} load highly on factor 1 (with correlations ranging from 0.828 to 0.920), while X_3, possibly X_5, and possibly X_{11} load highly on factor 2 (with (absolute) correlations ranging from 0.637 to 0.794), and X_6 seems to load highly on factor 3 (with a correlation of 0.667). However, particularly for factors 2 and 3 the high loadings are a bit ambiguous. So, let's 'rotate' this matrix to ease the interpretability, as shown in Figure 17.30.

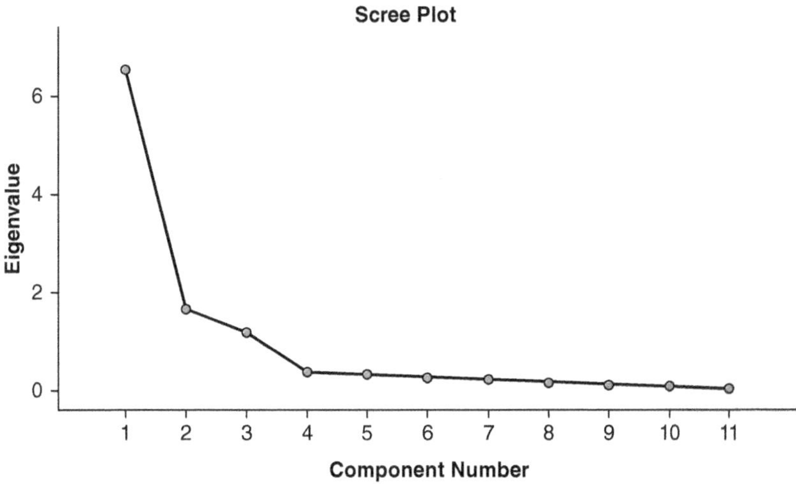

Figure 17.28 Scree plot in a factor analysis.

Using the varimax rotation procedure to obtain the simplest structure of the factor matrix, we obtain factor loadings which more clearly load highly on *one, and only one,* common factor. We can now clearly see that the variables with high loadings on each respective factor are:

- factor 1: X_1 (0.923), X_2 (0.790), X_4 (0.805), X_7 (0.861), X_8 (0.736), X_9 (0.901) and X_{10} (0.921)
- factor 2: X_3 (0.918) and X_{11} (0.850)
- factor 3: X_5 (0.876) and X_6 (0.874).

While our initial thoughts are unchanged for factor 1, note how X_5 was initially thought to 'belong' to factor 2, but after rotation it is clearly assigned to factor 3. Rotation has been a great help with factor interpretation!

Let's now look at the factor loading plot in Figure 17.31. Because we have extracted three factors, we can view the factor loadings reported in the rotated component matrix as coordinates in three-dimensional space. Hence when plotted we obtain a three-dimensional scatter plot, with the coordinates plotted along the *x*-axis, *y*-axis and *z*-axis. Admittedly, a two-dimensional view of a three-dimensional plot can be tricky to make sense of by eye – it depends how good your eyes are at seeing perspective!

Component Matrix[a]

	Component		
	1	2	3
Ambition	.881	-.017	-.318
Drive	.876	.137	-.084
Experience	.339	.794	.321
Grasp	.919	-.025	.001
Honesty	.426	-.650	.496
Likeability	.577	-.290	.667
Lucidity	.892	-.149	-.137
Potential	.920	.012	.140
Salesmanship	.904	.057	-.247
Self-confidence	.828	-.279	-.353
Suitability	.622	.637	.253

Extraction Method: Principal Component Analysis.
a. 3 components extracted.

Figure 17.29 Component matrix of factor loadings (correlations) between input variables and extracted factors.

The plot shows each variable with coordinates close to 0 for two axes (two low factor loadings), and close to 1 for one axis (one high factor loading). If you can make sense of the factor loading plot, great, if not then the list of variables highly loaded on each factor may be preferable to help name each factor. Note that for four or more factors we would not be able to produce a factor loading plot, since we can only plot in a maximum of three dimensions.

Using either the rotated component matrix (Figure 17.30) or the factor loading plot (Figure 17.31), we now attempt to name each factor. The factors are described, respectively, by:

- factor 1: ambition, drive, grasp, lucidity, potential, salesmanship and self-confidence
- factor 2: experience and suitability
- factor 3: honesty and likeability.

The choice of factor names is inevitably subjective, but let's go with factor 1 as *assertiveness*, factor 2 as *expertise* and factor 3 as *character*. Otherwise, we could elect to use surrogate variables (the observed variable most highly correlated with each factor), which would be 'ambition' for factor 1 (correlation of 0.923), 'experience' for factor 2 (correlation of 0.918), and 'honesty' for factor 3 (correlation of 0.876). However, as a personal preference (or personal bias!), I like the 'assertiveness', 'expertise' and 'character' nomenclature. Indeed, Righthome could make practical use of an 'assertiveness' factor, given the nature of the role of a sales negotiator. Note how the purpose of the analysis helps to guide this choice of factors versus surrogate variables.

We now turn to the component score coefficient matrix in Figure 17.32. Using standardised variable notation, we see that the three respective factor scores may be calculated as follows:

$$\begin{aligned}\text{Assertiveness} = F_1 = {} & 0.245X_1' + 0.142X_2' - 0.134X_3' + 0.124X_4' - 0.099X_5' - 0.170X_6' \\ & + 0.183X_7' + 0.066X_8' + 0.215X_9' + 0.269X_{10}' - 0.059X_{11}',\end{aligned}$$

$$\begin{aligned}\text{Expertise} = F_2 = {} & -0.076X_1' + 0.084X_2' + 0.533X_3' + 0.034X_4' - 0.135X_5' + 0.116X_6' \\ & - 0.079X_7' + 0.102X_8' - 0.012X_9' - 0.224X_{10}' + 0.443X_{11}',\end{aligned}$$

$$\begin{aligned}\text{Character} = F_3 = {} & -0.154X_1' - 0.050X_2' - 0.022X_3' + 0.059X_4' + 0.550X_5' + 0.556X_6' \\ & + 0.006X_7' + 0.137X_8' - 0.129X_9' - 0.097X_{10}' - 0.001X_{11}'.\end{aligned}$$

These $m = 3$ factor scores can now be used instead of the original $k = 11$ variables in subsequent multivariate analyses (such as a multiple regression or a discriminant analysis). By construction, since we used the varimax rotation procedure, these factor scores are *uncorrelated* and hence there is no risk of multicollinearity if these served as independent variables. Note that we can check that these are uncorrelated by producing a correlation matrix of the factor scores, as seen in Figure 17.33.

We now assess the factor model fit by examining the residuals provided in Figure 17.34. The top half of this matrix table shows the values of the reproduced correlations. The bottom half shows the residuals (the *differences* between the original correlations and the reproduced correlations). As seen in the footnote to the reproduced correlations table, 10 out of 55 (18%) of the residuals exceed the (absolute value) threshold of 0.05. Plotting the residuals in Figure 17.35, it can be seen that none are especially extreme. Subjectively, the residuals do not seem 'too' large such that overall the model fit is pleasing and we should feel happy to use the results of this factor analysis.

We conclude by thinking about how Righthome can use the results of this factor analysis to inform its interview short-list decision-making. First, let's see how the $n = 48$ applicants score on the three factors of assertiveness, expertise and character in Figure 17.36.

Noting the factor loadings and the signs in the component score coefficient matrix, we can deduce that (assuming respondents rated themselves on each attribute accurately in the questionnaire):

- the *higher* the assertiveness score, the *more* assertive the individual is (an assumed highly desirable trait for a sales negotiator)

Rotated Component Matrix[a]

	Component		
	1	2	3
Ambition	.923	.144	.077
Drive	.790	.370	.176
Experience	.059	.918	-.045
Grasp	.805	.283	.342
Honesty	.207	-.202	.876
Likeability	.219	.224	.874
Lucidity	.861	.112	.290
Potential	.736	.373	.430
Salesmanship	.901	.244	.102
Self-confidence	.921	-.110	.168
Suitability	.355	.850	.085

Extraction Method: Principal Component Analysis.
Rotation Method: Varimax with Kaiser Normalization.

a. Rotation converged in 5 iterations.

Figure 17.30 Rotated component matrix of factor loadings (correlations) between input variables and extracted factors.

- the *higher* the expertise score, the *more* experienced/suitable the individual is for the role (an assumed proven track record in this job role)
- the *higher* the character score, the *more* honest/likeable the individual is (perhaps desirable to build rapports with buyers and sellers).

The hiring managers will need to consider how desirable each attribute is (is assertiveness more important than expertise and character?) and then can short-list for interview those individuals who best fit the ideal person description. Note that the factor scores are being used for *screening purposes* – hiring based solely on these would be ill-advised, as a strong performance at interview would likely be required to secure the keys to the job, if not the property!

17.5 CHAPTER OVERVIEW

This chapter has explored a powerful data reduction technique known as factor analysis. In essence, factor analysis exploits the correlations between a large set of observed variables and seeks to extract a smaller number of underlying factors, or constructs, which explain a large proportion of the observed variation. These factors entail a (small) loss of information, but with the benefit of a reduction in the dimensionality of the dataset. In practice many constructs are latent, or hidden, and cannot be directly observed. By computing factor scores we have a means of quantifying these latent constructs for use in subsequent analyses. We have seen how SPSS facilitates factor analysis with ease, and much focus has been on determining the appropriate number of factors, as well as issues of interpretability and model fit.

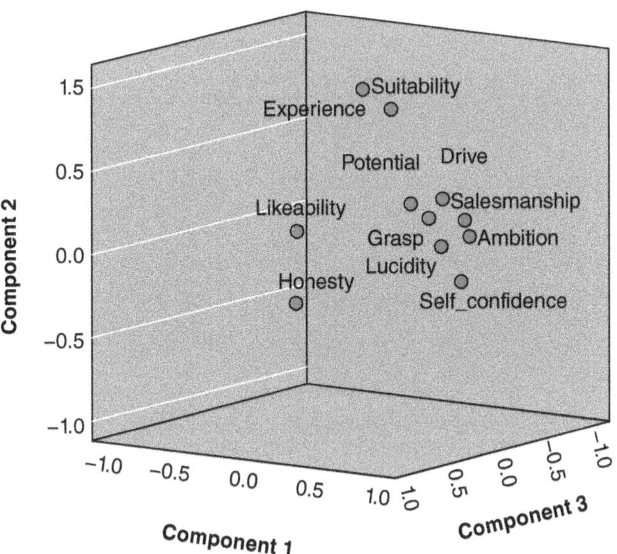

Figure 17.31 Factor loading plot based on the rotated component matrix.

Component Score Coefficient Matrix

	Component		
	1	2	3
Ambition	.245	-.076	-.154
Drive	.142	.084	-.050
Experience	-.134	.533	-.022
Grasp	.124	.034	.059
Honesty	-.099	-.135	.550
Likeability	-.170	.116	.556
Lucidity	.183	-.079	.006
Potential	.066	.102	.137
Salesmanship	.215	-.012	-.129
Self-confidence	.269	-.224	-.097
Suitability	-.059	.443	-.001

Extraction Method: Principal Component Analysis.
Rotation Method: Varimax with Kaiser Normalization.
Component Scores.

Figure 17.32 Component score coefficient matrix for a factor analysis.

Correlations

		Assertiveness	Expertise	Character
Assertiveness	Pearson Correlation	1	.000	.000
	Sig. (2-tailed)		1.000	1.000
	N	48	48	48
Expertise	Pearson Correlation	.000	1	.000
	Sig. (2-tailed)	1.000		1.000
	N	48	48	48
Character	Pearson Correlation	.000	.000	1
	Sig. (2-tailed)	1.000	1.000	
	N	48	48	48

Figure 17.33 Correlation matrix of factor scores from a factor analysis.

Reproduced Correlations

		Ambition	Drive	Experience	Grasp	Honesty	Likeability	Lucidity	Potential	Salesmanship	Self-confidence	Suitability
Reproduced Correlation	Ambition	.878[a]	.796	.183	.810	.229	.301	.832	.766	.875	.846	.456
	Drive	.796	.793[a]	.379	.801	.242	.409	.772	.795	.821	.716	.610
	Experience	.183	.379	.849[a]	.292	-.212	.180	.140	.366	.273	-.054	.798
	Grasp	.810	.801	.292	.845[a]	.409	.538	.823	.845	.829	.767	.555
	Honesty	.229	.242	-.212	.409	.851[a]	.766	.409	.454	.226	.359	-.023
	Likeability	.301	.409	.180	.538	.766	.863[a]	.467	.621	.341	.323	.343
	Lucidity	.832	.772	.140	.823	.409	.467	.837[a]	.800	.833	.829	.425
	Potential	.766	.795	.366	.845	.454	.621	.800	.866[a]	.798	.709	.615
	Salesmanship	.875	.821	.273	.829	.226	.341	.833	.798	.882[a]	.820	.536
	Self-confidence	.846	.716	-.054	.767	.359	.323	.829	.709	.820	.888[a]	.247
	Suitability	.456	.610	.798	.555	-.023	.343	.425	.615	.536	.247	.856[a]
Residual[b]	Ambition		-.016	.012	-.026	-.014	.045	-.075	.003	-.015	-.004	-.022
	Drive	-.016		-.042	-.087	.038	-.016	-.075	-.007	-.006	-.012	.012
	Experience	.012	-.042		.007	.057	-.039	.007	-.018	-.017	.070	-.105
	Grasp	-.026	-.087	.007		-.023	-.036	.059	.031	-.047	-.046	-.027
	Honesty	-.014	.038	.057	-.023		-.121	-.053	-.038	.014	.051	.026
	Likeability	.045	-.016	-.039	-.036	-.121		.016	-.015	.021	-.021	-.016
	Lucidity	-.075	-.075	.007	.059	-.053	.016		-.023	-.015	-.021	-.009
	Potential	.003	-.007	-.018	.031	-.038	-.015	-.023		-.045	-.037	-.041
	Salesmanship	-.015	-.006	-.017	-.047	.014	.021	-.015	-.045		-.020	.022
	Self-confidence	-.004	-.012	.070	-.046	.051	-.021	-.021	-.037	-.020		.003
	Suitability	-.022	.012	-.105	-.027	.026	-.016	-.009	-.041	.022	.003	

Extraction Method: Principal Component Analysis.

a. Reproduced communalities

b. Residuals are computed between observed and reproduced correlations. There are 10 (18.0%) nonredundant residuals with absolute values greater than 0.05.

Figure 17.34 Reproduced correlation matrix for a factor analysis.

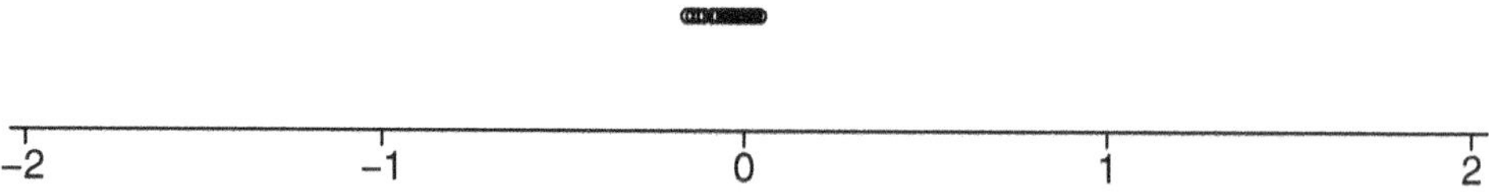

Figure 17.35 Plot of the residuals from a factor analysis.

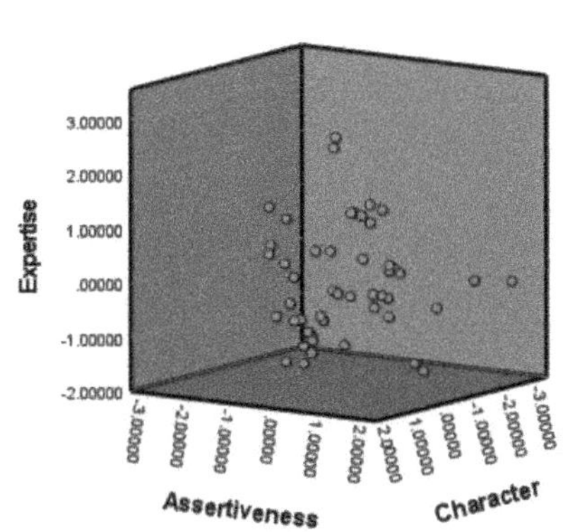

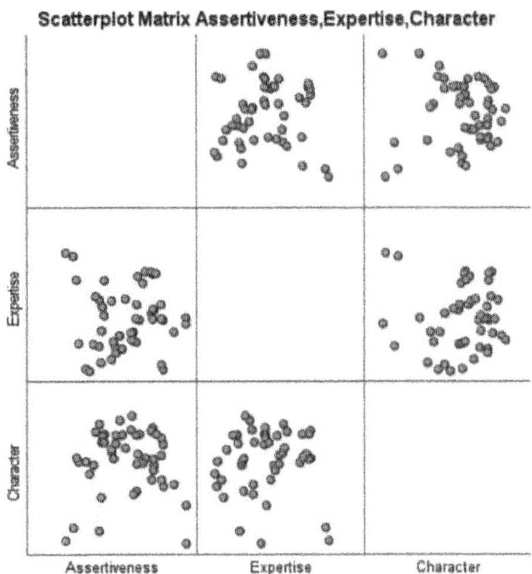

Figure 17.36 Exploratory analysis of the applicants' factor scores.

17.6 KEY VOCABULARY

Bartlett's test of sphericity
Communality
Correlation matrix
Data reduction
Factor
Factor analysis
Factor loading (plot)
Factor rotation
Factor score
Kaiser-Meyer-Olkin (KMO) statistic
Multivariate
Residual
Scree plot
Surrogate variable
Varimax

17.7 EXERCISES

17.7.1 Test your understanding

1 What is a multivariate random variable? Provide an example.

2 For each of the following, what 'factors' influence your purchasing decision? Briefly explain why in each case.

   (a) Shopping for food.
   (b) Booking a holiday destination.
   (c) Choosing where to live.

3 Suppose you are a clothing retailer interested in people's degree of fashion consciousness. How would you define fashion consciousness? Is it directly observable? If not, identify a plausible set of observed variables that you would expect to be highly correlated with fashion consciousness.

4 In what sense does factor analysis facilitate 'data reduction'?

5 Have you taken a Myers–Briggs personality test yet? If yes, do you agree with the result? If no, have a go! Whichever test you take, can you identify which personality trait is linked to each survey question?

6 To run a factor analysis, should the observed variables be correlated or uncorrelated? Briefly explain why.
7 How are observed variables 'standardised'?
8 What is a factor loading?
9 What is a communality?
10 For what purpose could factor scores be used, and why?
11 What is a 'good' value for the Kaiser–Meyer–Olkin statistic?
12 What does Bartlett's test of sphericity actually test?
13 When reducing k observed variables to m underlying factors, with $m < k$, how can the value of m be determined?
14 What does a scree plot show?
15 At a high level, what is meant by 'factor rotation'?
16 What is the connection, if any, between the rotated component matrix and the factor loading plot?
17 How are factors scores calculated?
18 When might you recommend use of a surrogate variable instead of an extracted factor?
19 In the context of factor analysis, what is a 'residual' and how is it calculated?
20 On what basis might a residual be deemed 'good' or 'bad'? 'Well, James, it depends' may feature in your answer, but explain what it depends on!

17.7.2 Practice with SPSS

Head over to the companion website for SPSS examples and screencasts!

18

CLUSTER ANALYSIS

Chapter contents

Chapter level: *Intermediate*

Source: Photo by Padrinan via Pixabay.

Key concepts

- Distinct clusters
- Hierarchical clustering
- Characteristic profiles

Chapter value

Cluster analysis can facilitate market segmentation such that similar consumer groups can be identified.

Key takeaway

Different clustering procedures and distance measures should be tested to check robustness of cluster results.

Chapter outline

Digital natives and digital immigrants. Those who grew up in the information age and those born in an analogue era. One can think of these two 'tribes' as *clusters*, that is, groups comprised of 'similar' individuals who share some traits, in this case their comfort level with technology. These two example clusters can be partitioned further, such as Millennials, Gen Z and Gen Alpha for the natives (clustered by age ranges/years of birth), with Gen X and the Baby Boomers for the immigrants.

Our objective with cluster analysis is to discover *naturally occurring groups* of customers, firms or relevant 'objects' based on a set of observed variables without knowing the actual cluster membership in advance. Once identified, clusters can be *profiled* according to useful criteria, such as on an attitudinal, behavioural or sociodemographic basis. Market segmentation, market opportunities or positioning, and identifying test markets are all possible applications of cluster analysis.

Learning outcomes

After completing this chapter, you should be able to:

- explain the purpose of cluster analysis in terms of data reduction and summarisation
- explain different clustering procedures
- conduct a hierarchical cluster analysis in SPSS
- judge the appropriate number of clusters and determine characteristic profiles of clusters.

Motivational case: Off the peg, on the money

Straight2Wardrobe is a new 'fast-fashion' company that would like to regularly use promotions to attract budget-conscious consumers. Its founder is an entrepreneur who decided to carry out some exploratory research to identify any distinct market segments related to brand loyalty and appetite for promotions.

How can the founder identify possible market segments to facilitate optimal brand positioning of Straight2Wardrobe to capture maximum market share?

18.1 INTRODUCTION

When faced with large datasets, it is usual to begin with some exploratory research – getting a 'feel' for the data ahead of performing more complex analysis. Using techniques introduced in previous chapters, good starting points are to:

- examine the distribution of each variable to detect any *outliers* (extreme observations, whose presence may exert distorting effects if not excluded), using histograms or box plots (univariate) and scatter plots (bivariate) (see Chapters 3 and 11)

- compare statistical attributes of distributions, using *descriptive statistics* such as the mean and standard deviation of variables (see Chapter 2)
- *standardise* variables if comparisons are sought and the variables have very different scales of measurement (see Chapter 2)
- explore *possible relationships* between variables, using cross-tabulations, side-by-side box plots, and scatter plots – if causality is expected, then analysis of variance and linear regression techniques can be used (see Chapters 12–14).

All of the above can be considered initial exercises in data reduction, since the data are simplified and summarised. In Chapter 17 we looked at *variable reduction* using factor analysis, essentially summarising k observed variables with m common factors, or m surrogate variables, with $m < k$.

In this chapter our goal is *observation reduction*, by searching for natural groups of observations. Whereas factor analysis looked at data reduction columnwise, cluster analysis is concerned with data reduction rowwise. With n (individual) observations, we hope to combine these into homogeneous groups, known as clusters.

One size fits all, or none?

Caps, T-shirts, socks and other apparel are sometimes advertised as 'one size fits all', designed to fit anyone and everyone. In practice, heads, torsos and feet come in many different sizes, if not shapes. Uniform sizing makes production easier (no size differentiation settings needed), but it's impossible for any one-size-fits-all item to fit everyone perfectly.

'One size fits *all*?' No. 'One size fits *most*?' Perhaps. 'One size fits *some*?' Better. 'One size fits *median*?' Yes!

Grouping all people into a single group (i.e. a 'one-cluster solution') achieves *maximum data reduction* (i.e. simplicity - good), but *maximum variation within the group* (bad). Increasing the number of groups and catering to the needs of each group separately achieves a bit more complexity (bad), but reduced variation within each group (good).

Take socks. Given a size choice of XS, S, M, L and XL, everyone's feet should be able to find a good-fitting pair! Happy feet.

18.2 CLUSTER ANALYSIS

With n observations or cases, our objective is to assign each to one of c mutually exclusive and collectively exhaustive clusters, where $c < n$. When $c = 1$, this is akin to a one-size-fits-all strategy, which as noted above is optimal only for the few, not for the many.

The clusters should be *homogeneous within each cluster*, so that a cluster consists of similar cases, and *heterogeneous between clusters*, so that each cluster is sufficiently distinct. Hence members of one cluster should be dissimilar from members in all other clusters.

In a business context, suppose the 'cases' are consumers. We can then treat each cluster as a distinct *market segment*. Knowledge of the relative segment sizes helps to judge the market composition and possible market size for different goods and services. Profiles of each segment would help with brand/product positioning to best cater for the needs of each consumer segment. Consider the following examples.

Example 18.1

Netflix can divide its subscribers into various 'taste clusters', establishing which types of movies and television shows appeal most to which audiences. This can help with decisions on which new shows to commission, as well as pushing the most appropriate recommendations to keep eyes glued to screens and subscription revenues flowing.

Example 18.2

Insurance companies with 'black box' car insurance policies can monitor driving behaviour (such as acceleration, braking and turning) via GPS tracking of car journeys. Driver profiles can be derived (ultra-cautious 'Sunday drivers', road-rage-prone 'angry drivers', risky 'speed merchants', etc.), allowing more accurate pricing of policies to reflect the different risks of claims posed by different driver groups. Admittedly, there may be a degree of *self-selection bias* in the type of driver who would welcome having a black box 'spy' monitoring their every (mirrors, signal) manoeuvre!

Example 18.3

Clustering shoppers in terms of, say, 'shopaholics', 'bargain hunters' and 'shopaphobes' can help retailers push new product lines, promotions, etc. in a targeted way.

18.3 CLUSTERING PROCEDURES

Clustering can be performed in one of two ways.

- Hierarchical clustering – in an *agglomerative* sense, cases are 'merged' together using one of many different possible methods, such that we transition from $c = n$ clusters each of size 1, to a $c = 1$ cluster with all cases merged into a single cluster (think one size fits all).
- Non-hierarchical clustering – cases are *partitioned* into a pre-determined number of clusters according to a specified criterion. We will note this approach only in brief.

18.3.1 Hierarchical clustering

Ahead of forming clusters, we consider how to measure the *distance* between cases. A distance measure is necessary to judge how similar/dissimilar cases are and whether they should/should not be combined into a common cluster.

A popular choice of distance measure is *Euclidean distance*, which is the straight line distance between any two cases, reported on an interval scale of measurement.

Euclidean distance

Suppose each case is measured on k different observed variables, $X_1, X_2, ..., X_k$. The **Euclidean distance** between any two cases, i and j, denoted by δ_{ij}, whose measurements are $(x_{i1}, x_{i2}, ..., x_{ik})$ and $(x_{j1}, x_{j2}, ..., x_{jk})$, respectively, is

$$\delta_{ij} = \sqrt{\sum_{p=1}^{k}(x_{ip} - x_{jp})^2}.$$

Example 18.4

When $k = 2$, such as the latitude and longitude coordinates of two distribution centres ($i = 1, j = 2$, say), the Euclidean distance between them is given by (good old Pythagoras' theorem!)

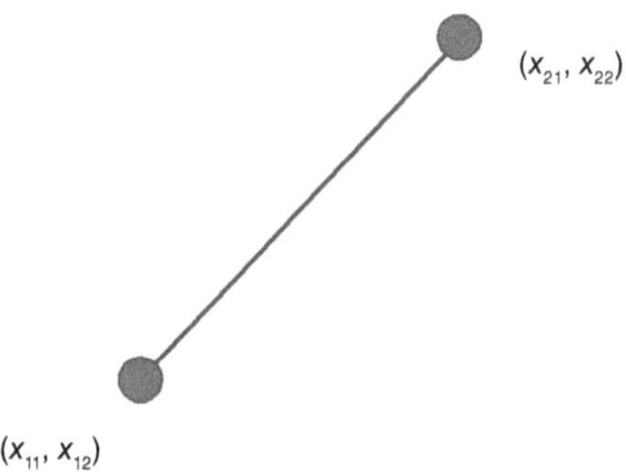

$$\delta_{12} = \sqrt{\sum_{p=1}^{k}(x_{1p} - x_{2p})^2} = \sqrt{(x_{11} - x_{21})^2 + (x_{21} - x_{22})^2}.$$

Two possible alternatives (these are not exhaustive) to Euclidean distance are:

- squared Euclidean distance:

$$\delta_{ij} = \sum_{p=1}^{k} (x_{ip} - x_{jp})^2$$

- Chebyshev distance:

$$\delta_{ij} = \max_{\forall p} |x_{ip} - x_{jp}|.$$

Dealing with binary observations

Euclidean distance is appropriate for measurable variables, that is, quantitative observations. Often, though, we may deal with *binary observations*, taking values 0 or 1. For example, a customer either possesses an attribute (1), or they don't (0). Suppose four customers are described based on a set of five binary variables as follows:

Variable	Customer 1	Customer 2	Customer 3	Customer 4
New customer (yes = 1, no = 0)	0	0	1	1
Orders online (yes = 1, no = 0)	1	1	1	0
Requests priority delivery (yes = 1, no = 0)	1	0	1	0
Recommends products (yes = 1, no = 0)	1	0	0	0
Returns products (yes = 1, no = 0)	0	1	0	0

Using Euclidean distance is inappropriate when we have binary observations. Instead, any relationship between individual cases may be summarised by way of a *contingency table* (previously seen in Chapter 11). For example, looking at customer 1 and customer 2, we determine the *frequency* of each contingency pair:

	Customer 2 (=0)	Customer 2 (=1)
Customer 1 (=0)	1 ($f_{0,0}$)	1 ($f_{1,0}$)
Customer 1 (=1)	2 ($f_{0,1}$)	1 ($f_{1,1}$)

Similarity between any two cases is identified by how many common attributes they share, that is, when both are type '0' or '1'. A natural choice of similarity measure would be

$$\frac{f_{0,0} + f_{1,1}}{f_{0,0} + f_{1,0} + f_{0,1} + f_{1,1}}.$$

Using this approach, the measure of similarity between customers 1 and 2 is 2/5 = 0.40. Similarity measures for all four customers may be presented in a similarity matrix as follows:

	Customer 1	Customer 2	Customer 3	Customer 4
Customer 1	1	0.40	0.60	0.20
Customer 2	0.40	1	0.40	0.40
Customer 3	0.60	0.40	1	0.60
Customer 4	0.20	0.40	0.60	1

Note that, by construction, the similarity matrix is *symmetric*. A *correlation matrix* is a good example of a similarity matrix. Stronger correlations imply stronger (linear) relationships. A correlation matrix would be useful if we wanted to cluster variables.

Clustering may be performed either using a *distance measure* or a *similarity measure*.

With hierarchical clustering, at sequential stages the most similar cases are merged together. An agglomeration schedule (reported by SPSS) represents an 'audit trail' of how the cases have been combined, starting with $c = n$ clusters (each of size 1), culminating in $c = 1$ cluster (containing all n cases). A dendrogram is a visualisation (also reported by SPSS) showing how the clusters developed.

Hierarchical clustering algorithm

The algorithm by which hierarchical clustering works is as follows.

1. Begin with $c = n$ clusters, each of size 1, and an $n \times n$ distance matrix or similarity matrix.
2. Use the matrix to find the nearest pair of cases (using the distance matrix) or the most similar pair of cases (using the similarity matrix) and combine these into the same cluster.
3. Update the distance/similarity matrix. Rows and columns of the two merged cases are replaced with a single row and column for the newly formed cluster.
4. Repeat stages 2 and 3 a total of $n - 1$ times, culminating in $c = 1$ cluster containing all n cases.

Stage 3 of this algorithm is a little vague after the first iteration. Once a cluster has more than one member in it, how do we measure distance or similarity? We consider the following possible methods.

1. Single linkage uses a 'nearest neighbours' approach. The distance between two clusters is measured by taking the *shortest* distance between members of two clusters, as illustrated in Figure 18.1.

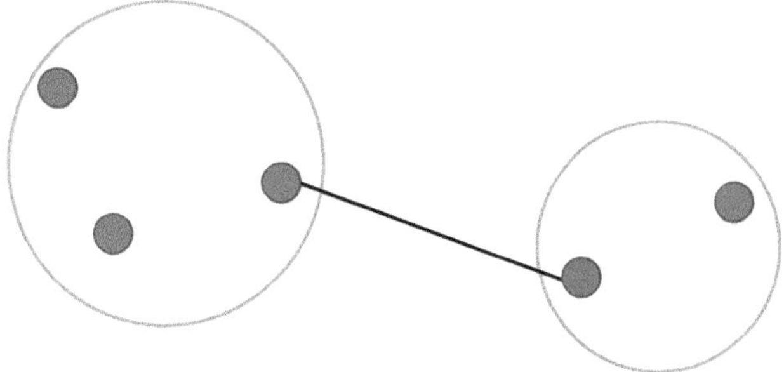

Figure 18.1 Single linkage clustering procedure.

2 **Complete linkage** uses a 'furthest neighbours' approach. The distance between two clusters is measured by taking the *furthest* distance between members of two clusters, as illustrated in Figure 18.2.

3 **Average linkage** uses an average approach, hence the name! The distance between two clusters is measured by taking the *average* distance (the arithmetic mean) between members of two clusters, as illustrated in Figure 18.3.

4 **Ward's method** works by minimising *intra-cluster variation*, that is, cases are combined to ensure the *smallest possible increase* in the new cluster's variance. Recall that we seek homogeneity (limited variation) within each cluster, but at each stage of hierarchical clustering we inevitably merge more distant cases each time, thereby increasing this within, or 'intra', cluster variation – Ward's method works to minimise this increase.

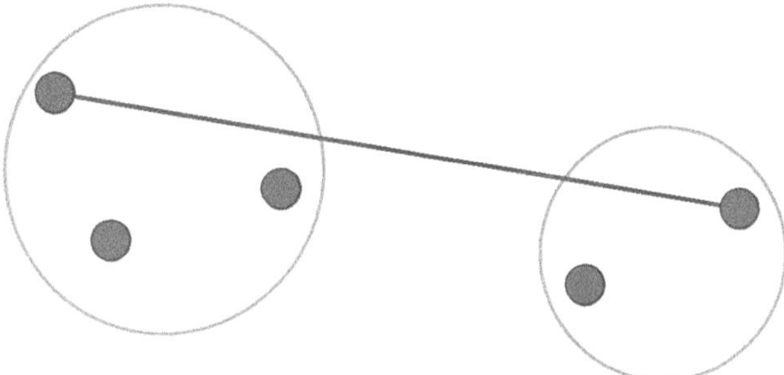

Figure 18.2 Complete linkage clustering procedure.

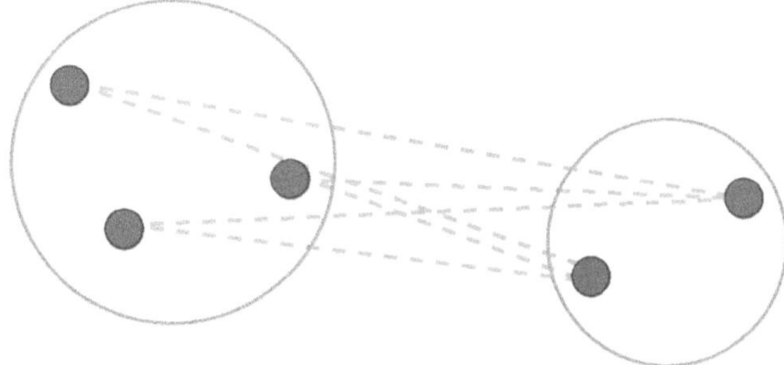

Figure 18.3 Average linkage clustering procedure.

5 **Centroid clustering** uses the 'nearest centroid' approach. The distance between two clusters is measured by taking the distance between the cluster centroids, that is, the averages of the variables. (Recall that the concept of the *centroid* was introduced in Chapter 16 when profiling different groups based on their discriminant scores.)

Which clustering method to use? Well, it is advisable to conduct a *sensitivity analysis* by experimenting with several clustering methods and assess the consistency of the cluster solutions. If similar (ideally the same) clusters emerge, then it is likely we have discovered naturally occurring groups due to the *robustness* of the results. If we end up with very different clusters from one method to another, that is, the clustering results are highly *sensitive* to the clustering method, then we face uncertainty about the 'true' groupings, so we should treat any alleged clusters with caution.

Note that when performing cluster analysis on variables with highly variable units of measurement, it is advisable to *standardise* the variable values as clustering solutions could be sensitive to different scales of measurement. Failure to standardise risks the variable with the largest order of magnitude ending up dominating the clustering procedure – bad!

The decision on the 'right' number of clusters is, like many decisions, subjective. Keep in mind, though, the objective of *homogeneity within clusters* and *heterogeneity between clusters*. The clusters should be useful from a practical perspective, such that (like the identification of factors in Chapter 17) the clusters are straightforward to profile – for example, based on usage characteristics and the demographic profiles of each cluster.

18.3.2 Non-hierarchical clustering

Also known as **k-means clustering**, non-hierarchical clustering is an alternative approach to its hierarchical counterpart. By (subjectively) pre-specifying the value of k, each case is then allocated to one of k clusters. The choice of k could be based on practical requirements – for example, the business analyst might have a target number of segments that they wish to identify, and could make practical use of. If k is too small, then the clustering is too broad, while if k is too large the gains from observation reduction are low.

Each case is identified by its coordinates (a multivariate observation) and, using the following algorithm, cases are allocated to the k clusters.

Non-hierarchical clustering algorithm

The algorithm by which non-hierarchical clustering works is as follows.

1. Cases are initially partitioned into k starting clusters, or k centroids (starting 'seeds') are initially specified.
2. Allocate each case to the cluster with the nearest centroid.
3. Update the centroids.
4. Repeat stages 2 and 3 until there are no more reallocations of cases.

However, our focus will be on hierarchical clustering, easily performed using SPSS.

18.4 CLUSTER ANALYSIS: FULL EMPIRICAL EXAMPLE

Market segmentation is important for businesses to understand the different groups of consumers that they serve. Meeting the needs, desires and wants of different constituent groups can assist with customer acquisition, customer satisfaction, and hence customer retention.

Suppose a random sample of 10 consumers were asked their level of agreement on a nine-point Likert scale (1 = strongly disagree, 9 = strongly agree) with the following statements:

- 'I am unwilling to switch brands' (X_1).
- 'The price is important in my purchasing decisions' (X_2).
- 'The brand is important in my purchasing decisions' (X_3).
- 'I shop frequently' (X_4).

The raw data are shown in Figure 18.4.

We will run a cluster analysis to see if we can reduce these $n = 10$ cases to a smaller number of c clusters, where $c < 10$. Note that since all four survey questions were answered on the same nine-point Likert scale, there is no need to standardise the variables.

To perform cluster analysis in SPSS using hierarchical clustering, proceed as follows.

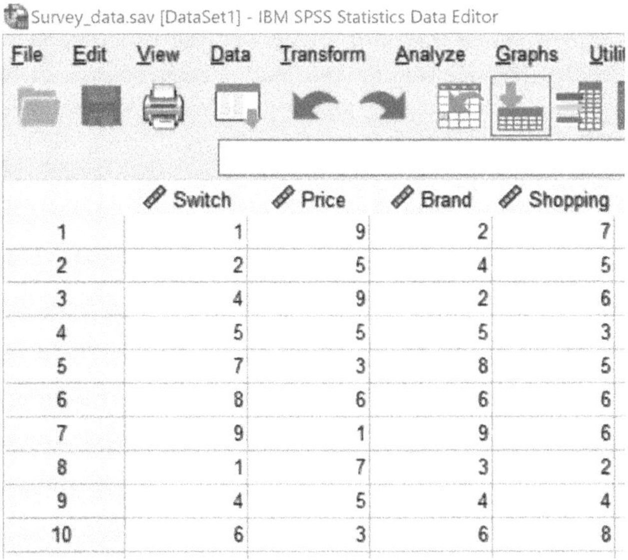

Survey_data.sav [DataSet1] - IBM SPSS Statistics Data Editor

File Edit View Data Transform Analyze Graphs Utili

	Switch	Price	Brand	Shopping
1	1	9	2	7
2	2	5	4	5
3	4	9	2	6
4	5	5	5	3
5	7	3	8	5
6	8	6	6	6
7	9	1	9	6
8	1	7	3	2
9	4	5	4	4
10	6	3	6	8

Figure 18.4 Survey responses from a random sample of 10 consumers.

- **Analyze > Classify > Hierarchical Cluster....**
- Move the relevant variables into the `Variables` box – here the above four variables, X_1, X_2, X_3, X_4.
- In the `Cluster` box, check `Cases` (default option). In the `Display` box, check `Statistics` and `Plots` (default options).

- Click on `Statistics...`. In the pop-up window, check `Agglomeration schedule` and `Proximity matrix`. In the `Cluster Membership` box check `Range of solutions` with sensible values for the minimum and maximum number of clusters. (Here we will experiment with a minimum of $c = 2$ and a maximum of $c = 4$.) Click on `Continue`.
- Click on `Plots...`. In the pop-up window, check `Dendrogram`. In the `Icicle` box check `All clusters` (default). In the `Orientation` box check `Vertical`. Click `Continue`.
- Click on `Method...`. For `Cluster Method` select your chosen clustering method (here we will use `Ward's method`). In the `Measure` box check `Interval` and select your chosen distance measure (here we will use `Euclidean distance`). Click on `Continue`.
- Click on `Save...`. In the pop-up window, check `Range of solutions` and enter the minimum and maximum number of clusters previously specified (here 2 and 4, respectively). Click on `Continue`.
- Click on `OK`.

Let's first look at the updated Data View in Figure 18.5. We see the assignment of each of the $n = 10$ cases to one of four clusters (in the `CLU4_1` column, with a mixture of 1s, 2s, 3s and 4s), to one of three clusters (in the `CLU3_1` column, with a mixture of 1s, 2s and 3s), and to one of two clusters (in the `CLU2_1` column, with a mixture of 1s and 2s). Of course, some detective work will be required to decide which is the 'best' number of clusters.

Turning to the output window, we first examine the proximity matrix, as shown in Figure 18.6. The proximity matrix reports how far apart each pair of observations is based on the distance measure specified when running the cluster analysis. Recall that we opted for the Euclidean distance measure for this example, and the proximity matrix indicates the Euclidean distance between each pair of cases. Note the zero entries on the leading diagonal, since this represents the distance between a case and itself!

*Survey_data.sav [DataSet1] - IBM SPSS Statistics Data Editor

File Edit View Data Transform Analyze Graphs Utilities Extensions Window Help

	Switch	Price	Brand	Shopping	CLU4_1	CLU3_1	CLU2_1
1	1	9	2	7	1	1	1
2	2	5	4	5	2	2	1
3	4	9	2	6	1	1	1
4	5	5	5	3	2	2	1
5	7	3	8	5	3	3	2
6	8	6	6	6	4	3	2
7	9	1	9	6	3	3	2
8	1	7	3	2	2	2	1
9	4	5	4	4	2	2	1
10	6	3	6	8	4	3	2

Figure 18.5 Updated Data View following a cluster analysis.

The matrix is symmetric, since $\delta_{ij} = \delta_{ji}$. As indicated at the bottom of the matrix, this is a *dissimilarity matrix*, that is, smaller (larger) distances indicate more similar (dissimilar) cases.

Proximity Matrix

	Euclidean Distance									
Case	1	2	3	4	5	6	7	8	9	10
1	.000	5.000	3.162	7.550	10.583	8.660	13.342	5.477	6.164	8.832
2	5.000	.000	5.000	3.742	6.708	6.481	9.539	3.873	2.236	5.745
3	3.162	5.000	.000	5.916	9.055	6.403	11.747	5.477	4.899	7.746
4	7.550	3.742	5.916	.000	4.583	4.472	7.550	5.000	1.732	5.568
5	10.583	6.708	9.055	4.583	.000	3.873	3.162	9.274	5.477	3.742
6	8.660	6.481	6.403	4.472	3.873	.000	5.916	8.660	5.000	4.123
7	13.342	9.539	11.747	7.550	3.162	5.916	.000	12.329	8.367	5.099
8	5.477	3.873	5.477	5.000	9.274	8.660	12.329	.000	4.243	9.274
9	6.164	2.236	4.899	1.732	5.477	5.000	8.367	4.243	.000	5.292
10	8.832	5.745	7.746	5.568	3.742	4.123	5.099	9.274	5.292	.000

This is a dissimilarity matrix

Figure 18.6 Proximity matrix from a cluster analysis.

Note that the two nearest cases (by far!) are 4 and 9, reported as $\delta_{49} = \delta_{94} = 1.732$, indicating that these will be the first two cases to be combined into a common cluster (of size 2). In passing, note how similar their survey responses were (seen in Figure 18.4):

$$X_4 = (5\ 5\ 5\ 3) \quad \text{and} \quad X_9 = (4\ 5\ 4\ 4).$$

In contrast, the two furthest apart cases are 1 and 7, reported as $\delta_{17} = \delta_{71} = 13.342$, due to very different survey responses:

$$X_1 = (1\ 9\ 2\ 7) \quad \text{and} \quad X_7 = (9\ 1\ 9\ 6).$$

Clearly, for large numbers of observations, the proximity matrix becomes very large so typically would not be reported. Nevertheless, when reviewing the agglomeration schedule (next) it can be worthwhile to cross-reference this with the proximity matrix.

Hierarchical clustering procedures base the agglomeration by combining cases which are in closest proximity to each other. So, our attention now moves to the agglomeration schedule, shown in Figure 18.7.

Ward Linkage

Agglomeration Schedule

	Cluster Combined			Stage Cluster First Appears		
Stage	Cluster 1	Cluster 2	Coefficients	Cluster 1	Cluster 2	Next Stage
1	4	9	.866	0	0	4
2	5	7	2.447	0	0	7
3	1	3	4.028	0	0	8
4	2	4	5.732	0	1	6
5	6	10	7.794	0	0	7
6	2	8	10.430	4	0	8
7	5	6	13.266	2	5	9
8	1	2	18.057	3	6	9
9	1	5	28.607	8	7	0

Figure 18.7 Agglomeration schedule from a cluster analysis.

The agglomeration schedule gives information on the cases being combined at each stage of a hierarchical clustering process. We begin with all of the $n = 10$ cases as individual clusters each of size 1, that is, $c = n = 10$ initially. At the first stage, SPSS combines the two cases which are closest together based on the distance measure used (Euclidean distance in our case). We noted above that cases 4 and 9 were most similar, and these are the first two cases to be combined as reported in 'Stage 1'. This means that after stage 1 we now have $c = 9$ clusters: 8 of size 1, and 1 of size 2 (with cases 4 and 9).

At stage 2, cases 5 and 7 are combined, such that now we have $c = 8$ clusters: 6 of size 1, and 2 of size 2 (with cases 4 and 9, and 2 and 7, respectively). The process continues until we have one cluster with all of the $n = 10$ cases within it. The right-hand columns report when a previously combined case first appeared. For example, case 4 was first combined in stage 1 (with case 9) and next appeared in stage 4 (when combined with case 2, forming a cluster of size 3, containing cases 2, 4 and 9).

Note that we specified Ward's method as the clustering method, so cases were combined at each stage to *minimise the increase in intra-cluster variation*. Inevitably, this means that while the number of clusters decreases stage by stage (good), the intra-cluster variances increase stage by stage (bad). We face a trade-off.

Our main challenge in cluster analysis is deciding on the appropriate number of clusters. There are a few aids that we can consider to help guide us in this decision. First, we can use the agglomeration schedule. The `Coefficients` column provides a (scaled) measure of how close the cases are at each stage of the clustering. As we advance through the stages of hierarchical clustering, we have to combine clusters which are further and further apart. When there is a 'large' increase in the `Coefficients` column, at that stage we are combining somewhat distant clusters and so we may wish to halt the agglomeration just before this happens – otherwise we combine distant cases which we might be unwilling to consider as being sufficiently 'similar' or 'homogeneous'.

Here we see a particularly large increase in the `Coefficients` column between stages 8 and 9 (from 18.057 to 28.607), suggesting it might be wise to stop after stage 8, which would mean a two-cluster solution.

What other 'evidence' should we consider?

Since we asked SPSS to consider a range of cluster solutions based on our desire to identify an approximate number of clusters (in our example, a minimum of two clusters and a maximum of four clusters), we can examine the *cluster membership box* in Figure 18.8 which reports to which cluster each individual case is assigned, for each type of solution. Note that these results also appeared as new columns in the Data View (see Figure 18.5).

From the cluster membership box (Figure 18.8), we see the following:

- If we settle on a four-cluster solution, we have:
    - cluster 1 members 1 and 3 (20% of the total cases)
    - cluster 2 members 2, 4, 8 and 9 (40% of the total cases)
    - cluster 3 members 5 and 7 (20% of the total cases)
    - cluster 4 members 6 and 10 (20% of the total cases).
- If we settle on a three-cluster solution, we have:
    - cluster 1 members 1 and 3 (20% of the total cases)
    - cluster 2 members 2, 4, 8 and 9 (40% of the total cases)
    - cluster 3 members 5, 6, 7 and 10 (40% of the total cases).

  Note that the previous clusters 3 and 4 have been merged to give (the new) cluster 3.

Cluster Membership

Case	4 Clusters	3 Clusters	2 Clusters
1	1	1	1
2	2	2	1
3	1	1	1
4	2	2	1
5	3	3	2
6	4	3	2
7	3	3	2
8	2	2	1
9	2	2	1
10	4	3	2

Figure 18.8 Cluster membership from a cluster analysis.

- If we settle on a two-cluster solution, we have:
  - cluster 1 members 1, 2, 3, 4, 8 and 9 (60% of the total cases)
  - cluster 2 members 5, 6, 7 and 10 (40% of the total cases).

  Note that the previous clusters 1 and 2 have been merged to give (the new) cluster 1, with the (old) cluster 3 becoming the (new) cluster 2.

If we assume the sample of $n = 10$ is *representative* of the population (here the population of all consumers), then the above percentages represent estimates of the market share of each type of consumer. Admittedly, we should caveat this by noting that the sample size is *very* small, hence representativeness is highly uncertain, such that the market share estimates are likely to be very imprecise. With a (much) larger dataset the market share estimates would be (much) more accurate.

However, we could use these percentages as a criterion for deciding on the appropriate number of clusters if we had a specific requirement for equal/similar/minimum cluster sizes or proportions.

Next we look at the icicle plot (so-called due to its features resembling icicles, if you squint) in Figure 18.9. The icicle plot shows the cluster compositions for all possible cluster solutions, in this example from 1 to 10 clusters. The vertical axis details the number of clusters and the individual cases are at the top of the plot (the numbers correspond to the survey respondents in this instance). The icicles indicate the split between cluster solutions in terms of which observations are included in each cluster. For example, for two clusters, the shortest icicle is between cases 5 and 8. So a two-cluster solution would have the following clusters (agreeing with the cluster membership box in Figure 18.8):

- cluster 1 (on the right), 1, 2, 3, 4, 8 and 9.
- cluster 2 (on the left), 5, 6, 7 and 10.

For three clusters, the next shortest icicle is between cases 2 and 3, hence splitting cluster 1 to give the following clusters (also agreeing with the cluster membership box):

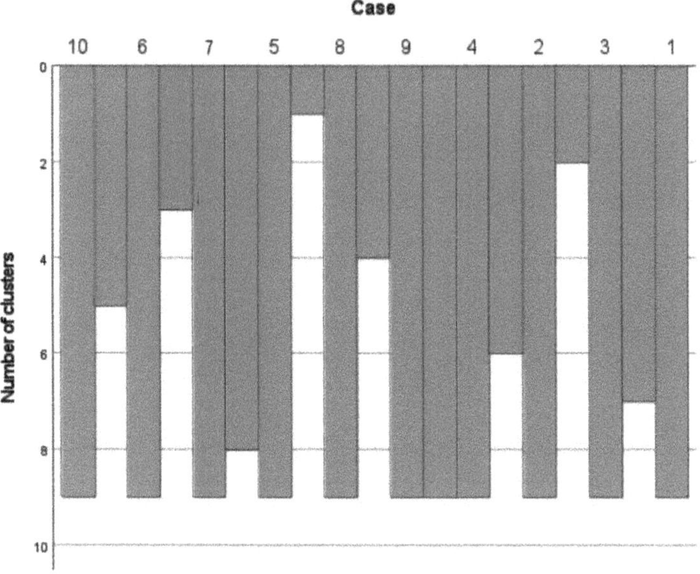

Figure 18.9 Icicle plot from a cluster analysis.

- cluster 1 (on the right), 1 and 3.
- cluster 2 (in the centre), 2, 4, 8 and 9.
- cluster 3 (on the left), 5, 6, 7 and 10.

Similarly, for four clusters, the next shortest icicle is between cases 6 and 7, etc.

When n is small, as in this example, the icicle plot gives a visual sense of the *relative cluster sizes*, which could be a criterion for judging the appropriate number of clusters.

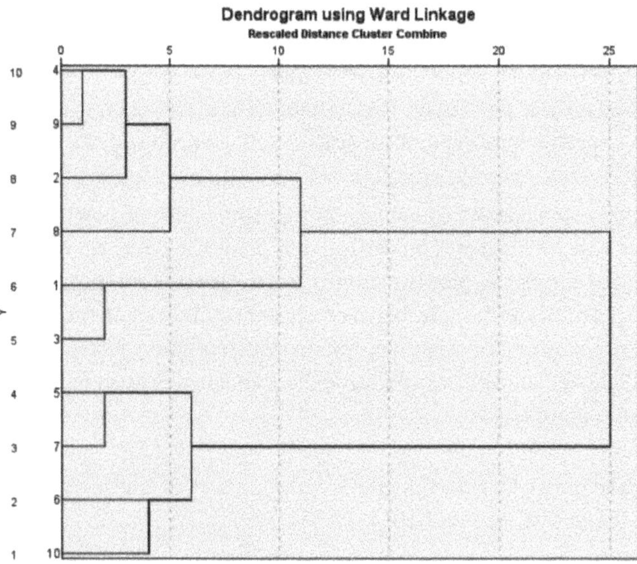

Figure 18.10 Dendrogram from a cluster analysis.

We now turn to the *dendrogram* in Figure 18.10. The dendrogram provides a convenient way to determine the appropriate number of clusters. Although the final decision is subjective, the dendrogram clearly shows the proximity when cases are combined. On the left-hand side we see the individual cases (the numbers correspond to the survey respondents). The horizontal axis is a rescaled distance measure showing the (rescaled) distance when combining occurs. The vertical lines in the diagram depict the combining of cases – simply trace back the cluster members to the left-hand side. The further to the right a vertical line occurs, the more *dissimilar* the two clusters being merged are (which, remember, is undesirable). Judgement is required, but we can use the rescaled distance axis to judge which vertical lines are 'acceptable', that is, those which are not too far to the right.

Using the dendrogram in Figure 18.10, it seems reasonable to identify three distinct clusters with members as follows:

- cluster 1 (middle of the vertical axis), 1 and 3.
- cluster 2 (top of the vertical axis), 2, 4, 8 and 9.
- cluster 3 (bottom of the vertical axis), 5, 6, 7 and 10.

Most importantly, any clusters we settle on must be of practical use. They need to be distinct in meaningful ways. Each cluster must have a clear characteristic profile, which can be obtained by examining the group centroids. Given that we have saved the cluster membership in the Data View, we can obtain the means of each variable for each cluster in SPSS as follows.

Use **Analyze > Compare Means > Means...**, then move the variables used for clustering (here X_1 to X_4) into the `Dependent List:`, and move the different cluster solutions (here the Ward's method variables) to the `Independent List:`. Under `Options...` keep the default `Cell Statistics` of `Mean` (to give the centroid values), `Number of Cases` (to give the cluster sizes) and `Standard Deviation` (to judge the degree of homogeneity/heterogeneity of the clusters). Click on `Continue`, and then click on `OK`.

Willingness to switch Importance of price Importance of brand Frequency of shopping * Ward Method

Ward Method		Willingness to switch	Importance of price	Importance of brand	Frequency of shopping
1	Mean	2.50	9.00	2.00	6.50
	N	2	2	2	2
	Std. Deviation	2.121	.000	.000	.707
2	Mean	3.00	5.50	4.00	3.50
	N	4	4	4	4
	Std. Deviation	1.826	1.000	.816	1.291
3	Mean	8.00	2.00	8.50	5.50
	N	2	2	2	2
	Std. Deviation	1.414	1.414	.707	.707
4	Mean	7.00	4.50	6.00	7.00
	N	2	2	2	2
	Std. Deviation	1.414	2.121	.000	1.414
Total	Mean	4.70	5.30	4.90	5.20
	N	10	10	10	10
	Std. Deviation	2.830	2.584	2.378	1.814

Figure 18.11 Descriptive statistics for a four-cluster solution.

First, let's examine the profiles of a four-cluster solution, shown in Figure 18.11. Since the survey questions were answered on a nine-point Likert scale (from strongly disagree to strongly agree), we should interpret the means of each variable with respect to this scale. Any means close to 1 or 9 will be useful in helping to choose a name for each cluster. The magnitude of standard deviation values should also be judged with respect to the nine-point scale (a standard deviation of 0.000 shows that all variable values for that cluster are the same, i.e. the within-cluster cases score identically for the variable). Note the cluster sizes of 2, 4, 2 and 2 reflect the 20%, 40%, 20% and 20% figures described earlier in terms of market share estimates.

A reminder of the original survey questions:

- 'I am unwilling to switch brands' (X_1).
- 'The price is important in my purchasing decisions' (X_2).
- 'The brand is important in my purchasing decisions' (X_3).
- 'I shop frequently' (X_4).

We are now in a position to (attempt to) profile the clusters as follows:

- Cluster 1: Consumers who are very price-conscious, caring little for brands and willing to switch brands. Suggested name: *bargain hunters*.
- Cluster 2: Consumers who score 'moderate' means on all variables, with no clear distinguishing features. Suggested name: *general shoppers*.
- Cluster 3: Consumers who are extremely attached to brands and very unwilling to switch, with price not a key factor. Suggested name: *brand loyalists*.
- Cluster 4: Similar to cluster 3, but marginally less attached to brands, and shop more frequently. Suggested name: *brand-loving shopaholics*.

The distinction between clusters 3 and 4 seems very mild. They clearly share similar passions for brands, such that we might see little benefit from treating these as different market segments. Let's see how a three-cluster solution compares by looking at Figure 18.12. Unsurprisingly, the two similar brand-loving clusters have been merged, so our cluster profiles are now:

Willingness to switch Importance of price Importance of brand Frequency of shopping * Ward Method

Ward Method		Willingness to switch	Importance of price	Importance of brand	Frequency of shopping
1	Mean	2.50	9.00	2.00	6.50
	N	2	2	2	2
	Std. Deviation	2.121	.000	.000	.707
2	Mean	3.00	5.50	4.00	3.50
	N	4	4	4	4
	Std. Deviation	1.826	1.000	.816	1.291
3	Mean	7.50	3.25	7.25	6.25
	N	4	4	4	4
	Std. Deviation	1.291	2.062	1.500	1.258
Total	Mean	4.70	5.30	4.90	5.20
	N	10	10	10	10
	Std. Deviation	2.830	2.584	2.378	1.814

Figure 18.12 Descriptive statistics for a three-cluster solution.

- Cluster 1: Consumers who are very price-conscious, caring little for brands and willing to switch brands. Suggested name: *bargain hunters*. (As before.)
- Cluster 2: Consumers who score 'moderate' means on all variables, with no clear distinguishing features. Suggested name: *general shoppers*. (As before.)
- Cluster 3: Consumers who are very attached to brands and unwilling to switch, who shop frequently, with price not a very important factor. Suggested name: *brand-loyal shopaholics*.

If we were content with these three clusters, then we could view these as three distinct segments for marketing purposes. Bargain hunters would likely respond well to promotions and discounts, with 20% of consumers estimated to be of this type (assuming a representative sample, caveated by the very small n). Brand-loyal shopaholics (estimated to be 40% of all consumers) are our ideal type of consumer once we have attracted them – their love of a brand and lack of price sensitivity mean these are a highly lucrative segment for us. General shoppers are, well, general, so we would wish to think about ways of migrating them into brand-loyal shopaholics – admittedly, this is perhaps easier said than done!

For completeness, let's see whether a two-cluster solution is a practical improvement by looking at Figure 18.13. We see that the bargain hunters and general shoppers have been merged together. Improved data reduction ($c = 2$ instead of $c = 3$) has come at a cost of greater heterogeneity *within* this newly formed cluster (notice the increased standard deviations for X_2, X_3 and X_4). Given that two-thirds of the members of this cluster (4 out of 6) do *not* consider price to be especially important, such consumers would not necessarily be that receptive to promotions and discounts (although who would refuse a discount when offered?!) so, on balance, the three-cluster solution is preferred.

If we had demographic information on the consumers (such as age, gender, etc.) this would enable us to have a sense of *who* the different shopper types are.

Willingness to switch Importance of price Importance of brand Frequency of shopping * Ward Method

Ward Method		Willingness to switch	Importance of price	Importance of brand	Frequency of shopping
1	Mean	2.83	6.67	3.33	4.50
	N	6	6	6	6
	Std. Deviation	1.722	1.966	1.211	1.871
2	Mean	7.50	3.25	7.25	6.25
	N	4	4	4	4
	Std. Deviation	1.291	2.062	1.500	1.258
Total	Mean	4.70	5.30	4.90	5.20
	N	10	10	10	10
	Std. Deviation	2.830	2.584	2.378	1.814

Figure 18.13 Descriptive statistics for a two-cluster solution.

18.5 CLUSTER ANALYSIS: FURTHER EXAMPLE

Let's now see how we can identify market segments for Straight2Wardrobe, including a look at demographic profiling.

A reminder that Straight2Wardrobe is a new 'fast-fashion' company that would like to regularly use promotions to attract budget-conscious consumers. Its founder is an entrepreneur who decided to carry out some exploratory research to identify any distinct market segments related to brand loyalty and appetite for promotions.

A short questionnaire was completed by a sample of n = 25 people. The following seven statements required a response on a seven-point Likert scale, ranging from 1 = strongly disagree to 7 = strongly agree.

- 'I am more likely to buy brands with a promotion' (X_1).
- 'Gamified promotions are fun' (X_2).
- 'I spend more money with brands when they offer a promotion' (X_3).
- 'I feel more emotionally connected to a brand when it offers a promotion' (X_4).
- 'I find brands more appealing when they offer a promotion' (X_5).
- 'I am more likely to notice a brand when it offers a promotion' (X_6).
- 'I am more loyal to a brand once it's offered a promotion' (i.e. I don't switch to other brands afterwards) (X_7).

In addition to responding to the above statements, each surveyed consumer reported their:

- age, in years
- gender (coded as 1 = male and 0 = female, with all 25 respondents identifying as either male or female)
- income, in thousands (pounds sterling)

under the assurance of anonymity to avoid non-response or response bias!

Cluster analysis should be conducted based on attitudinal or behavioural characteristics of consumers (here, the Likert-scale responses), and *not* the demographic or income variables – these should be used only for building characteristic profiles of any identified clusters.

Suppose we use the Euclidean distance measure, and the complete linkage clustering method (select `Furthest neighbor` for the cluster method in SPSS). The $n \times n = 25 \times 25$ proximity matrix is too large to show (and of limited direct interest), so we jump straight to the agglomeration schedule, shown in Figure 18.14.

We see quite a large jump in the `Coefficients` column between stages 23 and 24, signalling that a two-cluster solution seems appropriate (i.e. the cluster combining should end after stage 23).

As n increases, icicle plots and dendrograms become harder to read, but these are just about interpretable for n = 25. First, the icicle plot is shown in Figure 18.15. A two-cluster solution would have roughly equal-sized segments. *Ceteris paribus*, similar-sized groups are desirable, but a (very) small group may be of interest if it was a highly lucrative market segment. For example, first class and business class airline passengers are far fewer in number, but far more profitable than those in economy class (often those 'turning left' subsidise those 'turning right').

Now let's consider the dendrogram in Figure 18.16. While highly subjective, this also suggests a two-cluster solution, or at least not a one-cluster solution! Ultimately, we need to consider the practical applicability of any alleged clusters. So, we now check whether there are any obvious characteristic profiles for a two-cluster solution. For this, we will also draw upon the age, income and gender variables.

Complete Linkage

Agglomeration Schedule

Stage	Cluster Combined		Coefficients	Stage Cluster First Appears		Next Stage
	Cluster 1	Cluster 2		Cluster 1	Cluster 2	
1	4	14	1.414	0	0	8
2	10	12	2.236	0	0	8
3	8	25	2.449	0	0	15
4	11	16	2.449	0	0	7
5	1	18	2.828	0	0	13
6	2	5	2.828	0	0	13
7	11	21	3.000	4	0	18
8	4	10	3.000	1	2	12
9	7	23	3.317	0	0	11
10	9	17	3.606	0	0	21
11	6	7	3.606	0	9	17
12	4	19	3.742	8	0	15
13	1	2	4.123	5	6	17
14	3	22	4.472	0	0	20
15	4	8	4.472	12	3	21
16	20	24	4.583	0	0	19
17	1	6	5.000	13	11	22
18	11	13	5.099	7	0	19
19	11	20	5.916	18	16	22
20	3	15	6.325	14	0	23
21	4	9	6.325	15	10	23
22	1	11	6.633	17	19	24
23	3	4	7.681	20	21	24
24	1	3	10.724	22	23	0

Figure 18.14 Agglomeration schedule from a cluster analysis.

We now examine Figure 18.17. With reference to the seven-point Likert scale, cluster 1 scores on average approximately 3.00–3.50 across the attributes, while cluster 2 scores on average approximately 5.00–6.00. Hence the second cluster seems the more receptive market segment for a new discounting fast-fashion company, namely:

- they respond to gamified promotions
- they gravitate to brands with promotions
- they are loyal to brands with promotions, spending more.

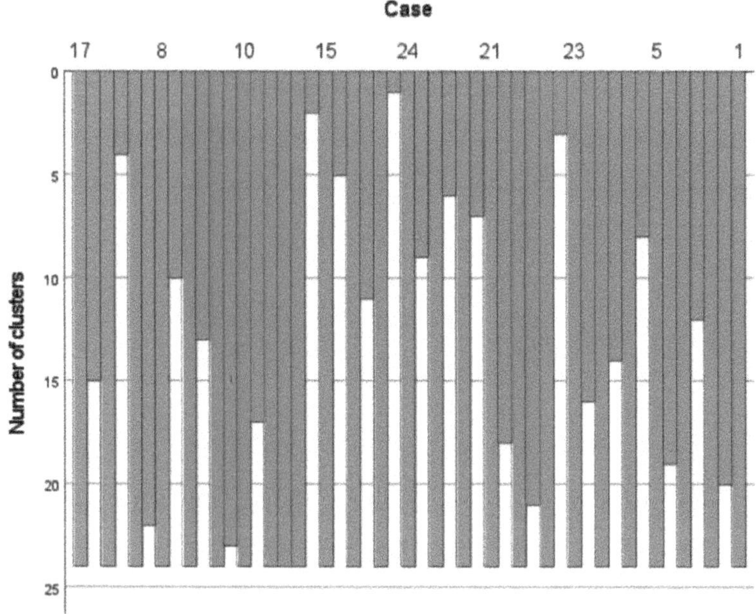

Figure 18.15 Icicle plot from a cluster analysis.

Examining the descriptive statistics of the two clusters demographically, cluster 1 is older (mean age of 54.08), and has higher income (mean income of 62,690 in the relevant currency), relative to cluster 2 (27.33 and 29,500, respectively). There is no discernible difference in terms of gender composition, with both clusters being very balanced (given the binary nature of the gender variable here, a mean of 0.50 would equate to an equal male–female split).

To reiterate, the age, gender and income (demographic and socioeconomic) variables were *not* used to perform the clustering technique, rather they are used to profile the two identified clusters.

Straight2Wardrobe's entrepreneur founder should look to target younger consumers who seem to be very receptive to promotions. Interestingly, gamification could be explored as a means to engage with these (primarily Gen Z and Gen Alpha) digital natives!

18.6 CHAPTER OVERVIEW

This chapter has looked at data reduction using cluster analysis. The objective is to identify naturally occurring groups (for businesses, usually of consumers) who share similarities within groups, but distinct differences between groups. Such groups can then be viewed as market segments, allowing goods and services to be tailored to the needs of different consumer groups. There is no single right approach to cluster analysis – there exist different ways of measuring the distance between cases (necessary to determine how similar/dissimilar they are) as well as a choice of clustering methods in hierarchical clustering (necessary to determine how cases are combined). In practice, a selection of distance measures and clustering methods should be tested and the robustness of any derived clusters assessed. Simple descriptive statistics (mean and standard deviation) may then be used to establish characteristic profiles of each segment, for which appropriate marketing strategies can be developed.

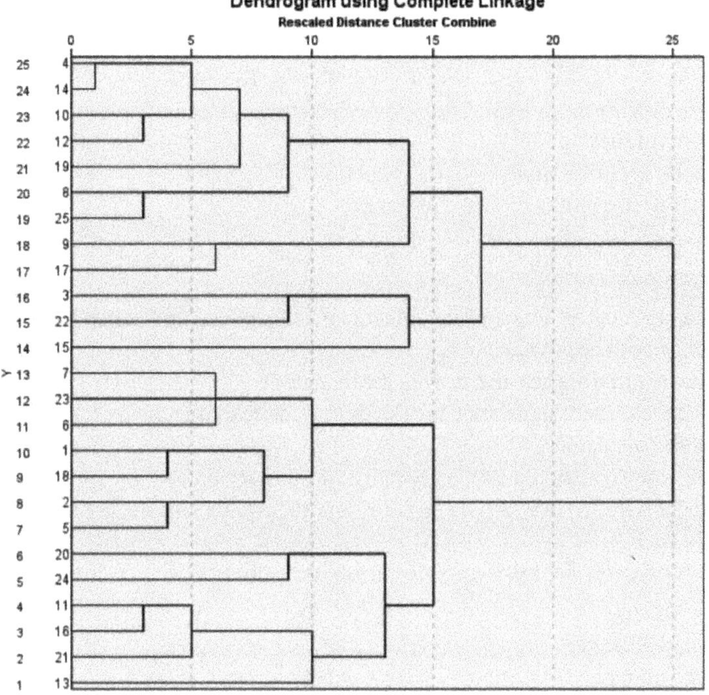

Figure 18.16 Dendrogram from a cluster analysis.

18.7 KEY VOCABULARY

Agglomeration schedule
Average linkage
Centroid clustering
Characteristic profile
Chebyshev distance
Cluster
Cluster analysis
Complete linkage
Data reduction
Dendrogram
Euclidean distance
Hierarchical clustering
Icicle plot
k-means clustering
Non-hierarchical clustering
Similarity matrix
Single linkage
Squared Euclidean distance
Ward's method

Complete Linkage		I am more likely to buy brands with a promotion	Gamified promotions are fun	I spend more money with brands when they offer a promotion	I feel more emotionally connected to a brand when it offers a promotion	I find brands more appealing when they offer a promotion	I am more likely to notice a brand when it offers a promotion	I am more loyal to a brand once it's offered a promotion (i. e. I don't switch to other brands afterwards)	Age	Gender	Income in 000s
1	Mean	3.15	3.46	3.54	3.38	3.15	3.54	3.00	54.08	.46	62.69
	N	13	13	13	13	13	13	13	13	13	13
	Std. Deviation	1.144	1.391	1.330	1.325	1.405	1.050	1.291	10.805	.519	14.250
2	Mean	5.75	5.67	5.67	5.83	5.08	6.17	5.58	27.33	.50	29.50
	N	12	12	12	12	12	12	12	12	12	12
	Std. Deviation	.965	1.155	1.435	1.115	1.505	1.030	1.084	4.716	.522	5.486
Total	Mean	4.40	4.52	4.56	4.56	4.08	4.80	4.24	41.24	.48	46.76
	N	25	25	25	25	25	25	25	25	25	25
	Std. Deviation	1.683	1.686	1.734	1.734	1.730	1.683	1.763	15.954	.510	20.044

Figure 18.17 Descriptive statistics for a two-cluster solution.

18.8 EXERCISES

18.8.1 Test your understanding

1. Identify possible forms of exploratory analysis which could be undertaken prior to more complex techniques.
2. In what sense is cluster analysis 'data reduction'?
3. How similar or dissimilar should clusters be:
   (a) within each cluster?
   (b) between each cluster?
4. How do hierarchical and non-hierarchical clustering procedures differ? Outline the algorithm for each approach.
5. What is Euclidean distance and how is it calculated?
6. Are there any alternative distance measures to Euclidean distance? If so, what are they and how are they calculated?
7. How would you construct a similarity matrix for binary data?
8. What is the difference between a similarity matrix and a dissimilarity matrix? Provide an example of each.
9. Distinguish between the following clustering techniques:
   (a) single linkage
   (b) complete linkage
   (c) average linkage
   (d) Ward's method
   (e) centroid clustering.
10. What use is an agglomeration schedule?
11. What use is an icicle plot?
12. What use is a dendrogram?
13. How is the 'right' number of clusters determined? 'Well, James, it depends' may feature in your answer, but explain what it depends on!
14. How would you go about building a characteristic profile for candidate clusters?
15. Should you only perform cluster analysis once, with only one distance measure and one clustering technique? Briefly justify your view.

18.8.2 Practice with SPSS

Head over to the companion website for SPSS examples and screencasts!

19

CONSTRAINED OPTIMISATION MODELS

Chapter contents

Chapter level: *Advanced*

Source: Photo by Jon Tyson via Unsplash.

Key concepts

- Decision variables
- Sensitivity analysis
- Conjoint analysis

Chapter value

Given choice, we always want the best. In practice we face constraints, so we solve for what is best subject to these.

Key takeaway

Sensitivity analysis is vital to understand how robust or sensitive optimal solutions are to changes in the model.

Chapter outline

Choice. It's meant to be a luxury. In decision-making, having a range of options available may seem appealing, but ultimately a choice has to be made. We would naturally seek to make the *best* choice, where 'best' means *optimal* in some sense - for example, choosing production levels to *maximise* 'good' things like profits, or *minimise* 'bad' things like costs. However, finite resources (such as time, money and raw materials) mean in practice we have to operate under various *constraints* (such as a deadline, a fixed budget or technological limits). So, we need to factor all constraints into our decision-making, giving rise to *constrained optimisation models*. In essence, we will pursue the best choice possible, while not exceeding any imposed limits.

Deadlines shift. Budgets change. Technology evolves. What if our constraints become tighter or looser? Well, our decisions can be *sensitive* to the degree of restrictions we face. As such, we can perform a *sensitivity analysis* to determine how an optimal solution itself may change due to revised constraints. We can even judge our maximum willingness to pay to loosen a binding constraint.

A special application of constrained problems in marketing is that of *conjoint analysis*. This attempts to quantify the relative importance of different characteristics of a product to a consumer, allowing marketers to understand what maximises customer satisfaction, allowing products and marketing to be presented in an optimal way.

Learning outcomes

After completing this chapter, you should be able to:

- construct simple constrained optimisation models algebraically and in spreadsheet form
- use Microsoft Excel's Solver add-in to derive optimal solutions for constrained optimisation problems
- perform and interpret a sensitivity analysis of optimal solutions
- present the conjoint analysis model and estimate model parameters using a two-stage process.

Motivational case: Doing the (best) splits

Stylish Chairs is a specialist in wooden chairs. It has focused exclusively on 'standard' chairs to date, but the company has been keen to diversify its product range by entering the 'deluxe' market where profit margins are higher as deluxe items command higher prices.

Market research has shown a growing consumer appetite for the deluxe product sector, albeit it is expected that the market for standard chairs will continue to be at least double that of deluxe chairs for the foreseeable future.

Wooden chairs are wood-intensive to produce and the company has a limited supply of wood available, although it would consider purchasing additional wood, if profitable to do so, and all wood is sustainably sourced.

How should the company split production between the different chair types?

19.1 INTRODUCTION

Linear programming models – don't worry, nothing to do with computer programming! – are a class of constrained optimisation models based on a set of linear equations. Linear programming represents a very common type of quantitative business model due to its wide applicability. Whenever a business operates in an environment of *finite resources* we can consider this a constrained optimisation exercise.

Optimisation problems can be one of three types:

- *maximising a value* – for example, a manufacturer choosing the optimal product mix to maximise profits
- *minimising a value* – for example, a logistics company choosing delivery routes to minimise transportation costs
- *achieving a fixed value* – for example, allocating a fixed research and development budget across competing projects.

To wait, or not to wait?

Expect the unexpected. The vulnerability of one of the world's busiest shipping channels was laid bare when the *Ever Given* container ship unexpectedly blocked the Suez Canal in March 2021. Wedged into a bank of the canal, it immediately brought one of the world's critical shipping arteries to a standstill. Images of a tiny digger valiantly trying to free the 200,000-tonne giant comically conveyed the futility of the rescue effort, but this was no laughing matter.

Minimising the shipping distance between Europe and Asia, the Suez Canal running through Egypt is the obvious quickest shipping route. However, *given* the grounding, very quickly a traffic jam of container ships started to build. Freight companies had to make a decision (Figure 19.1):

- wait it out for an unknown length of time, hoping for a swift reopening of the Suez Canal
- reroute via the Cape of Good Hope in South Africa, adding 3500 nautical miles to the trip and a further 8.5-day expected journey time (increasing transportation costs in terms of fuel and crew wages), but with greater certainty regarding destination arrival time.

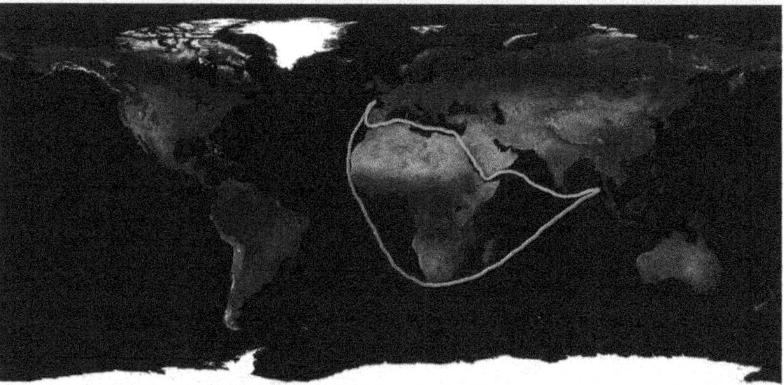

Figure 19.1 The two feasible shipping routes between Asia and Europe.

Here the nautical routes impose fixed constraints (we cannot simply shift continents to open up a quicker route!) and shipping managers needed to balance minimising freight delays and transportation costs.

Fortunately, within a week the *Ever Given* was freed, unblocking the Suez plumbing, allowing global trade to resume happy *ever (given)* after. The end.

19.2 OPTIMISATION MODELS

We now consider the components of optimisation models. Each consists of several common parts.

- Decision variables. These are the variables whose values are under the control of the decision-maker, that is, they are *free to choose these*. Decision variables are critical in optimisation models, since they determine everything else. For example, in manufacturing, the quantities of different goods to produce would be decision variables since management can decide the amounts of each good.
- Objective function. This is the function which returns the key variable to be optimised, whether maximised, minimised, or imposed to be a fixed value. For example, a manufacturer targets maximising its total profit (which in part will be affected by its production levels) which can be calculated using a profit function (where profit equals total revenue minus total cost).
- Constraints. These may be physical (such as factory space), logical (such as non-negative quantities) or economic restrictions (such as budget to be spent on raw materials), which vary depending on the nature of the problem. Constraints *must* be satisfied, either *binding* (with no slack) or *non-binding* (with some slack).

Decision variables, the objective function and constraints all need to be related. This is achieved using an algebraic model – a *system of equations* connecting all model variables together. Once an algebraic model is constructed, we will need to *solve the model* to find the optimal solution; that is, the optimal values of the decision variables, based on solving a set of simultaneous equations – simultaneous, because all equations and constraints must hold *at the same time*.

Rather than having to resort to figuring out mathematical solutions with copious amounts of algebra (you may recall solving a pair of simultaneous equations by hand back in school), fortunately we can call on Microsoft Excel to solve linear programming problems using the Solver add-in. Note that Excel has its own terminology when working with optimisation models as follows.

- Changing cells. These are spreadsheet cells which contain values of the *decision variables*.
- Objective cell. This is the spreadsheet cell which contains the formula for the *objective function*.
- Constraints. These are restrictions imposed on the values in the *changing cells*.
- Non-negativity. This is a special type of constraint forcing specified cells to contain *non-negative numbers* (useful for real-world variables which cannot be negative, like quantities).

19.2.1 Solving optimisation problems

Initially, some brainstorming is required to *develop the optimisation model* – specifically, to:

- determine the decision variables, objective function and all constraints
- model how everything is related, that is, develop algebraic expressions to connect all variables together.

The second step is to *optimise*, whereby we seek the *optimal solution*. In practice, there may be many *feasible* solutions, such that all constraints are satisfied, giving us a choice of possibilities for the decision variables. However, we want to identify the solution which is the *best* – for example, in a maximisation problem we are looking for the solution which maximises the value of the objective function. We have the following classification:

- A **feasible solution** is a solution which satisfies *all* of the constraints.
- The **feasible set** is the set of *all* feasible solutions, such that any feasible solution is viable in practice.
- An **infeasible solution** violates *at least one* of the constraints, such that it is impossible to use an infeasible solution in practice.
- The **optimal solution** is the feasible solution which optimises the objective function, and hence is the *best solution*.

The third step is to perform a **sensitivity analysis** – the extent to which the final solution is *sensitive* to parameter values and constraints used in the model. We will consider sensitivity analysis in more depth later. For now, we will focus on developing an optimisation model and subsequently optimise it.

19.3 PRODUCT MIX

A frequent problem in business is that of *product mix*, which means deciding how much to produce of each of n products. The simplest such problem is when there are only two products to choose between (i.e. $n = 2$). Coincidentally, we can now help solve Stylish Chairs' production dilemma.

Example 19.1

Consider a profit-maximising manufacturer deciding on its optimal product mix between two types of chair: standard chairs and deluxe chairs. Each chair is made exclusively from wood, with no additional factor inputs (for the sake of simplicity). A standard chair is made using 15 kg of wood, while a deluxe chair is made from 20 kg of wood. The manufacturer has a total of 5000 kg of wood available for production. (Don't be alarmed - the wood is sustainably sourced!)

Standard chairs generate a profit of £50 each, while deluxe chairs generate a profit of £80 each, since deluxe products are sold at higher prices with a greater profit margin. Given estimates about product demand from consumers based on previous purchasing behaviour, the number of standard chairs should be at least double the number of deluxe chairs. Usually only those with higher levels of disposable income can afford deluxe ranges such that there is a smaller market for the deluxe type.

Assume that every chair produced is ultimately sold. As chairs are not perishable, unlike foodstuffs, unsold stock may simply be held as inventory until sufficient consumer demand is generated for them to be sold. For simplicity, assume storage costs are negligibly small, and as such can be ignored.

We define the *decision variables* as follows:

- x = quantity of standard chairs to produce
- y = quantity of deluxe chairs to produce.

So, the manufacturer needs to determine the production quantities x and y with the objective of maximising profits. While deluxe chairs have a higher profit margin (£80 > £50), they are also more wood-intensive and the manufacturer expects demand for standard chairs to be at least double that of deluxe chairs.

Total profit is calculated as the unit (i.e. per chair) profit multiplied by the quantity produced (since we assume every chair produced is ultimately sold). Algebraically, the *objective function* is

$$50x + 80y,$$

since £$50x$ is the profit from standard chairs, and £$80y$ is the profit from deluxe chairs. Adding these together naturally gives the total profit.

Without any constraints the manufacturer would wish to produce an *infinite* number of each type of chair, which would lead to infinite profits! However, we live in a world of finite resources - in this case, there are only 5000 kg of wood available for production. So, this is a *constrained* optimisation problem (constrained by wood and consumer preferences for chair types), not an *unconstrained* one!

The linear programming problem is

$$\max_{x,y} 50x + 80y,$$

that is, choose x and y to maximise $50x + 80y$, subject to the wood constraint (total wood used in production cannot exceed the total amount available),

$$15x + 20y \leq 5000 \Rightarrow y \leq 250 - 0.75x,$$

and the production constraint (the number of standard chairs should be at least double the number of deluxe chairs),

$$x \geq 2y \Rightarrow y \leq 0.5x.$$

Note how the wood and production constraints are *linear* in x and y, with both constraints rearranged to leave just y on the left-hand side.

We also require *non-negativity* constraints, since we can never produce a negative quantity of chairs! Hence we must have that

$$x \geq 0 \text{ and } y \geq 0.$$

(Continued)

While our preference will be to use Solver to solve linear programming problems, since we only have $n = 2$ decision variables we can actually solve this problem *graphically*. Indeed, such a visual representation may help you to conceptualise such constrained optimisation problems.

A graphical representation of the problem is as follows (Figure 19.2):

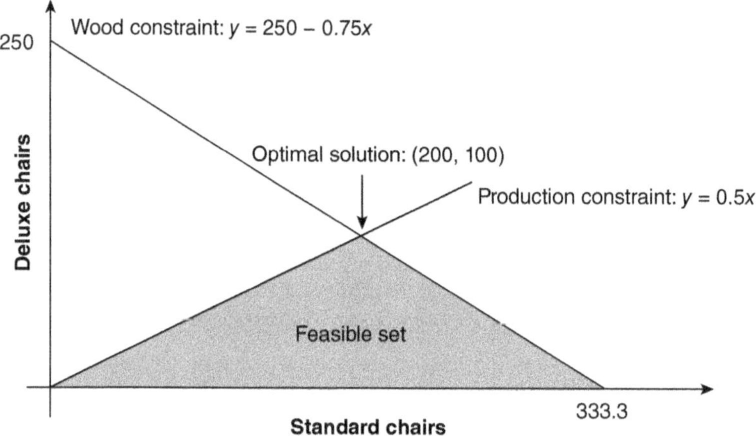

Figure 19.2 Graphical solution of product mix problem for Example 19.1.

Production levels of standard chairs and deluxe chairs are shown on the x-axis and y-axis, respectively. Given the non-negativity constraints ($x \geq 0$ and $y \geq 0$) we only need to draw in quadrant I (i.e. top right with respect to the origin). When the wood and production constraints are written as equalities (with '=' rather than '≤') these linear constraints are drawn with the lines $y = 250 - 0.75x$ (wood) and $y = 0.5x$ (production) as shown.

Since the actual constraints are $y \leq 250 - 0.75x$ and $y \leq 0.5x$, all feasible solutions must be *on or below* each constraint line (and not beyond the x- and y-axes, due to the non-negativity constraints). As such the *set of feasible solutions* is indicated, meaning that *any* point in the feasible set is a possible product mix (the coordinates of any point represent the production quantities, x and y). However, which point is profit-maximising?

The maximum (and minimum) values of the objective function will lie at a *corner* of the feasible set. The two lines *intersect* when both constraint equations are true, hence when

$$15x + 20y = 5000 \text{ and } x = 2y.$$

This happens at the point (200, 100). We can find the values of the objective function at each corner by substitution into the objective function, $50x + 80y$. The three corners of the feasible set are:

- (0, 0), with profit of $50x + 80y = £0$ (which is the minimum profit, i.e. when nothing is produced!)
- ($333.\dot{3}$, 0), with profit $50x + 80y = £16,666.67$ (which is when only standard chairs are produced)
- (200, 100), with profit $50x + 80y = £18,000$ (which is the maximum profit achievable).

We see that the optimal solution is £18,000, which is obtained by making 200 standard chairs and 100 deluxe chairs. Note that all constraints are satisfied: production levels are non-negative, standard chair production is double that of deluxe chairs (satisfying that production is *at least* double), and we have not exceeded the amount of wood available since the total wood used in production is

$$15 \times 200 + 20 \times 100 = 5000 \text{ kg}.$$

For this optimal solution, all constraints are *binding*, meaning that there is no slack - for instance, there is no unused wood.

What about using Solver instead? Well, no problem at all! Consider the following spreadsheet model:

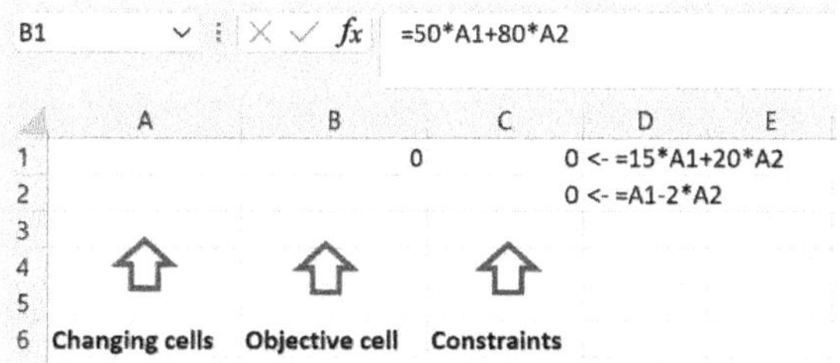

Cells A1 and A2 are the *changing cells*, that is, the values of x and y (where the solutions $x = 200$ and $y = 100$ will be returned). Cell B1 is the *objective cell*, with formula =50*A1+80*A2 representing the objective function $50x + 80y$ visible in the formula bar. Cells C1 and C2 contain the left-hand sides of the *constraint equations*, with formulae =15*A1+20*A2 (being the left-hand side of the wood constraint $15x + 20y \leq 5000$) and =A1-2*A2 (being the left-hand side of the rearranged production constraint $x \geq 2y$ given by $x - 2y \geq 0$).

With the Solver add-in loaded, we need to populate it with the required constraints, as well as specifying the location of the value returned by the objective function and the type of constrained optimisation problem being conducted (maximisation of profit in this case). Opening the `Solver Parameters` dialog box, we populate it as follows:

Solver Parameters

Set Objective: $B$1

To: Max Min Value Of: 0

By Changing Variable Cells:
$A$1:$A$2

Subject to the Constraints:
$C$1 <= 5000
$C$2 >= 0

Add Change Delete Reset All Load/Save

Make Unconstrained Variables Non-Negative

Select a Solving Method: Simplex LP Options

Solving Method
Select the GRG Nonlinear engine for Solver Problems that are smooth nonlinear. Select the LP Simplex engine for linear Solver Problems, and select the Evolutionary engine for Solver problems that are non-smooth.

Help Solve Close

(Continued)

This shows the following:

- `Set Objective` is set to `$B$1`, since this is what we have designated to be the *objective cell* where the value of the profit function is to be returned.
- `To` is set to `Max`, since we want to *maximise* the objective function (you can see how Solver handles minimisation problems and achieving a fixed value with the `Min` and `Value Of:` options).
- `By Changing Variable Cells` is set to `$A$1:$A$2`, identifying the cells where the solution should be returned, that is, the *changing cells* we have specified as being the values of x and y.
- `Subject to the Constraints` lists `$C$1 <= 5000` and `$C$2 >= 0` as the *full constraints* for wood ($15x + 20y \leq 5000$) and production ($x - 2y \geq 0$), respectively.
- `Make Unconstrained Variables Non-Negative` is checked as we wish to impose *non-negativity* on x and y.

We will not consider the 'solving methods' in this text. Rather, we stick with the default `Simplex LP` approach. Clicking on `Solve` then yields the solution:

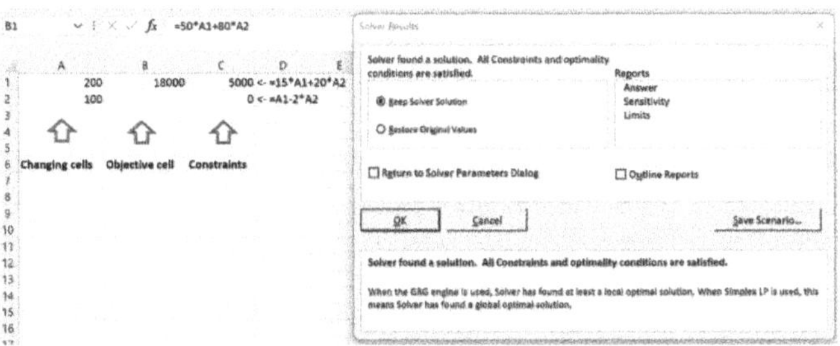

Success! Solver has solved the problem! We see the optimal solution of $x = 200$ and $y = 100$ in cells `A1:A2`. With these values present, the maximum profit of £18,000 is returned in cell `B1`. Cell `C1` confirms that all 5000 kg of wood are used, while cell `C2` confirms that x is at least double that of y - more specifically since the value is 0, then x is *exactly* double y.

If we select the `Answer` report, we obtain a summary of the model solution as a new worksheet:

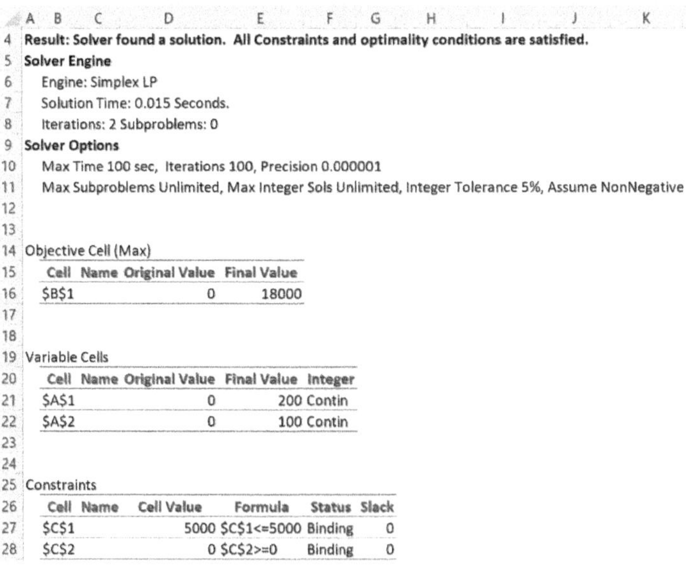

Result: Solver found a solution. All Constraints and optimality conditions are satisfied.

Solver Engine

Engine: Simplex LP

Solution Time: 0.015 Seconds.

Iterations: 2 Subproblems: 0

Solver Options

Max Time 100 sec, Iterations 100, Precision 0.000001

Max Subproblems Unlimited, Max Integer Sols Unlimited, Integer Tolerance 5%, Assume NonNegative

Objective Cell (Max)

Cell	Name	Original Value	Final Value
$B$1		0	18000

Variable Cells

Cell	Name	Original Value	Final Value	Integer
$A$1		0	200	Contin
$A$2		0	100	Contin

Constraints

Cell	Name	Cell Value	Formula	Status	Slack
$C$1		5000	$C$1<=5000	Binding	0
$C$2		0	$C$2>=0	Binding	0

Notice that the final values of the objective function and variable cells are tabulated, and the status of each constraint is reported to be binding, with zero slack.

19.4 SENSITIVITY ANALYSIS

In Example 19.1 we determined that the profit-maximising product mix achieves a total profit of £18,000. Is it possible for the manufacturer to generate profits *greater than* this amount? Yes, but only if at least one aspect of the model *changes*.

Suppose we were to make recommendations to the chair manufacturer so that it could increase profits beyond the amount of £18,000. Possible recommendations could be:

- increase profit margins per chair based on marketing efforts
- increase the supply of wood available, subject to the price of wood
- relax the production constraint to increase demand for deluxe chairs due to their higher profit margin (this would likely relate to the marketing efforts).

More specifically, of interest is to what extent the optimal solution of $x = 200$ and $y = 100$ is *sensitive* to changes in the optimisation model. We are now in a position to examine the `Sensitivity` report, which can be requested from the `Solver Results` dialog box upon solving the original problem. We obtain:

	A	B	C	D	E	F	G	H
1	**Microsoft Excel 16.0 Sensitivity Report**							
2	**Worksheet: [Linear-programming-example.xlsx]Example**							
3								
4	Variable Cells							
5				**Final**	**Reduced**	**Objective**	**Allowable**	**Allowable**
6		**Cell**	**Name**	**Value**	**Cost**	**Coefficient**	**Increase**	**Decrease**
7		$A$1		200	0	50	10	90
8		$A$2		100	0	80	1E+30	13.33333333
9								
10	Constraints							
11				**Final**	**Shadow**	**Constraint**	**Allowable**	**Allowable**
12		**Cell**	**Name**	**Value**	**Price**	**R.H. Side**	**Increase**	**Decrease**
13		$C$1		5000	3.6	5000	1E+30	5000
14		$C$2		0	-4	0	333.3333333	500

We begin analysing the `Variable Cells` table. The `Objective Coefficient` column reports 50 and 80, which are the profit margins of standard and deluxe chairs, respectively. These enter the linear programming model as the coefficients on x and y in the objective function:

$$50x + 80y.$$

The allowable increase and allowable decrease tell us by how much the respective coefficient could change *before* the optimal solution ($x = 200$ and $y = 100$) would change. For example, the profit on standard chairs of £50 per unit could take any value in the range [–£40, £60] and the optimal production levels of $x = 200$ and $y = 100$ would remain unchanged. The value –£40 is because we are allowed to decrease 50 by a maximum of 90 units; £60 because we may increase 50 by a maximum of 10 units. Of course, a negative coefficient does not make commercial sense since this would mean selling standard chairs at a loss! However, we could increase the price of standard chairs by £10, resulting in a profit margin of £60 and the optimal product mix would remain the same. Note, however, that although the x and y values do not change, the maximum profit realised *would* change, since the objective coefficient on x would have changed. Total profit would now be:

$$60 \times 200 + 80 \times 100 = £20{,}000,$$

which is £2,000 more than previously. It is important, though, that the constrained optimisation problem is about choosing the *quantities* to produce, not the profit achieved (although we wish to maximise profit, this amount is simply a consequence of the decision variables).

For deluxe chairs, the allowable increase is infinite (showing as 1E+30, which is 1×10^{30} – Excel's way of showing infinity) and the allowable decrease is 13.3. So, the optimal solution of $x = 200$ and $y = 100$ would remain for any deluxe chair profit margin in the range [£66.67, £∞). While the infinite coefficient may seem strange, recall that this is a *constrained* problem, with there being a finite amount of wood and the requirement that at least twice as many standard chairs are produced as deluxe chairs. As such, this constrains the maximum number of deluxe chairs which can be produced, and therefore there is no (upper) limit to how much deluxe chairs can be sold for, giving rise to the possibility of an infinite profit margin on deluxe chairs. In practice, though, if the price of deluxe chairs were too high (above consumers' maximum willingness to pay) then our *assumption* that every chair produced is ultimately sold would be unrealistic. Effective marketing, and a strong brand image, may permit a small increase in deluxe chair prices, and hence their profit margin, but there would inevitably be an upper bound. Clearly, there is scope to extend the model by placing an upper bound on the realistic profit margins of each type of chair.

The reduced cost is applicable for any decision variable with an optimal solution value of *zero* (which is not the case here since $x = 200 > 0$ and $y = 100 > 0$). In such instances, the reduced cost tells us by how much the respective objective coefficient must change until the associated decision variable has a non-zero solution.

Next, we consider the `Constraints` table. Here, the shadow price indicates the change in the optimal value of the objective function when the right-hand side of a constraint changes by *one unit*. Consider the wood constraint. Suppose we increase the amount of wood available by 1 kg, such that now 5,001 kg are available (*ceteris paribus*). Solving, we now get:

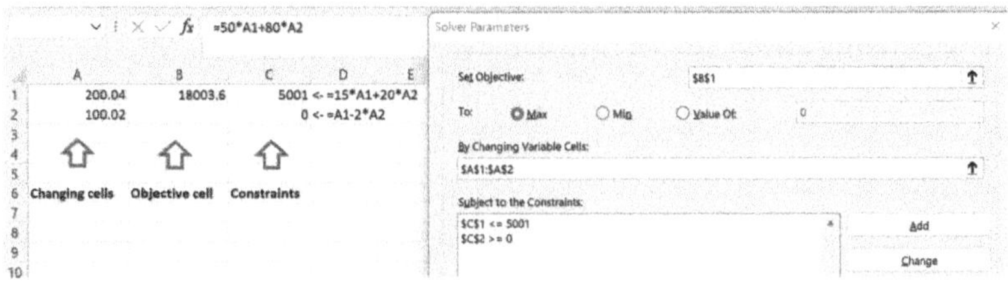

and we see that the optimal solution has changed to $x = 200.04$ and $y = 100.02$, with the maximum profit having increased by the reduced cost of 3.6 to £18,003.60. Admittedly, in practice we cannot produce non-integer quantities of either type of chair, but if instead quantities had been expressed in terms of thousands of units, then it would be meaningful: 200,040 standard chairs and 100,020 deluxe chairs, with a much healthier profit of £18,003,600!

While £18,003.60 is greater than the previous solution of £18,000, to achieve this we required an additional kilogram of wood (note that the original wood constraint was binding, with no slack). Understandably, with more wood available, we could produce more chairs, but wood is not free. So, should the manufacturer buy an additional kilogram of wood to achieve an extra £3.60 in profit? Well, James, it depends...on the cost of wood!

Whenever a resource constraint is binding in the optimal solution, the shadow price has an important interpretation as the *maximum willingness to pay* for an additional unit of a resource, such as wood here.

If the price of wood was:

- *less than* £3.60 per kilogram, then the manufacturer would *definitely wish to purchase* it as its cost is less than the benefit in terms of extra profit
- *equal to* £3.60 per kilogram, then the manufacturer would be *indifferent about purchasing* it as its cost would exactly offset the benefit in terms of extra profit
- *more than* £3.60 per kilogram, then the manufacturer would *definitely not wish to purchase* it as its cost is more than the benefit in terms of extra profit – the wood is too expensive.

Shadow prices are non-zero when a constraint is binding, that is, when the final value equals the constraint's right-hand side, meaning there is no slack. When a constraint is non-binding in an optimal solution, then there is slack so the shadow price would be zero, since we would not be prepared to pay any amount for an additional unit of a resource if we already have some spare resource available – we would choose to exhaust the slack first before contemplating paying for any additional resource units.

We also see that there are allowable increases and decreases shown in the `Constraints` table. These have a different interpretation than those applied to the objective coefficients. In the context of the constraints, the allowable increases and decreases inform us by how much the right-hand side of the respective constraint can be changed *until* the binding constraints change.

19.5 CONJOINT ANALYSIS

Having introduced Solver, we now look to apply it in a special marketing context, known as conjoint analysis. This statistical technique models a product as a *bundle* of different characteristics. Conjoint analysis can be used to ascertain the *relative importance* attached by consumers to these different characteristics such that the contribution of each to the consumer's overall satisfaction, or preference rating, is quantifiable. Rank orders of the characteristics can then be determined for different demographic segments, allowing marketing communications to be tailored for maximum impact by emphasising the principal benefits of a product that would be expected to appeal most to a specific consumer. After all, to whet consumers' appetites and persuade them to part with their money, it is advisable to raise their awareness of the features that appeal most to them, rather than what appeals least to them!

Conjoint analysis works by treating each characteristic as a categorical, or qualitative, variable, with different *levels* (such that there are at least two levels for each variable characteristic).

Example 19.2

Mobile phones can be thought of as a bundle of characteristics, such as:

- brand (Apple, Huawei, Samsung, Sony, etc.)
- price (in whatever currency)
- model year (year of production)
- mobile operating system (Android, iOS, Linux, Windows)
- cellular technology (3G, 4G and 5G)
- camera resolution (various megapixel (MP) specifications)
- internal memory (various GB limits)
- condition (new, refurbished, used).

This is not necessarily a collectively exhaustive list of characteristics, nonetheless different consumers would be expected to value some of these more than others. Price-conscious consumers would place more weight on price (and possibly condition), whereas social media influencers may place a premium on the camera resolution.

19.5.1 Data collection

To conduct conjoint analysis we have to survey consumers and record their preference *ratings*, not rankings, of products with different combinations of levels of the various characteristics. Why ratings, not rankings? Well, conjoint analysis employs linear regression, such that the preference values will be the dependent variable, which needs to be measurable (achieved with ratings), not categorical (which would result from rankings).

How many preference ratings are required? Ideally, we would like each respondent to evaluate every possible combination of characteristic levels. However, for large numbers of different specifications this could be very time-consuming and we would likely encounter a degree of non-response or refusal of a respondent to complete an entire set of preference ratings.

Suppose a product is modelled as a bundle of n characteristics. Let the ith characteristic, for $i = 1, 2, \ldots, n$, have c_i different levels. The total number of combinations of different levels is

$$\prod_{i=1}^{n} c_i = c_1 \times c_2 \times \cdots \times c_n$$

which can quickly result in a (very!) large number of total combinations due to the multiplication (indicated by the product operator, $\prod$).

Example 19.3

Consider the $n = 8$ characteristics of mobile phones listed in Example 19.2. We have:

- $i = 1$: brand, with $c_1 = 4$ (assuming only the brands Apple, Huawei, Samsung and Sony)
- $i = 2$: price, with $c_2 = 3$ (assuming 'low price', 'medium price' and 'high price')
- $i = 3$: model year, with $c_3 = 6$ (assuming 2018, 2019, 2020, 2021, 2022, 2023)
- $i = 4$: mobile operating system, with $c_4 = 4$ (Android, iOS, Linux, Windows)
- $i = 5$: cellular technology, with $c_5 = 3$ (3G, 4G and 5G)
- $i = 6$: camera resolution, with $c_6 = 4$ (assuming '< 5 MP', '5-9.9 MP', '10-20 MP', '> 20 MP')
- $i = 7$: internal memory, with $c_7 = 8$ (assuming < 4 GB, 4 GB, 8 GB, 16 GB, 32 GB, 64 GB, 128 GB, ≥ 256 GB)
- $i = 8$: condition, with $c_8 = 3$ (new, refurbished, used).

In total there are:

$$\prod_{i=1}^{8} c_i = 4 \times 3 \times 6 \times 4 \times 3 \times 4 \times 8 \times 3 = 82,944$$

different combinations! Clearly, far too many for a single respondent to evaluate.

In practice, we would like as many preference ratings as possible, without risking respondent fatigue and drop-out. Division of labour is possible if we could identify different consumer segments and ensure as many different bundles of characteristics were rated as possible by people within a given segment. The idea being that those within the same segment should have homogeneous (i.e. similar) tastes and preferences.

Conjoint analysis model

Using the double summation operator introduced in Section 11.2.2, the model may be expressed as

$$\text{preference rating of } X = \sum_{i=1}^{n} \sum_{j=1}^{c_i} \alpha_{ij} x_{ij}$$

where

- X is a specific bundle of characteristics
- α_{ij} is the **part-worth contribution** towards the preference rating due to the jth level (for $j = 1, 2, \ldots, c_i$) of the ith characteristic (for $i = 1, 2, \ldots, n$)
- $x_{ij} = 1$ if the jth level of the ith characteristic is present, and 0 otherwise
- c_i is the number of levels of the ith characteristic
- n is the number of product characteristics.

(Continued)

The *importance* of the *i*th characteristic, denoted by I_i, is defined in terms of the *range* of the part-worth contributions, α_{ij}, across the levels of the *i*th characteristic, such that

$$I_i = \max(\alpha_{ij}) - \min(\alpha_{ij})$$

for $i = 1, 2, ..., n$. The *relative* importance of the *i*th characteristic is obtained by *normalising* I_i by calculating its **importance weighting**, W_i, such that

$$W_i = \frac{I_i}{\sum_{i=1}^{n} I_i}, \quad \text{where} \sum_{i=1}^{n} W_i = 1.$$

Note that the part-worths, α_{ij}, represent the part of the total preference rating associated with the *j*th level of the *i*th characteristic. The overall preference rating is simply the *sum* of the contributions from each level. For each α_{ij} we have the following possibilities:

- $\alpha_{ij} > 0$ when the *j*th level of the *i*th characteristic is considered *favourably* by the consumer, that is, having a positive effect on the preference rating. The more favourable, the more (positive) the value of α_{ij}.
- $\alpha_{ij} = 0$ when the consumer is *indifferent* to the *j*th level of the *i*th characteristic, that is, it has no effect on the preference rating.
- $\alpha_{ij} < 0$ when the *j*th level of the *i*th characteristic is considered *unfavourably* by the consumer, that is, having a negative effect on the preference rating. The less favourable, the more (negative) the value of α_{ij}.

The more important a characteristic is to a consumer, the more sensitive the consumer is to the specific level of that characteristic, since I_i increases in the range of the part-worths, by definition. Hence the larger the difference between the maximum and minimum α_{ij} for a characteristic, the larger the value of its importance, I_i. In turn, the greater I_i is relative to the other importance values, this will result in a greater importance weighting, W_i.

While we will continue to use preference rating of a product bundle, conjoint analysis would work perfectly well with other potential dependent variables, such as *intention to purchase* (the more desirable a particular characteristic is, the greater the intention to purchase would be).

Example 19.3 demonstrated how the total number of different combinations can escalate very quickly due to multiplication. So, to illustrate conjoint analysis we will keep things manageable by focusing on just three characteristics (i.e. we set $n = 3$). Is this oversimplification? Well, let's suppose we had previously undertaken market research that suggested the top three characteristics which seemed to matter to a specific segment of consumers. Perhaps these were frequently mentioned in a focus group, say.

Example 19.4

Focus group studies of a consumer segment (based on sociodemographic attributes such as age and income group) suggested that the top three characteristics of a mobile phone which mattered to them were price, cellular technology and condition. We define the following:

- price is the first characteristic, $i = 1$, with levels
  - $j = 1$: 'low price'
  - $j = 2$: 'medium price'
  - $j = 3$: 'high price',

hence $c_1 = 3$

- cellular technology is the second characteristic, $i = 2$, with levels
  - $j = 1$: 3G
  - $j = 2$: 4G
  - $j = 3$: 5G,

hence $c_2 = 3$

- condition is the third characteristic, $i = 3$, with levels
  - $j = 1$: new
  - $j = 2$: refurbished
  - $j = 3$: used,

hence $c_3 = 3$.

We model preference ratings as

$$\text{preference rating of } X = \sum_{i=1}^{3}\sum_{j=1}^{c_i} \alpha_{ij}x_{ij}$$

$$\begin{aligned} &= \alpha_{11}x_{11} + \alpha_{12}x_{12} + \alpha_{13}x_{13} && \text{(price contribution, } i = 1\text{)} \\ &\quad + \alpha_{21}x_{21} + \alpha_{22}x_{22} + \alpha_{23}x_{23} && \text{(cellular technology contribution, } i = 2\text{)} \\ &\quad + \alpha_{31}x_{31} + \alpha_{32}x_{32} + \alpha_{33}x_{33} && \text{(condition contribution, } i = 3\text{)} \end{aligned}$$

where we have expanded the double summation operator. This shows how the total preference rating of X is an aggregate of contributions from each of the three characteristics - a price contribution, a cellular technology contribution and a condition contribution.

To see this, recall that $x_{ij} = 1$ if the jth level of the ith characteristic is present, and 0 otherwise. So, for a given X, for the ith characteristic only one of x_{1i}, x_{2i}, and x_{3i} will be 1, with the other two being 0.

For example, a high-price, 4G, new phone will have:

- $x_{11} = 0$ (because it *is not* low price)
- $x_{12} = 0$ (because it *is not* medium price)
- $x_{13} = 1$ (because it *is* high price)
- $x_{21} = 0$ (because it *is not* 3G)
- $x_{22} = 1$ (because it *is* 4G)
- $x_{23} = 0$ (because it *is not* 5G)
- $x_{31} = 1$ (because it *is* new)

(Continued)

- $x_{32} = 0$ (because it *is not* refurbished)
- $x_{33} = 0$ (because it *is not* used)

and so, substituting, we have

$$\text{preference rating of } X = \sum_{i=1}^{3}\sum_{j=1}^{c_i} \alpha_{ij} x_{ij}$$

$$\begin{aligned} &= \alpha_{11} \times 0 + \alpha_{12} \times 0 + \alpha_{13} \times 1 && \text{(price contribution, } i = 1\text{)} \\ &\quad + \alpha_{21} \times 0 + \alpha_{22} \times 1 + \alpha_{23} \times 0 && \text{(cellular technology contribution, } i = 2\text{)} \\ &\quad + \alpha_{31} \times 1 + \alpha_{32} \times 0 + \alpha_{33} \times 0 && \text{(condition contribution, } i = 3\text{)} \\ &= \alpha_{13} + \alpha_{22} + \alpha_{31}. \end{aligned}$$

So, we can see that the preference rating for X, where X is a high-price, 4G, new phone simplifies to the sum of α_{13} (the preference for a high price), α_{22} (the preference for 4G), and α_{31} (the preference for new).

Similarly, we can deduce that

$$\text{preference rating of } X = \alpha_{12} + \alpha_{21} + \alpha_{33}$$

would refer to a medium-price, 3G, used mobile phone, while:

$$\text{preference rating of } X = \alpha_{11} + \alpha_{23} + \alpha_{32}$$

would refer to a low-price, 5G, refurbished mobile phone - admittedly this may not be a readily available combination in practice, but it would likely have a high preference rating!

So far, so good. But what on earth are the *values* of the parameters $\alpha_{11}, \alpha_{12}, \ldots, \alpha_{33}$?! An excellent question. Answer: we need to *estimate* them based on preference rating data! We will actually need to undertake a two-stage process combining linear regression and Solver.

The linear regression stage will make use of dummy variables (introduced in Chapter 14). For each characteristic one of the levels needs to be designated as the *reference category*. The reference category could be *any* of the c_i categories. Without loss of generality (since we could use any reference category), we will use the *first* level in each case as the reference category.

Example 19.5

Extending Example 19.4, we need to define three pairs of dummy variables. 'Three' because there are three characteristics, and 'pairs' since each characteristic has three levels, with one (the first) used as the reference category, leaving each of the other two requiring a dummy variable.

More generally, when the ith characteristic has c_i levels, it is coded in terms of $c_i - 1$ dummy variables to avoid the 'dummy-variable trap', as discussed in Chapter 14.

We define:

- X_1, X_2 = the dummy variables representing price
- X_3, X_4 = the dummy variables representing cellular technology
- X_5, X_6 = the dummy variables representing condition.

Using the first level as the reference category in each case, the dummy variable codes are therefore:

	Price dummies		Cellular technology dummies		Condition dummies	
	X_1	X_2	X_3	X_4	X_5	X_6
Level 1 (reference category)	0	0	0	0	0	0
Level 2	1	0	1	0	1	0
Level 3	0	1	0	1	0	1
Interpretation of '1'	medium price	high price	4G	5G	refurbished	used

Dummy-variable regression

The **dummy variable regression** model is

$$\text{preference rating of } X = \beta_0 + \sum_{i=1}^{k} \beta_i X_i + \varepsilon,$$

where k is the total number of required dummy variables, given by

$$k = \sum_{i=1}^{n} (c_i - 1).$$

Example 19.6

Extending Example 19.5, we have six dummy variables, $X_1, X_2, \ldots, X_6$, because

$$k = \sum_{i=1}^{3} (c_i - 1) = (c_1 - 1) + (c_2 - 1) + (c_3 - 1) = (3-1) + (3-1) + (3-1) = 6$$

so the regression model is

$$\text{preference rating of } X = \beta_0 + \beta_1 X_1 + \beta_2 X_2 + \beta_3 X_3 + \beta_4 X_4 + \beta_5 X_5 + \beta_6 X_6 + \varepsilon$$

and the corresponding *estimated model* would be

$$\widehat{\text{preference rating}} \text{ of } X = \hat{\beta}_0 + \hat{\beta}_1 X_1 + \hat{\beta}_2 X_2 + \hat{\beta}_3 X_3 + \hat{\beta}_4 X_4 + \hat{\beta}_5 X_5 + \hat{\beta}_6 X_6.$$

In order to estimate the β_i coefficients in the dummy-variable regression model, we will need preference rating data from at least one respondent. This would involve asking the respondent to evaluate their preference ratings for different bundle combinations. When there are many characteristics with a (very) large number of combinations, such as in Example 19.3, then we would definitely need a large number of respondents (from the same consumer segment) to have an adequate number of combinations evaluated. For example, 100 respondents each evaluating 20 different combinations would produce 2000 preference ratings. We would be satisfied with that!

Example 19.7

Extending Example 19.6, since there are only 3 × 3 × 3 = 27 possible combinations (three characteristics, each with three levels), it will suffice to have one respondent evaluating all 27 possibilities.

Suppose their responses (rating mobile phones on a 0–100 scale) were as follows:

	Characteristic			
Mobile phone no.	Price	Cellular technology	Condition	Preference rating
1	Low	3G	New	81
2	Low	3G	Refurbished	73
3	Low	3G	Used	65
4	Low	4G	New	86
5	Low	4G	Refurbished	77
6	Low	4G	Used	71
7	Low	5G	New	98
8	Low	5G	Refurbished	92
9	Low	5G	Used	86
10	Medium	3G	New	76
11	Medium	3G	Refurbished	66
12	Medium	3G	Used	55
13	Medium	4G	New	77
14	Medium	4G	Refurbished	63
15	Medium	4G	Used	50
16	Medium	5G	New	83
17	Medium	5G	Refurbished	71
18	Medium	5G	Used	61
19	High	3G	New	62
20	High	3G	Refurbished	47
21	High	3G	Used	35
22	High	4G	New	68
23	High	4G	Refurbished	55

		Characteristic		
Mobile phone no.	Price	Cellular technology	Condition	Preference rating
24	High	4G	Used	40
25	High	5G	New	69
26	High	5G	Refurbished	57
27	High	5G	Used	46

We can see that this respondent (unsurprisingly) has the greatest preference for a low-price, 5G, new phone (no. 7), and the least preference for a high-price, 3G, used phone (no. 21).

There is clearly significant *variation* in preference ratings, suggesting conjoint analysis will be worthwhile to determine the relative importance of different characteristics, and how each level affects this particular consumer's preference ratings.

We proceed to convert the preference rating data into *dummy-variable form*, which will allow us to estimate the dummy-variable regression. Applying the dummy variables defined in Example 19.5, we have

			Dummy variables				
Mobile phone no.	X_1	X_2	X_3	X_4	X_5	X_6	Preference rating
1	0	0	0	0	0	0	81
2	0	0	0	0	1	0	73
3	0	0	0	0	0	1	65
4	0	0	1	0	0	0	86
5	0	0	1	0	1	0	77
6	0	0	1	0	0	1	71
7	0	0	0	1	0	0	98
8	0	0	0	1	1	0	92
9	0	0	0	1	0	1	86
10	1	0	0	0	0	0	76
11	1	0	0	0	1	0	66
12	1	0	0	0	0	1	55
13	1	0	1	0	0	0	77
14	1	0	1	0	1	0	63
15	1	0	1	0	0	1	50
16	1	0	0	1	0	0	83
17	1	0	0	1	1	0	71
18	1	0	0	1	0	1	61
19	0	1	0	0	0	0	62

(Continued)

Mobile phone no.	Dummy variables X_1	X_2	X_3	X_4	X_5	X_6	Preference rating
20	0	1	0	0	1	0	47
21	0	1	0	0	0	1	35
22	0	1	1	0	0	0	68
23	0	1	1	0	1	0	55
24	0	1	1	0	0	1	40
25	0	1	0	1	0	0	69
26	0	1	0	1	1	0	57
27	0	1	0	1	0	1	46

We then run the dummy-variable regression. Don't be put off by the name, this is simply a multiple linear regression where all of the independent variables are dummy variables. Running the regression in Excel returns the following results:

	A	B	C	D	E	F	G
1	SUMMARY OUTPUT						
2							
3	*Regression Statistics*						
4	Multiple R	0.973916445					
5	R Square	0.948513241					
6	Adjusted R Square	0.933067213					
7	Standard Error	4.080214228					
8	Observations	27					
9							
10	ANOVA						
11		*df*	*SS*	*MS*	*F*	*Significance F*	
12	Regression	6	6134	1022.333333	61.40823137	7.85002E-12	
13	Residual	20	332.962963	16.64814815			
14	Total	26	6466.962963				
15							
16		*Coefficients*	*Standard Error*	*t Stat*	*P-value*	*Lower 95%*	*Upper 95%*
17	Intercept	86.92592593	2.077543395	41.84072696	5.98717E-21	82.59224634	91.25960551
18	x1	-14.11111111	1.923431433	-7.336425343	4.32425E-07	-18.12331877	-10.09890345
19	x2	-27.77777778	1.923431433	-14.44178217	4.83292E-12	-31.78998544	-23.76557012
20	x3	3	1.923431433	1.559712475	0.134512241	-1.012207663	7.012207663
21	x4	11.44444444	1.923431433	5.950014255	8.08485E-06	7.432236782	15.45665211
22	x5	-11	1.923431433	-5.71894574	1.34863E-05	-15.01220766	-6.987792337
23	x6	-21.22222222	1.923431433	-11.03352158	5.9055E-10	-25.23442988	-17.21001456

where the estimated β_i values are highlighted. Hence the estimated regression model is

$$\widehat{\text{preference rating}} \text{ of } X = 86.926 - 14.111X_1 - 27.778X_2 + 3.000X_3 + 11.444X_4 - 11.000X_5 - 21.222X_6$$

since

$$\hat{\beta}_0 = 86.926,\ \hat{\beta}_1 = -14.111,\ \hat{\beta}_2 = -27.778,\ \hat{\beta}_3 = 3.000,\ \hat{\beta}_4 = 11.444,\ \hat{\beta}_5 = -11.000,\ \hat{\beta}_6 = -21.222,$$

reporting the estimated coefficients to three decimal places. In passing, we see that $R^2 = 0.9485$, that is, an impressive 94.85% of the variation in the preference ratings for this respondent can be explained by the model. Examining the *p*-values (in column E), we note that all the dummy variables are *(highly) statistically significant*, with the exception of β_3, but I think we can 'excuse' that minor imperfection.

Ultimately, our objective is to estimate the part-worths (the α_{ij}), which are *not* the same as the estimated β_i in the dummy-variable regression. However, we can leverage the latter to recover estimates of the former. To achieve this, recall the interpretation of the coefficient of a dummy variable (Chapter 14) – it represents the expected difference in the dependent variable between the level associated with the '1' of the dummy variable and the reference category.

Therefore, due to the dummy-variable coding used, where the first level has been used as the reference category, we can now relate the estimated regression coefficients to the estimated part-worths.

Example 19.8

Extending Example 19.7, for the price characteristic we have

$$\hat{\alpha}_{12} - \hat{\alpha}_{11} = \hat{\beta}_1 \Rightarrow \hat{\alpha}_{12} - \hat{\alpha}_{11} = -14.111 \quad (19.1)$$

and

$$\hat{\alpha}_{13} - \hat{\alpha}_{11} = \hat{\beta}_2 \Rightarrow \hat{\alpha}_{13} - \hat{\alpha}_{11} = -27.778. \quad (19.2)$$

However, as things stand, we are unable to solve for *three* unknowns ($\hat{\alpha}_{11}, \hat{\alpha}_{12}$ and $\hat{\alpha}_{13}$) using only *two* equations. So we need to 'engineer' a third equation by imposing the *constraint*

$$\hat{\alpha}_{11} + \hat{\alpha}_{12} + \hat{\alpha}_{13} = 0. \quad (19.3)$$

Equations (19.1)-(19.3) can be solved simultaneously to obtain the part-worth estimates $\hat{\alpha}_{11}, \hat{\alpha}_{12}$ and $\hat{\alpha}_{13}$. Hence we have a *constrained optimisation* set-up.

Similarly, for the cellular technology characteristic we have

$$\hat{\alpha}_{22} + \hat{\alpha}_{21} = \hat{\beta}_3 \Rightarrow \hat{\alpha}_{22} + \hat{\alpha}_{21} = 3.000 \quad (19.4)$$

and

$$\hat{\alpha}_{23} + \hat{\alpha}_{21} = \hat{\beta}_4 \Rightarrow \hat{\alpha}_{23} + \hat{\alpha}_{21} = 11.444, \quad (19.5)$$

and we impose the constraint

$$\hat{\alpha}_{21} + \hat{\alpha}_{22} + \hat{\alpha}_{23} = 0. \quad (19.6)$$

(Continued)

Equations (19.4)-(19.6) can be solved simultaneously to obtain the part-worth estimates $\hat{\alpha}_{21}, \hat{\alpha}_{22}$ and $\hat{\alpha}_{23}$.

Likewise, for the condition characteristic we have

$$\hat{\alpha}_{32} + \hat{\alpha}_{31} = \hat{\beta}_5 \Rightarrow \hat{\alpha}_{32} + \hat{\alpha}_{31} = -11.000 \quad (19.7)$$

and

$$\hat{\alpha}_{33} + \hat{\alpha}_{31} = \hat{\beta}_6 \Rightarrow \hat{\alpha}_{33} + \hat{\alpha}_{31} = -21.222, \quad (19.8)$$

and we impose the constraint

$$\hat{\alpha}_{31} + \hat{\alpha}_{32} + \hat{\alpha}_{33} = 0. \quad (19.9)$$

Equations (19.7)-(19.9) can be solved simultaneously to obtain the part-worth estimates $\hat{\alpha}_{31}, \hat{\alpha}_{32}$ and $\hat{\alpha}_{33}$.

These three three-equation systems can be solved simultaneously using Solver as follows:

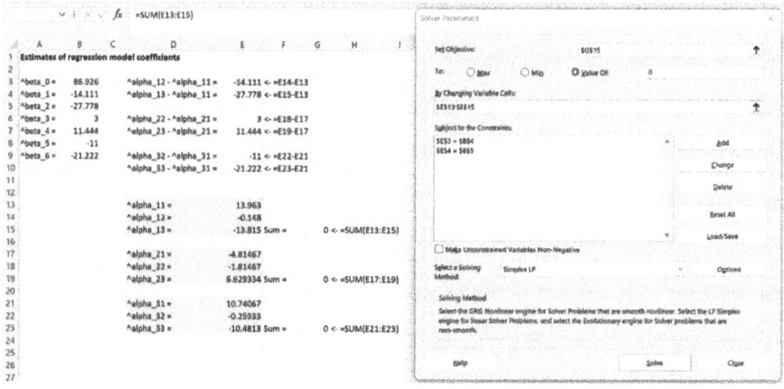

from which we have (values highlighted)

$$\hat{\alpha}_{11} = 13.963, \quad \hat{\alpha}_{12} = -0.148, \quad \hat{\alpha}_{13} = -13.815$$

for the estimated part-worths of the price characteristic. Note how Solver has been used. The left-hand side of the third constraint (19.3) has been used as the objective function, such that cell `G15` has been set as the objective cell and the solution forces this to take the value 0 (i.e. the right-hand side). Solver is then free to change the values in cells `E13:E15` which have been designated as the decision variable cells, that is, the values of $\hat{\alpha}_{11}, \hat{\alpha}_{12}$ and $\hat{\alpha}_{13}$, respectively. Equations (19.1) and (19.2) then form the two constraints of the problem, as specified in the `Subject to the Constraints` box.

Similarly, we can employ Solver to obtain

$$\hat{\alpha}_{21} = -4.815, \quad \hat{\alpha}_{22} = -1.815, \quad \hat{\alpha}_{23} = -6.629$$

for the estimated part-worths of the cellular technology characteristic. Likewise,

$$\hat{\alpha}_{31} = 10.741, \quad \hat{\alpha}_{32} = -0.259, \quad \hat{\alpha}_{33} = -10.481$$

for the estimated part-worths of the condition characteristic.

At this point, let us think about the appeal of the third equation constraints, that is, equations (19.3), (19.6) and (19.9). By forcing the part-worths for the *i*th characteristic to sum to *zero*, either *all* of the part-worths are zero (indicating the characteristic has no effect on a consumer's preference rating, regardless of level), or *at least one* part-worth is positive (indicating the characteristic's level has a positive effect on a consumer's preference rating) and *at least one* part-worth is negative (indicating the characteristic's level has a negative effect on a consumer's preference rating), as at least one negative value is required to offset at least one positive value in order for the part-worths to sum to zero.

Example 19.9

Extending Example 19.8, for the price characteristic, we have:

$$\hat{\alpha}_{11} = 13.963, \quad \hat{\alpha}_{12} = -0.148, \quad \hat{\alpha}_{13} = -13.815.$$

Since $\hat{\alpha}_{11} > 0$, the low price level is positively rated by this consumer. $\hat{\alpha}_{12} \approx 0$, so the medium price level is viewed with near indifference, while $\hat{\alpha}_{13} < 0$, so the high price level is negatively rated. Overall this seems reasonable - customers generally prefer low prices to high prices!

For the cellular technology characteristic, we have

$$\hat{\alpha}_{21} = -4.815, \quad \hat{\alpha}_{22} = -1.815, \quad \hat{\alpha}_{23} = 6.629.$$

Since $\hat{\alpha}_{23} > 0$, 5G is positively rated by this consumer. $\hat{\alpha}_{21} < \hat{\alpha}_{22} < 0$, so 3G and 4G are viewed negatively, with 3G being the least preferred. Overall this seems reasonable - customers generally prefer the latest technology!

For the condition characteristic, we have

$$\hat{\alpha}_{31} = 10.741, \quad \hat{\alpha}_{32} = -0.259, \quad \hat{\alpha}_{33} = -10.481.$$

Since $\hat{\alpha}_{31} > 0$, new mobile phones are positively rated by this consumer. $\hat{\alpha}_{32} \approx 0$, so refurbished mobile phones are viewed with near indifference, while $\hat{\alpha}_{33} < 0$, so used mobile phones are negatively rated. Overall this seems reasonable - customers generally prefer new things rather than second-hand!

The *relative magnitudes* of the part-worth estimates then allow us to determine the importance of each characteristic, and in turn the relative importance weightings. We now compute these for the mobile phone example.

Example 19.10

Extending Example 19.9, the importance values are computed as the range of the part-worths for each characteristic.

For the price characteristic (beware the double negatives!),

$$I_1 = \max(\alpha_{1j}) - \min(\alpha_{1j}) = \hat{\alpha}_{11} - \hat{\alpha}_{13} = 13.963 - (-13.815) = 27.778.$$

For the cellular technology characteristic,

$$I_2 = \max(\alpha_{2j}) - \min(\alpha_{2j}) = \hat{\alpha}_{23} - \hat{\alpha}_{21} = 6.629 - (-4.815) = 11.444.$$

For the condition characteristic,

$$I_3 = \max(\alpha_{3j}) - \min(\alpha_{3j}) = \hat{\alpha}_{31} - \hat{\alpha}_{33} = 10.741 - (-10.481) = 21.222.$$

Since

$$\sum_{i=1}^{3} I_i = 27.778 + 11.444 + 21.222 = 60.444,$$

we can now normalise the I_i to derive the *relative importance weightings*. For price,

$$W_1 = \frac{I_1}{\sum_{i=1}^{3} I_i} = \frac{27.778}{60.444} = 0.460.$$

For cellular technology,

$$W_2 = \frac{I_2}{\sum_{i=1}^{3} I_i} = \frac{11.444}{60.444} = 0.189.$$

For condition,

$$W_3 = \frac{I_3}{\sum_{i=1}^{3} I_i} = \frac{21.222}{60.444} = 0.351.$$

So, this consumer cares most about the price of a mobile phone, with 46.0% importance, followed by the condition, with 35.1% importance, and finally the cellular technology, with 18.9% importance.

What bundle of characteristics would make this consumer euphoric? Well, noting the estimated part-worths, this is easy: a low price, 5G, new phone would be their preferred bundle. This would give them the *best* of all three worlds!

Suppose an advertisement is to be developed - perhaps a 20-second television commercial aired at a time likely to be seen by the consumer segment represented by the respondent who provided the preference rating data. What should the key message be? With only 20 seconds of airtime to play with, it would not be possible to discuss more than, say, two characteristics. Based on these importance weightings, emphasising the price (assuming it's a low price!) and condition (assuming the phones are new!) would be the optimal messaging content, with reference to cellular technology relegated from the messaging altogether as this seems not to matter much to this type of consumer.

19.6 CHAPTER OVERVIEW

This chapter has introduced constrained optimisation models whereby a specific objective is sought, such as maximising or minimising the objective, subject to real-world imposed constraints. Microsoft Excel Solver is a useful add-in to provide numerical solutions to such problems, once the correct spreadsheet model has been created. We have seen how to perform a sensitivity analysis, which enables us to see how sensitive the optimal solution is to a change in circumstance(s), such as a model parameter. It also allows us to determine our maximum willingness to pay for additional units of input resources. Finally, we demonstrated how constrained optimisation could be applied in the field of conjoint analysis – quantifying the relative importance different consumer segments attach to product characteristics.

19.7 KEY VOCABULARY

Algebraic model
Allowable increase/decrease
Changing cells
Conjoint analysis
Constraint
Decision variables
Dummy variables
Dummy-variable regression
Feasible set
Feasible solution
Importance weighting
Infeasible solution
Linear programming
Non-negativity
Objective cell
Objective function
Optimal solution
Part-worth contribution
Reduced cost
Sensitivity analysis
Shadow price
Solver

19.8 EXERCISES

19.8.1 Test your understanding

1 What are the three types of optimisation problems? Provide a real-world example of each.
2 Explain the role each of the following has in an optimisation model:

(a) decision variables
(b) objective function
(c) constraints.

3 Following on from Question 2, what terminology does Excel use when working with optimisation models?
4 What is the difference between a feasible solution and a feasible set?
5 In what sense is the 'optimal solution' to a constrained optimisation problem optimal?
6 For a product mix model involving two products, say X and Y:

(a) what are the decision variables?
(b) what is the objective function?
(c) what sorts of constraints could feature?

Note you may assume any parameter values you wish.

7 What is meant by a 'binding solution'?

8 Explain the purpose of Solver.
9 In a sensitivity analysis report, what do the following terms mean?

   (a) Allowable increase.
   (b) Allowable decrease.
   (c) Reduced cost.
   (d) Shadow price.

10 What is the purpose of conjoint analysis?
11 If a product has $n = 10$ characteristics, each with four levels, what is the total number of combinations of different levels?
12 The conjoint analysis model is

$$\text{preference rating of } X = \sum_{i=1}^{n}\sum_{j=1}^{c_i} \alpha_{ij} x_{ij}.$$

Define all terms in this model.

13 How is the importance of a characteristic defined, and how can importance weightings for each characteristic be derived from the importance values?
14 For a conjoint analysis with $n = 2$ characteristics each with four levels, determine a full set of dummy-variable codes which could be employed to run a dummy-variable regression.
15 For a conjoint analysis with $n = 5$ characteristics, each with three levels, what is the total number of dummy variables required to run the dummy-variable regression?
16 For a conjoint analysis with $n = 3$ characteristics, each with three levels, write down the full set of equations which would need to be solved in order to estimate all part-worths.
17 A profit-maximising manufacturer is deciding on its optimal product mix between two types of table: light tables (x) and heavy tables (y). Each table is made exclusively from (sustainably sourced) wood, with no additional factor inputs. A light table is made using 30 kg of wood, while a heavy table is made from 40 kg of wood. The manufacturer has 8000 kg of wood available for production.

Light tables generate a profit of £60 each, while heavy tables generate a profit of £100 each. Given estimates about product demand from consumers, the number of light tables should be at least double the number of heavy tables.

   (a) Formulate the manufacturer's decision as a linear programming problem, explaining the purpose of each equation.
   (b) Solve this linear programming problem graphically and by solving a pair of simultaneous equations, making sure you clearly indicate the set of feasible production bundles on your graph.
   (c) Briefly discuss any recommendation(s) that you would make to this table manufacturer so that it could increase profits beyond the amount you calculated in part (b).

18 Consider Example 19.7. For all 27 mobile phone combinations, record your personal preference ratings for each (on a 0–100 scale), and then run a full conjoint analysis to establish the relative importance of each characteristic for you. Are the results consistent with your own opinion about these characteristics?

19.8.2 Practice with Excel

Head over to the companion website for Excel examples and screencasts!

20

MONTE CARLO SIMULATION

Chapter contents

Chapter level: ***Advanced***

Source: Photo by WikiImages via Pixabay.

Key concepts

- Expected outcome and risk
- Random number generation
- Quantile function

Chapter value

Simulation models offer a safe space for experimentation to judge what is likely to happen in practice.

Key takeaway

Monte Carlo simulation does not tell you what to do, rather by quantifying risk you can make a risk-informed decision.

Chapter outline

Universe or multiverse? One world or many worlds? Cosmologists may argue over such matters, but on this planet we live in one present, with one past, but with one *unknown* future. Decisions taken in the present will affect the future, but the precise outcomes cannot be known with certainty today. *Monte Carlo simulation* allows us to simulate many possible future worlds by modelling one or more random inputs - moving away from 'deterministic' models to 'stochastic' models.

Turnover, profits, investment returns and more can be simulated to produce a *distribution of outcomes* - a frequency distribution of the realised outcomes in each of many future possible worlds. Computing the mean of this distribution allows us to form an *expectation* of the outcome variable of interest, while the standard deviation quantifies the *risk* associated with the decision.

Monte Carlo simulation does *not* tell us what to do, rather it allows us to make an informed decision commensurate with our personal *risk appetite*. Risk-averse decision-makers may judge a project as being too risky to proceed with, while risk-lovers may relish the prospect of proceeding due to the adrenaline rush. Note, though, that an individual's risk tolerance may depend on the monetary amount at stake. Risking £1, no problem; risking £1 billion, less trivial!

Learning outcomes

After completing this chapter, you should be able to:

- explain the mechanics of simulation models
- use a pseudo-random number generator in Excel to perform simulations, including applications of some common probability distributions such as the normal and exponential
- discuss the distinction between a simulation and its analytical counterpart.

Motivational case: To launch, or not to launch?

Paraphernalia is a retailer of assorted products that it manufactures. To keep its product line fresh and desirable for consumers, it periodically introduces new product lines. However, any new product has uncertain revenues, uncertain costs, and hence uncertain profits.

The marketing team has conducted some market research into possible demand (and hence sales revenues) of a new product which it expects to be normally distributed each quarter. Costs are also uncertain, due to some raw materials being sourced from abroad, subject to a small risk of supply chain disruption and exchange rate fluctuations, such that an exponential distribution is assumed.

How should managment decide whether to launch the new product?

20.1 INTRODUCTION

A (good!) simulation model is designed to imitate a real-life system by representing the main features of reality, while ignoring unnecessary details (as per our definition of a 'model' in Chapter 1 – it seems we have come full circle). This allows us to experiment with different inputs and set-ups to see what *might* happen as a consequence. Simulation models may be physical (such as testing Formula One car aerodynamics in a wind tunnel) or housed within a computer (such as modelling GDP growth rates under different monetary policy decisions on interest rates). The key advantage of a simulation model is that it provides an *entire distribution of results* from simulating the system a large number of times, which is more useful than just a single result.

Monte Carlo or bust!

Monte Carlo simulation derives its name from the playground of the rich and famous. A ward of the Principality of Monaco, Monte Carlo is famed for its glitz, glamour and gambling. The *Casino de Monte-Carlo* is home to games of chance such as baccarat, craps and roulette - random outcomes separate the winners and losers. Random outcomes are central to the Monte Carlo simulation technique.

As simulations are not 'real', our simulated world provides a *safe space* for experimentation – a nightmare outcome encountered in a simulated world is better than in reality! Simulation models allow managers to answer what-if questions without actually changing (or building) a physical system. However, don't necessarily expect reality to always coincide with your simulation-driven expectations!

Gone with the wind?

Scuderia Ferrari is an iconic Formula One team. To win races, the 'prancing horse' needs a fast car and the right strategy. Aerodynamic efficiency helps with the former, albeit less so at the Monaco Grand Prix with the tight street circuit, passing the Casino de Monte-Carlo.

Unfortunately, for several seasons poor *calibration* of their wind tunnels meant that what were promising results from new experimental parts in the simulated environment of the wind tunnel often produced the opposite effects when the parts were introduced at circuits. Great expectations quickly morphed into on-track disappointment for the fabled *Tifosi*, and team sponsors!

When the simulated world deviates from the real world, nasty surprises can result. *Forza Ferrari*, but only with good calibration.

Every simulation model contains at least one *random* input: a random variable which is modelled using a suitable probability distribution. Each different set of values for the uncertain input quantities is called a scenario. Simulation models allow businesses to generate many scenarios, each leading to a particular outcome of interest, such as profit. This approach is illustrated in Figure 20.1.

Probability distributions for uncertain inputs

⇓

Simulation model

⇓

Probability distributions for important outputs

Figure 20.1 Flow diagram illustrating a Monte Carlo simulation.

Simulations are used in a variety of business settings. Simulation models can be employed to:

- investigate how *sensitive* a system is to changes in its operating conditions
- *improve* a system
- find a *robust* system design
- try out *different strategies* which otherwise in practice would be prohibitively expensive and/or risky.

Example 20.1

Suppose that from our research and development portfolio there are several products we could release, but we have to select just one due to the cap on our marketing budget. Which one should we choose? How much revenue will a new product generate? Which logistics will be best for our new supply chain?

Simulation can enable us to test different products to determine which is the best product to be released in the market. Of course, we would need to define what 'best' means, such as in terms of revenue generation or market penetration.

We would prefer a product which sells well under tough market conditions, such as during a recession or a cost-of-living crisis.

Example 20.2

Suppose we have to design a schedule of arrivals and departures for a new airport. What is the best schedule for the airport? Again, we would need to define what 'best' means, such as minimising the turnaround times of aircraft - airlines want their planes in the air, not sitting idle on the tarmac.

We would prefer an airport schedule which can deal with delays and disruptions, such as bad weather affecting itineraries.

In simulating systems, we make an abstraction of the real world. This means we need to represent a system's main features, conceptualising the system and building a model using a set of equations relating all variables and parameters together. This model is then implemented, such as in Excel, and validated. We may then run many simulations, which is our experimental stage. The insights derived from our simulation results can then be used to improve a system. This is graphically represented in Figure 20.2.

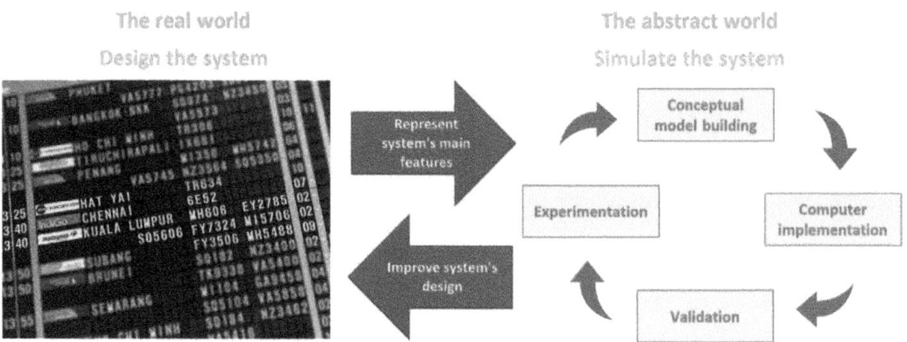

Figure 20.2 Linking the real world and the abstract world.

Source: Unsplash - flight board highlighting Hat Yai, Chennai, and Kuala Lumpur (Published on December 4, 2017).

Example 20.3

Consider an airline manufacturer which uses a wind tunnel to test new aircraft designs. When designing a system in the real world we seek to represent the system's main features in the abstract world. In this instance, building a 1:k scale model of an aircraft (for a suitable positive value of $k > 1$, where $k = 1$ is the full-scale, i.e. life-size version) should retain the aerodynamic features of the real aircraft, allowing different set-ups to be tested with the aim of optimising the aircraft (e.g. in t\erms of aerodynamic efficiency) such that after running simulations in the wind tunnel we can then improve the aircraft's design back in the real world.

20.1.1 Static versus dynamic simulation models

We can make a distinction between *static* and *dynamic* simulation models.

Static simulation models are stable, or stationary, in nature.

Example 20.4

Possible problems analysed with static simulation models include:

- development/launch of a new product to market (possible output variables of interest: market share, sales, revenues, costs)
- managing a large infrastructure project (possible output variables of interest: risks of delays and going over budget). Fun fact: hosting the Olympic Games is considered the most complex peacetime project in the world.
- building up an investment portfolio (possible output variables of interest: returns, risks)
- making a series of sequential decisions (possible output variables of interest: probabilities of scenarios, outcomes).

Dynamic simulation models can be thought of as having 'moving parts'.

Example 20.5

Possible problems analysed with dynamic simulation models include:

- scheduling a fleet of aircraft (possible output variables of interest: turnaround times, runway utilisation)
- planning the layout of supermarkets (possible output variables of interest: footfall flow, congestion, queue lengths)
- designing call centres (possible output variables of interest: service waiting times, staffing levels)
- positioning road tolls or speed cameras along motorways (possible output variables of interest: revenue collection, reduction of speeding).

20.2 BASICS OF SIMULATION

Suppose a company wants to analyse the following corporate investment in a project which involves an uncertain revenue and an uncertain cost. What is the *expected value* of profit and the *risk* that it generates a loss? Assume that the revenues and costs are statistically independent, and that the possible outcomes of these variables and their corresponding probabilities are:

Revenue (in £ millions)	Cost (in £ millions)
50 (with probability 0.2)	80 (with probability 0.2)
80 (with probability 0.4)	60 (with probability 0.6)
100 (with probability 0.4)	30 (with probability 0.2)

To conduct a Monte Carlo simulation, we proceed as follows.

1 Sample from a *random number generator* for each input variable.
2 Represent each possible input variable value to a range of (random) numbers according to the above probability distributions.
3 For each input variable generate a random number, then from the random number map it to the respective revenue/cost.
4 Calculate the outcome variable (which here will be profit = revenue – cost) and record it.
5 Repeat steps 3 and 4 until the desired number of simulations is reached.
6 Draw a histogram of the outcome variable values and compute the *mean* and *standard deviation*, which represent the expected outcome and risk of the outcome, respectively.

Suppose we conduct 20 simulations and obtain the following results:

Simulation no.	Revenue (in £m)	Cost (in £m)	Profit (in £m)	Simulation no.	Revenue (in £m)	Cost (in £m)	Profit (in £m)
1	50	60	–10	11	80	60	20
2	80	60	20	12	80	60	20
3	80	60	20	13	50	60	–10
4	80	60	20	14	80	60	20

Simulation no.	Revenue (in £m)	Cost (in £m)	Profit (in £m)	Simulation no.	Revenue (in £m)	Cost (in £m)	Profit (in £m)
5	80	30	50	15	80	60	20
6	80	80	0	16	50	80	-30
7	100	60	40	17	80	30	50
8	80	80	0	18	50	30	20
9	80	80	0	19	100	60	40
10	80	60	20	20	80	60	20

To estimate the expected value of profit, based on the 20 simulation results, we calculate the *average* profit obtained

$$\frac{-10+20+\cdots+20}{20}=16.5 \Rightarrow £16.5\text{m},$$

and the risk that the investment generates a loss is estimated to be the *percentage* of occurrences when a loss occurred in the 20 simulations. In this case three simulations (nos. 1, 13 and 16) resulted in a loss, hence we would estimate the probability of a loss to be

$$\frac{3}{20}=0.15 \text{ or } 15\%.$$

Here, the number of simulations refers to the *sample size* of the Monte Carlo simulation. Taking a *relative frequency* approach to probability (discussed in Section 4.5), we would expect sample proportions of particular events from n simulations to converge to their corresponding 'population' proportions (i.e. actual probabilities) as $n \to \infty$.

In this corporate investment example it is actually possible to derive the analytical solution for the expected profit, thanks to our simplifying assumption of statistically independent revenues and costs. Recall from Chapter 4 that if A and B are independent events, then the *joint probability* is given by

$$P(A \cap B) = P(A)\, P(B).$$

The theoretical distribution of profit can be derived as follows:

(Revenue, Cost) pair	Probability of (Revenue, Cost) pair	Resulting profit
(£50m, £80m)	0.2 × 0.2 = 0.04	−£30m
(£50m, £60m)	0.2 × 0.6 = 0.12	−£10m
(£50m, £30m)	0.2 × 0.2 = 0.04	£20m
(£80m, £80m)	0.4 × 0.2 = 0.08	£0m
(£80m, £60m)	0.4 × 0.6 = 0.24	£20m
(£80m, £30m)	0.4 × 0.2 = 0.08	£50m
(£100m, £80m)	0.4 × 0.2 = 0.08	£20m
(£100m, £60m)	0.4 × 0.6 = 0.24	£40m
(£100m, £30m)	0.4 × 0.2 = 0.08	£70m

So, we see that there are only seven *distinct* values for profit (three of the (Revenue, Cost) pairs result in the same profit of £20m). Note that two of these nine values are negative, indicating a loss. Therefore, we may write out this *discrete* probability distribution of profit as follows:

Profit	−£30m	−£10m	£0m	£20m	£40m	£50m	£70m
P(Profit)	0.04	0.12	0.08	0.36	0.24	0.08	0.08

We know that the expected value of a discrete random variable is simply a *probability-weighted average*. Therefore, the analytical solution for the expected profit is

$$E(\text{Profit}) = (-£30\text{m} \times 0.04) + (-£10\text{m} \times 0.12) + \cdots + (£70\text{m} \times 0.08) = £24\text{m}.$$

Remember, an expected value is not necessarily a possible outcome. Rather, expectations should be viewed as *long-run averages*. Clearly, £24m is not a member of the *sample space*: it is not a possible value of the profit variable in this setting. We would *never* realise a profit of £24m if we undertook this investment. If we are very lucky, we realise the best (Revenue, Cost) pair of (£100m, £30m), resulting in the maximum possible profit of £70m, while if we are very unlucky, we realise the worst (Revenue, Cost) pair of (£50m, £80m), resulting in the maximum possible loss of £30m.

When we ran $n = 20$ simulations, we calculated a sample mean of £16.5m and a 15% estimated probability of a loss. Contrast these with the theoretically derived expected value of £24m and the probability of a loss of 0.04 + 0.12 = 0.16 or 16%. So we see that the loss probability estimate is not far off (15% versus 16%), but the simulated expected value differs considerably (£16.5 versus £24m).

Suspecting that $n = 20$ simulations is too few, let's increase n. We would expect that as $n \to \infty$, there should be *convergence* of the mean of the simulated profits to £24m, convergence of the loss probability to 16%, indeed the convergence of *all* simulated distribution attributes (e.g. the standard deviation, and the entire distribution of outcomes) to the 'true' values.

Suppose we run $n = 5000$ simulations. Cell `M28` in Figure 20.3 estimates the expected profit based on the sample mean of the 5000 simulated profits. This figure is approximately £24m (£23.996m). The probability of a loss is estimated to be 16.44% (cell `M30`), very close to the 'true' value of 16%.

Should we undertake the investment? Well, James, it depends! While the expected profit is positive (if the expected profit was negative this would indicate an expected loss), this fails to take into account the *risk* of the investment. Cell `M30` shows the *proportion* of losses in the run of 5000 simulations, which is our estimate of the probability of a loss. Depending on your appetite for risk, you may or may not choose to undertake the investment. We may even wish to take into account the *magnitude* of the loss. Losing £10m is bad, losing £30m could result in bankruptcy!

Remember, Monte Carlo simulation does *not* tell you what to do. Rather, it allows you to make a *risk-informed* decision.

20.2.1 To simulate, or not to simulate?

Why bother conducting simulations if we know the 'true' mean, as calculated using the theoretical distribution of profit above? Well, of course, if we *know* the true value of some quantity then there is no need to estimate it. However, in the *real world*, problems are much more complex than in the simple corporate investment example above, such that determining the true value analytically is often far too complicated to do! Instead, in such situations we can perform Monte Carlo simulations confident in the convergence of sample statistics to their (unknown) theoretical counterparts for a large enough number of simulations. In the corporate investment example, $n = 5000$ simulations clearly leads to a reasonable degree of convergence such that, based on the simulation results, we would predict an expected profit of (approximately) £24m.

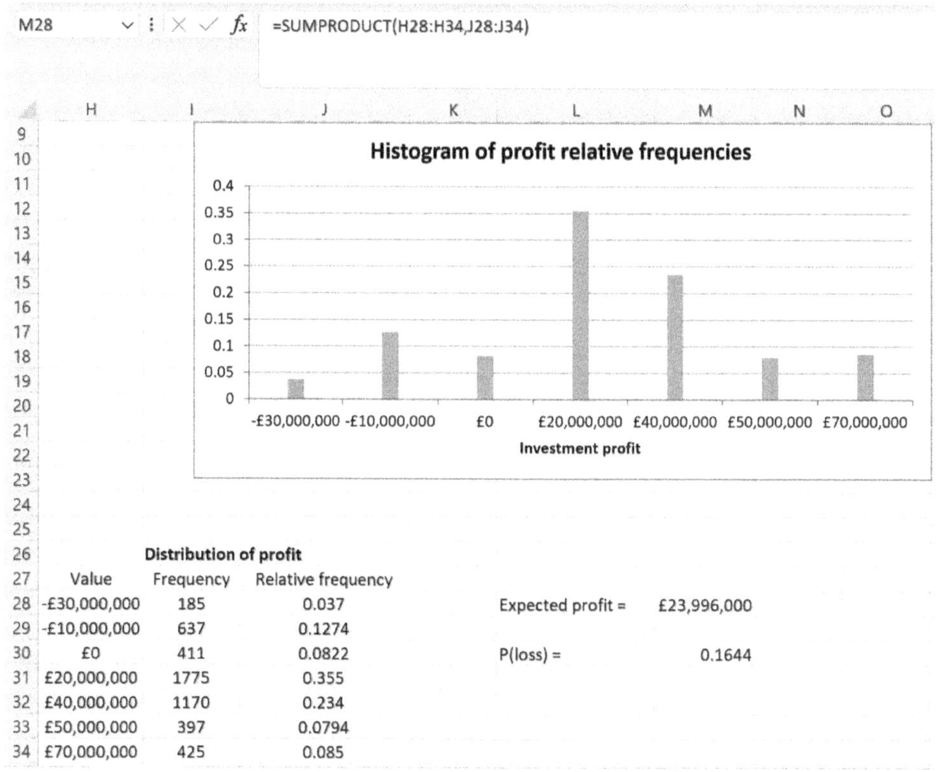

Distribution of profit

Value	Frequency	Relative frequency
-£30,000,000	185	0.037
-£10,000,000	637	0.1274
£0	411	0.0822
£20,000,000	1775	0.355
£40,000,000	1170	0.234
£50,000,000	397	0.0794
£70,000,000	425	0.085

Figure 20.3 Output distribution from $n = 5000$ simulations for the corporate investment example.

20.3 PROBABILITY DISTRIBUTIONS FOR INPUT VARIABLES

A major difference between the constrained optimisation models in Chapter 19 and the simulation models covered here is that the former are *deterministic*, meaning there is no randomness nor uncertainty – the system of equations is solved analytically – whereas the latter are *stochastic*, meaning randomness is introduced by making each of the input variables a *random* variable. As such, at least one of the input variable cells in a simulation spreadsheet model contains *random numbers*.

Each time the spreadsheet recalculates (in Excel, press the F9 key to recalculate), the random numbers *change*, and the new random values of the inputs produce new values of the outputs.

Technically speaking, input cells do not contain random numbers; they contain *probability distributions*.

Chapter 5 covered probability distributions extensively. Recall that a probability distribution indicates the possible values of a variable and the probabilities of those values. It is necessary to choose an appropriate probability distribution for each specific problem based on the real-world attributes, or stylised facts, of each variable in practice. General characteristics of probability distributions include:

- discrete versus continuous (or even a mixture of each)
- symmetric versus skewed
- restricted sample space versus unrestricted (such as $x \geq 0$, i.e. non-negative valued only, versus $-\infty < x < \infty$).

How to choose the probability distribution? Usually we do not try to invent new distributions from scratch. Instead, we use one of many existing standard distributions. There is a large number of such distributions, such that for most purposes we can find a suitable standard distribution. Note, however, that there is no single 'right answer' as to which distribution(s) to use. You must decide the most appropriate probability distribution which, in your opinion, most closely captures the variable's actual real-world attributes (its stylised facts).

Your choice of probability distributions in Monte Carlo simulation models has the potential to significantly influence the results, that is, the results may be *sensitive* to the choice. The idea of conducting a *sensitivity analysis* is not new – it was introduced in Chapter 19 in the context of constrained optimisation models (whereby we considered how sensitive decision variables were to, say, changes in the objective function coefficients). In the context of simulation models, a sensitivity analysis can be conducted by:

- changing the parameter values of the probability distributions of input variables
- changing the (family of) probability distributions used to model input variables.

Appendix B provides a library of several probability distributions, summarising the following:

- the probability mass function (discrete), $p(x)$, or probability density function (continuous), $f(x)$, which determines the shape of the probability distribution
- the cumulative distribution function, $F(x)$, which recall returns $P(X \leq x)$ – an alternative view of the probability distribution
- the sample space – the possible values of X
- the parameter space – the possible values of the parameter(s) of the probability distribution
- the expected value, $\mathrm{E}(X)$ – the central tendency/location of the probability distribution
- the variance, $\mathrm{Var}(X)$ – the spread/dispersion of the probability distribution.

20.4 PSEUDO-RANDOM NUMBER GENERATORS

Monte Carlo simulation models require random inputs which are obtained using random numbers. How do we obtain random numbers? Using a random number generator. Strictly speaking, the random number generators in Excel (and other software packages) are *pseudo*-random number generators since they are algorithmic ('pseudo' means 'not real', but applied here can be thought of as meaning 'as if' or 'resembling'). This means that if we knew the algorithm and the 'seed' (the starting point of the algorithm) we could predict with certainty which 'random' numbers would be returned, which is to say that the numbers are actually deterministic as they are generated according to the algorithm, as opposed to magic. However, for practical purposes, these 'deterministic' numbers have the appearance of being random (and would satisfy statistical requirements for randomness), so appear 'as if' or 'resembling' random numbers, hence pseudo-random!

In simulation models we require random numbers drawn from specific probability distributions, those used to represent the random input variables. To achieve this, we make use of the *cumulative distribution function*, $F(x)$, which (recall from Chapter 5) is

$$F(x) = P(X \leq x).$$

Since $F(x)$ is a probability, it must be the case that $0 \leq F(x) \leq 1$ (remember that probabilities are always between 0 and 1, inclusive). So, this motivates our approach to random number generation from *any* probability distribution provided we know $F(x)$. We simply generate a random number between 0 and 1, then treat this as the randomly generated cumulative probability, $F(x)$. We then just need to *invert* the function $F(x)$ to recover the random number x from the desired probability distribution. The inverse function, $F^{-1}(x)$, is known as the *quantile function*.

20.4.1 Random number generation in Excel

In Excel, we may obtain a random number between 0 and 1 using the `=RAND()` function, as shown in Figure 20.4. In practice this means returning a value from the *continuous uniform distribution* over [0, 1], that is, sampling at random from Uniform[0, 1]. Since all values in this unit interval are *equally likely*, there is no selection bias in the value which is returned, so we may think of the returned random number as an unbiased (i.e. fair) randomly generated value of $F(x)$.

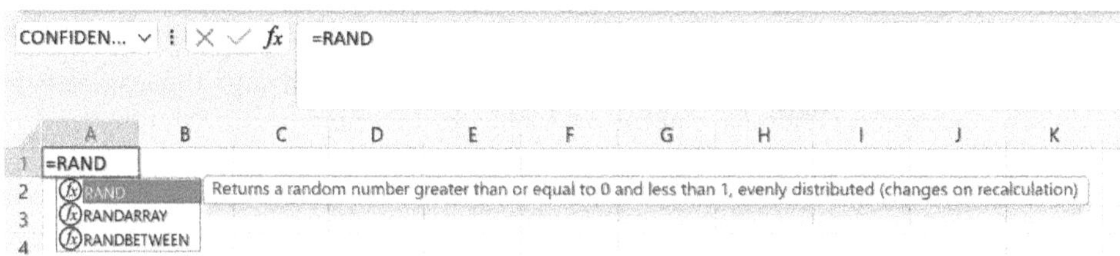

Figure 20.4 Calling the Excel function `=RAND()`.

Technical note (as per Chapter 7)

Algorithmically, how can we generate (pseudo-)random numbers from Uniform[0, 1]? Answer: use a **congruential generator**.

Define a sequence $\{x_i\}$ and set (for some integer values a, b, M and x_0):

$x_{i+1} = (ax_i + b) \bmod M.$

It is then the case that $U_i = x_i/M \sim$ Uniform[0, 1], that is, U_i is a random drawing from the continuous uniform distribution over the unit interval [0, 1].

For large M, the numbers obtained by the algorithm above satisfy all the properties of random samples from the Uniform[0, 1] distribution. They are hence called **pseudo-random numbers.**

Let's now consider how to obtain random revenues and costs for our earlier corporate investment problem. Recall the probability distributions of revenues and costs, respectively.

Revenue (in £m)	Cost (in £m)
50 (with probability 0.2)	80 (with probability 0.2)
80 (with probability 0.4)	60 (with probability 0.6)
100 (with probability 0.4)	30 (with probability 0.2)

By using Excel's `=RAND()` function, we can randomly select a number equally likely to be between 0 and 1, represented by Figure 20.5.

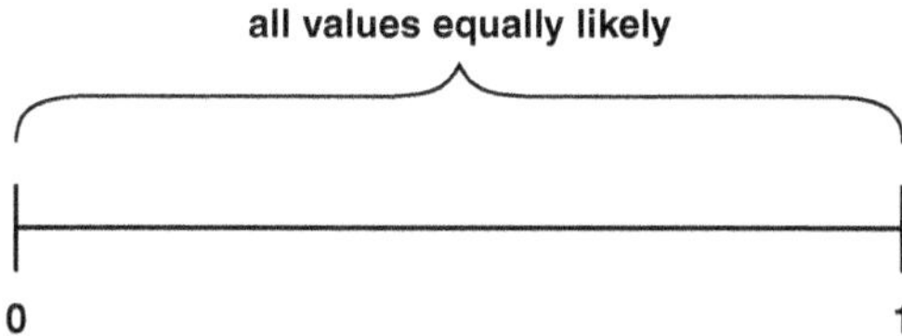

Figure 20.5 Excel's `=RAND()` function ensures all values between 0 and 1 are equally likely to be returned.

Given the probability distribution of revenues, we could simulate revenues depending on the value returned by `=RAND()` according to Figure 20.6 which ensures each revenue value occurs with the required probability. For example, there is a 20% chance that `=RAND()` returns a value in the interval [0, 0.2], which would be mapped to a revenue of £50m.

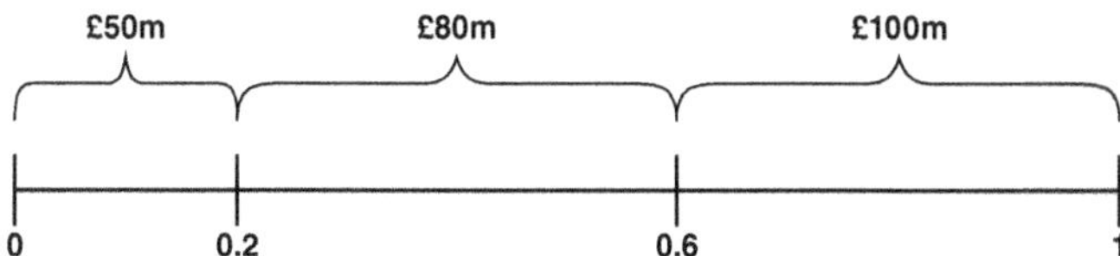

Figure 20.6 Mapping possible revenues to ranges of values in [0, 1] according to the probability distribution of revenues.

Similarly, for costs, we could map these to ranges of values in [0, 1] as shown in Figure 20.7.

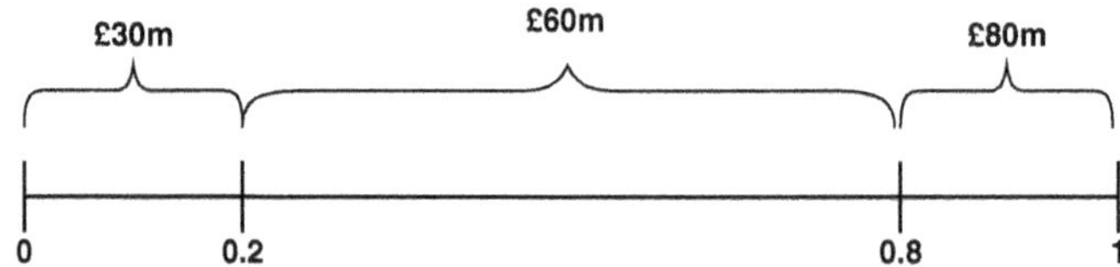

Figure 20.7 Mapping possible costs to ranges of values in [0, 1] according to the probability distribution of costs.

Suppose for the first simulation we had random numbers for revenues and costs of 0.1467 and 0.7672 (returned by `=RAND()`), mapping to revenues of £50m and costs of £60m, respectively. This corresponds to

Revenue = £50m, Costs = £60m ⇒ Profit = –£10m (a loss).

Suppose for the second simulation we had random numbers for revenues and costs of 0.3384 and 0.2056, respectively (again returned by `=RAND()`). This corresponds to

Revenue = £80m, Costs = £60m ⇒ Profit = £20m.

We now look at demonstrating random number generation from the *exponential distribution* in Excel. First, a technical exposition.

Technical note

For any continuous random variable X, its distribution function, $F(x)$, is strictly increasing over its sample space, S. The inverse function, $F^{-1}(x)$, known as the **quantile function**, is strictly increasing on [0, 1], such that $F^{-1}(x)$ maps [0, 1] to S.

Let $U \sim$ Uniform[0, 1] be a continuous uniform random variable over [0, 1]. Its distribution function is

$$F_U(u) = \begin{cases} 0 & \text{for } u < 0 \\ u & \text{for } 0 \le u \le 1 \\ 1 & \text{for } u > 1. \end{cases}$$

Let $X = F_X^{-1}(U)$. Its distribution function is:

$$F_X(x) = F_U((F_X^{-1})^{-1}(x)), \quad \text{for } x \in S,$$

which can be used to simulate random samples from a required probability distribution by simulating values of u from Uniform[0, 1], and then view $X = F_X^{-1}(U)$ as a random draw from $F_X(x)$.

Example 20.6

Suppose we wanted to include 'customer waiting time', X, as an input variable in a Monte Carlo simulation. If we assumed X had an exponential distribution with parameter λ, then $X \sim \text{Exp}(\lambda)$. The cumulative distribution function is (see Appendix B)

$$F(x) = \begin{cases} 0 & \text{for } x < 0 \\ 1 - e^{-\lambda x} & \text{for } x \geq 0. \end{cases}$$

The *quantile function* (i.e. the inverse distribution function) is (solving for x):

$$F^{-1}(u) = \frac{1}{\lambda} \ln\left(\frac{1}{1-u}\right), \quad \text{for } 0 \leq u \leq 1.$$

Therefore, if $U \sim \text{Uniform}[0, 1]$, then

$$\frac{1}{\lambda} \ln\left(\frac{1}{1-U}\right) \sim \text{Exp}(\lambda). \tag{20.1}$$

So, use =RAND() to generate a value of U, then use (20.1) to return the value of X for a given value of λ.

Consider the following simulation results.

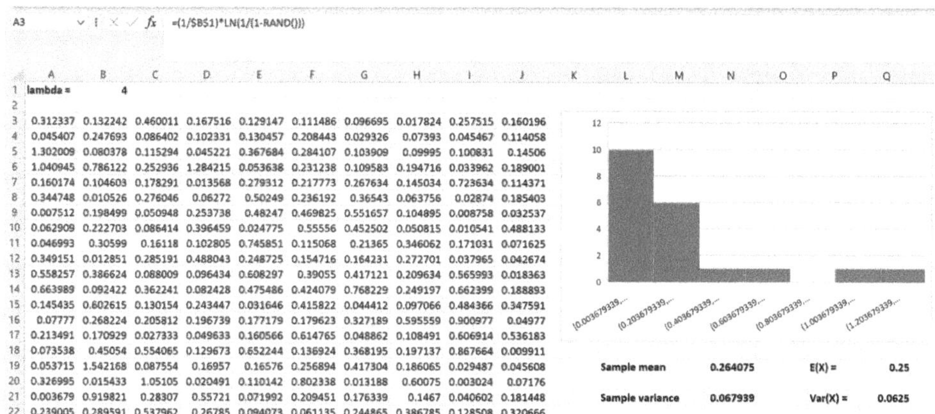

A3 =(1/$B$1)*LN(1/(1-RAND()))

	A	B	C	D	E	F	G	H	I	J
1	lambda =	4								
2										
3	0.312337	0.132242	0.460011	0.167516	0.129147	0.111486	0.096695	0.017824	0.257515	0.160196
4	0.045407	0.247693	0.086402	0.102331	0.130457	0.208443	0.029326	0.07393	0.045467	0.114058
5	1.302009	0.080378	0.115294	0.045221	0.367684	0.284107	0.103909	0.09995	0.100831	0.14506
6	1.040945	0.786122	0.252936	1.284215	0.053638	0.231238	0.109583	0.194716	0.033962	0.189001
7	0.160174	0.104603	0.178291	0.013568	0.279312	0.217773	0.267634	0.145034	0.723634	0.114371
8	0.344748	0.010526	0.276046	0.06272	0.50249	0.236192	0.36543	0.063756	0.02874	0.185403
9	0.007512	0.198499	0.050948	0.253738	0.48247	0.469825	0.551657	0.104895	0.008758	0.032537
10	0.062909	0.222703	0.086414	0.396459	0.024775	0.55556	0.452502	0.050815	0.010541	0.488133
11	0.046993	0.30599	0.16118	0.102805	0.745851	0.115068	0.21365	0.346062	0.171031	0.071625
12	0.349151	0.012851	0.285191	0.488043	0.248725	0.154716	0.164231	0.272701	0.037965	0.042674
13	0.558257	0.386624	0.088009	0.096434	0.608297	0.39055	0.417121	0.209634	0.565993	0.018363
14	0.663989	0.092422	0.362241	0.082428	0.475486	0.424079	0.768229	0.249197	0.662399	0.188893
15	0.145435	0.602615	0.130154	0.243447	0.031646	0.415822	0.044412	0.097066	0.484366	0.347591
16	0.07777	0.268224	0.205812	0.196739	0.177179	0.179623	0.327189	0.595559	0.900977	0.04977
17	0.213491	0.170929	0.027333	0.049633	0.160566	0.614765	0.048862	0.108491	0.606914	0.536183
18	0.073538	0.45054	0.554065	0.129673	0.652244	0.136924	0.368195	0.197137	0.867664	0.009911
19	0.053715	1.542168	0.087554	0.16957	0.16576	0.256894	0.417304	0.186065	0.029487	0.045608
20	0.326995	0.015433	1.05105	0.020491	0.110142	0.802338	0.013188	0.60075	0.003024	0.07176
21	0.003679	0.919821	0.28307	0.55721	0.071992	0.209451	0.176339	0.1467	0.040602	0.181448
22	0.239005	0.289591	0.537962	0.26785	0.094073	0.061135	0.244865	0.386785	0.128508	0.320666

Sample mean	0.264075	E(X) =	0.25
Sample variance	0.067939	Var(X) =	0.0625

Here we choose $\lambda = 4$ (cell B1) and generate a random sample of $n = 200$ observations. Cell A3 shows the application of (20.1) to generate the first random drawing from Exp(4). The cell range A3:J22 shows all values, where the value returned by =RAND() (corresponding to U in (20.1)) *changes* each time. Also shown are the histogram of the 200 values, which resembles an exponential density function, and the sample mean (cell N19) and sample variance (cell N21), which are both close to their respective theoretical counterparts:

$$E(X) = \frac{1}{\lambda} = \frac{1}{4} = 0.25 \text{ and } \text{Var}(X) = \frac{1}{\lambda^2} = \frac{1}{4^2} = 0.0625.$$

20.5 SIMULATING FROM COMMON PROBABILITY DISTRIBUTIONS IN EXCEL

Excel has in-built quantile functions for the normal and binomial distributions. We briefly review these.

20.5.1 Normal distribution

Excel function: `NORM.INV`

`=NORM.INV(probability, mean, standard_dev)` returns the inverse of the normal cumulative distribution for the specified mean and standard deviation, where:

- `probability` is a probability corresponding to the normal distribution, a number between 0 and 1 inclusive
- `mean` is the arithmetic mean of the distribution
- `standard_dev` is the standard deviation of the distribution, a positive number.

Excel function: `NORM.S.INV`

`=NORM.S.INV(probability)` returns the inverse of the standard normal cumulative distribution (has a mean of 0 and a standard deviation of 1), where:

- `probability` is a probability corresponding to the normal distribution, a number between 0 and 1 inclusive.

Example 20.7

Substituting `RAND()` for `probability` in the above Excel functions allows for random drawings from the respective normal distribution. Note that `=NORM.S.INV(probability)` is equivalent to `=NORM.INV(probability, 0, 1)`.

Suppose we choose $\mu = 7$ (cell `B1`) and $\sigma = 3$ (cell `F1`). For $n = 200$, a simulated distribution is as follows:

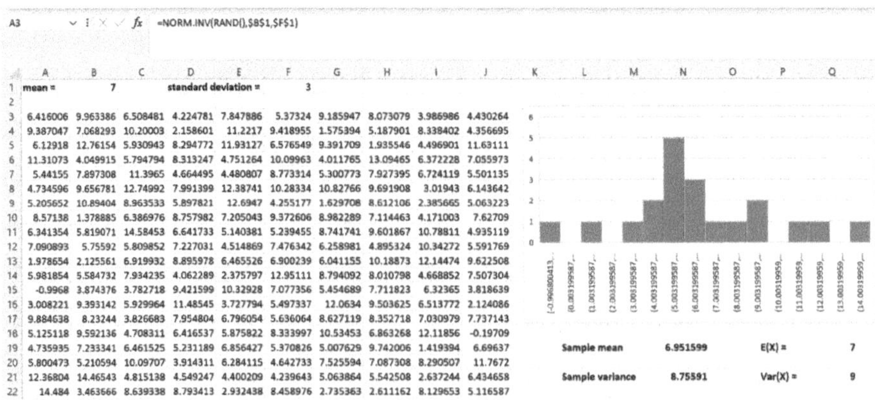

A3 =NORM.INV(RAND(),$B$1,$F$1)

	A	B	C	D	E	F	G	H	I	J
1	mean =	7		standard deviation =		3				
2										
3	6.416006	9.963386	6.508481	4.224781	7.847886	5.37324	9.185947	8.073079	3.986986	4.430264
4	9.387047	7.068293	10.20003	2.158601	11.2217	9.418955	1.575394	5.187901	8.338402	4.356695
5	6.12918	12.76154	5.930943	8.294772	11.93127	6.576549	9.391709	1.935546	4.496901	11.63111
6	11.31073	4.049915	5.794794	8.313247	4.751264	10.09963	4.011765	13.09465	6.372228	7.055973
7	5.44155	7.897308	11.3965	4.664495	4.480807	8.773314	5.300773	7.927395	6.724119	5.501135
8	4.734596	9.656781	12.74992	7.991399	12.38741	10.28334	10.82766	9.691908	3.01943	6.143642
9	5.205652	10.89404	8.963533	5.897821	12.6947	4.255177	1.629708	8.612106	2.385665	5.063223
10	8.57138	1.378885	6.386976	8.757982	7.205043	9.372606	8.982289	7.114463	4.171003	7.62709
11	6.341354	5.819071	14.58453	6.641733	5.140381	5.239455	8.741741	9.601867	10.78811	4.935119
12	7.090893	5.75592	5.809852	7.227031	4.514869	7.476342	6.258981	4.895324	10.34272	5.591769
13	1.978654	2.125561	6.919932	8.895978	6.465526	6.900239	6.041155	10.18873	12.14474	9.622508
14	5.981854	5.584732	7.934235	4.062289	2.375797	12.95111	8.794092	8.010798	4.668852	7.507304
15	-0.9968	3.874376	3.782718	9.421599	10.32928	7.077356	5.454689	7.711823	6.32365	3.818639
16	3.008221	9.393142	5.929964	11.48545	3.727794	5.497337	12.0634	9.503625	6.513772	2.124086
17	9.884638	8.23244	3.826683	7.954804	6.796054	5.636064	8.627119	8.352718	7.030979	7.737143
18	5.125118	9.592136	4.708311	6.416537	5.875822	8.333997	10.53453	6.863268	12.11856	-0.19709
19	4.735935	7.233341	6.461525	5.231189	6.856427	5.370826	5.007629	9.742006	1.419394	6.69637
20	5.800473	5.210594	10.09707	3.914311	6.284115	4.642733	7.525594	7.087308	8.290507	11.7672
21	12.36804	14.46543	4.815138	4.549247	4.400209	4.239643	5.063864	5.542508	2.637244	6.434658
22	14.484	3.463666	8.639338	8.793413	2.932438	8.458976	2.735363	2.611162	8.129653	5.116587

Sample mean	6.951599	E(X) =	7
Sample variance	8.75591	Var(X) =	9

Note that the histogram looks (approximately) like a bell curve, and the sample mean (cell N19) of $\bar{x} = 6.952 \approx 7 = \mu$, and that the sample variance (cell N21) $s^2 = 8.756 \approx 9 = \sigma^2$. Hence the statistical attributes of the simulated values closely resemble those of the 'parent' $N(7, 9)$ distribution.

20.5.2 Binomial distribution

Excel function: BINOM.INV

`=BINOM.INV(trials,probability_s,alpha)` returns the smallest value for which the cumulative binomial distribution is less than or equal to a criterion value, where:

- `trials` is the number of independent trials
- `probability_s` is the probability of success on each trial
- `alpha` is the criterion value.

Example 20.8

Substituting `RAND()` for `alpha` in the above Excel function allows for random drawings from the binomial distribution for the specified number of trials, `trials`, and probability of success, `probability_s`.

Suppose we choose 10 trials (cell B1) and probability of success of 0.6 (cell F1). For $n = 200$, a simulated distribution is as follows:

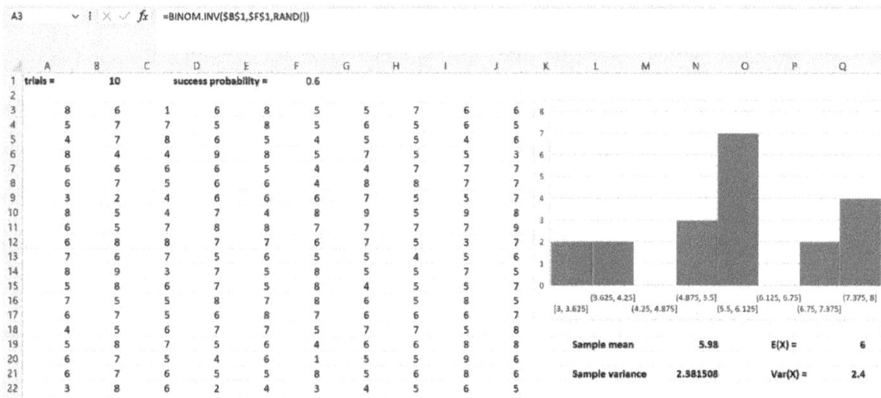

A3 =BINOM.INV($B$1,$F$1,RAND())

	A	B	C	D	E	F	G	H	I	J
1	trials =	10		success probability =		0.6				
2										
3	8	6	1	6	8	5	5	7	6	6
4	5	7	7	5	8	5	6	5	6	5
5	4	7	8	6	5	4	5	5	4	6
6	8	4	4	9	8	5	7	5	5	3
7	6	6	6	6	5	4	4	7	7	7
8	6	7	5	6	6	4	8	8	7	7
9	3	2	4	6	6	6	7	5	5	7
10	8	5	4	7	4	8	9	5	9	8
11	6	5	7	8	8	7	7	7	7	9
12	6	8	8	7	7	6	7	5	3	7
13	7	6	7	5	6	5	5	4	5	6
14	8	9	3	7	5	8	5	5	7	5
15	5	8	6	7	5	8	4	5	5	7
16	7	5	5	8	7	8	6	5	8	5
17	6	7	5	6	8	7	6	6	6	7
18	4	5	6	7	7	5	7	7	5	8
19	5	8	7	5	6	4	6	6	8	8
20	6	7	5	4	6	1	5	5	9	6
21	6	7	6	5	5	8	5	6	8	6
22	3	8	6	2	4	3	4	5	6	5

Sample mean	5.98	E(X) =	6
Sample variance	2.381508	Var(X) =	2.4

Note that in 200 simulations, we never encountered $x = 0$, since this has probability

$$P(X = 0) = (1 - \pi)^{10} = 0.4^{10} \approx 0.0001,$$

which is highly unlikely to occur in a sample of just 200. Note also the sample mean (cell N19) of $\bar{x} = 5.98 \approx 6 = 10 \times 0.6 = n\pi = E(X)$ and the sample variance (cell N21) of $s^2 = 2.382 \approx 2.4 = 10 \times 0.6 \times 0.4 = n\pi(1 - \pi) = Var(X)$. Hence the statistical attributes of the simulated values closely resemble those of the 'parent' Bin(10, 0.6) distribution.

20.6 SIMULATION CASE STUDY

Paraphernalia is deciding whether to launch a new product line with uncertain revenues, uncertain costs, and hence uncertain profits.

Market research has indicated possible demand levels such that it is assumed that revenues will be normally distributed. In the first quarter, expected revenues are £5000, with an assumed standard deviation of £1800. In subsequent quarters the expected revenue is assumed to be the actual revenues achieved in the previous quarter, with the *same* standard deviation. This is an adaptive expectations approach, since the expected revenue is updated each quarter to reflect the most recent actual revenue (the £5000 is an assumed starting value).

Costs are assumed to follow an exponential distribution, with an expected value of £4000, which is a rate parameter of 0.00025 (since $E(X) = 1/\lambda = 4000$ leads to $\lambda = 0.00025$).

The simulation model shown in Figure 20.8 was constructed, with 10,000 simulations (the results of the first five simulations are shown in rows 15–19).

G15 fx =NORM.INV(RAND(),D15,$B$7)

	A	B	C	D	E	F	G	H	I	J	K	L	M	N	O
1	**Simulating quarterly profits**														
2															
3	**Assume quarterly revenues are normally distributed**			**Assume quarterly costs are exponentially distributed**											
4															
5	Revenues in Q1			Costs each quarter											
6	Mean	5,000		Lambda	0.00025										
7	Standard deviation	1,800													
8				**Q1 revenue**	**Q1 costs**	**Q1 profit**	**Q2 revenue**	**Q2 costs**	**Q2 profit**	**Q3 revenue**	**Q3 costs**	**Q3 profit**	**Q4 revenue**	**Q4 costs**	**Q4 profit**
9	Revenues in Q2 through Q4		**Average**	5,012	4,032	980	5,015	4,067	948	5,057	3,994	1,063	5,045	4,046	999
10	Mean	The previous quarter	**Standard deviation**	1797	4015	4398	2557	4011	4762	3133	3990	5068	3608	4049	5392
11	Standard deviation	Unchanged	**Minimum**	-1,512	0	-43,717	-4,793	0	-27,921	-7,233	0	-30,009	-9,845	1	-47,065
12			**Maximum**	11,689	46,660	10,998	15,275	32,415	13,621	18,347	33,576	16,700	20,324	53,224	19,519
13															
14			Simulation run	Q1 revenue	Q1 costs	Q1 profit	Q2 revenue	Q2 costs	Q2 profit	Q3 revenue	Q3 costs	Q3 profit	Q4 revenue	Q4 costs	Q4 profit
15			1	6,898	893	6,005	5,119	5,123	-4	5,252	6,519	-1,267	5,432	231	5,201
16			2	6,229	3,044	3,186	8,521	588	7,933	6,582	3,579	3,003	8,488	4,942	3,547
17			3	3,717	1,722	1,995	-1,029	7,371	-8,399	-1,089	851	-1,940	-1,795	8,331	-10,126
18			4	1,780	214	1,566	508	2,518	-2,010	-32	5,519	-5,551	-683	2,200	-2,883
19			5	3,012	2,761	251	2,837	11,893	-9,057	431	22,877	-22,446	2,299	9,098	-6,799

Figure 20.8 Results of a Monte Carlo simulation for Paraphernalia.

For example, cell G15 simulates the Q2 revenue from the $N(6898, 1800^2)$ distribution, using the realised Q1 revenue (cell D15) as the expected revenue in Q2, while the standard deviation remains at 1800. As shown in the formula bar, the Excel function used is

```
=NORM.INV(RAND(),D15,$B$7)
```

(where the standard deviation cell reference has dollar signs to lock the referenced cell (B7) when the formula is copied to other cells).

Costs are simulated from the exponential distribution. For example, the Excel function used in cell E15 is

```
=(1/$E$6)*LN(1/(1-RAND())).
```

A quarter's profits (the output variable of interest) are then calculated as revenues – costs, such as cell F15 which is =D15-E15.

Descriptive statistics (mean, standard deviation, minimum and maximum) of each quarter's revenues, costs and profits for the 10,000 simulation results are shown in the cell range D8:O12.

Notice that our simulation model is not really satisfactory. For example, taking simulation no. 3, we see nonsensical values for revenues (these are negative in Q2, Q3 and Q4, but logically the minimum revenues can be is zero, i.e. no sales). Why did we obtain such an outcome? Well, we applied an *adaptive expectations* approach to quarterly revenue, whereby we used the previous quarter's realised revenue as the new expected value. In simulation no. 3, by chance revenues in Q1 were quite low (the random drawing from $N(5000, 1800)$ returned 3717 in cell `D17`), hence the Q2 revenue is simulated from $N(3717, 1800)$.

Now, recall the *empirical rules* (see Section 5.15.3) such that for a normal distribution there is (approximately) a 95% probability of being within *two* standard deviations of the mean, and (approximately) a 99.7% probability of being within *three* standard deviations of the mean. Here

$$\mu \pm 2\sigma \Rightarrow 3717 \pm 2 \times 1800 \Rightarrow (117, 7317)$$

and

$$\mu \pm 3\sigma \Rightarrow 3{,}717 \pm 3 \times 1800 \Rightarrow (-1683, 9117).$$

So, there is a non-negligible probability (about 2.5%) of the Q2 simulated revenue being less than £117, and about a 0.15% chance of being less than –£1683. As seen in cell `G17`, we actually obtained –£1029, which defies our logical floor of £0.

In turn, the Q3 revenue is simulated from $N(-1029, 1800)$, returning –£1089 in cell `J17`, and in turn the Q4 revenue is simulated from $N(-1089, 1800)$, returning –£1795 in cell `M17`.

Costs are also problematic. While the average costs hover around £4000 (consistent with the theoretical mean of an exponential distribution with $\lambda = 0.00025$, since $E(X) = 1/\lambda$), we observe occasions across the 10,000 simulation runs of costs of £0 (the minimum observed quarterly costs, such as in cells `E11`, `H11` and `K11`), which seems implausible, while costs achieved a maximum of £53,224 (encountered in Q4, see cell `N12`). We are perhaps less concerned with such large costs – perhaps due to extremely volatile markets for raw materials, or even a pandemic inducing a stratospheric rise in shipping costs.

(**Not-so-fun fact**: Due to the Covid-19 pandemic causing shipping freight costs to spiral upwards, some businesses with time-sensitive cargo to transport would even switch to airfreight, costing upwards of £10 per kilogram! To ensure customers receive their goods on time and keep them happy, incurring a loss to maintain goodwill and ensure customer retention may be the lesser evil. So, extremely high costs (and indeed a pandemic) may be rare, but are at least plausible.)

So, it seems our first attempt at a simulation model may achieve an A for effort, but an F for commercial realism. In any model-building exercise we should not expect to achieve perfection on our first attempt. Tweaking and refining the model will be necessary, and in practice take some time.

Our problems centred around the unrealistic minimum values sometimes returned for the simulated revenues and costs. We can easily accommodate this issue by revising our simulation model to place a *floor* on each variable, that is, fix a *minimum value*. For revenues, this could be £0 or, if we had confirmed pre-orders for the product, a guaranteed minimum level of revenue. Similarly, we can define a minimum value for costs (perhaps negotiated with our suppliers to lock in a minimum cost – but costs could be expected to rise due to *force majeure*, i.e. unforeseen circumstances, such as a surge in shipping costs following a pandemic).

We could make one additional improvement. The standard deviation of revenues has been held constant throughout at £1800. However, with our use of adaptive expectations, as realised revenues increase, we might wish to increase the standard deviation (higher revenues should perhaps be associated with a larger standard deviation, as there is greater potential for fluctuations in subsequent revenues). Also, lower realised revenues indicate a lack of consumer appetite for the product, so future revenues are unlikely to vary much, so a lower standard deviation would seem sensible.

G15 fx =IF(D15=0,0,MAX(NORM.INV(RAND(),D15,$B$7*D15/$B$6),0))

	A	B	C	D	E	F	G	H	I	J	K	L	M	N	O	P
1	**Simulating quarterly profits**															
2																
3	**Assume quarterly revenues are normally distributed**			**Assume quarterly costs are exponentially distributed**												
4																
5	Revenues in Q1			Costs each quarter												
6	Mean	5,000		Lambda	0.00025											
7	Standard deviation	1,800														
8				**Q1 revenue**	**Q1 costs**	**Q1 profit**	**Q2 revenue**	**Q2 costs**	**Q2 profit**	**Q3 revenue**	**Q3 costs**	**Q3 profit**	**Q4 revenue**	**Q4 costs**	**Q4 profit**	**Total profit**
9	Revenues in Q2 through Q4		**Average**	4,992	4,472	520	4,987	4,475	512	5,016	4,442	575	5,056	4,463	593	2,201
10	Mean	The previous quarter	**Standard deviation**	2796	3766	4169	2618	3740	4553	3211	3647	4832	3726	3666	5210	12333
11	Standard deviation	Update to reflect	**Minimum**	0	2,000	-39,670	0	2,000	-33,097	0	2,000	-29,730	0	2,000	-42,399	-59,130
12		realised revenues	**Maximum**	12,059	43,757	9,054	19,283	37,818	15,922	22,299	35,058	20,299	71,018	46,038	69,018	61,511
13																
14			Simulation run	Q1 revenue	Q1 costs	Q1 profit	Q2 revenue	Q2 costs	Q2 profit	Q3 revenue	Q3 costs	Q3 profit	Q4 revenue	Q4 costs	Q4 profit	Total profit
15			1	3,235	2,000	1,235	4,555	2,669	1,886	4,370	2,123	2,247	5,065	2,984	2,081	7,449
16			2	5,759	2,215	3,544	5,392	4,938	454	7,034	2,000	5,034	4,820	3,539	1,281	10,312
17			3	4,462	7,141	-2,679	4,435	5,365	-930	3,933	6,434	-2,502	3,434	2,000	1,434	-4,678
18			4	1,077	5,416	-4,339	836	2,000	-1,164	0	2,000	-2,000	0	2,000	-2,000	9,502
19			5	6,699	8,452	-1,753	9,648	3,095	6,553	7,370	2,752	4,618	10,473	2,592	7,881	17,299

Figure 20.9 Results of a revised Monte Carlo simulation for Paraphernalia.

Consider the updated simulation model shown in Figure 20.9. Immediately, we see the 'correction' of the nonsensical revenue and cost values previously seen. For example, quarterly revenue is never negative (see cells `D11`, `G11`, `J11` and `M11`). It is sometimes zero, but that would simply indicate no demand for the new product (perhaps it failed to capture consumer attention, or just proved an unpopular product). Costs never drop below £2000 (see cells `E11`, `H11`, `K11` and `N11`) while they can be considerable (capturing, for example, unforeseen shocks to shipping costs). What Excel formulae were used? We consider a couple of examples.

- Cell `G15`:

```
=IF(D15=0,0,MAX(NORM.INV(RAND(),D15,$B$7*D15/$B$6),0))
```

returns the larger (maximum) of the simulated normal random variable and zero (using the `MAX` function), provided the previous quarter achieved non-zero revenues (using the `IF` function). Concerning the normal distribution parameters, note that the mean of the previous quarter's revenue, `D15`, reflects adaptive expectations, and note that the standard deviation has been updated to reflect how Q1 realised revenues differed from expectations. In this case, the actual Q1 revenues of £3235 (cell `D15`) were below expectations of £5000 (cell `B6`). As revenues underperformed in Q1, we then adjust the standard deviation parameter *downwards* by multiplying the original £1800 (cell `B7`) by the ratio $3235/5000 < 1$.

- Cell `H15`:

```
=MAX((1/$E$6)*LN(1/(1-RAND())),2000)
```

simulates Q2 costs based on the exponential distribution, but with a minimum cost of £2000 imposed (using the `MAX` function).

We now turn to decision-making. Should *Paraphernalia* proceed to launch the new product line? Well, James, it depends! Of course, to assist with our decision-making we should look, say, at the simulated distribution of annual profit. This is shown in Figure 20.10.

Ultimately, whether we wish to proceed or not depends on our risk appetite. While there is a chance of a healthy profit (the maximum total profit for the year based on the 10,000 simulation runs was £61,511; see cell P12 in Figure 20.9), there is a significant downside risk. Indeed, the worst case scenario among these simulations is an annual *loss* of £59,130.

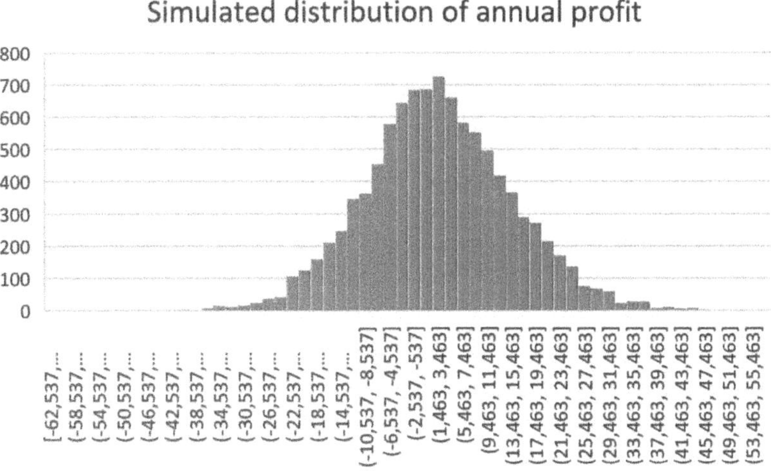

Figure 20.10 Histogram of the simulated annual profit for *Paraphernalia*.

Remember that Monte Carlo simulation does *not* tell you what to do, but allows risk-based decision-making to be undertaken.

By no means is our model perfect. For example, take simulation no. 4. Suppose we viewed Q1 as our pilot quarter. If revenue failed to achieve a minimum sales target, say £2000, then we would consider removing the product line entirely. If so, we would have an effective 'stop loss' of £4339 and discontinue the product line, rather than letting the run of poor sales continue which, as we see in simulation no. 4, ultimately leads to an annual loss of £9502, which is significantly worse than a loss of 'only' £4339.

Should you wish, feel free to experiment with the simulation model, adding whatever assumptions or realistic features you see fit. See how sensitive profits are to your choices!

20.7 CHAPTER OVERVIEW

This chapter has introduced the concept of Monte Carlo simulation. The idea is to incorporate uncertainty of input variables in a simulation by modelling each input variable as a probability distribution. Each simulation can then be thought of as a possible future world. In practice we run many simulations to represent the many possible future worlds which could occur. As the future is uncertain (it hasn't happened yet), we do not know which *specific* future world will occur, but we can observe the distribution of possible outcomes to assist with our decision-making. Simple descriptive statistics of output distributions, such as the mean and standard deviation, allow us to derive expectations and quantify risks, respectively. Remember that the results of a Monte Carlo simulation do *not* tell you what to do! Rather, by appreciating the risks associated with each decision, you can make a risk-based decision.

20.8 KEY VOCABULARY

Abstraction
Adaptive expectations
Analytical solution
Congruential generator
Expected outcome
Monte Carlo simulation
Probability distribution
Pseudo-random numbers
Quantile function
Random number generator
Risk
Scenario
Simulation model
What-if questions

20.9 EXERCISES

20.9.1 Test your understanding

1 What is the purpose of a simulation model?
2 Produce a flow diagram illustrating a Monte Carlo simulation.
3 How are the real world and abstract world related? What happens in the abstract world?
4 What is the difference between a static simulation model and a dynamic simulation model?
5 List the six steps for conducting a Monte Carlo simulation in practice.
6 On what basis would you choose a probability distribution for an input variable in a simulation model?
7 What does the Excel function `=RAND()` do?
8 Why is the Excel function `=RAND()` useful in simulation models?
9 What are pseudo-random numbers?
10 What is a quantile function and how can it be used to simulate random samples from a specified probability distribution?
11 State the in-built Excel quantile functions for the normal and binomial distributions. Include their arguments.
12 When might you wish to employ adaptive expectations in a simulation model? Provide a practical example.
13 What is the 'right' number of simulations to perform? 'Well, James, it depends' may feature in your answer, but explain what it depends on!
14 Consider the simulation case study in Section 20.6. Discuss any changes you would propose making to this simulation model, briefly justifying your choice(s).
15 A business wants to conduct a Monte Carlo simulation to model its profits over the next 5 years. The model will include the following two input variables:

(a) consumer demand for its most popular product each year
(b) whether a new competitor begins trading each year.

For each of these two variables suggest an appropriate probability distribution that you would recommend is used to model it, briefly justifying your choice of distribution in each case.

16 You are employed as a financial analyst and your team has run many simulation models to estimate the profitability of various projects. If you had to choose just two measures of the distribution of any important output variable, such as net profit, to report, which two would you choose and why? Are there any drawbacks to only using your two chosen measures?

17 For each probability distribution in Appendix B, identify one possible real-world input variable of a simulation model which could arguably be assumed to follow the distribution.

18 The triangular distribution is a continuous probability distribution which has three parameters:

(a) the minimum, a
(b) the maximum, b
(c) the mode, c

such that $a \leq c \leq b$. Explain why this could be a useful probability distribution for an input variable in a simulation model.

20.9.2 Practice with Excel

Head over to the companion website for Excel examples and screencasts!

APPENDIX A
COMMON EXCEL FUNCTIONS

A.1 USING EXCEL FUNCTIONS

Functions are pre-defined formulae. Excel is equipped with numerous in-built functions, so you can perform many calculations easily. This appendix lists some useful functions – but note the content is far from exhaustive!

You use functions by specifying *arguments* (values) and the type of arguments you use is specific to the function being implemented. The order in which you position the elements in a function is called the *syntax* (similar to the role grammar plays in a language). The standard syntax is

```
=FunctionName(arguments)
```

Many functions are built into Excel, but some are part of the *Analysis ToolPak* add-in which must be installed in your version of Excel. To check if the ToolPak is installed on your computer, go to the `Data` tab in the Toolbar in Excel. If `Data Analysis` appears in the ribbon, the ToolPak has already been installed. An example is shown in Figure A.1.

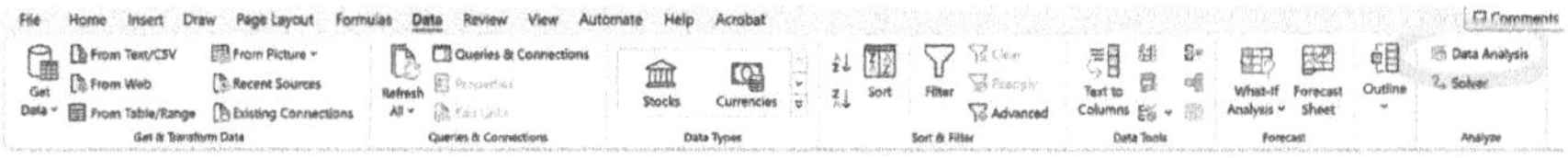

Figure A.1 Excel ribbon with Data Analysis ToolPak installed.

If not, click the Office button in the top left and select `Excel Options`. Choose `Add-Ins` and highlight the `Analysis ToolPak` in the list and click on `Go`. Check the box next to Analysis ToolPak and click on `OK`.

You are strongly encouraged to experiment with the functionality of Excel, as you are likely to use it in your future studies and employment.

A.2 DESCRIPTIVE STATISTICS

Chapter 2 introduced descriptive statistics. These allow us to summarise a key attribute of a dataset numerically and include *measures of central tendency* (mean, median and mode) and *measures of dispersion* (such as standard deviation and variance). Below are some common Excel functions related to descriptive statistics.

- `=AVERAGE(number1, number2, ...)` returns the arithmetic mean of a set of numbers.
- `=CORREL(array1, array2)` returns the correlation coefficient of two cell ranges, `array1` and `array2`.
- `=COUNT(number1, number2, ...)` counts the number of cells in a list which contains numbers.
- `=COVAR(array1, array2)` returns the covariance (the average of the products of deviations for pairs of data points) located in `array1` and `array2`.
- `=FREQUENCY(data_array, bins_array)` calculates how often values appear in a range of values and to get a vertical array of numbers, where:
    - `data_array` is a range or reference to a set of values for which you want to count frequencies
    - `bins_array` is a range or reference to intervals into which you want to assemble the values in `data_array`.
- `=LARGE(array, k)` returns the *k*th largest value in a dataset in `array`.
- `=MAX(number1, number2, ...)` returns the largest value in a set of numbers.
- `=MEDIAN(number1, number2, ...)` returns the median of a set of numbers.
- `=MIN(number1, number2, ...)` returns the smallest value in a set of numbers.
- `=MODE(number1, number2, ...)` returns the most frequently occurring, or repetitive, value in a range of data. Excel returns `#N/A` if no most frequent number exists.
- `=PERCENTILE(array, k)` returns the *k*th percentile of an array's value.
- `=QUARTILE(array, k)` returns the *k*th quartile of a set of numbers. Note the median is when $k = 2$.

- `=RANK(number, ref, order)` returns the rank of a number in a list, where:
    - `number` specifies the number whose rank you are seeking
    - `ref` specifies a range of, or a reference to, a list of numbers
    - `order` specifies a number distinguishing how to rank numbers.
- `=SKEW(number1, number2, ...)` returns the skewness of a distribution.
- `=SMALL(array, k)` returns the *k*th smallest value in a dataset in `array`.
- `=STDEV(number1, number2, ...)` returns the standard deviation based on *sample data*.
- `=STDEV.P(number1, number2, ...)` returns the standard deviation based on *population data*.
- `=TRIMMEAN(array, percent)` returns the mean of the inside of a dataset where `percent` specifies the fractional number of data points to leave out of the calculation.
- `=VAR(number1, number2, ...)` returns the variance based on *sample data*.
- `=VAR.P(number1, number2, ...)` returns the variance based on *population data*.

A.3 DISCRETE DISTRIBUTIONS

Chapter 5 introduced probability distributions. Common discrete probability distributions include the discrete uniform, binomial and Poisson distributions. Appendix B summarises their statistical properties and examples of modelling applications (among other distributions). Below are some common Excel functions related to these common discrete distributions.

- `=RANDBETWEEN(bottom, top)` returns any integer between `bottom` and `top` with equal probability.
- `=BINOM.DIST(number_s, trials, probability_s, cumulative)` is a function which returns the individual term binomial distribution probability, where:
    - `number_s` is the number of successes in the trials
    - `trials` is the number of independent trials
    - `probability_s` is the probability of success on each trial
    - `cumulative` is a logical value: for the cumulative distribution function, use TRUE; for the probability (mass) function, use FALSE.
- `=BINOM.INV(trials, probability_s, alpha)` returns the smallest value for which the cumulative binomial distribution is less than or equal to a criterion value, where:
    - `trials` is the number of independent trials
    - `probability_s` is the probability of success on each trial
    - `alpha` is the criterion value.
- `=POISSON.DIST(x, mean, cumulative)` returns the Poisson distribution, where:
    - `x` is the number of events
    - `mean` is the expected numeric value, a positive number
    - `cumulative` is a logical value: for the Poisson cumulative probability, use TRUE; for the Poisson probability mass function, use FALSE.

A.4 CONTINUOUS DISTRIBUTIONS

Chapter 5 introduced probability distributions. Common continuous probability distributions include the continuous uniform, exponential and normal distributions. Appendix B summarises their statistical properties and examples of modelling applications (among other distributions). Below are some common Excel functions related to these common continuous distributions.

- `=RAND()` returns a random number greater than or equal to 0 and less than 1, evenly distributed (changes on recalculation).
- `=EXPON.DIST(x, lambda, cumulative)` returns the exponential distribution, where:
    - `x` is the value of the function, a non-negative number
    - `lambda` is the parameter value, a positive number
    - `cumulative` is a logical value for the function to return: the cumulative distribution function = TRUE; the probability density function = FALSE.
- `=NORM.DIST(x, mean, standard_dev, cumulative)` returns the normal cumulative distribution for the specified mean and standard deviation, where:
    - `x` is the value for which you want the distribution
    - `mean` is the arithmetic mean of the distribution
    - `standard_dev` is the standard deviation of the distribution, a positive number
    - `cumulative` is a logical value: for the cumulative distribution function, use TRUE; for the probability density function, use FALSE.
- `=NORM.S.DIST(z, cumulative)` returns the standard normal cumulative distribution (has a mean of zero and a standard deviation of one), where:
    - `z` is the value for which you want the distribution
    - `cumulative` is a logical value: for the cumulative distribution function, use TRUE; for the probability density function, use FALSE.
- `=NORM.INV(probability, mean, standard_dev)` returns the inverse of the normal cumulative distribution for the specified mean and standard deviation, where:
    - `probability` is a probability corresponding to the normal distribution, a number between 0 and 1 inclusive
    - `mean` is the arithmetic mean of the distribution
    - `standard_dev` is the standard deviation of the distribution, a positive number.
- `=NORM.S.INV(probability)` returns the inverse of the standard normal cumulative distribution (has a mean of 0 and a standard deviation of 1), where:
    - `probability` is a probability corresponding to the normal distribution, a number between 0 and 1 inclusive.
- `=STANDARDIZE(x, mean, standard_dev)` returns a normalised value from a distribution characterised by a mean and standard deviation, where:
    - `x` is the value you want to normalise
    - `mean` is the arithmetic mean of the distribution
    - `standard_dev` is the standard deviation of the distribution, a positive number.

A.5 STATISTICAL INFERENCE

Chapters 9 and 10 introduced confidence intervals and hypothesis testing, respectively. Below are some common Excel functions related to statistical inference.

- `=CONFIDENCE.NORM(alpha, standard_dev, size)` is used to get the confidence interval for the mean of a population, where:
  - `alpha` is the significance level you use to compute the confidence level
  - `standard_dev` is the standard deviation for the range (it is assumed to be a known value)
  - `size` is the size of the sample.
- `=NORM.DIST(x, mean, standard_dev, cumulative)` is used to get the normal cumulative distribution for the specified mean and standard deviation, where:
  - `x` specifies the value for which you want the distribution
  - `mean` specifies the arithmetic mean of the distribution
  - `standard_dev` is the standard deviation of the distribution
  - `cumulative` specifies the form of the function.
- `=NORM.INV(probability, mean, standard_dev)` is used to get the inverse of the normal cumulative distribution for the specific mean and standard deviation, where:
  - `probability` specifies a probability relating to the normal distribution
  - `mean` specifies the arithmetic mean of the distribution
  - `standard_dev` is the standard deviation of the distribution.
- `=NORM.S.DIST(z)` is used to get the standard normal cumulative distribution function for value `z`.
- `=NORM.S.INV(probability)` is used to get the inverse of the standard normal cumulative distribution for probability `probability`.
- `=STANDARDIZE(x, mean, standard_dev)` is used to get a normalised value from a distribution distinguished with specified mean and standard deviation, where:
  - `x` specifies the value you want to normalise
  - `mean` specifies the arithmetic mean of the distribution
  - `standard_dev` is the standard deviation of the distribution.
- `=T.DIST(x, degrees_freedom, tails)` is used to get the Student's *t* distribution, where:
  - `x` specifies the numeric value to use to evaluate the distribution
  - `degrees_freedom` specifies an integer denoting the number of degrees of freedom
  - `tails` specifies the number of distribution tails to return.
- `=T.INV(probability, degrees_freedom)` is used to get the inverse of the Student's *t* distribution for the specified degrees of freedom, where:
  - `probability` specifies the probability corresponding to the two-tailed Student's *t* distribution
  - `degrees_freedom` specifies the number of degrees of freedom to identify the distribution.

- `=T.TEST(array1, array2, tails, type)` is used to get the probability associated with a Student's *t* test, where:
  - `array1` specifies the first dataset
  - `array2` specifies the second dataset
  - `tails` specifies the number of distribution tails
  - `type` specifies the type of *t* test to carry out.
- `=Z.TEST(array, x, sigma)` is used to get the two-tailed *p*-value of a *z* test, where:
  - `array` specifies the range of data against which to test *x*
  - `x` specifies the value to test
  - `sigma` specifies the population standard deviation.

APPENDIX B
COMPENDIUM OF PROBABILITY DISTRIBUTIONS

Source: Photo by T-Tide via Pixabay.

This appendix presents a compendium (or 'library') of theoretical probability distributions. Each may be used as an *approximating model* of particular real-world phenomena. When choosing a probability distribution, we seek one which adequately captures the *stylised facts* or *real-world attributes* of the variable being modelled.

More specifically, in statistical inference we will treat observations

$$x_1, x_2, \ldots, x_n$$

(the sample, of size n) as values of a random variable X, which has some probability distribution (the population distribution). How to choose the probability distribution? Usually we do not try to invent new distributions from scratch. Instead, we use one of many existing standard distributions. There are many such distributions, such that for most purposes we can find a suitable standard distribution.

This appendix may be used as a reference resource of many families of probability distributions of discrete and continuous random variables. Some of these distributions are presented in Chapter 5. In this compendium, the following are provided (where appropriate) for each distribution:

- summary of the distribution
- business application examples
- notation for the distribution
- sample space (the possible values the variable may take)
- parameter space (the possible values of the parameter(s) of the distribution)
- probability mass function, $p(x)$ (if discrete) or probability density function, $f(x)$ (if continuous)
- cumulative distribution function, $F(x)$
- example plots
- mean, $\mathrm{E}(X)$
- variance, $\mathrm{Var}(X)$.

B.1 DISCRETE UNIFORM DISTRIBUTION

Summary: Assigns equal (i.e. the same, or 'uniform') probabilities to each member of its sample space.

Business application examples: Useful to model discrete input random variables in Monte Carlo simulations (see Chapter 20) when only the minimum, a, and maximum, b, possible values are known, with no knowledge of the relative probabilities of each outcome – can be considered as the 'I don't know' distribution!

Notation: $X \sim \text{Uniform}\{a, b\}$.

Sample space: $\{a, a+1, \ldots, b-1, b\}$.

Parameter space: $a < b$, where a and b are integers.

Probability mass function:

$$p(x) = \begin{cases} \dfrac{1}{b-a+1} & \text{for } x = a, a+1, \ldots, b-1, b \\ 0 & \text{otherwise.} \end{cases}$$

Cumulative distribution function:

$$F(x) = \begin{cases} 0 & \text{for } x < a \\ \dfrac{\lfloor x \rfloor - a + 1}{b-a+1} & \text{for } x = a, a+1, \ldots, b-1, b \\ 1 & \text{for } x > b \end{cases}$$

where $\lfloor x \rfloor$ denotes the 'floor function' which returns the largest integer less than or equal to x. For example, $\lfloor 3.6 \rfloor = 3$.

Example plots: Figure B.1 shows the pmf and cdf of $X \sim \text{Uniform}\{1, 10\}$, i.e. $a = 1$ and $b = 10$.

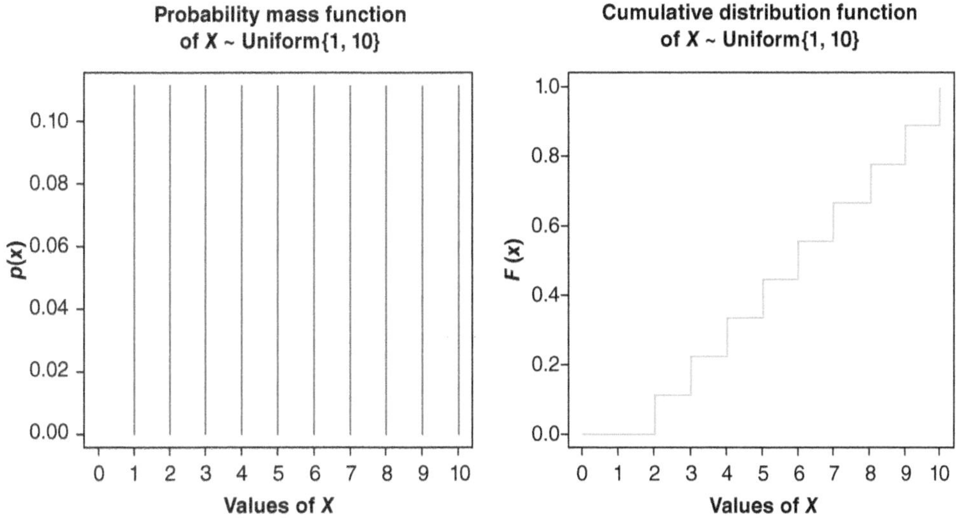

Figure B.1 The pmf and cdf of $X \sim \text{Uniform}\{1, 10\}$.

Mean: $\text{E}(X) = \dfrac{a+b}{2}$.

Variance: $\text{Var}(X) = \dfrac{(b-a+1)^2 - 1}{12}$.

B.2 BERNOULLI DISTRIBUTION

Summary: Assigns probabilities π and $1 - \pi$ to the only two possible outcomes, often referred to as 'success' and 'failure', respectively, although these do not necessarily have to represent 'good' and 'bad' outcomes, respectively.

Business application examples: π can represent a market share, while in opinion research (Chapter 8) π can represent a proportion, such as of satisfied customers.

Notation: $X \sim \text{Bernoulli}(\pi)$.

Sample space: $\{0, 1\}$.

Parameter space: $0 \leq \pi \leq 1$.

Probability mass function:

$$p(x) = \begin{cases} \pi^x (1-\pi)^{1-x} & \text{for } x = 0,1 \\ 0 & \text{otherwise.} \end{cases}$$

Cumulative distribution function:

$$F(x) = \begin{cases} 0 & \text{for } x < 0 \\ 1 - \pi & \text{for } 0 \le x < 1 \\ 1 & \text{for } x \ge 1. \end{cases}$$

Example plots: Figure B.2 shows the pmf and cdf of $X \sim$ Bernoulli(0.70), i.e. $\pi = 0.70$.

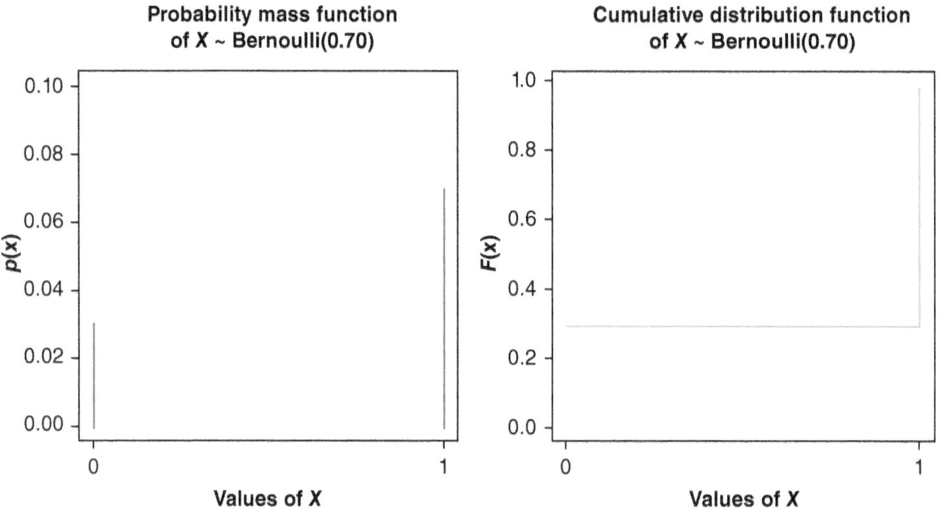

Figure B.2 The pmf and cdf of $X \sim$ Bernoulli(0.70).

Mean: $E(X) = \pi$.

Variance: $Var(X) = \pi(1 - \pi)$.

B.3 BINOMIAL DISTRIBUTION

Summary: Assigns probabilities to the number of successes in n independent trials each with only two possible outcomes with a constant probability of success, π.

Business application examples: Number of customers who purchase a product, request a refund or recommend a product; number of defective items in a batch of manufactured goods; number of respondents to a market research survey.

Notation: $X \sim \text{Bin}(n, \pi)$.

Sample space: $\{0, 1, 2, \ldots, n\}$.

Parameter space: $n \in \{0, 1, 2, \ldots\}$ and $0 \le \pi \le 1$.

Probability mass function:

$$p(x) = \begin{cases} \binom{n}{x} \pi^x (1-\pi)^{n-x} & \text{for } x = 0,1,2,\ldots,n \\ 0 & \text{otherwise} \end{cases}$$

where $\binom{n}{x} = \frac{n!}{x!(n-x)!}$ is the binomial coefficient.

Cumulative distribution function:

$$F(x) = \begin{cases} 0 & \text{for } x < 0 \\ \sum_{i=0}^{\lfloor x \rfloor} \binom{n}{i} \pi^i (1-\pi)^{n-i} & \text{for } 0 \leq x < n \\ 1 & \text{for } x \geq n. \end{cases}$$

Example plots: Figure B.3 shows the pmf and cdf of $X \sim \text{Bin}(10, 0.75)$, i.e. $n = 10$ and $\pi = 0.75$.

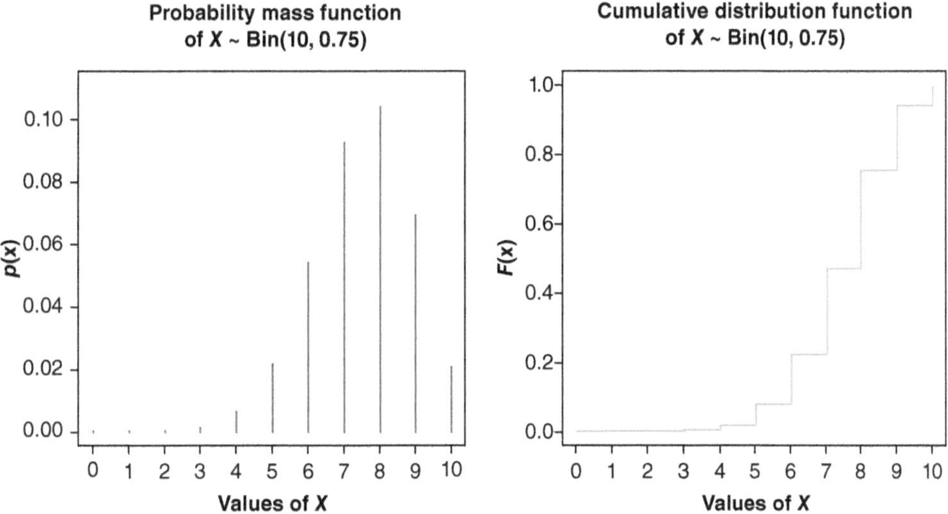

Figure B.3 The pmf and cdf of $X \sim \text{Bin}(10, 0.75)$.

Mean: $E(X) = n\pi$.

Variance: $\text{Var}(X) = n\pi(1 - \pi)$.

Note: The special case when $n = 1$ corresponds to the Bernoulli(π) distribution, and the sum of n independent and identically distributed Bernoulli(π) random variables has a Bin(n, π) distribution.

B.4 POISSON DISTRIBUTION

Summary: Used to model the number of occurrences of events over a fixed interval, typically in space or time.

Business application examples: Customers arriving at a service counter; number of insurance claims which a particular policyholder makes in a year; machine breakdowns per unit of time.

Notation: $X \sim \text{Pois}(\lambda)$.

Sample space: $\{0, 1, 2, \ldots\}$.

Parameter space: $\lambda > 0$.

Probability mass function:

$$p(x) = \begin{cases} \dfrac{e^{-\lambda}\lambda^x}{x!} & \text{for } x = 0,1,2,\ldots \\ 0 & \text{otherwise} \end{cases}$$

Cumulative distribution function:

$$F(x) = \begin{cases} 0 & \text{for } x < 0 \\ e^{-\lambda}\sum_{i=0}^{\lfloor x \rfloor} \dfrac{\lambda^i}{i!} & \text{for } x \geq 0. \end{cases}$$

Example plots: Figure B.4 shows the pmf and cdf of $X \sim \text{Pois}(3)$, i.e. $\lambda = 3$.

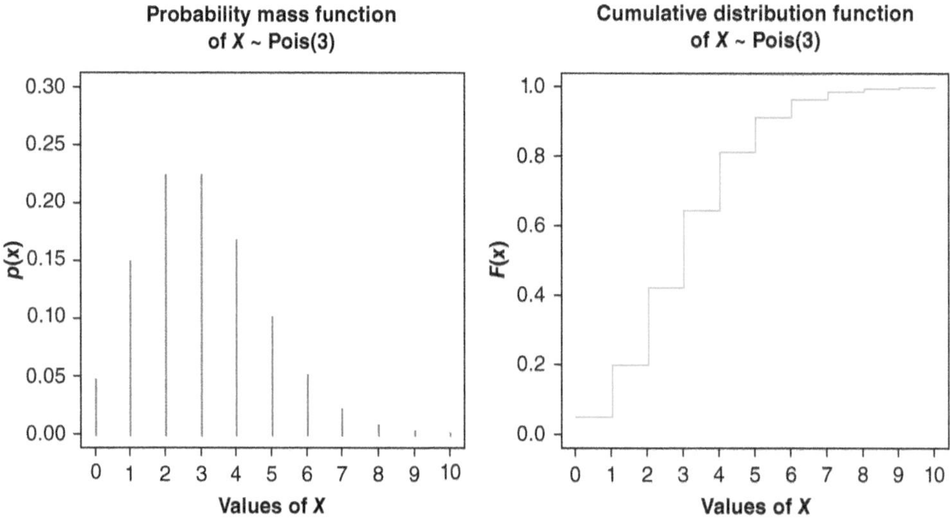

Figure B.4 The pmf and cdf of $X \sim \text{Pois}(3)$.

Mean: $E(X) = \lambda$.

Variance: $Var(X) = \lambda$.

B.5 GEOMETRIC DISTRIBUTION

Summary: Represents the number of failures before the first success in a set of independent and identically distributed Bernoulli trials.

Business application examples: Consumer feedback; quality control in manufacturing processes.

Notation: $X \sim Geo(\pi)$.

Sample space: $\{0, 1, 2, \ldots\}$.

Parameter space: $0 < \pi \leq 1$.

Probability mass function:

$$p(x) = \begin{cases} (1-\pi)^x \pi & \text{for } x = 0,1,2,\ldots \\ 0 & \text{otherwise.} \end{cases}$$

Cumulative distribution function:

$$F(x) = \begin{cases} 0 & \text{for } x < 0 \\ 1-(1-\pi)^{\lfloor x \rfloor + 1} & \text{for } x \geq 0. \end{cases}$$

Example plots: Figure B.5 shows the pmf and cdf of $X \sim Geo(0.3)$, i.e. $\pi = 0.3$.

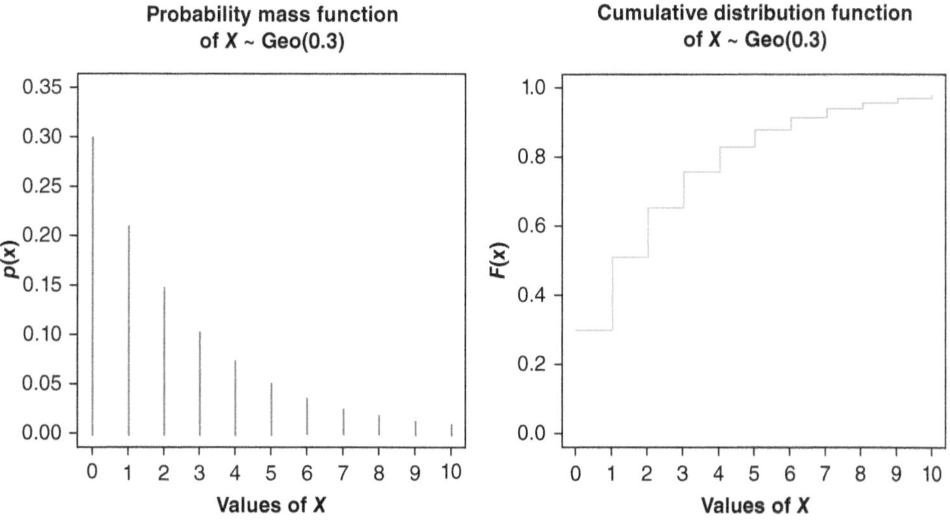

Figure B.5 The pmf and cdf of $X \sim Geo(0.3)$.

Mean: $E(X) = \frac{1-\pi}{\pi}$.

Variance: $\text{Var}(X) = \frac{1-\pi}{\pi^2}$.

B.6 CONTINUOUS UNIFORM DISTRIBUTION

Summary: Assigns probability equally (i.e. uniformly, hence the name) over its sample space.

Business application examples: The special case of $X \sim \text{Uniform}[0, 1]$, when the sample space is the unit interval, is used in business simulations of random samples from distributions, by treating a random drawing from Uniform[0, 1] as a randomly drawn value of a distribution function. Inverting the distribution function recovers the (simulated) random drawing from the desired distribution.

Notation: $X \sim \text{Uniform}[a, b]$.

Sample space: $[a, b]$.

Parameter space: $-\infty < a < b < \infty$.

Probability density function:

$$f(x) = \begin{cases} \frac{1}{b-a} & \text{for } a \le x \le b \\ 0 & \text{otherwise.} \end{cases}$$

Cumulative distribution function:

$$F(x) = \begin{cases} 0 & \text{for } x < a \\ \frac{x-a}{b-a} & \text{for } a \le x \le b \\ 1 & \text{for } x > b. \end{cases}$$

Example plots: Figure B.6 shows the pdf and cdf of $X \sim \text{Uniform}[0, 5]$, i.e. $a = 0$ and $b = 5$.

Mean: $E(X) = \frac{a+b}{2}$.

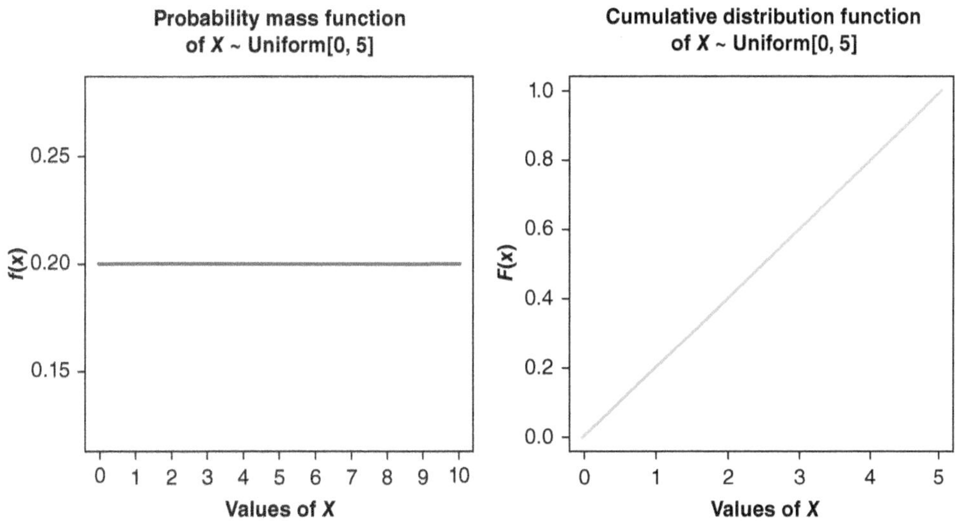

Figure B.6 The pdf and cdf of $X \sim$ Uniform[0, 5].

Variance: $\mathrm{Var}(X) = \dfrac{(b-a)^2}{12}.$

B.7 EXPONENTIAL DISTRIBUTION

Summary: Used to model the time between occurrence of Poisson process events.

Business application examples: Arises in reliability theory and queuing theory.

Notation: $X \sim \mathrm{Exp}(\lambda)$.

Sample space: $x \geq 0$.

Parameter space: $\lambda > 0$.

Probability density function:

$$f(x) = \begin{cases} \lambda e^{-\lambda x} & \text{for } x \geq 0 \\ 0 & \text{otherwise} \end{cases}$$

Cumulative distribution function:

$$F(x) = \begin{cases} 0 & \text{for } x < 0 \\ 1 - e^{-\lambda x} & \text{for } x \geq 0. \end{cases}$$

Example plots: Figure B.7 shows the pdf and cdf of $X \sim \text{Exp}(2)$, i.e. $\lambda = 2$.

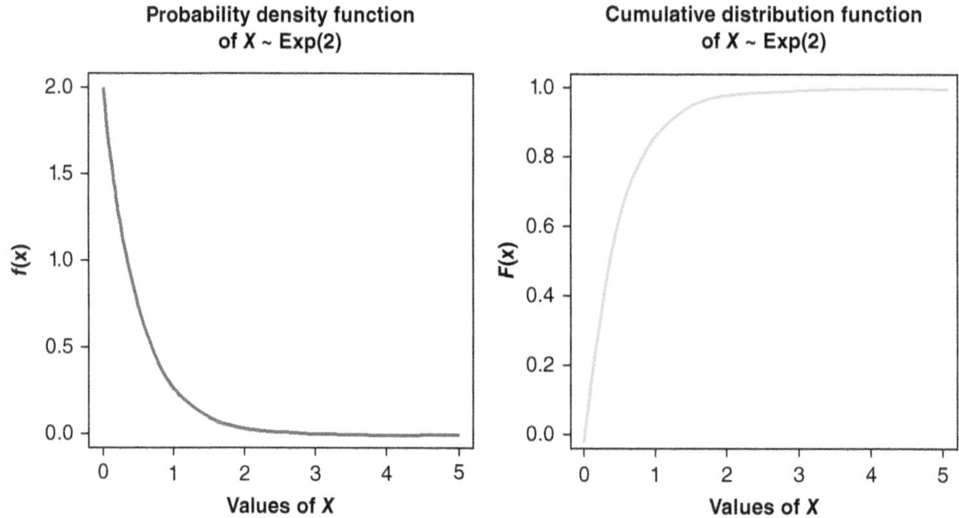

Figure B.7 The pdf and cdf of $X \sim \text{Exp}(2)$.

Mean: $\text{E}(X) = \frac{1}{\lambda}$.

Variance: $\text{Var}(X) = \frac{1}{\lambda^2}$.

B.8 NORMAL DISTRIBUTION

Summary: The familiar bell-shaped curve, which is often used as a distribution assumption in modelling. It is completely specified by its mean, μ, and its variance, σ^2.

Business application examples: Many business variables have distributions which are approximately normal, such as weights of various products. The normal distribution has extremely convenient mathematical properties, which make it a useful default choice of distribution in many contexts, and is often a distributional assumption in many applications (such as in Chapters 10, 12 and 13).

Notation: $X \sim N(\mu, \sigma^2)$.

Sample space: $-\infty < x < \infty$.

Parameter space: $-\infty < \mu < \infty$ and $\sigma^2 > 0$.

Probability density function:

$$f(x) = \frac{1}{\sqrt{2\pi\sigma^2}} \exp\left(-\frac{(x-\mu)^2}{2\sigma^2}\right) \quad \text{for} -\infty < x < \infty.$$

Cumulative distribution function: The distribution function of a normal random variable does not have a closed form.

Example plots: Figure B.8 shows the pdf and cdf of $X \sim N(5, 1)$, i.e. $\mu = 5$ and $\sigma^2 = 1$.

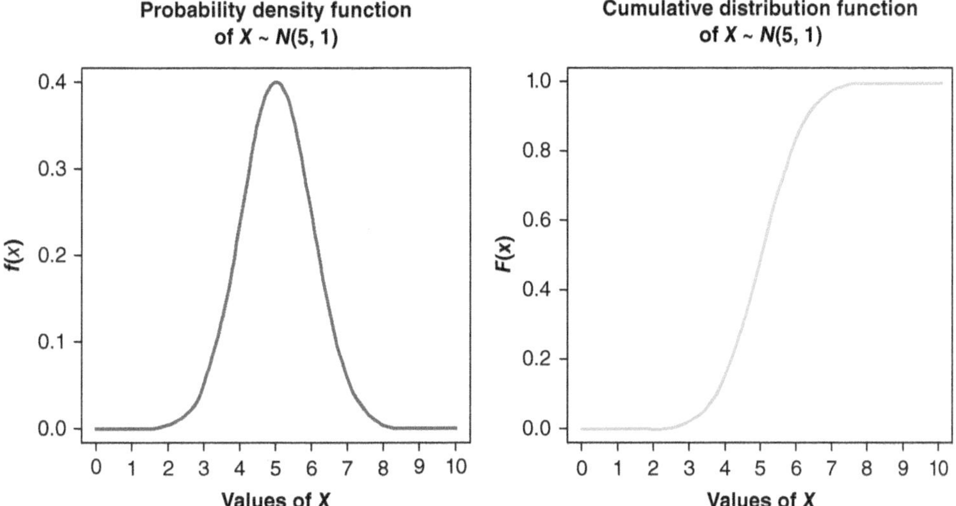

Figure B.8 The pdf and cdf of $X \sim N(5, 1)$.

Mean: $E(X) = \mu$.

Variance: $\text{Var}(X) = \sigma^2$.

Note: An important special case is the standard normal distribution with $\mu = 0$ and $\sigma^2 = 1$, denoted $Z \sim N(0, 1)$. X and Z are related through the linear transformation

$$Z = \frac{X - \mu}{\sigma} \quad \Leftrightarrow \quad X = \mu + \sigma Z.$$

The distribution function of Z is denoted by Φ, such that if $Z \sim N(0, 1)$, then

$$\Phi(z) = F(z) = P(Z \leq z).$$

INDEX